RESEARCH METHODS IN SPORT STUDIES AND SPORT MANAGEMENT

A Practical Guide

Research Methods in Sport Studies and Sport Management

A Practical Guide

A. J. Veal and Simon Darcy

Routledge
Taylor & Francis Group

LONDON AND NEW YORK

This edition first published 2014
by Routledge
2 Park Square, Milton Park, Abingdon, Oxon, OX14 4RN

and by Routledge
711 Third Avenue, New York, NY 10017

Routledge is an imprint of the Taylor & Francis Group, an informa business

British Library Cataloguing in Publication Data
A catalogue record for this book is available from the British Library

Library of Congress Cataloging-in-Publication Data
Veal, Anthony James.
   Research methods in sport studies and sport management : a practical guide /
A. J. Veal and Simon Darcy.
      pages cm.
   ISBN 978-0-273-73669-1
 1. Sports--Research--Methodology.   2. Sports--Management.   I. Title.
   GV706.8.V43 2013
   796.07--dc23
                                                            2013030695

ISBN13: 978-0-415-73385-4 (hbk)
ISBN13: 978-0-273-73669-1 (pbk)
ISBN13 978-1-315-77666-8 (ebk)

Typeset in Palatino and Helvetica Neue
by
Servis Filmsetting Ltd, Stockport, Cheshire

List of figures		xxi
List of tables		xxvii
List of case studies		xxviii
Preface		**xxx**
I	**Introduction**	**1**
1.	Introduction to research: what, why and who?	3
2.	Approaches to research in sport	31
3.	Starting out – research plans and proposals	57
4.	Research ethics	105
5.	The range of research methods	127
6.	Reviewing the literature	167
II	**Data collection**	**197**
7.	Secondary data sources	199
8.	Observation	225
9.	Qualitative methods: introduction and data collection	251
10.	Questionnaire surveys: typology, design and coding	277
11.	Experimental research	343
12.	The case study method	369
13.	Sampling: quantitative and qualitative	387
III	**Data analysis**	**407**
14.	Analysing secondary data	409
15.	Analysing qualitative data	425

16.   Analysing quantitative and survey data   455
17.   Statistical analysis   497

IV   **Communicating results**   **547**
18.   Research reports and presentations   549

     Index   571

Detailed chapter contents

List of figures   xxi
List of tables   xxvii
List of case studies   xxviii
Preface   xxx

I   Introduction and Preparation   1

1   Introduction to research: what, why and who?   3

Introduction   3
What is research?   5
    Research defined   5
    Scientific research   5
    Social science research   5
    Descriptive, explanatory and evaluative research   6
Why study research?   8
    In general   8
    Research in policy-making, planning and management
        processes   9
Who does research?   14
    Academics   15
    Students   16
    Government, commercial and non-profit organisations   16
    Managers   17
    Consultants   18
Who pays?   18
Research outputs   19
    Academic journal articles   20
    Professional journal articles   21
    Conference papers/presentations   21
    Books   21
    Policy/planning/management reports   21

Terminology   24
Using this book   25
Summary   25
Test questions   26
Exercises   26
Resources   27
References   27

2   Approaches to research in sport   31

Introduction   31
Disciplinary traditions   31
Approaches, dimensions, issues, terminology   34
   Ontology, epistemology, methodology   35
   Positivist, post-positivist, interpretive and critical
      approaches/paradigms   36
   Descriptive, explanatory and evaluative research   37
   Qualitative and quantitative research   38
   Pragmatism   40
   Participatory research   41
   Theoretical and applied research   41
   Reflexivity   41
   Empirical and non-empirical research   42
   Induction and deduction   43
   Experimental and naturalistic methods   46
   Objectivity and subjectivity   48
   Primary and secondary data   48
   Self-reported and observed data   48
   Validity, reliability and trustworthiness   49
Summary   51
Test questions   51
Exercises   52
Resources   52
References   53

3   Starting out – research plans and proposals   57

Introduction   57
Planning a research project   57
   Select a topic   59
   Review the literature   65
   Devise conceptual framework   67
   Decide research question(s)   76
   List information requirements   79
   Decide research strategy   80
   Obtain ethics clearance   82

Conduct research   84
Communicate findings   84
Store data   85

The research process in the real world   85

Research proposals   86
Introduction   86
Self-generated research proposals   87

Responsive proposals – briefs and tenders   91

Summary   97

Test questions   97

Exercises   98

Resources   98

References   99

4   Research ethics   105

Introduction   105

Institutional oversight of research ethics   106

Ethics in the research process   107

Ethical issues in research   110
Social benefit   110
Researcher competence   111
Free choice   111
Informed consent   113
Risk of harm to the subject   116
Honesty/rigour in analysis, interpretation and reporting   120
Authorship and acknowledgements   121

Access to research information   122

Summary   123

Test questions   123

Exercises   124

Resources   124

References   125

5   The range of research methods   127

Introduction – horses for courses   127

The range of major research methods   128
Scholarship   128
Just thinking   129
Existing sources 1: using the literature/systematic reviews   129
Existing sources 2: secondary data   130
Observation   130
Qualitative methods   131
Questionnaire-based surveys   132

Experimental method   134
Case study method   134

Subsidiary/cross-cutting techniques   135
Action research   135
Big data   137
Conjoint analysis   137
Content analysis   138
Coupon surveys/conversion studies   138
Delphi technique   139
Discourse analysis   139
En route/intercept/cordon surveys   139
Epidemiology   140
Experience sampling method (ESM)   140
Historical research   141
Longitudinal studies   141
Mapping techniques   141
Media reader/viewer/listener surveys   142
Meta-analysis   142
Netnography   143
Network analysis   143
Panel studies   144
Projective techniques   144
Psychographic/lifestyle research   144
Q methodology   146
Quantitative modelling   146
Repertory grid   146
Scales   147
Time-use surveys   148
Web-based research   148

Multiple/mixed methods   149
Triangulation   149
Counting heads   150
Mixed methods   151

Choosing methods   151
The research question or hypothesis   151
Previous research   152
Data availability/access   152
Resources   152
Time and timing   152
Validity, reliability, trustworthiness and generalisability   153
Ethics   153
Uses/users of the findings   153

Summary   154

Test questions   155

Exercises   156

Resources   156

References   159

6	**Reviewing the literature**	**167**
	Introduction – an essential task	167
	The value of bibliographies	168
	Searching: sources of information	169
	Library catalogues	169
	Specialist indexes and databases	170
	Searching on the Internet	171
	Google Scholar	171
	Published bibliographies	171
	General sport publications	172
	Reference lists	172
	Beyond sport	172
	Unpublished research	173
	Obtaining copies of material	173
	Compiling and maintaining a bibliography	174
	Reviewing the literature	174
	Types of literature review	175
	Reading critically and creatively	176
	Summarising	178
	Meta-analysis/interpretation/evaluation/review	179
	Referencing the literature	181
	The purpose of referencing	181
	Recording references	181
	Referencing and referencing systems	182
	The author/date or Harvard system	184
	Footnote or endnote system	186
	Comparing two systems	188
	Referencing issues	189
	Second-hand references	189
	Excessive referencing	190
	Latin abbreviations	190
	Summary	190
	Test questions	191
	Exercises	191
	Resources	192
	References	193
II	**Data collection**	**197**
7	**Secondary data sources**	**199**
	Introduction	199
	Measuring sport activity	199
	Types of engagement	200
	Counting heads	202

Introduction to secondary sources   204
    Advantages and disadvantages of using secondary data   205
    Types of secondary data   206
Administrative/management data   206
    Management data   206
National sport participation surveys   207
    The national sport participationsurvey phenomenon   207
    Validity and reliability of national sport participation surveys 210
    Sample size   211
    Main question – participation reference period and duration   211
    Age range   213
    Social/demographic characteristics   214
    The importance of sport participation surveys   214
    National time-use surveys   214
Elite sport performance   215
Economic data   216
    Household expenditure   216
The population census   216
    The modern population census   217
    Uses of census data   217
Documentary sources   218
Opportunism   219
Summary   219
Test questions   220
Exercises   220
Resources   220
References   222

8   Observation   225
Introduction   225
    Types of observational research: quantitative and qualitative   226
Possibilities   226
    Children's play/physical activity   227
    Sport activity patterns   228
    Informal sport areas   228
    Visitor profiles   230
    Deviant behaviour   230
    Mystery shopping   232
    Complementary research   232
    Everyday life   233
    Social behaviour   233
Main elements of observational research   233
    Step 1: Choice of site(s)   234
    Step 2: Choice of observation point(s)   234
    Step 3: Choice of observation time-period(s)   235
    Step 4: Continuous observation or sampling?   235

Step 5: Count frequency   236
Step 6: What to observe   236
Step 7: Division of site into zones   237
Step 8: Recording information   238
Step 9: Conducting the observation   238
Step 10: Analysing data   239

Use of technology   241
Automatic counters   241
GPS   242
Aerial photography   243
Still photography and video: visual research   243
Time-lapse photography   243
Just looking   244

Summary   244

Test questions   245

Exercises   245

Resources   246

References   247

9   Qualitative methods: introduction and
     data collection   251

Introduction   251
The nature of qualitative methods   251

Merits, functions, limitations   252

The qualitative research process   254

The range of qualitative methods – introduction   255

In-depth interviews   256
Nature   256
Purposes and situations   257
Checklist   258
The interviewing process   258
Recording   261

Focus groups   262
Nature   262
Purposes   262
Methods   262

Participant observation   263
Nature   263
Purposes   263
Methods   263

Analysing texts   264
Nature   264
Novels and other literature   264
Mass media coverage   265
Film   265
Internet   265

Biographical research	**265**
Nature	265
Biography/autobiography/personal narrative	266
Oral history	266
Memory work	266
Personal domain histories	266
Ethnography and mixed methods	**267**
Validity and reliability, trustworthiness	**267**
Summary	**268**
Test questions	**269**
Exercises	**269**
Resources	**270**
References	**271**
10 Questionnaire surveys: typology, design and coding	**277**
Introduction	**277**
Definitions and terminology	278
Roles	278
Merits	279
Limitations	280
Interviewer-completion or respondent-completion?	**282**
Types of questionnaire survey	283
The household questionnaire survey	**283**
Nature	283
Conduct	284
Omnibus surveys	285
Time-use surveys	286
National surveys	286
The street survey	**286**
Nature	286
Conduct	287
Quota sampling	287
The telephone survey	**288**
Nature	288
Conduct	288
Representativeness and response levels	289
National surveys	290
The mail survey	**290**
Nature	290
The problem of low response rates	290
Mail and user/site/visitor survey combos	295
Discussing/analysing non-response	295
E-surveys	**295**
Nature and conduct	295
Advantages and disadvantages	296
User/on-site/visitor surveys	**296**
Nature	296

Conduct   297
The uses of user surveys   298
User/site/visitor and mail/e-survey combo   300

Captive group surveys   300
Nature   300
Conduct   300

Questionnaire design   301
Introduction – research problems and information
    requirements   301
Example questionnaires   302
General design issues   303
Types of information   308
Respondent characteristics   314
Attitude/opinion questions   320
Market segments   322
Ordering of questions and layout of questionnaires   322

Coding   325
Pre-coded questions   325
Open-ended questions   325
Recording coded information   326

Validity of questionnaire-based data   328
Threats to validity   328
Checking validity   330

Conducting questionnaire surveys   332
Planning fieldwork arrangements   332
Conducting a pilot survey   335

Summary   336

Test questions   337

Exercises   337

Resources   338

References   339

11   Experimental research   343

Introduction   343

Principles of experimental research   344
Components   344
The classic experimental design   344

Validity   345
Threats to validity   346
Field experiments versus laboratory experiments   347

Quasi-experimental designs   347
Types of quasi-experimental design   347
Experiments and projects   348

Experimental methods in sport research   349
Training/coaching   349
Sport policy/management experimental projects   352
Psychological/perceptual studies   355

Equipment   356
Experimenting with research methods   357
Children's play   359
Other examples of use of experimental methods   360

Summary   362

Test questions   363

Exercises   363

Resources   364

References   365

12   The case study method   369

Introduction   369

Definitions   370
What is the case study method?   370
What the case study method is not   370
Scale   371

Validity and reliability   372

Merits of the case study approach   374

Design of case studies   374
Defining the unit of analysis   374
Selecting the case(s)   375
Data gathering   375

Analysis   376

Case studies in practice   377

Test questions   382

Exercises   382

Summary   382

Resources   383

References   384

13   Sampling: quantitative and qualitative   387

Introduction   387

The idea of sampling   387

Samples and populations   388

Representativeness   389
Random sampling   389
Sampling for household surveys   389
Sampling for telephone surveys   390
Sampling for site/user/visitor surveys   391
Sampling for street surveys and quota sampling   392
Sampling for mail surveys   393
Sampling for complex events   393
Sampling and random assignment in experimental research   394

Sample size   394
    1. Level of precision – confidence intervals   395
    2. Level of detail of proposed analysis   398
    Budget   399
    Reporting sample size issues   399
    Confidence intervals applied to population estimates 400
    Sample size and small populations   400

Weighting   401

Sampling for qualitative research   403

Test questions   404

Summary   404

Resources   405

References   405

Exercises   405

Appendix 13.1   Suggested appendix on sample size and
confidence intervals   406

III   Data analysis   407

14   Analysing secondary data   409

Introduction   409

Examples of secondary data analysis   409

Summary   422

Resources   423

Exercises   423

References   424

15   Analysing qualitative data   425

Introduction   425
    Data collection and analysis   425
    Data storage and confidentiality   426
    Case study example   427

Manual methods of analysis   430
    Introduction   430
    Reading   430
    Emergent themes   430
    Mechanics   432
    Analysis   432

Qualitative analysis using computer software – introduction 434
    Interview transcripts   435

NVivo   435
    Introduction   435
    Starting up   435
    Creating a new project   436

Saving 436
Attributes 436
Cases and their attributes 436
Importing documents 439
Linking cases and documents 439
Setting up a coding system 439
Modelling 441
Coding text 441
Project summary 441
Analysis 441
Case study 447

Summary 451

Test questions 452

Exercises 452

Resources 453

References 453

16   Analysing quantitative and survey data 455

Introduction 455

Survey data analysis and types of research 456
Descriptive research 456
Explanatory research 456
Evaluative research 457
Overlaps 458
Reliability 458

Spreadsheet analysis 458

Statistical Package for the Social Sciences (SPSS) 460

Preparation 462
Cases and variables 462
Specifying variables 463
Starting up 468
Entering information about variables – Variable View window 468
Saving work 470
Entering data – Data View window 470

SPSS Statistics procedures 471
Starting an analysis session 471
Descriptives 472
Frequencies 474
Checking for errors 475
Multiple response 476
Recode 476
Mean, median and mode – measures of central tendency 478
Presenting the results: statistical summary 481
Crosstabulation 481
Weighting 483
Graphics 485

The analysis process   489
Summary   489
Test questions   490
Exercises   490
Resources   490
References   491
Appendix 16.1   Frequencies Output File   492

17   Statistical analysis   497

Introduction   497
The statistics approach   498
    Probabilistic statements   498
    The normal distribution   498
    Probabilistic statement formats   499
    Significance   501
    The null hypothesis   502
    Dependent and independent variables   502
Statistical tests   503
    Types of data and appropriate tests   503
    Chi-square   504
    Comparing two means: the t-test   509
    A number of means: one-way analysis of variance (ANOVA)   513
    A table of means: factorial analysis of variance (ANOVA)   517
    Correlation   518
    Linear regression   524
    Multiple regression   529
    Multivariate analysis   532
In conclusion   534
Summary   535
Test questions   536
Exercises   536
Resources   536
References   537
Appendix 17.1   Details of example data file used – questionnaire, variable
details and data   539
Appendix 17.2   Statistical formulae   545

IV   Communicating results   547

18   Research reports and presentations   549

Introduction   549
Written research reports   549
    Getting started   550

Report components 550
Main body of the report – technical aspects 555
Main body of the report – structure and content 560
Research reports: conclusion 565

Other media 566
Oral presentations 566
Use of 'PowerPoint'-type software 567

Summary 568

A final comment 568

Resources 569

References 569

Test questions/exercises 569

Index 569

List of figures

1.1	Physical exercise and sport	4
1.2	Types of research	6
1.3	Why study research?	9
1.4	Examples of policies, plans and management	10
1.5	The rational-comprehensive planning/management process	11
1.6	Example of planning/management tasks and associated research	12
1.7	Who does research?	15
1.8	Managers and research	17
1.9	Who pays?	18
1.10	Research report formats	19
1.11	Refereed journals in sport	20
2.1	Disciplines and examples of research questions	33
2.2	Terminology: approaches/dimensions/issues	34
2.3	Circular model of the research process	43
3.1	Elements in the research process	58
3.2	Examples of research topics from different sources	59
3.3	Reasons for revisiting theories/propositions/observations from the literature	61
3.4	Purposes of research	64
3.5	Roles of the literature in research	66
3.6	Development of a conceptual framework	69
3.7	Exploration of relationships between concepts – example	70
3.8	Concept map example	71
3.9	Examples of concepts – definition and operationalisation	72
3.10	Conceptual framework as quantifiable model	73
3.11	Exercise – fitness – stress – hardiness and health	74

3.12	Conceptual framework: performance evaluation	74
3.13	Conceptual framework: market research study	75
3.14	Conceptual framework: customer service quality study	76
3.15	The research question vs. the hypothesis	77
3.16	Information needs	79
3.17	Research strategy components	80
3.18	Example research budget	82
3.19	Example of research programme diagrammatic representation	83
3.20	Example of research project timetable	83
3.21	The research process in the real world	86
3.22	Research proposal checklist: self-generated research	88
3.23	Research proposal checklist: responsive research	93
4.1	Ethics in the research process	108
4.2	Information for research participants: checklist	114
4.3	Example of a consent form	115
4.4	Ethics guidelines for anonymous questionnaire-based surveys	116
4.5	Personally identifiable data	119
5.1	The range of major methods	128
5.2	Qualitative data collection methods	132
5.3	Types of questionnaire-based survey	134
5.4	Subsidiary, cross-cutting and multiple techniques/methods	136
5.5	Action research process	137
5.6	A simple network	143
5.7	Examples of psychographic/lifestyle categories	145
5.8	Repertory grid – example	147
5.9	Scales for sport-related topics	148
5.10	Triangulation	150
5.11	Considerations in selecting a research method	151
6.1	The roles of the literature in research	168
6.2	Sources of information	169
6.3	Types of literature review	175
6.4	Questions to ask when reviewing the literature	177
6.5	Making sense of the literature	179
6.6	Standard/generic reference formats	182
6.7	Examples of reference formats	183
6.8	Reference systems: features, advantages, disadvantages	189
7.1	Typology of individual engagement with sport	200

7.2	Measuring sport/physical activity	201
7.3	Local/non-local participants	202
7.4	Counting heads in sport: sources and methods	203
7.5	Advantages and disadvantages of using secondary data	205
7.6	Types of secondary data	206
7.7	Management data	207
7.8	National sport participation surveys: composite publications coverage	208
7.9	National sport participation survey details	209
7.10	Participation rates in sports by reference period, persons aged 16+, England	212
7.11	Time use, Britain and Australia	215
7.12	Measures of national performance in multi-sport international sport events	216
7.13	Census data: levels of availability	217
7.14	Census data available	218
7.15	Documentary sources	219
8.1	Types of observational research	226
8.2	Situations for observational research	227
8.3	Pattern of conflict at the Bathurst 'Bike Races', 1985	231
8.4	Steps in an observation project	234
8.5	Counts of site use	236
8.6	Observed use of a sports centre	237
8.7	Observation recording sheet: counts	238
8.8	Park usage pattern	240
9.1	Sequential and recursive approaches	255
9.2	Qualitative methods: summary	256
9.3	Questions, responses and interview types	257
9.4	Example of a checklist for in-depth interviewing	259
9.5	Interviewing interventions – Whyte (1982)	261
10.1	The use of questionnaire surveys compared with other methods – examples	280
10.2	Interviewer-completion compared with respondent-completion	282
10.3	Types of questionnaire survey – characteristics	284
10.4	Factors affecting mail survey response	291
10.5	Mail survey follow-ups	293
10.6	Mail survey response pattern	293
10.7	Types of e-survey	296

10.8	Questionnaire design process	302
10.9	Question wording: examples of good and bad practice	307
10.10	Open-ended vs. pre-coded questions – example	307
10.11	Example of range of replies resulting from an open-ended question	309
10.12	Range of information in sport questionnaires	310
10.13	Economic status/occupational/socio-economic groupings	315
10.14	Household type and visitor group type	317
10.15	Life-cycle stages	318
10.16	Housing information	319
10.17	Opinion/attitude question formats	321
10.19	Coding open-ended questions – example	326
10.20	Completed questionnaire	327
10.21	Data from 15 completed questionnaires	329
10.22	Questionnaire surveys: threats to validity	330
10.23	Fieldwork planning tasks	333
10.24	Pilot survey purposes	336
11.1	Classic experimental design	345
11.2	Threats to validity of experiments	346
11.3	Quasi-experimental research designs	348
11.4	Types and contexts of experiments in sport research	349
11.5	Experimental model of policy projects	353
11.6	Survey respondent groups – Hammitt and McDonald	358
12.1	The case study method: demographic and geographic levels	371
12.2	Case-study research: theory and policy	373
12.3	Trends in swimming participation, Australia, 2001–10	378
13.1	The normal curve and confidence intervals	396
13.2	Selected qualitative sampling methods	403
14.1	Income inequality and sport participation, European countries, 2009	411
14.2	Estimating likely demand for a sport facility: approach	413
14.3	Facility utilisation	416
14.4	Catchment/market area	417
15.1	Circular model of research in qualitative and quantitative contexts	426
15.2	Outline conceptual framework for a qualitative study of activity choice	427
15.3	Interview transcript extracts	428

15.4	Developed conceptual framework for qualitative study of activity choice	431
15.5	'Crosstabulation' of qualitative data	433
15.6	NVivo procedures covered	436
15.7	Create NVivo project – procedure	437
15.8	Attributes – procedure	438
15.9	Cases and attributes – procedure	438
15.10	Importing documents – procedure	440
15.11	Linking documents and cases – procedure	440
15.12	Setting up a coding system – procedure	442
15.13	Modelling – procedure	443
15.14	Coding text – procedure	444
15.15	Activity Choice project summary	445
15.16	Coding query – procedure	446
15.17	Matrix coding query – procedure	447
16.1	Research types and analytical procedures	456
16.2	Questionnaire survey data: spreadsheet analysis	459
16.3	Questionnaire survey data: spreadsheet analysis steps	461
16.4	Survey analysis – overview	462
16.5	Variable names, labels and values	464
16.6	Starting an *SPSS Statistics* session	468
16.7	Blank Variable View and Data View windows	469
16.8	Variable View window with variable names and labels	470
16.9	Data View window with data from 15 questionnaires/cases	471
16.10	Starting an SPSS analysis session	472
16.11	Descriptives procedure and output	473
16.12	Frequencies for one variable: procedure and output	475
16.13	Multiple Response procedure and output	477
16.14	Recode procedure and output	479
16.15	Means procedures and output	480
16.16	Campus Sporting Life Survey 2011: statistical summary	482
16.17	Crosstabs procedures and output	484
16.18	Data types and graphics	485
16.19	Graphics procedures and output	486
17.1	Drawing repeated samples and the normal distribution	500
17.2	Dependent and independent variables	503
17.3	Types of data and types of statistical test	504
17.4	Alternative expressions of hypotheses	505

17.5	Chi-square test – procedures	506
17.6	Distribution of chi-square assuming null hypothesis is true	507
17.7	Presentation of chi-square test results	509
17.8	Chi-square and t distributions	510
17.9	Comparing means: t-test: paired samples: procedures	511
17.10	Comparing means: t-test: independent samples – procedure	512
17.11	Comparing ranges of means – procedures	513
17.12	Comparing means and variances	514
17.13	One-way analysis of variance – procedures	516
17.14	A table of means – procedures	517
17.15	Factorial analysis of variance – procedures	519
17.16	Relationships between variables	520
17.17	Correlation	522
17.18	Correlation matrix – procedures	523
17.19	Regression line	525
17.20	Regression analysis – procedures	526
17.20	Regression analysis – procedures	526
17.21	Regression line – curve fit – procedure	527
17.22	Regression: curve fit, non-linear – procedures	528
17.23	Multiple regression – procedures	530
17.24	Structural equation modelling	531
17.25	Binary and scale variable graphic	531
17.26	Simple manual factor analysis	533
17.27	Plots of 'clusters'	534
17.28	Dendrogram	534
18.1	Types of research report	551
18.2	Report style and components	552
18.3	Example list of contents for a research report on student sport	554
18.4	Main body of report: technical aspects	556
18.5	Dot-point list example	556
18.6	Table and commentaries	559
18.7	Conventional academic article structure	561
18.8	Report as narrative – structure	564

List of tables

8.1   Observed use of a park   239

8.2   Estimating daily visit numbers from count data   241

10.1 Participation in sport/physical recreation activities
      by reference period, Britain, 1987   312

12.1 Trends in swimming participation, adults aged 15+,
      Australia, 2001–10   397

13.1 Confidence intervals related to sample size   398

13.2 Necessary sample sizes to achieve given
      confidence intervals   398

13.3 Sample size and population size: small populations   400

13.4 Interview/usage data from a site/visitor survey   401

13.5 Weighting   402

13.6 Selected qualitative sampling methods   402

14.1 Inequality and sport participation data, European
      countries, 2009   410

14.2 Basketball participation by age   413

14.3 Estimating demand for basketball   414

14.4 Facility utilisation data   415

14.5 Medals, population and GDP, London 2012 Olympic
      Games, top ten countries   418

14.6 Scores on nine measures of national performance,
      London 2012 Olympic Games   420

14.7 Nine measures of performance rank, London 2012
      Olympic Games   420

15.1 Psychological contract framework classification   449

15.2 Examples of psychological contract quotations   450

List of case studies

2.1	Tennis vs. golf – inductive and deductive approach	44
3.1	Example of successful self-generated research proposal	89
3.2	Example of a successful response to a research brief	94
4.1	Examples of ethical issues in sport research	109
6.1	Example of a meta-analysis methodology	180
8.1	Observing riots	231
10.1	Example questionnaires	304
11.1	Training patterns and performance	350
11.2	Visual and auditory cues and behaviour	350
11.3	Pre-competition stress	352
11.4	Sport participation promotion projects: review	353
11.5	Sport and crime reduction	354
11.6	Psychological/perceptual studies	355
11.7	Players and sporting equipment	356
11.8	Experiments with research methods	357
11.9	Children's physical play experiments	360
11.10	Discrete choice experiment: sport facility preferences of soccer attendees	361
12.1	Activity profile: swimming	377
12.2	Nike, advertising and women	379
12.3	Leisure, sport, lifestyle and the new middle class	380
12.4	The Beckham brand	381
12.5	Sponsorship	381
14.1	The Spirit Level and sport	409
14.2	Estimating likely demand for a sport facility	411
14.3	Facility utilisation	415

14.4   Facility catchment area   416

14.5   Olympic medals   417

14.6   The colour red and sporting success   420

15.1   Activity choice qualitative study   427

15.2   Using psychological contract to understand
        volunteer management in community sport clubs   448

Preface

The preparation of this book was prompted by the growing significance of courses in sport studies and sport management, both as stand-alone degrees and as majors in broader degrees. The aim is to introduce research methods both as a skill required by students planning a professional career in the public or private sport sector and as initial preparation for those embarking on research degrees. We seek to provide a 'how to do it' text and also to offer an understanding of how research findings are generated in order to assist students and practising managers to become knowledgeable consumers of the research of others.

Three software packages are used to demonstrate quantitative and qualitative data analysis (Excel, SPSS and NVivo). The particular packages selected did not arise as the result of a 'consumer test' of available packages, but are simply the packages with which we are familiar and which have been available to the students in the universities where we have taught. We can vouch for the usefulness of the packages demonstrated but are not in a position to compare the packages used with others available.

Regarding presentational style: we have sought, in the interests of readability, to reduce the amount of overt referencing in the body of the text, with references to literature offering examples of the use of various methods and techniques being provided in case studies or in the Resources sections at the end of each chapter.

The book is modelled on an existing text, *Research Methods for Leisure and Tourism: A Practical Guide* (Veal, 2011), following the same chapter structure, with much generic material in common and demonstration data sets and exercises adapted to apply to sport. An advantage of this is that in those institutions where sport studies students are taught together with leisure and tourism studies students, the specialist students can use their own subject-specific version of the text with relevant examples and source material.

Readers may wish to consult the online material available which includes:

● copies of all diagrams, tables and some dot-point lists in PowerPoint files;

● copies of statistical and qualitative data sets used in the book, plus others;

- extended versions of some case studies;
- errata – which will be corrected in reprints following discovery.

A. J. Veal
Simon Darcy
Sydney, December 2013

Reference
Veal, A. J. (2011) *Research Methods for Leisure and Tourism: A Practical Guide, Fourth edn*. Harlow, UK: Financial Times Prentice Hall.

Acknowledgements

We are grateful to the following for permission to reproduce copyright material:

Figures
Figure 7.10 from Shibli, S., & Bingham, J. (2005) Measuring the sporting success of nations. In Henry, I. (ed.), *Transnational and Comparative Research in Sport* (pp. 59–81). London: Routledge.; Figure 17.24 adapted from *Principles and Practice of Structural Equation Modelling*, Second Edition, Guilford Press (Kline, R. B. 2005).

Tables
Table 14.1 from *The Spirit Level: Why More Equal Societies Almost Always do Better*, Allen Lane (Wilkinson, R., & Pickett, K. 2009), Reproduced by permission of Penguin Books Ltd.

In some instances we have been unable to trace the owners of copyright material, and we would appreciate any information that would enable us to do so.

Part

Introduction and Preparation

This part of the book contains six chapters:

- Chapter 1, 'Introduction to research: what, why and who?' and Chapter 2, 'Approaches to research in sport', set the context, for research generally and for the background to research in the field of sport.

- Chapter 3, 'Starting out – research plans and proposals', considers the all-important process of designing a research project and provides a framework for the various components of research discussed in the rest of the book.

- Chapter 4 introduces the topic of the ethical conduct of research, which relates to moral as well as legal and administrative issues.

- Chapter 5, 'The range of research methods', provides an overview of the range of social science research methods and techniques used in sport contexts, and which are discussed in more detail in the rest of the book.

- Chapter 6 discusses the fundamental task of reviewing the literature, that is, examining existing published and unpublished research relevant to the project in hand.

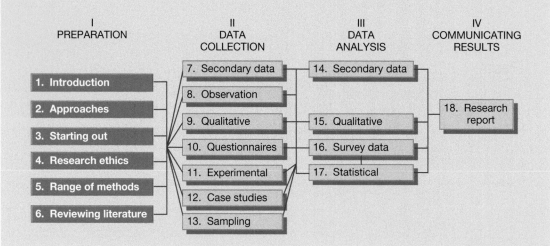

Introduction to research: what, why and who?

Introduction

Information, knowledge and understanding concerning the natural, social and economic environment have become the very basis of cultural and material development in contemporary societies and economies. Recent controversies over the research basis of global climate change predictions offer a dramatic demonstration of this. An understanding of how information and knowledge are generated and utilised and an ability to conduct or commission research relevant to the requirements of an organisation can therefore be seen as key skills for managers in any industry sector and a key component of the education of the modern professional. Research is, however, not just a set of disembodied skills; it exists and is practised in a variety of social, political and economic contexts. The purpose of this book is to provide an introduction to the world of social research in the context of sport, as an industry sector, a public policy concern and a field of academic enquiry and reflection. The aim is to provide a practical guide to the conduct of research and an appreciation of the role of research in the policy-making, planning and management processes of the sport sector and to foster a critical understanding of existing theoretical and applied research.

The focus of the book is sport. While research methodology can be seen as universal, various fields of research – including sport studies – have developed their own methodological emphases and bodies of experience. In some fields of enquiry scientific laboratory experiments are the norm, while in others social surveys are more common. While most of the principles of research are universal, a specialised text such as this reflects the traditions and practices in its field of focus and draws attention to examples of relevant applications of methods and the particular problems and issues which arise in such applications.

The field of sport is a large one, encompassing a wide range of individual and collective human activity. Sport can be defined as physical activity which is rule-based and competitive. Competition can be between individuals or teams or between individuals/teams and the environment, as in mountaineering and hunting. However, it overlaps with exercise activity, such as jogging or recreational swimming, which is neither rule-based nor competitive. Furthermore, some public policies and related research are concerned with the idea of exercise more broadly conceived, including exercise undertaken in non-leisure contexts, including domestically based work (e.g. gardening), travel (walking and cycling) and physical activity in workplaces (e.g. walking or lifting), as indicated in Figure 1.1. Sport can be viewed as an activity engaged in by individuals and groups, but also as a service industry involving public sector, non-profit and commercial organisations and facilities as diverse as small commercial gyms and major sport stadia. There is also a major overlap with the emerging field of *events studies*, with sporting events such as the Olympic Games and the soccer World Cup being among the largest peacetime events in the world. This is a major component of the phenomenon of *sport tourism* which covers active involvement in sporting activity – as in a skiing holiday – and passive involvement, such as travelling to attend a major sporting event as a spectator or fan.

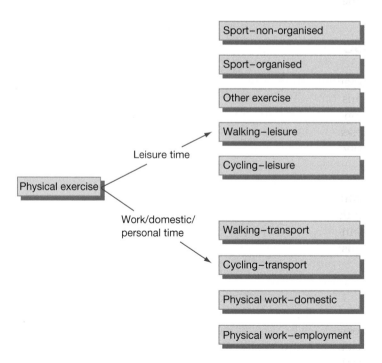

Figure 1.1 Physical exercise and sport

Most of the book is concerned with *how* to do research, so the aim of this opening chapter is to introduce the 'what, why and who' of research. What is it? Why study it? Who does it?

What is research?

Research defined

What is research? The sociologist Norbert Elias defined research in terms of its aims, as follows:

> The aim, as far as I can see, is the same in all sciences. Put simply and cursorily, the aim is to make known something previously unknown to human beings. It is to advance human knowledge, to make it more certain or better fitting ... the aim is ... discovery. *Elias (1986: 20)*

Discovery – making known something previously unknown – could cover a number of activities, for instance the work of journalists or detectives. Elias, however, also indicates that research is a tool of 'science' and that its purpose is to 'advance human knowledge' – features which distinguish research from other investigatory activities.

Scientific research

Scientific research is conducted within the rules and conventions of science. This means that it is based on logic and reason and the systematic examination of evidence. Ideally, within the scientific model, it should be possible for research to be *replicated* by the same or different researchers and for similar conclusions to emerge (although this is not always possible or practicable). It should also contribute to a cumulative body of knowledge about a field or topic. This model of scientific research applies most aptly in the physical or natural sciences, such as physics or chemistry, and in the biological sciences. In the area of *social science*, which deals with people as individuals and social beings with relationships to groups and communities, the pure scientific model must be adapted and modified, and in some cases largely abandoned.

Social science research

Social science research is carried out using the methods and traditions of social science. Social science differs from the physical or natural sciences in that it deals with *people* and their social behaviour, and people are less predictable than non-human phenomena. People can be aware of the research being conducted about them and are not therefore purely passive subjects; they can react to the results of research and change their behaviour accordingly. While the fundamental behaviour patterns of non-human phenomena are relatively constant and universal, people in different parts of the world and at different times behave differently. The social world is constantly changing, so it is rarely possible to produce exact replications of research at different times or in different places and obtain similar results.

Descriptive, explanatory and evaluative research

Elias' term *discovery* can be seen as, first, the process of finding out – at its simplest, therefore, research might just *describe* what exists. But to 'advance human knowledge, to make it more certain or better fitting' requires more than just the accumulation of information or facts. The aim is also to provide *explanation* – to explain why things are as they are, and how they might be. In this book, we are also concerned with a third function of research, namely *evaluating* – that is, judging the degree of success or value of policies or programmes. Three types of research can be identified corresponding to these three functions, as shown in Figure 1.2. In some cases particular research projects concentrate on only one of these, but often two or more of the approaches are included in the same research project.

1. Descriptive research

Descriptive research is very common in the sport area, for three reasons: the relative newness of the field, the changing nature of the phenomena being studied, and the frequent separation between research and action.

Since sport is a relatively new field of study, there is a need to map the territory. Much of the research therefore seeks to discover, describe or map patterns of behaviour in areas or activities which have not previously been studied in the field or for which information needs to be updated on a regular basis. It might therefore be described as *descriptive*. In some texts this form of research is termed *exploratory*. But because the other categories of research, including explanatory and evaluative, can also at times be exploratory, the term descriptive is used here.

1. Descriptive research	finding out, describing what is
2. Explanatory research	explaining *how* or *why* things are as they are (and using this to predict)
3. Evaluative research	evaluation of policies and programmes

Figure 1.2 Types of research

One of the reasons why descriptive research is required is that sport is constantly changing over time, for example:

- the popularity of different sports changes;
- the sporting preferences of different social groups (for example young people or women) change;
- new forms of sport are introduced, such as indoor versions of sports such as soccer and cricket;
- new technologies are introduced, for example hi-tech swimsuits;
- new/additional facilities are provided; and
- new policy initiatives are taken, for example in marketing or training of coaches.

A great deal of research effort in the field is therefore devoted to tracking – or monitoring – changing patterns of behaviour. Hence the importance in sport of secondary data sources, that is, data collected by other organisations, such as government statistical agencies **(see Chapter 7)**. A complete understanding and explanation of these changing patterns would be ideal, so that the future could be predicted, but this is only partially possible, so providers of sport services must be aware of changing social and market conditions whether or not they can be fully explained or understood; they are therefore reliant on a flow of descriptive research to provide up-to-date information.

Descriptive research is often undertaken because that is what is commissioned. For example, a company may commission a *market profile* study or a local council may commission a *sport and recreation needs* study from a research team – but the actual use of the results of the research, in marketing or planning, is a separate exercise with which the research team is not involved: the research team may simply be required to produce a descriptive study.

2. *Explanatory research*

Explanatory research moves beyond description to seek to explain the patterns and trends observed; for example, explanations might be required for:

- the falling popularity of a particular sport;
- community opposition to the hosting of a major sporting event;
- the fact that some social groups have particularly low levels of participation in sport.

Such questions raise the thorny issue of *causality:* the aim is to be able to say, for example, that there has been an increase in A because of a corresponding fall in B. It is one thing to discover that A has increased while B has decreased; but to establish that the rise in A has been *caused* by the fall in B is often a much more demanding task. To establish causality, or the likelihood of causality, requires the researcher to be rigorous in the collection, analysis and interpretation of data. It also generally requires some sort of theoretical framework to relate the phenomenon under study to wider social, economic and political processes. The issue of causality and the role of theory in research are discussed further in later chapters.

Once causes are, at least partially, understood the knowledge can be used to *predict*. This is clear enough in the physical sciences: we know that heat causes metal to expand (explanation) – therefore we know that if we apply a certain amount of heat to a bar of metal it will expand by a certain amount (prediction). In the biological and medical sciences this process is also followed, but with less precision: it can be predicted that if a certain treatment is given to patients with a certain disease then it is *likely* that a certain proportion will be cured. In the social sciences this approach is also used, but with even less precision. For example, economists have found that demand for goods and services, including sport goods and services, responds to price levels: if the price of a product or service is reduced then sales will generally increase. But this does not always happen because there are so many other factors involved – such as variation in quality and the success of brand marketing. Human beings make their own decisions and are far less predictable than non-human phenomena. Nevertheless, prediction is a key aim of much of the research that takes place in the area of sport.

3. Evaluative research

Evaluative research arises from the need to make judgements on the success or effectiveness of policies or programmes – for example whether a particular sporting facility or programme is meeting required performance standards or whether a particular promotion campaign has been cost-effective. In the private sector the level of sales and profit are the main criteria used for such evaluations, although additional ratios may also be used. In the public and non-profit sectors, where facilities or services are not usually intended to make a cash profit, research is required to assess community benefits and even, in some cases such as the use of public open space for physical exercise, to assemble data as elementary as levels of use. Evaluative research is highly developed in some areas of public policy, for example education, but is less well developed in the field of sport.

Why study research?

In general

Why study research? Research and research methods might be studied for a variety of reasons, as summarised in Figure 1.3.

1. Understanding research reports, etc.
2. To conduct academic research projects
3. Management tool in:
   - policy-making
   - planning
   - management (individual team/facility/organisation)
   - evaluation

Figure 1.3 Why study research?

- First, it is useful to be able to *understand* and *evaluate* research reports and articles encountered in an academic, professional or managerial context. It is advantageous to understand the basis and limitations of such reports and articles.

- Second, many readers of this book may engage in research in an academic environment, where research is conducted for its own sake, in the interests of the pursuit of knowledge – for example for a thesis.

- Third, most readers will find themselves conducting or commissioning research for professional reasons, as managers or consultants. It is therefore particularly appropriate to consider the role of research in the policy-making, planning and management process.

Of course, for many readers of this book, the immediate challenge is to complete a research-related project as part of an undergraduate or postgraduate programme of study. This book should, of course, assist in this task, but it is a means to an end, not an end in itself. Research projects conducted as part of a curriculum are seen as a learning process to equip the student as a professional consumer, practitioner and/or commissioner of research in professional life.

Research in policy-making, planning and management processes

All organisations, including those in the sport industries, engage in policy-making, planning and managing processes to achieve their goals. A variety of terms is used in this area and the meanings of terms vary according to the context and user. In this book:

- *policies* are considered to be the statements of principles, intentions and commitments of an organisation;

- *plans* are detailed strategies, typically set out in a document, designed to implement policies in particular ways over a specified period of time;

- *management* is seen as the process of implementing policies and plans.

Level	Governing body of sport	Community sport centre	Sport club
Policy	Host world championships	Maximise use by all age-groups	Develop junior competition
Plan	a. Develop key facilities b. Prepare/submit a bid	Two-year plan to increase visits by older people by 50%	Prepare strategy plan to recruit teams/ coaches and secure venues/sponsorship
Management	(If successful) Manage the championship event	Implement daily morning keep-fit sessions for older people	Implement the strategy

Figure 1.4   Examples of policies, plans and management

Although planning is usually associated in the public mind with national, regional and local government bodies, it is also an activity undertaken by the private sector. Organisations such as developers of bowling alleys or sport tourism venues are all involved in planning, but their planning activities are less public than those of government bodies. Private organisations are usually only concerned with their own activities, but government bodies often have a wider responsibility to provide a planning framework for the activities of many public and private sector organisations. Examples of policies, plans and management activity in sport contexts are given in Figure 1.4.

Both policies and plans can vary enormously in detail, complexity and formality. Here the process is considered only briefly in order to examine the part played by research. Of the many models of policy-making, planning and management processes that exist, the *rational-comprehensive* model, a version of which is depicted in Figure 1.5, is the most traditional, 'ideal' model. It is beyond the scope of this book to discuss the many alternative models which seek to more accurately reflect real-world decision-making, but guidance to further reading on this issue is given in the Resources section at the end of the chapter. Suffice it to say here that these alternatives are often 'cut-down' versions of the rational-comprehensive model, emphasising some aspects of this model and de-emphasising, or omitting, others. Thus some reflect the view that it is virtually impossible to be completely *comprehensive* in assessing alternative policies; some reflect the fact that political interests often intervene before 'rational' or 'objective' decisions can be made; while others elevate community/stakeholder consultation to a central rather than supportive role. In nearly all cases the models are put forward as an *alternative* to the rational-comprehensive model, so the latter, even if rejected, remains the universal reference point.

In most of these models a research role remains – sometimes curtailed and sometimes enhanced. It is rare that all of the steps shown in Figure 1.5 are followed through in the real world. And it is also rare for research to inform the

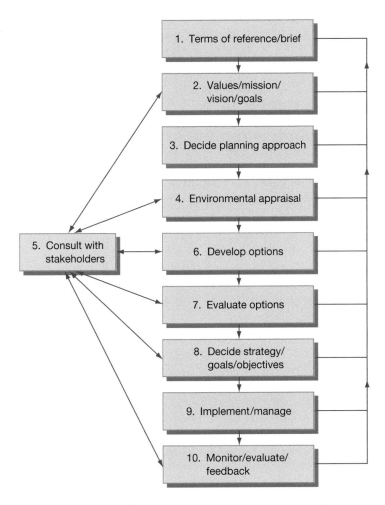

Figure 1.5   The rational-comprehensive planning/management process

process in all the ways discussed below. The steps depicted provide an agenda for discussing the many roles of research in policy-making, planning and management processes. Two examples of how the process might unfold in sport contexts are given in Figure 1.6.

1. *Terms of reference/brief:* The 'terms of reference' or 'brief' for a particular planning or management task sets out the scope and purpose of the exercise. Research can be involved right at the beginning of this process, in assisting in establishing the terms of reference. For example, existing research on low levels of sport participation in a community may result in a government policy initiative to do something about it.

2. *Values/mission/goals:* Statements of the mission or goals of the organisation may already be in place if the task in hand is a relatively minor one, but if it is a major undertaking, such as the development of a strategic plan for

| Steps in the process (see Figure 1.5) | Young people and sport in a local community | |
	Policy/planning/ management	Associated research
1. Terms of reference	Increase young people's participation in sport	Existing research indicates 40% participation rate.
2. Set goal	Increase participation level to 60% over 5 years	–
3. Decide planning approach	Needs-based, demand-based, etc: for discussion, see Veal (2010: Chapter 7)	As below.
4. Environmental appraisal	Consider existing supply–demand situation	Existing programmes and infrastructure fully used.
5. Consult stakeholders	Consult sporting clubs, schools, young people	Survey of groups: indicates support among all groups and confirms feasibility.
6. Develop options	a. Publicity campaign b. Free vouchers c. Build more community facilities d. Provide support to clubs/ schools e. Train leaders/coaches/ teachers	Review of experience of each option in other regions, based on published accounts and a survey.
7. Evaluate options	Evaluate options a–e	Each option costed; on basis of survey evidence, estimate made of cost-effectiveness of each option.
8. Decide strategy	Options c and d adopted	Options c and d recommended.
9. Implement/manage	Implement options c and d	–
10. Monitor/evaluate/ feedback	Assess success in terms of increased participation. Continue programme: increase resources for training coaches/leaders	Survey indicates participation increase to 45% after 1 year, but shortage of coaches/leaders.

Figure 1.6 **Example of planning/management tasks and associated research**

the whole organisation, then the development of statements of mission and goals may be involved. It is very much a task for the decision-making body of an organisation (such as the board, committee or council) to determine its mission and/or goals; research may be directly involved when consultation with large numbers of stakeholders is involved, as discussed under step 5.

3. *Decide planning approach:* Like research, a range of different methodologies and approaches is available for policy-making and planning, including: adopting externally specified fixed standards of provision; aiming to maximise opportunity; resource-based planning; meeting defined demand; meeting the requirements/requests of stakeholders; meeting unmet 'needs'; providing social or economic benefits; and aiming to increase participation (Veal, 2010: Chapter 7). The method/approach selected will determine the type of research to be carried out during the policy-making/planning process: for example, a needs-based approach will require a definition of need and a method for collecting information on needs, while resource-based planning will require identification of the range of built and/or environmental resources to be included, for example in an outdoor sport/recreation strategy, and processes for data gathering and evaluation.

4. *Environmental appraisal:* An environmental appraisal involves the gathering of relevant information on the physical, social, economic and organisational context of the task in hand. Information may relate to the organisation's internal workings or to the outside world, including actual and potential clients, and the activities of governments and competitors and physical resources. Such information may be readily to hand and may just need collation, or it may require extensive research.

5. *Consult with stakeholders:* Consultation with *stakeholders* is considered vital by most organisations and, indeed, is a statutory requirement in many forms of public sector planning. Stakeholders can include employees, clients, visitors, members of the general public, members of boards and councils, and neighbouring or complementary organisations. Research can be a significant feature of such consultation, especially when large numbers of individuals or organisations are involved.

6. *Develop options:* In order to develop a plan or strategy, consideration must be given to what policy options are available to pursue the goals of the organisation, their feasibility, their likely contribution to the achievement of the goals and the best way to implement them. Research can be involved in the process of *identifying* alternative policy or planning options, for example, by providing data on the extent of problems or on stakeholder preferences.

7. *Evaluate options:* Deciding on a strategy involves selecting a course or courses of action from among all the possible options identified. This choice process may involve a complex process requiring research to *evaluate* the alternatives. Typical formal evaluation techniques include cost–benefit analysis, economic impact analysis and environmental and social impact analysis, and the use of the *importance-performance* technique or *conjoint analysis* (see Resources section).

8. *Decide strategy/goals/objectives:* Evaluation processes rarely produce a single best solution or course of action. Thus, for example, option A may be cheaper than option B, but option B produces better outcomes. Final decisions on which strategy to pursue must be taken by the governing body of the organisation – the board, committee or council – based on political and/or personal values. A strategy should involve clear statements of what the strategy is intended to achieve (goals), with measurable outcomes and time-lines (objectives).

9. *Implement/manage:* Implementing a plan or strategy is the field of management. Research can be involved in day-to-day management, for example in investigating improved ways of deploying resources, and in providing continuous feedback on the management process, for example in the form of customer surveys. However, the line between such research and the monitoring and evaluation process is difficult to draw.

10. *Monitor/evaluate:* Monitoring progress and evaluating the implementation of strategies is clearly a process with which research is likely to be involved. The process comes full circle with the feedback step. The data from the monitoring and evaluation step can be fed back into the planning or management cycle and can lead to a revision of any or all of the decisions previously made. The monitoring and evaluation process may report complete success, it may suggest minor changes to some of the details of the policies and plans adopted, or it could result in a fundamental re-think, going 'back to the drawing board'.

Who does research?

This book is mainly concerned with how to conduct research, but it also aims to provide an understanding of the research process which will help the reader to become a knowledgeable, critical consumer of the research carried out by others. In reading reports of research, it is useful to bear in mind *why* the research has been done and to a large extent this is influenced by *who* did the research and *who paid* for it to be done. Who does research is important because it affects the nature of the research conducted and hence has a large impact on what constitutes the *body of knowledge* which students of sport must absorb and which sport managers draw on.

Sport research is undertaken by a wide variety of individuals and institutions, as listed in Figure 1.7. The respective roles of these research actors are discussed in turn below.

Group	Motivation/purpose
Academics	Part of the job description. Knowledge for its own sake and/or to engage with industry/profession and/or benefit society.
Students	Coursework students: projects as learning medium and/or part of professional training. Research students: adding to knowledge and training/qualification for a research/academic career.
Government, commercial and non-profit organisations	Research to inform policy, monitor performance and aid in decision-making. Relevant to the idea of 'evidence-based policy'.
Managers	Research to inform policy, monitor performance and aid in decision-making.
Consultants	Research under contract to government, commercial and non-profit organisations.

Figure 1.7 **Who does research?**

Academics

Academics are members of the paid academic staff of academic institutions, including professors, lecturers, tutors and research staff – in North American parlance: *the faculty*. In most academic institutions, professors and lecturers are expected, as part of their contract of employment, to engage in both research and teaching. Typically a quarter or third of an academic's time might be devoted to research and writing. Promotion and job security depend partly (some would say mainly) on the achievement of a satisfactory track record in published research. Publication can be in various forms, as discussed under 'outputs' below.

Some research arises from academic interest and some arises from immediate problems being faced by sport organisations. Much published academic research tends to be governed by the concerns of the various theoretical disciplines, such as sociology, economics or psychology, which may or may not coincide with the day-to-day concerns of the sport industry. In fact, part of the role of the academic researcher is to 'stand apart' from the rest of the world and provide disinterested analysis, which may be critical and may not be seen as particularly supportive by those working in the industry. However, what may be seen by some as overly critical and unhelpful, or just plain irrelevant, may be seen by others as insightful and constructive.

Applied disciplines such as the fields of urban planning, business management, marketing or financial management focus specifically on aspects of the policy, planning and management process. While academic research in these areas can also be critical rather than immediately instrumental, it is more likely to be driven by the sorts of issues which concern the industry. Generally academics become involved in funded research of a practically orientated nature when their own interests coincide with those of the agency concerned. For instance, an academic may be interested in ways of measuring what motivates people to engage in certain sporting activities and this could coincide with a sport organisation's need for research to assist in developing a marketing strategy. Academics who specialise in applied areas are very often in a better position to attract funding from industry sources.

Students

PhD and master's degree students are major contributors to research. Theses (or dissertations to use the term more common in North America) produced in recent years are mostly available in digital form and university libraries generally subscribe to various thesis databases **(see Chapter 6)**.

In the science area, research students often work as part of a team, under the direction of a supervisor who may determine what topics will be researched by individual students within a particular research programme. In the social sciences this approach is less common, with students having a wider scope in their selection of research topic.

PhD theses are the most significant form of student research, but research done by master's degree and graduate diploma students and even undergraduates in the form of projects and honours theses can be a useful contribution to knowledge. Sport is not generally well endowed with research funds, so even, for example, a small survey conducted by a group of undergraduates on a particular sport in a particular locality, or a thorough review of an area of literature, may be of considerable use or interest to others.

Government, commercial and non-profit organisations

Government, commercial and non-profit organisations conduct or commission research to inform policy, monitor performance or aid in decision-making. A term coined to describe this relationship between policy and research is *evidence-based policy* (Pawson, 2006). Some large organisations have their own in-house research organisations – for example, the Office for National Statistics in the UK and the Australian Bureau of Statistics in Australia. Commercial organisations in sport tend to rely on consultants for their social, economic and market research, although sport equipment manufacturers may conduct their own scientific research for product development.

Research reports from these organisations can be important sources of knowledge, especially of a more practically orientated nature. For example, in nearly every developed country some government agency takes responsibility for conducting nation-wide surveys of sport participation rates (Cushman *et al.*, 2005) **(see Chapter 7)**. This is descriptive research which few other organisations would have the resources or incentive to undertake.

- Current customers/members
- Market research: potential customers/community
- Environmental appraisal
- Organisational performance – Sales – Efficiency – Staff performance/motivation
- Competitors
- Products
  - Existing
  - New

Figure 1.8 Managers and research

Managers

Professionals in sport who recognise the full extent of the management, policy-making and planning process see research as very much part of their responsibilities. Managers may find themselves carrying out research on a range of types of topic, as indicated in Figure 1.8. Since many of the readers of this book will be actual or trainee managers, this is an important point to recognise.

Successful management depends on good information. Much information – for example sales or team performance figures – is available to the manager as a matter of routine and does not require *research*. However, the creative utilisation of such data – for example to establish market trends or seasonal patterns – may amount to research. Other types of information can only be obtained by means of specific research projects. In some areas of sport management even the most basic information must be obtained by research. For example, while managers of stadia or swimming pools routinely receive information on the level of use of their facilities from sales figures or bookings, this is not the case for the manager of a network of sport playing pitches leased to clubs. To gain information on the number of users of this type of facility it is necessary to conduct a specific data-gathering exercise. Such data gathering may not be very sophisticated and some would say that it does not qualify as *research*, being just part of the management information system, but in the sense that it involves *finding out*, sometimes *explaining*, and the deployment of specific techniques and skills, it qualifies as research for the purposes of this book.

Most managers need to carry out – or commission – research if they want information on their users or customers, for example where they come from (the 'catchment area' of the facility) or their socio-economic characteristics. Research is also a way of finding out about customers' evaluations of the facility or service.

It might be argued that managers do not themselves need research skills since they can always commission consultants to carry out research for them. However, managers will be better able to commission good research and evaluate the results if they are familiar with the research process themselves. It is also the case that few managers in sport work in an ideal world where funds exist to commission all the research they would like; often the only way managers can get research done is to do it using their own and colleagues' 'in-house' skills and time.

Consultants

Consultants offer their research and advisory services to government, commercial and non-profit organisations and industries. Some consultancy organisations are large, multinational companies involved in accountancy, management and project development consultancy generally, and who often establish specialised units covering the sport/leisure/events/tourism field. Examples are PricewaterhouseCoopers and Ernst and Young. But there are also many much smaller, specialised organisations in the consultancy field. Some academics operate consultancy companies as a 'sideline', either because of academic interest in a particular area or to supplement incomes or both. Self-employed consultancy activity is common among practitioners who have taken early retirement from sport industry employment.

Who pays?

Most research requires financial support to cover the costs of paying full-time or part-time research assistants, to pay for research student scholarships, to pay interviewers or a market research firm to conduct interviews, or to cover travel costs or the costs of equipment. Research is funded from a variety of sources, as indicated in Figure 1.9.

- *Unfunded:* Some research conducted by academics requires little or no specific financial resources over and above the academic's basic salary – for example theoretical work and the many studies using students as subjects.

- *University internal funds:* Universities tend to use their own funds to support research which is initiated by academic staff and where the main motive is the 'advancement of knowledge'. Most universities and colleges have research funds for which members of their staff can apply.

- Unfunded
- University internal funds
- Government-funded research councils
- Private trusts
- Industry – public, commercial or non-profit

Figure 1.9 Who pays?

● *Government-funded research councils:* Governments typically establish organisations to fund scientific research – for example the UK Economic and Social Research Council or the Australian Research Council or the National Health and Medical Research Council. These or similar bodies often also provide scholarships for research students.

● *Private trusts:* Many private trusts or foundations also fund research – for example the Ford Foundation and the Leverhulme Trust. Trusts have generally been endowed with investment funds by a wealthy individual or from a public appeal.

● *Industry:* Funds may come from the world of practice – for instance from a government department or agency, from a commercial company or from a non-profit organisation such as a governing body of a sport. In this case the research will tend to be more practically orientated. Government agencies and commercial and non-profit organisations fund research to solve particular problems or to inform them about particular issues relevant to their interests.

Research outputs

Research on sport planning/management is presented in many forms and contexts. Some of these are listed in Figure 1.10 and discussed briefly below. The formats are not all mutually exclusive: a number of them may arise in various aspects in a single research project.

- Academic journal articles
- Professional journal articles
- Conference presentations/papers
- Books
- Policy/planning/management reports
  - Position statements
  - Market profiles
  - Market research
  - Market segmentation/lifestyle/psychographic studies
  - Feasibility studies
  - Sport needs studies
  - Tourism strategies/marketing plans
  - Forecasting studies
  - Impact studies

Figure 1.10 Research report formats

Academic journal articles

Publication of research in academic journals is considered to be the most prestigious form in academic terms because of the element of *refereeing* or *peer review*. Articles submitted to such journals are assessed (refereed) on an anonymous basis by two or three experts in the field, as well as the editors. Editorial activity is overseen by a board of experts in the field, whose names are listed in the journal. Figure 1.11 contains a listing of refereed journals in the sport area.

In addition, sport features in a number of journals in cognate areas, such as leisure studies, tourism and events, and in mainstream disciplinary journals, such as in sociology, economics and psychology.

Academic research and publication is, to a large extent, a 'closed system'. Academics are the editors of the refereed journals and serve on their editorial advisory boards and referee panels. They therefore determine what research is acceptable for publication. Practitioners therefore very often find published academic research irrelevant to their needs – this is hardly surprising since much of it is not designed for the practitioner but for the academic world. Students training to become professional practitioners in the sport area should not therefore be surprised to come across scholarly writing on sport which is not suit-

- *European Sport Management Quarterly*
- *International Journal of Sport Management and Marketing*
- *International Journal of Sport Policy and Politics*
- *International Journal of Sport Psychology*
- *International Journal of Sports Marketing and Sponsorship*
- *International Review for the Sociology of Sport*
- *Journal of Applied Sport Psychology*
- *Journal of Sport and Social Issues*
- *Journal of Sport Behaviour*
- *Journal of Sport Economics*
- *Journal of Sport History*
- *Journal of Sport Management*
- *Review of Sport and Leisure*
- *Sociology of Sport Journal*
- *SportScience* (online)
- *Sport in Society*
- *Sport, Education and Society*
- *Sport Management Review*
- *Sport Marketing Quarterly*
- *Sporting Traditions*
- *The Sport Psychologist*

Figure 1.11 Refereed journals in sport

able for direct practical application to policy, planning and management. This does not mean that it is irrelevant, but simply that it does not necessarily focus explicitly on immediate practical problems.

Professional journal articles

Journals published by professional bodies for their members rarely publish original research, but may publish summaries of research of immediate relevance to practitioners.

Conference papers/presentations

Some academic conferences publish the papers presented in a hard-copy or on-line set of *proceedings.* In some cases such papers have been peer reviewed and have a similar status to academic journals, but this is rare in sport. Typically research presented at conferences will also be published in journals or book form.

Books

Academic books can be divided into *textbooks*, like this one, and *monographs*, which may present the results of a single empirical research project or research programme, may be largely theoretical or may be a mixture of the two. Textbooks are not expected to present original research but may provide summaries and guides to research. Edited books with chapters contributed by a number of authors may be closer to the textbook model, or, if they contain original research, may be closer to the monograph model.

Policy/planning/management reports

Research conducted by commercial bodies is usually confidential but that conducted by government agencies is generally available to the public, increasingly via the Internet. Such reports can invariably be found on the websites of national agencies, such as sport councils or tourism commissions and government departments, and local councils. Such reports can take a variety of forms.

Position statements

Position statements are similar to the *environmental appraisals* discussed above in relation to the rational-comprehensive planning model. They are compilations of factual information on the current situation with regard to a topic or issue of concern, and are designed to assist decision-makers to become knowledgeable about the topic or issue and to take stock of such matters as current policies, provision levels and demand. For example, if a local authority wishes to develop new policies for sport in its area, a position statement might be prepared listing the sport clubs in the area and their memberships, the commercial outlets for sport and all facilities, their ownership, size, quality and usage, and patterns of participation among the resident population.

Market profiles

Market profiles are similar to position statements, but relate specifically to current and potential consumers and suppliers of a product or service. If an organisation wishes to start a project in a particular sport market it will usually require a profile of that market sector. How big is it, in terms of sales? What are its growth prospects? Who are the customers? What sub-sectors does it have? How profitable is it? Who are the current suppliers? Such a profile will usually require considerable research and can be seen as one element in the broader activity of market research.

Market research

Market research is a more encompassing activity than a market profile. Research on the actual or potential market for a product or service can take place in advance of a service being established but also as part of the ongoing monitoring of the performance of an operation. Market research seeks to establish the scale and nature of the current market – the number of people who use or are likely to use the product or service, their expenditure and their characteristics – and actual and potential customer requirements, attitudes and motivations.

Market segmentation/lifestyle/psychographic studies

Traditionally market researchers attempted to classify consumers into sub-markets or segments on the basis of their product preferences, including sporting activities, and their socio-demographic characteristics such as age, gender, occupation and income. Later they sought to classify people using not only these background social and economic characteristics but also data on their attitudes, values and behaviour. Such *lifestyle segments* may be developed as part of any survey-based research project, but there are also commercially developed systems which survey companies may apply to a range of market research projects.

Feasibility studies

Feasibility studies investigate not only current consumer characteristics and demands, as in a market profile, but also future demand and such aspects as the financial viability and environmental impact of proposed developments or investment projects. The decision whether or not to build a new sport facility or product is usually based on a feasibility study.

Sport/recreation needs studies

Sport/recreation needs studies are a common type of research in local planning, covering sport and informal outdoor recreation, such as visiting parks. If 'leisure' rather than 'recreation' is used, arts/cultural activities may be involved. These are comprehensive studies, usually carried out for local councils, examining levels of provision and use of facilities and services, levels of participation in recreational activities, and views and aspirations of the population concerning their own recreation preferences and desired provision. In some cases a needs study also includes a recreation or sport and recreation 'plan', which makes recommendations on future provision; in other cases the plan is in a separate document. It has been argued that so-called recreation needs studies are not *needs* studies at all, since they do not investigate what people need, but what they *want*, would *like to do* or *might do* in the future (Veal, 2010: 45–56).

Tourism strategies/tourism marketing plans

Tourism strategies/tourism marketing plans are the tourism equivalent of the sport/recreation needs study. They often cover sporting activity, for example if they include snow sports, adventure recreation, water sports or special events. Indeed, the area of sport tourism is a significant and growing sector. Rather than referring to the *needs* of the local population, tourism strategies or marketing plans refer to the tourism *demands* of non-local populations to be accommodated in a destination area. Such tourism studies usually consider the capacity of the host area to meet the demands of a projected number of tourists, in terms of accommodation, transport, existing and potential attractions and acceptable levels of environmental impacts.

Forecasting studies

Forecasting studies form a key input to many plans. They might provide, for example, projections of demand for a particular sport or group of sports (e.g. water sports) over a ten-year period. Forecasting is intrinsically research based and can involve predicting the likely effects of future population growth and change, the effects of changing tastes, changing levels of income or developments in technology.

Impact studies

Large built developments typically require an environmental impact study to be undertaken as part of the process of gaining approval from planning agencies, covering matters such as noise, traffic generation and impacts on wildlife and cultural heritage. A common occurrence in the case of major events, particularly sporting and cultural events, is the conduct of an economic impact study to demonstrate that the costs incurred by the hosting of an event will be, or has been, offset by benefits, such as the generation of income and jobs and other types of legacy.

Dissemination

Some of these types of documents are published, particularly when public agencies are involved, when they are typically made available on agency websites, often with invitations for public comment. In same cases, such as position statements and forecasting studies, they are inputs into later documents, such as strategic plans. Some may also appear, in summary form, in academic publications, in articles and as case studies in textbooks.

Terminology

Like any field of study and practice, research methods has its own distinct terminology, some of which is familiar to the wider community and some of which is not. Most terms and expressions will be introduced and defined in the appropriate chapters which follow; but some are common to the whole research process and two key ones are described here.

Subject is used to refer to people providing information or being studied in a research project. For example, if a social survey involves interviews with a sample of 200 people, it involves 200 subjects. Some researchers prefer to use of the term participant, believing that subject implies subjective, suggesting a hierarchical relationship between the researcher and the researched. The term 'case' is sometimes used, particularly when the phenomenon being researched is not individual people – for example, organisations, countries, destinations, sports.

Variable refers to a characteristic, behaviour pattern or opinion which varies from subject to subject. Thus, for example, age, income, level of exercise or sport preferences are all variables. An independent variable is one which is controlled by forces outside the context of the study, and influences dependent variables within the scope of the study. Thus, for example, in a study of outdoor sport the weather would be an independent variable while the number of people who play soccer is a dependent variable. In another context, such as the study of climate, the weather could be a dependent variable influenced by such independent variables as the behaviour of the sun and the temperature of the oceans.

Using this book

The aim in compiling this book has been to be as comprehensive as possible, to cater for a wide range of potential users and to provide guidance in relation to the diversity of material and issues which readers are likely to encounter in their own reading and research practice. Most users will therefore be selective in their use of the various parts of the book, depending on their interests, needs and time available. Often this process of selection will be guided by a teacher or supervisor. The various summary tables and detailed table of contents and index are designed to aid the process of selection and the use of the book as a reference work. It should be emphasised that substantial sections of the book are designed as a working manual to be used alongside actual research activity: this applies particularly to the detailed outline of the research process **(Chapter 3)** and to the analysis chapters involving computer software **(Chapters 15–17)**.

In Part I, a great deal of material of a general nature is covered. Just a limited number of sporting examples or illustrations are given, but references are provided to some in the Resources sections and users of the book are encouraged to explore their own examples and applications in the questions and exercises. The uses of specific methods are referred to in illustrative examples in case studies in Parts II and III (see listing in the book's list of contents).

Summary

This chapter addresses the 'What?' of research in defining and introducing the concept of research and describes three types of research with which this book is concerned: descriptive, explanatory and evaluative. The 'Why?' of research is discussed primarily in the context of policy-making, planning and management, since the majority of the users of the book will be studying for a vocational qualification. The links between research and the various stages of policy-making, planning and management are discussed using the rational-comprehensive model as a framework, and attention is drawn to the variety of forms that research reports can take in the management environment. 'Who?' conducts research is an important and often neglected aspect of research: in this chapter, the respective research roles of academics, students, governmental and commercial organisations, consultants and managers are discussed. Finally, there is an introduction to the various formats in which research results may be published, from academic journal articles to a variety of management-related reports.

Test questions

1. What is the difference between research and journalism?

2. Outline the differences between descriptive, explanatory and evaluative research; suggest sport-related examples of each.

3. Summarise the potential role of research in three of the ten steps in the 'rational-comprehensive' model of the policy-making/planning/management process presented in this chapter.

4. Name three of the 13 formats which research reports might take, as put forward in this chapter, and outline their basic features.

5. Outline three of the six topics, as put forward in this chapter, on which managers might conduct or commission research, giving your own sport-related examples.

6. Why does academic research often appear to be irrelevant to the needs of practitioners?

Exercises

1. Choose a sport organisation with which you are familiar and outline ways in which it might use research to pursue its objectives.

2. Choose a sport organisation and investigate its research activities. What proportion of its budget does it devote to research? What research has it carried out? How are the results of the research used, by the organisation or others?

3. Take an edition of a sport journal, such as one of those listed on page 20, and ascertain, for each article: why the research was conducted; how it was funded; and who or what organisations are likely to benefit from the research and how.

4. Repeat exercise 3, but using an edition of a journal outside the sport field, for example a sociology journal or a physics journal.

5. Using the same journal edition as in 3 above, examine each article and determine whether the research is descriptive, explanatory or evaluative.

Resources

- Evaluative research: Atkinson (2012: 74–80), Coalter (2007, 2010), Jennings (2011), Mertens (2009), Pollard (1987), Riddick and Russell (1999), Shadish *et al.* (1991), Veal (2010: Chapters 12, 13).

- Exploratory research: Stebbins (1997).

- Evidence-based policy: Atkinson (2012: 80–5), Coalter (2007), Downward *et al.* (2009), Solesbury (2002), Pawson (2006), Ruiz (2004).

- Feasibility studies: Westerbeek *et al.* (2005), Stewart (2012).

- Importance-performance technique: Howat *et al.* (1996), Martilla and James (1977), Rial *et al.* (2008), Zhang *et al.* (2011).

- Models of planning and policy-making: introductory discussions: Parsons (1995: 248ff), Veal (2010: Chapters 7–8).

- Research in the planning process: Getz (2003).

- Segmentation/psychographics/lifestyle: Funk (2002), Mullin *et al.* (2007), Pitts *et al.* (1994), Salome and Van Bottenburg (2012).

- Sport forecasting: Bauman *et al.* (2010), Mallios (2000), Stekler *et al.* (2010), Veal *et al.* (2012).

- Theory, research and practice: sport management: Doherty (2013), Irwin and Ryan (2013).

- Terminology: Atkinson (2012).

- Tracking change in sport/physical recreation participation: Nicholson *et al.* (2011), Veal (2003), Cushman *et al.* (2005).

References

Atkinson, M. (2012) *Key Concepts in Sport and Exercise Research Methods.* London: Sage.

Bauman, A., Owen, N. and Rushworth, R. L. (2010) Recent trends and socio-demographic determinants of exercise participation in Australia. *Community Health Studies*, 14(1), 19–26.

Coalter, F. (2007) *A Wider Role for Sport? Who's Keeping the Score?* London: Routledge.

Coalter, F. (2010) The politics of sport-for-development: limited focus programmes and broad gauge problems? *International Review for the Sociology of Sport*, 45(3), 295–314.

Cushman, G., Veal, A. J. and Zuzanek, J. (eds) (2005) *Free Time and Leisure Participation: International Perspectives.* Wallingford, UK: CABI.

Doherty, A. (2013) Investing in sport management: the value of good theory. *Sport Management Review*, 16(1), 5–11.

Downward, P., Dawson, A. and Dejonghe, T. (2009) *Sports Economics: Theory, Evidence and Policy.* Oxford: Butterworth-Heinemann.

Elias, N. (1986) Introduction. In N. Elias and E. Dunning *Quest for Excitement: Sport and Leisure in the Civilising Process.* Oxford: Basil Blackwell, 19–62.

Funk, D. (2002) Consumer-based marketing: the use of micro-segmentation strategies for understanding sport consumption. *International Journal of Sports Marketing and Sponsorship*, 4(3), 231–56.

Getz, D. (2003) Sport event tourism: planning, development and marketing. In S. Hudson (ed.) *Sport and Adventure Tourism.* Binghampton, NY: Haworth, 49–88.

Howat, G., Absher, J., Crilley, G. and Milne, I. (1996) Measuring customer service quality in sports and leisure centres. *Managing Leisure*, 1(2), 77–89.

Irwin, R. L. and Ryan, T. D. (2013) Get real: using engagement with practice to advance theory transfer and production. *Sport Management Review*, 16(1), 12–16.

Jennings, G. (2011) Evaluation research methods in leisure, recreation and tourism research. In E. Sirakaya-Turk, M. Uysal, W. E. Hammitt and J. J. Vaske (eds) *Research Methods for Leisure, Recreation and Tourism.* Wallingford, UK: CABI, 140–61.

Mallios, W. S. (2000) *The Analysis of Sports Forecasting: Modelling Parallels between Sports Gambling and Financial Markets.* London: Kluwer.

Martilla, J. A. and James, J. C. (1977) Importance-performance analysis. *Journal of Marketing*, 41(1), 77–9.

Mertens, D. M. (2009) *Transformative Research and Evaluation.* New York: Guilford Press.

Mullin, B. J., Hardy, S. and Sutton, W. A. (2007) *Sport Marketing.* Champaign, IL: Human Kinetics.

Nicholson, M., Hoye, R. and Houlihan, B. (eds) (2011) *Participation in Sport: International Policy Perspectives.* Abingdon, UK: Routledge.

Parsons, W. (1995) *Public Policy.* Cheltenham, UK: Edward Elgar.

Pawson, R. (2006) *Evidence-based Policy: A Realist Perspective.* London: Sage.

Pitts, B. G., Fielding, L. and Miller, L. (1994) Industry segmentation theory and the sport industry: developing a sport industry segment model. *Sport Marketing Quarterly*, 3(1), 15–24.

Pollard, W. E. (1987) Decision making and the use of evaluation research. *American Behavioral Scientist*, 30(6), 661–76.

Rial, A., Rial, J., Varela, J. and Real, E. (2008) An application of importance-performance analysis (IPA) to the management of sport centres. *Managing Leisure*, 13(3–4), 179–88.

Riddick, C. C. and Russell, R. V. (1999) *Evaluative Research in Recreation, Park, and Sport Settings: Searching for Useful Information.* Champaign, IL: Sagamore.

Ruiz, J. (2004) *A Literature Review of the Evidence Base for Culture, the Arts and Sport Policy*. Edinburgh: Social Research, Scottish Executive, available at: www.scotland.gov.uk/Resource/Doc/17002/0023718.pdf (Accessed May 2013).

Salome, L. and Van Bottenburg, M. (2012) Are they all daredevils? Introducing a participation typology for the consumption of lifestyle sports in different settings. *European Sport Management Quarterly*, 12(1), 19–42.

Shadish, W. R., Jr, Cook, T. D. and Leviton, L. C. (1991) *Foundations of Program Evaluation: Theories of Practice*. Newbury Park, CA: Sage.

Solesbury, W. (2002) The ascendancy of evidence. *Planning Theory and Practice*, 3(1), 90–6.

Stebbins, R. A. (1997) Exploratory research as an antidote to theoretical stagnation in leisure studies. *Society and Leisure*, 20(2), 421–34.

Stekler, H. O., Sendor, D. and Verlander, R. (2010) Issues in sports forecasting. *International Journal of Forecasting*, 26(3), 606–21.

Stewart, B. (2012) *Sport Funding and Finance*. London: Routledge.

Veal, A. J. (2003) Tracking change: leisure participation and policy in Australia, 1985–2002. *Annals of Leisure Research*, 6(3), 246–78.

Veal, A. J. (2010) *Leisure, Sport and Tourism: Politics, Policy and Planning*. Wallingford, UK: CABI.

Veal, A. J., Toohey, K. and Frawley, S. (2012) The sport participation legacy of the Sydney 2000 Olympic Games and other international sporting events hosted in Australia. *Journal of Policy Research in Tourism, Leisure and Events*, 4(2), 155–84.

Westerbeek, H., Smith, A., Turner, P., Emry, P., Green, C. and Van Leeuwen, L. (2005) *Managing Sport Facilities and Major Events*. Sydney: Allen & Unwin.

Zhang, J. J., Lam, E. T. C., Cianfrone, B. A., Zapalac, R. K., Holland, S. and Williamson, D. P. (2011) An importance-performance analysis of media activities associated with WNBA game consumption. *Sport Management Review*, 14(1), 64–78.

Approaches to research in sport

Introduction

The aim of this chapter is to introduce a range of disciplines and paradigms within which sport research is conducted. The chapter examines:

● *Disciplinary traditions*: reviews of a number of academic disciplines and their approaches to sport research, including sociology, economics, geography, psychology, social psychology, history and philosophy.

● *Terminology: approaches, dimensions, issues:* examination of a number of mainly dichotomous concepts which characterise research approaches and methods.

Disciplinary traditions

The bulk of published sport research has arisen, not from the demands of the sport industries, but from the interests of academics who owe allegiance to a particular discipline. Here we examine, very briefly, the contributions by academic disciplines that have been particularly significant in the field, namely:

- sociology and cultural studies
- economics
- geography/environmental studies
- psychology/social psychology
- history and anthropology
- political science.

Disciplines are characterised by the particular aspect or dimension of the universe with which they are concerned, the theories which they develop for explanation and the distinctive techniques they use for conducting research. Some commentators refer to sport studies as a discipline, but, since it does not meet the criteria for a free-standing discipline, in this book it is seen as a multidisciplinary, cross-disciplinary or interdisciplinary *field of study*.

- *Multidisciplinary* means that research from a number of disciplines is used – for example the economics and the sociology of sport.
- *Cross-disciplinary* means that issues, theories, concepts and methods which are common to more than one discipline are involved – for example the *cross-disciplinary dimensions* discussed later in this chapter.
- *Interdisciplinary* refers to sub-fields of research which do not fit neatly into any particular discipline – for example time-budget research.

When reading in the area of sport studies it should be noted that not all commentators keep the wide mix of disciplines consistently in mind. For example, when making comments on 'sport studies' they may in fact be discussing only 'the sociology of sport'.

We should also note other fields of study which are generally longer established than sport studies and which are sometimes referred to as disciplines, sometimes as 'applied disciplines' and sometimes as fields of study. These include:

- physical education
- management
- marketing
- planning.

Despite the importance of these fields of study for professional practitioners in the sport sectors, they are not examined separately in this chapter because, for research purposes, they generally draw, to varying degrees, on the methods associated with the six disciplines listed above.

The relationships between sport research and the six disciplines are summarised in Figure 2.1, which presents examples of descriptive, explanatory and evaluative research topics/questions addressed by each discipline in relation to sport.

Descriptive	Explanatory	Evaluative
Sociology		
• What proportions of the population and of various socio-economic groups participate in specified sports activities? • What are the trends in the numbers playing team sports over the last ten years?	• Why do members of middle-class, highly educated groups make greater use of sport facilities than members of other groups? • What factors influence trends in individual sports as compared with team sports?	• To what extent have policies designed to boost women's participation in sport been successful? • How successful was the hosting of an international sporting event in increasing employment and incomes?
Geography/environment		
• What is the spatial area from which most users of a particular sport facility travel? • What impacts does a particular golf resort have on the environment?	• What is the relative importance of distance and travel time in affecting use of a particular sport facility?	• How effective is the local council in meeting the sport demands of all neighbourhoods in its area? • How effective is the local tourism strategy in protecting the environment from the impacts of sport tourism in the area?
Economics		
• What proportion of household expenditure is devoted to sports goods and services? • What proportion of the labour force works in the sport sector?	• What is the relationship between level of income and expenditure on sport? • What is the relationship between travel cost and level of visits to a sport facility?	• What are the costs and benefits of hosting the Olympic Games? • What has been the economic impact of developing a sport-tourism project at destination X?
Psychology/social psychology		
• What satisfactions do people obtain from engaging in sport? • What is the level of stress among teenagers regarding body image?	• To what extent is Maslow's hierarchy of need theory relevant to sport? • Does sporting activity relieve stress? If so, how lasting is this?	• How effective has a youth sports programme been in enhancing participants' self-esteem? • How effective has a marketing policy been in boosting sport participation?
History/anthropology		
• How has the role of sport in shaping national identity changed over the last 25 years? • What is the history of the Olympic Games?	• What was the influence of marketing and sponsorship on sport over the last 25 years? • What has caused the growth in sport gambling over the last 25 years?	• How successful have public policies to increase physical activity been over the last 25 years? • Over the last 25 years, have governments helped or hindered the development of sport?
Political/policy science		
• What are the sport/physical recreation policies of the major political parties? • What proportion of publicly owned sports facilities are managed by commercial contract?	• How has changing political philosophy affected sport policies in the last two changes of government? • How is power exercised in sport contexts?	• How effective are policies directed at 'inclusion' in increasing sport participation? • How effective have joint public–private partnerships been in sport development?

Figure 2.1 Disciplines and examples of research questions

Approaches, dimensions, issues, terminology

A number of approaches, dimensions, issues and associated terminology recur in the research literature and discourses on research, and at least a basic understanding of them is necessary if the literature and the discourses are to be understood. They are listed in Figure 2.2. Those terms which arise in pairs, X and Y, are often presented in the literature as X *versus* Y. But X and Y are not always opposed to one another; they are often complementary, so here the form X *and* Y is used. It is not possible to analyse all the terms and concepts in detail in this introductory chapter, especially given that definitions

Pairs/groups	Brief definition of terms	Associated terms
Ontology	Way of looking at the world	Paradigm, philosophy
Epistemology	Relationship between researcher and the subject of research	
Method	Ways of gathering and analysing data	Technique
Positivist	Hypotheses are tested using objectively collected factual data which, if successful, produces scientific laws	Scientific method, logical empiricist, functionalist, objectivist
Post-positivist	Hypotheses found to be consistent (or not) with the data deemed to be 'not falsified', establishing probable facts or laws	
Interpretive	People provide their own accounts or explanation of situation/behaviour	Phenomenology, phenomenography, symbolic interaction, intersubjectivity, ethnography, subjectivist, grounded theory
Critical	Research influenced by beliefs/values critical of the status quo in society	Standpoint, emancipatory, transformative
Constructivist	People construct their own views of reality and the researcher seeks to discover this	Social constructivism
Descriptive	Seeks to describe what is	Exploratory
Explanatory	Seeks to explain causal relationships between phenomena	Predictive
Evaluative	Seeks to test policy/management outcomes against benchmarks	Evidence-based
Qualitative	Research in which words (and possibly images, sounds) are the medium	
Quantitative	Research in which numbers are the main medium	
Pragmatism	No commitment to particular research approaches: emphasis on *experience* and *practicality* as key criteria	Mixed methods, eclecticism, *bricolage*
Participatory	Researcher and subjects jointly influence the pattern of research	Action research (see Chapter 5)

Figure 2.2   Terminology: approaches/dimensions/issues

Pairs/groups	Brief definition of terms	Associated terms
Theoretical	Research which results in general propositions about how things/people behave	Pure
Applied	Use of research to address particular policy/ management issues	Evidence-based
Experimental	Research where the researcher seeks to control all variables	Controlled experiment
Naturalistic	Research where subjects are researched in their 'natural' environment where the researcher's control is minimal	Real-life context
Reflexive	The process of examining the relationship between the researcher and the subject of the research	Intersubjective
Empirical	Research involving data – quantitative or qualitative or both	
Non-empirical	Research involving only theory and the literature	Theoretical
Inductive	Hypotheses/explanations/theories are generated from examination of the data	Exploratory
Deductive	Data collected to test *a priori* hypotheses	Hypothetical-deductive, confirmatory
Primary data	Data gathered by the researcher for the current project	
Secondary data	Use of existing data gathered by other people/ organisations for other purposes	
Self-reported	Subjects' own accounts of activity/behaviour	
Observed	Researcher's observation of subjects' activity/ behaviour	Unobtrusive
Validity	The research accurately identifies/measures what is intended	
Reliability	Repetition of the research would produce similar findings	
Trustworthiness	Trust which can be placed in qualitative research	

Figure 2.2 *(continued)*

vary in the literature. The coverage is quite extensive and can be viewed as a reference source for future consultation. Additional sources are provided in the Resources section of the chapter.

Ontology, epistemology, methodology

Ontology, epistemology and methodology are frequently encountered in discussions of research approaches, particularly in sociology.

● *Ontology* refers to the nature of reality assumed by the researcher – in the positivist paradigm (see below) the researcher assumes that the 'real world' being studied is as seen by the researcher, while in interpretive and similar approaches the researcher's perspective is not privileged: emphasis is placed on the varying views and realities as perceived by the people being studied.

- *Epistemology* refers to the relationship between the researcher and the phenomenon being studied – again the distinction is most sharply drawn between the positivist and interpretive stance, with the former seeking to adopt an objective, distanced stance, while the interpretive researcher is more subjective and engaged with the subjects of the study.

- *Methodology* refers to the ways by which knowledge and understanding are established: research methods. For example, the method used in the classic positivist approach is the controlled experiment (as discussed below), which is only possible in certain sport research contexts. The quantitative and qualitative divide, as discussed below, also offers distinctive methodologies. Ideally the choice of method in a study should be closely influenced by the ontological and epistemological perspectives used.

Positivist, post-positivist, interpretive and critical approaches/paradigms

The positivism, post-positivism and interpretive and critical approaches refer to *paradigms* in the social sciences which are ways of looking at the theoretical/research world.

- *Positivism* is a framework of research, similar to that adopted by the natural scientist, in which the researcher sees the phenomena to be studied from the outside, with behaviour to be explained on the basis of data and observations objectively gathered by the researcher, using theories and models developed by the researcher. The classic positivist approach uses the *hypothetical-deductive* model, a deductive process (as discussed below), to test a pre-established hypothesis. If successful, this results in the establishment of 'laws' – for example, Newton's laws of motion. Many commentators in the social sciences are highly suspicious of such attempts to translate natural science approaches into the social world, arguing that it is inappropriate to draw conclusions about the causes and motivations of *human* behaviour on the basis of the type of evidence used in the natural sciences. Anthony Giddens (1974: 2) pointed out that in the social sciences by the 1970s the term 'positivist' had almost become a term of abuse.

- *Post-positivism* is distinguished from the classic positivist approach by some writers (e.g. Guba and Lincoln, 2006) as an approach in which hypotheses found to be consistent with the data are deemed to be 'not falsified'; researchers do not claim to have discovered the 'truth' but to have established *probable* facts or laws which are useful until such time as they are supplanted by new theories/laws which provide a fuller or more comprehensive explanation of the available data.

- *Interpretive* approaches to research place reliance on people providing their own explanations of their situation or behaviour. The interpretive researcher tries to 'get inside' the minds of subjects and see the world from their point of view. This of course suggests a more flexible approach to data collection, usually involving qualitative methods and generally an inductive approach. A number of variations exist within this category, as indicated in the 'associated terms' column in Figure 2.2 **(these are discussed in Chapter 9)**.

- *Critical* approaches to research are influenced by particular sets of beliefs or values which are critical of the *status quo* in society: the most common in sport are neo-Marxist perspectives, which are critical of the capitalist system, and various feminist perspectives, which are critical of the economic, social and political inequality between men and women. There are numerous other perspectives which researchers may adopt or causes with which they may be associated. One term used for research shaped by such commitments is *standpoint research* (Hartsock, 1999), related particularly to feminism, while Karla Henderson (2009) has used the term '*just* research' to refer to research which is not only *about* diversity and inclusiveness but is committed to it. Other terms include *emancipatory* research (Antonio, 1989), which is committed to emancipation of society from oppressive forces; and *transformative* research, which is seen as a 'metaphysical umbrella' (Mertens, 2009: 13) for a number of areas of research which are committed to transforming society to achieve social justice in areas such as gender, race, class and disability.

Along with parallel debates on quantitative and qualitative research, there is much debate in sport studies on the relative merits, suitability and appropriateness of the above alternative approaches to research. However, since sport researchers are generally all using a combination of theory and empirical evidence to draw conclusions about sport phenomena, the question arises as to how great the underlying, as opposed to surface, differences are between these approaches. Allen Lee (1989) has explored this issue and, using the terms 'subjectivist' and 'objectivist', argues that a subjectivist case study in organisation studies has similarities to the classic scientific experiment, which is usually seen as positivist and quantitative.

Descriptive, explanatory and evaluative research

In Chapter 1 the differences between descriptive, explanatory and evaluative research were discussed and it is appropriate to raise the issue again here.

- *Descriptive* research aims to describe, as far as possible, what is. The focus is not on explanation. Another term which might be used here is *exploratory*, although exploratory research could also extend to attempts at explanation.

- *Explaining* the patterns in observed or reported data usually involves establishing that one phenomenon is caused by another, and the aim of research is to identify these causal relationships. For example, where descriptive research might show that a sport is losing participants, explanatory research would seek to establish whether this was caused by, for example, competition from another sport or changing demographics. Explanation can often provide the basis for *prediction.*

- *Evaluative* research seeks to assess the success of policy or management action – for example, the effects of a marketing campaign.

These issues raise the question of *causality:* whether or not A causes B. Labovitz and Hagendorn (1971: 4) state that there are 'at least four widely accepted scientific criteria for establishing causality. These criteria are association, time priority, nonspurious relation and rationale.'

- *Association* is a 'necessary condition for a causal relation' – that is, A and B must be associated in some way, for example, A increases when B decreases. 'There are two characteristics of an association that generally strengthen the conclusion that one variable is at least a partial cause of another. The first is magnitude, which refers to the size or strength of the association … The second … is consistency. If the relation persists from one study to the next under a variety of conditions, confidence in the causal nature of the relation is increased' (Labovitz and Hagendorn, 1971: 5).

- *Time priority* means that for A to be the cause of B, then A must take place before B.

- *Non-spurious relationships* are defined as associations between two variables that 'cannot be explained by a third variable' (Labovitz and Hagendorn, 1971: 9). This means that it must be established that there is no third factor, C, which is affecting both A and B.

- *Rationale* means that statistical or other evidence is not enough; the conclusion that A causes B is not justified simply on the basis of an observed relation; it should be supported by some plausible, theoretical or logical explanation to suggest how it happens.

Qualitative and quantitative research

Much sport research involves the collection, analysis and presentation of statistical information. Sometimes the information is innately quantitative – for example the numbers of people engaging in a list of sport activities in a year, the amount of money spent by spectators at sport events or the average income of a group of people. Sometimes the information is qualitative in nature but is presented in quantitative form – for instance numerical scores obtained by asking people to indicate levels of satisfaction with different services, where the scores range from 1, 'very satisfied', to 5, 'very dissatisfied'.

The *quantitative* approach to research involves numerical data. It relies on numerical evidence to draw conclusions or to test hypotheses. To be sure of the reliability of the results it is often necessary to study relatively large numbers of people and to use computers to analyse the data. The data can be derived from questionnaire surveys, from observation involving counts or measurements, or from administrative sources, such as ticket sales data from a sport facility.

There can be said to be three approaches to quantitative research:

a. *Hypothetical-deductive:* quantitative research conforms to the hypothetical-deductive model discussed under positivism above. Invariably statistical methods and tests, such as chi-square tests, t-tests, analysis of variance, correlation or regression **(outlined in Chapter 17)**, are used. This model is implicit in many discussions of quantitative methods.

b. *Statistical:* quantitative research makes use of statistical methods but is not necessarily hypothetical-deductive. It can be descriptive, exploratory and/ or deductive.

c. *Inductive:* quantitative research is based on numerical data, but makes little or no use of statistical tests: its most sophisticated statistical measure is usually the percentage and sometimes means/averages. This type of quantitative research is more common in policy-related sport research: it is more informal than type (a) or type (b) and is closer in approach to qualitative methods.

The *qualitative* approach to research is generally not concerned with numbers but typically with information in the form of words, conveyed orally or in writing. In addition to words, it may also involve images and sounds. Definitions offered in the literature often go beyond this minimalist definition to include types of methods which are often associated with qualitative research but, arguably, are not exclusive to the approach. Thus, for example, Denzin and Lincoln (2005: 3) include in their definition the proposition that qualitative research practices 'transform the world', when clearly any type of research *may* seek to achieve this. Similarly, they state that qualitative research involves a 'naturalistic' (see below) approach, when clearly qualitative methods may be deployed in non-naturalistic settings (e.g. a laboratory) and quantitative research may take place in 'naturalistic' settings (e.g. quantitative measurement of athlete performance).

Qualitative research methods generally make it possible to gather a relatively large amount of information about the research subjects, which may be individuals, groups, places/facilities, events or organisations. But the collection and analysis processes typically place a practical limit on the number of subjects which can be included. The approach involves obtaining a full and rounded account and understanding of the behaviour, attitudes and/ or situation of a few individuals, as opposed to the more limited amount of information which might be obtained in a quantitative study of a large sample of individuals. No claim is therefore made that the sample studied in a qualitative study is representative of a larger population, so that the findings cannot be generalised to the wider population, although this principle is often breached in practice.

The methods used to gather qualitative information include observation, informal and in-depth interviewing, participant observation and analysis of texts. Research studying groups of people using non-quantitative, anthropological approaches is referred to as *ethnographic* research or *ethnographic fieldwork*. Such methods were initially developed by anthropologists, but have been adapted by sociologists for use in their work on contemporary communities.

The question of the differences between, and respective merits of, quantitative and qualitative methods is one of the most discussed methodological issues in social research. The discussion is often led by proponents of qualitative methods who generally portray themselves as pioneering a novel approach in the face of opposition from proponents of 'traditional' quantitative methods. While the debate between protagonists of qualitative and quantitative research can become somewhat partisan, it is now widely accepted that the two approaches complement one another. Leading proponents of qualitative methods, Guba and Lincoln (1998: 195), have stated: 'From our perspective, both qualitative and quantitative methods may be appropriate with any research paradigm.'

Quantitative research is often based on initial qualitative work and it is possible that the two approaches are moving closer together in one respect, as computers are now being used to analyse qualitative data **(as outlined in Chapter 15)**.

Pragmatism

As an approach to research, *pragmatism* emerged in philosophy at the beginning of the twentieth century, and involved the proposition that the criterion for valid knowledge should not be based on theoretical or logical rigour alone but also on experience in the real world and practical usefulness in solving real-world problems. In the social sciences it has come to refer to an approach to research which is not committed, *a priori*, to either the post-positivist or interpretive paradigm but may combine them in different parts of the same research exercise. For example, a project might involve a survey of sport participation with quantified results, but also some in-depth interviews with participants and non-participants, which adds complexity to the notion of 'participation', even challenging the definition used in the survey. That the approach may involve the use of quantitative and/or qualitative methods has also led to the use of the term 'mixed methods'. Another related term is *bricolage*, a French word referring to the work of a handyman/woman, who is multi-skilled and assembles a miscellany of tools and materials ('bits and pieces') to do the job in hand.

Participatory research

Typically, the researcher takes total responsibility for the design, conduct and reporting of the research. Some researchers, however, work in fields where the subjects of the research may be involved with the researchers in directing the research in a cooperative manner. This can happen in exploratory research in relatively informal environments, such as community groups, but also in open-ended, diagnostic research involving organisations. The approach over-laps with the concept of action research, in which the research is part of a pro-cess for bringing about change, with which the researcher is actively involved. Action research is discussed further in Chapter 5.

Theoretical and applied research

Theoretical research seeks to draw conclusions about the class of phenomena being studied which can be applied to that class of phenomena as a whole, not just the cases or subjects included in the study. Indeed, some theoretical research is non-empirical (see below), so it does not involve the direct study of cases or subjects, but relies on the existing research literature and local analysis.

Applied research, however, is less universal in its scope: it does not necessar-ily seek to create wholly *new* knowledge about the world but to apply exist-ing theoretical knowledge to particular problems or issues. Such problems or issues may arise in particular policy, planning or management situations. Policy studies, planning and management are themselves fields of study which have developed a body of theory. Because they are related to areas of practice they can be seen as *applied disciplines*. In these fields, therefore, there can be such a thing as *applied theory*. The rational-comprehensive model of manage-ment portrayed in Figure 1.5 is an example of a context for considering the dif-ference between theoretical and applied research: research which might seek to develop or elaborate the model in general would be theoretical, whereas research which simply used the model as a framework for examining a prob-lem in a particular group or organisation would be called applied. In some discussions of this dimension the term 'pure' is used rather than 'theoretical'.

Reflexivity

A reflexive approach to research involves explicit and self-aware consideration of the relationship between the researcher and the researched. As Charlotte Davies (1997: 3) points out, all research involves a degree of reflexivity. Thus, for example, in particle physics the very act of measurement can only be achieved by the researcher causing physical interference with the particle being measured and this becomes the focus of the research methodology. In questionnaire-based research, interaction between the researcher and the respondent is in the form of the asking of questions: different wording of the questions and the manner in which they are posed affect the answers given. Reflexivity is most often considered in the context of qualitative research, and the deeper the involvement of the researcher with the research subjects the more relevant it becomes, the most extreme being participant observation. Thus reflexivity may be related to physical relationships, to culture or power, or to a variety of forms of social interaction. In social research, reflexivity is sometimes referred to as intersubjectivity (McLaughlin and Torres, 2011, 1993).

In methodologies closer to the classic scientific model, the aim is generally to minimise the impact of the researcher on the research subjects, and descriptions of measures taken to achieve this are confined to the 'methods' section of the research report, although it may be revisited in the conclusions, particularly if the results are less than clear-cut and might be improved in future by changes in the research design. But in interpretive studies involving methods such as participant observation, discussion of the relationship between the researcher and the researched can be a major part of the analysis and reporting process.

Empirical and non-empirical research

The dichotomy here should probably be between *purely* empirical research, if such a thing exists, and *purely* theoretical research. Empirical research involves the collection and/or analysis of data, which may be quantitative or qualitative, primary or secondary. The research is informed by observations or information from the 'real world'. It is, however, rare for any research project to be exclusively empirical – it is usually informed by some sort of theory or conceptual framework **(see Chapter 3)**, however implicit.

It is possible for the researcher to become carried away with data and their analysis and to forget the theory which should make them *meaningful*. The disparaging term 'mindless empiricism' is sometimes used to describe such a situation. Similarly, theoretical research with no reference to information about the 'real world', however contested the description of that might be, is likely to be of limited value. Typically – and ideally – theoretical and empirical research coexist and enhance each other; indeed, most research projects have complementary theoretical and empirical components.

A review of the contents of one or two editions of the main sport studies journals will reveal the existence of both sorts of research – and the contributions which each can make. While the empirical studies provide some of the building blocks of a great deal of research and knowledge, non-empirical contributions are needed to review and refine ideas and to place the empirical work in context. A book like this inevitably devotes more space to empirical methods, because they involve more explicit, technical processes which can be described and taught. It cannot, however, be too strongly stressed that a good review of the literature or a thoughtful piece of writing arising from deep, insightful, inspirational thinking about a subject can be worth a thousand, unthinking, surveys or experiments!

Induction and deduction

Induction and deduction refer to alternative approaches to explanation in research. It has been noted that research involves *finding out* and *explaining*. Finding out might be called the 'what?' of research. Explaining might be called the 'how?' and the 'why?' of research.

Finding out involves description and gathering of information. Explaining involves attempting to understand that information: it goes beyond the descriptive. Appropriate research methods can facilitate both these processes. Description and explanation can be seen as part of a circular model of research as illustrated in Figure 2.3.

The research process can work in two ways:

- *Deductive:* The process starts at point A1 and moves via observation/description (B) to analysis/testing (C) which confirms or disproves the hypothesis (D1). The process is deductive: it involves *deduction*, where the process is based on prior logical reasoning and available evidence from observation or the research literature resulting in a hypothesis to be tested.

- *Inductive:* The process may begin with a question, at point A2, or it may begin with observation/description, at point B in the diagram; it then moves from analysis (C) to answering, or failing to answer, the question. The process is *inductive*: the explanation is *induced* from the data; the data come first and the explanation later.

The concept of a *hypothesis* begins the deductive process. A hypothesis is a proposition about how something might work or behave – an explanation which may or may not be supported by data, or possibly by more detailed or

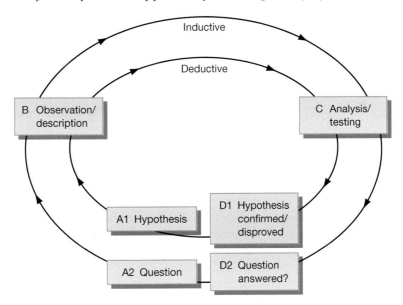

Figure 2.3   Circular model of the research process

rigorous argument. A hypothesis may be suggested from informal observation and experience of the researcher or from examination of the existing research literature. As we shall see **(Chapter 3)**, not all research projects involve the use of hypotheses, which are associated with the classic positivistic or *hypothetical-deductive* model as discussed above.

The terms *theory* or *model* could also be included at point D1; when more elaborate hypotheses or a number of interrelated hypotheses are involved, the term theory or model may be used. A theory or model can be similar to a hypothesis, in being propositional, or it may have been subjected to empirical validation – that is, testing against data. A research project may involve a single circuit or a number of circuits of the process, possibly in both directions. Theory and models can also arise out of the inductive process if, for example, the question was a 'why?' question.

Case study 2.1 illustrates the concepts of induction and deduction using an example of the relative popularity of two sport activities.

Case study 2.1	Tennis vs. golf – inductive and deductive approach

The relative popularity of tennis and golf could be studied using an inductive or deductive approach to research and explanation.

A. Inductive

A descriptive survey shows that more people play tennis than play golf. This is just a piece of information; we cannot explain why this is so without additional information and analysis. If the research also reveals that it costs more to play golf than to play tennis then we could offer the explanation that relative popularity is related to price.

However, qualitative information from the survey might also indicate that more people consider tennis as being fun to play than consider golf to be fun. This suggests that tennis is intrinsically more attractive than golf for many people and its popularity is not related to price but to intrinsic enjoyment.

On the other hand, the research might indicate that there are more tennis courts available than golf courses in the particular community being studied, suggesting that, if there were more golf courses available, golf would be more popular – implying that popularity is related to availability of facilities.

In this example, a series of possible explanations is being *induced* from the data. In its most fully developed form the explanation amounts to a theory. In this case a theory of sport participation might be developed, relating levels of participation to costs of participation, intrinsic satisfactions and supply of facilities, perceived attractiveness of the activity and facilities and so on.

B. Deductive

On the basis of reading and existing theory on leisure activities generally, the following two hypotheses are put forward.

H1: if sport A is more expensive to play than sport B, then sport B will be more popular than sport A.

H2: if more facilities are available for sport B than for sport A, then sport B will be more popular than sport A.

To test these hypotheses a research project is designed to collect information on:

a. the levels of participation in the two sports – tennis and golf;

b. the costs of participating in the two sports;

c. the availability of facilities for the two sports in the study area.

The two hypotheses would then be tested using the data collected. The data collection and outcomes are limited by the hypotheses put forward. In this example the idea of 'intrinsic motivation', which featured in the inductive approach, was not identified; in this case the research is guided from the beginning by the initial hypotheses. The process is deductive.

In practice, data are rarely collected without at least an informal explanatory model in mind – otherwise how would the researcher know what data to collect? So there is always an element of deduction in any research. And it is not possible to develop hypotheses and theories without at least some initial information on the topic in hand, however informally obtained; so there is always an element of induction. Thus most research is partly inductive and partly deductive.

There is a tendency, particularly among writers on qualitative methods, to associate quantitative methods with a deductive approach and qualitative methods with inductive approaches (e.g. Atkinson, 2012). But quantitative research can be, and often is, inductive. For example:

● *Factor analysis* **(see Chapter 17)** is a highly quantitative data manipulation technique which seeks to identify a manageable number of meaningful 'factors' from a large number of variables, such as might be generated from a questionnaire. The technique can be used as an *exploratory* (i.e. inductive) tool, to discover what, if any, factors might exist in the data, and as a *confirmatory* (i.e. deductive) tool, to confirm the existence of hypothesised factors.

● *Structural equation modelling* (SEM) is also a highly quantitative technique **(see Chapter 17)**; in his book on the technique, Rex Kline notes that computer programs used to analyse data for SEM require the researcher to provide in advance specifications of the model to be tested and observes:

> These specifications reflect the researcher's hypotheses, and in total they make up the model to be evaluated in the analysis. In this sense SEM could be viewed as confirmatory [i.e. deductive]. That is, the model is given at the beginning of the analysis, and one of the main questions to be answered is whether it is supported by the data. But, as often happens in SEM, the data may be inconsistent with the model, which means that the researcher must either abandon the model or modify the hypotheses on which it is based. The former option is rather drastic. In practice, researchers more often opt for the second choice, which means the analysis now has a more exploratory [i.e. inductive] nature as revised models are tested with the same data. *(Kline, 2005: 10)*

Whether hypotheses or theories containing the explanation are put forward at the start of a research project or arise as a result of exploratory data analysis, they represent the key creative part of the research process. Data collection and analysis can be fairly mechanical but interpretation of data and the development of explanations requires at least creativity and, at best, inspiration!

Experimental and naturalistic methods

The experiment is the classic scientific research method: the popular image of the scientist is someone in a white coat in a laboratory, conducting experiments. In the experimental method of research the scientist aims to control the environment of the subject of the research and measure the effects of controlled change. Knowledge based on the experimental method progresses on the basis that, in a controlled experimental situation, any change in A must have been brought about by a change in B because everything except A and B have been held constant. The experimental researcher therefore aims to produce conditions such that the research will fulfil the requirements for causality discussed above.

In the world of human beings, with which the social scientist deals, there is much less scope for experiment than in the world of inanimate objects or animals with which natural scientists deal. Some situations do exist where experimentation with human beings in the field of sport can take place. For example, it is possible to experiment with:

● variations in design of an exercise or coaching programme;

● willing subjects in game-playing or decision-making tasks under different conditions, or responding to 'stimuli', such as photographs or videos;

● management situations, for instance varying prices or advertising strategies in relation to sport events.

But many areas of interest to the sport researcher are not susceptible to controlled experiment. For instance, the researcher interested in the effect of income levels on sport participation rates cannot take a group of people and vary their incomes in order to study the effects on their sport participation behaviour – it would be difficult to find people on executive salaries willing voluntarily to spend a year living on a student grant in the interests of research! Furthermore, unlike the natural scientist experimenting with rats, it is not possible to find two groups of humans identical in every respect except for their level of income. Even more fundamentally, it is of course not possible to vary people's social class or race. In order to study these phenomena it is necessary to use *non-experimental* methods; that is, it is necessary to study differences between people as they exist.

So, for example, in order to study the effects of income on sport participation patterns it is necessary to gather information on the sport behaviour patterns of a range of people with different levels of income. But people differ in all sorts of ways, some of which may be related to their level of income and some not. For example, two people with identical income levels can differ markedly in terms of their personalities, their family situation, their physical health and so on. So, in comparing the behaviour of two groups of people, it is difficult to be sure which differences arise as a result of income differences and which as a result of other differences. The results of the research are therefore likely to be less clear-cut than in the case of the controlled experiment.

One term used for studying people in their normal environment, that is, not in a laboratory, is *naturalistic*. In a fully naturalistic study the researcher would be as unobtrusive as possible so as not to interfere in any way with the normal behaviour of the research subjects. Unlike the laboratory experiment, where as many variables as possible are controlled, the naturalistic researcher would be taking a *holistic* or *systematic* view, in which all relevant known and unknown variables are in operation simultaneously. As Lincoln and Guba (1985: 8) put it, in naturalistic research: 'first, no manipulation on the part of the inquirer is implied and, second, the inquirer imposes no *a priori* units on the outcome'.

Some observational methods seek to achieve this. Interviews of various types may begin to interfere with the normal or 'natural' behaviour of the subject: the asking of a question can be seen as a sort of loosely controlled experiment. But interviews which take place in a subject's home or at a sport site or holiday destination are more naturalistic than a focus group session in the office of a market research company which is closer to the experiment end of the experimental–naturalistic continuum. For some types of naturalistic research project, quite extensive interaction may be required between the researcher and the subjects being researched in order to gain an understanding of behaviour in the subject's normal/natural environment.

The experimental method is dealt with in Chapter 11. The other methods **(discussed in Parts II and III)** can all be seen as naturalistic but varying in their degrees of naturalism.

Objectivity and subjectivity

As indicated in Chapter 1 and in the discussion of the experimental method above, the classical stance of the researcher in the natural science research model is as an objective observer. Experiments are set up to prove or disprove a hypothesis. If the data from the experiment are consistent with the hypothesis, the latter is accepted as reflecting the real world until such time as new evidence emerges which is inconsistent with the hypothesis, which is then rejected or modified. In practice, absolute objectivity is impossible since the researcher's selection of one research topic rather than any one of a thousand others suggests a value position: the researcher's choice implies that the selected topic is, in some way, more important than the others. If the research has been funded from a trust or government grant-giving body, the application will invariably have been required to demonstrate the 'social benefits' of the research. When moving into the social science area it becomes even more difficult to maintain the classic objective stance: thus much research on sport is conducted because the researcher is convinced of the value of sporting activity to society as a whole or to particular groups within society. Nevertheless, researchers typically seek to be as objective as possible and to report honestly on the results of empirical enquiry **(see Chapter 4)**.

Primary and secondary data

In planning a research project it is advisable to consider whether it is necessary to go to the expense of collecting new information (*primary* data, where the researcher is the first user) or whether existing data (*secondary* data, where the researcher is the secondary user) will do the job. Sometimes existing information is in the form of research already completed on the topic or a related topic; sometimes it arises from non-research sources, such as administration. A fundamental part of any research project is therefore to scour the existing published – and unpublished – sources of information for related research or data. Existing research might not obviate the need for the originally proposed research or data, but it may provide interesting ideas and points of comparison with the proposed research.

Even if the research project is to be based mainly on new information it will usually be necessary also to make use of other, existing, information – such as official government statistics or financial records from a sport facility or service. Such information is generally referred to as *secondary data*, as opposed to the *primary data*, which is the new data to be collected in the proposed research. The topic of secondary data is dealt with in Chapter 7.

Self-reported and observed data

The best, and often the only, sources of information about people's sport behaviour or attitudes are individuals' own reports about themselves. Much sport research therefore involves asking people about their past activity, attitudes and aspirations, by means of an interviewer-administered or respondent-completed questionnaire **(Chapter 10)** or by means of informal, in-depth, semi-structured or unstructured interviews **(Chapter 9)**. In some cases information can be gathered from written sources, such as diaries, letters or biographies.

There are some disadvantages to this approach, mainly that the researcher is never sure just how honest or accurate people are in responding to questions. In some instances people may deliberately or unwittingly distort or 'bend' the truth – for instance in understating the amount of alcohol they drink or overstating the amount of exercise they take. In other instances they may have problems of recall – for instance in remembering just how much time they spent engaging in exercise some months ago – or even yesterday! In biomedical research, which relies a great deal on subjects/patients accurately reporting such things as symptoms and behaviour, study of the design and practice of such data collection has come to be referred to as the 'science of self-report' (Stone *et al.*, 2000).

For some types of information an alternative to relying on self-report is for the researcher to *observe* behaviour. For instance, to find out how people use the equipment in a gym it would probably be better to watch them than to try to ask them about it. Patterns of movement and crowding, for example at a sport stadium, can be *observed*. Sometimes people leave behind evidence of their behaviour – for instance the most used beaches are likely to be those where the most litter is dumped. Generally these techniques are referred to as *observational* or *unobtrusive* techniques **(dealt with in Chapter 8)**. Clearly observation does not provide direct information on motives, attitudes and aspirations or past behaviour.

Validity, reliability and trustworthiness

The quality of research and the trust which can be placed in it depends on the methods used and the care with which they have been deployed. Two dimensions are generally considered in this context: validity and reliability.

Validity is the extent to which the information presented in the research truly reflects the phenomena which the researcher claims it reflects. *External validity* refers to generalisability or representativeness: to what extent can the results be generalised to a population wider than the particular sample used in the study? This will depend on how the members of the sample are selected **(see Chapter 13)**. *Internal validity* refers to how accurately the characteristics of the phenomena being studied are represented by the variables used and the data collected – sometimes referred to as *measurement* or *instrument* (e.g. questionnaire) *validity* – and the extent to which the study identifies and measures all the relevant variables.

Sport research is fraught with difficulties in this area, mainly because empirical research is largely concerned with people's behaviour and with their attitudes, and for information on these the researcher is, in the main, reliant on people's own reports in the form of responses to questionnaire-based interviews and other forms of interview. These instruments are subject to a number of imperfections, which means that the validity of sport data can rarely be as certain as in the natural sciences. For example, data on the number of people who have participated in an activity at least once over the last month (a common type of measure used in sport research) covers a wide range of different types of involvement, from the person who participates for two hours every day to the person who had an unplanned engagement with the activity just once for a few minutes. So the question of what is a *participant* can be complex. More detailed questioning to capture such complexity can be costly to undertake on a large scale and can try the patience of interviewees, thus increasing the risk that responses will be inaccurate or incomplete.

Reliability is the extent to which research findings would be the same if the research were to be repeated at a later date or with a different sample of subjects. Again it can be seen that the model is taken from the natural sciences where, if experimental conditions are appropriately controlled, a replication of an experiment should produce identical results wherever and whenever it is conducted. This is rarely the case in the social sciences, because they deal with human beings in differing and ever-changing social situations. While a single person's report of his or her behaviour may be accurate, when it is aggregated with information from other people it presents a snapshot picture of a group of people, which is subject to change over time, as the composition of the group changes, or as *some* members of the group change their patterns of behaviour. Further, identical questions asked of people in different locations, even within the same country or region, are likely to produce different results, because of the varying social and physical environment. This means that the social scientist, including the sport researcher, must be very cautious when making general, theoretical, statements on the basis of empirical research. While measures can be taken to ensure a degree of generalisability, strictly speaking, any research findings relate only to the subjects involved, at the time and place the research was carried out.

There is a considerable literature on validity and reliability, particularly related to experimental research and the use of scales **(see Chapter 5)**; sources are indicated in the Resources section at the end of the chapter.

It has been noted that the use of validity and reliability as criteria for assessing the quality of research arose from the positivist tradition and that they are therefore not always fully appropriate for non-positivist research approaches. In qualitative research in particular, the concepts of *trustworthiness* and *authenticity* have been introduced by Lincoln and Guba (1985) to replace validity and reliability. Trustworthiness has four components: credibility (paralleling internal validity), transferability (external validity), dependability (reliability) and confirmability (objectivity). Authenticity includes: fairness and ontological, educative, catalytic and tactical authenticity. Because qualitative studies draw on different traditions, and processes vary from study to study, a detailed explanation of the research process is advisable; as Karla Henderson (2006: 231) has put it: 'A thorough reporting of the process and the results of qualitative data collection and analysis is the key to justifying and assuring that trustworthiness exists in the study.'

Summary

The aim of this chapter is to provide an introduction to the disciplinary context and traditions of sport research and to introduce some of the general dimensions and concepts associated with social science research. It begins with a brief overview of the contributions of individual disciplines to sport research, covering: sociology, physical education, economics, psychology/social psychology, history and anthropology and political science. The review indicates that most of the disciplines contributing to sport research make use of a wide variety of research methods. The second part of the chapter covers a range of generic social science concepts and issues which arise in the literature and with which the sport researcher should be familiar. They are: ontology, epistemology and methodology; positivist, post-positivist, interpretive and critical approaches; descriptive, explanatory and evaluative research as discussed in Chapter 1; qualitative and quantitative research; theoretical and applied research; empirical and non-empirical research; induction and deduction; experimental and non-experimental research; primary and secondary data; self-reported and observed data; and validity and reliability.

Test questions

1. What are the basic differences between theoretical and applied research?

2. What are the basic differences between empirical and non-empirical research?

3. What are the basic differences between the inductive and deductive approach to research?

4. What are the basic differences between descriptive and explanatory research?

5. What are the basic differences between the positivist and interpretive approach to research?

6. What are the basic differences between experimental and non-experimental research?

7. What is the basic difference between primary and secondary data?

8. What is the basic difference between self-reported and observed data?

9. What are the basic differences between qualitative and quantitative research?

10. What are validity and reliability?

Exercises

1. Examine any issue of a sport studies refereed journal and classify the articles into disciplinary areas. Contrast the key questions which each article is addressing.

2. Using the same journal issue as in exercise 1, determine whether the articles are: a. empirical or non-empirical; b. deductive or inductive; c. positivist or interpretive.

3. Take an issue of a sport studies journal at two-yearly intervals over 10 or 12 years and summarise the apparent change over time in the topics addressed and methods used in the articles.

4. Select a sport-related thesis from your university's catalogue (they are generally listed separately and may be available in hard copy or electronically) and summarise and comment on the way the researcher has decided on, and explained, his or her adopted research approach.

5. On the website of a national government sport agency, locate a recent research report and identify the problem/issue being addressed and the approached used in researching it. How does this differ from the way the problem/issue might have been addressed in an academic journal?

Resources

- Action research: Greenwood and Levin (2007), see also Chapter 5 Resources section.

- *Bricolage:* Kincheloe (2001) – see also mixed methods, pragmatism and eclecticism.

- Disciplines and sport: Coalter (2010); Downward *et al.* (2009), King (2006), Love and Andrew (2012), Weed (2009), Wiggins and Mason (2006).

- Eclecticism: Hammersley (1996) – see also mixed methods, pragmatism and *bricolage.*

- Emancipatory theory: Antonio (1989).

- Ethnography and sport: Burke *et al.* (2008), Silk (2005), Sykes *et al.* (2005).

- Experimental method in sport research: Haerens and Tallir (2012) – see case studies in Chapter 11.

- Grounded theory: see Chapter 9 Resources section.

- Mind/concept maps of research methods: Crowe and Sheppard (2012).

- Mixed methods (qualitative and quantitative): general: Creswell (2009), Howe (1988), Mertens (2009), Teddlie and Tashakori (2009); in sport: Camerino *et al.* (2012), Rohm *et al.* (2006) – see also pragmatism, eclecticism, *bricolage.*

- Participatory research: Greenwood and Levin (2007), Heron and Reason (1997), see also Action research.

- Pragmatism: general: Greenwood and Levin (2007: 9–11, 59–63, 71–73), Howe (1988), Patton (1988); and sport: Giacobbi *et al.* (2005) – see also mixed methods, eclecticism, *bricolage.*

- Qualitative–quantitative research: Allwood (2012), Atkinson (2012: 164–9), Biddle *et al.* (2001), Borman *et al.* (1986), Bryman and Bell (2003: Chapters 21, 22), Howe (1988), Krenz and Sax (1986); women and physical activity: Henderson *et al.* (1999).

- Qualitative research methods and sport: Andrews *et al.* (2005), Hastie and Hay (2012), Plymire (2005), Silk *et al.* (2005); trends in use: Culver *et al.* (2003).

- Quantitative approaches: Biddle *et al.* (2001), Hale and Graham (2012), see Chapters 16 and 17.

- Reflexivity: Davies (1997), Donne (2006).

- The science of self-report: Stone *et al.* (2000).

- Standpoint research: Hartsock (1999).

- Transformative paradigm: Mertens (2009).

- Trustworthiness: Lincoln and Guba (1985), Guba and Lincoln (1998).

- Validity/reliability: Burns (1994: 206–28).

References

Allwood, C. M. (2012) The distinction between qualitative and quantitative research methods is problematic. *Quality and Quantity*, 46(5), 1417–29.

Andrews, D. L., Mason, D. S. and Silk, M. L. (eds) (2005) *Qualitative Methods in Sport Studies*. Oxford: Berg.

Antonio, R. J. (1989) The normative foundations of emancipatory theory: evolutionary versus pragmatic perspectives. *American Journal of Sociology*, 94(4), 721–48.

Atkinson, M. (2012) *Key Concepts in Sport and Exercise Research Methods*. London: Sage.

Biddle, S. J. H., Markland, D. and Gilbourne, D. (2001) Research methods in sport and exercise psychology: quantitative and qualitative issues. *Journal of Sports Sciences*, 19(10), 777–809.

Borman, K. M., LeCompte, M. D. and Goetz, J. P. (1986) Ethnographic and qualitative research design and why it doesn't work. *American Behavioral Scientist*, 30(1), 42–57.

Bryman, A. and Bell, E. (2003) Breaking down the quantitative/qualitative divide, and Combining quantitative and qualitative research. Chapters 21–22 of: *Business Research Methods*. Oxford: Oxford University Press, 465–94.

Burke, S. M., Sparks, A. C. and Allen-Collinson, J. (2008) High altitude climbers as ethnomethodologists making sense of cognitive dissonance: ethnographic insights from an attempt to scale Mt. Everest. *Sport Psychologist*, 22(4), 336–55.

Burns, R. B. (1994) *Introduction to Research Methods, Second edn.* Melbourne: Longman Cheshire.

Camerino, O., Castamer, M. and Anguera, M. T. (eds) (2012) *Mixed Methods in the Movement Sciences: Case Studies in Sport, Physical Education and Dance.* London: Routledge.

Coalter, F. (2010) The politics of sport-for-development: limited focus programmes and broad gauge problems? *International Review for the Sociology of Sport*, 45(3), 295–314.

Creswell, J. W. (2009) *Research Design: Qualitative, Quantitative and Mixed Methods Approaches, Third edn.* Thousand Oaks, CA: Sage.

Crowe, M. and Sheppard, L. (2012) Mind mapping research methods. *Quality and Quantity*, 46(5), 1493–504.

Culver, D. M., Gilbert, W. D. and Trudel, P. (2003) A decade of qualitative research in sport psychology journals: 1990–1999. *The Sport Psychologist*, 17(1), 1–15.

Davies, C. (1997) *Reflexive Ethnography: A Guide to Researching Selves and Others.* London: Routledge.

Donne, K. (2006) From outsider to quasi-insider at Wodin Watersports: a reflexive account of participant observation in a leisure context. In S. Fleming and F. Jordan (eds) *Ethical Issues in Leisure Research.* LSA Publication 90, Eastbourne, UK: Leisure Studies Association, 63–82.

Downward, P., Dawson, A. and Dejonghe, T. (2009) *Sports Economics: Theory, Evidence and Policy.* Oxford: Butterworth-Heinemann.

Giacobbi, P. R., Poczwardowski, A. and Hager, P. (2005) A pragmatic research philosophy for applied sport psychology. *The Sport Psychologist*, 19(1), 18–31.

Giddens, A. (ed.) (1974) *Positivism and Sociology.* London: Heinemann.

Greenwood, D. J. and Levin, M. (2007) *Introduction to Action Research: Social Research for Social Change, Second edn.* Thousand Oaks, CA: Sage.

Guba, E. G. and Lincoln, Y. S. (1998) Competing paradigms in qualitative research. In N. K. Denzin and Y. S. Lincoln (eds) *The Landscape of Qualitative Research: Theories and Issues.* Thousand Oaks, CA: Sage, 195–220.

Guba, E. G. and Lincoln, Y. S. (2005) Paradigmatic controversies, contradictions and emerging confluences. In N. K. Denzin and Y. S. Lincoln (eds) *Handbook of Qualitative Research, Third edn.* Thousand Oaks, CA: Sage, 191–216.

Haerens, L. and Tallir, I. (2012) Experimental research methods in physical education and sport. In K. Armour and D. Macdonald (eds) *Research Methods in Physical Education and Youth Sport*. London: Routledge, 149–62.

Hale, B. and Graham, D. (2012) Quantitative approaches. In K. Armour and D. Macdonald (eds) *Research Methods in Physical Education and Youth Sport*. London: Routledge, 95–105.

Hammersley, M. (1996) The relationship between qualitative and quantitative research: paradigm loyalty versus methodological eclecticism. In J. T. E. Richardson (ed.) *Handbook of Qualitative Research Methods for Psychology and the Social Sciences*. Leicester, UK: BPS Books, 159–74.

Hartsock, N. (1999) *The Feminist Standpoint Revisited, and Other Essays*. New York: Basic Books.

Hastie, P. and Hay, P. (2012) Qualitative approaches. In K. Armour and D. Macdonald (eds) *Research Methods in Physical Education and Youth Sport*. London: Routledge, 79–94.

Henderson, K. A. (2009) Just research and physical activity: diversity is more than an independent variable. *Leisure Sciences*, 31(2), 100–5.

Henderson, K. A., Ainsworth, B. E. and Stolarzcrk, L. M. (1999) Notes on linking qualitative and quantitative data: the Cross Cultural Physical Participation Study. *Leisure Sciences*, 21(3), 247–55.

Heron, J. and Reason, P. (1997) A participatory inquiry paradigm. *Qualitative Inquiry*, 3(3), 274–94.

Howe, K. R. (1988) Against the quantitative-qualitative incompatibility thesis: or dogmas die hard. *Educational Researcher*, 17(8), 10–16.

Humberstone, B. (2011) Embodiment and social and environmental action in nature-based sport: spiritual spaces. *Leisure Studies*, 30(4), 495–512.

Kincheloe, J. L. (2001) Describing the bricolage: conceptualizing a new rigor in qualitative research. *Qualitative Inquiry*, 7(6), 679–92.

King, S. (2006) Methodological contingencies in sports studies. In D. L. Andrews, D. S. Mason and M. L. Silk (eds) *Qualitative Methods in Sport Studies*. Oxford: Berg, 21–38.

Kline, R. B. (2005) *Principles and Practice of Structural Equation Modelling, Second edn*. New York: Guilford Press.

Krenz, C. and Sax, G. (1986) What quantitative research is and why it doesn't work. *American Behavioral Scientist*, 30(1), 58–69.

Labovitz, S. and Hagedorn, R. (1971) *Introduction to Social Research*. New York: McGraw-Hill.

Lee, A. S. (1989) Case studies as natural experiments. *Human Relations*, 42(2), 117–37.

Lincoln, Y. and Guba, E. G. (1985) *Naturalistic Inquiry*. Beverly Hills, CA: Sage.

Love, A. and Andrew, D. P. S. (2012) The intersection of sport management and sociology of sport research: a social network perspective. *Sport Management Review*, 15(2), 244–56.

McLaughlin, D. W. and Torres, C. R. (2011) Sweet tension and its phenomenological description: sport, intersubjectivity and horizon. *Sport, Ethics and Philosophy*, 5(3), 270–84.

Mertens, D. M. (2009) *Transformative Research and Evaluation*. New York: Guilford Press.

Patton, M. (1988) Paradigms and pragmatism. In D. Fetterman (ed.) *Qualitative Approaches to Evaluation in Educational Research*. Newbury Park, CA: Sage, 116–37.

Plymire, D. (2005) Qualitative methods in sport-media studies. In D. L. Andrews, D. S. Mason and M. L. Silk (eds) *Qualitative Methods in Sports Studies*. Oxford: Berg, 139–64.

Rohm, A. J., Milne, G. R. and McDonald, M. A. (2006) A mixed-method approach for developing market segmentation typologies in the sports industry. *Sport Marketing Quarterly*, 15(1), 29–39.

Rudd, A. and Johnson, R. B. (2010) A call for more mixed methods in sport management research. *Sport Management Review*, 13(1), 14–24.

Silk, M. L. (2005) Sporting ethnography: philosophy, methodology and reflection. In D. L. Andrews, D. S. Mason and M. L. Silk (eds) *Qualitative Methods in Sports Studies*. Oxford: Berg, 65–103.

Silk, M. L., Andrew, D. L. and Mason, D. S. (2005) Encountering the field: sports studies and qualitative research. In D. L. Andrews, D. S. Mason and M. L. Silk (eds) *Qualitative Methods in Sports Studies*. Oxford: Berg, 1–20.

Stone, A. A., Turkkan, J. S., Bachrach, C. A., Jobe, J. B., Kurtzman, H. S. and Cain, V. S. (2000) *The Science of Self-report: Implications for Research and Practice*. Mahwah, NJ: Lawrence Erlbaum.

Sykes, H., Chapman, J. and Swedberg, A. (2005) Performed ethnography. In D. L. Andrews, D. S. Mason and M. L. Silk (eds) *Qualitative Methods in Sports Studies*. Oxford: Berg, 185–202.

Teddlie, C. and Tashakkori, A. (eds) (2009) *Foundations of Mixed Methods Research: Integrating Quantitative and Qualitative Approaches in the Social and Behavioral Sciences*. Thousand Oaks, CA: Sage.

Weed, M. (2009) Progress in sports tourism research? A meta-review and exploration of futures. *Tourism Management*, 30(5), 615–28.

Wiggins, D. K. and Mason, D. S. (2006) The socio-historical process in sports studies. In D. L. Andrews, D. S., Mason and M. L. Silk (eds) *Qualitative Methods in Sport Studies*. Oxford: Berg, 39–64.

Starting out – research plans and proposals

Introduction

This chapter examines:

- stages in the planning of research projects;
- the formulation and presentation of research proposals and tenders.

Planning a research project

A research plan or proposal must summarise how a research project is to be conducted in its entirety; consequently, preparation of a plan or proposal involves examination of the whole research process from beginning to end. In this chapter, therefore, a certain amount of cross-referencing is required to later chapters, where particular elements of the process are dealt with in detail.

The research process can be envisaged in a number of ways, but for the purposes of discussion in this chapter it is divided into ten main elements, as shown in Figure 3.1. The enormous variety of approaches to research means that all research projects do not follow precisely the sequence as set out in the

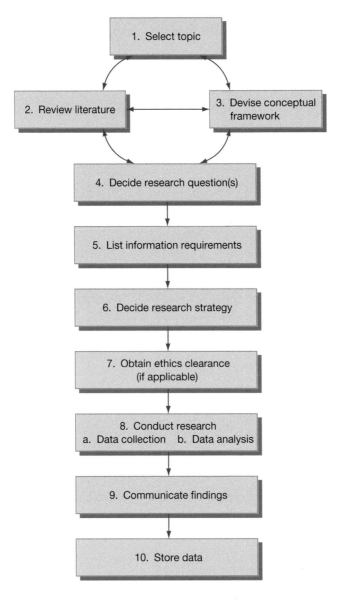

Figure 3.1   Elements in the research process

diagram. In particular, the first four elements depicted – selecting the topic, reviewing the literature, devising a conceptual framework and deciding the key research questions – rarely happen in the direct, linear way that the numbered sequence implies. There is generally a great deal of 'to-ing and fro-ing' between the elements. Hence, in Figure 3.1, these elements are depicted on a circle, implying that a number of circuits may be necessary before proceeding to element 5. To illustrate the process in operation, a case study is presented in summary at the end of this section. Each of the ten elements in Figure 3.1 is discussed in turn below.

Select a topic

How do research topics arise? They may arise from a range of sources, including: the researcher's personal interests; reading research literature; a policy or management problem; an issue of social concern; a popular or media issue; published research agendas; brainstorming, which may draw on a number of the above sources; and/or opportunism. Examples of topics arising from these sources are shown in Figure 3.2.

Personal interest

Personal interest can give rise to a research project in a number of ways. For example, the researcher may be personally involved in a particular sport or may be a member of a particular social group, based on gender, ethnicity or

Source of topic	Examples of topics
Personal interest (usually combined with one or more of the next seven sources)	• A particular sport – trends in participation, participants' motivations/satisfactions • A particular sporting event – history, impact • Different fitness training regimes – effectiveness • A particular professional group – its ethos, history and future
The literature	• Does Csikzentmihayli's (1990) idea of 'flow' apply to participation in sport X? • How do different theories of management apply in sport management? • What is known about participation in 'extreme' sports?
Policy/management	• Why are visits to sport facility X declining? • What market segments should be used to develop a strategy for promoting sport X? • What are the sport provision needs of community X?
Social	• The impact of increasingly sedentary lifestyles on health • Sport and at-risk youth • The role of sport in a third-world community
Popular/media	• Are performance-enhancing drugs harmful? • How significant is racism in sport? • Is public money spent on major sporting events like the Olympics justified?
Published research agendas	• The following examples of research agendas include a number of potential research topics: e.g. Australian Sports Commission (2004), Brownson *et al.* (2008), Tomlinson *et al.* (2005), Weed (2009).
Brainstorming	• Conduct a 'brainstorm' session on any of the above topics/sources – a means of exploring the potential of all of the above.
Opportunism	• Government-collected sport participation data provide the opportunity to undertake some demand forecasting; membership of a sporting club offers an opportunity to conduct participant-observer research.

Figure 3.2 Examples of research topics from different sources

occupation, and so be personally aware of certain pertinent issues or problems. Using personal interest as a focus for research has advantages and disadvantages. The advantage lies in the knowledge of the phenomenon which researchers already have, the possibility of access to key individuals and information sources, and the high level of motivation which is likely to be brought to the research. Pirkko Markula and Jim Denison (2005) suggest that personal experience is a way into the process of exploring potential topics for research in sport. The disadvantage is that the researcher may be unduly biased and may not be able to view the situation 'objectively'; familiarity with the subject of the research may result in too much being taken for granted so that the researcher can't 'see the wood for the trees'.

While a particular personal interest in the research topic may be referred to in writing up a research project – generally in a Foreword or Preface rather than in the main body of the report – it is often not mentioned in formal reports of research, such as journal articles. On the other hand, for some types of qualitative or 'standpoint' research **(see Chapter 2)**, the researcher's personal relationship with the subjects of the research may be an important aspect of the methodology.

Personal interest may be a component in the process of selecting a research topic, but does not alone generally provide a sufficient rationale or focus for a research project; it is necessary to develop additional criteria for selection of a specific topic from among the other sources discussed below.

The research literature

The research literature is the most common source of topics for academic research. A researchable topic derived from reading of the literature can take a variety of forms. It may arise from an informal scanning of the literature which stimulates a spark of interest in a topic, or it may arise from a more critical and focused reading. Much reported research is very specific to time and place, so that even a widely accepted theory might be subject to further testing and exploration. Thus it may be that a certain theory or theoretical proposition has never been tested empirically, or it merits further empirical testing for a variety of reasons, as set out in Figure 3.3.

Clearly, therefore, identifying a topic from the literature requires a special, *questioning*, exploratory approach to reading research literature: the aim is not just to identify what the literature *says*, but also what it does *not* say or the *basis* for assertions made or conclusions reached. The process of critically reviewing the literature is discussed further below under element 2 of the research process **(and in Chapter 6)**. If the research literature is to be the main source of ideas for a research topic then the first two elements of the research process, selecting a topic and reviewing the literature, are effectively combined.

A policy or management issue/problem

Policy or management topics are often specified by an organisation, but students or academics interested in policy or management issues can also identify

Reason	The theories/propositions/ observations history	Examples
Geographical	May have been tested only in one country/region	• Theory established using US data could be tested in another country. • Behaviour patterns of urban residents – are they replicated in rural areas?
Social	May have been established on the basis of the experience of one social group only	• Theory based on men's experience – does it apply to women? • Theory tested on middle-class subjects – does it apply to working-class people?
Temporal	May be out of date	• Theory on youth culture established in the 1980s – is it still valid?
Contextual	May have been established in fields other than sport	• Foucault's (1979) theories on power are based on studies in a hospital – are they relevant in sport (e.g. Markula and Pringle, 2006)?
Methodological	May have been tested using only one methodology	• Conclusions from a qualitative study could be tested quantitatively.
Disciplinary	May have been researched in the context of only one discipline	• How does social inequality (sociology) play out in spatial terms (geography)?

Figure 3.3   **Reasons for revisiting theories/propositions/observations from the literature**

such topics. For example: sport demand forecasting is conducted not only by, and at the behest of, government and commercial sport bodies but also by academics; and surveys of users of sport facilities or cost–benefit analyses of programmes and projects can be conducted by interested academics as well as sport service organisations. The difference between industry-sponsored and academically initiated research is that:

• academically initiated research results will often be made public, will generally be presented so as to highlight their more general implications rather than the particular application to the facility or programme being studied, and will be concerned as much with the *methodology* of the study as with its substantive findings;

• industry-sponsored research results, on the other hand, may often not be made public, the wider implications of the research might not be examined and the methodology, while it must be sound, will often not be of particular interest to the sponsoring organisation.

In some cases academics involved with one or more industry-sponsored projects, the results of which have been reported to the sponsoring organisation, may publish academic articles highlighting particular features for a wider readership.

Research sponsored by government bodies lies somewhere in between these two situations: the results of the research may be very specific, but will often not be confidential.

It is common for an organisation requiring research on a particular policy or management topic to outline its requirements in a *brief* or set of *terms of reference* for a funded research or consultancy project. Research organisations – usually consultants – are then invited to respond in the form of a competitive *tender* to conduct the project. This type of procedure has its own set of practices and conventions, as discussed later in the chapter under 'Responsive proposals – briefs and tenders'.

Social concern

Social concern – of the researcher and/or sections of society at large – can give rise to a wide range of research topics. For example, concern for certain deprived or neglected groups in society, such as at-risk youth, can lead to research on the sport needs or behaviour of members of such groups. Concern for the environment can lead to research on the environmental impact of sport activities in sensitive areas, for example hunting or rock climbing. Often such research is closely related to policy or management issues, but the research may have a more limited role, seeking to highlight problems rather than necessarily seeking to devise solutions.

Popular/media

A popular issue can inspire research that seeks to explore popular beliefs or conceptions, especially where it is suspected that these may be inaccurate or contestable. 'Popular' usually means 'as portrayed in the media'. For example, this might be seen as the motivation for much research on media portrayals of such phenomena as sporting crowd violence and 'alienated youth' (Rowe, 1995: 4) or major controversial sport developments, such as facilities to host international sporting events.

Published research agendas

From time to time public agencies, professional bodies or individual academics publish 'research agendas', based on an assessment, often made by a committee, of the research needs of a field of study. The following are some examples:

● Australian Sports Commission (2004): social research agenda for sport in Australia;

● Brownson *et al.* (2008): developing a research agenda for the promotion of physical activity;

● European Platform for Sport Innovation (2008): strategic sports research agenda for Europe.

Often the aim of the body initiating the agenda is to implement the published research agenda itself, but in other cases the idea is for researchers in the field generally – including students – to respond by adopting topics in the agenda for their own research. Students looking for research topics know that if their topic is selected from such a published list, then there will be at least a few people 'out there' who will be interested in the results!

Brainstorming

Brainstorming involves a group of two or more people bouncing ideas off one another in discussion in pursuit of inspiration or solutions to a problem. Typically this might be done with the aid of a whiteboard or flipchart (or suitable software) to write down ideas as they emerge. It can be seen as a separate source of ideas for a research topic or a way of refining ideas from any or all of the other sources discussed.

Opportunism

Sometimes an idea for research is prompted for opportunistic reasons: for example, a data source or access to a site becoming available. Various government surveys and other data collected for policy and administrative purposes and used for limited and internal policy-related or administrative purposes present constant opportunities for secondary analysis **(this is discussed further in Chapter 7)**. Membership of an organisation or a visit to sport facility or event provides the opportunity for participant observation and the availability of organisational or personal archives may provide an opportunity for historical research. In all these cases, as well as considering the nature and quality of the available data, one or more of the above rationales have to be brought into play to establish whether conducting a project using the data can be justified.

Selecting the topic

What makes a viable research topic? There is no single, or simple, answer to this question. In general it is not the topic itself which is good or bad but the way the research is conceptualised (see element 3 of the research process) and how the research question or questions are framed (element 4). A key question is whether the topic has already been researched by someone else – hence the need for a review of the literature, as discussed in element 2. But even when a topic has already been researched there is invariably scope for further research – sometimes this is pointed out by the original researcher in concluding comments.

Thus the first four elements of the research process – select topic, review literature, conceptualise, define research questions – form an iterative, often untidy, process, which is invariably difficult and challenging and sometimes frustrating. But it is essential to get this stage right or the rest of the research effort may be wasted.

Type of purpose/motivation	Features
Pursue knowledge for its own sake	Academic/scientific criteria – but may combine with others below
Ideologically driven: • conservative • reformist • social-democratic • environmental • radical/critical • neo-liberal • neo-Marxist • radical-feminist • anti-globalist	• defence/acceptance of the status quo • need to improve the status quo • a more egalitarian society • sustainability • need for radical change to status quo • defence/extension of the market • demonstration of class conflict/exploitation • demonstration of patriarchy/women's oppression • demonstration of undesirable features of global market trends
Policy/management: • Critical • Instrumental	• Critiques current policy/management – may reflect one or more radical/critical stances above • Accepts, at least by implication, the broad philosophy or organisational milieu in which the study is taking place

Figure 3.4   Purposes of research

The purpose of research

The *purposes* of a research project can shape the choice of topic and the subsequent research design. Three types of purpose are discussed here, namely: knowledge for its own sake; ideological/political purposes; and policy/management purposes. Their key features are summarised in Figure 3.4. These purposes or motivations for research are often not explicitly stated in research reports, but are generally implicit. They affect the choice of topic and the overall shaping of the research process.

Knowledge for its own sake. The classic purpose of research is to 'add to knowledge' for its own sake, or for the general good as judged by the researcher. Some researchers continue to be driven by this goal in all or some of their research, and work in an institutional environment where it can be pursued. Much unfunded research undertaken by academics in their own time is of this nature. But even in such a 'pure' situation, other, less noble, although not necessarily illegitimate, purposes may be involved – for example personal career advancement.

Ideological/political. Many academic researchers are motivated in whole or in part by an ideological or political agenda. It could be said that *all* researchers are so motivated to a certain extent, and in certain areas of the social sciences this is a valid point. Thus many social scientists might be described as *reformist*, in that they are motivated by a general desire for a more equitable or just society and their research will tend to be at least consistent with such a goal, if not centrally concerned with it. For example, much sport research is concerned with equality and inequality of access to sport opportunities. Similarly, environmental protection and sustainability is often an implicit or explicit concern.

If none of these concerns is apparent, but the research is dealing with social issues, the implicit stance may be taken as *conservative* – implying contentment with the political, social and/or economic *status quo*. In contrast, some researchers are guided by one or more of a number of ideological positions which seek fundamental change in society and might be described as *radical* or *critical*. The concept of *standpoint research* has already been noted **(Chapter 2)**. On the right of the political spectrum is radical 'New Right' thinking which endorses market processes and seeks their extension, and might be termed *neo-liberal*. There is relatively little research in sport studies with this outlook, although it is implicit in some research which is concerned with the use of sport as a vehicle for economic development.

By contrast, there are researchers who, in the words of Yvonna Lincoln (2005: 165), are 'committed to seeing social science used for democratic and liberalizing social purposes'. Researchers on the left with, for example, neo-Marxist beliefs are often explicit about the political purpose of research. Thus, for example, Helen Lenskyj (2008: 6), in her book on the Olympic Games, states that her 'radical approach' is 'not neutral' and that she approaches the topic 'from a social justice and equity perspective, in order to develop an analysis of interlocking systems of oppression, particularly classism, racism, and sexism, and their impacts on disadvantaged populations in Olympic bid and host cities'.

Policy/management. The purpose of policy or management-related research seems obvious enough: to address policy or management problems. But the stance adopted can vary and can be affected by the ideological positions outlined above. Some research might be seen as *critical*, in that it steps outside the policy or management milieu of the public or private sector organisations being studied and adopts a reformist or, as in the case of Lenskyj above, leftist stance when it critiques processes such as privatisation or 'managerialism' or seeks to demonstrate the inequitable outcomes of certain policies or management practices. Research which seeks to make management systems more efficient or profitable and generally accepts the broad philosophical stance of the organisational milieu being studied can be seen as *instrumental*.

Review the literature

Introduction

The process of reviewing the existing research literature is sufficiently important for a complete chapter to be devoted to it in this book **(Chapter 6)**. 'Reviewing the literature' is a somewhat academic term referring to the process of identifying and engaging with previously published research relevant to the topic of interest. The process can play a number of roles, as listed in Figure 3.5 **(and discussed further in Chapter 6)**.

In many cases the review undertaken in the early stages of the research has

- Entire basis of the research
- Source of ideas on topics for research
- Source of information on research already done by others
- Source of methodological or theoretical ideas
- Basis of comparison
- Source of information that is an integral/supportive part of the research

Figure 3.5 Roles of the literature in research

to be seen as a preliminary or interim literature review only, since time does not always permit a thorough literature review to be completed at the start of a project. Part of the research programme itself may then be to explore the literature further. Having investigated the literature as thoroughly as possible, it is usually necessary to proceed with the research project in the hope that all relevant material has been identified. Exploration of the literature will generally continue for the duration of the project. Researchers always run the risk of coming across some previous – or contemporaneous – publication which will completely negate or upstage their work just as they are about to complete it. But that is part of the excitement of research! In fact, unlike the situation in the natural sciences, the risk of this happening in the sport field is minimal, since research in this area can rarely be replicated exactly. In the natural sciences research carried out in, say, California can reproduce exactly the findings of research carried out in, say, London. In sport research, however, this is rarely the case – a set of research procedures carried out in relation to individuals or organisations in California could be expected to produce very different results from identical procedures carried out in London – or even New York – simply because sport research is involved with unique people in varying social settings.

Conducting the review

Where possible, attempts should be made to explore not just published research – the *literature* – but also unpublished and ongoing research. This process is very much hit and miss. Knowing what research is ongoing or knowing of completed but unpublished research usually depends on having access to informal networks, although some research organisations produce registers of ongoing research projects. Once a topic of interest has been identified it is often clear, from the literature, where the major centres for such research are located and to discover, from direct approaches or from websites, annual reports or newsletters, what research is currently being conducted at those centres. This process can be particularly important if the topic is a 'fashionable' one. However, in such cases the communication networks are usually very active, which eases the process. In this respect, papers from conferences and seminars are usually better sources of information on current research than books and journals, since the latter have long gestation periods, so that the research reported in them is generally based on work carried out two or more years prior to publication.

A review of the literature should be concluded with a *summary* which provides an overview of the field, its substantive and methodological merits and deficiencies or gaps, and an indication of how such conclusions are related to the research task in hand **(see Chapter 6)**.

What discipline?

In an academic context, especially for undergraduate or graduate projects, it is helpful to consider what *discipline(s)* the project relates to. In some cases this is obvious because the project is linked to a particular disciplinary unit – for example, marketing. In other cases the project is a capstone exercise in a degree course which may draw on one or more of any of the subjects studied in the course. Often, the fact that a topic does not have an obvious disciplinary label results in student researchers failing to draw on available disciplinary theories and frameworks and failing to take the opportunity to demonstrate the knowledge they have gained during the course of their studies. For example, if the research topic is to do with the subject of *golf*, searching library catalogues and databases using the keyword 'golf' will undoubtedly produce a certain amount of useful material. But consideration of whether the focus of the study is to be on golf management, golf marketing, the social context of golf or the motivations or training regimes of golf players opens up the possibility of applying generic theories and relating the research to comparable studies of other phenomena in the area of management, planning, sociology, psychology and human movement, respectively. An important question to ask is, therefore: What disciplinary field(s) is this research related to? What theories and ideas can be drawn from the literature in this discipline or these disciplines?

Devise conceptual framework

The idea of a conceptual framework

The development of a conceptual framework is arguably the most important part of any research project and also the most difficult. And it is the element which is the weakest in many research projects. A *conceptual framework* involves *concepts* involved in a study and the *hypothesised relationships between them.*

In this discussion the term conceptual framework has been used to cover a wide range of research situations. Thus such a term can be used in applied research when the framework adopted might relate to such activities as planning or marketing. In such cases, ideas for conceptual frameworks may readily be found in the planning or marketing literature. When the research is more academically orientated, the term *theoretical framework* might equally well be used. Miles and Huberman, in their book on *Qualitative Data Analysis*, describe conceptual frameworks as follows:

> A conceptual framework explains, either graphically or in narrative form, the main things to be studied – the key factors, constructs or variables – and the presumed

relationships among them. Frameworks can be rudimentary or elaborate, theory-driven or commonsensical, descriptive or causal. *(Miles and Huberman, 1994: 18)*

Different types of research – descriptive, explanatory or evaluative **(see Chapter 1)** – tend to call for different styles of conceptual framework. *Descriptive research* rarely requires an elaborate conceptual framework, but clear definitions of the concepts involved are required. In some cases this can nevertheless be a considerable undertaking; for example, if the descriptive task is concerned with levels of physical activity, considerable thought will need to be given on the question of just how this is to be measured **(see Chapter 7)**. Both *explanatory* and *evaluative* research call for well-developed conceptual frameworks which form the basis for the explanation or evaluation work required from the research.

One reaction to this discussion of conceptual frameworks is to observe that the approach seems inconsistent with the inductive approach **(see Chapter 2)**, in which theory is derived from the data rather than data being used to test pre-existing theory. In particular, it seems inconsistent with apparently more open-ended approaches such as grounded theory and informal, flexible approaches used in qualitative research. However, as Miles and Huberman indicate, conceptual frameworks are just as vital for qualitative research as for quantitative – arguably more so. In the context of qualitative research, Karla Henderson uses the term 'working hypothesis' to indicate that an initial framework may lack detail and may be subject to change as the research unfolds:

> A researcher conducting an inductive qualitative study should have a broad research question, conceptual framework, or working hypothesis in mind when beginning a project and, subsequently, as data collection begins … however, a researcher must be willing to let the working hypothesis metamorphose as the study progresses. *(Henderson, 2006: 79)*

In fact, a conceptual framework need not be a straitjacket: it can be a flexible, evolving device. In qualitative research, theory development and data collection and analysis are often intertwined, rather than being sequential **(see Chapter 9)**. But the researcher rarely starts with an absolutely blank conceptual framework – there is usually some sort of rudimentary framework drawn from the literature or other sources. At the minimum there will be an initial list of relevant concepts with which the researcher is concerned and without which it is difficult to know what questions to ask or what issues to explore. In some cases the researcher may start with a framework from the literature which is seen as unsatisfactory in some way: the aim of the research is then not to validate the framework but to do the opposite and replace it with an improved – and possibly very different – model. The conceptual framework drawn up at the beginning of the research project can be seen as the 'first draft'. As data gathering and analysis proceeds, further drafts will emerge, incorporating new insights arising from the research. The developing conceptual framework becomes the focus of the research process. As Miles and Huberman (1994: 298) put it: 'many qualitative analysts would not start with a conceptual framework, but rather aim to end up with one'.

The concepts identified and the framework within which they are set determines the whole course of the study. In exploring the conceptual framework for the study the researcher is asking: What's going on here? What processes are at work or likely to be at work? Sometimes the framework is developed from individual reflection or 'brainstorming' and sometimes it arises from the literature; indeed, an existing framework from the literature might well be adopted for application in a new situation. Where a number of areas of literature have been reviewed to provide the basis for the research, the skill is to draw the theoretical ideas together into a common framework – even if the aim is to show the incompatibility between two or more perspectives. Such links, of course, should be clearly and fully explained in the exposition of the framework.

Devising a conceptual framework

The development of a conceptual framework can be thought of as involving four elements, as depicted in Figure 3.6. The element 'Identification of concepts' should, perhaps, be the starting point, but this is rarely the case: the tendency is to think about relationships first, and then identify and define the concepts involved, as this becomes necessary. In fact the exercise is generally *iterative* – that is, it involves going backwards and forwards, or round and round, between the various elements until a satisfactory solution is reached. The four elements are discussed in turn below.

1. *Explore/explain the relationships.* Relationships may represent power relationships, other influencing factors (e.g. role models), money or information flows or simply a sequence of elements in a temporal process. The postulated relationships correspond to the theory – however tentative – which underpins the conceptual framework. Explaining a conceptual framework may be a lengthy and complex process, especially when links with the literature are involved. The example in Figure 3.7 is very simple. It shows the progression from a simple statement (Stage A) to a more complex statement or series of statements (Stage C) as the ideas develop. In the example, the statements are

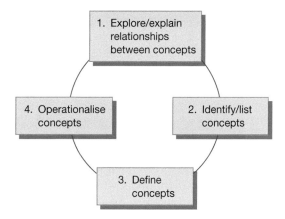

Figure 3.6 Development of a conceptual framework

Stage	Statements/hypotheses *(concepts are in italics)*
A	*Participation* in a sporting activity arises as a result of an individual (or group/household/family) decision-making process.
B	Whether or not a person participates could depend on a variety of *events and circumstances*, for example: ● the *availability of and access to facilities* may be good or bad; ● *advertising and promotion* may vary in quantity and influence; ● the *cost* of participation may be high or low; ● a *chance event*, such as meeting up with a group of friends or seeing an activity on television, may trigger the desire to *participate*.
C	Whether or not individuals participate will also depend on their *characteristics*, such as: ● *age/gender*; ● *income*; ● *personality*; ● *physical characteristics*; and ● *past experience* in participating in that or similar experiences.

Figure 3.7 Exploration of relationships between concepts – example

expressed in the form of hypotheses; they could alternatively be expressed as questions, for example: 'To what extent is the decision influenced by income?'

One aid to the development of a conceptual framework is to use the device of a *concept map*, sometimes referred to as a *mental map* or *relevance tree*. While some concept maps are more self-evident than others, a concept map is only an optional aid – a full narrative discussion and explanation always forms the core of the conceptual framework. A concept map merely illustrates or summarises the discussion.

Concept mapping can be seen as a form of visual 'brainstorming' and can be done alone or as part of a group exercise. The idea is to write down all the concepts which appear to be relevant to a topic, in any order which they come to mind. This can be done on one or more pieces of paper, on 'Post-It' notes, a board or flipchart, or on a computer screen using suitable software (for example, in Microsoft Word, go to 'Insert' and insert a 'Text Box': right-click for menus to produce a variety of shapes and colours). Then begin to group the concepts and indicate linkages between them. This is likely to involve a process of trial and error. Figure 3.8 illustrates diagrammatically the framework described verbally in Figure 3.7. Three versions of the concept map correspond to the three stages in Figure 3.7.

The concept map then, depicts concepts – usually shown in boxes or circles – and the *relationships* between concepts, which are usually represented by lines between the concepts, with or without directional arrows. Different types of concept might be represented by different-shaped boxes. The concepts and their relationships are explained in the accompanying text (Figure 3.7). The key relationships identified at stages A, B and C in the process are labelled accordingly.

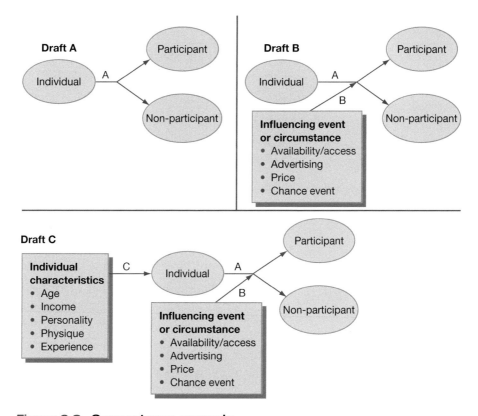

Figure 3.8   Concept map example

2. *Identify/list concepts.* Concepts are general representations of the phenomena to be studied – the 'building blocks' of a study. Concepts emerge in the discussion of relationships and the concept mapping process: here we formally identify, recognise and list them. They might involve types of individuals (e.g. manager, player), groups of individuals (e.g. team, community) or organisations (e.g. club, government) and/or their characteristics or actions. The first column of Figure 3.9 lists the concepts encountered in Figures 3.7 and 3.8.

3. *Define concepts.* Concepts must be clearly defined for research purposes. Dictionary definitions or definitions from the research literature may be used, but it is often necessary to be selective or adaptive. Column 2 of Figure 3.9 includes suggested definitions for the concepts listed there. Definitions might be very rudimentary in the early stages of the exercise and become more detailed and complex with time: as we talk about 'X' we have to clarify exactly what we mean by 'X'.

4. *Operationalise concepts.* The terminology used to describe the process of *operationalisation* depends on whether a concept is quantitative or qualitative in nature or in its treatment:

● Quantitative: operationalisation involves deciding *how the concept might be measured.*

Concept (see Figure 3.8)	Definition	Operationalisation
1. Participant	Person who engages in a sport or exercise activity in leisure time	Participation in sport/exercise activity at least once in a week
2. Event circumstance		
a. Availability/access	Preferred type of sport facility at affordable price available in home community	Range of facilities within 30 minutes' travel time at or below various 'benchmark' costs, e.g. £5, £10, £25
b. Advertising/promotion	Sport advertising/ promotion to which individual is exposed	Individual's recall of a specified list of advertisements/promotions in last 3 months
c. Cost	Total cost of sport experience	Costs of activity: a. per season (if applicable); b. per visit; c. for equipment/clothing
d. Chance event/viewing	Unplanned occurrence or viewing on media which affects decision to participate	Events which individual claims affected recent decisions to participate: experience, advice from friend/relative, item read or seen in the media
3. Individual characteristics	Individual attributes (which influence sport decisions), for example:	
	a. Age	a. Age last birthday
	b. Gender	b. Male/female
	c. Income	c. Annual household income before tax
	d. Personality	d. Results of Myers–Briggs test
	e. Physical characteristics	e. e.g. height, BMI
	f. Past sport experience	f. Sport activities undertaken in last year (from checklist)

Figure 3.9 Examples of concepts – definition and operationalisation

- Qualitative: the operationalisation process involves deciding how the concept might be *identified, described or assessed* when conducting qualitative research, such as in-depth interviews.

Examples of operationalisation of concepts are shown in column 3 of Figure 3.9. Most of the concepts listed lend themselves to quantification and measurement, at least in part, but concepts 2a, 2b and 2d have qualitative characteristics and could be treated either way. The question of measurement is discussed more fully in Part II of the book **(particularly in Chapter 7)**.

To some extent operationalisation involves thinking ahead as to how information about a concept might, in practice, be gathered: it is an indication of the practical implications of the definition. Often arbitrary or pragmatic choices have to be made in order to operationalise the project. For example, should 'sport participation' involve 'regular' participation being counted as 'participation' or is 'once a week' adequate? These may be arbitrary decisions, or decisions based on the need to gather data which is comparable to other, existing, data, for example official guidelines on exercise requirements.

Models

A conceptual framework might also be called a *model*, particularly when the research is quantitative in nature. For example, the relationship between sport participation and a person's social and economic circumstances could be expressed in quantitative modelling terms as shown in Figure 3.10. A survey of sport participation would identify various groups with different levels of income and participation, and statistical analysis could be used to 'calibrate' the equation, that is, find values for the 'parameters' a and b, so that the level of participation of a particular group could be predicted once the average income of that group was known. In Figure 3.10, hypothetical parameters of 0.2 and 0.31 are presented to illustrate the approach and an example is given of how such an equation might be used to estimate or predict participation frequency of groups with given income levels, now or in the future. The technicalities of the statistical process are not pursued further here, but are touched on again when the technique of regression is discussed **(in Chapter 17)**. More complex models could be developed, including, concepts such as people's age, occupation, the price of participation, and so on.

Examples of conceptual frameworks in sport studies

Fitness and health. Roth *et al.* (1989) examined the relationship between a person's self-perceived health status (which is known to be a good indicator of objective health status) and four variables, measured as follows:

- level of exercise – frequency, duration and intensity of participation in 15 activities;

Conceptual framework/theory	The average frequency of sport participation of a particular group is positively related to the group's average level of income
Concepts/variables	S = frequency of participation in sport per year N = annual income in £'000s
Relationship/equation	S = a + bN
Example of calibrated equation (value of a and b found from survey-based research)	S = 0.2 + 0.31 N
Use of the equation for prediction (assume N = £30k)	S = 0.2 + 0.31 × 30 = 0.2 + 9.3 = 9.5 times a year

Figure 3.10   Conceptual framework as quantifiable model

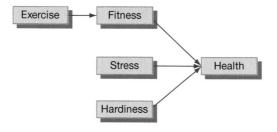

Figure 3.11   Exercise – fitness – stress – hardiness and health

Source: Simplified version of Roth *et al.* (1989: Fig. 1)

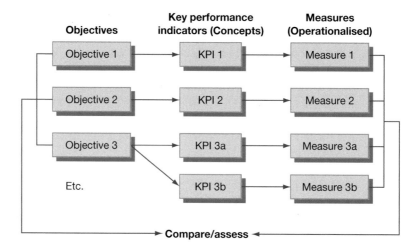

Figure 3.12   Conceptual framework: performance evaluation

- fitness level – a score based on self-assessment of 12 fitness and exercise capacity items;

- stress – exposure to 'stressful life experiences' through a 'life experience survey' questionnaire;

- hardiness – a number of scales related to alienation, security and locus of control.

Using structural equation modelling **(discussed in Chapter 17)**, they established a model as shown in Figure 3.11 with, as might be expected, level of exercise affecting fitness, which in turn affects health.

Management/policy: performance evaluation. In many cases research is part of a specific management task, of the sort discussed at the end of Chapter 1 and listed in Figure 1.8. In these cases the conceptual framework for the research may be part of a wider task. Often the 'research question' is clear from the beginning, because it is to resolve the management problem or task. Planning, marketing

Aim: to assess the size and nature of the market for a potential new sports facility.

Strategy (concepts are indicated in italics): 1. to obtain information on the general level of *demand* for *this type of facility* in the community at large, and the *market profile* of users of existing similar facilities, using national or regional data; 2. to estimate the *current level of demand* and *future level of demand* for this type of facility in the specified *market area*, based on *local demand*; 3. to assess *existing provision* of this type of facility in the locality and the likely *market share* which it might attract; 4. to conduct a consumer study of *quality* of existing provision to guide developers on the design of the proposed new facility.

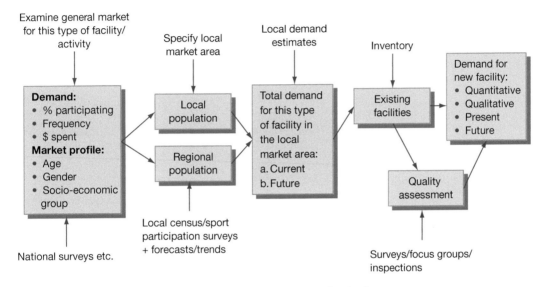

Figure 3.13 Conceptual framework: market research study

or management frameworks from the applied literature may be used as the basis for the research framework. Figure 3.12 presents a generic concept map of research which might be conducted for performance evaluation, as indicated in Step 8 of the rational-comprehensive model of the management process shown in Figure 1.4. Typically, the progress towards achievement of objectives in a corporate plan or strategy is measured by *key performance indicators* (KPIs), measures for which must often be obtained by some sort of research. Thus, for example, an objective to increase event visitor numbers would have associated with it a KPI which would call for periodic measurement of the number of event visitors.

Management/policy: market research. Figure 3.13 concerns a market research study for a proposed new facility or attraction.

Management/policy: customer service. Figure 3.14 concerns a customer service quality study using the SERVQUAL approach. The latter is similar to what is sometimes referred to as the *importance-performance* approach (see Resources section).

Aim: To assess customers' satisfaction with a leisure/tourism facility/service

Strategy (concepts in italics): Use the SERVQUAL approach to customer service quality measurement (see Parasuraman *et al.*, 1985; Howat *et al.*, 2003; Martin and O'Neill, 2010), which compares customers' *expectations* concerning various *attributes of service quality* with customers' assessment of actual *performance* of the service in regard to those attributes. The *difference* or *disconfirmation* between the two assessments provides information for managers on areas of service quality which require *management action*.

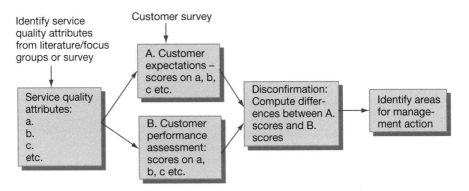

Figure 3.14   Conceptual framework: customer service quality study

Decide research question(s)

Research question, problem or hypothesis?

The focus of a research project might be expressed as a *question*, a *problem* or a *hypothesis*:

- A question requires an answer.

- A problem requires a solution.

- A hypothesis is expressed as a statement, which must be shown to be 'true' (consistent with the evidence), or 'false' (not consistent with the evidence).

The differences and relationships between the question-based approach and the hypothesis-based approach are illustrated in Figure 3.15, which uses the *problem* of declining visitor numbers at a sport facility as an illustrative example. Two versions are offered, version A, the simple version, and the more complex version B, involving exploration of a range of possible answers in the question form and testing a range of hypotheses in the hypothesis form. In each case the left-hand column uses the question form and the right-hand column uses the hypothesis form.

The hypothesis format is more common in the natural sciences while the research question format is more common in the social sciences. The latter

Research question	Hypothesis
A. Simple version	
1. Pose *research question:* Why have visitor levels at facility X declined in the last two years?	1. State hypothesis: Visitor levels declined in the last two years at facility X because of the attraction of newer, better value facilities.
2. Conduct research.	
3. *Answer:* Because of the attraction of newer, better value sites.	2. Conduct research.
	3. Result: Consistent with the evidence.
B. More detailed version	
1. *Pose research question:* Why have visitor levels at facility X declined in the last two years?	1. *Develop hypotheses:* Brainstorm/ review literature/make enquiries as to range of possible reasons for decline in attendances.
2. *Develop research strategy* Brainstorm/review literature/make enquiries as to range of possible reasons for decline in visits. Compile list of possible reasons:	2. *Formulate/state hypotheses:* Visit levels have declined because of:
a. attraction of newer, better value facilities	a. attraction of newer, better value facilities
b. declining income in local catchment	b. declining disposable income in lo-cal catchment
c. boom in competing sports	c. boom in competing sports
d. decline in quality of the facility	d. decline in quality of the facility, or
e. increase in prices.	e. increase in prices.
	… or a combination of the above.
3. *Conduct research:* Collect evidence/data to discover which reasons are plausible.	3. *Conduct research:* Collect evidence/ data and test all five hypotheses.
4. *Answer:* Because of the attraction of newer, better value facilities.	4. *Results:* a. Consistent with evidence; b. Not consistent; c. Not consistent; d. Not consistent; e. Not consistent.

Figure 3.15   The research question vs. the hypothesis

lends itself to descriptive and inductive research, while the former is more appropriate for explanatory and deductive research **(see Chapter 2)**. For most of the book the research question format is assumed, but the hypothesis format is integral to certain forms of statistical analysis and so is used in Chapter 17.

Specific starting point

In some cases the research *topic* selected by the researcher is quite specific from the beginning and is initially expressed in the form of a question: the subsequent literature review and the conceptual framework are then the process by which this specific issue is analysed and placed in the context of existing knowledge. This is demonstrated in the example used in Figure 3.15 on declining visitor numbers at a site.

Decision-making models

The conceptual framework can involve *decision-making models*, that is, the research is designed to explore the causal factors and processes involved in people's decisions to participate in an activity or visit a facility, in order to discover how others might be persuaded to participate or visit. The literature review would involve a review of similar existing models and a review of existing research on the various factors which influence people to choose a destination or visit a sport site.

Area of interest

In other cases the topic is initially quite vague: it is an area of interest without a very specific focus. In such cases the literature review and the process of developing a conceptual framework help to focus the topic and determine what exactly should be researched. The aim is to focus the research on one or more very specific questions which can be answered by the research. This is inevitably an iterative process; a question that looks simple and answerable, once subject to thought, reading and analysis, often develops into many questions which become conceptually too demanding to deal with in one project or which cannot be managed in the time and with the resources available. In such a situation a smaller part of the problem must be isolated for research. This does not mean that the complex, 'big picture' must always be ignored – there is always a case, when writing up a research project, for setting it in its wider context and explaining how and why the particular focus was adopted.

Research questions or objectives?

Often research projects have a set of practical *objectives* but these should not be confused with research *questions*. Nor should objectives be confused with the list of *tasks* necessary to conduct the research – as discussed under *research strategy* below. Thus, for example, to say that the purpose of this research is 'to conduct a survey of a group of clients' is to confuse ends with means. The survey, in this case, is being conducted for a purpose, to answer the research question(s), not as an end in itself. Of course, a research question can be embedded in an objective; thus it is possible to say that 'the objective of this research is to answer the following question: Why are attendances falling?'

The one possible exception to this rule is the sort of research project which is aimed at establishing a database for a range of possible future uses. For example, the national statistics office of most countries conducts the Population Census every five or ten years as a service to a multitude of users who use the data for a wide range of purposes **(see Chapter 7)** – so 'conducting a census of the population' could be said to be the objective of the research project. But even in this case, most of the possible future uses are known: the project assumes at least a prior range of policy-orientated research questions, related to trends in ageing, educational needs, health matters, and so on. Few sport researchers find themselves in this sort of 'open-ended' data collection situation: data should generally not be collected for their own sake or in the hope that they 'might come in useful'.

Primary and secondary questions

In most situations the idea of *primary* and *secondary* or *subsidiary* questions is helpful. The subsidiary questions are necessary steps towards answering the primary question. For example, in Figure 3.14, a number of unknowns are indicated in the diagrams, which could be turned into subsidiary research questions. Thus, in Figure 3.14 the 'market profile' could be translated into the subsidiary question: 'What is the profile of existing visitors to this type of attraction?' Compiling an inventory of existing competing local attractions presupposes the subsidiary question: 'What are the existing competing local attractions for the proposed development?'

List information requirements

The research question(s) and the conceptual framework should give rise to a list of *information requirements.* In some cases these are quite clear and the likely sources of information are straightforward. For example, in the case of the market research study in Figure 3.13, each of the concepts suggests the need for data to determine its nature or to measure it. This is illustrated in Figure 3.16, which indicates the information needs for the market research study. It also suggests some likely sources for this information. But some types of information can be

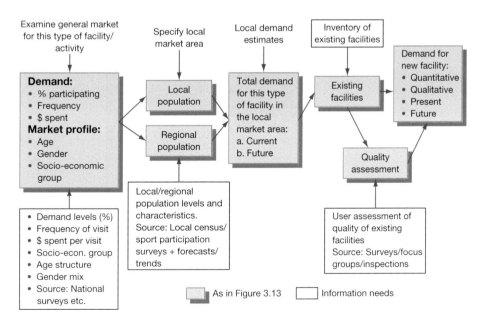

Figure 3.16 Information needs

obtained from a variety of sources, so the decision on the source of the information is a separate issue and is discussed further below. The information needs are only indicated in abbreviated form in Figure 3.16: for example, a 'market profile' for a particular type of attraction could involve more than just age, gender and socio-economic group. This is clearly linked to the idea of 'operationalising' concepts, as discussed above.

Decide research strategy

Development of a *research strategy* involves making decisions on a number of aspects of the research process, as listed in Figure 3.17.

a. Project elements/stages

Often a research project will involve a number of different elements, or 'subprojects' – for example gathering of primary and secondary data or data gathering in different locations or in different time-periods. This is clearly illustrated in the project shown in Figure 3.13, where there is an initial 'sub-project' to establish the nature of the market generally, a second sub-project to assess the nature and scale of the local market base, then a third sub-project to estimate demand for the proposed facility in relation to existing facilities. A project may involved detailed designed of stages one at a time, particularly when one part is dependent on the findings from another. For example, stage 1 might involve some fieldwork in a particular location and, depending on the outcomes of stage 1, stage 2 might involve more in-depth work in the same location or conducting work in a second location.

b. Information-gathering techniques to be used

It is at this stage that alternative information-gathering techniques are considered. While the *operationalisation of concepts* and the identification of *information needs* processes may already have indicated certain types of information source, it is here that the detail is determined. For each item in the list of information needs, a range of sources may be possible. Judgement is required to determine just what techniques to use, particularly in the light of time and resources available, or likely to be made available.

---

a. Identify project elements/stages

b. Decide information-gathering techniques to be used

c. Decide data analysis techniques to be used

d. Decide budget

e. Draw up timetable

Figure 3.17   Research strategy components

A further review of the literature can be valuable at this stage, concentrating particularly on techniques used by previous researchers, and asking such questions as whether their chosen methods were shown to be limiting or even misguided and whether lessons can be learned from past errors.

The range of information-gathering methods which are most likely to be considered at this stage consists of those covered in the following chapters of this book, namely:

- utilisation of existing information, including published and unpublished research and secondary data **(Chapters 6 and 7)**;

- observation **(Chapter 8)**;

- qualitative methods: including ethnographic methods, participant observation, informal and in-depth interviews, group interviews or focus groups **(Chapter 9)**;

- questionnaire-based surveys: including household face-to-face surveys, street surveys, telephone surveys, e-surveys, user/site surveys, postal surveys **(Chapter 10)**;

- experimental methods **(Chapter 11)**;

- the case study approach **(Chapter 12)**.

These individual techniques are not discussed further here since they are covered in general terms in Chapter 4 and in detail in subsequent chapters, as indicated.

Where the process of information gathering involves going out into the field – for instance to conduct interviews or to undertake observation – the planning of *fieldwork* needs to be considered. In the case of experimental research the proposed programme of experiments would be considered here, including consideration of location. If the proposed research does not involve primary data collection, this will not be a consideration. Where extensive data collection is involved, the organisation of fieldwork may be complex, involving recruitment and training of field staff (e.g. interviewers or observers), obtaining of permissions, including ethics committee clearance in universities **(see Chapter 4)**, and organisation of data processing and analysis.

c. *Approach to data analysis*

Data analysis may be simple and straightforward and may follow fairly logically from the type of information collection technique to be used. This is particularly the case when the research is descriptive in nature. In some cases, however, the analysis of data may be complex and particular thought needs to be given to the time and the skills which will be required to undertake the analysis. Consideration must be given to the format of the data which will be collected and just how its analysis will answer the research questions posed. The planned analysis procedures have implications for data collection. Where

Item*	Cost, £
Printing of questionnaires (500)	250
Interviewers (2 × 60 hrs@ £17/hr, gross)	2040
Data preparation (75 hrs@ £17/hr, gross)	1275
Travel to site (researcher and interviewers)	1500
Total	5065

Figure 3.18   Example research budget

* NB. the salary of the main researcher is not included

qualitative data are to be collected, for example using in-depth interviews, thought must be given as to how the results of the interviews will be analysed. Details of analysis methods which are appropriate and possible for different data collection techniques are discussed in subsequent chapters in Part III of the book, but it must be borne in mind that when planning a project, full consideration should be given to the time and resources required not only for the *collection* of data but also for its *analysis* **(as discussed in Part III).**

d. Budget and e. Timetable

In some situations key aspects of the research budget and timetable are fixed. For example, students generally have only their own labour available and no other resources and may be required to submit a report by a specified date. Research consultants usually have an upper budgetary limit and a fixed completion date. In other situations, for example when seeking a grant for research from a grant-giving body, or permission to conduct an 'in-house' project, the proposer of the research is called upon to recommend both budget and timetable. Whatever the situation, the task is never easy, since there is rarely enough time or money available to conduct the ideal research project, so compromises invariably have to be made. An example of a research budget is presented in Figure 3.18.

The research strategy and timetable can be represented in various graphical formats; examples are shown in Figures 3.19 and 3.20.

Obtain ethics clearance

Ethical behaviour is important in research, as in any other field of human activity. Certain ethical considerations, concerned with such matters as plagiarism and honesty in reporting of results, arise in all research, but additional issues arise when the research involves human subjects, in both the biological and social sciences. The principles underlying 'research ethics' are universal – they concern things like honesty and respect for the rights of individuals.

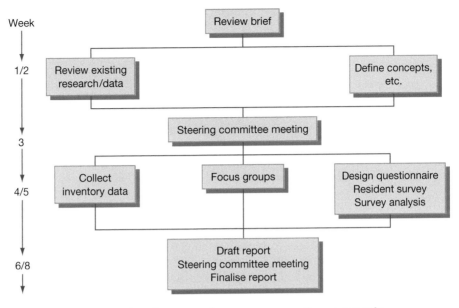

Figure 3.19 Example of research programme diagrammatic representation

Week:	1	2	3	4	5	6	7	8
Review literature								
Secondary data analysis								
Conduct survey								
Analyse survey								
Focus groups								
Meetings with clients	*			*		*		*
Write up report								

Figure 3.20 Example of research project timetable

Professional groups, such as market researchers, have established explicit 'codes of ethics' to which members are obliged to adhere. Most universities now have codes of ethics enforced by ethics committees. Typically, under-graduate and graduate projects are covered by a generic code of behaviour, but research proposals for theses and funded research by academics which involve humans or animals must be individually submitted for approval by the University Ethics Committee before the research can proceed **(research ethics are considered in more detail in Chapter 4).**

Conduct research

Element 8 of the research process is divided into two components: a. data collection and b. data analysis. These two components have not been presented as two sequential elements because in some research approaches, particularly qualitative methods, they are often intertwined; in other cases there are multiple data collection/analysis tasks in a single research project, with some being contingent on the results of others.

Actually conducting the research is what the rest of the book is about, so it is not discussed in detail here. However, it cannot be stressed enough that good research will rarely result if care is not taken over the preparatory processes discussed in this chapter. In a more positive vein, good preparation can ease the rest of the research process considerably. Often inexperienced researchers move too rapidly from stage 1, selecting the topic, to stage 8, conducting the research. This can result in the collection of data which are of doubtful use, and the researcher being presented with a problem of making sense of information which has been laboriously collected, but does not fit into any framework. If the above process is followed, every item of information collected should have a purpose, since it will have been collected to answer specific questions or test specific hypotheses. This does not, of course, mean that the unexpected will not happen and 'serendipitous' findings may not arise, nor is it intended to ignore methodologies in which the framework–strategy–data collection/analysis relationships are iterative in nature: it is intended to ensure that the core intellectual structure of the research is 'front of mind'.

It might be thought that inductive research, 'grounded theory' and various forms of qualitative research require less preparation, but in practice this is rarely the case. In qualitative research it is certainly true that there is often a more fluid, evolutionary structure to the research design **(see Chapter 9)**, but a sound preparatory base is still vital.

Communicate findings

The question of writing up of research results is not discussed in detail here because the whole of the final chapter of the book is devoted to the topic. Unlike the conduct of the empirical components of research, which inexperienced researchers invariably rush into too quickly, beginning the writing up of results is often delayed too long, so that insufficient time is left to complete it satisfactorily. An outline of the research process, as presented here, can itself be part of the problem, in that it implies that the writing-up process comes right at the end. In fact, the writing of a research report can begin almost as soon as the project begins, since all the early stages, such as the review of the literature and the development of the conceptual framework, can be written up as the project progresses.

Store data

Data, in the form of questionnaires, images and audio and video tapes/disks, in various hard-copy and electronic formats, must be securely stored during the conduct of a project and for a period of time after its conclusion. Particular ethical and legal issues arise in the case of personally identifiable data **(these are discussed in Chapter 4)**. These matters are generally affected by legislation relating to privacy and rights of access to personal records. Some data may also be subject to freedom of information laws.

Research organisations, such as universities, generally have policies on the minimum length of time for which research materials, such as hard-copy and electronic copies of questionnaires and experimental observations, must be stored after completion of research projects, typically five years. Given the length of time sometimes taken for results to be published, this is seen as a necessary precaution in case errors are detected in published results which may need to be checked back to original data sources – for example the errors can arise from miscoding of questionnaires or in transferring of data from notes or other sources into electronic form. Given that researchers may move on from institutions before the minimum storage time-period elapses, it is clearly necessary for institutions to have organised archiving and disposal systems. Of course, the ease of electronic storage means that this form of the data will generally be stored indefinitely. Re-analysis of data at a later stage and replication of research for comparative purposes often arise. In the case of longitudinal research **(see Chapter 5)**, this is intrinsic to the method. This means that the data as stored should be easily accessible and readable by the original researcher and possibly others.

The research process in the real world

As noted in the introduction, the research process rarely proceeds in the ordered way depicted in Figure 3.1 and in the above discussion. The ten-element process is an idealised framework which underpins the actual process. It is also the sort of process which has to be outlined when planning the allocation of time in a project and when seeking funding. The idea that the process might not be entirely uni-directional is indicated by the fact that the first four elements are shown as connected in a circular process. Figure 3.21 shows some additional examples of iterative components of the process and additional events which might occur during the course of research causing revisions of any element. In some more inductive research processes, iteration between the data and the research questions and conceptual framework is intrinsic to the approach and this can be conveyed verbally and diagrammatically in research proposals. This is particularly the case with qualitative methods **(see Chapter 9)**.

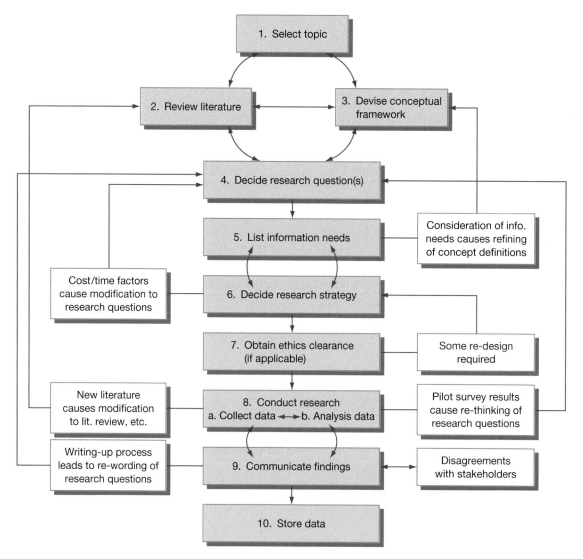

Figure 3.21 The research process in the real world

Research proposals

Introduction

Research proposals of two broad kinds are discussed here:

- *self-generated* – proposals of the sort prepared by students seeking approval for research for a project or thesis on a topic of their own choosing or by academics seeking funds for a research project of their own devising;

- *responsive* – proposals prepared by consultants responding to research briefs prepared by potential clients, sometime simulated in the teaching environment with student projects for real or hypothetical client organisations.

Planners and managers seeking 'in-house' resources to conduct research fall somewhere between the two situations described.

In each case the proposal is a written document, which may also be supported by an oral presentation, and which must be convincing to the person or persons who will decide whether the research should go ahead. The writers of a research proposal are faced with the difficult task of convincing the decision-makers of:

- the value of the research;

- the soundness of the proposed approach;

- the valuable and original insights which they will bring to the project; and

- their personal capability to conduct the research.

In some cases the decision-makers will be experts in the field, while in other cases they may be non-experts, so care must be taken to ensure that the proposal is understandable to all concerned. Clarity of expression and succinctness are often the key qualities looked for in these situations.

Self-generated research proposals

Academic research proposals, for student theses/projects or for academics seeking funding, must not only describe what research is to be done and how, but also provide a rationale for the choice of topic. This may be in part related to the declared research strategy and areas of strength of the host organisation. The topic and its treatment must be seen to be appropriate, in terms of scale and complexity, to the particular level of project involved, be it an undergraduate project, a PhD thesis or a funded project involving a team of researchers over a number of years.

In general, the academic research proposal must cover the material dealt with in this chapter. In some cases considerable work will already have been completed before the proposal is submitted. This could apply in the case of a PhD proposal, which might be based on as much as a year of preparatory work, or a proposal from an experienced academic who has been working in a particular field for a number of years. In such cases, the proposal may present considerable completed work on elements 1 to 6 of the research process. The funding being sought may only be required to conduct the fieldwork part of the research and write up the results – elements 7 to 9 of the process. In other cases, little more than the selection of the topic may have been completed and the proposal outlines a programme of funding to undertake elements 2 to 9 of the process. Some proposals contain a preliminary review of the literature with a proposal to undertake more as part of the project. Some proposals are very clear about the conceptual framework to be used, while in other cases only speculative ideas are presented. While bearing in mind, therefore, that there can be substantial differences between proposals of various types, the checklist in Figure 3.22 is offered as a guide to the contents of a proposal. A summary of a successful self-generated proposal, covering elements 1–6 is provided in Case study 3.1.

Item	Fig. 3.1	Element
1 Background and justification for selection of topic	1	3
2 (Preliminary) review of the literature	2	3
3 Conceptual/theoretical framework/theoretical discussion	3	3
4 Statement of research questions or hypotheses	4	3
5 Outline of data/information requirements and research strategy	5, 6	3
6 Details of information collection methods: structured by the research strategy, but including:	6	
• outline of any additional literature to be reviewed		6
• summary of any secondary data sources to be used		7
• outline of primary empirical tasks to be conducted – qualitative and/or quantitative, including, as appropriate		7–12
• sample/subject selection methods (Chapter 13)		13
• justification of sample sizes		13
• procedures to ensure quality		7–12
7 Consideration of ethical implications	7	4
8 Details of data analysis methods	6	9, 11, 12, 14–17
9 Timetable or work/tasks	6d	3
10 Budget, where applicable, including costing of each element/ stage/task	6	3
11 Report/thesis chapter outline or indication of number and type of publications	9	18
12 Other resources, researcher skills/experience/'track record' (necessary when seeking funds)	6d	3

Figure 3.22 Research proposal checklist: self-generated research

Case study 3.1	Example of successful self-generated research proposal

This is a summary of Frawley *et al.* (2009), a research grant application to the University of Technology, Sydney, Faculty of Business Internal Grants programme. Results of the research can be found in Frawley and Cush (2011) and Veal *et al.* (2012).

'Sport For All' and Major Sporting Events

Introduction: Sport for All

'Sport for All' is a collective term used to describe a range of policies adopted by governments to promote active participation in sport in the community. The origins of the Sport for All movement lie with the Council of Europe in the 1960s but it is now espoused by governments worldwide and by the International Olympic Committee (IOC).

One among many measures adopted by governments to promote Sport for All is to support participation in, and the hosting of, major sporting events, such as the Olympic Games and the Commonwealth Games. Among the claimed public benefits of such events is inspiring people to themselves participate in sport, a process referred to as the 'trickle down' effect.

Research questions

Three issues are addressed in the proposed research:

1. Effectiveness of the 'trickle down' effect. Whether this effect actually works, and if so, whether it is cost-effective, is unknown. The evidence available on the effectiveness of the policy is at best anecdotal. The proposed research is concerned with the question of whether or not the trickle down effect works.

2. Cost-effectiveness of the 'trickle down' effect. Public expenditure costs of supporting the Olympic Games has been related to the number of medals won, but if the 'trickle down' effect works, part of these costs should be set against the values of the social benefits of increased community participation in sport.

3. Administrative support to ensure the 'trickle down' effect. It seems likely that in some cases the trickle could work without intervention by sporting organisations or government – for example in the case of people taking up individual activities which require little infrastructure. In other cases, such as team sports, increased participation may depend on sporting organisations' activities.

Existing research

There is a small but growing literature on the 'legacy' of major sporting events in host countries, particularly the Olympic Games, but very little of it is concerned with the mass sport participation legacy (De Moragas *et al.*, 2003). Exceptions are:

- Cashman (1999), who lists mass sport participation as just one of nine types of legacy;
- Hogan and Norton (2000), who note the lack of federal government emphasis on mass participation compared with elite sport;
- a 2001 review by the Australian Sports Commission which concluded that the evidence is not clear on whether the trickle down effect was in operation in Australia following the Sydney 2000 Olympic Games;
- an analysis by the Australian Bureau of Statistics (Vanden Heuvel and Conolly, 2001) which suggested that a trickle down effect following the Sydney 2000 Olympic Games could not be discounted;
- a preliminary analysis by Veal (2003) which suggests a mixed picture among Olympic and non-Olympic sports, with some showing increases in participation in Australia after 2000, some a decline and some being stable;
- a study by Hindson *et al.* (1994) relating to New Zealand's participation in the 1992 Barcelona Summer Olympic Games and the Albertville Winter Olympic Games, which indicated very little impact on participation; and
- a report by Sust (1994) on a specific programme developed in Barcelona around the time of the 1992 Olympics to encourage children's participation in sport.

The above research, while for the most part soundly based, is deficient in a number of respects:

1. it tends to deal with only the immediate post-Sydney Olympics period, giving no indication of the sustainability of any detected changes in participation levels;
2. it tends to deal with sport as a whole, but not individual Olympic and non-Olympic sports;
3. there is no consideration of state/region-specific or city-specific participation levels;
4. there has been little research on sporting club and sporting organisations' activities;
5. there has been no consideration of costs of supporting major sporting events compared with the potential benefits of increased participation;
6. Australian work has concentrated almost entirely on the Sydney 2000 Olympics.

The proposed research is designed to overcome the first four of these deficiencies. Additional funding may be sought to address items 5 and 6.

Research plan

- The study will draw on data from the annual Exercise, Recreation and Sport Surveys (ERASS) conducted by the Standing Committee on Recreation and Sport (SCORS), over the period 2001–2005 and the 1999, 2000 and 2002 Australian Bureau of Statistics Participation in Sport and Physical Activities (PSPA) surveys to examine whether, in regard to sport participation as a whole, there is evidence for a sustained 'trickle down' effect in Australia, pre and post the Sydney 2000 Olympics, from 1998 to 2003.

- Using the same data sources, participation in individual Olympic and non-Olympic sports will be examined over the same period to determine whether there is evidence for a trickle down effect for individual sports.

- The published ERASS and PSPA reports contain state-specific data, but special tabulations will be obtained of state data broken down by metropolitan/non-metropolitan area, which yields data on capital cities – particularly Sydney, where the 2000 Games took place. While sample size limits the detail of this analysis, Steps 1 and 2 will be replicated using NSW and Sydney data to determine whether there is stronger evidence for any 'trickle down' effect in the host state/city.

- On the basis of item 3, five Olympic sports will be selected to examine the activities of governing bodies and clubs in regard to marketing and promotion activities before, during and after the Sydney 2000 Olympics. For each sport, this will involve examination of annual reports, interviews with officials of national (some Sydney-based and some Canberra-based) and state sporting governing bodies and interviews with managers of selected sport clubs.

Responsive proposals – briefs and tenders

A *brief* is an outline of the research which an organisation wishes to have undertaken. Consultants wishing to be considered to undertake the project must submit a written, costed proposal or *tender*. Usually briefs are prepared by an organisation with a view to a number of consultants competing to obtain the contract to do the research. In some cases potential consultants are first asked, possibly through an advertisement, to indicate their *expression of interest* in the project. This will involve a short statement of the consultants' capabilities, their track record of previous consultancies and the qualifications and experience of staff available.

In some cases public bodies maintain a register of accredited consultants with particular interests and capabilities, who may be invited to tender for particular projects. In the light of such statements of interest or information in the register, a *shortlist* of consultants is sent the full brief and invited to submit a detailed proposal. In very large projects some financial compensation may be provided to shortlisted candidates to cover the costs of the work taken to prepare a more detailed tender. The successful tender is not usually selected on the basis of price alone (the budget is in any case often a fixed sum indicated in the brief) but on the quality of the submitted proposal and the track record of the consultants.

Briefs vary in the amount of detail they provide. Sometimes they are very detailed, leaving little scope for consultants to express any individuality in their proposals. In other cases they are very limited and leave a great deal of scope for consultants to indicate proposed methods and approaches. Client organisations experienced in commissioning research can produce briefs which are clear and 'ready to roll'. In other situations, potential tenderers may find it necessary to clarify the client's meanings and intentions. For example, a client might ask for a study of the 'sport needs' of a community – in which case it would be necessary to clarify the client's view of the of the term 'sport' – for example whether non-organised activity is to be included, or various forms of non-competitive activity, such as walking or fitness activity. If a client asks for the 'effectiveness' of a programme to be assessed, it may be necessary to clarify whether a statement of objectives or a list of performance criteria for the programme already exists, or whether that must be developed as part of the research.

Paradoxically, problems can arise when client organisations are over-specific about aspects of their requirements but vague about other aspects. For example, an organisation may ask for a 'user survey' or 'visitor survey' to be conducted. It is not easy to decide what should be included in such a survey without information on the management or policy issues which the resultant data are intended to address. Is the organisation concerned about declining attendances? Is it wanting to change its 'marketing mix'? Is it concerned about the particular mix of clientele being attracted? Is it concerned about future trends in demand? It would be preferable in such a situation for the client to indicate the nature of the management issue and leave the tenderer to suggest the most suitable research approach to take, which might or might not include a survey.

Sometimes there is a hidden agenda which the potential researcher would do well to become familiar with before embarking on the research. For example, research can sometimes be used as a means to defuse or delay difficult management decisions in an organisation. An example would be where a sport service is suffering declining attendances because of poor maintenance of facilities and poor staff attitudes to customers; this is very clear to anyone who walks through the door, but the management decides to commission a 'market study', in the hope that the answer to their problem can be found 'out there' in the market – when in fact the problem is very much 'in here', and their money might be better spent on improving maintenance and staff training than on research!

A situation where the client's requirements may seem vague is when the research is not related to immediate policy needs but to possible future needs or simply to satisfy curiosity. For example, a manager of a sport facility might commission a visitor survey (perhaps because there is spare money in the current year's budget) without having any specific policy or management problems in mind. In that case the research will need to specify hypothetical or potential policy or management issues and match the data specifications to them.

What should a proposal contain? The first and golden principle is that it should *address the brief.* It is likely that the brief will have been discussed at great length in the commissioning organisation; every aspect is likely to be of importance to some individual or section in the organisation, so *all* aspects should be addressed in the proposal. So if the brief lists, say, four objectives, it would be advisable for the proposal to indicate very clearly how each of the four objectives will be met. A proposal must therefore indicate the following:

- What is to be done.
- How is it to be done.
- When will it be done.
- What will it cost.
- Who will do it.

A typical responsive proposal might include elements as shown in Figure 3.23, and an example covering elements 1–6 is presented in Case study 3.2.

Item	Fig. 3.1	Element
1. Brief summary of key aspects of the proposal, including any unique approach and particular skills/experience of the consultants		
2. Re-statement of the key aspects of the brief and interpretation/ definition of key concepts		
3. Conceptual framework/theoretical discussion	3	3
4. Research strategy – methods/tasks	6	3
5. Details of information collection methods – structured by the research strategy, but including:	5, 6	
• outline of any additional literature to be reviewed	2	6
• summary of any secondary data sources to be used		7
• outline of fieldwork to be conducted – qualitative and/or quantitative		7–12
• sample/subject selection methods		13
• sample sizes and their justification		13
• procedures to ensure quality		
6. Timetable of tasks, including interim reporting/meetings with clients/draft and final report submission	6	3
7. Budget: Costing of each element/stage/task	6	3
8. Chapter outline of report and, if appropriate, details of other proposed reporting formats – e.g. interim reports, working papers, articles	9	18
9. Resources available, staff, track record		3

Figure 3.23   **Research proposal checklist: responsive research**

Case study 3.2   Example of a successful response to a research brief

In 2009 the Australian Sports Commission published a call for 'expressions of interest' for a project concerned with *Sport and active recreation participation and non-participation for people with disability*. Five main tasks were listed in this brief:

1. identify the full range of factors that prevent people with disability from participating in sport and physical recreation;
2. identify and provide an understanding of the benefits people with disability derive from participating in sport and physical recreation;
3. identify the attitudes and perceptions that influence the participation of people with disabilities in sport and physical recreation;
4. identify the key messages that would be most effective at influencing the participation of people with disability in sport and physical recreation;
5. identify the extent and range of opportunities currently being provided by the disability service or sport and recreation provider.

A submission from a team at the University of Technology, Sydney was successful. While the submission addressed all five of the tasks listed above, here we summarise the response to the first one only.

Submission from the University of Technology, Sydney team: Identification of the full range of factors that prevent people with disability from participating in sport and physical recreation[1]

Context

- During the last twenty years, many Western countries have adopted their own disability discrimination legislation, which includes the right to cultural life. This was reinforced by the UN *Convention on the Rights of Persons with Disabilities* (United Nations, 2006).
- Researchers concur that historically there has been systematic discrimination against people with disability concerning access to sport and recreation both in Australia and internationally (Barnes *et al.*, 2010).
- An area where the effect is stark is sport and active recreation where the participation rate of people with disability is some 15 per cent lower than for the general population (Australian Bureau of Statistics, 2006).
- Participation is a complex interaction between intrapersonal, interpersonal and structural factors (Jackson and Scott, 1999). If access to sport and active recreation is constrained, inhibited or denied then the benefits of involvement in these activities cannot be realised (Liu, 2009).

- Recent research confirms that people with disability participate in sport and active recreation at a significantly lower rate than the rest of the population (Liu, 2009; Robertson and Emerson, 2010) and that sport practices often reflect historical factors (Cashman and Darcy, 2008).

- It was not until the launch of the Exercise Recreation and Sport Survey in 2001 (Australian Sports Commission, 2001–2009) that detailed annual sport participation data were collected in Australia. However, the survey has not identified people with disability.

- Much of the above research presents descriptions of lower participation rates but does not explain why people with disability participate less than the general population.

Constraints

Leisure constraints research has investigated constraints on leisure participation generally (Crawford and Godbey, 1987; Jackson and Scott, 1999) and three categories of constraint have been identified:

1. intrapersonal constraints – lack of skills, self-confidence, encouragement or information about opportunities for leisure that affect preference or level of interest in a particular type of leisure activity;
2. interpersonal constraints – associated with other individuals, including lack of leisure partners or lack of social interaction skills; and
3. structural constraints – those that exist between individual preferences and participation in a leisure activity, including lack of finances, lack of transportation, limited abilities, lack of time or architectural barriers.

A review of the literature on sport participation and non-participation and disability and sport constraints suggests four major gaps or omissions:

- People with disability are treated as a homogeneous group rather than a number of discrete groups with different access needs.

- The degree of disability is likely to have a major impact on participation but is untested in the constraint literature.

- Disability studies theory involving social model approaches (Barnes *et al.*, 2010) and 'impairment effects' (Thomas, 2004) have not been incorporated into constraint research.

- No studies on constraints to participation in sport and active recreation have been undertaken for people with disability.

Research questions

The following research questions are suggested:

1. What are the comparative sport and active recreation participation and non-participation rates of people with disability in Australia?

2. What constraints to sport participation do people with disability them-selves identify?

3. What effect does disability type (mobility, hearing, vision and cognitive) have on the constraints faced?

4. What effect does the level of support need (independent, low, moderate, high and very high) have on the constraints faced?

Research design and methods

- The proposed research design is an online survey based, for comparative purposes, on the Exercise, Recreation and Sport Survey design, together with questions on constraints, socio-demographic profile, disability type and support needs.

- It will be delivered in eight formats for the different types of disability: 1. an online questionnaire compliant with World Wide Web Consortium (W3C) accessibility standards; 2. in hard copy (for participants without Internet access); 3. in large print (for participants with a visual impair-ment); 4. easy text (people who are blind or vision impaired/blind who use screen readers); 5. Braille (for blind participants); online questionnaire with embedded Auslan (Australian Sign Language) video clips (for deaf and hearing impaired); 6. telephone-assisted completion (for people who had trouble completing online or hard copy); 7. an online questionnaire designed specifically for participants with mental health constraints; 8. an easy English version for administration by a third-party attendant or sup-porter for people with limited literacy or other forms of moderate to very high support needs.

Findings

The findings of the study can be found in Darcy *et al.* (2011).

Note

1 A number of references to the literature included in the original have been deleted from this summary.

References

See Resources section.

Summary

This chapter covers the process of planning a research project and preparing a research proposal. It is structured around ten 'elements':

1. selecting the topic;

2. reviewing the literature;

3. devising a conceptual framework;

4. deciding the research questions;

5. listing information needs;

6. deciding a research strategy;

7. obtaining ethics clearance (where relevant);

8. conducting the research;

9. reporting the findings; and

10. storing the data.

The term 'elements' is used rather than 'stages' or 'steps', since the ten elements do not always occur in the precise order indicated. In particular, the first four elements listed take place in a variety of orders, often in an iterative process. The overview of the research process is followed by a discussion of research proposals – self-generated proposals, where the researcher initiates the research, and responsive proposals, which are prepared in response to a research brief from a commissioning organisation.

Test questions

1. In this chapter, it is suggested that a research topic might arise from eight different sources – what are the eight sources?

2. What is a concept?

3. What is meant by 'operationalisation' of a concept?

4. What is a conceptual framework?

5. What is the difference between a research question and a hypothesis?

6. What are the differences between a self-generated research proposal and a responsive research proposal and what implications do they have for the content of the two types of proposal?

Exercises

1. Over the next week, watch the sports news on one television channel and read the sports section of the major newspaper of your city. Excluding results of competition, identify a research topic that emerges from the contemporary issues discussed in the media for the week.

2. Select three articles from an issue of a sport journal and identify the basis of their choice of research topic.

3. Select any article from a copy of a sport journal and: a. identify the key concepts used in the article; b. draw a simple concept map to show how the concepts are related.

4. Draw a concept map for a possible research project on either: a. the effects of American culture on sport in another country of your choice; or b. the effects of the ageing of the population on trends in sport participation in Western countries.

5. Write a case study, similar in structure and length to case study 3.1, on a topic of your own choice.

Resources

The best reading material for this chapter would be examples of successful research grant applications and proposals written in response to tenders. Completed research reports, whether academic or non-academic, vary in the amount of detail they provide about the development of the process.

- *Approaches to sport research:* Mondello and Pederson (2003), Weed (2009).

- *Concepts in sport:* Atkinson (2012), Caudwell *et al.* (2009), Masteralexis *et al.* (2011).

- *Stages in the research process:* Most general and specific research methods texts deal with the stages in the research process, for example: Andrew *et al.* (2011: 29–44), Gratton and Jones (2010: 16), Long (2007: 17).

- *Concept mapping:* Brownson *et al.* (2008), Nicholls and Ntoumanis (2010).

- *Conceptual frameworks:*

    o general: Miles and Huberman (1994: 18–22), Pearce (2012: 28–49)

    o generated from qualitative research: Johnston *et al.* (1999: 263–74)

- adolescent girls and sport/recreational choice: James and Embrey (2005)
- developing sport skills: Weissensteiner *et al.* (2009)
- environmental influences on walking and cycling: Pikora *et al.* (2003)
- policy for international elite sporting success: De Bosscher *et al.* (2006)
- psychological connection to sport: Funk and James (2001)
- sport and consumer behaviour: Kim and Trail (2011)
- sport sponsorship: Lamont *et al.* (2011)
- sport events: Mazodier *et al.* (2012)
- sport marketing: Fullerton and Merz (2008)
- sport tourism: Wäsche and Woll (2010)
- recreation participation: Brandenburg *et al.* (1982).

- *Importance-performance analysis:* Howat *et al.* (1996), Rial *et al.* (2008), Veal (2010: Chapter 13), Zhang *et al.* (2011).
- Purposes of research: Newman *et al.* (2003).
- *Research strategies/agenda:*
  - Australian sport: Australian Sports Commission (2004)
  - USA – physical activity: Brownson *et al.* (2008)
  - Europe – sport: European Platform for Sport Innovation (EPSI) (2008)
  - UK – lifestyle sports: Tomlinson *et al.* (2005)
  - General: promotion of walking for exercise: Owen *et al.* (2004).
- *Topic selection:* Andrew *et al.* (2011: 29–44).

References

Andrew, D. P. S., Pederson, P. M. and McEvoy, C. D. (2011). *Research Methods and Design in Sport Management.* Champaign, IL: Human Kinetics.

Atkinson, M. (2012) *Key Concepts in Sport and Exercise Research Methods.* London: Sage.

Australian Bureau of Statistics (2006) *General Social Survey* (Cat. No. 9155.0). Canberra: Australian Bureau of Statistics.

Australian Sports Commission (2001–2009) Exercise, Recreation and Sport Survey (ERASS), available at: www.ausport.gov.au/information/casro/ERASS (Accessed May 2013).

Australian Sports Commission (2004) *Statement of Intent: Social Research Agenda, 2004–2008.* Canberra: ASC, available at: www.ausport.gov.au/information/nsr/about_us (Accessed May 2013).

Barnes, C., Mercer, G. and Shakespeare, T. (2010) *Exploring Disability: A Sociological Introduction, Second edn.* Malden, MA: Polity Press.

Brandenburg, J., Greiner, W., Hamilton-Smith, E., Scholten, H., Senior, R. and Webb, J. (1982) A conceptual model of how people adopt recreation activities. *Leisure Studies*, 1(3), 263–76.

Brownson, R. C., Kelly, C. M. *et al.* (2008) Environmental and policy approaches for promoting physical activity in the United States: a research agenda. *Journal of Physical Activity and Health*, 5(4), 488–503.

Cashman, R. (1999) Legacy. In R. Cashman and A. Hughes (eds) *Staging the Olympics: The Event and its Impact.* Sydney: University of New South Wales Press, 183–94.

Cashman, R. and Darcy, S. (eds) (2008) *Benchmark Games: The Sydney 2000 Paralympic Games.* Petersham, NSW: Walla Walla Press/Australian Centre for Olympic Studies.

Caudwell, J., Wheaton, B., Wagg, S. and Brick, C. (2009) *Key Concepts in Sports Studies.* London: Sage.

Crawford, D. W. and Godbey, G. (1987) Reconceptualising barriers to family leisure. *Leisure Sciences*, 9(2), 119–28.

Csikszentmihalyi, M. (1990) *Flow: The Psychology of Optimal Experience.* New York: Harper and Row.

Darcy, S., Taylor, T., Murphy, A. and Lock, D. (2011) *Getting Involved in Sport: The Participation and Non-Participation of People with Disability in Sport and Active Recreation.* Canberra: Australian Sport Commission, available at: www.ausport.gov.au/participating/disability/resources/research_and_reports/disability_participation_research (Accessed May 2013).

De Bosscher, V., De Knop, P., Van Bottenburg, M. and Shibli, S. (2006) A conceptual framework for analysing sports policy factors leading to international sporting success. *European Sport Management Quarterly*, 6(2), 185–215.

De Moragas, M., Kennett, C. and Puig, N. (eds) (2003) *The Legacy of the Olympic Games, 1984–2000: International Symposium, Lausanne, 14–16 Nov. 2002.* International Olympic Committee, Lausanne.

European Platform for Sport Innovation (EPSI) (2008) *Building a Future of European Sports Innovation.* Brussels: EPSI, available at: http://epsi.eu/strategic-research-agenda/ (Accessed June 2012).

Foucault, M. (1979) *Discipline and Punish.* Harmondsworth, UK: Penguin.

Frawley, S. and Cush, A. (2011) Major sporting events and participation legacy: the case of the 2003 Rugby World Cup. *Managing Leisure*, 16(1), 65–76.

Frawley, S., Veal, A. J., Cashman, R. and Toohey, K. (2009) *'Sport For All' and Major Sporting Events: Introduction to the Project.* School of Leisure, Sport and Tourism Working Paper 5, Sydney: University of Technology, Sydney, available at: www.business.uts.edu.au/lst/research/research_papers.html (Accessed May 2013).

Fullerton, S., and Merz, G. R. (2008) The four domains of sports marketing: a conceptual framework. *Sports Marketing Quarterly*, 17(1), 90–108.

Funk, D. C. and James, J. (2001) The Psychological Continuum Model: a conceptual framework for understanding an individual's psychological connect to sport. *Sport Management Review*, 4(2), 119–50.

Gratton, C. and Jones, I. (2010) *Research Methods for Sport Studies, Second edn.* London: Routledge.

Henderson, K. A. (2006) *Dimensions of Choice: A Qualitative Approach to Recreation, Parks, and Leisure Research, Second edn.* State College, PA: Venture.

Hindson, A., Gidlow, B. and Peebles, C. (1994) The 'trickle-down' effect of top-level sport: myth or reality? A case-study of the Olympics. *Australian Journal of Leisure and Recreation*, 4(1), 16–24, 31.

Hogan, K. and Norton, K. (2000) The 'price' of Olympic gold. *Journal of Science and Medicine in Sport*, 3(2), 203–18.

Howard, K. and Sharp, J. A. (1983) *The Management of a Student Research Project.* Aldershot, UK: Gower.

Howat, G., Absher, J., Crilley, G. and Milne, I. (1996) Measuring customer service quality in sports and leisure centres. *Managing Leisure*, 1(2), 77–89.

Howat, G., Crilley, G., Mikilewicz, S., Edgecombe, S., March, H., Murray, D. and Bell, B. (2003) Service quality, customer satisfaction and behavioural intentions of Australian aquatic centre customers, 1999–2001. *Annals of Leisure Research*, 5, 52–65.

Jackson, E. L. and Scott, D. (1999) Constraints to leisure. In E. L. Jackson and T. L. Burton (eds) *Leisure Studies: Prospects for the Twenty-First Century.* State College, PA: Venture, 299–332.

James, K. and Embrey, L. (2005) Adolescent girls' leisure: a conceptual framework highlighting factors that can affect girls' recreational choices. *Annals of Leisure Research*, 5(1), 14–26.

Johnston, L. H., Corban, R. M. and Clarke, P. (1999) Multi-method approaches to the investigation of adherence issues within sport and exercise: qualitative and quantitative techniques. In S. J. Bull (ed.) *Adherence Issues in Sport and Exercise.* Chichester, UK: John Wiley, 263–88.

Kartakoullis, N., Karlis, G. and Karadakis, M. (2009) Sports for all philosophy: the evolution in Cyprus and the transfer from a sport to a health orientation. *International Journal of Sport Management, Recreation and Tourism*, 3(1), 47–60.

Kim, Y. K. and Trail, G. (2011) A conceptual framework for understanding relationships between sport consumers and sport organisations: a relationship quality approach. *Journal of Sport Management*, 25(1), 57–69.

Lamont, M., Hing, N. and Gainsbury, S. (2011) Gambling on sport sponsorship: a conceptual framework for research and regulatory review. *Sport Management Review*, 14(3), 246–57.

Lenskyj, H. J. (2008) *Olympic Industry Resistance.* Albany, NY: State University of New York Press.

Lincoln, Y. (2005) Institutional review boards and methodological conservatism: the challenge to and from phenomenological paradigms. In N. K.

Denzin and Y. S. Lincoln (eds) *Handbook of Qualitative Research, Third edn.* Thousand Oaks, CA: Sage, 165–90.

Liu, Y. D. (2009) Sport and social inclusion: evidence from the performance of public leisure facilities. *Social Indicators Research*, 90(2), 325–37.

Long, J. (2007) *Researching Leisure, Sport and Tourism: The Essential Guide.* London: Sage.

Markula, P. and Denison, J. (2005) Sport and personal narrative. In D. L. Andrews, D. S. Mason and M. L. Silk (eds) *Qualitative Methods in Sports Studies.* Oxford: Berg, 165–84.

Markula, P. and Pringle, R. (2006) *Foucault, Sport and Exercise.* London: Routledge.

Martin, D. S. and O'Neill, M. (2010) Scale development and testing: a new measure of cognitive satisfaction in sports tourism. *Event Management*, 14(1), 1–15.

Masteralexis, L., Barr, C. and Hums, M. (2011) *Principles and Practice of Sport Management.* Sudbury, MA: Jones & Bartlett Learning.

Mazodier, M., Quester, P. and Chandon, J. L. (2012) Unmasking the ambushers: conceptual framework and empirical evidence. *European Journal of Marketing*, 46(1/2), 192–214.

Miles, M. B. and Huberman, A. M. (1994) *Qualitative Data Analysis, Second edn.* Thousand Oaks, CA: Sage.

Mondello, M. J. and Pedersen, P. M. (2003) A content analysis of the *Journal of Sports Economics. Journal of Sports Economics*, 4(1), 64–73.

Newman, I., Ridenour, C. S., Newman, C. and DeMarco, G. M. P. (2003) A typology of research purposes and its relationship to mixed methods. In A. Tashakkori and C. Teddlie (eds) *Handbook of Mixed Methods in Social and Behavioral Research.* Thousand Oaks, CA: Sage, 167–88.

Nicholls, A. R. and Ntoumanis, N. (2010) Traditional and new methods of assessing coping in sport. In A. R. Nicholls (ed.) *Coping in Sport: Theory, Methods and Related Constructs.* Hauppauge, NY: Nova Science Publishers, 35–51.

Nicholson, M. and Hoye, R. (2012) *Sport and Social Capital.* London: Routledge.

Owen, N., Humpel, N., Leslie, E., Bauman, A. and Sallis, J. F. (2004) Understanding environmental influences on walking: review and research agenda. *American Journal of Preventive Medicine*, 27(1), 67–76.

Parasuraman, A., Zeithaml, V. A. and Berry, L. L. (1985) A conceptual model of service quality and implications for future research. *Journal of Marketing*, 49(4), 41–50.

Pearce, D. (2012) *Frameworks for Tourism Research*, Wallingford, UK. CABI.

Pikora, T., Giles-Corti, B., Bull, F., Jamrozik, K. and Donovan, R. (2003) Developing a framework for assessment of the environmental determinants of walking and cycling. *Social Science and Medicine*, 56(6), 1693–703.

Rial, A., Rial, J., Varela, J. and Real, E. (2008) An application of importance-performance analysis (IPA) to the management of sport centres. *Managing Leisure*, 13(3–4), 179–88.

Robertson, J. and Emerson, E. (2010) Participation in sports by people with intellectual disabilities in England: a brief report. *Journal of Applied Research in Intellectual Disabilities*, 23(6), 616–22.

Roth, D. L., Wiebe, D. J., Fillingim, R. B. and Shay, K. A. (1989) Life events, fitness, hardiness, and health: a simultaneous analysis of proposed stress-resistant effects. *Journal of Personality and Social Psychology*, 57(1), 136–42.

Rowe, D. (1995) *Popular Cultures: Rock Music, Sport and the Politics of Pleasure.* London: Sage.

Sust, F. (1995) The sports legacy of the Barcelona Games. In M. De Moragas and M. Botella (eds) *The Keys to Success: The Social, Sporting, Economic and Communications Impact of Barcelona '92.* Barcelona: Centre d'Estudis Olímpics i de l'Esport, Universitat Autònoma de Barcelona, 261–5.

Thomas, C. (2004) Disability and impairment. In J. Swain, S. French, C. Barnes and C. Thomas (eds) *Disabling Barriers – Enabling Environments.* London: Sage, 21–8.

Tomlinson, A., Ravenscroft, N., Wheaton, B. and Gilchrist, P. (2005) *Lifestyle Sports and National Sport Policy: An Agenda for Research.* London: Sport England, available at: www.academia.edu/197074/Lifestyle_Sports_and_National_Sport_Policy_An_Agenda_for_Research.

United Nations (2006) *Convention on the Rights of Persons with Disabilities.* New York: United Nations General Assembly, available at: www.un.org/disabilities/convention/conventionfull.shtml (Accessed May 2013).

Vanden Heuvel, A. and Conolly, L. (2001) *The Impact of the Olympics on Participation in Australia: Trickle Down Effect, Discouragement Effect or No Effect?* Adelaide, National Centre for Culture and Recreation Statistics, Australian Bureau of Statistics (discussion paper available via www.abs.gov.au).

Veal, A. J. (2003) Tracking change: leisure participation and policy in Australia, 1985–2002. *Annals of Leisure Research*, 6(3), 245–7.

Veal, A. J. (2010) *Leisure, Sport and Tourism: Politics, Policy and Planning.* Wallingford, UK: CABI.

Veal, A. J., Frawley, S. and Toohey, K. (2012) The sport participation legacy of the Sydney 2000 Olympic Games and other international sporting events hosted in Australia. *Journal of Policy Research in Tourism, Leisure and Events*, 4(2), 155–84.

Wäsche, H. and Woll, A. (2010) Regional sports tourism networks: a conceptual framework. *Journal of Sport and Tourism*, 15(3), 191–214.

Weed, M. (2009) Progress in sports tourism research? A meta-review and exploration of futures. *Tourism Management*, 30(5), 615–28.

Weissensteiner, J., Abernethy, B. and Farrow, D. (2009) Towards the development of a conceptual model of expertise in cricket batting: a grounded theory approach. *Journal of Applied Sport Psychology*, 21(3), 276–92.

Zhang, J. J., Lam, E. T. C., Cianfrone, B. A., Zapalac, R. K., Holland, S. and Williamson, D. P. (2011) An importance-performance analysis of media activities associated with WNBA game consumption. *Sport Management Review*, 14(1), 64–78.

Research ethics

Introduction

Ethical behaviour is important in research, as in any other field of human activity. Ethical considerations, concerned with such matters as plagiarism and honesty in reporting of results, arise in all research, but additional issues arise when the research involves human and animal subjects, in both the social and biological sciences. Increasingly, ethical issues also arise in relation to research which may have an impact on the physical environment. The underlying principles of research ethics are universal: they concern things like honesty and respect for the rights of individuals and animals and the integrity of ecosystems. The issue came to the fore at the end of the Second World War when details were revealed of horrific experiments which had been conducted on prisoners in the Nazi concentration camps, and certain medical experiments conducted in the United States in the 1960s and 1970s without the consent of the subjects (Loue, 2002). These events raised questions not only about the ethical conduct of research but also the use of findings from research conducted unethically.

The result has been the establishment of international, national, professional and institutional codes of research ethics and their oversight by regulatory organisations. The scope of contemporary concerns in the area of research ethics is demonstrated in a document on the responsible conduct of research published in 2007 by a consortium of national research funding organisations and universities; it covered:

- honesty and integrity;

- respect for human research participants, animals and the environment;

- good stewardship of public resources used to conduct research;

- appropriate acknowledgement of the role of others in research;

- responsible communication of research results (NHMRC *et al.*, 2007: 13).

In this chapter we consider:

- the institutional oversight of research ethics

- ethics in the research process

- ethical issues in research, including:

  - researcher competence;
  - subjects' freedom to participate or not;
  - informed consent;
  - risk of harm to subjects;
  - honesty/rigour in analysis, interpretation and reporting;
  - authorship and acknowledgements;
  - access to research information.

Institutional oversight of research ethics

Most universities now have their own codes of research ethics enforced by ethics committees or boards. Typically, undergraduate and graduate projects are covered by a generic code of behaviour, but research proposals for student theses and funded and unfunded research by academics which involve human or animal subjects must be individually submitted for approval by the University Ethics Committee.

Codes of research ethics have intrinsic value in protecting the rights of humans and animals involved in research, but they also serve a professional and organisational function. Researchers may be subject to litigation and can lose professional indemnity if they are not seen to have adhered to the appropriate code of ethics. A related consideration is the question of public relations and the standing of organisations responsible for the research within the community. Some practices may be ethical, but still give offence, so the value of the data collected using such practices must be weighed against the ill-will which may be generated.

In universities and other research institutions, research projects involving human or animal subjects are subject to approval by an ethics committee. Some universities have established ethics committees to cover the whole of the university, but more usually at least two committees, cover human- and animal-related research, respectively. In some cases committees are faculty or division based. Typically the approval process involves the completion of an 'Application for Ethics Approval Form' which must provide full details of the rationale for the research, the methods to be used and qualifications of the researchers involved. The *National Ethics Application Form* of the Australian National Health and Medical Research Council (NHMRC, nd), which is a model for the use of Australian research institutions, runs to over 450 items of information.

When ethics committees are faculty/division specific, a researcher would expect committee members to be familiar with the research methods being used, but with university-wide committees there is a possibility that committee members might not be familiar with research methods being used by colleagues from very different disciplines, especially newer methods. This is believed by some to be the case with some qualitative methods which reflect a very different epistemology from the positivist approach of the natural sciences. This issue is argued by Yvonna Lincoln (2005) who notes 'increased scrutiny' from research committees in the United States 'largely in response to failures in biomedical research', but spilling over into the social sciences and resulting in '… multiple rereviews of faculty proposals for qualitative research projects and' … rereviews and denials of proposed student research (particularly dissertation research) that utilise action research … methods, research in the subjects' own settings (e.g. high schools), and/or research which is predominantly qualitative in nature' (Lincoln, 2005: 167). This is just one example of the expression of unease about the growing significance of a formalised ethics bureaucracy in universities and the spread of their influence from natural sciences into social sciences, as expressed, for example, by Haggerty (2004).

Ethics in the research process

Research ethics can be examined in regard to three dimensions: the nature of the ethical issue, the stage or component of the research process where the issues arise and whether the research subject is anonymous or identified.

Regarding the nature of the ethical issue: most codes of ethics and ethical practice are based on the 'golden rule' which relates to all human conduct and is endorsed by most religions, that is, that you should treat others as you yourself would wish to be treated. More specifically, the general principles usually invoked in codes of research ethics are that:

- the research should be *beneficial to society;*

- researchers should be suitably *qualified* and/or *supervised* to conduct the research;

- subjects should take part *freely;*
- subjects should take part only on the basis of *informed consent;*
- no *harm* should befall the research subjects;
- data should be *honestly* and *rigorously analysed, interpreted* and *reported.*

These issues arise in different stages/components of the research process, as summarised in Figure 4.1.

Regarding anonymous versus personally identifiable data, in much primary empirical sport research, for example on-site questionnaire-based surveys and much observational research, data are collected and stored anonymously: the researcher never knows the names of the subjects, so names are not recorded in any form. However, in some cases the names and contact details of individual subjects are known to the researcher and may be recorded in hard copy or electronically as part of the data from the research.

Examples of the ways these three dimensions relate to one another are shown in Case study 4.1. It can be seen that the question of identifiable subjects relates not only to the storage and reporting of results components of the research. The ethical issues are discussed in turn below.

	Stage in the research process					
Ethical issue	Design/ organisation	Data collection	Data analysis/ interpretation	Storing data during project	Reporting	Storing data after project
Social benefit	●					
Researcher competence	●					
Subjects' freedom of choice		●				
Subjects' informed consent		●				
Risk of harm to subjects – anonymous		●				
Risk of harm to subjects – identifiable		●	●	●	●	●
Honesty/rigour in analysis/ interpretation			●			
Honesty/rigour in reporting					●	

Figure 4.1 **Ethics in the research process**

Case study 4.1   Examples of ethical issues in sport research

A. Status of the participant observer in an outdoor adventure setting

Keith Donne (2006) conducted research for a PhD thesis as a participant observer at a water sports outdoor adventure centre involving a study of young people aged 14–16 years, who used the centre, and the professional instructors who worked at the centre. Among ethical issues he identifies during the experience were the following:

- In order to gain access to facilities involving contact with children it was necessary for the researcher to undergo an official police check to ensure that he had no prior criminal record.
- Donne describes the role he chose to play at the centre. Centre staff – mainly instructors – knew he was conducting research but it was necessary for him to indicate an appropriate level of expertise in water sports since he knew that 'appearing too knowledgeable could have resulted in confrontational situations' with the staff, while 'any pretence of incompetence' could have identified him as a liability. He had personal skills in sailing and windsurfing, was a qualified kayak and canoe instructor and had competed at high level in canoe slalom. He decided to pose as 'an enthusiastic learner with a basic understanding and competence'. This mild level of deception was considered justified in the interests of successfully conducting the research.
- Early on, Donne recognised two instructors at the centre whom he had taught in the past and who would be aware of his skill level, and he had to take them into his confidence regarding his 'enthusiastic learner' role.
- When one of the centre instructors, who had been reluctant to be interviewed for the research, challenged Donne to a canoe race, he accepted but then regretted having done so because it placed him in a dilemma as to whether he should deliberately lose the race to secure the instructor's cooperation with the research.

B. Exposure by association in autobiographical research on élite sport coaching

Robyn Jones et al. (2006) discuss the example of a doctoral thesis on the relationship between an élite athlete (the researcher) and his coach, using the autobiographical method. The relationship between the two had deteriorated over time, with negative views expressed about the coach in the thesis. While a pseudonym was used for the coach, the author of the thesis was clearly identified and so, for people familiar with the athletics scene, the coach could be identified 'by association'. This was pointed out by one of the thesis examiners. The paper, involving the student and thesis supervisors, describes how the problem was dealt with in the final, approved, version of the thesis.

Ethical issues in research

Social benefit

Research on nuclear and chemical weaponry has given rise to the proposition that research should only be supported if its social benefits can be demonstrated. Such an assessment is, of course, subjective. Thus, during the Cold War, it was argued that research on nuclear weapons could be defended on the grounds that peace was maintained as long as each side – the West and the communist bloc – matched each other's weapons, in terms of technological sophistication as well as quantity, so that neither side would risk attacking the other: the principal of mutually assured destruction (MAD). In contemporary sport research the issues are not as dramatic, but can arise in relation to funding sources: for example, should research funding be accepted from tobacco companies or from companies with questionable environmental practices?

Policy/practice-related research

Ethics issues can arise in policy-related research commissioned by government, commercial or non-profit organisations when such organisations see research as supporting their particular political/policy, interest-group or commercial, actual or planned activities. This has become a live issue in research commissioned by governments to justify public investment in major sport events. Not only can this result in research which is designed to produce certain desired results, but it can result in policy-making being based on possibly inappropriate instrumental factors rather than intrinsic factors.

Push polls

In 1995 the US National Council on Public Polls issued the following media release about:

> a growing and thoroughly unethical political campaign technique, commonly called 'push polls', masquerading as legitimate political polling ... A 'push poll' is a telemarketing technique in which telephone calls are used to canvass vast numbers of potential voters, feeding them false and damaging 'information' about a candidate under the guise of taking a poll to see how this 'information' affects voter preferences. In fact, the intent is to 'push' the voters away from one candidate and toward the opposing candidate. This is clearly political telemarketing, using innuendo and, in many cases, clearly false information to influence voters; there is no intent to conduct research.
>
> These telemarketing techniques damage the electoral process in two ways. They injure candidates, often without revealing the source of the information. Also, the

results of a 'push poll', if released, give a seriously flawed and biased picture of the political situation. *(National Council on Public Polls, 1995)*

Push polling typically takes place in marginal electorates where a successful telephone campaign can have a significant impact on the election outcome. A typical push poll question would be of the following format: 'Given that candidate X could increase income tax by 50 per cent, whereas candidate Y is committed to no increases in income tax, how does this affect your voting intentions?' The results of the poll are of less interest than the planting of the false or misleading information about candidate X in the listener's mind.

Push polling occurs in the political realm and would rarely be relevant to sport, but it highlights the ethical dimension of the use of the 'leading question' **(discussed further in Chapter 10)**.

Researcher competence

Research ethics guidelines require that those undertaking research have appropriate levels of training, qualifications and experience, including familiarisation with ethical issues.

Occasionally, cases in which unqualified individuals are found to have been practising as doctors and even as surgeons attract media publicity. The community is shocked that unqualified people should be undertaking such important work and the individuals are duly prosecuted. Such cases represent the extreme of public ethical concern because of the level of risk of harm involved. But the issue of professional competence, while less clear-cut in other areas, is nevertheless applicable. In sport research a researcher who is not competent, through training and/or experience, to conduct research runs the risk of:

● wasting the resources of the funding organisation;

● wasting the time of subjects;

● abusing the goodwill of subjects;

● misleading the users of the research results; and/or

● damaging the reputation of the research organisation.

Free choice

It seems obvious that subjects should not be coerced to become involved in research projects, but there are some grey areas. Some of these are institutional and some are intrinsic to the design and nature of the research.

Captive groups

In universities, students are often used as subjects in research. In some places students are *required* to be available for a certain amount of experimental or survey work conducted by academic staff, and in some cases they receive study credit for this involvement. Although, invariably, students are able to opt out of such activities, there could be moral pressure on them to conform and possibly fear of sanctions if they do not. Clearly it would be unethical for the university to allow such undue moral pressure to be brought to bear.

Other captive-group cases involve classes of schoolchildren, members of sporting organisations or medical patients, whose participation is agreed to by the person in charge. Again, while opting out may be possible, in practice it may be difficult and the subject may be, to all intents and purposes, coerced. As a consequence, education authorities generally place strict controls on the amount and type of research which may be carried out using schoolchildren. Research in prisons and mental and other hospitals raises similar questions about genuine freedom of choice on the part of the subject.

Children

Research involving children raises particular ethical issues. At what age are children able to give informed consent to being involved in research? How does this relate to parents' or carers' rights and obligations? If children below a certain age are not deemed to be able to give consent on their own behalf, in what circumstances, if any, is it appropriate for carers to give consent on the child's behalf? Are there situations where the risk of physical or emotional harm is greater for children than for adults involved with similar research processes?

In general it is believed that particular care should be taken in conducting research involving children because they typically see adults – including researchers – as figures of authority. Thus they may be less likely than adults to exercise their right to non-cooperation. This is not only a human rights issue but can also raise validity issues if children see questions as some sort of performance test and/or feel a need to please the questioner by answering or behaving in certain ways.

Where institutions are involved, such as play centres or schools, those organisations will have their own guidelines, particularly in regard to the requirements for parental permission.

Official surveys

The principle of freedom of choice is constantly infringed by governments: it is an offence, for example, not to complete the Population Census forms or to refuse cooperation with a number of other official surveys. In these cases, the 'social benefit' argument relating to the need for accurate and complete data is considered to outweigh the citizen's right to refuse to give information.

Observation

In the case of some types of research where large numbers of subjects are involved – for example studies of traffic flows, pedestrian movements or crowd behaviour – choice on the part of the subject is impossible. In many observational research situations, if the subjects knew that they were being observed they might well modify their behaviour, and so invalidate the research. These considerations might apply in research ranging from people's interpersonal behaviour in a gym through to research on the milieu of prostitution, gambling or drinking. This would apply particularly in situations where anti-social, and even illegal, behaviour may be involved.

Participant observation

The problem of freedom to participate arises particularly in research using participant observation where **(see Chapter 9)** the researcher is a participant in the phenomenon being studied. Examples are presented in Case study 4.1. The whole basis of such research may rely on the researcher being accepted and trusted by the group being investigated: this may not be forthcoming if it is known that the participant is a researcher. If the researcher does 'come clean', there is the risk – even the likelihood – of the subjects modifying their behaviour, thus invalidating the research. To what extent is it ethical for researchers to disguise their identity to the people they are interacting with and studying – in effect to lie about their identity? When researchers are involved with groups engaging in illegal and/or anti-social activities, for example recreational or performance-enhancing drug-taking or some youth gangs, where do their loyalties lie? In some research methodologies a different approach is adopted, and fully informed interaction between researcher and subjects is embraced and becomes part of the analysed and reported research.

If it is accepted that research of this type is permissible, despite the lack of freedom of consent, the issue of confidentiality in reporting, as discussed below, becomes even more critical.

Informed consent

In experimental research, where there is a risk, however remote, of physical harm to the subject (for example where allergies might be involved, or a risk of muscle strain, or even of heart attack), it is clearly necessary for subjects to be fully aware of the risks involved in order to be able to give their *informed consent* to participate. The level of risk of harm is a matter of judgement, and often only the researcher is fully aware of the extent of risk involved in any given research procedure. This raises the question of the extent to which the subject can ever be 'fully informed'. Subjects can never be as fully informed as the researcher. A judgement has to be made about what is reasonable.

In the traditional science laboratory setting, verbal and written explanations of the nature of the research are given to the potential subjects and they are asked to sign a document indicating their agreement to being involved in the research. A checklist regarding the sort of information which should be provided to potential participants is provided in Figure 4.2 and an example of a consent form is provided in Figure 4.3. In the case of a single, anonymous questionnaire-based survey, verbal consent is generally considered adequate, but if names are recorded and lengthy and/or repeated interviews or other types of activity are involved, written consent is advisable.

A researcher could, of course, 'go through the motions' of following this procedure but abuse it by providing misleading information about the level of risk – itself an unethical practice. Hence the need for clear guidelines and monitoring of these matters.

In addition to risks of physical or mental harm, there may also be a moral dimension. For example, some people may object to being involved in research which is being conducted for certain public, political or commercial organisations. So being informed also involves being informed about the purpose of the research and the nature of the sponsor or beneficiary.

In some cases the status of the researcher is ambivalent, for example when students engaged in a project as part of their learning process in a university course conduct the project on behalf of a real client organisation, or when part-time students conduct research for a university assignment using their

- Name of organisation conducting the research

- Purpose of the research

- Sponsoring/funding organisation if applicable

- Participants and how they are being selected

- What is required from participants:
  - nature of involvement (interviews, focus groups, etc.)
  - time required for each session
  - number of sessions
  - time-period over which sessions will take place

- Any risks to the participant

- Voluntary nature of participation

- Right of participant to refuse to answer any questions or withdraw at any stage without giving reasons

- Privacy and security of data

- Ways in which data will be used

- Contact details for research project supervisor

Figure 4.2   Information for research participants: checklist

---

University of xxxxxxx School of Sport

Exercise research project

CONSENT FORM

I confirm that I have read and understood the research project information
sheet for the 'Exercise research project' and have had any questions
answered to my satisfaction.   _____

I understand that my participation in the study is entirely voluntary and I
may cease to take part at any time without giving reasons.   _____

I agree to take part in the study as described in the information sheet.   _____

I agree to interviews/discussion sessions being recorded.   _____

I agree that anonymous quotations from interviews/discussions may be
used in publications.   _____

Name: _____ Date: _____

Signature: _____

Researcher's name: _____ Date:_____

Signature: _____

Figure 4.3 Example of a consent form

fellow employees as subjects or conduct research on competitors. It is clearly
unethical for students to identify themselves only as students and not to identify to their informants the organisation which will be the beneficiary of the
research.

But again there are some grey areas. In some cases the research would be
invalidated if subjects knew its purpose in detail. For example, responses could
be affected if the subjects knew that a survey was being carried out to see how
respondents reacted to interviewers of differing race or gender. In some attitu-
dinal research, for example on potentially sensitive topics such as race or sex, it
may be thought that responses would be affected if respondents were told too
much about the research and therefore placed 'on their guard' to give 'correct'
answers. Clearly such deception raises ethical issues and judgements have to be
made about whether the value of the research justifies the use of mild deception.

In some cases the provision of detailed information to informants, and
obtaining their written consent, is neither practicable nor necessary. Thus the
typical sport participation survey:

● is anonymous,

● involves only a short interview (e.g. 3 or 4 minutes),

● involves fairly innocuous, non-personal questions, and

● takes place at a facility/site with the agreement of the management or
authorities.

In this type of situation most respondents are not interested in detailed explanations of the research. Most adults are familiar with the survey process and
their main concern is that if they are to take part, the interview should not take

up too much of their time! Potential respondents can become impatient with attempts to provide detailed explanations of the research and would prefer to 'get on with it'. Often questions about the purpose of the survey, if they arise at all, do so later during the interview process, when the respondent's interest has been stimulated. A suggested set of guidelines for such survey situations is provided in Figure 4.4.

Risk of harm to the subject

There may be a risk of harm to the subject in the collection of data, in its storage and handling and in publication. Such risks should obviously be eliminated or minimised, for the sake of the subjects, the researcher and sponsoring organisations and, indeed, the whole research process.

Data collection process

The risk of harm in data collection arises particularly in medical/biological research, where a subject's physical health may be put at risk by an experimental procedure. The risk of injury may arise in sport-related experimenting and testing, for example in cases of excessive exertion. Assuming there is appropriate screening and selection of subjects, for example checking on health status, this risk should be minimised by appropriate briefing of subjects and clear explanation and implementation of informed consent procedures.

---

1. Interviewers should be identified with a badge including their given name and the name of the organisation involved (the host/client organisation or university).
2. Interviewers should be fully briefed about the project so that they can answer questions if asked.
3. If a respondent-completion ('handout') questionnaire is used, a brief description of the purpose of the project should be provided on the questionnaire (typically two or three lines so that it takes just a few seconds to read), with contact telephone numbers of supervisors for those requiring more information.
4. Interviewers approaching potential respondents should introduce themselves and seek cooperation using wording such as the following: 'We are conducting a survey of users of ..., would you mind answering a few questions?'
5. Telephone numbers of supervisors should be available and can be given to respondents if required.
6. A short printed handout may be available with more information for those respondents who are interested.
7. Respondents should not be pressured if they refuse to answer a question or wish to terminate the interview at any time.

Figure 4.4   Ethics guidelines for anonymous questionnaire-based surveys

Risks of harm can also arise in psychological research, where stress and distress can be caused, and in socio-psychological research where interpersonal relationships could be damaged.

Anxiety during the data collection process may arise if the subject has concerns about how the data are to be used. This may relate to themselves and their own privacy, which relates to data storage, handling and publication, as discussed below. The harm which may potentially arise if privacy is breached could vary from mild embarrassment to disruption of relationships with friends, colleagues or employers, to loss of reputation and/or position. Concerns may also relate to moral principles, for example the use of data by certain types of corporation or governments, which relates to the 'fully informed' issue discussed above. In this case the potential harm is the affront to the subject's moral principles. Both concerns relate to the right of the subject to refuse to answer questions and/or withdraw from the process at any stage.

Data storage and handling

Data storage and handling involve not only hard-copy materials, such as questionnaires and records of experimental results, but also digital material, such as audio and video recordings, transcripts and coded data files. Typically hard-copy data may be kept for several years as the project progresses and the publication process unfolds, and for a minimum period of time after the completion of the project specified by research organisations, typically about five years. Digital data today are likely to be stored indefinitely. The term 'handling' is used as well as storage because, while data may be stored securely in a formal sense, there are issues about who has access to it at the various stages (e.g. coding, data computer entry, transmission) and whether they are aware of and adhere to confidentiality commitments.

Hard-copy data should be protected by an appropriately secure form of storage and digital data by password-protected access.

The risk of harm to the subject due to the way data are stored and handled is affected by whether the information is provided entirely anonymously or the subject's name and/or contact details are known to the researcher and/or recorded. There is an in-between situation which can be termed *partial anonymity*. These three situations are discussed in turn below.

Anonymous subjects. Even in an anonymous situation, informants may be reluctant to give certain types of information to 'a complete stranger'. Where such sensitivity is encountered, the usual approach is to stress the voluntary and anonymous nature of the information-giving process, while respecting the respondent's right to refuse to provide certain types of information.

Partial anonymity. Often research participants are not randomly drawn from the population but are members of a community or organisation. While the community or organisation may not be named in the publication, as discussed below, it may be named in the stored data, and it is possible that individuals or groups could be identified by their position – for example the president, secretary, coach, head teacher, team captain, or competition winner. Participants may therefore have concerns about the security of the data, particularly if they have revealed information about themselves or expressed views about others which they would like to be kept confidential.

Much digital information is anonymous because of use of identification numbers rather than names but, somewhere there will be a list linking names and identification numbers, so the security and confidentially of that list becomes important.

In addition to written information, observational research may involve photography and video material which may involve invasion of people's privacy if they are recognised, even in the most innocent-seeming activities.

Identified subjects. Privacy is a valued right in Western society and such rights are generally enshrined in laws, which vary in detail between jurisdictions. People can be offended and suffer stress if their affairs are made public or divulged to certain third parties. There is therefore an obligation on the researcher to ensure confidentiality of any personally identifiable data which have been collected.

Situations where personally identifiable data inevitably arise and the nature of the confidential data are summarised in Figure 4.5, together with suggested means to reduce risk.

Some routine methods for maintaining individuals' privacy, such as keeping lists of names separate from actual data and use of pseudonyms, are indicated, but these measures may not always prevent research subjects from being offended in ways discussed further below. An important principle, but one that is difficult to prescribe in detail, is that the researcher should be aware of research subjects' sensitivities, whether they be personal, professional, cultural or organisational.

In some research projects the naming of individuals is inevitably involved – for example where the number of subjects is small and they are key figures associated with particular high-profile organisations or communities. Where interviews are conducted with such individuals, care must be taken to adopt the journalist's practice of checking whether information is being given 'on the record' or 'off the record'. Thus, in interviews, particularly where sensitive matters arise, it is wise to ask named informants whether they are prepared to be quoted.

In reporting results, the use of false names or numbers to identify individuals, organisations, events, places and communities is the obvious solution. However, this is not always sufficient. The use of false names may protect identities from the world at large, but for those 'in the know', the places and the people involved in the research project may be all too easily identifiable – the partial anonymity situation discussed above (occasionally this issue can be carelessly exacerbated by the author's own list of 'acknowledgements' if it clearly identifies people, organisations and places!) Particular care should be taken when dealing with members of close-knit communities: the researcher should be aware of cultural and interpersonal sensitivities within such communities. Such issues are further highlighted in certain types of qualitative research where the research methodology involves gaining the trust and confidence of research subjects. It would be unethical to betray such trust and confidence.

When data are confidential, measures must be taken to protect that confidentiality through ensuring the security of the raw data, such as interview

Research method	Who is identified?	Identifying information	Why identify?	Issues re storage or publication	Methods to reduce risk
Postal surveys – quantitative	Sampled members of general public or of organisations	Names + addresses	Intrinsic to method	Storage	List of names and addresses kept separate from questionnaires and destroyed at end of data collection.
Telephone surveys – quantitative	Sampled members of general public or of organisations	Telephone numbers	Intrinsic to method + quality control	Storage	As above.
Interviews – qualitative – individuals	Private individuals	Name + possibly telephone no./address	Intrinsic to method	Both	Use of pseudonyms; be aware of sensitivities.
Interviews – qualitative – individuals in organisational roles	Individuals in identifiable public offices (e.g. mayor) or corporate roles (e.g. managing director)	Names, positions, organisation/place/contact details	Intrinsic to method	Both	Use pseudonyms for individuals, place or organisation, but not always possible. Clarify 'on record'/'off record'; be aware of sensitivities.
Interviews – qualitative – small groups	Members of small groups (e.g. a team, a club or a small business)	Names (possibly addresses, tel. nos., surnames may not be involved)	Intrinsic to method	Both, but mainly publication	Use of pseudonyms for individuals, group and place, but not always possible. Clarify 'on record'/'off record'; be aware of sensitivities.
Ethnographic — variety of subjects and qualitative methods	Individuals, separately or as members of a group	Names (possibly addresses, tel. nos., surnames may not be involved)	Intrinsic to method	Mainly publication	Use of pseudonyms, but issue may lie in betraying confidence/trust. Be aware of sensitivities.
Longitudinal research: quantitative and qualitative	Same subjects are contacted to be studied at intervals over a number of weeks, months, years	Names, addresses, tel. nos.	Intrinsic to method	a Storage b Both	Storage: Keep names etc. separate from data. Publication: use pseudonyms.

Figure 4.5 Personally identifiable data

recordings/transcripts/questionnaires. Specific freedom of information and privacy laws invariably cover the storage of and access to personally identifiable data, including allowing individuals access to their own records and the right to have inaccuracies corrected.

Data can be stored with code-numbers or false names, with a key to the code-numbers or names being kept securely in a place apart from the data.

Mail surveys are an in-between case. If returned questionnaires do not have any identification, there is no way of identifying non-respondents in order to send reminders. Sending reminders to *everyone* is costly and an irritation to those who have already responded. One solution is to place an identifying number on the provided return *envelope* rather than on the questionnaire, with an assurance that the number will not be transferred to the questionnaire. In some situations a third party, such as a legal firm, is used to receive the questionnaires and pass them on to the researcher in anonymous form.

As noted above, care must be taken in any acknowledgments not to inadvertently reveal identities. Confidentiality issues often arise with regard to the relationship between the researcher and the organisation funding the research. In particular, if the funding organisation 'owns' the data, the researcher may wish to protect the confidentiality of informants by *not* passing on to the sponsoring organisation any information which could identify informants by name.

Publication

Many of the considerations discussed above in relation to data storage and handling also apply in the case of publication of results. Any undertaking given to individuals or organisations in regard to anonymity should be respected and steps should be taken to avoid inadvertent breaches of confidentiality. Typically issues do not arise at the publication stage with individuals in quantitative research, particularly if they were anonymous from the start. But if the subjects were drawn from a particular geographical community or an organisation, unintended embarrassment could arise. General readers would generally not be able to make the identification, or would not be concerned they could. People in the academic or policy community familiar with the research may be able to make the identification, as might interested residents or members of the organisation. So the researcher must be prepared, in ethical terms, for the possibility of such identification and take this into account when writing the research report.

Honesty/rigour in analysis, interpretation and reporting

The falsification of research results is clearly unethical. There have been some notorious cases in the natural sciences where experimental results have been falsified.

A common practice in quantitative research is to exclude 'outliers' from the analysis. Thus, for example, if a survey of physical recreation found that all respondents participated three times a week or less except for two who participated ten times a week, these two might be termed 'outliers' and excluded from the analysis because they would distort averages. This is generally seen as ethical as long as it is stated in the research report that it has taken place. The same principle could, of course, apply in qualitative research, although identifying an 'outlier' would be a more complex task.

Researchers are concerned about reporting 'negative findings' or non-findings. This typically does not arise with descriptive research – what is, is – or in evaluative research – the performance of the programme/organisation is as found. The difficulty arises with explanatory research when no apparent 'explanation' is found. But negative findings are of interest and use if the research has been carefully designed. Thus if the interest is in the effect on variable X of 15 different independent variables and none of them is found to have a significant influence, then this would generally be of interest, in that it suggests that other variables must be at work. In the case of qualitative research, of course, the fact that the 15 variables are not influential in one study does not preclude them being influential in another study, since the findings would not be generalisable.

In some cases, negative findings are the result of a limited sample size: there may be an effect, but the small sample size makes it impossible to be confident about it – it is statistically insignificant. With a larger sample a small but significant relationship may have been found. But such findings may be relevant for later studies when considering required sample sizes and may be taken into account in systematic reviews of research, or meta-analyses **(see Chapter 6)**, which aggregates the findings of many similar studies. This may seem like purely practical rather than ethical matters but, arguably, there is an ethical obligation to report all the findings of research which might contribute to the development of knowledge.

Authorship and acknowledgements

Authorship

A clear ethical principle is that all those involved with a research project should receive appropriate acknowledgement of their contribution in any publication. Acknowledgement of funding sources, named informants or collaborators and anonymous research subjects may be made in a footnote or in a preface or acknowledgements section. Difficulties can arise in the case of claims for joint authorship, especially in academic research where careers are dependent on such matters. Judgements have to be made as to whether a research assistant, who may be a research student, has simply undertaken routine work for payment or whether he or she has contributed intellectually to the research.

Typically in team research situations, the name of the leader of the team, or 'principal investigator', is placed first in the list of authors but, where the leadership is shared, names may appear in alphabetical order or may be rotated in different publications in a research programme.

Plagiarism

Plagiarism – the use of others' data or ideas without due acknowledgement and, where appropriate, permission – is clearly unethical and is also covered by copyright and intellectual property laws.

Use and abuse of research results in policy/practice

The policy/practice dimension discussed under 'social benefit' also arises here. If research findings do not provide the support which the commissioning governmental or other body seeks, it may 'cherry pick' or misrepresent the results, ignore the research or seek to actively suppress it. While the unethical conduct in this instance is being committed by the commissioning body, it has implications for the researchers, whether they are employed by the organisation or are private or academic consultants. The issue arises as to whether to go public in some way.

Access to research information

Some of the controversies surrounding climate research in recent years have highlighted the issue of rights of access to research information. We have already referred to individuals' rights of access to personal information about them held by public and other corporate bodies, as covered by freedom of information and privacy legislation. But such legislation also covers the public rights of access to information held by public bodies, for example on decision-making processes, a right which is regularly pursued by journalists. While the provisions of legislation vary between jurisdictions, the common principle is that information held by public bodies is *not secret* unless publication would threaten individual privacy, commercial property rights or national security, or the costs of compiling information and making it publicly available would be prohibitive. In theory, such provisions apply to research data gathered with the support of public funds and/or held by public research institutions and have implications for the way data sets are stored and the length of time for which they are kept. As noted above, since most research data in the social sciences are held in digital form, they are, for the most part, potentially storable indefinitely.

It might be thought that if the results of research have been published, there should be no further interest in the raw data but, as Montford (2010: 134, 379–83) and Mann (2012) discuss in the case of climate research, in the natural sciences *replication* is a key criterion in assessing validity; however, as data sets become increasingly complex and expensive to compile, the only way of checking and replicating some types of published research is through access to the authors' original data. Some scientific journals are therefore requiring public (website) archiving of data sets and of the computer code used to analyse them as a condition of publication.

Summary

This chapter considers the ethical, and legal, dimensions of conducting research. It is noted that in universities and other research organisations the responsible and ethical conduct of research is regulated by codes of conduct and ethics committees. In this chapter we consider mainly issues arising in research involving human subjects. In the biological and physical sciences consideration is also given to involvement with animals and, increasingly, environmental dimensions. Ethical considerations arise in all components of the research process, including design, data collection, data storage and handling, analysis and interpretation, and publication. A number of questions must be answered satisfactorily for a research project to be judged to be ethical: Is the research likely to be of social benefit? Are the researchers involved competent to conduct the research? Are the subjects involved participating voluntarily, without compulsion? Are the subjects taking part fully informed about the purposes and nature of the research – have they given 'informed consent'? Is the risk of harm to subjects at an acceptably low level? Has the analysis and interpretation of data and reporting of the results been undertaken honestly and rigorously? Have all those involved been suitably acknowledged or, where appropriate, included among the authors?

Test questions

1. What are the main ethical issues which arise in research?

2. What is 'informed consent' and what measures must be taken to ensure it? For which groups in society is 'informed consent' likely to be a particularly significant issue?

3. What are the 'grey areas' where participation in research may not be voluntary?

4. What are the main possible sources of harm to participants in social science research?

5. How does the concept of confidentiality arise in the research process?

6. What is plagiarism?

Exercises

1. Identify the research ethics code of practice and processes in operation: a) in the institution at which you are studying and b) nationally and determine the extent to which they might apply to class-based student research exercises.

2. In an approved project involving interviewing of school students on their sporting activities, a few of the respondents let you know that they take illegal drugs and indicate indirectly who supplies them. Do you tell anyone or maintain confidentiality? Do you include the finding, anonymously, in your research report?

3. Christensen's (1980) critique of Moeller *et al.* (1980a) relates to a survey conducted in a park, but the ethical issues could also rise in such a survey conducted in a sport facility. Examine the response of Moeller *et al.* (1980b) and discuss.

4. You are the chief executive officer of a national sport organisation and a sportswear company has offered a generous sponsorship deal for five years. The deal requires the organisation to give the sponsor annual access to the membership database for research purposes. How would you respond to the proposal?

Resources

Websites

Research ethics guidelines:

- Market Research Society (UK): www.mrs.org.uk/standards/codeconduct.htm

- Social Research Association (UK): http://the-sra.org.uk/wpcontent/uploads/ethics03.pdf

- NHMRC/ARC/Universities Australia guidelines: www.nhmrc.gov.au/_files_nhmrc/file/publications/synopses/r39.pdf

- University of Technology, Sydney: for undergraduate and postgraduate students: www.gsu.uts.edu.au/policies/hrecguide.html.

Publications

- Research ethics generally: Haggerty (2004), Israel and Hay (2006), Loue (2002).

- Research ethics guidelines: Saunders *et al.* (2000: 459–62).

- Research ethics, ethics committees and qualitative research: Lincoln (2005).

- Research ethics in sport: McFee (2009), Tomlinson and Fleming (1997); in leisure: Fleming and Jordan (2006); in survey research: Moeller *et al.* (1980a, 1980b), Christensen (1980).

- Climate change: Mann (2012), Montford (2010).

- Informed consent: Olivier and Olivier (2001).

References

Christensen, J. E. (1980) A second look at the informal interview. *Journal of Leisure Research*, 12(2), 183–6.

Donne, K. (2006) From outsider to quasi-insider at Wodin Watersports: a reflexive account of participant observation in a leisure context. In S. Fleming and F. Jordan (eds) *Ethical Issues in Leisure Research*. LSA Publication 90, Eastbourne, UK: Leisure Studies Association, 63–82.

Fleming, S. and Jordan, F. (eds) (2006) *Ethical Issues in Leisure Research*. LSA Publication 90, Eastbourne, UK: Leisure Studies Association.

Haggerty, K. D. (2004) Ethics creep: governing social science research in the name of ethics. *Qualitative Sociology*, 27(4), 391–414.

Israel, M. and Hay, I. (2006) *Research Ethics for Social Scientists*. Los Angeles, CA: Sage.

Jones, R. L., Potrac, P., Haleem, H. and Cushion, C. (2006) Exposure by association: anonymity and integrity in autobiographical research. In S. Fleming and F. Jordan (eds) *Ethical Issues in Leisure Research*. LSA Publication 90, Eastbourne, UK: Leisure Studies Association, 45–62.

Lincoln, Y. (2005) Institutional review boards and methodological conservatism: the challenge to and from phenomenological paradigms. In N. K. Denzin and Y. S. Lincoln (eds) *Handbook of Qualitative Research, Third edn*. Thousand Oaks, CA: Sage, 165–90.

Loue, S. (2002) *Textbook of Research Ethics: Theory and Practice*. New York: Kluwer.

Mann, M. E. (2012) *The Hockey Stick and the Climate Wars: Dispatches from the Front Lines*. New York: Columbia University Press.

McFee, G. (2009) *Ethics, Knowledge and Truth in Sports Research*. London: Routledge.

Moeller, G. H., Mescher, M. A., More, T. A. and Shafer, E. L. (1980a) The informal interview as a technique for recreation research. *Journal of Leisure Research*, 12(2), 174–82.

Moeller, G. H., Mescher, M. A., More, T. A. and Shafer, E. L. (1980b) A response to 'A second look at the informal interview'. *Journal of Leisure Research*, 12 (2), 187–88.

Montford, A. W. (2010) *The Hockey Stick Illusion: Climategate and the Corruption of Science*. London: Stacey International.

National Council on Public Polls (1995) *Push Polls*. Press release, 25 May, Clifton, NJ: NCPP, available at: www.ncpp.org/?q=node/41 (Accessed May 2013).

National Health and Medical Research Council (NHMRC) (nd) *National Ethics Application Form*. Canberra: NHMRC, available at: www.neaf.gov.au/default.aspx (Accessed May 2013).

National Health and Medical Research Council (NHMRC)/Australian Research Council (ARC) and Universities Australia (2007) *Australian Code for the Responsible Conduct of Research*. Canberra: Australian Government (website, see above).

Olivier, S. and Olivier, A. (2001) Informed consent in sport science. *SportScience*, 5(1), online journal, available at: www.sportsci.org/jour/0101/so.htm (Accessed May 2013).

Saunders, M., Lewis, P. and Thornhill, A. (2000) *Research Methods for Business Students*. Harlow, UK: Financial Times-Prentice Hall.

Tomlinson, A. and Fleming, S. (eds) (1997) *Ethics, Sport and Leisure*. Aachen, Germany: Meyer & Meyer Verlag.

The range of research methods

Introduction – horses for courses

In this chapter the range of alternative research methods and criteria for their use are examined in broad terms, as an introduction to the methods and techniques to be covered in more detail in subsequent chapters. The chapter has four main sections:

- *major methods:* a range of major methods used in sport research, including the roles of scholarship, 'just thinking', the use of the research literature, secondary data, observation, qualitative methods and questionnaire-based surveys;

- *subsidiary and cross-cutting methods:* approaches and techniques which are subsidiary to one or more of the major methods, in that they are a variation on or an application of the major method or cut across a number of the major methods;

- *multiple methods:* including triangulation, counting heads and mixed methods; and

- *choice of method:* the process of selecting a research method for a particular purpose.

Choosing appropriate research methods is clearly vital. In this book we espouse the principle that every technique has its place; the important thing is for researchers to be aware of the limitations of any particular method and to take these into account when reporting research results. A *horses for courses* approach is adopted; techniques are not intrinsically *good* or *bad*, but are considered to be *appropriate* or *inappropriate* for the task in hand. Further, it is maintained that it is not a question of good or bad techniques which should be considered, but good or bad *use* of techniques.

The range of major research methods

The range of major methods to be examined is listed in Figure 5.1 and discussed below.

Scholarship

Although the dividing line between *scholarship* and *research* can be difficult to draw, it is useful to consider the differences between the two. Scholarship involves being well informed about a subject and also thinking critically and creatively about a subject and the accumulated knowledge on it. Scholarship therefore involves *knowing the literature*, but also being able to synthesise it, analyse it and critically appraise it. Scholarship is traditionally practised in the role of teacher, but when the results of scholarship are published they effectively become a contribution to research.

Method	Brief description
Scholarship	Being well read about a topic and thinking deeply and creatively about it
Just thinking	The thinking part of scholarship
Existing sources 1: using the literature/ systematic reviews	Identifying, summarising and evaluating the research literature – part of all research but can be the sole method used in a project
Existing sources 2: secondary data	Re-use of data originally collected by another organisation for other purposes
Observation	Direct looking at behaviour or use of still or video cameras
Qualitative methods	Range of methods where the data gathered are in the form of words, as opposed to quantitative methods, where data are in the form of numbers
Questionnaire-based surveys	Methods using a formal, printed schedule of questions to gather data – the main quantitative method in sport research
Experimental method	The researcher controls the environment of the phenomenon being studied, holding all variables constant except those which are the focus of the research
Case study	The focus of the research is on one or a small number of cases, and typically a number of data-gathering and analysis methods is used

Figure 5.1   The range of major methods

Research involves the generation of new knowledge. Traditionally this has been thought of as involving the gathering and presentation of new data – empirical research – but clearly this is not a necessary condition for a contribution to be considered research. New insights, critical or innovative ways of looking at old issues, or the identification of new issues or questions – the fruits of scholarship – are also contributions to knowledge. Indeed, the development of a new framework or *paradigm* for looking at a field can be far more significant than a minor piece of empirical work using an outmoded paradigm.

Just thinking

There is no substitute for thinking! Creative, informed thinking about a topic can be the only process involved in the development and presentation of a piece of research, although it will usually also involve consideration of the literature, as discussed below.

But even when data collection is involved, the difference between an *acceptable* piece of research and an *exceptional* or *significant* piece of research is usually the quality of the creative thought that has gone into it. The researcher needs to be creative in:

● identifying and posing the initial questions or issues for investigation;

● conceptualising the research and developing a research strategy;

● analysing data; and

● interpreting and presenting findings.

Texts on research methods, such as this, can provide a guide to mechanical processes, but creative thought must come from within the individual researcher – in the same way that the basics of drawing can be taught but *art* comes from within the individual artist.

Existing sources 1: using the literature/ systematic reviews

There is virtually no research that can be done which would not benefit from some reference to the existing literature and for most research such reference is essential. It is possible for a research project to consist only of a review of the literature: in comparatively new areas of study, such as sport, especially when they are multidisciplinary as sport studies is, there is a great need for the consolidation of existing knowledge which can come from good literature reviews. In the science area, a *systematic review* of research on a specific topic is seen as a research method in its own right: this is discussed further in Chapter 6, where examples in the sport area are also listed.

The review of the literature often plays a key role in the formulation of research projects; it indicates the state of knowledge on a topic and is a source of, or stimulant for, ideas, both substantive and methodological.

A review of the literature can be important even when it uncovers no literature on the topic of interest. To establish that *no* research has been conducted on a particular topic, especially when the topic is considered to be of some importance to the field, can be a research finding of some significance in its own right. The literature review process is discussed in detail in Chapter 6.

Existing sources 2: secondary data

Clearly, if information is already available which will answer the research questions posed, then it would be wasteful of resources to collect new information for the purpose. As discussed in Chapter 7, large quantities of information are collected and stored by government and other organisations as routine functions of policy-making, management and evaluation, including sales figures and visitor numbers, income and expenditure, staffing, accident reports, crime reports and travel, sport participation and health data. Such data are referred to as *secondary* data, because their primary use is administrative and research is only a secondary use. Even when such data are not ideal for the research at hand, they can often provide answers to some questions more quickly and at less cost than the collection of new data.

Secondary data need not be quantitative. Historians, for example, use diaries, official documents, records or newspaper reports as sources – such sources may be seen as secondary, since they were not initially produced for research purposes, but for historians themselves some of them are described as primary sources. In policy research such documents as the annual reports or minutes of meetings of organisations might be utilised.

In some cases data have been collected for research as opposed to administrative purposes but may not have been fully analysed, or they may have been analysed only in one particular way for a particular purpose, or even not analysed at all. Secondary analysis, or re-analysis, of research data is a potentially fruitful, but widely neglected, activity.

Observation

The technique of observation is discussed in Chapter 8. Observation has the advantage of being unobtrusive – indeed, the techniques involved are sometimes referred to as *unobtrusive* techniques (Kellehear, 1993). Unobtrusive techniques involve gathering information about people's behaviour without their knowledge. While in some instances this may raise ethical questions **(see Chapter 4)**, it clearly has certain advantages over techniques where subjects are aware of the researcher's presence and may therefore modify their behaviour, or where reliance must be placed on subjects' own recall and description of their behaviour, which can be inaccurate or distorted.

Observation may be the only possible technique to use in certain situations, for example when researching illicit activity, which people may be reluctant to talk about, or when researching the behaviour of young children (for example their play patterns) who may be too young to interview.

Observation is capable of presenting a perspective on a situation which is not apparent to the individuals involved. For example, the users of a crowded part of a venue may not be aware of the uncrowded areas available to them – the uneven pattern of use of the site can only be assessed by observation.

Observation is therefore an appropriate technique to use when knowledge of the presence of the researcher is likely to lead to unacceptable modification of subjects' behaviour, and when mass patterns of behaviour not apparent to individual subjects are of interest.

Qualitative methods

As discussed in Chapter 2, qualitative methods stand in contrast to *quantitative* methods. The main difference between the two groups of techniques is that quantitative methods involve numbers – quantities – whereas qualitative methods rely on words, and sometimes images, as the unit of analysis. In the case of qualitative techniques the information collected does not generally lend itself to statistical analysis, and conclusions are not based on such analysis.

In consequence there is a tendency for qualitative techniques to involve the gathering of large amounts of relatively detailed information about relatively few cases (people, organisations, facilities, programmes, locations) and for quantitative techniques to involve the gathering of relatively small amounts of data on relatively large numbers of cases. It should be emphasised, however, that this is just a *tendency*. It is possible, for example, for a quantitative research project to involve the collection of, say, 500 items of data on only 20 people and for a qualitative research project to involve the collection of relatively little information on, say, 200 people. Conversely, some questionnaire-based surveys designed to collect quantitative data can involve questionnaires many pages long, which take an hour or more to administer and can collect hundreds of items of data from each respondent. The difference in the two approaches lies in the nature of information collected and the way it is analysed.

In what situations are qualitative techniques used? They tend to be used when one or more of the following situations apply:

- when the focus of the research is on meanings and attitudes (although these can also be studied quantitatively);

- when the situation calls for exploratory theory building rather than theory testing;

- when the researcher accepts that the concepts, terms and issues must be defined by the subjects themselves and not by the researcher in advance;

- when interaction between members of a group is of interest.

Data collection methods	Alternative names/ variations	Description
In-depth interviews	Informal, semi-structured or un-structured interviews	One-on-one interviews with a relatively small sample of individuals, interviewed at length, possibly on more than one occasion, typically using a checklist of topics rather than a formal questionnaire.
Focus groups	Group interviews	Discussions with groups of people (typically 6–12) led by a facilitator.
Observation*	Unobtrusive techniques	The phenomenon of interest is examined by the naked eye or by use of still or video camera.
Participant observation	–	The researcher becomes a participant in the phenomenon being studied.
Biographical methods	Auto-ethnography	Research subjects are invited to provide their own accounts of events etc., in written or recorded oral form.
Analysis of texts	Content analysis,* hermeneutics	Analysis and interpretation of the content of published or unpublished texts. May also involve audio-visual materials (images, TV, film, music, radio).
Ethnography	Field research (in anthropology)	Studying groups of people using a mixture of the above methods.
Netnography	Web-based, online, virtual research	Ethnographic research based on internet activity.

Figure 5.2   Qualitative data collection methods

*can also be quantitative

Qualitative techniques are not appropriate when the aim of the research is to make general statements about large populations, especially if such statements call for quantification.

Figure 5.2 summarises a range of types of qualitative data collection method and these are discussed in more detail in Chapter 9.

Questionnaire-based surveys

A questionnaire is a printed or electronic list of questions. In a questionnaire-based survey the same questionnaire is used to interview a sample of respondents. The term questionnaire-*based* survey is used because such surveys can take two formats:

- *interview format*, in which an interviewer, in a face-to-face situation or via the telephone, reads out the questions from the questionnaire and records the answers; and

- *respondent-completion format*, in which the respondent reads the questions and writes answers on the questionnaire or on-screen, and no interviewer is involved.

In many discussions of research methods in the literature, 'questionnaires' and 'interviews' are presented as alternatives; this is clearly misleading, since interviews may be conducted using a questionnaire. A more accurate distinction would be made between questionnaires and informal, in-depth or unstructured interviews, as discussed above.

Questionnaire-based surveys are popular in sport research, partly because the basic mechanics are relatively easily understood and mastered, but also because so much sport research calls for the sorts of general, quantified statement referred to above. Thus for example, governments want to know how many people engage in sport generally or in specific sports; managers of sport facilities want to know what proportion of customers are dissatisfied with a service and marketers want to know how many people are in a particular sport market segment. All these examples come from practical policy/management situations, which emphasises that most of the resources for survey research come from the public or private sector of the sport industries. Academic papers are very often a secondary spin-off from research which has been sponsored for such specific, practical purposes.

Unlike qualitative techniques, where the researcher can begin data collection in a tentative way, return to the subjects for additional information and gradually build the data and concepts and explanation, questionnaire-based surveys require researchers to be very specific about their data requirements from the beginning, since they must be committed irrevocably to a questionnaire.

A further key feature of questionnaire-based surveys is that they depend on respondents' own accounts of their behaviour, attitudes or intentions. In some situations – for example in the study of 'deviant' behaviour or in the study of activities which are socially approved (e.g. playing sport) or disapproved of (e.g. smoking or drinking excessively) – this can raise some questions about the validity of the approach, since the accuracy and honesty of responses may be called into question.

Questionnaire-based surveys are used when quantified information is required concerning a specific population and when individuals' own accounts of their behaviour and/or attitudes are acceptable as a source of information. Questionnaire surveys nevertheless may be used to gather qualitative as well as quantitative data by the inclusion of open-ended questions, as discussed in Chapter 10 – although this is not a view shared by all researchers (see, for example, Dupuis, 1999: 45).

Type	Alternative name	Description
Household survey	Community survey or social survey	People are selected on the basis of where they live and are interviewed in their home.
Street survey	Quota or intercept survey	People are selected by stopping them in the street, in shopping malls, etc.
Telephone survey		Interviews are conducted by telephone.
Online survey	Web-based survey	Respondents complete screen-based questionnaire online.
Mail survey	Postal survey	Questionnaires are sent and returned by mail.
Site or user survey	Visitor survey, customer survey, intercept survey	Users of a sport/recreation facility or site are surveyed on site.
Captive group survey	–	Members of groups such as classes of schoolchildren, members of a club or employees of an organisation are surveyed.

Figure 5.3   Types of questionnaire-based survey

Questionnaire surveys can be divided into six types, as shown in Figure 5.3 and considered in more detail in Chapters 10 and 16.

Experimental method

The experimental method is the traditional approach of the natural sciences, although 'quasi-experimental' studies are widely used in policy-related areas, as discussed in Chapter 11. The method involves the researcher controlling the environment in order to study the effects of specified variables, typically in a laboratory setting. The principles of the method were discussed in Chapter 2 and are addressed in more detail in Chapter 11.

Case study method

A case study involves the study of an example – a case – of the phenomenon being researched. The aim is to seek to understand the phenomenon by studying single examples. Cases can consist of individuals, groups of individuals, communities, organisations or whole countries. Invariably multiple methods are used, including historical/documentary research, the use of secondary data, interviews and, in the case of communities, questionnaire-based or qualitative surveys. The case study method and its use in sport studies are discussed further in Chapter 12.

Subsidiary/cross-cutting techniques

The somewhat inelegant term 'subsidiary and cross-cutting' is used to describe a number of techniques which are subsidiary to one or more of the major methods discussed above, in that they are a variation on or an application of the major method (e.g. Delphi technique, which uses questionnaires) or cut across a number of major methods (e.g. action research, which can use any or all of the major methods). The techniques discussed here are listed in Figure 5.4 and discussed in turn below, and an indication is given of how they relate to the pattern of the book. The brief descriptions presented here do not provide a basis for implementing the various techniques, but they indicate their general nature and possibilities. Guides to further information are provided in the Resources section. It should be noted that the emphasis here is on forms of data collection or combined collection and analysis processes. Particular forms of data analysis are presented in Part II of the book.

Action research

The common image of research is as a detached process reporting objectively on what is discovered. When a researcher is personally committed to the topic under investigation, whether that be self-interest related, such as the fortunes of a company, or a social cause, like saving the environment, efforts are still generally made to abide by the rules of science, for ethical reasons or because of the general belief that sound research is more likely to be effective in supporting a cause. Some types of research can, nevertheless, be deliberately designed to involve the researcher in the topic and are intended to be overtly part of the process of bringing about change – such research is termed 'action research'. Typically, action research is also distinguished by being conducted on behalf of, and in association with, one or more organisations, or stakeholders. Indeed, some definitions envisage the action research process as happening within a corporate organisation, with the researcher 'embedded' in the organisation for the duration of the project.

The action research process shown in Figure 5.5 indicates that researchers are involved in the 'action' stages of the process as well as the research stage and there may be various feedback loops in the process as research is conducted to assist the campaign for change and to evaluate outcomes.

There are similarities with the conventional management research process within an organisation, where Step 3 is an internal resource allocation and implementation process. It can also be seen as a quasi-experimental process. Action research is not constrained as to methods or techniques. There is a tendency to see it as a form of qualitative research, but in their introductory text on the subject Greenwood and Levin state:

Technique	Brief description
Subsidiary and cross-cutting techniques/methods	
Action research	Research committed to social outcomes, typically involving collaboration with a client organisation.
Big data	Analysis of very large electronic/digital data-sets: for example, organisations with a large customer base can analyse data from electronic records of customer activity to reveal patterns of behaviour of use in marketing.
Conjoint analysis	A process for studying people's choice processes by asking them to express preferences for hypothetical products with different combinations of attributes.
Content analysis	Quantitative study of printed/written documents or static/moving images (see also qualitative methods).
Coupon surveys/ conversion studies	Analysis of returns from 'special offer', 'two for the price of one' etc. vouchers/advertisements.
Delphi technique	Process in which a sample of experts responds to questions about future events in repeated rounds, ideally to achieve consensus.
Diary methods	see Time-use studies.
Discourse analysis	Examination of the ways in which language is used in the treatment of a topic, typically in social/ political contexts and/or in the popular and/or academic print and other communications media.
En route/intercept/ cordon surveys	Survey conducted with visitors entering, leaving or travelling to or from a site/destination.
Epidemiology	The study of geographical distributions of variables (e.g. health status) among the population.
Experience sampling method (ESM)	Subjects are 'beeped' or contacted electronically several times a day to record activities/feelings etc. as they go about day-to-day activities.
Historical research	Research on past events.
Longitudinal studies	The same sample of subjects is repeatedly surveyed, typically over a number of years.
Mapping techniques	Subjects provide graphic representation of components of a problem/issue, typically collaborative.
Media reader/viewer/ listener surveys	Media report on surveys which readers/listeners have been invited to take part in, typically online or via automated phone-in.
Meta-analysis	Examination and summary of a number of studies on the same topic, typically with a key outcome measure such as a correlation coefficient.
Multiple classification analysis	Analytical techniques used to group subjects on the basis of comparable behaviour patterns, tastes and socio-demographic (lifestyle) characteristics.
Netnography	Research on Internet activity.
Network analysis	Study of links between individuals and/or organisations involved in an activity.
Panel studies	A sample of individuals recruited to a 'panel' who may take part in several surveys over a period of time.
Projective techniques	Subjects are asked to respond to hypothetical scenarios.
Psychographic/lifestyle studies	Research which gathers data on a wide range of attitudes, values and socio-demographic characteristics and analyses them to determine distinctive psychographic/lifestyle groups or market segments.
Q methodology	Process in which subjects rank scale items depicted on cards.
Quantitative modelling	Quantitative method in which relationships between two or more variables are assessed statistically.
Repertory grid/laddering	Pairs of contrasting descriptors for the phenomenon being studied are elicited from respondents to form constructs, and scores on the constructs are analysed to form a perceptual picture.
Scales	Development and use of batteries of 'stimulus items' (statements/questions, features, etc.) to be responded to via Likert-type scales.
Time-use surveys	Survey in which respondents complete a detailed 1–2-day diary of activities.
Web-based research	Research on, or using, the Internet – see also 'netnography'.
Multiple methods	
Triangulation (also termed 'mixed methods'	Two or more methods used to focus on the same phenomenon, providing confirmation or differing insights.
Counting heads	A management task involving various research approaches, needed in situations where usage/ visitor numbers are not available from ticket sales.

Figure 5.4 Subsidiary, cross-cutting and multiple techniques/methods

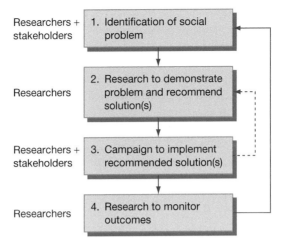

Figure 5.5 Action research process

> it is wrong to think of action research as 'qualitative' research, yet a great many conventional researchers and far too many action researchers make this error. … An action research process must use qualitative, quantitative and/or mixed-method techniques wherever and whenever the conditions and subject an action research team deals with require. (*Greenwood and Levin, 2007: 98*)

Action research is less usual in the sport context than in some areas of social policy, such as housing or ethnic affairs.

Big data

'Big data' is a form of secondary data analysis using very large electronic/digital data sets. Thus, for example, commercial or public organisations with a large customer base, often running into millions, can make use of the data which has accumulated from on-line and other electronic purchasing records to discover patterns of behaviour and socio-demographic, geographic and temporal relationships which may be of use in marketing. One of the market phenomena identified by this research activity is the 'long tail': the observation, which applies particularly to cultural products like books and recorded music, that, while best-sellers and block-busters attract most of the publicity, the bulk of the market is accounted for by hundreds or thousands of titles which sell very few copies, and may even be only marginally economic (Anderson 2011).

Conjoint analysis

Conjoint analysis is a methodology used to explore people's decision-making processes, including choosing a brand of equipment or a holiday destination. In particular, it seeks to discover how various features of products are evaluated by the consumer and how this evaluation influences choices. One way of doing this would be to examine people's actual selections against the attributes of a range of existing products, and there is research which adopts this approach, but it is a complex, 'messy', and possibly expensive, process. Furthermore, such research would be constrained by the available products and their features. In conjoint analysis subjects are asked to express their preferences among a range of hypothetical products with varying combinations of features. The more distinct features are considered and the more levels or categories exist for each feature, the more combinations there will be for consideration. For example, four features, each with four levels/categories, produces 256 different combinations. Selecting combinations for inclusion in a study and analysing the results is the complex mathematical task undertaken by conjoint analysis. The detail is beyond the scope of this book, but further reading is indicated in the Resources section and the approach is discussed again in Chapter 11 under the heading of 'Discrete choice experiments'.

Content analysis

In some fields of enquiry the focus of research is textual – for example the content of organisations' annual reports, politicians' speeches or the coverage of sport in the media. The analysis and interpretation of the content of published or unpublished texts is referred to as *content analysis*, often when the analysis is quantitative, or *hermeneutics*, when the analysis is of a more qualitative nature. The technique has not traditionally been widely used in sport studies, but with the development of postmodernism and the widening of the scope of *text* to include a wide variety of cultural products such as company documents, advertising material, websites and letters, the approach is attracting increasing attention. Some examples of quantitative studies are listed in the Resources section and qualitative approaches are discussed in Chapter 9.

Coupon surveys/conversion studies

In marketing research, use can be made of information from the responses of the public to advertising coupons – that is, where the public is invited in an advertisement to write, telephone or log on for information on a product. The data can be used to indicate the level of interest in the product on offer (compared with other products or with the same product in previous periods) and also to indicate the geographical spread of the interested public. The question then arises as to the extent to which people who respond to such advertising actually become customers. Thus conversion studies are designed to examine the extent to which enquirers *convert* to become customers (Woodside and Ronkainen, 1994).

Delphi technique

The Delphi technique (named after the classical Greek 'Delphic oracle') is a procedure involving the gathering and analysing of information from a panel of experts on future trends in a particular field of interest. The experts in the field (e.g. sport or tourism) complete a questionnaire indicating their views on the likelihood of certain developments taking place in future; these views are then collated and circulated to panel members for further comment, a process which might be repeated a number of times before the final results are collated. The technique is used in some areas of business and technological forecasting, and has been used to a limited extent in sport. In this book the technique is not examined explicitly, but to some extent it involves questionnaire design and analysis, as covered in Chapters 10 and 16. A thorough state-of-the-art review has recently been provided by Donohue and Needham (2009).

Discourse analysis

Discourse analysis refers to research on the use of language in relation to a topic/issue in popular and/or academic texts and other communications media. The way language is used, consciously or unconsciously, in relation to a phenomenon, shapes popular and official conceptualisations of that phenomenon. For example, the public view of a sport event is likely to be affected if it is invariably accompanied by the descriptor 'over-budget' or 'taxpayer-funded'. The conscious adoption of one term rather the another – for example, English cricket fans referring to themselves as the 'Barmy Army' – signals an intent on the part of the users. In the organisational context, the process is the stock-in-trade of public relations practitioners or 'spin merchants'. Research on this dimension of human interaction typically involves analysis of media and official broadcast and print material on a topic over a period of time.

En route/intercept/cordon surveys

En route surveys (Steen *et al.*, 2008) arise in tourism research, so they are only likely to be relevant to sport in the context of sports tourism. Such surveys may be conducted in aeroplanes, at airports or while travelling by car (when travellers are waved into lay-bys for survey purposes with the assistance of police). In this book this type of survey, which invariably involves a questionnaire, is considered to be a special case of site or user surveys, as discussed in Chapter 10. Since respondents are 'intercepted' at or near a destination, site or attraction, the term *intercept survey* is sometimes used, and if all approaches to the destination, site or attraction are covered, the term *cordon* survey may be used.

Epidemiology

Epidemiology is a medical term and is concerned with the spread/distribution of disease among the population. It is relevant to sport particularly because of the link between sport/exercise and health. In this type of research, large-scale national or regional surveys might be used, for example to study patterns of participation in physical activity related to health data from the survey (self-assessed) or from national/regional aggregate data on health. Another setting where the approach is used is in the study of sports injuries, when general practitioners may be co-opted to gather data from patients on such matters as injuries, sports played, general fitness and training/playing regime (see, for example, Hägglund *et al.*, 2005).

Experience sampling method (ESM)

ESM was pioneered by Mihaly Csikszentmihalyi and his colleagues at the University of Chicago in 1977 (Csikszentmihalyi and Larson, 1977) and can be seen as a development of the time-budget survey/diary method. Alternative names for the technique are *ecological momentary assessment* (EMA) (Smyth and Stone, 2003) and *ambulatory assessment*.

An ESM study typically takes place over a few days, during which, on about eight occasions each day, study participants are alerted by some electronic device – a pager in the early examples, later by watches programmed to 'beep' at certain times and most recently by mobile telephone. When alerted, or as soon as practically possible thereafter, the study participant completes a short questionnaire in a booklet carried with the participant at all times or, in recent versions, responds to questions via text-message. Information is gathered on activities being undertaken, where and with whom, and attitudes and feelings. The method has the advantage of recording activities and feelings in real time and in the 'natural' environment of the subject, rather than relying on recall at a later date in a different environment. While the amount of information which can be elicited in any one episode is limited, the cumulative amount of information gathered, together with any information included in a preliminary conventional questionnaire, can be substantial.

The research approach made possible by ESM has been characterised as *idiographic*, based on the Greek word *idios*, meaning specific to an individual (Conner *et al.*, 2009). This is in contrast to *nomothetic* research, based on the Greek word *nomos*, meaning law, which seeks to establish general scientific laws of behaviour based on studies of a number of individuals. However, unlike qualitative research, which is often idiographic, ESM is generally quantitative in nature since it gathers data from individuals on repeated occasions.

Further developments in this type of electronically aided research are:

● the Electronically Activated Recorder (EAR) in which the subject wears a small microphone and recording device which is automatically activated for short periods (for example for 30 seconds, 12 times per hour) thus providing a record of the environments the subject experiences and conversational interaction with people – this has been used in psychological research to track social interaction (Mehl *et al.*, 2001) but there are no known examples in sport or tourism;

- digital tracking using the global positioning system **(discussed in Chapter 8)**.

The details of the method are not pursued further in this book, but references to examples of its use, generally and in sport, are provided in the Resources section.

Historical research

History is of course a major discipline with its own approaches to research. Historical research arises in the sport research environment in a least two contexts: biographical research **(discussed as a qualitative approach in Chapter 9)** and case-study research **(discussed in Chapter 12)**. It can also be seen as a form of secondary data analysis, since historians are invariably dependent on documents contemporary to a period, which were originally compiled for other purposes. As a discipline, history is part of the humanities, although in the context of sport research it clearly extends into the social sciences when history is presented as a partial explanation for contemporary phenomena, for example in research on the Olympic Games. Compared with the social science literature, in historical literature there is tendency for the question of method to be played down or taken for granted. While historical accounts are generally conducted in a scholarly manner, with detailed reference to sources, just how the source material has been used and analysed is not always clear: thus there is rarely a 'methods' section in historically based articles. Historical methods are not pursued in this book, but some sources are indicated in the Resources section.

Longitudinal studies

Longitudinal studies involve surveying the same sample of individuals periodically over a number of years (Young *et al.*, 1991). Such studies are, of course, expensive because of the need to keep track of the sample members over the years, and the need to have a large enough sample at the beginning to allow for the inevitable attrition to the sample over time. They are, however, ideal for studying social change and the combined effects of social change and ageing. There are numerous cases of longitudinal studies of the effects of exercise, for example in rehabilitation – see Resources section.

Mapping techniques

One of the issues in sport planning and marketing is the extent to which the public are well informed about available facilities and services. This is partly related to information coming through the media, formal marketing activities and personal networks, but can also relate to people's spatial perception of the neighbourhood, city or region in which they live. For example, people are likely to be familiar with their immediate neighbourhood and the route to their place of work or school, but are likely to be less familiar with areas on the other side of town. This can apply particularly to people without cars, notably young people and the elderly. Information on people's 'perceptual space' can be elicited by inviting them to draw 'perceptual maps' of their city.

The idea of spatial perception and mapping can be extended to other mental processes, so that the process becomes similar to the development of conceptual frameworks or 'concept maps' **(see Chapter 3)**. An example is the 'mapping' of athletes' views of banned performance-enhancing substances undertaken by Pan and Baker (1998).

Media reader/viewer/listener surveys

Newspapers, magazines, and radio and television stations often run opinion-poll-type surveys among their readers, viewers or listeners, often web-based. At the local level the public's views on an issue may be canvassed by the inclusion of some sort of form in a newspaper, which readers may fill in and return, and radio and television stations often run 'phone-in' polls on topical issues. The results of these exercises have entertainment value, but should not generally be taken seriously. This is mainly because there is no way of knowing whether either the original population (the readers/listeners/viewers who happen to read, hear or view the item) or the sample of respondents are representative of the population as a whole. In most cases they are decidedly unrepresenta-tive, in that the audiences and readership of particular media outlets tend to have particular socio-economic characteristics and only those with pronounced views, one way or the other, are likely to become involved in the survey pro-cess. These exercises should not, of course be confused with surveys sponsored by the media but conducted by reputable survey companies, such as Newspoll or AC Nielsen.

Meta-analysis

Meta-analysis – or systematic reviewing – combines features of a literature review and secondary data analysis and involves a quantitative appraisal of the findings of a number of research projects on the same topic. The technique is suitable for the sort of research where findings are directly comparable from one study to another – for example when the key findings are expressed in terms of correlation and regression coefficients between particular variables **(see Chapter 17)**. In a meta-analysis, the reported findings of a large number of individual research projects in the same area provide the basis for further exploration and analysis of the area. Typically, because many studies are involved and must be compared on a common basis, only relatively simple relationships can be examined. Examples of meta-analysis in the sport area are given in the Resources section.

A less formal approach to cross-project appraisal is the *consensus study* in which a group of researchers review the accumulated research on a topic and seek to reach a consensus on the state of knowledge – the most well known of these in recent years being the reviews of the UN Intergovernmental Panel on Climate Change (2013) **(discussed further in Chapter 6)**.

Netnography

The Internet, and the social network phenomenon in particular, are increasingly significant as means of communication. They are therefore key potential sources of information about people's attitudes, values, tastes and behaviour, which is of interest to marketers and social and cultural researchers. A set of practices and associated literature have grown up in this area, referred to as *netnography* or *virtual research*. Sources are indicated in the Resources section.

Network analysis

Many human activities operate through networks involving nodes and links between them, including transport systems, electricity supply systems and telecommunications. A science has developed around this idea and has been used to optimise the design of networks. Figure 5.6 shows a simple network represented in analogue and digital format, with the numbers indicating the size of the flows between the nodes (e.g. traffic flows, financial flows, communication). Analysis can be confined to graphical formats and can involve qualitative approaches, but it is clear that this situation lends itself to mathematical analysis, which is not pursued here. In terms of data collection, the method involves the identification of the relevant nodes (organisations, destinations) in the system and measuring the extent of links between them. The approach has similarities to the notion of *sociometry* as used in psychotherapy and education research (see Oppenheim, 2000: 254–9; Dayton, 2005).

Major sporting events, particularly multi-sport events such as the Olympic or Commonwealth Games, clearly involve networks, including the major

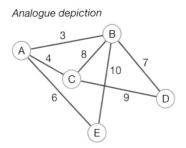

Analogue depiction   *Digital depiction*

	A	B	C	D	E
A	0	3	4	0	6
B	3	0	8	7	10
C	4	8	0	9	0
D	0	7	9	0	0
E	6	10	0	0	0

Figure 5.6   A simple network

sponsoring organisation, individual sports, and numerous organisations in the host community (Wäsche and Woll, 2010). Everyday sport and leisure activity also involves networks, among individuals and groups. The phenomenon of the social networking website is the latest manifestation of this, and, indeed, when network analysis is applied at the individual and small group level it is referred to as *social network analysis*. Numerous surveys of leisure facility and service users over many years have illustrated the importance of friendship networks when they discovered that 'word of mouth' is a far more significant source of information for most people than any form of advertising. Social network analysis is not common in sport and leisure studies, but has been explored by Patricia Stokowski (1994; Stokowski and Lee, 1991).

Panel studies

Market research companies often maintain *panels* of individuals for some of their surveys. Panels are made up of a representative cross-section of the public who agree to be on call for a series of surveys over a period of time. Often some financial reward is paid to panel members, but this cost is offset by the savings in not having to select and contact new samples of respondents for every survey. While managing such panels presents particular problems, the range of survey methods which can be used with panels – by telephone, by mail or by face-to-face interview – is the same as for normal one-off samples. Panel studies can therefore be seen as a particular form of household questionnaire survey.

Projective techniques

Projective techniques might be termed 'what if?' techniques, in that they involve subjects responding to hypothetical – projected – situations. For example, subjects might be asked to indicate how they might spend a particular sum of money if given a free choice, or how they might spend additional leisure time if it were made available, or they might be invited to respond to photographs of particular facilities. While the technique can become elaborate and specialised, in this book it is considered to be an extension of questionnaire-based surveys, and possibly of focus-group interviews and experimental methods.

Psychographic/lifestyle research

Psychographic research **(see Chapter 1)** involves gathering data on a wide range of attitudes and socio-demographic characteristics of people and analysing the data to establish groupings or market segments with common characteristics, typically using statistical techniques such as factor and cluster analysis **(discussed in Chapter 17)**. A number of commercial market research or survey/consultant organisations offer psychographic/lifestyle systems to clients to classify survey respondents into segments seen as more meaningful than those based on the usual age, gender and social class:

- The VALS typology (Values, Attitudes and Life Styles), developed in the United States, classifies people into nine segments, as shown in Figure 5.7. This system has been widely used in market research.

- The ACORN (A Classification of Residential Neighbourhoods) was developed in Britain by the commercial survey company CACI, and is based on socio-demographic data from census collection areas **(see Chapter 7)** so, since it does not contain attitude data it must be classified as a lifestyle rather than a psychographic system. It has five segments divided into 17 sub-segments, as shown in Figure 5.7, and has been used in sport research, notably in the annual Sport England Active People Survey, as discussed in Chapter 7.

Examples of the use of psychographic/lifestyle segmentation in the sport sector are listed in the Resources section.

It should be noted that the term 'lifestyle sports' is used to refer to a number of sporting activities which are also referred to as 'extreme', 'alternative' or 'action' sports. These include surfing, skateboarding, snowboarding and certain 'adventure sports' (Wheaton, 2004). This is, however, a somewhat different use of the term 'lifestyle' and does not involve a systematic classification of lifestyles across the society.

VALS*	ACORN†	
1. Survivor	1. Wealth achievers	A. Wealthy executives
2. Sustainer		B. Affluent greys (older people)
3. Belonger		C. Flourishing (well-off) families
4. Emulator	2. Urban prosperity	D. Prosperous professionals
5. Achiever		E. Educated urbanites (young urban professionals)
6. I-Am-Me		F. Aspiring singles (mainly urban area students)
7. Experiential	3. Comfortably off	G. Starting out (young couples)
8. Socially conscious		H. Secure families
9. Integrated		I. Settled suburbia (older couples in suburbs)
		J. Prudent pensioners
	4. Moderate means	K. Asian communities
		L. Post-industrial families (older skilled)
		M. Blue-collar roots (manual workers)
	5. Hard-pressed	N. Struggling (low-income) families
		O. Burdened singles (elderly and single parents)
		P. High-rise hardship
		Q. Inner city adversity

Figure 5.7 Examples of psychographic/lifestyle categories

* Values, Attitudes and Lifestyles: Strategic Business Insights (2009)
† A Classification of Residential Neighbourhoods: CACI Ltd (2006)

Q methodology

Q methodology was developed in the 1930s by physicist/psychologist William Stephenson to examine people's subjective opinions of phenomena. It involves five steps:

1. Definition of the 'concourse', the scope of the phenomenon to be studied – typically in the form of a set of attitude statements **(see Chapter 10)**, but sometimes photographs.

2. Development of the 'Q-sample' or 'Q-set' of stimulus items – typically a set of cards, each containing one of the statements/photographs.

3. Selection of the 'person-sample', 'P-sample or 'P-set' – the sample of individuals to be involved in the study.

4. Q-sorting – individuals sort the cards into piles arranged along a spectrum – for example from strongly agree to strongly disagree, scored as in a Likert scale **(see Chapter 10)**. Subjects are required to arrange cards on a provided template in the shape of a bell-shaped 'normal curve' (as shown in Figure 17.1a).

5. Analysis and interpretation – this involves factor analysis of the data **(see Chapter 17)** to discover themes.

Computer software packages, such as 'PQ Method' are available to analyse the data. Examples of applications in sport-related studies are indicated in the Resources section.

Quantitative modelling

The techniques discussed in this chapter are mostly distinguished primarily by their data collection procedures and in some cases by both their data collection and analysis procedures. Quantitative modelling is distinguished by an approach to theory and data analysis: the data used are quantitative, but may have been collected by one or more of a variety of methods (e.g. observation, questionnaires, documentary records, experiment). The idea of quantitative modelling was discussed briefly in Chapter 3, where it is noted that hypotheses concerning the relationships between variables may be expressed and tested in the form of models/equations. This approach to research is considered further in Chapter 17, particularly in connection with linear and multiple regression.

Repertory grid

The repertory grid technique was developed by psychologist George Kelly in the 1950s and is used from time to time in sport research. It can be seen as a formalisation and quantification of the conceptual form of perceptual mapping.

Friendly						Threatening
Cool						Uncool
Expensive						Cheap
Etc.						

Figure 5.8   Repertory grid – example

Research subjects are asked to indicate a range of qualities of the phenomenon being studied and then the opposite of that quality – for example friendly: threatening; cool: uncool; expensive: cheap. A number of these bi-polar constructs are elicited – typically up to about 20 – and presented in a grid, as shown in Figure 5.8. Subjects then indicate on the grid where the study object fits on each construct; for example, for the first construct, whether it is closer to the friendly end or the threatening end. This information can be scored and analysed using graphic and/or statistical analyses such as factor analysis **(see Chapter 17)** at the individual level and/or collectively. Sport-related examples are listed in the Resources section.

Scales

A scale is a numerical index used to measure concepts which are generally not intrinsically quantitative. Typically subjects are asked to respond to questions on a number of factors using rating scales and the scores are combined to produce a scale or index of the phenomenon of interest. In Chapter 10 the development and use of customised scales in questionnaires is discussed, but it is quite common for researchers to make use of standardised scales which have been developed by others. The advantage of the use of existing scales is that researchers are not continually 'reinventing the wheel' by devising their own measure of a particular phenomenon. Widely used scales have generally been subject to considerable testing to ensure validity – that is, that they measure what they are intended to measure. Further, the use of common measures facilitates comparability between studies. The disadvantage is, of course, that any fault in the scale validity may be replicated across many studies and a fixed scale may not fully reflect different socio-economic environments or change over time.

The use of such scales is widespread, particularly in psychology and related disciplines:

● The most well-known is personality indicators, such as the Myers–Briggs personality scale.

● Researchers in the area of sport and exercise often make use of scales related to physical and mental health, such as that developed by Ware, Kosinski and Keller (1994).

● The *Marketing Scales Handbook*, published in a number of volumes by the American Marketing Association (Bruner and Hensel, 1992), lists hundreds

Listed in Bruner and Hensel (1992)

| 261 | Sports activeness | 262 | Sports enthusiasm |

Listed in Bruner, James and Hensel (2001)

217	Involvement (televised soccer match)	307	Satisfaction (with health club)
259	Pressure to be thin	323	Sensation-seeking
285	Quality of service (stadium)	345	Service quality (health club)

Other scales

Life Satisfaction Index: Neugarten *et al.* (1961)
Locus of Control Scale: Levenson (1974)
Physical and mental health: Ware *et al.* (1994)
Sport Commitment Model: Scanlan *et al.*, 1993a, 1993b
Sport consumption/motivation: Trail and James (2002)
Sport events: Martin and O'Neill (2010)
Sport motivation: Pelletier *et al.* (1995)
Sport spectators: Bouchet *et al.* (2011)
Team identification: Theodorakis *et al.* (2010)

Figure 5.9 Scales for sport-related topics

of scales used in marketing research, most relating to generic topics, such as consumer motivation and attitudes, but others relating to specific settings.

A selection of relevance to sport is listed in Figure 5.9.

Time-use surveys

There is a long tradition of investigating people's allocation of time between such categories as paid work, domestic work, sleep and leisure, including sport (Szalai, 1972; Pentland *et al.*, 1999). Such studies involve survey respondents keeping a detailed diary of activity for one or two days. Time-use surveys are conducted periodically in most economically developed countries. Examples of studies drawing on such data and focusing on sport are provided in the Resources section. Time-use – or time-budget – research is basically a special case of the household survey **(and some reference is made to it in that context in Chapter 10)**.

Web-based research

The Internet, and the social network phenomenon in particular, are increasingly significant as means of communication. They are therefore key potential sources of information about people's attitudes, values, tastes and behaviour, which is of interest to marketers and social and cultural researchers. A set of practices and associated literature has grown up in this area, referred to as *netnography* or *virtual research*, noted above. Research on websites themselves and on their users can also be quantitative. Sources and examples are indicated in the Resources section.

Multiple/mixed methods

Many research methods involve the use of more than one method or technique (Rudd and Johnson, 2010). Two multi-method situations are discussed here: triangulation and counting heads, along with the general idea of 'mixed methods'. The case study method is also a multi-method approach but, as it is also considered to be a primary method in its own right, it is discussed separately above **(and in Chapter 12)**.

Triangulation

Triangulation gets its name from the land surveying method of fixing the position of an object by measuring it from two different positions, with the object of study being the third point of the triangle. In research, the triangulation method involves the use of more than one research approach in a single study to gain a broader or more complete understanding of the issues being investigated. The methods used are often complementary in that the weaknesses of one approach are complemented by the strengths of another. Triangulation often utilises both qualitative and quantitative approaches in the same study. Duffy (1987: 131) has identified four different ways that triangulation can be used in research, namely:

● analysing data in more than one way;

● using more than one sampling strategy;

● using different interviewers, observers and analysts in the one study; and

● using more than one methodology to gather data.

   If triangulation methods are to be used in a study the approaches taken will depend on the imagination and the experience of the researcher. However, it is important that the research question is clearly focused and not confused by the methodology adopted, and that the methods are chosen in accordance with their relevance to the topic. In particular, the *rationale* for using triangulation should be outlined in reporting the research. In particular, the possible weaknesses of one method and the ways in which the additional method has been used to overcome such a weakness should be explained. This is clearly relevant to the issue of validity and reliability **(discussed in Chapter 2)**.

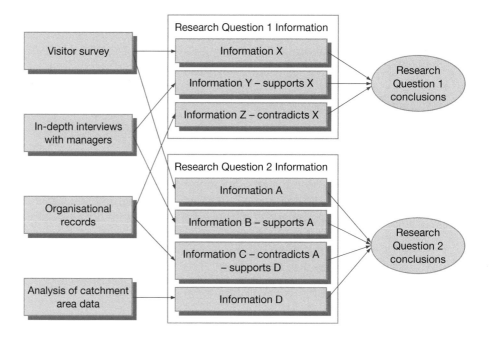

Figure 5.10 Triangulation

Often triangulation is claimed in a study because more than one data source and/or analytical method has been used to address different aspects of the research question, or even different research questions. However, it is when the different data/methods address the *same* question that true triangulation can be said to have occurred. Figure 5.10 presents an example where four data collection methods are used to address two research questions. A research report on a project where triangulation is claimed should therefore compare and contrast the findings from the multiple methods. Whether the multiple methods produce similar or different findings should then be an issue for discussion.

Counting heads

In virtually all sport management/policy contexts there is a requirement for information on visitor numbers for planning and management purposes. This calls for what is colloquially referred to as 'counting heads' or, in seated venues, counting 'bums on seats'. In many cases the required information is generated automatically by the ticket sales process. But there are also situations where ticket numbers are not available, for example: facilities such as playing fields, where bookings are made on behalf of a club; informal areas, such as beaches, bicycle tracks or rock-climbing sites. In these situations a variety of data collection methods may be available from which one or more may be selected. The methods/sources can be divided into administrative, survey-based and direct counts. Thus assembling data concerning one site or destination involves consideration of methods. **This issue is addressed initially in Chapter 7, and** information provided in Figures 7.2 and 7.3 is cross-referenced in Chapters 8 and 10.

Mixed methods

Mixed methods has emerged as the term to describe the conscious process of using two or more methods in the same project, particularly combining qualitative and quantitative approaches. In our discussion of planning and designing research projects it should be clear that this is seen as a quite routine rather than an exceptional situation. Nevertheless, there is a specific literature growing up around the concept, and examples are indicated in the Resources sections of this chapter **(and in Chapter 2)**.

Choosing methods

The process of choosing appropriate research methods for a research task is part of the whole process of planning and designing a research project **(as considered in Chapter 3)**. Here a number of considerations which should be borne in mind are discussed, as listed in Figure 5.11 and discussed in turn below.

The research question or hypothesis

Much of the decision on how to research a topic is bound up in the basic research question or hypothesis. The 'research question' can take a variety of forms **(see Chapter 3)**, but generally it will point the researcher in the direction of certain data sources – for example in relation to participants, employees, customers or organisations. Certain types of data also suggest certain types of analysis.

- The research question or hypothesis
- Previous research
- Data availability/access
- Resources
- Time
- Validity, reliability, trustworthiness
- Generalisability
- Ethics
- Uses/users of the findings

Figure 5.11   Considerations in selecting a research method

Previous research

If the proposed research is closely keyed into the literature and previous research, the methods used in earlier research are likely to influence the choice of methods. The aim may be to replicate the methodology used in previous studies to achieve comparability, to improve on the methods used, or to deliberately adopt a contrasting methodology.

Data availability/access

In some cases an obvious existing data source presents itself, and may even have prompted the research in the first place **(termed opportunistic research in Chapter 2)**. For example:

- a set of archives of an organisation can provide the basis for historical research;

- official survey-based data which have been published but only superficially analysed could be analysed in more depth;

- access to a sample of people, such as the workforce or customer-base of a company, members of a sports club or members of an informal interest group can be seen as a research opportunity too good to miss.

In other cases, *lack* of access shapes the research – for example, ethical or practical issues may preclude some research on children, so data may have to be gathered from parents.

Resources

Clearly the resources of staff and money will have a major effect on the type and scale of the research to be conducted.

Time and timing

Time and timing are always a limitation. Most research projects have a time limit. Timing in relation to external events or routines is also often a factor: for example, research using the current year's attendance data must be completed quickly if it is to be used to influence next year's strategic planning, and empirical research on events, such as a sporting events, is constrained by their timing.

Validity, reliability, trustworthiness and generalisability

Validity, reliability, trustworthiness and generalisability are key considerations in all research. As discussed earlier **(see Chapter 2)**:

- *validity* is the extent to which the data collected truly reflect the phenomenon being studied;

- *reliability* is the extent to which research findings would be the same if the research were to be repeated at a later date, or with a different sample of subjects;

- *trustworthiness* is sometimes used in place of the above in qualitative research;

- *generalisability* refers to the extent to which the results of the research findings apply to other subjects, other groups and other conditions: the extent to which this is required as an outcome of the research will influence the choice of method.

Ethics

Ethical issues also limit choices of research method. Reference has already been made to ethical issues surrounding research on children **(further examples are discussed in Chapter 4)**.

Uses/users of the findings

The uses and users of the research are often taken for granted, but they are an important factor in shaping research. If substantial investment or changes in practice will depend on the results of the research, a more extensive and thorough-going project will be required than if the research is to be used only to generate ideas for further exploration. When life-and-death issues are at stake – for example in medical research on the effects of a treatment for a disease – much more precision is needed in the results than if, for example, a company merely wishes to know the socio-economic characteristics of its customers.

Summary

This chapter complements Chapter 3 in setting out in brief the range of research methods available to the sport researcher. It reinforces the message of Chapter 3, that research methods should ideally be selected on the basis of their suitability to answer the research questions posed, not on the basis of some prior preference for a particular method. Initially the 'major' research methods are reviewed, namely:

- scholarship;

- 'just thinking';

- the use of existing information – the literature and secondary data;

- observation;

- qualitative methods;

- questionnaire-based surveys;

- case-study method; and

- experimental method.

The first two are included to emphasise that research is not just about deploying techniques, but also involves being well informed about the field and *thinking* about the problems and issues being researched in theoretical and practical terms. The other major methods foreshadow subsequent chapters which deal with them in detail.

The middle section of the chapter briefly introduces a number of approaches and techniques which are subsidiary to one or more of the major methods, in that they are a variation on, or an application of, the major method, or cut across a number of the major methods. The approaches and techniques covered are:

- action research;

- big data;

- conjoint analysis;

- content analysis;

- coupon surveys/conversion studies;

- Delphi technique;

- diary methods;

- discourse analysis;

- en route/intercept surveys;
- experience sampling method;
- historical research;
- longitudinal studies;
- mapping techniques;
- media reader/viewer/listener surveys;
- meta-analysis;
- network analysis;
- panel studies;
- projective techniques;
- psychographic/lifestyle research;
- Q methodology;
- quantitative modelling;
- repertory grid/laddering;
- scales;
- time-use surveys.

In the next section of the chapter consideration is given to 'multiple methods', with a discussion of the concept of *triangulation*, *counting heads* and *mixed methods.*

Finally, factors to be considered in selecting research methods are examined.

Test questions

1. What is 'scholarship'?
2. Define each of the following:
   a. Action research
   b. Big data
   c. Conjoint analysis
   d. Content analysis
   e. Coupon surveys/conversion studies
   f. The Delphi technique
   g. Diary methods
   h. Discourse analysis

i.   En route/intercept surveys

j.   Epidemiological research

k.   Experience sampling method

l.   Historical research

m. Longitudinal studies

n.   Mapping techniques

o.   Media reader/viewer/listener surveys

p.   Meta-analysis

q.   Netnography

r.   Network analysis

s.   Panel studies

t.   Projective techniques

u.   Psychographic/lifestyle research

v.   Q methodology

w. Quantitative modelling

x.   Repertory grid/laddering

y.   Scales

z.   Time-use surveys.

3. What is triangulation and why is it used in research?

4. What does counting heads involve?

Exercises

Exercises involving the major methods and subsidiary and cross-cutting methods arise in the subsequent chapters.

Resources

Websites

- Experience sampling method: Society for Ambulatory Assessment: www.ambulatory-assessment.org; software sites: www.experience-sampling.org, http://myexperience.sourceforge.net

- Longitudinal: UK Longitudinal Studies Centre: www.iser.essex.ac.uk/survey/ulsc, Australian Longitudinal Study of Women's Health: www.alswh.org.au.

- Meta-analysis: the Cochrane Collaboration: www.cochrane.org.

- Q methodology: www.qmethod.org/about.php.

- Time use: Centre for Time Use Research, USA: www.timeuse.org, International Association for Time Use Research: www.iatur.org.

Publications

- Major methods: Armour and Macdonald (2012) **(and see Resources sections of Chapters 6–12)**.

- Action research: Blodgett *et al.* (2011), Chalip (1997), Frisby *et al.* (2005), Greenwood and Levin (2007), McNiff and Whitehead (2002), Reason and Bradbury (2001).

- Big Data: Anderson (2011), Mayer-Schönberger and Cukier (2013).

- Community studies: Wynne (1986, 1998), Waldren (1996, 1997).

- Conjoint analysis: Cosper and Kinsley (1984), Claxton (1994), Jones (1991).

- Content analysis: media coverage of sport: Capranica (2005), Toohey (1997); Internet: McDaniel and Sullivan (1998).

- Counting heads: Gartner and Hunt (1988); **(see Chapter 8)**.

- Coupon surveys/conversion studies: Perdue and Botkin (1988), Schwarz and Hunter (2012).

- Delphi technique: general and tourism: Mallen *et al.* (2010), Hsu and Sandford (2007); in sport: Murray and Jarman (1987); recreational walking/cycling influences: Pikora *et al.* (2003).

- Discourse analysis: Gee (2010); critical discourse analysis: Locke (2004).

- En route surveys: Gartner and Hunt (1988), Hurst (1994).

- Epidemiological research: and sport injuries: Hägglund *et al.* (2005).

- Experience sampling method: Conner *et al.* (2009), Csikszentmihayli and Larson (1977), Hektner *et al.* (2006); in sport/exercise: Gauvin and Szabo (1992) and Stein *et al.* (1995).

- Historical research: Wiggins and Mason (2006); on the Olympic Games: see Veal (2010).

- Longitudinal studies: in the social sciences: Young *et al.* (1991); in sport: Cresswell and Eklund (2007); the Australian Longitudinal Study on Women's Health includes questions on sport/leisure and a number of publications has resulted, for example: Brown *et al.* (2009); an up-to-date list of papers emerging from the project can be found on the project website listed above.

- Mental maps – see perceptual mapping.

- Meta-analysis: general: Card (2011), Glass *et al.* (1981), Littell *et al.* (2008); sport-related: Priest *et al.* (2008); sport legacy of the Olympic Games: Weed *et al.* (2009).

- Methodological debate: see Kelly (1980), Henderson (2006), Rojek (1989), Borman *et al.* (1986), Krenz and Sax (1986), Bryman and Bell (2003: 465–78 – Chapter 21: 'Breaking down the quantitative/qualitative divide,') Dupuis (1999).

- Mixed methods: Camarino *et al.* (2012: esp. Chapter 2), Creswell and Piano Clark (2007), Henderson *et al.* (1999), Rohm *et al.* (2006), Rudd and Johnson (2010), Vergeer and Lyle (2007).

- Netnography: general: Kozinets (2009); marketing: Xun and Reynolds (2010); sport-related: Berger *et al.* (2008).

- Network analysis: leisure: Stokowski (1994); sport tourism: Wäsche and Woll (2010); sport management: Sallent *et al.* (2011); sociometry: Oppenheim (2000: 254–5); squash centre friendships: Jenkins *et al.* (1977).

- Panel surveys: Kasprzyk *et al.* (1989), Rose (2000).

- Perceptual mapping: Buzan (1994), Crowe and Sheppard (2012); sport consumers and sponsorship: Martin and Carroll (1994); banned substances: Pan and Baker (1998).

- Projective techniques: Semeonoff (1976), Oppenheim (2000: Chapter 12).

- Psychographic/lifestyle research: general: Strategic Business Insights (2009), CACI Ltd (2006); sport spectators: Bouchet *et al.* (2011); sport participants: Rohm *et al.* (2006); sport politics: Ahlfeldt *et al.* (2010).

- Qualitative methods – see Chapters 9 and 15 references.

- Q methodology: principles: McKeown and Thomas (1988); sport/exercise: Annear *et al.* (2009), Farquhar and Meeds (2007).

- Repertory grid: Kelly (1955); sport-related: Balduck *et al.* (2009), Feixas *et al.* (1989).

- Scales: see Figure 5.9 listing.

- Textual analysis: Prior (2003); sport: Rowe (2004), Delaney and Eckstein (2008); television coverage: Billings and Tyler Eastman (2002); print media coverage: Stone and Horne (2008); corporate sport advertising: Carty (1997) – see Case study 12.2.

- Time-use studies: general: Szalai (1972), Pentland *et al.* (1999); leisure: Zuzanek and Veal (1998); youth and physical activity: Dunton *et al.* (2010); children and physical activity: Ridley *et al.* (2006).

- Triangulation: Bryman and Bell (2003: 482–4), Duffy (1987).
- Web-based research: Scholl and Carlson (2012).

References

Ahlfeldt, G. M., Maennig, W. and Ölschläger, M. (2010) *Lifestyles and Preferences for (Public) Goods: Professional Football in Munich.* Hamburg Contemporary Economic Discussions No. 30, Faculty of Economic and Social Sciences, University of Hamburg, available at: http://hdl.handle.net/10419/42230 (Accessed May 2013).

Anderson, C. (2011) *The Long Tail: How Endless Choice is Creating Unlimited Demand, Revised edn.* New York: Random House.

Annear, M. J., Gidlow, B. and Cushman, G. (2009) Neighbourhood deprivation and older adults' preferences for and perceptions of active leisure participation. *Annals of Leisure Research*, 12 (2), 96–128.

Armour, K. and Macdonald, D. (eds) (2012) *Research Methods in Physical Education and Youth Sport.* London: Routledge.

Balduck, A-L., Van Rossem, A. and Buelens, M. (2010) Identifying competencies of volunteer board members of community sports clubs. *Nonprofit and Voluntary Sector Quarterly*, 39(2), 213–35.

Berger, I. E., O'Reilly, N., Parent, M. M., Séguin, B. and Hernandez, T. (2008) Determinants of sport participation among Canadian adolescents. *Sport Management Review*, 11(3), 277–307.

Billings, A. C. and Tyler Eastman, S. (2002) Selective representation of gender, ethnicity and nationality in American television coverage of the 2000 Summer Olympics. *International Review for the Sociology of Sport*, 37(3/4), 351–70.

Blodgett, A. T., Schinke, R. J. and Peltier, D. (2011) May the circle be unbroken: the research recommendations of Aboriginal community members engaged in participatory action research with university academics. *Journal of Sport and Social Issues*, 35(3), 264–83.

Borman, K. M., LeCompte, M. D. and Goetz, J. P. (1986) Ethnographic and qualitative research design and why it doesn't work. *American Behavioral Scientist*, 30(1), 42–57.

Bouchet, P., Bodet, G., Bernache-Assallant, I. and Kada, F. (2011) Segmenting sport spectators: construction and preliminary validation of the Sporting Event Experience Search (SEES). *Sport Management Review*, 14(1), 42–53.

Brown, W. J., Heesch, K. and Miller, Y. (2009) Life events and changing physical activity patterns in women at different life stages. *Annals of Behavioral Medicine*, 37(3), 294–305.

Bruner, G. C. and Hensel, P. J. (1992) *Marketing Scales Handbook: A Compilation of Multi-Item Measures.* Chicago, IL: American Marketing Association.

Bruner, G. C., James, K. E. and Hensel, P. J. (2001) *Marketing Scales Handbook: A Compilation of Multi-Item Measures Volume III*. Chicago, IL: American Marketing Association.

Bryman, A. and Bell, E. (2003) Breaking down the quantitative/qualitative divide, and Combining quantitative and qualitative research. Chapters 21–22 of *Business Research Methods*. Oxford: Oxford University Press, 465–94.

Buzan, T. (1994) *The Mind Map Book: How to Use Radiant Thinking to Maximise your Brain's Untapped Potential*. New York: Dutton.

CACI Ltd (2006) *ACORN User Guide*. London: CACI Ltd, available at: www.caci.co.uk/financialacorn.aspx (Accessed May 2013).

Camarino, O., Castaner, M. and Anguera, M. T. (eds) (2012) *Mixed Methods Research in the Movement Sciences*. London: Routledge.

Capranica, L. (2005) Newspaper coverage of women's sports during the 2000 Sydney Olympic Games: Belgium, Denmark, France, and Italy. *Research Quarterly for Exercise and Sport*, 76(2), 212–33.

Card, N. A. (2011) *Applied Meta-Analysis for Social Science Research*. New York: Guilford Press.

Carty, V. (1997) Ideologies and forms of domination in the organization of the global production and consumption of goods in the emerging postmodern era: a case study of Nike Corporation and the implications for gender. *Gender, Work and Organization*, 4(4), 189–201.

Chalip, L. (1997) Action research and social change in sport: an introduction to the special issue. *Journal of Sport Management*, 11(1), 1–7.

Claxton, J. D. (1994) Conjoint analysis in travel research: a manager's guide. In J. R. B. Ritchie and C. R. Goeldner (eds) *Travel, Tourism and Hospitality Research, Second edn*. New York: John Wiley, 513–522.

Conner, T. S., Tennen, H., Fleeson, W. and Barrett, L. F. (2009) Experience sampling methods: a modern idiographic approach to personality research. *Social and Personality Psychology*, 3(3), 292–313.

Cosper, R. and Kinsley, B. L. (1984) An application of conjoint analysis to leisure research: cultural preferences in Canada. *Journal of Leisure Research*, 16(3), 224–33.

Cresswell, S. L. and Eklund, R. C. (2007) Athlete burnout: a longitudinal qualitative study. *Sport Psychologist*, 21(1), 1–20.

Creswell, J. W. and Piano Clark, V. L. (2007) *Designing and Conducting Mixed Methods Research*. Thousand Oaks, CA: Sage.

Crowe, M. and Sheppard, L. (2012) Mind mapping research methods. *Quality and Quantity*, 46(6), 1493–504.

Csikszentmihalyi, M. and Larson, R. (1977) The ecology of adolescent activity and experience. *Journal of Youth and Adolescence*, 6(3), 281–94.

Dayton, T. (2005) *The Living Stage: A Step-by-step Guide to Psychodrama, Sociometry and Experiential Group Therapy*. Deerfield Beach, FL: Health Communication Books.

Delaney, K. and Eckstein, R. (2008) Local media coverage of sports stadium initiatives. *Journal of Sport and Social Issues*, 32(1), 72–93.

Donohue, H. M., and Needham, R. D. (2009) Moving best practice forward: Delphi characteristics, advantages, potential problems, and solutions. *International Journal of Tourism Research*, 11(4), 415–37.

Duffy, M. E. (1987) Methodological triangulation: a vehicle for merging qualitative and quantitative research methods. *IMAGE: Journal of Nursing Scholarship*, 19(1), 130–3.

Dunton, G. F., Berrigan, D. and Ballard-Barbash, R. (2010) Adolescents' sport and exercise environments in a U.S. time use survey. *American Journal of Preventive Medicine*, 39(2), 122–9.

Dupuis, S. (1999) Naked truths: towards a reflexive methodology in leisure research. *Leisure Sciences*, 21(1), 43–64.

Farquhar, L. K. and Meeds, R. (2007) Types of fantasy sports users and their motivations. *Journal of Computer-Mediated Communication*, 12(4), article 4, online journal, available at: http://jcmc.indiana.edu/vol12/issue4/farquhar.html (Accessed May 2013).

Feixas, G., Marti, J. and Villegas, M. (1989) Personal construct assessment of sports teams. *International Journal of Personal Construct Psychology*, 2(1), 49–54.

Frisby, W., Reid, C. J., Millar, S. and Hoeber, L. (2005) Putting 'participatory' into participatory action research. *Journal of Sport Management*, 19(4), 367–86.

Gartner, W. and Hunt, J. D. (1988) A method to collect detailed tourist flow information. *Annals of Tourism Research*, 15(1), 159–72.

Gauvin, L. and Szabo, A. (1992) Application of the Experience Sampling Method to the study of the effects of exercise withdrawal on well-being. *Journal of Sport and Exercise Psychology*, 14(4), 361–74.

Gee, J. P. (2010) *An Introduction to Discourse Analysis*. London: Routledge.

Glass, G. V., McGaw, B. and Smith, M. L. (1981) *Meta-Analysis in Social Research*. Beverly Hills, CA: Sage.

Greenwood, D. J. and Levin, M. (2007) *Introduction to Action Research*. Thousand Oaks, CA: Sage.

Hägglund, M., Walden, M., Bahr, R. and Ekstrand, J. (2005) Methods for epidemiological study of injuries to professional football players: developing the UEFA model. *British Journal of Sports Medicine*, 39(6), 340–6.

Hektner, J. M., Schmidt, J. A. and Csikszentmihayli, M. (eds) (2006) *Experience Sampling Method: Measuring the Quality of Everyday Life*. Thousand Oaks, CA: Sage.

Henderson, K., Ainsworth, B. E. and Stolarzcyk, L. M. (1999) Notes on linking qualitative and quantitative data: the cross-cultural physical activity participation study. *Leisure Sciences*, 21(3), 247–55.

Henderson, K. A. (2006) *Dimensions of Choice: A Qualitative Approach to Recreation, Parks, and Leisure Research, Second edn*. State College, PA: Venture.

Hsu, C.-C. and Sandford, B. A. (2007) The Delphi technique: making sense of consensus. *Practical Assessment, Research and Evaluation*, 12(10), 1–8.

Hurst, F. (1994) En route surveys. In J. R. B. Ritchie and C. R. Goeldner (eds) *Travel, Tourism and Hospitality Research, Second edn*. New York: John Wiley, 453–72.

Jenkins, C., Knapp, B., and Bonser, K. (1977) *Squash at Rugby Sports Centre: an Exploratory Study, Research Working Papers 2*. London: Sports Council.

Jones, R. A. (1991) Enhancing marketing decisions using conjoint analysis: an application in public leisure services. *Society and Leisure*, 14(1), 69–84.

Kasprzyk, D., Duncan, G., Kalton, G. and Singh, M. P. (1989) *Panel Surveys*. New York: John Wiley & Sons.

Kellehear, A. (1993) *The Unobtrusive Researcher: A Guide to Methods*. Sydney: Allen & Unwin.

Kelly, G. A. (1955) *The Psychology of Personal Constructs*. New York: Norton.

Kelly, J. R. (1980) Leisure and quality: beyond the quantitative barrier in research. In T. L. Goodale and P. A. Witt (eds) *Recreation and Leisure: Issues in an Era of Change*. State College, PA: Venture, 300–14.

Kozinets, R. V. (2009) *Netnography: Doing Ethnographic Research Online*. London: Sage.

Krenz, C. and Sax, G. (1986) What quantitative research is and why it doesn't work. *American Behavioral Scientist*, 30(1), 58–69.

Levenson, H. (1974) Activism and powerful others: distinction within the concept of internal-external control. *Journal of Psychology and Aging*, 1(1), 117–26.

Littell, J. H., Corcoran, J. and Pillai, V. (2008) *Systematic Reviews and Meta-Analysis*. Oxford: Oxford University Press.

Locke, T. (2004) *Critical Discourse Analysis*. London: Continuum.

Mallen, C., Adams, L., Stevens, J. and Thompson, L. (2010) Environmental sustainability in sport facility management: a Delphi study. *European Sport Management Quarterly*, 10(3), 367–89.

Martin, D. S. and O'Neill, M. (2010) Scale development and testing: a new measure of cognitive satisfaction in sports tourism. *Event Management*, 14(1), 1–15.

Martin, J. H. and Carroll, J. (1994) Using a perceptual map of the consumer's sport schema to help make sponsorship decisions. *Sport Marketing Quarterly*, 3(3), 27–33.

Mayer-Schönberger, V., and Cukier, K. (2013) *Big Data: a Revolution that will Transform How we Live, Work and Think*. London: John Murray.

McDaniel, S. R. and Sullivan, C. B. (1998) Extending sports experience: mediations in cyberspace. In L. A. Werner (ed.) *MediaSport*. London: Routledge, 266–81.

McKeown, B. and Thomas, D. (1988) *Q Methodology*. Newbury Park, CA: Sage.

McNiff, J. and Whitehead, J. (2002) *Action Research: Principles and Practice*. London: Routledge/Falmer.

Mehl, M. R., Pennebaker, J. W., Crow, D. M., Dabbs, J. and Price, J. H. (2001) The Electronically Activated Recorder (EAR): a device for sampling naturalistic daily activities and conversations. *Behavior Research Methods, Instruments, and Computers*, 33(4), 517–23.

Murray, W. F. and Jarman, B. O. (1987) Predicting future trends in adult fitness using the Delphi approach. *Research Quarterly for Exercise and Sport*, 58(2), 123–31.

Myers, N. D., Chase, M. A., Pierce, S. W. and Martin, E. (2011) Coaching efficacy and exploratory structural equation modelling: a substantive-methodological synergy. *Journal of Sport and Exercise Psychology*, 33(2), 779–806.

Neugarten, P. L., Havighurst, R. J. and Tobin, S. S. (1961) The measurement of life satisfaction. *Journal of Gerontology*, 16(1), 134–43.

Oppenheim, A. N. (2000) *Questionnaire Design, Interviewing and Attitude Measurement: New Edition*. London: Pinter.

Pan, D. W. and Baker, J. A. W. (1998) Perceptual mapping of banned substances in athletics. *Sport and Social Issues*, 22(2), 170–82.

Pelletier, L. G., Fortier, M. S., Vallerand, R. J. and Tuson, K. M. (1995) Toward a new measure of intrinsic motivation. Extrinsic motivation and amotivation in sports: the Sport Motivation Scale (SMS). *Journal of Sport and Exercise Psychology*, 17(1), 35–53.

Pentland, W. E., Harvey, A. S., Powell Lawton, M. and McColl, M. A. (eds) (1999) *Time Use Research in the Social Sciences*. New York: Kluwer/Plenum.

Perdue, R. R. and Botkin, M. R. (1988) Visitor survey versus conversion study. *Annals of Tourism Research*, 15(1), 76–87.

Pikora, T., Giles-Corti, B., Bull, F., Jamrozik, K. and Donovan, R. (2003) Developing a framework for assessment of the environmental determinants of walking and cycling. *Social Science and Medicine*, 56(6), 1693–703.

Priest, N., Armstrong, R., Dyle, J. and Waters, E. (2008) *Policy Interventions Implemented Through Sporting Organisations to Promote Healthy Behaviour Change*. Oxford: The Cochrane Collaboration, available at: www.cochrane.org (Accessed May 2013).

Prior, L. (2003) *Using Documents in Social Research*. London: Sage.

Quested, E. and Duda, J. L. (2011) Antecedents of burnout among elite dancers: a longitudinal test of basic needs theory. *Psychology of Sport and Exercise*, 12(2), 159–167.

Reason, P. and Bradbury, H. (eds) (2001) *Handbook of Action Research: Participative Inquiry and Practice*. London: Sage.

Ridley, K., Olds, T. S. and Hill, A. (2006) The multimedia activity recall children and adolescents (MARCA): development and evaluation. *International Journal of Behavioral Nutrition and Physical Activity*, 3(10), 1–11.

Rohm, A. J., Milne, G. R. and McDonald, M. A. (2006) A mixed-method approach for developing market segmentation typologies in the sports industry. *Sport Marketing Quarterly*, 15(1), 29–39.

Rojek, C. (1989) Leisure and recreation theory. In E. L. Jackson and T. L. Burton (eds) *Understanding Leisure and Recreation: Mapping the Past and Charting the Future*. State College, PA: Venture, 69–88.

Rose, D. (ed.) (2000) *Researching Social and Economic Change: The Uses of Household Panel Studies*. London: Routledge.

Rowe, D. (ed.) (2004) *Critical Readings: Sport, Culture and the Media*. Maidenhead, UK: Open University Press.

Rudd, A. and Johnson, R. B. (2010) A call for more mixed methods in sport management research. *Sport Management Review*, 13(1), 14–24.

Sallent, O., Palau, R. and Guia, J. (2011) Exploring the legacy of sport events on sport tourism networks. *European Sport Management Quarterly*, 11(4), 397–421.

Scanlan, T. K., Simons, J. P. and Carpenter, P. J. (1993a) An introduction to the Sport Commitment Model. *Journal of Sport and Exercise Psychology*, 15(1), 1–15.

Scanlan, T. K., Carpenter, P. J. and Schmidt, G. W. (1993b) The Sport Commitment Model: measurement development for the youth-sport domain. *Journal of Sport and Exercise Psychology*, 15(1), 16–38.

Scholl, H. J. and Carlson, T. S. (2012) Professional sports teams on the Web: a comparative study employing the information management perspective. *European Sport Management Quarterly*, 12(2), 137–60.

Schwarz, E. and Hunter, J. (2012) *Advanced Theory and Practice in Sport Marketing, Second edn.* Oxford: Routledge.

Semeneoff, B. (1976) *Projective Techniques.* London: John Wiley.

Smyth, J. M. and Stone, A. A. (2003) Ecological momentary assessment research in behavioral medicine. *Journal of Happiness Studies*, 4, 35–52.

Steen, J. K. S., Denstadli, J. M. and Rideng, A. (2008) Skiers' sense of snow: tourist skills and winter holiday attribute preferences. *Tourism Analysis*, 13(5–6), 605–14.

Stein, G. L., Kimiecik, J. C., Daniels, J. and Jackson, S. A. (1995) Psychological antecedents to flow in recreational sport. *Personality and Social Psychology*, 21(2), 125–35.

Stokowski, P. A. (1994) *Leisure in Society: A Network Structural Perspective.* London: Mansell.

Stokowski, P. A. and Lee, R. G. (1991) The influence of social network ties on recreation and leisure: an exploratory study. *Journal of Leisure Research*, 23(1), 95–113.

Stone, J. and Horne, J. (2008) The print media coverage of skiing and snowboarding in Britain: does it have to be downhill all the way? *Journal of Sport and Social Issues*, 32(1), 94–112.

Strategic Business Insights (2009) *The VALS Survey.* Menlo Park, CA: Strategic Business Insights, available at: www.strategicbusinessinsights.com/vals/presurvey.shtml (Accessed May 2013).

Szalai, A. (ed.) (1972) *The Use of Time: Daily Activities of Urban and Suburban Populations in Twelve Countries.* The Hague: Mouton.

Theodorakis, N. D., Dimmock, J., Wann, D. and Barlas, A. (2010) Psychometric evaluation of the Team Identification Scale among Greek sport fans: a cross-validation approach. *European Sport Management Quarterly*, 10(3), 289–305.

Toohey, K. (1997) Australian television, gender and the Olympic Games. *International Review for the Sociology of Sport*, 32(1), 19–29.

Trail, G. T. and James, J. D. (2002) The motivation scale for sport consumption: assessment of the scale's psychometric properties. *Journal of Sport Behavior*, 24(1), 108–27.

United Nations Intergovernmental Panel on Climate Change (UNIPCC) (2013) *Climate Change 2013: The Physical Science Basis.* Geneva: UNIPCC, available at: www.ipcc.ch.

Veal, A. J. (2010) *The Olympic Games: A Bibliography.* School of Leisure and Tourism Studies, University of Technology, Sydney, On-line Bibliography 5, available at: www.business.uts.edu.au/olympic/downloads/olympic_bib_update2.pdf (Accessed May 2013).

Vergeer, I. and Lyle, J. (2007) Mixed methods in assessing coaches' decision-making. *Research Quarterly for Exercise and Sport*, 78(3), 225–35.

Ware, J. E., Kosinski, M. and Keller, S. D. (1994) *SF 36 Physical and Mental Health Summary Scales: A User's Manual.* Boston, MA: The Health Institute, New England Medical Centre.

Wäsche, H. and Woll, A. (2010) Regional sports tourism networks: a conceptual framework. *Journal of Sport and Tourism*, 15(3), 191–214.

Weed, M., Coren, E. and Fiore, J. (2009) *A Systematic Review of the Evidence Base for Developing a Physical Activity and Health Legacy from the London 2012 Olympic and Paralympic Games.* Canterbury, UK: Centre for Sport, Physical Education and Activity Research, Canterbury Christ Church University, available at: www.canterbury.ac.uk/social-applied-sciences/ (Accessed May 2013).

Wheaton, B. (ed.) (2004) *Understanding Lifestyle Sports.* London: Routledge.

Wiggins, D. K. and Mason, D. S. (2006) The socio-historical process in sports studies. In D. L. Andrews, D. S. Mason and M. L. Silk (eds) *Qualitative Methods in Sport Studies.* Oxford: Berg, 39–64.

Woodside, A. G. and Ronkainen, I. A. (1994) Improving advertising conversion studies. In J. R. B. Ritchie and C. R. Goeldner (eds) *Travel, Tourism and Hospitality Research, Second edn.* New York: John Wiley, 481–7.

Wynne, D. (1986) Living on 'The Heath'. *Leisure Studies*, 5(1), 109–16.

Wynne, D. (1990) Leisure, lifestyle and the construction of social position. *Leisure Studies*, 9(1), 21–34.

Xun, J. and Reynolds, J. (2010) Applying netnography to market research: the case of the online forum. *Journal of Targeting, Measurement and Analysis for Marketing*, 18(1), 17–31.

Young, C. H., Savola, K. L. and Phelps, E. (1991) *Inventory of Longitudinal Studies in the Social Sciences.* Newbury Park, CA: Sage.

Zuzanek, J. and Veal, A. J. (eds) (1998) Time pressure, stress, leisure participation and well-being. Special issue of *Loisir et Société/Society and Leisure*, 21(2).

Reviewing the literature

Introduction – an essential task

The aim of this chapter is to explain the importance, for any research project, of reviewing previous research and being aware of existing writing – the literature – on a topic. In addition, the chapter indicates general sources of information on sport studies literature, sets out the mechanics of compiling bibliographies and recording bibliographical references and considers the *process* of reviewing the literature for research purposes.

Reviewing existing research or writing on a topic is a vital step in the research process. The field of sport studies comprises relatively new areas of academic enquiry which are wide-ranging and multidisciplinary in nature. Research is not so plentiful in the field that we can afford to ignore research which has already been completed by others. As discussed briefly in Chapters 3 and 5, the literature can serve a number of functions, as indicated in Figure 6.1.

The aim of research of an academic nature is to add to the body of human knowledge. In most societies that body of knowledge is generally in written form – the literature. To presume to add to the body of knowledge it is necessary to be familiar with what knowledge exists and to indicate precisely how the proposed or completed research relates to it. In research which is of a consultancy or policy nature, where the *primary* aim is not to add to knowledge but to use research to assist directly in the solution of policy, planning or management problems, a familiarity with existing knowledge in the area is still vital. Much time and valuable resources can be wasted in 'reinventing the wheel' to devise suitable methodologies to conduct a project, or in conducting projects

1. The entire basis of the research
2. Source of ideas on topics for research
3. Source of information on research already done by others
4. Source of methodological or theoretical ideas
5. Source of confirmation or comparison between your research and that of others
6. Source of information that is an integral or supportive part of the research – for example statistical data on the study area population

Figure 6.1 The roles of the literature in research

with inadequate methodologies, when reference to existing work could provide information on tried and tested approaches.

The fifth role listed in Figure 6.1 refers to confirmatory or comparative engagement with the literature, which is particularly applicable in the case of the grounded theory approach to research. In this approach, the practice can be to conduct fieldwork and a certain amount of data analysis or interpretation before conducting any substantial literature review **(as noted in Chapter 3)**. In such a situation, the researcher discovers whether the literature confirms or contradicts the research conducted so far or compares and contrasts the research conducted, and the conclusion drawn, with the literature, in an iterative manner. This process can, however, arise in any sort of research. Even when a research project is initiated with a substantial initial literature review, unexpected findings, or simply the detail of the findings, may give rise to further examination of the literature.

Identifying relevant literature is often a demanding task. It involves a careful search for information on relevant published and, if necessary, unpublished work; obtaining copies of relevant items and reading them; making a list of useful items to form a *bibliography*; and assessing and summarising aspects which are salient for the research proposal or the research report in hand.

The value of bibliographies

This chapter focuses on reviewing the literature in relation to planned research projects, but the development of a bibliography can be a useful end in itself. It might be thought that modern electronic search methods have made the compilation and publication of bibliographies on specific topics obsolete, but this is not the case. While electronic databases are continually developing, they are still incomplete, especially with regard to:

● older published material;

● 'ephemeral' material, such as conference papers and reports and working papers not published by mainstream publishers (grey literature);

- chapters from edited collections of papers;

- relevant content which is not mentioned in abstracts or keywords.

More importantly, electronic databases do not provide an *evaluation* of material: they do not always distinguish between a substantial research paper and a lightweight commentary with no original content. Further, not all databases are full-text, so electronic systems will only be able to identify items on the basis of their titles or, in some cases, key words and abstracts. A database may not indicate, for example, whether a report on 'sport' includes data on a specific activity, such as golf, or how broadly 'sport' is defined. A great deal of useful work can therefore still be done in compiling bibliographies on specific topics, thus helping to consolidate the 'state of the art' and saving other researchers a great deal of time and trouble in searching for material.

Examples of published bibliographies in the sport area are listed in the Resources section at the end of the chapter and considerable scope exists for the development of similar bibliographies on other topics.

A bibliography can be just a list of references, or it can be extended by the inclusion of keywords and abstracts or by some form of classification, for example by methodology. Further analysis and commentary on content takes us into the realm of the *literature review*, the *systematic review* and *meta-analysis*, which are discussed separately below.

Searching: sources of information

Where can the researcher look for information on existing published research on a topic? In this section a number of sources are examined, as listed in Figure 6.2.

Library catalogues

Modern libraries have computerised catalogues which are accessible via terminals within the library and also from remote locations via the Internet. These online catalogues include information on:

- Library catalogues
- Specialist indexes and databases
- Searching the Internet
- Google Scholar
- Published bibliographies
- General sport studies books
- Reference lists
- Beyond sport

Figure 6.2 **Sources of information**

- the library's own physical holdings;

- online materials, including online versions of journals, e-books and bibliographical databases and statistical database sites such national governmental statistical offices;

- in some cases, access to other university and public library catalogues.

Many of the online materials are, like lending rights, available only to registered library members, such as students or academic staff.

Searches can be made on the basis of the titles of publications or using key words assigned to them by the library. This can be very helpful as a starting point in establishing a bibliography. But it is *only* a starting point, particularly for the researcher with a specialist interest.

If search words such as *sport* or *exercise* are used, the typical computerised catalogue will produce an enormous number of references, running to thousands, and far too many to be manageable. But if more specialised terms, such as *female golfers* or *motor sport fans*, are entered, the catalogue will produce few references, sometimes none at all. Whether a large or small number of references are produced, a proportion will be of a 'popular' nature, concerned with, for example, how to play golf or biographies of golfers, although some databases will distinguish between refereed academic journals and other sources. 'Popular' material may be of interest to some researchers, but will be of little use if the researcher is interested in such aspects as levels of participation in golf, or the socio-economic characteristics of golfers.

A library catalogue cannot indicate, for instance, whether a general report on *sport* includes any reference to a specific sport activity. And of course the catalogue will not necessarily identify publications which, while they deal with one topic, provide a suitable methodology for studying other topics. Such material can only be identified by actually reading – or at least perusing – original texts.

Catalogues of a library's own physical holdings do not contain references to individual articles in journals, individual chapters in books which are collections of readings, or individual papers in collections of conference papers. But integrated within library online catalogues is access to Internet sources provided by specialist organisations, such as EBSCO, Informaworld and Ingenta, and online services provided by journal publishers.

Specialist indexes and databases

Specialist indexes and databases are online resources generally accessed via subscribing libraries. Examples in the sport area are as follows:

- SPORTDiscus is the most comprehensive reference and full-text source for some 500 sport and sport medicine journals.

- The ISI Web of Knowledge (formerly Social Sciences Citation Index) is a comprehensive listing of papers from thousands of social science journals, cross-referenced by author and subject. In addition, items of literature referred to by authors in papers are themselves listed and cross-referenced, so that further writings of any cited author can be followed up. The index includes references to a considerable amount of sport material.

The advantage of using this type of database is that they ensure a level of reliability by dealing mainly with peer-reviewed material as discussed later in this chapter.

Searching on the Internet

Direct searching on the Internet using a search engine such as Google is second nature to computer users. Such searches are clearly effective when searching for organisational websites, but are a rather blunt tool for searching for published material compared with the specialist sources discussed above. Extreme caution should be exercised in using Internet sources. Thus, for example, while *Wikipedia* can be a useful source, its anonymous nature and frequent lack of source references are such that it should only be used as a route to other, more fully authenticated sources. Some key specialist websites are listed in the Resources section.

Google Scholar

The Google Scholar website stores bibliographical information related to authors. It does not contain a complete bibliography for the individuals listed, but just those items which have been referenced – or 'cited' – by other authors. It therefore has a similar structure to the ISI Web of Knowledge mentioned above. For example, entering the name of the well-known sport author Jennifer Hargreaves produces a long list of her publications, arranged in order of number of citations. The first is her book *Sporting Females* (1994), which, in September 2013, had received 1019 citations. Clicking on the book title provides details of the book and clicking on the citation number brings up a list of the 1019 publications in which the book has been cited. This is an effective way of identifying other publications on the topic of women and sport. The database can also be searched using key words.

Published bibliographies

Reference has already been made to the value of bibliographies on particular topics. Libraries usually have a separate section for bibliographies and it may be worth browsing in that section, especially when the topic of interest is interdisciplinary. While many bibliographies have been published in hard-copy form over the years (see Resources section for examples), the trend recently has been to publish these resources online.

General sport publications

The researcher should be aware of publications which contain information on specific activities or aspects of sport. For example, Chapter 7 discusses national sport participation surveys which contain information on as many as a hundred sport activities and a number of background items such as age and income. They are therefore a source of basic statistical information on many topics of interest.

General introductory books on sport may have something to say on the topic of interest or may provide leads to other sources of information via the index and bibliography. In addition, specialist encyclopaedias typically include bibliographic references. Some examples are:

- *Encyclopedia of International Sports Studies* (Bartlett, Gratton and Rolf, 2006)

- *Encyclopedia of Exercise, Sport and Health* (Brukner, Khan and Kron, 2003)

- *Encyclopedia of the Modern Olympic Movement* (Findling and Pelle, 2004)

- *Encyclopedia of Women and Sports* (Sherrow, 1996)

- *Encyclopedia of World Sport: From Ancient Times to the Present* (Levinson and Christensen, 1996).

Searching through such texts, using the contents pages or the index, can be a somewhat 'hit and miss' process, but can often be rewarded with leads which could not be gained in any other way. Even scanning through the contents pages of key journals may produce relevant material which would not be identified by conventional searches.

Reference lists

Most importantly, the lists of references in the books and articles identified in initial searches will often lead to useful material. Researchers interested in a particular topic should be constantly on the alert for sources of material on that topic in anything they are reading. Sometimes key items are encountered when they are least expected. The researcher should become a 'sniffer dog' obsessed with 'sniffing out' anything of relevance to the topic of interest. In a real-world research situation this process of identifying as much literature as possible can take months or even years. While a major effort should be made to identify material at the beginning of any research process, it will also be an ongoing exercise, throughout the course of the project.

Beyond sport

Lateral thinking is also an aid to the literature search task. The most useful information is not always found in the most obvious places. Sport studies is an interdisciplinary area of study, not a discipline in its own right – it does not have a set of research methods and theories uniquely its own. Much is to be gained from looking outside the immediate area of sport studies. For example, if the research involves measurement of *attitudes* then certain *psychological* literature will be of interest; if the research involves the study of sport *markets* then general *marketing* journals may be useful sources and if the research involves the sporting activities of *older people* then *gerontology* journals should be consulted.

Unpublished research

Where possible, attempts should be made to explore not just published research – the *literature* – but also unpublished and ongoing research. This process is very much hit and miss. Knowing what research is ongoing or knowing of completed but unpublished research usually depends on having access to informal networks, although some organisations produce registers of ongoing research projects, typically on their websites. Once a topic of interest has been identified, it is often clear, from the literature, where the major centres for such research are located and to discover, from direct approaches or from websites, annual reports or newsletters, what research is currently being conducted at those centres. This process can be particularly important if the topic is a 'fashionable' one. However, in such cases the communication networks are usually very active, which eases the process. In this respect, papers from conferences and seminars are usually better sources of information on current research than books and journals, since the latter have long gestation periods – the research reported in them is generally based on work carried out two or more years prior to publication.

Obtaining copies of material

If material is not available via a particular library, in hard copy or online, it can often be obtained through the *inter-library loan* service. This is a system through which loans of books and reports can be made between one library and another. In the case of older journal articles not available online, the service usually involves the provision of a digital copy. In theory, any item published in a particular country should be available through this system since it is connected with national copyright libraries – such as the British Lending Library in Boston Spa or the National Library in Australia – where copies of all published items must be lodged by law. Practices vary from library to library; in academic libraries the service is often available to postgraduate students but undergraduate students may only access it through a member of the academic staff.

For researchers working in metropolitan areas the other obvious source of material is specialist libraries, particularly of government agencies. For example, in London, the Sport England library is a major resource for sport researchers. In metropolitan areas and some other regions there is also often a cooperative arrangement between municipal reference libraries such that particular libraries adopt particular specialist areas – so it can be useful to discover which municipal library service specialises in sport.

Compiling and maintaining a bibliography

What should be done with the material once it has been identified? First, a record should be made of everything which appears to be of relevance. The researcher is strongly advised to start a file of every item of literature used. This can be of use not only for the current research project but also for future reference – a personal bibliography can be built up over the years. Such record keeping can be done using cards, but is best done on a computer, using a word-processor or a database program, which can also store key words. This has the attraction that when there is a need to compile a bibliography on another topic in future, a start can be made from your personal bibliography by getting the computer to copy designated items into a new file. In this way the researcher only ever needs to type out a reference once!

Bibliographic computer packages, such as *Endnote*, *Mandeley*, *RefWorks*, *Zotero* and *Pro-Cite*, store reference material in a standard format, but will automatically compile bibliographies in appropriate formats to meet the requirements of different report styles and the specifications of different academic journals.

It takes only seconds to record *full details* of a reference when it is first identified. If this practice is adopted, hours of time and effort can be saved in not having to chase up details of references at a later date. Not only should the details be recorded accurately, as set out below, but a note should be made on the database about the availability of the material – for example the library catalogue reference, or the fact that the item is *not* in the library, or that a photocopy or digital copy has been taken. Needless to say, storage of downloaded material on the researcher's computer should be organised in a suitable way, and backed up. Some universities provided free online to such packages to students and online bibliographical databases allow references to be imported directly into these package systems (Rohmann, 1999).

Reviewing the literature

Reviewing the literature on a topic can be one of the most rewarding – and one of the most frustrating – of research tasks. It is a task where a range of skills

- Inclusive bibliography
- Inclusive/evaluative/systematic reviews/meta-analyses
- Exploratory
- Instrumental
- Content analysis/hermeneutics

Figure 6.3 Types of literature review

and qualities needs to be employed – including patience, persistence, insight and lateral thinking.

Types of literature review

The review of the literature can play a number of roles in a research project, as outlined above, and this leads to a number of approaches to conducting a review, as listed in Figure 6.3.

Inclusive bibliography

The *inclusive* approach to reviewing the literature seeks to identify everything that has been written on a particular topic. The compilation of such a bibliography may be a significant achievement in itself, independent of any research project with which it may be connected. It becomes a resource to be drawn on in the future by others. Such a bibliography does not amount to a 'review' of the literature if there is no accompanying commentary, although classification of entries into categories (e.g. books, articles, government reports), time-periods, methodologies or sub-topics can be seen as the beginning of such a process. In some cases bibliographies merely list the reference details; in other cases they include abstracts of the contents – in which case they are referred to as *annotated* bibliographies. A number of examples of comprehensive bibliographies are listed in the Resources section.

Inclusive/evaluative review/systematic reviews/meta-analyses

The *inclusive/evaluative* approach or *systematic review* takes the inclusive approach a stage further by providing a commentary on the literature in terms of its coverage and its contribution to knowledge and understanding of the topic. When this type of exercise is undertaken by a panel of researchers appointed by a governmental or other organisation, it may be referred to as a 'consensus study'. The most well-known study of this type in recent years has been the series of reports by the United Nations Intergovernmental Panel on Climate Change which evaluated the results of thousands of scientific publications to draw conclusions regarding climate change and its causes (UNIPCC, 2013).

An even more formalised quantitative approach to analysing the literature is known as *meta-analysis or the systematic review* and involves a systematic, quantitative appraisal of the findings of a number of research projects focused on the same topic. The technique is suitable for the sort of research where findings are directly comparable from one study to another – for example when the key research findings are expressed in terms of correlation or regression coefficients **(see Chapter 17)**. In this approach the reported findings of the research themselves become the subject of research and the number of reported projects can become so large that it is necessary to *sample* from them in the same way that individuals are sampled for empirical research. The meta-analysis approach is discussed in more detail below.

Exploratory review

The *exploratory* approach is more focused and seeks to discover existing research which might throw light on a specific research question or issue. This is very much the classic literature review which is the norm for academic research and best fits the model of the research process **outlined in Chapter 3**. Comprehensiveness is not as important as the focus on the particular question or issue. The skill in conducting such a review lies in keeping the question or issue in sight, while 'interrogating' the literature for ideas and insights which may help shape the research. The reviewer needs to be open to useful new ideas, but must not be sidetracked into areas which stray too far from the question or issue of interest.

Instrumental review

Here the focus of the research is a management issue and the literature is used as a source of suitable ideas on how the research might be tackled. The criterion for selection of literature is not to present a picture of the state of knowledge on the topic, but merely to identify a useful methodology for the project in hand.

Content analysis and hermeneutics

Content analysis and hermeneutics are techniques which involve detailed analysis of the contents of a certain body of literature or other documentary source as *texts*. The texts might be, for example, novels, media coverage of a topic, politicians' speeches or the contents of advertising. Content analysis tends to be quantitative, involving, for example, counting the number of occurrences of certain phrases. Hermeneutics tends to be qualitative in nature, the term being borrowed from the traditional approach to analysis and interpretation of religious texts. The essence of this approach is discussed in Chapter 9, in relation to the analysis of in-depth interview transcripts.

Reading critically and creatively

Reviewing the literature for *research* purposes involves reading the literature in a certain way. It involves being concerned as much with the methodological aspects of the research (which are not always well reported) as the substantive content. That is, it involves being concerned with *how* the conclusions are arrived at as well as with the conclusions themselves. It involves being critical – questioning rather than accepting what is being read. The task is as much to ascertain what is *not* known, as it is to determine what *is* known. This is different from reading for other purposes, such as some essay-writing, when a particular substantive critical issue may be being explored, but the research basis or overall scope of the literature being discussed may not be an issue.

As material is being read, a number of questions might be asked, as set out in Figure 6.4. The questions relate both to individual items and to the body of literature as a whole.

It can be helpful to be conscious of the appropriate way in which the contents of an item of literature should be reported. A number of styles of reporting are used, including:

- Smith believes… thinks… is of the opinion…

- Smith argues…

- Smith establishes…

- Smith observes…

- Smith speculates…

- Smith puts forward the possibility that…

- Smith concludes…

---

a. *Individual items*
   - What is the (empirical) basis of this research?
   - How does the research relate to other research writings on the topic?
   - What theoretical framework is being used?
   - What geographical area does the research refer to?
   - What social group(s) does the research refer to?
   - When was the research carried out and is it likely still to be empirically valid?
b. *In relation to the literature as a whole*
   - What is the *range* of research that has been conducted?
   - What *methods* have generally been used and what methods have been neglected?
   - What, in summary, does the existing research tell us?
   - What, in summary, does the existing research *not* tell us?
   - What contradictions are there in the literature – either recognised or unrecognised by the authors concerned?
   - What are the *deficiencies* in the existing research, in substantive or methodological terms?

Figure 6.4 Questions to ask when reviewing the literature

An author's opinion or beliefs may be important if the author is someone who deals in opinions and beliefs, such as a politician or cleric, but we generally expect more than just statements of belief from academic literature. An academic may be influenced by particular ideological or religious beliefs – for example, some writers are personally committed to the philosophical idea of 'Olympism' associated with the Olympic Games (e.g. Powell, 1994), while others are firmly opposed to it (e.g. Bale and Christensen, 2004). A review of the literature should convey accurately the basis of the material presented, whether it be opinion, the result of argument or presentation of empirical evidence, informal observation or speculation. The type of literature being summarised is therefore important: newspaper and popular and professional magazine articles are not subject to the same checks and balances as academic journal articles; and reports emanating from sport organisations or from politically motivated organisations cannot always be relied on to tell 'the truth, the whole truth and nothing but the truth'. Of course, such material may appear in a literature review, but its status and the way it is reported and interpreted should be treated with caution and subtlety.

Care should be taken when referring to textbooks, such as this one, which may contain some original contributions from the author, but will mostly contain summaries of the state of knowledge in a field, with some material attributed to specific sources and some not. Generally, in a research report, particularly a thesis, original scholarly sources rather than textbooks should be referred to where possible.

As regards the substantive content of the literature, a major challenge for a reviewer is to find a framework to classify and analyse it. In the case of an inclusive review, literature might be classified chronologically, by geographical origin or by discipline. For other types of review, themes or issues are likely to be more important. Reviewing the literature in this way can be similar to the development of a conceptual framework for a research project **(see Chapter 3)**. Some sort of diagrammatic, concept map, approach, as indicated in Figure 6.5, may be helpful. Such a diagram might be devised before starting a review, or may be developed, inductively, as the review progresses.

Summarising

A review of the literature should draw *conclusions* and *implications for the proposed research programme.* It is advisable to complete a review by presenting a *summary* which addresses the second set of questions in Figure 6.4. This summary should lead logically to the research project in hand. It should make clear to the reader just how the proposed research relates to the existing body of literature – whether it is seeking to:

● add to the body of knowledge in a unique way;

● fill a gap in knowledge;

● update existing knowledge;

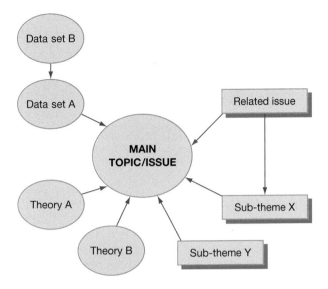

Figure 6.5 **Making sense of the literature**

- correct or contradict some aspect of existing knowledge; or
- use ideas from the literature as a source of ideas or comparison.

When a large amount of literature with similar format is being reviewed, it may be helpful to summarise it in a tabular quasi-meta-analytical form, using headings such as: geographical area covered, sample size, independent variables used, year of survey.

Meta-analysis/interpretation/evaluation/review

Meta-analysis and related approaches such as systematic reviews, treat the literature review process as a project in its own right, with research publications being treated rather like observations in an empirical study. The alternative formats for this type of project are as follows:

- meta-analysis – research projects under review have common format with quantitative outcomes, which are aggregated;
- meta-interpretation – meta-analysis for qualitative research;
- meta-evaluation – focus of the review is on methodology used in projects;
- meta-review – a review of other reviews of varying types.

In the case of meta-analysis, precise conclusions are typically drawn about the field of research on the topic being studied, so it is considered necessary to detail the steps taken to identify the literature included in the evaluation, in the same way that the process of selecting a sample of human subjects for a study would be described. An example is shown in Case study 6.1 and references to further examples are listed in the Resources section.

Case study 6.1	Example of a meta-analysis methodology
Study	**Meta-analysis of the effectiveness of interventions (exercise programmes) to promote physical activity, related to context (alone/at home or group/organised environment).**
Authors	Burke *et al*.
Date	2006
Databases searched	PsycINFO, PsycARTICLES, MEDLINE-OVID, SPORTDiscus
Keywords used	Physical activity interventions; exercise; aerobic; adherence; attendance; home-based exercise; exercise class; group exercise
Additional manual search	Following up references in existing review studies (five sources identified) and searching 13 identified journals
Initial number of studies identified	148
Criteria for inclusion	1. Study must compare two or more physical activity contexts 2. Must include a statistical measure of the effectiveness of context in promoting physical activity.
Net number of studies included	44
Combined number of study subjects	4578
Total population of effect sizes	1046
Effect sizes included	214
Exclusion criteria	Multiple endpoint measures, e.g. strength, balance, gait and flexibility in supervised and unsupervised programmes
Dependent variables identified (i.e. outcomes of participation in a programme)	102 variables in 5 categories: 1. adherence to programme; 2. social interaction; 3. quality of life; 4. physiological effectiveness; 5. functional effectiveness.
Independent variables (type of programme)	1. true group (group with organised interaction) 2. collective (group, but no organised interaction) 3. home-based with contact 4. home-based without contact.
Descriptive statistics	Context; Age of participants; Gender; Clinical referral status; Activity level; Intervention level; Selection of participants
Also included: Calculation of effect sizes; Effect sizes; standard deviations and confidence intervals; Discussion; Limitations	

A version of meta-analysis for qualitative research has been put forward, referred to as *meta-interpretation*. This process is 'iterative rather than pre-determined' and, rather than being based on statistical findings, it is based on the interpretations of data in the original studies (Weed, 2005).

Meta-evaluation may refer to a meta-analysis of evaluation studies, such as those which might evaluate policy interventions, or it may refer to a meta-analysis which concentrates on the methods and rigour of a range of studies rather than their substantive findings (Weed, 2008).

Referencing the literature

The purpose of referencing

What is the purpose of referencing? First, referencing is evidence of the writer's scholarship: it indicates that the particular research report is related to the existing body of knowledge. This is not only of importance to teachers marking student assignments or theses – it is part and parcel of the development of knowledge. Second, references enable the reader of the research report to check sources – either to verify the writer's interpretation of previous research or to follow up areas of interest.

Recording references

A number of standard or conventional formats exist for recording references to the literature. The conventions have been established by leading academic organisations and publishers. Guides are produced by organisations such as the American Psychological Association (2001) and Oxford University Press (2012), to which the reader is referred for more detail. The formats presented here do not conform to any one standard approach but offer a style which, if followed consistently, would be acceptable in many academic contexts. In what follows, the word *text* refers to the main body of the research report or article. It should be noted that, if bibliographic management systems such as *Endnote* and *Pro-Cite*, as discussed above, are used, references can be formatted in a variety of styles and automatically changed to suit publication requirements.

The general format recommended for recording references is as shown in Figure 6.6.

In some systems the date is put at the end, but when using the *author/date* or *Harvard* system, as discussed below, the date should follow the author name as indicated.

Note that the part of the reference which is in *italics* is the title which would be found in a library catalogue, that is, the name of the periodical, not the title of the article, and the title of the book, not the title of a chapter.

- *A book or report:*
  Author(s), Initials (Year) *Title of Book or Report in Italics.* Place of publication: Publisher.
- *An article from a periodical (journal/magazine/newspaper):*
  Author(s), Initials (Year) Title of article (lower case). *Title of Periodical in Italics,* Volume number (Issue number), Page numbers.

Figure 6.6   Standard/generic reference formats

Note that the *publisher* of a book is not the same as the *printer* of the book. In the case of this book, the *publisher* is Routledge, but the *printer* is TJ International. References do not need to refer to the printer. And note that it is *not* necessary to refer to the publisher in the case of periodicals.

Some examples of reference formats are set out in Figure 6.7 to illustrate the principles.

Particular note should be made that, in the book chapter example, the main reference is to the chapter author(s), not to the book editor(s).

Internet references are becoming increasingly common. One of the problems with this medium is that some sources disappear or their website address (URL) changes over time, so that it is difficult for the reader to follow them up. For individual publications it is often advisable to give the organisation's 'list of publications' address rather than the often long and complex address of the individual publication, which can be subject to change. The general principle to be followed is that an Internet reference should include all the details which would normally apply to hard-copy items, *plus* the website URL *and* the date accessed. The geographical place of publication is not always clear from the website, but can generally be found with a little effort. If accessing a journal article via the Internet, it is not necessary to give the website address unless the journal is known to be published only electronically. Published style guides are available for referencing in relation to this medium, for example *The Columbia Guide to Online Style* (Walker and Taylor, 1998).

Some guidelines suggest that newspaper articles should be referenced with the title of the article rather than, as here, with the author or the name of the newspaper. The important point to note is that, once a style is adopted, it should be consistent throughout the report.

Referencing and referencing systems

There are two commonly used referencing systems: the *author/date system,* sometimes referred to as the *Harvard system,* and the *footnote* or *endnote system.* These two systems are discussed in turn below.

1. A book	Toohey, K., and Veal, A. J. (2006) *The Olympic Games: A Social Science Perspective.* Wallingford, UK: CABI.
2. An edited book	Nicholson, M., and Hoye, R. (eds) (2011) *Sport and Social Capital.* Oxford: Butterworth-Heinemann.
3. A chapter from an edited book	Lock, D., Taylor, T., and Darcy, S. (2011) Soccer and social capital in Australia: social networks in transition. In M. Nicholson and R. Hoye (eds), *Sport and Social Capital.* Oxford: Butterworth-Heinemann, 317–38.
4. A published conference report	De Moragas, M., Kennett, C., and Puig, N. (eds) (2003) *The Legacy of the Olympic Games, 1984–2000: International Symposium, Lausanne, November, 2002.* Lausanne: International Olympic Committee.
5. A published conference paper	Cashman, R. (2003) What is 'Olympic legacy'? In M. de Moragas, C. Kennett and N. Puig (eds), *The Legacy of the Olympic Games, 1984–2000: International Symposium, Lausanne, November 2002.* Lausanne: International Olympic Committee, 31–42.
6. A government agency report, authored and published by the same agency	Sport England (1999) *Best Value Through Sport: Case Studie*s. London: Sport England.
7. A journal article	Veal, A. J., Toohey, K., and Frawley, S. (2012) The sport participation legacy of the Sydney 2000 Olympic Games and other international sporting events hosted in Australia. *Journal of Policy Research in Tourism, Leisure and Events*, 4(2), 155–84.
8. A newspaper article with named author (accessed online)	Rourke A. (2012) Paralympic Games: London needs to learn from Beijing and Sydney. *The Guardian*, 21 May. Retrieved, Oct. 2012, from <www.guardian.co.uk/sport/2012/may/21/paralympic-games-london-beijing-sydney>.
9. A newspaper item without a named author (hard copy access)	*Sun Herald* (1999) Rail-Banned Paralympian issues Games warning. November 11, p. 28.
10. An Internet source	Veal, A. J. (2012) *The Olympic Games: A Bibliography.* Sydney: Business School, University of Technology, Sydney, On-line Bibliography 5. Available at: <www.business.uts.edu.au/olympic/downloads/olympic_bib_update2.pdf>.

Figure 6.7 **Examples of reference formats**

The author/date or Harvard system

Basic features

In the author/date, or Harvard, system, references to an item of literature are made in the text using the author's name and the year of the publication, as in this book. At the end of the paper or report, references are listed in alphabetical order. In books, the list of references may be at the end of each chapter, as in this book, or at the end of the whole book. A sentence in a report using this system might look something like this:

> Researchers have examined the impact of the hosting of major sporting events on local communities from a number of perspectives, including, for example, the political perspective of Lenskyj (2000), the economic perspective of Preuss (2005) and the physical infrastructure perspective of Essex and Chalkley (2003).

Note that authors' initials are not used in these references (unless there are two authors with the same surname). A more informal style can be used by including and an author's first, or given, name, which can be appropriate when mentioning an author for the first time, and especially for particularly significant authors.

At the end of the report a list of references is provided, arranged in alphabetical order, as follows.

References

Essex, S. and Chalkley, B. (2003) The infrastructural legacy of the Summer and Winter Olympic Games: a comparative analysis. In M. De Moragas, C. Kennett and N. Puig (eds), *The Legacy of the Olympic Games, 1984–2000.* Lausanne: International Olympic Committee, 94–101.

Lenskyj, H. J. (2000) *Inside the Olympic Industry: Power, Politics and Activism.* Albany, NY: State University of New York Press.

Preuss, H. (2005) The economic impact of visitors at major multi-sport events. *European Sport Management Quarterly*, 5(3), 283–303.

Style variation

The style of presentation can be varied. For example, the above statement could be made drawing less explicit attention to specific authors:

> Researchers have examined the impact of the hosting of major sporting events on local communities from a number of perspectives, including, for example, political, economic and cultural perspectives (Lenskyj, 2000; Preuss, 2005; MacAloon, 2003).

Specifics and quotations

When referring to *specific points* from an item of literature, rather than making a general reference to the whole item, as above, page references should be given to the specific point of interest. This is particularly important when referring to a specific point from a substantial publication like a book. Thus, for example, while we might refer to the overall message of Lenskyj's book as above, if drawing attention to a particular for example:

> Lenskyj (2000: 180–183) is particularly critical of the coverage of the lead-up to the Sydney 2000 Olympic Games by the Sydney media.

Regrettably, however, few publications follow this practice.

When *quoting* directly from a source, page references should also be given:

> Essex and Chalkley (2003: 96) note the 'substantial investment in "non-Olympic" related infrastructure'.

A longer quotation (of about three lines or longer) should be indented in the page and handled like this:

> Essex and Chalkley note:

>> Most Olympic Games since 1984 have involved substantial investment in 'non-Olympic' related infrastructure, such as transport, hotel accommodation, cultural facilities, water and sewage systems and urban landscaping, which assist in the effective operation of the Games and assist in creating a favourable image of the host city. (Essex and Chalkley, 2003: 96)

Advantages and disadvantages

The author/date system is an 'academic' style. Its disadvantage is therefore that referencing is very 'up-front', even obtrusive, in the text. It is not an appropriate style for some practically orientated reports, particularly where the readership is not academic. Large numbers of references using this style tend to clutter the text and make it difficult to read. The system also has the disadvantage that it does not incorporate footnotes (at the foot of the page) or endnotes (at the end of the chapter). However, one view is that footnotes and endnotes are undesirable anyway – that if something is worth saying it is worth saying in the text. If notes and asides are nevertheless considered necessary, it is possible to establish a footnote system for this purpose in addition to using the author/date system for references to the literature only. This of course becomes somewhat complex. If a number of footnotes/endnotes are considered necessary, it is probably best to use the footnote/endnote style for everything, as discussed below.

The advantages of the author/date system are that it saves the effort of keeping track of footnote or endnote numbers; it indicates the date of publication to the reader; the details of any one item of literature have to be written out only once; and it results in a tidy, alphabetical list of references at the end of the document or chapter.

Footnote or endnote system

Basic features

The *footnote* style involves the use of numbered references in the text and a list of corresponding numbered references at the foot of the page, at the end of each chapter or at the end of the report or book. The term footnote originates from the time when the notes were invariably printed at the foot of each page – and this can be seen in older books. However, this came to be viewed as too complex to organise and too expensive to set up for printing, so it was generally abandoned in favour of providing a list of notes at the end of each chapter or at the end of the book. Consequently *endnotes* are now more common. Ironically, the advent of word-processing has meant that the placing of footnotes at the bottom of the page can now be done automatically by computer. Most word-processing packages offer this feature, automatically making space for the appropriate number of footnotes on each page and keeping track of their numbering and so on. Publishers have, however, generally adhered to the practice of placing the notes all together at the end of the chapter or book.

The actual number reference in the text can be given in brackets (1) or as a superscript:[1]. Using the footnote system, the paragraph given above appears as follows:

> Researchers have examined the impact of the hosting of major sporting events on local communities from a number of perspectives, including, for example, the political perspective of Lenskyj[1], the economic perspective of Preuss[2] and the physical infrastructure perspective of Essex and Chalkley[3].

The list of notes at the end of the report appear in the numerical order in which they appear in the text:

> Notes
> 1. Lenskyj, H. J. (2000) *Inside the Olympic Industry: Power, Politics and Activism.* Albany, NY: State University of New York Press.
> 2. Preuss, H. (2005) The economic impact of visitors at major multi-sport events. *European Sport Management Quarterly*, 5(3), 283–303.
> 3. Essex, S. and Chalkley, B. (2003) The infrastructural legacy of the Summer and Winter Olympic Games: a comparative analysis. In M. De Moragas, C. Kennett and N. Puig (eds), *The Legacy of the Olympic Games, 1984–2000.* Lausanne: International Olympic Committee, 94–101.

It can be seen that this format is less obtrusive in the text than the author/date system. In fact it can be made even less obtrusive by using only one footnote, as follows:

> Researchers have examined the impact of the hosting of major sporting events on local communities from a number of perspectives, including, for example, political, economic and cultural perspectives.[1]

At the end of the report the reference list then appears as follows:

Note
1. Lenskyj, H. J. (2000) *Inside the Olympic Industry: Power, Politics and Activism*. Albany, NY: State University of New York Press. Preuss, H. (2005) The economic impact of visitors at major multi-sport events. *European Sport Management Quarterly*, 5(3), 283–303. Essex, S. and Chalkley, B. (2003) The infrastructural legacy of the Summer and Winter Olympic Games: a comparative analysis. In M. De Moragas, C. Kennett and N. Puig (eds), *The Legacy of the Olympic Games, 1984–2000*. Lausanne: International Olympic Committee, 94–101.

Multiple references

It should never be necessary to write a reference out in full more than once in a document. Additional references to a work already cited can be made using *op. cit.* or references back to previous footnotes. For example, the above paragraph of text might be followed by:

Lenskyj also examines hidden costs, community resistance and corporate environmental credentials[2].

The footnote would then say:

2. Lenskyj, *op. cit.* (work cited)   OR   2. See footnote 1.

Specifics, quotations

Page references for specific references or quotations are given in the footnote rather than the text. So the Essex and Chalkley quotation given above would look like this:

Essex and Chalkley (2003) note the 'substantial investment in "non-Olympic" related infrastructure'.[1]

The footnote would then say:

1. Essex, S. and Chalkley, B. (2003) The infrastructural legacy of the Summer and Winter Olympic Games: a comparative analysis. In M. De Moragas, C. Kennett & N. Puig (eds), *The Legacy of the Olympic Games, 1984-2000*. Lausanne: International Olympic Committee, p. 96.

Further quotations from the same work might have footnotes as follows:

2. Essex and Chalkley, *op. cit.* p. 97.

A longer quotation (of about three lines or longer) would be indented in the page and handled like this:

Essex and Chalkley note:

> Most Olympic Games since 1984 have involved substantial investment in 'non-Olympic' related infrastructure, such as transport, hotel accommodation, cultural facilities, water and sewage systems and urban landscaping, which assist in the effective operation of the Games and assist in creating a favourable image of the host city.[1]

The footnote would then say:

> 1. Essex, S. and Chalkley, B. (2003) The infrastructural legacy of the Summer and Winter Olympic Games: a comparative analysis. In M. De Moragas, C. Kennett and N. Puig (eds), *The Legacy of the Olympic Games, 1984–2000.* Lausanne: International Olympic Committee, p. 96.

Further quotations from the same work might have footnotes as follows:

> 2. Essex and Chalkley, *op. cit.* p. 97.

Advantages and disadvantages of the footnote/endnote system

One of the advantages of the footnote system is that it is less obtrusive than the author/date system and it can accommodate authors' notes in addition to references to the literature, as discussed above. A disadvantage of the system is that it does not result in a tidy, alphabetical list of references. This diminishes the convenience of the report as a source of literature references for the reader. Some writers therefore resort to producing a bibliography in addition to the list of footnotes, resulting in extra work and space. Keeping track of footnotes or endnotes and their numbering in a long report is much less of a disadvantage than it used to be, since this can now be taken care of by the computer.

Comparing two systems

The features, advantages and disadvantages of the two systems, author/date and footnote/endnote, are summarised in Figure 6.8.

One way of combining the advantages of both systems is for the list of notes in a footnote/endnote system to consist of author/date references and then to provide an alphabetical list of references at the end of the report. So the list of footnotes for the above paragraph would then appear as follows:

Notes
1. Lenskyj, 2000.
2. Preuss, 2005.
3. Essex and Chalkley, 2003.

An alphabetical bibliography would then follow which would be the same as for the author/date system. This approach is particularly useful when making several references to the same document.

Feature	Harvard/Author-date	Footnote/Endnote
Reference in text	Author (date)	Number, e.g.:[1]
Reference format	Author (date) *Title.* Publishing details.	1. Author (date) *Title.* Publishing details (or date may be at end)
Reference list format	Alphabetical list at end of chapter or report	Numbered list at: <ul><li>foot of pages, or</li><li>end of chapters, or</li><li>end of report</li></ul>
Advantages	<ul><li>alphabetical bibliography</li><li>easy to use</li><li>date of publication conveyed in text</li></ul>	<ul><li>unobtrusive in text</li><li>can add other notes/comments</li></ul>
Disadvantages	<ul><li>obtrusive in text</li><li>can't include notes</li></ul>	<ul><li>can be difficult to use without computer</li><li>no alphabetical bibliography</li></ul>

Figure 6.8 Reference systems: features, advantages, disadvantages

Referencing issues

Second-hand references

Occasionally you make a reference to an item which you yourself have not read directly, but which is referred to in another document which you have read. This can be called a *second-hand* reference. It is misleading, somewhat unethical, and dangerous to give a full reference to the original if you have not read it directly yourself. The reference should be given to the second-hand source, *not* to the original. For example:

> Kerlinger characterises research as 'systematic, controlled, empirical, and critical investigation of hypothetical propositions about the presumed relations among natural phenomena' (quoted in Iso-Ahola, 1980: 48).

In this instance the writer has not read Kerlinger in the original but is relying on Iso-Ahola's quotation from Kerlinger. The Kerlinger source is not listed in the references; only the Iso-Ahola reference is listed. It is not only ethical to treat the second-hand reference this way; it is also safe, since any inaccuracy in the quotation then rests with the second-hand source.

In academic research reports – journal articles and theses – second-hand references should be avoided and every effort made to access and refer to the original source.

Excessive referencing

A certain amount of judgement must be used when a large number of references are being made to a single source. It becomes very tiresome when repeated reference is made to the same source on every other line of a report! One way to avoid this is to be very 'up-front' about the fact that a particular section of your literature review is based on a single source. For example, if you are summarising Preuss's work on the economics of the Olympic Games, rather than have large numbers of formal references to Preuss cluttering up the text, it may be preferable to a separate section of the report and announce it as follows:

> The Work of Preuss
> This section of the review summarises Preuss's (2005) work on the economics of the Olympic Games.

Subsequently, formal references need only be given when using specific quotations.

Latin abbreviations

A number of Latin abbreviations are used in referencing.

et al. If there are more than two authors of a work, the first author's name and *et al.* may be used in text references, but all authors should be listed in the bibliography: *et al.* stands for the Latin *et alia*, meaning 'and the others', and is generally presented in italics, although some publishers are now abandoning this practice.

op. cit. stands for the Latin *opere citato*, meaning 'in the work cited'.

ibid. In the footnote system, if reference is made to the same work in consecutive footnotes, the abbreviation *ibid.* is sometimes used, short for *ibidem*, meaning 'the same'.

Summary

This chapter provides an overview of the process of reviewing the literature, as a research tool in its own right and as an essential element of any research project. It is noted that a literature review can have a number of purposes and can take a number of forms, ranging from being the entire basis of a research project to being the source of ideas and methods for conducting a research project. The mechanics of searching for relevant literature is examined, including library catalogues, published bibliographies and indexes and electronic sources. The process of reviewing the literature is examined, addressing the sorts of questions which should be asked when conducting such a review for research purposes. Finally, the chapter reviews the process of referencing the literature, examining the characteristics and advantages and disadvantages of the author/date or 'Harvard' system and the footnote or endnote system.

Test questions

1. What are the potential uses of the literature review in research?

2. Name three different sources of bibliographical information and their advantages and limitations.

3. What is the difference between conducting a literature review for the purpose of writing an essay compared with providing the context for a research project?

4. What are the advantages and disadvantages of the author/date referencing system compared with the footnote/endnote system?

5. What is a 'second-hand' reference?

Exercises

1. Locate a systematic review of literature on a sport topic (e.g. from among those listed in the Resources section below) and summarise the methodology used and the main conclusions drawn.

2. Investigate your institutional library's available online bibliographic referencing packages, or open free online packages, and undertake training to use a selected package. Exercises below can then be undertaken using the package.

3. Compile an *inclusive* bibliography on a topic of your choice, using the Resources section of this chapter.

4. Choose a research topic and:

   a. investigate the literature using a library computerised catalogue and any other electronic database available to you;

   b. explore the literature via literary sources, such as reference lists and indexes in general textbooks, journal contents and lists of references in articles;

   c. compare the nature and extent of the bibliography arising from the two sources.

Resources

Websites

Endnote: http://endnote.com/

Mendeley: www.mendeley.com/

RefWorks: www.refworks.com/

Zotero: www.zotero.org/

Publications

Examples of bibliographies:

- on recreational use of beaches: Veal (1997).

- on the Olympic Games: Veal (2012).

- on leisure, sport and ethnicity: Geary *et al.* (1996).

Systematic reviews:

- systematic review methodology: Littell *et al.* (2008), Smith (2010), Weed (2005); including qualitative research: Thomas *et al.* (2004).

Examples of systematic reviews:

- burnout in sport: Goodger *et al.* (2007);

- consumer expenditure on sport and recreation: Pawlowski and Breuer (2011: 7–10);

- lifestyle as a concept: Veal (1993);

- mass sport participation: empirical studies: Downward and Rasciute (2010: 192–98);

- Paralympic Games: Misener *et al.* (2013)

- policy for international sporting success: De Bosscher *et al.* (2006);

- programmes to boost sport participation: Priest *et al.* (2008);

- sport and physical activity participation, qualitative research: Allender *et al.* (2006);

- sport-participation impact of the Olympic Games: Weed *et al.* (2009)

- sport psychology: Hutchison *et al.* (2011);

- sport tourism: Weed (2008);

- walking as exercise: Owen *et al.* (2004);

- young people and physical activity: Rees *et al.* (2006).

Meta-analysis/interpretation/evaluation:

- meta-analysis: generally: Glass *et al.* (1981), Littell *et al.* (2008); critique: Pawson (2006); sport: Hagger (2006), Hopkins (2004); sport and youth: Marshall *et al.* (2004).

- meta-interpretation: sport tourism: Weed (2005).

- meta-evaluation: sport tourism: Weed (2008).

- meta-review: sport tourism: Owen *et al.* (2004), Weed (2009).

Style manuals:

- American Psychological Association (APA) (2001) and www.apastyle.org.

- Australian: DCITA (2002).

- UK: Oxford University Press (2012).

- Electronic style manual: Walker and Taylor (1998); APA guidelines at: www.apastyle.org/elecref.html.

References

Allender, S., Cowburn, G. and Foster, C. (2006) Understanding participation in sport and physical activity among children and adults: a review of qualitative studies. *Health Education Research*, 21(6), 826–35.

American Psychological Association (APA) (2001) *Publication Manual of the American Psychological Association, Fifth edn.* Washington, DC: APA.

Bale, J., and Christensen, M. K. (eds) (2004) *Post-Olympism? Questioning Sport in the Twenty-first Century*. Oxford: Berg.

Bartlett, R., Gratton, C. and Rolf, C. G. (eds) (2006) *Encyclopedia of International Sports Studies*. London: Routledge.

Brukner, P., Khan, K. and Kron, J. (eds) (2003) *Encyclopedia of Exercise, Sport and Health*. Crows Nest, NSW: Allen & Unwin.

Burke, S. M., Carron, A. V., Eys, M. A., Ntoumas, N. and Estabrooks, P. A. (2006) Group versus individual approach? Meta-analysis of the effectiveness of interventions to promote physical activity. *Sport and Exercise Psychology Review*, 2(1), 13–29.

DCITA (2002) *Style Manual for Authors, Editors and Printers.* Brisbane: John Wiley.

De Bosscher, V., De Knop, P., Van Bottenburg, M. and Shibli, S. (2006) A conceptual framework for analysing sports policy factors leading to international sporting success. *European Sport Management Quarterly*, 6(2), 185–215.

Downward, P. and Rasciute, S. (2010) The relative demands for sports and leisure in England. *European Sport Management Quarterly*, 10(2), 189–214.

Findling, J. E. and Pelle, K. D. (eds) (2004) *Encyclopedia of the Modern Olympic Movement.* Westport, CT: Greenwood Press.

Geary, C., Taylor, T., Toohey, K. and Lynch, R. (1996) *Leisure, Sport and Ethnicity: A Bibliography.* School of Leisure and Tourism Studies, University of Technology, Sydney, On-line Bibliography 6, available at: www.business .uts.edu.au/lst/research/publications/bibliographies/index.html (Accessed March, 2012).

Glass, G. V., McGaw, B. and Smith, M. L. (1981) *Meta-Analysis in Social Research.* Beverly Hills, CA: Sage.

Goodger, K., Gorely, T., Lavallee, D. *et al.* (2007) Burnout in sport: a systematic review. *Sport Psychologist*, 21(2), 127–51.

Hagger, M. S. (2006) Meta-analysis in sport and exercise research: review, recent developments, and recommendations. *European Journal of Sport Science*, 6(2), 103–15.

Hargreaves, J. (1994) *Sporting Females: Critical Issues in the History and Sociology of Women's Sports.* London: Routledge.

Hopkins, W. G. (2004) An introduction to meta-analysis. *Sportscience*, 8(1), 20–4.

Hutchison, A. J., Johnston, L. H. and Breckon, J. D. (2011) Grounded theory-based research within exercise psychology: a critical review. *Qualitative Research in Psychology*, 8(3), 247–72.

Levinson, D. and Christensen, K. (eds) (1996) *Encyclopedia of World Sport: From Ancient Times to the Present.* Santa Barbara, CA: ABCCLIO.

Littell, J. H., Corcoran, J. and Pillai, V. (2008) *Systematic Reviews and Meta-Analysis.* Oxford: Oxford University Press.

Marshall, S. J., Biddle, S. J. H. and Gorely, T. (2004) Relationships between media use, body fatness and physical activity in children and youth: a meta-analysis. *International Journal of Obesity*, 28(6), 1238–46.

Misener, L., Darcy, S., Legg, D. and Gilbert, K. (2013) Beyond Olympic legacy: understanding Paralympic legacy through thematic analysis. *Journal of Sport Management*, 27(4), 197–222.

Owen, N., Humpel, N., Leslie, E., Bauman, A. and Sallis, J. F. (2004) Understanding environmental influences on walking: review and research agenda. *American Journal of Preventive Medicine*, 27(1), 67–76.

Oxford University Press (2012) *New Oxford Style Manual.* Oxford: OUP.

Pawlowski, T. and Breuer, C. (2011) The demand for sports and recreational services: empirical evidence from Germany. *European Sport Management Quarterly*, 11(1), 5–34.

Pawson, R. (2006) Systematic obfuscation: a critical analysis of the meta-analytic approach. Chapter 3 of: *Evidence-based Policy: A Realist Perspective.* London: Sage, 38–72.

Powell, J. T. (1994) *Origins and Aspects of Olympism*. Champaign, IL: Stipes.

Priest, N., Armstrong, R., Doyle, J. and Waters, E. (2008) Interventions implemented through sporting organisations for increasing participation in sport. *Cochrane Database of Systematic Reviews*, 3, no pagination, available at: www.cochrane.org (Accessed May 2013).

Rees, R., Kavanagh, J., Harden, A. and Shepherd, J. (2006) Young people and physical activity: a systematic review matching their views to effective interventions. *Health Education Review*, 21(6), 806–25.

Rohmann, G. (1999) ProCite and EndNote: bibliographic management software. *Office Systems, Research Journal*, 17(1), 51–53.

Sherrow, V. (ed.) (1996) *Encyclopedia of Women and Sports*. Santa Barbara, CA: ABCCLIO.

Smith, M. F. (2010) Systematic review research strategy. Chapter 3 of *Research Methods in Sport*. Exeter, UK: Learning Matters, 44–64.

Thomas, J., Harden, A. and Oakley, A. (2004) Integrating qualitative research with trials in systematic reviews. *British Medical Journal*, 328(7446), 1010–12.

United Nations Intergovernmental Panel on Climate Change (UNIPCC) (2013) *Climate Change 2013: The Physical Science Basis*. Geneva: UNIPCC, available at: www.ipcc.ch (Accessed May 2013).

Veal, A. J. (1993) The concept of lifestyle: a review. *Leisure Studies*, 12(4), 233–52.

Veal, A. J. (1997) *Recreational Use of Beaches: Bibliography*. Business School, University of Technology, Sydney, On-line Bibliography 1, available at: www.business.uts.edu.au/management/research/publications/bibliographies/bibbeaches.pdf (Accessed May 2013).

Veal, A. J. (2012) *The Olympic Games: A Bibliography*. Business School, University of Technology, Sydney, On-line Bibliography 5, available at: www.business.uts.edu.au/olympic/downloads/olympic_bib_update2.pdf (Accessed May 2013).

Walker, J. R. and Taylor, T. (1998) *The Columbia Guide to Online Style*. New York: Columbia University Press.

Weed, M. (2005) Research synthesis in sport management: dealing with 'chaos in the brickyard'. *European Sport Management Quarterly*, 5(1), 77–90.

Weed, M. (2008) Sports tourism research 2000–2004: a systematic review of knowledge and a meta-evaluation of methods. In M. Weed (ed.) *Sport and Tourism: A Reader*. London: Routledge, 90–112.

Weed, M. (2009) Progress in sports tourism research? A meta-review and exploration of futures. *Tourism Management*, 30(5), 615–28.

Weed, M., Coren, E. and Fiore, J. (2009) *A Systematic Review of the Evidence Base for Developing a Physical Activity and Health Legacy from the London 2012 Olympic and Paralympic Games*. Canterbury, Kent: Centre for Sport, Physical Education and Activity Research, Canterbury Christ Church University, available at: www.canterbury.ac.uk/social-applied-sciences/ (Accessed May 2013).

Part

Data Collection

This part is concerned with six forms of data collection and the process of sampling, which is relevant to all empirical methods. The chapters are:

Chapter 7   Secondary data sources;

Chapter 8   Observation;

Chapter 9   Qualitative methods: introduction and data collection;

Chapter 10 Questionnaire surveys: typology, design and coding;

Chapter 11 Experimental methods;

Chapter 12 The case study method; and

Chapter 13 Sampling: quantitative and qualitative.

Specific chapters on data analysis are provided in Part III for secondary data, qualitative methods and questionnaire surveys.

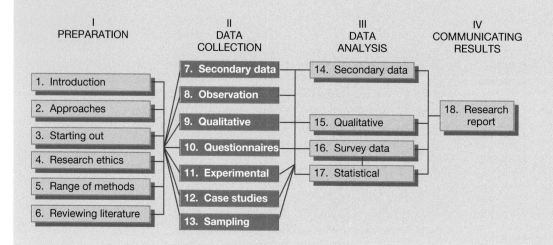

I
PREPARATION

II
DATA
COLLECTION

III
DATA
ANALYSIS

IV
COMMUNICATING
RESULTS

1. Introduction

2. Approaches

3. Starting out

4. Research ethics

5. Range of methods

6. Reviewing literature

7. Secondary data

8. Observation

9. Qualitative

10. Questionnaires

11. Experimental

12. Case studies

13. Sampling

14. Secondary data

15. Qualitative

16. Survey data

17. Statistical

18. Research report

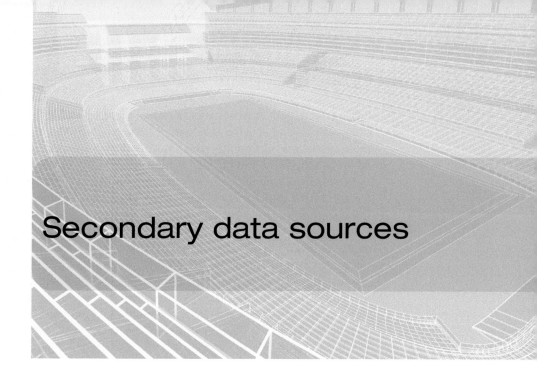

Secondary data sources

Introduction

Before giving specific consideration to secondary data sources, we address the issue of measurement in sport. This relates not only to secondary sources, but to any form of quantitative method, including quantitative forms of observation **(Chapter 8)**, the design of questionnaires **(Chapter 10)**, aspects of experimental methods **(Chapter 11)** and case study research **(Chapter 12)**. Therefore this initial section of the chapter can be seen as an introduction to the quantitative parts of Part II of the book. We consider the issue of measurement of sport in general, then address the topic of counting heads **(as raised in Chapter 5)**.

Measuring sport activity

Measurement in this sector can be considered in two ways: at the individual, spectator and community level, in terms of engagement/participation and social/cultural impact, and at the industry level, in terms of sales/income, economic scale and impact, and employment. These two areas are closely connected, in that it is individuals that make up both the markets/audiences and the industry labour force for sport.

Types of engagement

Engagement with sports varies along a spectrum from the full-time professional at one end, via the amateur and the committed, enthusiastic fan to the most casual and occasional, mediated audience member or consumer at the other, as represented in Figure 7.1.

Professional athletes, both full-time and part-time, are discussed in the industry section of the chapter. There is, however, considerable overlap between the part-time professional category and the active leisure and volunteer participants, with the latter categories often being a route of entry to professional status. It should be noted that the group of categories, amateur, hobbyist and volunteer, are referred to by Robert Stebbins (1992, 2007) as categories of 'serious leisure', a concept which has been subject to considerable research, including sporting examples.

Figure 7.2 presents a sevenfold typology of ways in which sport activity can be measured and the relationships between them.

A. The percentage *participation rate* is the most commonly used measure in sport policy and planning research: it indicates the proportion of the population participating or the proportions of particular social groups participating. This is particularly salient because of the public policy emphasis on equity and access.

B. The *number of participants* is equal to the participation rate multiplied by the population, so if the latter is rising, the number of participants can be rising even as the participation rate is falling.

C. The *volume of activity* is equal to the numbers of participants multiplied by frequency of participation and is one of the measures of greatest interest to sport facility managers because it indicates the number of tickets sold. This introduces the issue of the nature of the 'community' to which the measurements apply, and this is discussed further below.

Type of engagement	Mode of engagement	Examples
1. Professional	Full-time	Full-time professional athlete, official, manager
	Part-time	Part-time professional athlete
2. Active leisure	Amateur	Amateur athlete (organised/competitive/club-based)
	Hobbyist	Casual participant
3. Volunteer	Volunteer	Volunteer/unpaid coach, official, marshal
4. Spectator/audience/ fan/supporter	Committed live	Regular live spectator/supporter club member
	Occasional live	Occasional live spectator
	Mediated	Watching on TV/DVD, listening on radio, online, reading sport print-media

Figure 7.1　Typology of individual engagement with sport

Measure		Definition	Relationships	Example
A	Participation rate	The proportion of a defined population which engages in an activity in a given period of time		6 per cent of the adult population of community X go swimming at least once a week
B	Number of participants	Number of people in a defined community who engage in an activity in a given period of time	(A) × pop'n. or (C) ÷ frequency of visit	20,000 people in community X swim at least once a week
C	Volume of activity (visits)	The number of visits made to a venue, or games played in an activity, by members of a defined community over a specified time-period	(B) × visits/games per time-period	There are 1.2 million visits to swimming pools in community X (1 million by local residents) in a year
D	Time	The amount of time devoted to sport activity by an individual or a community, over a specified period	(C) × time per visit	The average retired person devotes 0.75 hours to sport or physical activity per day
E	Expenditure	Money spent per individual or a defined community on sport or particular sporting goods or services over a specified time-period	(C) × expenditure per visit	Consumer expenditure on sport in Britain is over £20 billion a year
F	Intensity	Rate of energy expenditure during exercise or the maximum rate that a body can transport and use oxygen (VO_2 max)	–	Elite male runners have VO_2 max of more than 80 millilitres per kilogram of bodyweight per minute
G	Employment	Engagement in a sporting activity involving payment	–	It is estimated that 4.5 million people are employed in sport in Europe

Figure 7.2   Measuring sport/physical activity

D. *Time* spent on an activity is particularly relevant in the sport policy context because of the concern over the amount of time people spend taking exercise compared with the amount of time they spend in sedentary activities.

E. *Expenditure* per visit and in total is, of course, the key measure for the private sector, and increasingly in the public sector.

F. *Intensity* refers to the amount of energy expended during exercise, usually measured by such indicators as oxygen uptake (VO_2 max). In social terms it may be reflected in allocation of time (item D) and money (item E), but also in the type of involvement, such as membership of and leadership in organisations, the time-span of the individual's involvement and peer esteem. In leisure studies it is partly captured by the idea of 'serious' leisure (Stebbins, 2007).

G. *Employment*, in the sport sector, in addition to paid employment a great deal of voluntary activity is involved in the running of clubs and even the largest of sporting events, such as the Olympic Games. While many such volunteers may view the involvement as leisure activity (and it is one form of the 'serious leisure' mentioned above), it is, in effect, unpaid work.

The definitions and examples in Figure 7.2 refer to time-periods and to unspecified study areas or 'communities', since all social research is temporally and geographically specific. Time is discussed further at various points in the chapter. Communities can vary from the very local, such as a neighbourhood, via villages, towns, cities, regions/states/provinces to nations and international regions, such as the European Union or South-East Asia. Measures of engagement for a community at any one of these levels can refer to residents of the community and to visitors from outside the community – tourists. This is illustrated visually in Figure 7.3. It should be borne in mind that some research methodologies, such as ticket sales at venues, include both categories of participant, while others, such as resident surveys, include only one category.

Counting heads

A key aspect of sport policy-making, planning and facility management is the identification of levels of use – 'counting heads' or, in the case of audiences and spectators, counting 'bums on seats' **(as noted in Chapter 5)**. Figure 7.4 shows a variety of sources of information on sport participant/visitor numbers in three

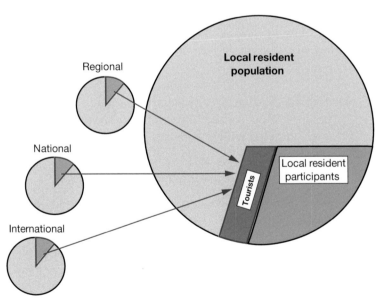

Figure 7.3   Local/non-local participants

Method	Data available	Additional data required to estimate numbers
Administrative – facility based		
1 Individual ticket sales	Ticket sales per time-period	–
2 Bookings data	Facility bookings per time-period	Group size (by sample observation)
3 Season ticket/annual pass sales	Annual/season ticket sales	No. of trips per time-period per ticket (by survey)
4 Membership records/ surveys	a. If member visits are automatically recorded: visits/ time-period b. If not: visits/time-period from member survey	a. – b. Number of members
5 Parking ticket sales data	Parking ticket sales per time-period	Vehicle occupancy (by sample observation)
Questionnaire-based surveys (see Chapter 10)		
6 Resident survey	% participating in activity and/ or visiting particular facilities or facility types, average frequency per time-period	Population (from census)
7 On-site visitor interview surveys	% commuters, neighbours**	Total visit numbers
On-site visitor counts (see Chapter 8) Automatic counters		
8 Automatic vehicle counters	Number of vehicles per time-period	Vehicle occupancy (by sample observations)
9 Automatic pedestrian coun-ters	Number of persons per time-period	–
10 Video/time-lapse cameras/aerial photography	Number of persons/vehicles/ craft present – sampled times, gives person/vehicle/ craft-hours	For vehicles/craft: vehicle occupancy For all: average length of stay (by survey)
Visual/manual counts		
11 Entrance or exit flows	Number of visitors per time-period	–
12 Spot counts of numbers present	Number of persons present – sampled times, gives person-hours	Average length of stay (by survey)

Figure 7.4   Counting heads in sport: sources and methods

* For more detailed discussion see Veal (2010a, Chapter 10)

** commuters and neighbours live in other council areas and use local facilities: commuters work in the study area and use facilities from workplace; neighbours use local facilities from home.

sections: administrative, or secondary, sources; questionnaire-based surveys; and direct, observational, counts.

Figure 7.4 clearly involves more than just secondary data but the full range of sources/methods is included here to make the point that none of these methods should be considered in isolation; indeed, for many estimation purposes data from different sources must be combined. Observation and survey methods are discussed in Chapters 8 and 10 where further reference is made to Figure 7.4.

Depending on how much information is gathered in the process, counting heads generally enables much more than presentation of numbers. It can facilitate examination, explanation of and extrapolation of: trends in usage; performance levels (e.g. costs or income per visit); market reach; and social/economic impact **(see Chapter 14)**.

Introduction to secondary sources

In this chapter we consider the use of existing sources of data, as opposed to the collection of new data which is the subject of most of the rest of the book. The chapter examines mainly published statistical sources, such as the census and national sport participation surveys, but other sources, such as archives and management data, are also included.

In undertaking research it is clearly wise to use existing information where possible, rather than embarking on expensive and time-consuming new data collection exercises. **(One aspect of this has already been touched on in Chapter 6 in relation to the use of the literature.)** In searching the literature the researcher may come across references to statistical or other data which are open to alternative analyses and interpretations or which may not have been fully analysed or exploited by their original collectors, because of their particular interests or limitations on time or money. In other cases, information may exist which was not originally collected for research purposes – for example the administrative records of a sport organisation – but which can provide the basis for research.

- *Primary* data are new data specifically collected in the current research project – the researcher is the *primary user* of such data.

- *Secondary data* already exist and were collected for some other (primary) purpose but can be used a second time in the current project – the researcher is the *secondary user*. Further analysis of such data is referred to as *secondary analysis*.

As with the literature, secondary data can play a variety of roles in a research project, from being the whole basis of the research to being a vital or incidental point of comparison. But to be seen as a research method in its own right in a project, the use of secondary data should contribute significantly to answering research questions or testing hypotheses.

Some secondary data are available in a very 'raw' form – for example organisational membership data; in such cases the dividing line between primary and secondary data becomes blurred. In other cases the data are highly processed, for example the results of national sport participation surveys. However, in such cases the data may still require considerable additional processing to be useful for the purpose in hand, and data from different sources may need to be combined in various ways. In a third category, the data available in published form are not adequate for the purpose in hand and fresh analysis of the raw data is required – for example involving accessing computer files of survey data for re-analysis. In this chapter we address just the sources of data **(data analysis is addressed in Chapter 14)**.

Advantages and disadvantages of using secondary data

Some advantages and disadvantages of using secondary data are listed in Figure 7.5.

A considerable amount of data on sport is collected on a regular basis at considerable cost, particularly by government agencies. Often the immediate policy requirements of the data are quite limited – for example to announce a global figure on the number of participants in sport in a country. In a sector where research funds are limited, it would seem unwise for the research community to waste such resources by failing to extract all possible research

---

Advantages
- Timing – data may be instantly available.
- Cost – cost of collecting new data avoided.
- Experience – the 'trial and error' experience of those who collected the original data can be exploited.
- Scale – secondary data may be based on larger samples than would otherwise be possible.
- Serendipity – inductive process of data analysis may yield serendipitous findings, which might not have arisen with primary, purpose-designed data collection.

Disadvantages
- Design – secondary data has been designed for another purpose, so may not be ideal for current project.
- Analysis limitations – if access to the raw data for re-analysis is not possible, opportunities for analysis/manipulation of the data for the current project may be limited.

Figure 7.5 Advantages and disadvantages of using secondary data

---

- Administrative/management data
- National sport participation surveys
- Economic surveys
- Elite sport performance data
- Documentary sources
- Opportunism

Figure 7.6 Types of secondary data

potential from them. This requires careful consideration of ways in which available data might be used, and often calls for a quasi-inductive approach to research, posing the question: what can these data tell us?

Types of secondary data

Six main sources of secondary data are listed in Figure 7.6 and discussed in turn below. The inclusion of national sport participation surveys might seem incongruous, since they are questionnaire-based surveys **(and so it might be thought that they should not be discussed in this chapter)**. But the class of surveys discussed here is large-scale and typically conducted on an annual basis so they take on the characteristics of 'official statistics'. The government agencies which commission them can be seen as the primary users, but they are also used by a variety of other organisations and individuals, including industry bodies and firms, other levels of government, consultants and academics. Where appropriate, reference is made to examples in Britain and Australia.

Administrative/management data

Management data

Most sport organisations generate routine data which can be of use for research purposes and many have *management information systems* specifically designed to produce data upon which assessments of the performance of the organisation are based. Examples of such data, which may be available on an hourly, daily, weekly, monthly, seasonal or annual basis, are listed in Figure 7.7. It is usually advisable to explore fully the nature, extent and availability of such data, and their potential utilisation, before embarking on fresh data collection. For example, **in Case study 3.1 in Chapter 3** the manager of a facility is concerned about declining levels of visits. Before initiating expensive procedures, such as surveys, to investigate the causes, it would be advisable to study the *available visitor data* to see whether the decline was across all services,

- Visitor numbers (in various categories)
- Visitor expenditure/income (in various categories)
- Bookings and facility utilisation
- Customer enquiries
- Membership numbers and details
- Customer complaints
- Results of visitor/customer surveys
- Expenditure of the organisation (under various headings)
- Staff turnover/absenteeism, etc.

Figure 7.7 Management data

and whether it was taking place at all times or only at certain times of the day, week, season or year.

Numerous agencies are involved in collection of management data for their own administrative purposes, and in most cases the information is available in the annual reports of those organisations, and sometimes on their websites. But generally the data made public are only presented in summary form and the detail remains unpublished. Collation of such information, for example as input to a local plan, therefore becomes a research project in its own right. And if information is required at national level, even in summary form, that also often requires considerable effort. There are some limited examples of such national collations, and examples are listed in the Resources section.

National sport participation surveys

The national sport participationsurvey phenomenon

In most developed countries, surveys of sport participation are conducted by government departments or agencies on a regular basis. In the United States such surveys have been conducted since the early 1960s, particularly on outdoor physical activities (Cordell *et al.*, 2005). Other countries began collecting sport participation data in the 1970s and 1980s. Each country has tended to adopt different design principles, particularly in the way 'participation' is defined, as discussed below, so that the findings between different countries are generally not comparable. A number of publications have, over the years, sought to bring together data on sport participation from a number of national surveys. Some of these are listed in Figure 7.8.

In Britain the *General Household Survey* (GHS), commissioned by government agencies and conducted by the Office for National Statistics and its predecessors, provided sport participation information every 3–5 years from 1973 to

	Kamphorst and Roberts (1989)	Cushman et al. (2005a)	European Commission (nd)	Nicholson et al. (2011)
Australia		•		•
Austria			•	
Belgium			•	
Bulgaria	•		•	•
Canada	•	•		•
China				•
Cyprus			•	
Czechoslovakia	•		•	
Denmark			•	
Estonia			•	
Finland	•	•	•	•
France	•	•	•	
Germany		•	•	•
Great Britain/UK	•	•	•	•
Greece			•	
Hong Kong		•		
Hungary			•	•
India	•			•
Ireland			•	
Israel		•		
Italy	•		•	
Japan	•	•		•
Latvia			•	
Lithuania			•	
Luxembourg			•	
Malta			•	
Netherlands	•	•	•	•
New Zealand	•	•		•
Nigeria	•			
Norway				•
Poland	•	•	•	
Portugal	•		•	
Romania			•	
Russia		•		
Singapore				•
Slovakia			•	
Slovenia			•	
South Africa				•
Spain		•	•	
Sweden			•	
USA	•	•		•

Figure 7.8   National sport participation surveys: composite publications coverage

2002 (Gratton and Veal, 2005). Since 2007 the Active People Survey, with a massive sample of 190,000, has been conducted annually by Sport England. The large sample size is necessary so that data can be made available for every local council, with a minimum sample size of 500, to be used in planning and annual performance monitoring. Figure 7.9 indicates the range of data available from the survey. The data are available online on the Sport England website (see Resources section).

The existence of this database demonstrates both the merits and drawbacks of secondary data. It is most unlikely that the £3–4 million a year which the Active People Survey costs to conduct would be available for purely research purposes: it is conducted to meet the policy requirements of Sport England.

Britain: Active People survey

Conducted by: Sport England
Sample size: 190,000
Participation data items
Sport and recreational physical activity
Walking – at least 30 mins (freq. in last 4 weeks, pace)
Cycling – as for walking
Other sport/recreation/physical activity – as for walking
Sports club membership
Competitive sports participation
Instruction/coaching in sport
Overall satisfaction with sports provision
Likelihood to do more sport: name one activity
Change in participation in last year: reason

Dates: Annual since 2007
Age-range: persons aged 16 and over
Socio-demographic data items
Gender/Age
Ethnic group
Education
Accommodation type
No. of children in household
Car/van availability
Disability
Current work status
Socio-economic status (10 questions)
Main income-earner occupation
Postcode

Australia: Exercise, Recreation and Sport Survey (ERASS)

Conducted by: Standing Committee on Recreation and Sport (SCORS)
Sample size: 13,000
Participation data items
Individual sport/physical activities participated in at least once in previous year.
For the above activities: number of times; whether organised by club etc. or informal
Of the above activities: Those participated in during previous 2 weeks: frequency, time spent.

Dates: Annual since 2001

Age-range: persons aged 15 and over
Socio-demographic data items
Gender, Age, Marital status
Parental status, no. children
Highest education qual.
Employment status, hours worked
Aboriginal
Language spoken at home
Postcode

Figure 7.9 National sport participation survey details

Sources: Britain: DCMS: www.sportengland.org/research/active_people_survey.aspx
Australia: Standing Committee on Recreation and Sport (SCORS): Exercise, Recreation and Sport Survey.
For further information, see Resources section.

This has implications for the design of the survey and the ways in which the data are analysed and published **(see Chapter 14)**.

In addition to the Active People Survey, the British government also conducts the annual Taking Part Survey, details of which can be found on the DCMS website (see Resources section). This survey seems to cover much the same ground as the Active People Survey, but with a much smaller, but still large, sample (27,000) which provides data down to the regional level but not to individual council level. The survey also covers children's participation.

In Australia the national government statistics agency, the Australian Bureau of Statistics (ABS), was responsible for the main sport and physical recreation participation surveys during the 1990s and continues to conduct such surveys from time to time. In addition, it conducts periodic surveys on participation in the arts, on children's sport participation and on sport-spectating. From 2001–2010, however, the main source of national and state-level sport and physical recreation participation data was the annual Exercise Recreation and Sport Survey (ERASS) conducted by the Standing Committee on Recreation and Sport (SCORS), which represents the Australian Sports Commission and the state governments' ministries of sport and recreation. Details are shown in Figure 7.9. Since 2011 the role has been resumed by the ABS.

National sport participation surveys are the main source of information available to researchers on overall participation levels in a range of sport activities. How they fit into the spectrum of methods for counting heads is discussed above. A number of issues arise in the use of these important databases, including questions of validity and reliability, sample size, the participation reference period used, the age range of the population covered, the range of activities included, and availability of information on the social characteristics of respondents. These topics are discussed in turn below.

Validity and reliability of national sport participation surveys

National sport surveys suffer from the limitation of all interview surveys in that they are dependent on respondents' own reports of their patterns of sport participation. How sure can we be, therefore, that the resultant data are accurate? We cannot be absolutely sure, as discussed in Chapter 10; however, a number of features of national surveys such as those discussed here lend credence to their reliability and value as sources of data:

- national government statistical organisations have an enviable reputation for quality and professionalism in their work;

- the surveys are often based on large sample sizes;

- the fact that there has been little dramatic variation in the findings of the various surveys over the years is reassuring (Cushman and Veal, 1993; Gratton and Tice, 1994) – erratic and unexplainable fluctuations in reported levels of participation would have led to suspicions that the surveys were unreliable, but this has generally not happened.

Some commentators have questioned the validity of participation surveys, conducting investigations which show that there is a tendency for respondents to exaggerate levels of participation substantially, at least in relation to some activities (Chase and Godbey, 1983; Chase and Harada, 1984). However, for some groups, some activities and some surveys there may also be under-reporting of levels of activity (Boothby, 1987). While national survey data, especially when sponsored by governments, have the imprimatur of being 'official statistics', they are subject to all the limitations of questionnaire-based surveys as discussed in Chapter 10.

Sample size

It is generally the case that the larger the sample size the more reliable and precise are the survey findings. The Australian survey discussed above is based on a samples of around 13,000 interviews and is therefore subject to only minimal 'statistical error' – a term explained in Chapter 13. The British survey, at 190,000, is much larger, in fact it would be unnecessarily large if its only purpose was to provide national-level data. But it is designed to provide data for each of the 350 local councils in England, giving most a sample of only 500, which is nevertheless subject to considerable margins of statistical error, as can be seen in Chapter 13 (Figure 13.1).

For many sporting activities covered in the surveys the proportion of the population participating is less than 1 per cent. However, even 1 per cent of the adult population of Britain is almost half a million people, so small percentages can represent large numbers of people. While this issue is discussed in more detail in Chapter 13, the constraints of a small sample size compared with a large sample size can be imagined from the following:

● Exercise, Recreation and Sport Survey, Australia: national sample size 13,000: 1% = 130

● Active People Survey, England: national sample size 190,000: 1% = 1900

● Active People Survey, England: sub-sample for one council area: 500: 1% = 5.

Main question – participation reference period and duration

The level of participation depends substantially on the 'reference period' used, that is, the period of time to which the participation relates. Thus, for example, the proportion of the population who have been swimming in the last 24 hours would be quite small, the proportion who have done so in the last month would be higher, while the proportion who have ever been swimming would be almost 100 per cent. Furthermore, in the case of physical activity, the *duration* of participation is important when considering the question of health benefits. Thus for physical activities, measuring only the proportion of participants who exercise sufficiently to gain health benefits (that is who have participated for at least a minimum prescribed time, such as 30 minutes on at least four days a week), would reduce the reported participation rate considerably. This is illustrated in Figure 7.10, which shows, for a number of sport activities:

- the proportion of the population participating at least once in the last year compared with the proportion in the last four weeks; and

- the proportion participating in the last month and, of those, people who have participated for at least 30 minutes in the last week.

It can be seen that the second measure in each case reduces the participation rate by at least half, and in some cases by two-thirds.

The published results from the Australian ERASS do not include the one-week measure for individual activities, but the proportion taking part in any form

Sports*	Participating at least once, 2002		Participating at least once, 2008–09[†]	
Reference period:	Last year	Last 4 weeks	Last month	Last week (>30 mins)
	%	%	%	%
Walking	45.9	34.9	na	na
Swimming	34.8	13.8	13.2	7.6
Cycling	19.1	9.0	9.3	4.5
Football	9.1	4.9	7.4	5.1
Athletics**	1.0	0.3	6.4	4.2
Golf	12.1	4.8	3.5	2.1
Badminton	6.4	1.8	2.4	1.3
Tennis	7.0	1.9	2.4	1.3
Squash	3.8	1.3	1.2	0.7
Cricket	2.4	0.6	1.0	0.5
Equestrian	3.5	1.9	1.0	0.8
Bowls	3.8	1.3	1.0	0.6

Figure 7.10　Participation rates in sports by reference period, persons aged 16+, England

* Activities with at least 1% participation in last month in 2008–09 included. ** 2002 definition is 'track and field' – 2008–09 includes all jogging, marathons etc. † National participation rates estimated from aggregated county figures.

Sources: For 2002: General Household Survey 2002: Office for National Statistics (2004); For 2008–09: Sport England: Active People Survey www.sportengland.org/research/active_people_survey/active.aspx

of exercise, recreation or sport activity in 2007–08 was 83.4 per cent while the proportion who participated at least three times a week was just 49.3 per cent.

The one-year reference period is becoming the international norm (Cushman *et al.*, 2005a: 284). This practice has the advantage of covering participation in all seasons of the year in one survey and including most infrequent participants. However, it has the disadvantage of introducing possible errors in respondents' recall of their activities over such a long time-period. Furthermore, for sport and physical exercise activity policy-makers are interested in minimum frequency and duration which produce health benefits, so a one-week or two-week measure is becoming an additional norm for this sector. Use of a shorter reference period has the advantage of increased accuracy of recall, but the disadvantage that seasonal variation must be covered by interviewing at different times of the year.

Age range

Sport participation surveys are restricted in terms of age range covered. Some include respondents as young as 12 years old, while some cover only those aged 18 and over. And some have upper age limits. The British and Australian surveys presented here cover people aged 16 and over. The reasons for not interviewing young children are threefold:

1. it may be difficult to obtain accurate information from very young children;

2. it may be considered ethically unacceptable to subject children to the sort of questioning which adults can freely choose to face or not **(see Chapter 4)**; and

3. there is a question as to when children are considered to be engaging in their own independent sport activities as opposed to being under the control of parents.

Some surveys present data on children from 'proxy' interviews, in which questions about children's activities are answered by parents: an example is the Australian Bureau of Statistics (2009) survey of children's participation in culture and sport activities. By contrast, the DCMS Taking Part Survey includes some data from direct interviews with children, but this is limited to children aged 11–15.

A lower age limit in the mid-teens has effects on the results, in that for some activities – for example swimming or cycling – young teenagers may be a significant proportion of total participants. For other activities – for example, golf or lawn bowls – the age limit may be less important because young people do not form a significant proportion of participants. When using data from sport participation surveys, particularly when seeking to compare results from different surveys, it is therefore important to bear in mind the age-range covered.

Social/demographic characteristics

In addition to the basic information on participation, national sport surveys generally include a wide range of background information on the people interviewed, including such variables as gender, occupation, age, education level reached, size of family or household unit and ethnicity or country of birth. This information can be used to examine levels of participation by different social groups from either an equity or a marketing point of view, and can also be used to predict demand, as future changes in the underlying social structure of the community affect patterns of demand **(this is explored in Chapter 14)**.

The importance of sport participation surveys

Sport participation surveys, despite their limitations, are the main source of information, not only on overall levels of participation but also on differences in participation between different groups in the community, such as the young and the old, men and women, and different occupational and income groups. Any sport researcher or professional should therefore be familiar with such key data sources.

National time-use surveys

Time-use, or time-budget, research became a significant focus of international social research with the conduct of the UNESCO-funded *Multinational Comparative Time-Budget Research Project* in the 1960s (Szalai, 1972). In Britain such surveys were conducted as long ago as the 1930s when the BBC used them to explore the public's patterns of use of broadcast media, while in Australia they date back to the 1970s. In recent years, time-use surveys have been of particular interest because of the belief that people are becoming increasingly time-pressured. The most recent UK time-use surveys which permit analysis of trends in time-use were conducted in 2001 and 2005. UK time-use surveys are conducted in association with 14 other European countries under the auspices of the Harmonised European Time Use Survey which makes data available online (see Resources section). The most recent in Australia were the 1997 and 2006 surveys conducted by the Australian Bureau of Statistics.

Time-use surveys ask respondents to keep a diary of their activities for one or two days, so they cover all aspects of time-use, including sport, and are a key source of information for sport studies. Compared with the participation surveys discussed above, the 'reference period' for a time-use survey is effectively one or two days. This overcomes the problem of recall accuracy involved in surveys which use longer recall periods, resulting in more reliable data, but drastically reduces the proportion of respondents engaging in any one type of activity. Apart from activities which large numbers of people engage in on most days, notably watching television and listening to the radio, time-use surveys are not ideal for studying individual sport activities; they are used to examine broad categories of time-use, as shown in Figure 7.11. It shows that

	Britain, 2005	Australia, 2006
	Hours per week, persons aged 15+	
Sleep	57.2	59.7
TV/video/radio/music	18.3	16.1
Sport/physical recreation	1.2	2.2
Other leisure	22.2	16.2
Paid work	19.8	24.1
Personal care	14.7	17.0
Domestic work/childcare	22.3	22.7
Travel and other	12.3	10.0
Total	168.0	168.0

Figure 7.11   Time use, Britain and Australia

NB. Some differences between Britain and Australia may be due to differences in activity definitions and some due to differing age-structure.

Sources: Britain: data from Office for National Statistics: Time Use Survey, 2005, available at: www.ons. gov.uk. Australia: data from Australian Bureau of Statistics *How Australians Use Their Time, 2006*, online resource at: www.abs.gov.au/ausstats/abs@.nsf/mf/4153.0

time spent on sport and physical recreation is just over one hour per week in Britain and just over two hours in Australia. It should, however, be noted that part of the difference between these two countries may be a reflection of the difference in age-structure, since the average age of the Australian population is lower than that of Britain.

Elite sport performance

One of the key issues in sport policy and management is the extent to which resources devoted to the support of elite sport, particularly at international level, are effective in achieving international success and, if so, whether this has its intended effects, such as the boosting of national prestige and inspiring grassroots participation. Addressing such issues raises questions of measurement and data.

Regarding elite sport performance: Shibli and Bingham (2005) show how the performance of a country at an international sporting event can be measured in a number of ways, as shown in Figure 7.12. The measures might be used to compare performance of one country over time, or to make international comparisons **(see examples for Chapter 14)**. Data on medals won at major sporting events can generally be found on the organising body's website, for example that of the International Olympic Committee (see Resources section). Additional data for the last two items in Figure 7.9 can be found on the websites of the national statistics agencies (see Resources section).

- Number of gold medals won
- Total number of medals won (gold, silver, bronze)
- Medal points won (points: gold = 3, silver = 2, bronze = 1)
- Number of athletes qualifying to take part
- Number of athletes in finals
- Number of athletes posting: season's best, personal best performance or breaking records
- Market share: country's % share of all medals or points awarded
- Cost (in terms of national government expenditure) per medal, by sport
- Each of the above related to national population and/or income

Figure 7.12   Measures of national performance in multi-sport international sport events

Source: Based on Shibli and Bingham (2005), except last item

Economic data

Household expenditure

In most developed countries surveys of *household expenditure* are conducted on a regular basis. In Britain the *Expenditure and Food Survey* is conducted annually while the Australian equivalent, the *Household Expenditure Survey*, is conducted every five years (see Resources section). These surveys collect information from a cross-section of families throughout their respective countries on their weekly expenditure on scores of items, many of which relate to sport. They provide the basis for the regular sport expenditure forecasting and market trend analysis reports produced by such organisations as the Sport Industries Research Centre at Sheffield Hallam University for the UK and Richard K. Miller and Associates for the United States (details in Resources section).

The population census

Historical sources indicate that the taking of a census of the whole population, for taxation and other purposes, is a long-standing practice of governments dating at least back to the Roman Empire. A well-known example is the *Domesday Book*, compiled by William the Conqueror for the whole of England in the eleventh century.

The modern population census

The *population census* is an important source of information and any aspiring sport manager or researcher should be fully aware of its content and its potential. A complete census of the population is taken in Britain by the Office for National Statistics (ONS) every 10 years; the latest was 2011, and before that 1991, 1981 and so on back to 1801. It is, however, likely that the 2011 census will be the last, as other forms of data may provide a cheaper means of assembling the required data (the 2011 census cost almost £500 million to conduct and analyse). Details of discussions on the future of the British Census can be found under 'Beyond 2011' on the ONS website (see Resources section below). In Australia, because the population is growing relatively rapidly, the Australian Bureau of Statistics undertakes a census every five years. It is a statutory requirement for householders (and hoteliers, hospital managers, boarding school principals and prison governors) to fill out a census form on 'census night', indicating the number of people, including visitors, in the building, and their age, gender, occupation and so on. Some people escape the net, for instance some people sleeping rough or illegal immigrants, but generally the information is believed to be reliable and comprehensive.

Data from the census are available at a number of levels, from national down to the level of Enumeration Districts (EDs) in the UK or Collection Districts (CDs) in Australia, as indicated in Figure 7.13. CDs are small areas, with populations of around 250 to 500, which a single census collection officer deals with. By adding together data from a few CDs, a sport facility manager can obtain data on the demographic characteristics of the population of the catchment area of the facility. An enormous amount of information is available on each of these areas, as listed in Figure 7.14.

Uses of census data

It can be seen that none of the census information is concerned directly with sport, so why should the census be of interest to the sport researcher? Among the uses **(which are explored further in Chapter 14)** are:

● planning sport facilities and conducting feasibility studies;

Britain	Australia
National	National
Regions	State
Counties	Postal codes
Local government areas	Local government areas
Parliamentary constituencies	State and federal Parliament electorates
Enumeration districts (EDs)	Collection districts (CDs)

Figure 7.13 **Census data: levels of availability**

Resident population
- Number of males/females
- Number/proportion in 5-year age-groups (and single years for under-20s)
- Numbers of people:
  - with different religions
  - by country of birth
  - speaking different languages
  - by country of birth of parents
- Numbers of families/households:
  - of different sizes
  - with different numbers of dependent children
  - which are single parent families
  - with various numbers of vehicles
  - living in different types of dwelling
- Numbers of people:
  - who left school at various ages
  - with different educational/technical qualifications
  - in different occupational groups
  - by working hours
  - unemployed

Figure 7.14 Census data available

- area management/marketing;
- facility performance evaluation;
- market segmentation.

Documentary sources

Documentary sources lie somewhere between literature and management/ administrative data as an information source for research. Typical examples are listed in Figure 7.15. Many such sources are important for historical research, either for a primarily historical research project or as background for a project with a contemporary focus. In some cases the documents are a focus of research in their own right – for example some research on women and sport has examined the coverage of women's sport in the media (e.g. Rowe and Brown, 1994). As the links between cultural and media studies and sport studies increase, so analysis of media content, including television, is likely to increase (Wenner, 1998).

- Minutes of committee/council/board meetings
- Correspondence of an organisation or an individual
- Archives (may include both of the above and other papers)
- Popular literature, such as novels, magazines
- Newspapers, particularly coverage of specific topics and/or particular aspects, such as editorials, advertising or correspondence columns
- Brochures and advertising material
- Diaries

Figure 7.15   Documentary sources

Opportunism

Secondary data often give rise to what might be called opportunistic research, as discussed in Chapter 3. This applies to many of the government-sponsored surveys discussed above: data exist and have been used by the collecting agency only for limited purposes, or in internal policy-making processes which are not in the public domain. Examples include:

- national profiles of sport participation, as in most of the chapters in Nicholson *et al.* (2011);

- the use of official data on sport participation to examine the validity of the claimed 'trickle down' effect of hosting major sporting events (Veal *et al.*, 2012);

- examination of sport participation and inequality **(see Case study 14.1).**

Summary

Following a discussion of measurement in sport studies, this chapter focusses on sources of secondary data, that is, data which have been collected by others for their own purposes but which might be utilised for current research purposes. There are potential cost and time-saving advantages to such a strategy and even an ethical dimension, which suggests that scarce resources should not be expended on new data collection if adequate data already exist. The chapter reviews a number of sources of secondary data commonly used in sport research, namely: national sport participation surveys; economic data on consumer expenditure; data on elite sport performance; the census of population;

management data; and documentary sources; **analysis of such data is discussed in Chapter 14**.

Test questions

1. What are the seven types of measurement of sport/physical activity identified at the beginning of the chapter?

2. What are the three sources of data for 'counting heads' identified at the beginning of the chapter?

3. What are the advantages and disadvantages of secondary data analysis?

4. What are some of the issues to be considered when using data from sport participation surveys?

5. What are the names of the main sport participation surveys conducted in your country?

6. The chapter lists nine sources of 'management data'. What are they?

7. The chapter lists seven types of 'documentary' source. What are they?

Exercises

NB. No exercises are offered for this chapter, but exercises using secondary data are presented in Chapter 14.

Resources

Websites

International:

- *Europe:* European Commission Eurobarometer surveys of sport participation (2004: Special Survey Report 213, 2009: Special Survey Report 334): http://ec.europa.eu/public_opinion/archives/eb_special_en.htm

- Harmonised European Time Use Survey: https://www.h2.scb.se/tus/tus/

- International Olympic Committee: www.olympic.org

UK:

- National statistics agency: Office for National Statistics: www.ons.gov.uk

- Sport/culture participation: Department for Culture, Media and Sport (DCMS) Taking Part Survey: https://www.gov.uk/government/publications/taking-part-2012-13-quarter-1-statistical-release. Note: dates in the URL will change in future

- Active People Survey: www.sportengland.org/research/active_people _survey.aspx

- Population census: www.statistics.gov.uk click on 'Population' for past census results and search on 'Beyond 2011' for discussions on future alternatives.

Australia:

- National statistics agency: www.abs.gov.au

- Exercise, Recreation and Sport Survey: www.ausport.gov.au/information/ casro

- Australian Bureau of Statistics data: www.abs.gov.au, search for 'Culture and Recreation'.

- Household Expenditure Survey: www.abs.gov.au

- Population census: www.abs.gov.au, click on 'Census'.

Annual industry/consumer expenditure surveys:

- UK annual sport/sport industry reviews: Sport Industry Research Centre, Sheffield Hallam University: www.shu.ac.uk/research/sirc/publications .html

- USA annual sport industry review: Richard K. Miller and Associates: www .rkma.com.

Publications

- Measurement: Trost and Rice (2012), Welk (2002); types of engagement/ involvement: ABS (2010).

- Facility use: national collation of local authority data, UK: Chartered Institute of Public Finance and Accountancy (CIPFA) (Annual) – data for individual councils on open space, golf courses, playing fields, swimming pools, cultural facilities: costs, income, use levels (some gaps for some data items).

- Sport participation surveys: Australia: Veal (2003); UK: Gratton and Veal (2005), Gratton *et al.* (2011); international: Nicholson *et al.* (2011), Cushman *et al.* (2005b) include data from sport and time-use surveys for 15 countries: see Figure 7.8; Eurobarometer special reports on sport (see websites above) include data on all members of the EU.

- Time-use surveys: Pentland *et al.* (1999).

- Documentary sources: Kellehear (1993).

References

Australian Bureau of Statistics (ABS) (2009) *Children's Participation in Cultural and Leisure Activities* (Cat. No. 4901.0). Canberra: ABS.

Australian Bureau of Statistics (ABS) (2010) *Involvement in Organised Sport and Physical Activity* (Cat. No. 6285.0). Canberra: ABS.

Boothby, J. (1987) Self-reported participation rates: further comment. *Leisure Studies*, 6(1), 99–104.

Chartered Institute of Public Finance and Accountancy (CIPFA) (Annual) *Culture, Sport and Recreation Statistics.* London: CIPFA.

Chase, D. R. and Godbey, G. C. (1983) The accuracy of self-reported participation rates. *Leisure Studies*, 2(2), 231–6.

Chase, D. and Harada, M. (1984) Response error in self-reported recreation participation. *Journal of Leisure Research*, 16(4), 322–9.

Cordell, H. K., Green, G. T., Leeworthy, V. R., Stephens, R., Fly, M. J. and Betz, C. J. (2005) United States of America: outdoor recreation. In G. Cushman, A.J. Veal and J. Zuzanek (eds) *Free Time and Leisure Participation: International Perspectives.* Wallingford, UK: CABI Publishing, 245–64.

Cushman, G. and Veal, A. J. (1993) The new generation of leisure surveys – implications for research on everyday life. *Leisure and Society*, 16(1), 211–20.

Cushman, G., Veal, A. J. and Zuzanek, J. (2005a) National leisure participation and time-use surveys: a future. In G. Cushman, A. J. Veal and J. Zuzanek (eds) *Free Time and Leisure Participation: International Perspectives,* Wallingford, UK: CABI Publishing, 283–92.

Cushman, G., Veal, A. J. and Zuzanek, J. (eds) (2005b) *Free Time and Leisure Participation: International Perspectives.* Wallingford, UK: CABI.

European Commission (nd) *The Citizens of the European Union and Sport: Special Eurobarometer Reports.* Brussels: European Commission (see website above).

Gratton, C. and Tice, A. (1994) Trends in sports participation in Britain, 1977–87. *Leisure Studies*, 13(1), 49–66.

Gratton, C. and Veal, A. J. (2005) Great Britain. In G. Cushman, A. J. Veal and J. Zuzanek (eds) *Free Time and Leisure Participation: International Perspectives.* Wallingford, UK: CABI, 109–26.

Gratton, C., Rowe, N. and Veal, A. J. (2011) International comparisons of sport participation in European countries: an update of the COMPASS project. *European Journal of Sport and Society*, 8(1–2), 99–116.

Kamphorst, T. J. and Roberts, K. (eds) (1989) *Trends in Sports: A Multinational Perspective.* Voothuizen, Netherlands: Giordano Bruno Colemborg.

Kellehear, A. (1993) *The Unobtrusive Researcher: A Guide to Methods.* Sydney: Allen & Unwin.

Nicholson, M., Hoye, R. and Houlihan, B. (2011) *Participation in Sport: International Policy Perspectives.* London: Routledge.

Office for National Statistics (2004) *Sport and Leisure: Results from the Sport and Leisure Module of the 2002 General Household Survey.* London: ONS.

Pentland, W. E., Harvey, A. S., Powell Lawton, M. and McColl, M. A. (eds) (1999) *Time Use Research in the Social Sciences.* New York: Kluwer/Plenum.

Rowe, D. and Brown, P. (1994) Promoting women's sport: theory, policy and practice. *Leisure Studies*, 13(2), 97–110.

Shibli, S. and Bingham, J. (2005) Measuring the sporting success of nations. In I. Henry (ed.) *Transnational and Comparative Research in Sport.* London: Routledge, 59–81.

Stebbins, R. A. (1992) *Amateurs, Professionals and Serious Leisure.* Montreal: McGill-Queen's University Press.

Stebbins, R. A. (2007) *Serious Leisure: A Perspective for Our Time.* New Brunswick, NJ: Transaction Publishers.

Szalai, A. (ed.) (1972) *The Use of Time: Daily Activities of Urban and Suburban Populations in Twelve Countries.* The Hague: Mouton.

Trost, S. G. and Rice, K. (2012) Measurement of physical activity. In K. Armour and D. Macdonald (eds) *Research Methods in Physical Education and Youth Sport.* London: Routledge, 163–73.

Veal, A. J. (2003) Tracking change: leisure participation and policy in Australia, 1985–2002. *Annals of Leisure Research*, 6(3), 246–78.

Veal, A. J., Frawley, S. and Toohey, K. (2012) The sport participation legacy of the Sydney 2000 Olympic Games and other international sporting events hosted in Australia. *Journal of Policy Research in Tourism, Leisure and Events*, 4(2), 155–84.

Welk, G. J. (ed.) (2002) *Physical Activity Assessments for Health-related Research.* Champaign, IL: Human Kinetics.

Wenner, L. (ed.) (1998) *MediaSport.* London: Routledge.

Observation

Introduction

The aim of this chapter is to draw attention to the importance of *looking* in research and to introduce some of the specific approaches of observational methods. It examines situations in which observation is particularly appropriate and outlines the main steps to be taken in designing and conducting an observation-based project. Observation is a neglected technique in sport research; nevertheless, while it is rarely possible to base the whole of a project on observation, the technique has a vital role to play, formally or informally, in most research strategies. Typically, observation is one of a number of techniques that may be used in a study, especially when 'head counting' is concerned **(as indicated in Figure 7.2)**.

The chapter is located in Part II of the book which is concerned with data collection, but there is no corresponding separate data analysis chapter in Part III. This is because, in the case of quantitative observation, data can readily be analysed using simple spreadsheet collation, calculation and graphics. In the case of qualitative observation, the field notes to be analysed are similar to any other field notes or interview transcripts, so are covered by the discussion of qualitative data analysis **(Chapter 15)**. Some case studies including analysis are, however, included here to demonstrate the outcomes of observational research.

Sometimes observational research is referred to as *unobtrusive* methods, since often there is generally no involvement with the observed subjects, who may not even be aware that they are being observed. But the term 'unobtrusive methods' is also used in relation to documentary sources, such as the media, organisational

Structured or systematic observation	Observation process subject to formal rules about what should be observed, how often, etc. – results typically recorded on forms and analysed quantitatively. Equivalent to the formal questionnaire-based survey in survey research.
Unstructured/naturalistic/ qualitative observation	No formal rules established; relatively informal recording or analysis procedures. Observer seeks to describe the phenomenon of interest and develop explanations and understandings in the process. Observational equivalent of the informal, in-depth interview.
Quasi-experimental observation	Researcher intervenes to change the environment and observes what happens – for example changing the design of a children's playground or a fitness circuit. May be structured or unstructured.
Participant observation	The researcher is a participant in the milieu being studied – for example a sport club or an event – rather than a separate, 'objective' researcher. May involve any of the above forms of observation. Discussed in Chapter 9.

Figure 8.1 Types of observational research

records and diaries (see Kellehear, 1993); in this book these sources are dealt with in the chapters on secondary data and qualitative methods. In this chapter we concentrate on direct visual engagement with sport activity and sites.

The chapter comprises three main sections:

● an overview of possible situations where observational methods might be used;

● a step-by-step examination of the typical observational research process; and

● the use of technology.

Types of observational research: quantitative and qualitative

Observation involves *looking*. It can take a number of forms, as indicated in Figure 8.1. Of importance here is that observational research can be quantitative, qualitative or a combination of both. There is also overlap with experimental methods and with participant observation **(see Chapters 9 and 11)**.

Possibilities

A number of types of situation or activity where observation is appropriate or necessary can be identified, as listed in Figure 8.2. These situations are discussed in turn below.

- Children's play/physical activity
- Sport activity patterns
- Informal sport areas
  - visit numbers – counting heads
  - spatial/functional patterns of use
- Visitor profiles
- Deviant behaviour
- Mystery shopping
- Complementary research
- Everyday life
- Social behaviour

Figure 8.2 Situations for observational research

Children's play/physical activity

There is some research which can only be tackled by means of observation. One example is children's physical play activity. With more sedentary lifestyles resulting in increased concerns about the negative health consequences of childhood obesity, this is a field of growing research interest. Such research is concerned with such issues as:

- extent to which play is physically active or passive;

- patterns of play in different environments;

- the types of equipment children of different ages prefer and/or which facilitate beneficial exercise;

- whether boys have different patterns of play from girls; and

- whether there are differences in play patterns between children from different cultural backgrounds.

It is unlikely that questions on these matters could be fully answered by interviewing children, particularly very young children. The obvious approach is to *observe* children at play and record their behaviour.

The System for Observing Fitness Instruction Time (SOFIT) (McKenzie *et al.*, 1991) is one of a number of available direct observation procedures designed to record children's activity levels during physical education programmes. The system involves recording, at 10-second intervals:

1. the activity level of students: 1. lying down; 2. sitting; 3. standing; 4. walking; 5. very active;

2. the lesson context: general content; knowledge content; motor content;

3. teacher involvement: prompting/encouraging; instructing; managing; observing; off-task.

The resultant data can be used to analyse the strategies which are most effective in promoting physical activity. A manual for the conduct of the system is available online (Mackenzie, 2009).

Sport activity patterns

Coaches typically observe and measure the activity of athletes with whom they work. Traditionally this was done with the naked eye and with the assistance of very basic equipment, such as distance and time measuring devices. While these basic approaches continue to be used, they are increasingly being complemented, and to some extent replaced, by technology, including video recording devices, physiological monitoring equipment and global positioning systems (GPS) linked to computers. Such devices can record and analyse athletes' movement patterns, associated energy expenditure and effectiveness.

Informal sport areas

Visit numbers: counting heads

Structured observation methods can be used to estimate the level of use of informal sport and recreation areas, such as beaches, ski areas, or rock climbing or fishing areas, where there is no admission charge and therefore no ticket sales data to inform managers and planners of levels of use, and where, typically, there are often few formal constraints on capacity or spatial usage patterns, such as fixed seating. In some cases, where a site includes a mixture of sporting and non-sporting activities, to identify sporting use it is necessary to distinguish between users on the basis of activity and this is discussed in the second half of the chapter.

As noted in the discussion of 'counting heads' **(Chapter 7)**, when playing fields are booked for a session or a whole season, average levels of actual use, in terms of numbers of training or match sessions and numbers of players involved in a given session, would need to be established by observational counts at a sample of sessions.

An indication of the level of use of sites may be required for a variety of reasons. For example:

- A public agency might decide that it would be useful, for political or public relations reasons, to be able to state the total number of visitors which a site or facility serves in a week or a year – in order to justify the level of taxpayers' money being spent on maintaining it.

- In management terms it is often useful to be able to relate the costs of maintaining a site to the number of visits which it attracts, as one of a number of inputs into decisions on how much money should be spent on different sites.

● In planning, the conversion of demand, in terms of numbers of participants and/or visits, into facility requirements requires information on typical use levels.

● A single-site manager might wish to compare levels of use over time to assess the impact of various marketing and other management measures.

● In a multi-purpose agency, such as a local council, performance is often measured by levels of use and costs across different types of facility. For those facilities without ticket sales data it becomes necessary to obtain an estimate by *observing* and *counting* the number of users.

Where the bulk of users arrive at a facility by private car and a charge is made for parking, indications of variations or trends in use levels may be provided by parking income, but this does not account for non-vehicular use and in some cases parking charges do not apply outside certain hours, or there may be season permit holders who are not recorded every time they enter. To account for all vehicular use it may be possible to install automatic vehicle counters to count the number of vehicles entering and leaving the site, as discussed later in the chapter. Vehicle counts, however, provide information on the number of *vehicles* using a site but not the number of *people*. To obtain estimates of the numbers of people it is necessary to supplement the vehicle counts by direct observation for a period of the time to ascertain the average number of persons in vehicles and, at some sites, to estimate the numbers arriving by foot or bicycle, who may not be recorded by the mechanical counting device. Manual methods of counting usage levels are discussed later in the chapter.

Spatial/functional patterns of use

Observation is useful not only for gathering data on the number of users of a site but also for studying the way people make use of a site. This is particularly important in relation to the design and layout of spaces, and their capacity. For instance, if people tend to use areas close to entrances and parking areas (which they often do in outdoor sites), then where those entrances and parking areas are positioned will affect the pattern of use of the site. Some users are influenced by particular site features, such as topography for BMX users or water qualities for anglers. This can be used as a management/design tool to influence the pattern of use of a site.

Buildings and open spaces for public use are often designed with either little or no consideration as to how people will actually use them, or on the basis of untested assumptions about how they will be used. In reality it is often found that people do not actually behave as anticipated by the designers and some spaces are underused while others are overcrowded, or spaces are not actually used for the activities for which they were designed or equipped.

Visitor profiles

Questionnaire-based site surveys are the typical means for researching demographic and group composition data which combine to provide a *visitor* or *user profile*. However, depending on the design of the questionnaire, and given that questionnaires in such situations are invariably quite brief, the information collected can miss vital features of the characteristics of the users of a site which can be identified by observation. For example, two sport venues could have identical user age/gender/group size profiles, but, because of the different types of programme offered, could attract very different crowds, in terms of fashion, lifestyle and behaviour. Even at a single venue an overall profile based on averages and percentages may hide the fact that it is used by a number of distinct user-groups. Questionnaire-based profiles may also miss distinctive usage patterns. For example, a sport centre survey may indicate that there are x% mothers with young children, or single elderly users, but fail to pick up the fact that these groups attend at particular times and meet together and socialise. Of course, a questionnaire survey could pick up these features if the questionnaire included appropriate questions and if the sample were large enough and the analysis sophisticated enough, but this is not always the case. In addition to being a research approach in its own right, observational research can be used as a preliminary process to identify features of the user profile so that appropriate questions can be included in a questionnaire.

Deviant behaviour

The notion of *deviant* behaviour is a contested one, with one person's 'deviance' being another person's 'acceptable behaviour'. The term covers such activities as the use of recreational and performance-enhancing drugs, illicit sports and rowdy crowd behaviour or other forms of 'rule-breaking' in sport settings. Deviant behaviour is a situation where observation is likely to be more fruitful than interviews. People are unlikely to tell an interviewer about their litter-dropping habits, their lack of adherence to the rules in a park, or their beer-can-throwing habits at a football match. Finding out about such things requires observation – usually of a covert nature! This, of course, raises ethical issues, such as people's rights to privacy **(see Chapter 4)**. Case study 8.1 shows parts of the results from a study of riots between police and 'bikie' gangs at a motor-sport event in New South Wales, Australia in the 1980s, indicating that the safety of the researchers can be at stake in observational research in some environments.

Case study 8.1   Observing riots

In their book, *The Dynamics of Collective Conflict*, Cunneen *et al.* (1989) present the results of their study of a series of violent conflicts, including pitched
battles, which took place between police and fans at the annual Bathurst
Motorcycle Grand Prix meetings in New South Wales, Australia, in the mid-
1980s. They used a variety of research methods, including observation, interviews, historical research and analysis of press and television reports, in an
attempt to understand the origins and nature of the conflicts between the
two groups and the role of the media, which reported the events and created images and interpretations for the consumption of the public and politicians. While media reports portrayed the fans as 'mindless hooligans' on
the rampage, detailed research revealed a history of suspicion between police
and 'bikies' and a picture of excessive and escalatory police response to the
carnivalesque behaviour of the crowd. There was no single explanation of
the riots – the meaning and interpretation of the events depended on who

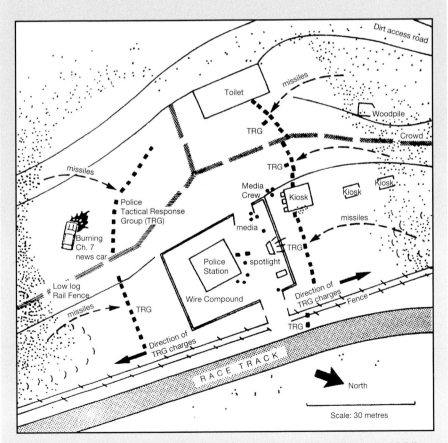

Figure 8.3   Pattern of conflict at the Bathurst 'Bike Races', 1985

was doing the interpretation – the police, the fans, the press or politicians. Figure 8.3 presents the results of detailed observation of the layout of the site and the parties involved in one of the pitched battles. Clearly it would be difficult to describe the scene entirely verbally – visual presentation of the results of the observational exercise is the obvious approach to adopt.

Mystery shopping

Mystery shopping is another potentially fruitful but underexploited use of observation. It involves a researcher playing the role of user/visitor/customer as a method of obtaining information on the quality of the experience enjoyed by users of a sport facility or product. The mystery shopper is required to make use of the facilities or services on offer on an *incognito* basis. The researcher has a checklist of features to observe – such as cleanliness, information availability and clarity, staff performance – and makes a report after using the facilities or services. Such an approach draws on the expertise of the observer to assess quality of service and to record details, for example related to safety, which might not be noticed by routine users. Again, ethical and industrial relations issues may arise in such a study because of the element of deception involved in a researcher playing the part of a customer, typically on behalf of management.

Complementary research

Observation can provide essential quantitative or qualitative complements to other research methods.

Quantitative

Observation involving counts of users can be a necessary complement to interview surveys to correct for variation in sampling rates. For instance, in a typical sport facility, two interviewers, working at a steady rate, may be able to interview virtually all (100 per cent) users in the less busy periods in the early morning but only manage to interview a small proportion of the users (say 5 per cent) during the busy lunch hour and afternoon periods. The final sample would therefore, in this case, over-represent early morning users and under-represent mid-day and afternoon users. If these two groups have different characteristics, the differential rate of sampling would be likely to have a biasing effect on, for example, the overall balance of views expressed by the users. Observational counts of the hourly levels of use can provide data to give an appropriate *weight* to the mid-day and afternoon users at the analysis stage. The process of weighting is described in more detail later in this chapter and **(see also Chapter 16)**.

Qualitative

Informal observation may be appropriate when the spatial behaviour is complex and takes place in ill-defined areas. An example is the behaviour of committed sports fans in such matters as loyalty to and defence of home 'territory' (Spaaij, 2008: 383–5) and the meanings attached to particular items and styles of clothing (Marsh *et al.*, 1978: 122–5). Informal observation may also provide complementary material for any study which is focused on a particular location or a type of location in order to set the research in context and provide some 'local colour'.

Everyday life

The idea of simply observing *everyday life* as an approach to studying society is particularly associated with Erving Goffman (1959), who was concerned with the ways individuals interact with one another in public and private places. One area in which these ideas have been applied is sports coaching, although the research on this topic reviewed by Jones *et al.* (2011, 2012) typically involved interviews as well as observation, with the latter often conducted as a component of a participant observation exercise.

Social behaviour

Observation has been used in sociological research to develop ideas and theories about social behaviour in specific milieux and generally. The research of Fiske (1983) and Grant (1984) on the use of beaches and Marsh and his colleagues (1978) on football fans are examples of this approach. These researchers use an interactive, inductive process to build explanations of social behaviour from what they observe. Very often a key feature of such studies is the way the researchers seek to contrast what they have observed with what has apparently been observed – or assumed to be taking place – by others, particularly those with influence or authority, such as officials, police and the media. Observational research can challenge existing stereotypical interpretations of events.

Main elements of observational research

Observation might seem to be essentially a simple research method with little 'technique' to consider. However, as with any research method, careful thought must go into the design, conduct and analysis stages of a project. In structured observation what is mainly required from the researcher is precision, painstaking attention to detail, and patience. In unstructured observation

---

1. Choice of site(s)
2. Choice of observation point(s)
3. Choice of observation time-period(s)
4. Continuous observation or sampling?
5. Number and length of sampling periods
6. Deciding what to observe
7. Division of site into zones
8. Determination of information-recording method
9. Conducting the observation
10. Analysing/interpreting data

Figure 8.4   Steps in an observation project

the same skills and attributes are required but, in addition, there is a need for a creative 'eye' which can perceive the significance and potential meanings of what is being observed and relate this to the research question. The main tasks in planning and conducting an observational project are as set out in Figure 8.4.

As with the 'elements of the research process' **(outlined in Chapter 3)**, it is difficult to produce a list of steps which will cover all eventualities. In particular, if the approach is unstructured rather than structured, then a number of the steps discussed here, particularly those concerning counting, may be redundant.

Step 1: Choice of site(s)

In the case of a provider-organisation's in-house or consultancy research the sites to be studied may be fixed; but where there is an element of choice some time should be devoted to inspecting and choosing sites which will offer the appropriate sport behaviour but also provide suitable conditions for observation and/or will be typical of the ranges of types of site to be studied.

Step 2: Choice of observation point(s)

Choice of observation points within a site is clearly important and needs to be done with care. Some sites can be observed in their entirety from one spot. In other cases a circuit of viewing spots must be devised. For structured observation – for example involving counting the number of people present or passing a particular point over a period of time – it may be vital to conduct the observation from the same point(s) in various study periods, but for unstructured observation this may not be a consideration; indeed, exploring and observing from different locations within a site may be desirable.

When unstructured but intensive observation of people's behaviour is involved, it may be necessary to choose observation points which are unobtrusive to avoid attracting attention, particularly in a confined space with relatively few people. This is related to the issue of the method of recording observations, as discussed in Step 8 below, since some forms of formal record-ing are more obvious than others.

Step 3: Choice of observation time-period(s)

The choice of time-period is important because of variations in use of a site, by time of the year, day of the week, time of day or weather conditions, according to external social factors such as public holidays, or internal factors, such as the type of programme – and hence of patron – offered on particular days at a sport facility. Observation to cover all time-periods may be very demanding in terms of resources, so some form of sampling of time-periods will usually be necessary.

Step 4: Continuous observation or sampling?

Decisions on whether to undertake continuous observation or to sample differ-ent time-periods will depend on the resources available and the nature of the site and the overall design of the project. The issue is particularly important if one of the aims of the research is to obtain an accurate estimate of the number of visitors to the site, when the terminology used to refer to the two approaches is *continuous counts* versus *spot counts*. It could, for example, be very expensive to place observers at the numerous gates of a large urban park for as much as 100 hours in a week to count the number of sporting users during all the time the park is open. Even if that were possible it is unlikely that resources would be available to cover a whole year – except using automatic mechanical devices. A sampling approach must be adopted in most observation projects. Having decided to sample, it is of course necessary to decide how often to do this. This is discussed further under Step 5.

   If counting is being undertaken there is also a decision to be made as to whether to count the number of people *entering* or *leaving* the site during speci-fied time-periods or the number of people *present* at particular points in time. Counting the number of people present is, a form of spot count. Counting the number of people entering or leaving over a period of time generally consti-tutes continuous counting, but if the time-periods are relatively short – for example half an hour or an hour – then the results can be seen as a form of spot count. Counting the number of people present at particular points in time is generally less resource intensive since it can be done by one person regardless of the number of entrances to the site, and can provide information on the spa-tial use of the site at the same time. Thus one person, at specified times, makes a circuit of the site and records the numbers of people present in designated zones (see Step 7).

   When unstructured observation is being undertaken it is more likely that continuous observation will be adopted since the aim will generally be to observe the dynamics of events and behaviour at the site. However, the ques-tion of when to undertake such observation in order to cover all aspects of the use of the site still needs careful consideration.

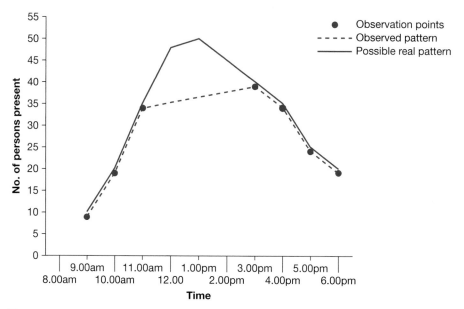

Figure 8.5   Counts of site use

Step 5: Count frequency

When the study involves counts of users, how often should the counts be undertaken? This will depend to a large extent on the rate of change in the level of use of the site. For example, the seven counts in Figure 8.5 are clearly insufficient since, if the broken line is the pattern of use observed in a research project, but the unbroken line is the true pattern, the research would have inaccurately represented the true situation. There is little advice that can be given to overcome this problem, except to sample frequently at the beginning of a project until the basic patterns of peaks and troughs in usage have been established; subsequently it may be possible to sample less often.

Step 6: What to observe

One approach to observing the spatial behaviour of visitors within a site is to record numbers of users present as indicated in Figure 8.6. In addition to observing numbers of people and their positions, it is possible to observe and record different types of activity or inactivity. It is also possible, to a limited extent, to record user characteristics. For instance, men and women could be separately identified and it is possible to distinguish between children and adults and to distinguish senior citizens, although, if a number of people are involved as counters, care will need to be taken over the dividing line between such categories as child, teenager, young adult, adult and elderly person. It is also possible, again with care, to observe the size of parties using a site, especially if they are observed arriving or leaving at a car park.

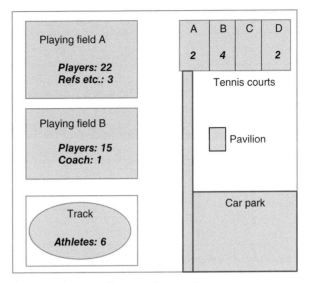

Figure 8.6 Observed use of a sports centre

These additional items of information would, of course, complicate the recording sheet and symbols would be necessary to record the different types of person on a map. Care needs to be taken not to make the data collection so complicated that it becomes too difficult for the observers to observe and collect, and leads to inaccuracies. This is one of those situations where it is necessary to consider carefully *why* the data are being collected and not to get carried away with data collection for its own sake.

The objectives of the research could be significantly more than just recording usage levels. More complex, qualitative, research, for example studying the interactions of participants in the use of a facility, may require an entirely different research strategy, since 'hanging around', with or without a clipboard or notebook, may not be acceptable. Participant observation, or the use of interviewing to gain an entrée to the facility, may be necessary.

Car registration numbers can be a useful source of information. First, they can provide information on where people have travelled from. Second, number plates can be used to trace the movement of vehicles within an area – for instance within a national park with a number of stopping points.

Step 7: Division of site into zones

In large sites it is advisable to divide the site into areas or zones and record the number of people and their activities within those zones, as indicated in Figure 8.6. The zones in this case refer to specific facilities.

Site	Observer	Date	Start time		Finish time	
	Skateboard Park	Track	Tennis Court A	Tennis Court B	Tennis Court C	Tennis Court D
Participants						
Referees etc.						
Spectators						
Comments						

Figure 8.7 Observation recording sheet: counts

Step 8: Recording information

Figure 8.7 provides an example of a counting sheet for recording usage information. The data collected using such a form are ideal for storage, manipulation and presentation in graphic form using a spreadsheet computer program as discussed in Step 10 below. Space is also provided for comments. In the case of unstructured observation, the 'comments' section could be much more extensive, perhaps requiring a separate sheet for each facility.

Step 9: Conducting the observation

In the case of a structured observational project, if the project has been well planned then the actual conduct should be straightforward. The main danger in a major project involving a lot of counting can be boredom, leading to inaccuracies in observing and recording data. It is therefore advisable to vary the work of those involved, with, where appropriate, data collectors being involved in alternate spells of behavioural observation and counting and, where possible, being switched between sites. Counting can be done manually or using a hand-held mechanical counter.

In the case of unstructured observational projects, more demands are placed on the observer. Such a project is, in effect, a visual form of the qualitative type of research **(see Chapter 9)**. The observer is required to observe and describe what is going on at the site, but must also engage directly with the research questions of the project in order to determine what to observe and what aspects of the observed scene should be described and recorded and at least begin the process of explanation.

Table 8.1 Observed sporting use of a park

	Inactive	Jogging	Skateboarding	Tennis	Total
	No. of people observed				
8 am	0	6	0	0	6
9 am	5	4	5	0	14
10 am	6	2	7	2	17
11 am	15	4	12	6	37
12 am	20	6	15	6	47
1 pm	22	12	17	10	61
2 pm	30	14	18	6	68
3 pm	25	10	15	6	56
4 pm	20	6	22	4	52
5 pm	22	12	19	12	65
6 pm	22	4	12	6	44
7 pm	10	0	12	4	26
Total	197	80	154	62	493
Average	16.4	6.7	12.8	5.2	41.1

Step 10: Analysing data

In some cases of structured observation, the visual presentation of the sort presented in Figure 8.6 constitutes the analysis. In other cases, data must be analysed and processed to present usable results. Four examples are presented here: presentation of usage patterns over the course of a day; estimating usage numbers from spot count data; weighting; and analysis of unstructured data.

Usage patterns

Consider the set of counts shown in Table 8.1, which relate to the numbers of active/non-active people present in a park, which opens at 8 a.m. and closes at 7 p.m. This pattern is illustrated graphically in Figure 8.8. This presentation may be sufficient for the project in hand, but it can be taken further, including converting the sample counts into an estimate of overall use numbers.

Estimating usage numbers

It is estimated in the example that there is an average of 41.1 people in the park, over a twelve-hour period, giving a total of 493 *visitor-hours*. The number of visitor-hours is a valid measure of use in its own right and could be used to compare different sites or to compare the performance of the same site over time. But, for example, twelve visitor-hours could result from:

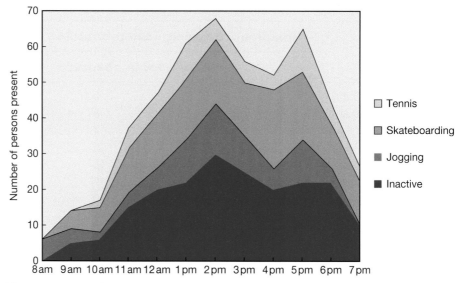

Figure 8.8   Park usage pattern

- one person visiting the park and staying all day;

- two people staying six hours each;

- twelve people staying one hour each; or

- twenty-four people staying half an hour each.

So if an estimate is required of the number of different *persons* visiting the park over the course of the day, additional information, on the *length of stay*, is necessary – this would usually be obtained from a questionnaire-based user survey, although it might possibly be obtained from detailed observation of a sample of groups. In the example in Table 8.2, the average length of stay for tennis players is 2 hours, so every user-hour represents 0.5 of a user, and the 62 user-hours indicate a total of 31 tennis players for the day. Thus the number of visitors is equal to the number of user-hours divided by the average length of stay.

Weighting

Details of user characteristics obtained from observation can be used as a check on the accuracy of sampling in interview surveys and may be used to *weight* the results of such surveys so that the final result is a better reflection of the characteristics of the users of the facility. This is similar to the time-of-day correction discussed above, but relates to the personal characteristics of users, rather than their time of use of the facility. For instance, if it was found by observation that half the users of a site were women but in an interview survey only a third of those interviewed were women, the women in the sample could be given a greater weighting at the analysis stage so that their views and attitudes would

Table 8.2 Estimating daily visit numbers from count data

	Data	Source	Inactive	Jogging	Skate-boarding	Tennis	Total
A	Avge no. of users present	Table 8.1	16.4	6.7	12.8	5.2	41.1
B	No. of hours open/day	Table 8.1	12.0	12.0	12.0	12.0	12.0
C	No. of user-hours	A x B	197.0	80.0	154.0	62.0	493.0
D	Average length of stay	User survey	0.5	0.3	2.0	2.0	1.6
E	No. of visits/day	C/D	394.0	267.0	77.0	31.0	769.0

receive due emphasis. **(The details of weighting are described more fully in Chapter 16.)**

Qualitative analysis

The raw form of the data from unstructured, qualitative, observation is likely to comprise a set of notes, possibly with some numbers, and probably with some diagrams. The immediate task for the researcher is therefore to ensure that these notes are in a readable form for future reference; this may involve writing or typing them out to provide a narrative. In the course of doing this, a start may be made on the analysis process. For example, the absence of a particular group of users on one occasion and their presence on another occasion may be linked to the absence or presence of another group or some other change in the environment. The result is therefore likely to be an extended set of notes which can be seen as comparable with sets of notes or transcripts from other forms of qualitative research. Similar approaches to analysis are therefore appropriate, including identification of themes and patterns. The inductive interaction between data collection, data analysis and theory development which applies to qualitative research generally also applies to unstructured observational research. The NVivo software **(see Chapter 15)** might also be used to analyse notes from observational research.

Use of technology

Automatic counters

Automatic counters are available for vehicles and pedestrians. Vehicle counters are based on one of four technologies:

- induction loop buried under the roadway: creates a magnetic field which detects vehicles passing through it – this option is relatively permanent and expensive due to installation costs;

- pressure pad or tube: vehicles passing over the pad or tube complete an electrical circuit – this is cheaper than induction loop, but limited life due to wear and tear;

- infra-red beam: vehicle is recorded when it breaks the beam – the cheapest option;

- CCTV (closed circuit television): software can be used to analyse the images and count vehicles passing in view of the camera.

In each case, the device is attached to computerised equipment which can produce a variety of reports for users, for example hourly, daily, weekly, monthly or annual counts and trend analysis. The technologies can generally detect vehicles of different types/sizes, for example motorcycles, passenger vehicles, heavy vehicles.

Infra-red beams and CCTV can also be used to count pedestrian movements. But because pedestrians do not necessarily cross the beam one at a time, the counters may have to be *calibrated* using some direct observational data collected for a sample period. For example, direct visual counts may reveal that, in a certain location, a count of 100 on the automatic counter may represent, say, 120 individuals.

Cyclists sometimes use roadways, where they may be picked up by traffic counters, or they may use exclusive cycleways, where infra-red devices can be used. Where they share paths with pedestrians, the mix of pedestrians and cyclists would need to be determined by calibration based on direct observation as discussed above.

One of the disadvantages of these devices is their fixed nature; one device can only monitor one route or pathway. Locating a device at every point or site entrance of interest may be expensive and moving them around on a roster may be costly. Again, calibration using a period of direct visual counts may be the solution. For example, if direct counts revealed that the main entrance to a site typically accounted for half of all visits, the counts from an automatic counter located at that entrance would need to be doubled to provide an estimate of total visits.

GPS

Global positioning systems, based on satellite technology, can be used to track the movement of people in space and this can clearly be applied in sporting contexts. Players can wear devices which record the distances they travel and speeds during the course of a training session or match, and this can be transmitted to a base computer in real time, as can be seen on some television sport broadcasts. Much of the early research in this field was methodological, testing satellite-based systems against traditional ground-based systems as used, for example, in sprint training. But in recent years the technology has proved itself and is used for substantive research, as indicated in the Resources section.

Aerial photography

The use of aerial photography is well developed in geography and geology, where a whole sub-discipline of *remote sensing* has developed using a variety of techniques. It can also be effective in sport research. Where large areas are concerned, such as coastlines and estuaries (e.g. sailing, fishing) or a multi-sport complex (e.g. Olympic Games sites) attracting large crowds or where access is difficult and use of the site is very scattered, aerial photography may be the only way of obtaining estimates of levels and patterns of use. In harbours and estuaries it is probably the best means of obtaining estimates of numbers of craft using the area, since, as they are generally moving about in random patterns, it can be difficult to count manually on a crowded waterway. Needless to say, a good quality camera is needed for such work.

Still photography and video: visual research

The value of ordinary, land-based, photography as an adjunct to direct observation should not be overlooked. Digital still photography and video editing software have made the incorporation of visual material into research increasingly easy. The level of crowding of a site, its nature, atmosphere and usage patterns can be conveyed to the reader of a report with the aid of photographs. Particular problems, for instance of erosion, or design faults, can be conveyed better visually than verbally – a picture speaks a thousand words. A 'photo-essay' can be composed around a number of themes or messages to convey simple research findings. Video can be used to record patterns of use of a site. As noted in relation to automatic counters and CCTV, software now exists to perform some types of analysis of digital images. The medium can provide a useful illustration of 'before' and 'after' situations, to illustrate the nature of problems on a site and the effect of measures to ameliorate the problems – for example congestion, erosion or littering.

A distinct tradition of 'visual research' has emerged in social research, which is based largely on photography and has its own journal, *Visual Sociology*, and a growing literature in sport (see Resources section).

Time-lapse photography

Time-lapse photography lies somewhere between still photography and video. A time-lapse camera can be set up to take pictures of a scene automatically, say, every ten seconds or every minute. The resultant sequence of pictures can then be projected as a film or video to show the speeded-up pattern of use of the area viewed. This is the technique used in wildlife documentaries which show a plant apparently growing before your eyes, but it can also be used to show the changing pattern of use of a sport site.

Just looking

Finally, we should not forget just how important it is to use our eyes in research, even if the research project does not involve systematic observational data collection. Familiarity with a sport activity or site helps in the design of a good research project and aids in interpreting data. Many studies have been based just on informal, but careful, observation. Not all useful information is in the form of numbers. Careful observation of what is happening in a particular sport situation, at a particular facility or type of facility or among a particular group of people can be a more appropriate research approach in some circumstances than the use of questionnaires or even informal interviews. The good researcher is all eyes.

Summary

This chapter is concerned with the neglected technique of observation – *looking* – as a tool for research in sport studies. It is noted that observation can be formalised or structured, involving counting of sporting site or facility users and strict time and space sampling methods, or it can be informal or unstructured. In general, observation is non-intrusive in the study site, but 'contrived observation', as in the experimental method, is also possible. Participant observation is a further type of observational research **(see Chapter 9)**. Observational research spans the quantitative/qualitative methodological spectrum and can therefore involve both quantitative and qualitative analysis methods. A number of sport or physical activity situations is described in which observation methods might be used, including: children's active play; the usage of informal sport/physical activity areas where no entrance fee is required and capacity and use patterns are not constrained by factors such as formal seating or booking systems; spatial and functional patterns of use of sites; user profiles; studying deviant behaviour; mystery shopping; research which is complementary to research conducted using other methods; everyday life; and social behaviour. The chapter outlines the observational research process in ten steps: 1. choice of study site(s); 2. choice of observation point(s); 3. choice of observation time-period(s); 4. deciding on continuous observation or sampling; 5. deciding on the number and length of sampling periods; 6. deciding what to observe; 7. division of the study site(s) into zones; 8. recording observational information; 9. conducting the observation; and 10. analysing data. Finally, brief consideration is given to various technological aids, including: automatic counters; GPS devices; and still, video and time-lapse cameras.

Test questions

1. Four types of observational research are identified at the beginning of the chapter. What are they?

2. A total of eight situations are described where observation is a suitable, and sometimes the *most* suitable, form of research. Name three of these situations and explain in each case why observation is a suitable research method.

3. What is the difference between spot counting and continuous counting?

4. In what forms can data from observational research be presented?

5. How can observational research findings assist in regard to weighting of survey data?

Exercises

1. Select an informal sport site and position yourself in an unobtrusive location, but where you can see what is going on. Over a period of two hours, record what happens. Write a report on: how the site is used; who it is used by; how many people use it; what conflicts there are, if any, between different groups of users; and how the design aids or hinders the activity which people engage in on the site.

2. Establish a counting system to record the number of people present in a sport site at hourly intervals during the course of a day. Estimate the number of visitor-hours at the site for the day.

3. In relation to exercise 2: conduct interviews with three or four visitors each hour, and ask them how long they have stayed, or expect to stay, at the site. Establish the average length of stay and, using this information and the data from exercise 2, estimate the number of persons visiting the site in the course of the day.

4. Use photographs to record examples of neglect or damage to sport sites known to you.

5. Choose a sport journal and identify a study that uses observation exclusively and one that uses observation as part of a mixed methods approach. Identify what is observed, how it is observed and how the results are analysed and presented.

Resources

- General/methodological: Adler and Adler (1994), Kellehear (1993), Wagner *et al.* (2010).

- Automated vehicle/pedestrian counters: Green Space (1998).

- Children: McKenzie (2002), Welk *et al.* (2000).

  - SOFIT (System For Observing Fitness Instruction Time): McKenzie (2009), McKenzie *et al.* (1991).

- GPS: Aughey (2011), Hartwig *et al.* (2008), Jennings *et al.* (2010).

- Measuring and Observation Tool in Sport (MOTS): Castellano *et al.* (2008).

- Mystery shopping: general: Dawson and Hillier (1995).

- Photography: Jones *et al.* (2012).

- Qualitative observation: Lofland and Lofland (1984), Moxham and Wiseman (2009).

- Sport-related studies using observation:

  - General: Birenbaum and Sagarin (1973);

  - Children: play: Child (1983); sport: Newland *et al.* (2012);

  - Sporting crowds/riots/hooliganism: Cunneen *et al.* (1989), Cunneen and Lynch (1988); football: Frosdick and Mars (2012), Gee (2010), Marsh *et al.* (1978), Pearson (2009);

  - Stadium security: Cieslak (2009);

  - Team sport movement patterns: Camerino *et al.* (2012: Chapter 2, 31–81);

  - Beach use: Fiske (1983), Grant (1984), Douglas *et al.* (1977);

  - Food environments at sport facilities: Chaumette *et al.* (2009).

- Structured vs. unstructured observation: Bryman and Bell (2003).

- Video: Arnberger and Eder (2008), Enomoto and Saito (2009), Frosdick (2010), Krahnstoever *et al.* (2009).

- Visual methods: Physical culture: Phoenix (2010); GPS vs. camera technology for measuring athlete movement: Duffield *et al.* (2010) **(see Case study 11.8c)**; sport coaching: Jones *et al.* (2012); Olympic Games: *Visual Sociology* (2012), special issue; Visual methods in physical cultures: *Qualitative Research in Sport and Exercise* (2010), special issue.

References

Adler, P. A. and Adler, P. (1994) Observational techniques. In N. K. Denzin and Y. S. Lincoln (eds) *Handbook of Qualitative Research.* Thousand Oaks, CA: Sage, 377–92.

Arnberger, A. and Eder, R. (2008) Assessing user interactions on shared recreational trails by long-term video monitoring. *Managing Leisure*, 13(1), 36–51.

Aughey, R. J. (2011) Applications of GPS technologies in field sports. *International Journal of Sports Physiology and Performance*, 6(2), 295–310.

Birenbaum, A. and Sagarin, E. (eds) (1973) *People in Places: The Sociology of the Familiar.* London: Nelson.

Bryman, A. and Bell, E. (2003) Breaking down the quantitative/qualitative divide, and Combining quantitative and qualitative research. Chapters 21–22 of *Business Research Methods.* Oxford: Oxford University Press, 465–94.

Camarino, O., Castaner, M. and Anguera, M. T. (eds) (2012) *Mixed Methods Research in the Movement Sciences.* London: Routledge.

Castellano, J., Perea, A., Alday, L. and Hernández Mendo, A. (2008) The measuring and observation tool in sports. *Behavior Research Methods*, 40(3), 898–905.

Chaumette, P., Morency, S., Royer, A., Lemieux, S. and Tremblay, A. (2009). The food environment at sports, recreational and cultural facilities in Quebec City: the current situation. *Canadian Journal of Public Health*, 100(4), 310–14.

Child, E. (1983) Play and culture: a study of English and Asian children. *Leisure Studies*, 2(2), 169–86.

Cieslak, T. J. (2009) Match day security at Australian sport stadia: a case study of eight venues. *Event Management*, 13(1), 43–52.

Cunneen, C. and Lynch, R. (1988) The social meaning of conflict in riots at the Australian Grand Prix motorcycle races. *Leisure Studies*, 7(1), 1–20.

Cunneen, C., Findlay, M., Lynch, R. and Tupper, V. (1989) *Dynamics of Collective Conflict: Riots at the Bathurst 'Bike Races'.* North Ryde, NSW: Law Book Co.

Dawson, J. and Hillier, J. (1995) Competitor mystery shopping: methodological considerations and implications for the MRS Code of Conduct. *Journal of the Market Research Society*, 37(4), 417–43.

Douglas, J. D., Rasmussen, P. K. and Flanagan, C. A. (1977) *The Nude Beach.* Beverly Hills, CA: Sage.

Duffield, R., Reid, M., Baker, J. and Spratford, W. (2010) Accuracy and reliability of GPS devices for measurement of movement patterns in confined spaces for court-based sports. *Journal of Science and Medicine in Sport*, 13(7), 523–5.

Enomoto, A. and Saito, H. (2009) AR display for observing sports events based on camera tracking using pattern of ground. In R. Shumaker (ed.) *Virtual and Mixed Reality: Third International Conference, VMR 2009, Proceedings.* New York: Springer, 421–30.

Fiske, J. (1983) Surfalism and sandiotics: the beach in Oz popular culture. *Australian Journal of Cultural Studies*, 1(2), 120–49.

Frosdick, S. (2010) Policing, safety and security in public assembly facilities. *International Journal of Police Science and Management*, 12(1), 81–9.

Frosdick, S. and Mars, G. (2012) 10 safety cultures in British sports grounds. In S. Frosdick and L. Walley (eds) *Sports and Safety Management*. Burlington, MA: Butterworth-Heinemann, 136–50.

Gee, C. J. (2010) Using a direct observation methodology to study aggressive behavior in ice hockey: the good, the bad, and the ugly. *Journal of Behavioral Health and Medicine*, 1(1), 79–90.

Goffman, I. (1959) *The Presentation of Self in Everyday Life*. Garden City, NY: Doubleday/Anchor.

Grant, D. (1984) Another look at the beach. *Australian Journal of Cultural Studies*, 2(2), 131–8.

Green Space (1998) *A Guide to Automated Methods for Counting Visitors to Parks and Green Spaces*. Reading, UK: Green Space, available at: www.green-space.org.uk (Accessed May 2013).

Hartwig, T. B., Naughton, G. and Searl, J. (2008) Defining the volume and intensity of sport participation in adolescent rugby union players. *International Journal of Sports Physiology and Performance*, 3(1), 94–106.

Jennings, D., Cormack, S., Coutts, A. J., Boyd, L. and Aughey, R. J. (2010) The validity and reliability of GPS units for measuring distance in team sport specific running patterns. *International Journal of Sports Physiology and Performance*, 5(3), 328–41.

Jones, R. L., Potrac, P., Cushion, C., Ronglan, L. T. and Davey, C. (2011) Erving Goffman: interaction and impression management. In R. L. Jones, P. Potrac, C. Cushion and L. T. Ronglan (eds) *The Sociology of Sports Coaching*. London: Routledge, 15–26.

Jones, R., Santos, S., Mesquita, I. and Gilbourne, D. (2012) Visual methods in coaching research: capturing everyday lives. In K. Armour and D. Macdonald (eds) *Research Methods in Physical Education and Youth Sport*. London: Routledge, 263–75.

Kellehear, A. (1993) *The Unobtrusive Researcher: A Guide to Methods*. Sydney: Allen & Unwin.

Krahnstoever, N., Tu, P., Yu, T., Patwardhan, K. and Doretto, G. (2009) Intelligent video for protecting crowded sports venues. Paper presented at the *Advanced Video and Signal Based Surveillance, 2009, Sixth IEEE International Conference*, Genoa, Italy, September, available at: http://ieeexplore.ieee.org (Accessed May 2013).

Lofland, J. and Lofland, L. H. (1984) *Analyzing Social Settings: A Guide to Qualitative Observation and Analysis, Second edn*. Belmont, CA: Wadsworth.

Marsh, P., Rosser, E. and Harré, R. (1978) *The Rules of Disorder*. London: Routledge.

McKenzie, T. L. (2002) Use of direct observation to assess physical activity. In G. J. Welk (ed.) *Physical Activity Assessments for Health-Related Research*. Champaign IL: Human Kinetics, 179–96.

McKenzie, T. L. (2009) *SOFIT: System for Observing Fitness Instruction Time: Generic Description and Procedures Manual.* San Diego, CA: Active Living Research, available at: www.activelivingresearch/node/11944 (Accessed May 2013).

McKenzie, T. L., Salis, J. F. and Nader, P. R. (1991) SOFIT: System for Observing Fitness Instruction Time. *Journal for Teaching in Physical Education*, 11(2), 195–205.

Moxham, C. and Wiseman, F. (2009) Examining the development, delivery and measurement of service quality in the fitness industry: a case study. *Total Quality Management and Business Excellence*, 20(5), 467–82.

Newland, B., Dixon, M. A. and Green, B. C. (2012) Engaging children through sport: examining the disconnect between program vision and implementation. *Journal of Physical Activity and Health*, 9(10).

Pearson, G. (2009) The researcher as hooligan: where 'participant' observation means breaking the law. *International Journal of Social Research Methodology*, 12(3), 243–55.

Phoenix, C. (2010) Seeing the world of physical culture: the potential of visual methods for qualitative research in sport and exercise. *Qualitative Research in Sport and Exercise*, 2(2), 93–108.

Spaaij, R. (2008) Men like us, boys like them: violence, masculinity, and collective identity in football hooliganism. *Journal of Sport and Social Issues*, 32(4), 369–92.

Qualitative Research in Sport and Exercise (2010) Special issue: Visual methods in physical cultures, 2(2).

Van der Zande, A. N. (1985) Distribution patterns of visitors in large areas: a problem of measurement and analysis. *Leisure Studies*, 4(1), 85–100.

Visual Sociology (2012) Special issue: Olympic Games, 10(1–2).

Wagner, U., Storm, R. K. and Hoberman, J. M. (2010) *Observing Sport: Modern System Theoretical Approaches.* Schorndorf, Germany: Hofmann.

Welk, G. J. (ed.) (2002) *Physical Activity Assessments for Health-Related Research.* Champaign IL: Human Kinetics.

Welk, G. J., Corbin, C. B. and Dale, D. (2000) Measurement issues in the assessment of physical activity in children. *Research Quarterly for Exercise and Sport*, 71(2), 59–73.

Qualitative methods: introduction and data collection

Introduction

This chapter addresses methods of research which involve the collection and analysis of *qualitative* information using the media of words, images or sounds, as distinct from numbers as used in quantitative methods. The chapter discusses the nature and advantages of qualitative methods, their role in research and the range of specific methods available, including in-depth interviews, group interviews/focus groups, participant observation, biographical methods and ethnographic approaches. The qualitative analysis of *texts* is also discussed.

For most qualitative research methods, data collection, analysis and interpretation are intermingled, rather than being functionally and temporally separated as is generally the case in quantitative methods. Nevertheless, distinct data collection and analysis processes can be identified and analysis procedures tend to have common characteristics across the range of qualitative data collection methods; qualitative data analysis is discussed in Part III of the book **(see Chapter 15)**.

The nature of qualitative methods

The term *qualitative* is used to describe research methods and techniques which use, and give rise to, qualitative rather than quantitative information, that is, information in the form of words, images and sounds rather than numbers. In general, the qualitative approach tends to collect a large amount of detailed (sometimes referred to as 'rich or 'thick') information about relatively few cases or subjects rather than the more limited information about a large number of cases or subjects which is typical of quantitative research. It is, however, possible to envisage qualitative research which actually deals with large numbers of cases. For example, a research project on sports spectators, involving observation and participation in spectator activity, could involve information relating, collectively, to tens of thousands of people.

Qualitative methods may be used for pragmatic reasons, in situations where formal, quantified research is not necessary or is not possible, but there are also theoretical grounds for using such methods. Qualitative research is generally based on the belief that the people personally involved in a particular (sporting) situation are best placed to describe and explain their experiences, motivations and world-view in their own words, and that they should be allowed to speak without the intermediary of the researcher and without being overly constrained by the framework imposed by the researcher. This identification of research methodology with a particular ontology can, however, be carried too far. For example, in the introduction to their book, *Qualitative Methods in Sports Studies*, Andrews, Mason and Silk (2006: 10) associate qualitative methods with particular political agendas. Any one political agenda can be pursued using a variety of research methods **(see discussion of action research in Chapter 5)**.

Merits, functions, limitations

Some of the merits of qualitative methods in the sport research context include (after Kelly, 1980) the following:

1. The method corresponds with a key aspect of the nature of the phenomenon being studied – that is, participation in sport is a qualitative experience for the individual.

2. The method 'brings people back in' to sport research and involves studying them 'in the round', as discussed by Maguire (1991). By contrast, quantitative methods tend to be very impersonal – *real* people with names and unique personalities do not generally feature.

3. The results of qualitative research are more understandable to people who are not statistically trained.

4. The method is better able to encompass personal change over time – by contrast, much quantitative research tends to look only at current behaviour as related to current social, economic and environmental circumstances, ignoring the fact that most people's behaviour is heavily influenced by their life history and experience.

5. Sport involves a great deal of face-to-face interaction between people – involving symbols, gestures, etc. – and qualitative research is well suited to investigating this.

6. Qualitative techniques are better at providing an understanding of people's needs and aspirations, although some researchers in the psychological field in particular might disagree with this proposition.

In this book it has been argued that different methods are not inherently good or bad, but just more or less appropriate for the task in hand. Thus, to some extent, the above comments relate to particular types of research with particular purposes. For example, qualitative methods would clearly be most appropriate if the focus of interest is: the qualitative experience of sport; personal sport histories; the use of symbols, gestures, etc. in sport contexts; people's sport needs and aspirations; and/or communicating with an audience without statistical training.

Peterson (1994), speaking from a market researcher's perspective, lists the potential uses of qualitative research as:

1. to develop hypotheses concerning relevant behaviour and attitudes;

2. to identify the full range of issues, views and attitudes which should be pursued in larger-scale research;

3. to suggest methods for quantitative enquiry – for example in terms of deciding who should be included in interview surveys;

4. to identify language used to address relevant issues (thus avoiding the use of jargon in questionnaires, or using it appropriately);

5. to understand how a buying decision is made – questionnaire surveys are not very good at exploring *processes;*

6. to develop new product, service or marketing strategy ideas – the free play of attitudes and opinions can be a rich source of ideas for the marketer;

7. to provide an initial screening of new product, service or strategy ideas;

8. to learn how communications are received – what is understood and how – particularly related to advertising.

On the grounds that qualitative methods are often used for certain purposes or in certain contexts, there is a tendency to associate them definitively with such purposes and contexts. For example, Hastie and Glotova (2012: 310) declare that 'qualitative research is, by definition, exploratory', while quantitative research is 'essentially conclusive'. It may often be the case that qualitative research is used for exploratory purposes and quantitative research is used to reach conclusions by testing theories, but it is not always the case. Quantitative secondary data analysis can be exploratory **(see Chapter 14)** and experimental research is often exploratory in nature **(see Chapter 11)**. Furthermore, qualitative research reports often draw quite strong conclusions (Olive and Thorpe, 2011).

While partisan proponents of qualitative methods are vigorous in promoting their virtues, like all methods, they also have their limitations. For example, Miles and Huberman, in their book on *Qualitative Data Analysis*, note the substantial increase in the prevalence of qualitative research in the social sciences, but caution:

> in the flurry of this activity, we should be mindful of some pervasive issues that have not gone away. These issues include the labour-intensiveness (and extensiveness over months or years) of [qualitative] data collection, frequent data overload, the distinct possibility of researcher bias, the time demands of processing and coding data, the adequacy of sampling when only a few cases can be managed, the generalizability of findings, the credibility and quality of conclusions, and their utility in the world of policy and action. (Miles and Huberman, 1994: 2)

The qualitative research process

Qualitative methods generally require, and enable, a more flexible, although no less rigorous, approach to overall research design and conduct than other approaches. Most quantitative research tends to be *sequential* in nature; the components of research **(see Chapter 3)** tend to be distinct and follow in a pre-planned sequence. This is inevitable because of the nature of the typical quantitative core primary data collection task. Much qualitative research involves a more fluid relationship between the various elements of the research – an approach which might be called *recursive.* In this approach hypothesis formation evolves as the research progresses, data analysis and collection take place concurrently and writing is also often evolutionary and ongoing, rather than a separate process which takes place at the end of the project. The two approaches are represented diagrammatically in Figure 9.1.

Although the sequential and recursive models are presented here in the context of a contrast between quantitative and qualitative methods, in fact both quantitative and qualitative methods can involve sequential and recursive approaches. Thus, it is possible for an essentially quantitative study to involve a variety of data sources and a number of small-scale studies, which build on one another in an iterative way. On the other hand, it is also possible for an essentially qualitative study to be conducted on a large scale, with a single data source – for example, a nation-wide study of managers of professional sports clubs, involving fairly standardised in-depth interviews.

An important philosophical perspective in the analysis of qualitative data is the concept of *grounded theory* developed by two sociologists, Barney Glaser and Anselm Strauss (1967). Grounded theory is concerned with the generation

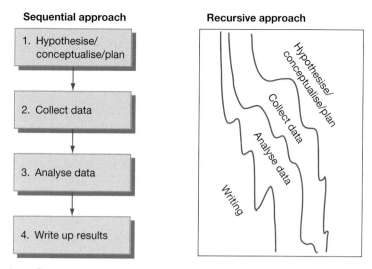

Sequential approach

1. Hypothesise/
   conceptualise/plan

2. Collect data

3. Analyse data

4. Write up results

Recursive approach

*Hypothesise/
conceptualise/plan*

Collect data

Analyse data

Writing

Figure 9.1 Sequential and recursive approaches

of theory from empirical research, as opposed to research that tests *a priori* theory. It is therefore inductive rather than deductive **(see Chapter 2)**. In this paradigm, theories and models should be *grounded* in real empirical observations rather than being governed by traditional methodologies and theories. In the generation of theory the researcher approaches the data with minimal pre-formed notions in mind, instead seeking to uncover patterns and contradictions through close examination of the data. To achieve this, the researcher needs to be very familiar with the data, the subjects and the cultural context of the research. The process is a complex and personal one.

One way in which qualitative research has been characterised is by referring to the researcher as the 'research instrument', in contrast to, for example, the survey method where the research instrument is a questionnaire.

The range of qualitative methods – introduction

Qualitative techniques commonly used in sport research and which are discussed in more detail in this chapter include: in-depth interviews; group interviews or focus groups; participant observation; textual analysis; biographical methods; and ethnography. The basic characteristics of these approaches are summarised in Figure 9.2.

As indicated above, while data collection and data analysis are, in practice, often difficult to separate in qualitative research, the discussions of individual methods below concentrate on data collection.

In-depth interviews	• Usually conducted with a relatively small number of subjects. • Interview guided by a *checklist* of topics rather than formal questionnaire. • Interviews often audio-recorded and notes or verbatim transcripts prepared. • Interviewing typically takes at least half an hour, and may extend over several hours. • Repeat/follow-up interviews possible.
Group interviews/ focus groups	• Interviews/discussions conducted with a group, typically from 5 to 12. • Process is managed by a *facilitator* who guides the discussion. • Interaction between subjects takes place as well as between facilitator and subjects. • Proceedings generally audio-recorded and notes or verbatim transcripts prepared.
Participant obser-vation	• Researcher gathers information by being an actual participant with the subjects being studied. • Researcher may be known by the subjects as a researcher or may be *incognito*.
Biographical re-search	• Focuses on individual full or partial life histories. • May involve in-depth interviews but also documentary evidence and subjects' own written accounts.
Textual analysis	• Analysis of the content of 'texts', including print and audio-visual media.
Ethnography and mixed methods	• Utilises a number of the above techniques rather than being a single technique – borrowed from anthropology.

Figure 9.2   Qualitative methods: summary

In-depth interviews

Nature

An in-depth interview, sometimes referred to as semi-structured, is character-ised by its length, depth and structure:

● *Length:* In-depth interviews tend to be much longer than questionnaire-based interviews, typically taking at least half an hour and sometimes sev-eral hours. The method may involve interviewing people more than once.

● *Depth:* As the name implies, the in-depth interview seeks to probe more deeply than is possible with a questionnaire-based interview. Rather than just asking a question, recording a simple answer and moving on, the in-depth interviewer typically encourages respondents to talk, asks supplementary questions and asks respondents to explain their answers.

● *Structure:* The in-depth interview is therefore less structured than a questionnaire-based interview. While questionnaire-based interviews may be seen as *structured*, in-depth interviews are seen as *semi-structured* or *unstructured*, as discussed further below. As a result, every interview in a qualitative study, although dealing with the same issues, will be different.

Arguably, interviews in general can be said to span part of a spectrum related to the extent to which the questions and their wording are fully pre-scribed in advance or not prescribed at all and the extent to which responses are pre-coded or open-ended. This is summarised in Figure 9.3, which shows that questionnaire-based and in-depth interviews overlap in the middle of the spectrum.

Purposes and situations

In-depth interviews tend to be used in three situations:

1. The subjects of the research may be relatively few in number, so a questionnaire-based, quantitative style of research would be inappropriate.

2. The information likely to be obtained from each subject is expected to vary considerably, and in complex ways. An example would be interviews with the management staff of a sports centre, or interviews with the coaches of different national sports teams. Each of these interviews would be different and would be a 'story' in its own right. In reporting the research it would be the unique nature and structure of each of these accounts which would be of interest – data on 'what percentage of respondents said what' would not be relevant.

3. A topic is to be explored as a preliminary stage in planning a larger study, possibly a quantitative study, such as a questionnaire-based survey.

Interview type	Question format	Responses	Interviewer/ interviewee interaction
Structured	Prescribed by questionnaire	Pre-coded and open-ended	Formal, consistent
Structured + semi-structured elements	Prescribed by questionnaire + supplementary	Open-ended	Mostly formal, consistent
Semi-structured	Checklist: question format not prescribed	Open-ended	Conversational, variable
Unstructured	Only the broad topic area is prescribed	Open-ended	Free-flowing conversational, variable

Figure 9.3   **Questions, responses and interview types**

Checklist

Rather than a formal questionnaire, the 'instrument' used for semi-structured in-depth interviews is often a *checklist* of topics to be raised, although a few key predetermined, prescribed questions may be included. For example, where a formal questionnaire might ask a question: 'Which of the following sports have you taken part in in the last year?', the informal interview checklist might simply include the words 'Recent sports'. The interviewer would shape the question according to the circumstances of a particular interview. If the interviewer is interested, for example, in the influence of childhood sport experiences on adult participation patterns, in some interviews it may be necessary to ask a specific question such as: 'What sports did you play as a child?' In other interviews, in response to the interviewer's initial question, the interviewee might talk at length and volunteer detailed information on childhood activity unprompted. It is then not necessary to ask the separate question. Thus in-depth interviews vary from interview to interview; they take on a life of their own.

The skill on the part of the interviewer is to ensure that all relevant topics are covered – even though they may be covered in different orders and in different ways in different interviews. This, however, assumes that the list of relevant topics is known from the beginning and is already covered by the checklist. In practice, the qualitative research allows the range of topics – and hence the content of the checklist – to evolve during the research process. New topics may emerge from interviewees themselves.

The design of the checklist should nevertheless be as methodical as the design of a formal questionnaire – in particular, the items to be included on the checklist should be based on the conceptual framework for the study and the resultant list of data needs, whether this be detailed or general in nature **(see Chapter 3)**. An example of a checklist is presented in Figure 9.4. The example given is in the form of a fairly terse list of topics. An alternative would be to include fully worded questions to initiate discussion of various topics, as would appear in a questionnaire; this may be advisable when a number of interviewers are involved. The problem with fully worded questions is that actually turning to the clipboard and reading out lengthy questions can interrupt the flow and informality of the interview. The more detailed the checklist, the more the interview would be described as *semi-structured*. If only a very brief checklist is used, or even none at all, the interview would be described as *unstructured*.

The interviewing process

Conducting a good in-depth interview could be said to require the skills of a good investigative journalist. As Dean and his colleagues put it:

> Many people feel that a newspaper reporter is a far cry from a social scientist. Yet many of the data of social science today are gathered by interviewing and observation techniques that resemble those of a skilled newspaper [reporter] … at work on

This is part of a checklist devised in connection with a study of people's participation in, and attitudes towards, sport.

Current sports/exercise	How often? Why?
Explore each one – compare	Where? – Home/away from home
	Who with?
	Meaning/importance
	Type of involvement/level achieved
Activities would like to do	Why?
Meaning 'to you' of:	'Fitness', 'sport'
Constraints:	Home
	Work – time/energy/colleagues
	Family roles
	Physical – build, health etc.
	Being a woman/man
	Being a parent
	Money/costs
	Car/transport
Past sport activity (why changes?)	At school, at college/univ.
	With family
Facilities	Locally favourite
	Use/non-use – why?
	Access
Clubs/associations	Membership/access/value
Personality	Skills
Dislikes	Aspirations

Figure 9.4 Example of a checklist for in-depth interviewing

the study of, say, a union strike or a political convention. It makes little sense for us to belittle these less rigorous methods as 'unscientific'. We will do better to study them and the techniques they involve so that we can make better use of them in producing scientific information. (*Dean, Eichhorn and Dean, quoted in McCall and Simmons, 1969: 1*)

There are two approaches to conducting an in-depth interview: standardised and informal or unstructured.

Standardised approach

The standardised approach is one in which the emphasis in 'semi-structured' is on the 'structured' and where elements of the traditional scientific approach are replicated. The interaction between researcher and subject is, as far as possible, similar for all subjects. So prescribed questions are used, although the interviewer also improvises, depending on the flow of the interview. In this case, an important skill in interviewing is to avoid becoming so taken up in the conversational style of the interview that the interviewee is 'led' by the interviewer. The interviewer avoids agreeing – or disagreeing – with the interviewee or suggesting answers. This is more difficult than it sounds, because in normal conversation we tend to make friendly noises and contribute to the discussion. In this situation the interviewer is torn between the need to maintain a friendly conversational atmosphere and the desire *not* to influence the interviewee's responses. Some of the carefully planned sequencing of questions which is built into formal questionnaires must be achieved by the interviewer being very sensitive and quick thinking. For example, having discovered that the respondent does not go to sports matches, the interviewer should not lead the respondent by saying: 'Is this because it is too expensive?' Rather, the interviewee should be asked a more open question, such as: 'Why is that?' If the interviewee does not mention cost, but cost is of particular interest in the study, then the respondent might be asked a question such as: 'What about ticket prices?' But this would be only *after* the interviewee has given his or her own unprompted reasons for not attending sports matches.

An important skill in interviewing of this sort is not to be afraid of silence. Some questions puzzle respondents and they need time to think. The interviewer does not have to fill the space with noise under the guise of 'helping' the interviewee. The interviewee is allowed time to ponder. The initiative can be left with the respondent to ask for an explanation if a question is unclear. While it is pleasant to engender a conversational atmosphere in these situations, the semi-structured interview is in fact different from a conversation. The interviewer is meant to listen and encourage the respondent to talk – not to engage in debate.

Informal or unstructured approach

A more informal or unstructured approach is favoured by some researchers. Sherry Dupuis (1999), for example, sees the semi-structured approach as inappropriately seeking to reflect the positivist paradigm in qualitative research. She argues that using qualitative methods should involve full interaction with research informants, so interviewers should be free to engage in a relatively free-flowing two-way conversation with interviewees. But she also makes the further point that, if this is to happen, then much more detail about this aspect of the research process should be reported in research accounts than is usually the case. Thus, for example, information gained by means of a full two-way conversation and exchange of views with a forthcoming interviewee is arguably different in nature from information gained from an interview where the interviewee is more reserved.

Distinction between standardised and informal approaches

The distinction between the standardised and informal interview approaches can be seen as corresponding to the *phenomenographic* and *phenomenological*

1. 'Uh-huh'	A non-verbal response which merely indicates that the interviewer is still listening and interested.
2. 'That's interesting'	Encourages the subject to keep talking or expand on the current topic.
3. Reflection	Repeating the last statement as a question – e.g. 'So you don't like sport?'
4. Probe	Inviting explanations of statements – e.g. 'Why don't you like sport?'
5. Back-tracking	Remembering something the subject said earlier and inviting further information – e.g. 'Let's go back to what you were saying about your school days'.
6. New topic	Initiating a new topic – e.g. 'Can we talk about other activities – what about sport spectating?'

Figure 9.5   Interviewing interventions – Whyte (1982)

approach to research (Ryan, 2000: 125). In the former, researchers adopt a minimalist approach to intervention in the interview and subsequently analyse and interpret the output – typically in the form of a transcript – in the same way that any text would be analysed. In the latter, researchers/interviewers are more active in eliciting responses to assist them in achieving an understanding of the interviewee's world-view during the course of the interview.

Whyte (1982) provides a sort of hierarchy in interviewer responses which vary in their degree of *intervention* in the interview. He sees this as the interviewer exercising varying degrees of *control* over the interview. Beginning with the least intrusive style of intervention, Whyte's list is as shown in Figure 9.5. It should be noted that, except for the sixth of these responses, the interviewer is essentially drawing on what the subject has already said and is inviting her or him to expand on it.

Recording

Sound or video recording of in-depth interviews is common, although in some cases it might be felt that such a procedure could inhibit respondents. If recording is not possible then notes must be taken during the interview or immediately afterwards. There can be great value in producing complete *verbatim* (word for word) transcripts of interviews from recordings. This is a laborious process – one hour of interview taking as much as six hours to transcribe, but online services now exist which use voice-recognition technology to transcribe digitised recordings automatically **(see Resources section)**. Transcripts can be used to analyse the results of interviews in a more methodical and complete manner than is possible with notes.

Focus groups

Nature

The idea of interviewing groups of people together rather than individually is becoming increasingly popular in market, community and political research. In this technique the interviewer becomes the *facilitator, convenor* or *discussion leader* rather than an interviewer as such. The aim of the process is much the same as in an in-depth interview, but in this case the participants interact with one another as well as with the researcher/facilitator.

Purposes

The technique can be used:

- when a particular group is important in a study but is so small in number that members of the group would not be adequately represented in a general community questionnaire-based survey – for example members of minority ethnic groups or people with particular disabilities;

- when the interaction/discussion process itself is of interest – for example in testing reactions to a proposed new product, or when investigating team behaviour;

- as an alternative to the in-depth interview, when it may not be practical to arrange for individual in-depth interviews but people are willing to be interviewed as a group – for example some youth groups or members of some ethnic communities.

Methods

A group will usually comprise between five and twelve participants. They may be chosen from a 'panel' of people who make themselves available to market researchers for this sort of exercise, or they may be chosen because they are members of a particular group of interest to the research – for example members of a sports club or local residents in a particular area. The members of the group may or may not be known to one another.

The usual procedure is to audio-record the discussion and for the researcher to produce a written summary from the recording.

Many of the same considerations apply here as in the in-depth interview situation: the process is informal but the facilitator still has a role in guiding the discussion and ensuring that all the aspects of the topic are covered. In addition, in the group interview, the facilitator has the task of ensuring that all members of the group have their say and that the discussion is not dominated by one or two vociferous members of the group.

Participant observation

Nature

In participant observation the researcher becomes a participant in the social process being studied. The classic study of this type is Whyte's *Street Corner Society* (1955), in which the researcher spent several years living with an inner city US Italian community. In sport, elements of participant observation are common in many types of research. Many studies of individual sports and sports clubs are by participants in the sport and/or members of a club. Traditionally, the process has involved considerable interaction of the researcher with the people being researched, and personal involvement of the researcher in a sport, particularly in team and competitive situations, provides an ideal environment for studying a sport over an extended period of time.

Purposes

In many cases, some sort of participant observation is the only way of researching particular phenomena – for instance it would be difficult to study what really goes on in a drug sub-culture, some youth sub-cultures or sport fan groups, using a questionnaire and clipboard. Becoming part of the group and immersed in its activities is the obvious way of studying the group.

Methods

Participant observation raises a number of practical/tactical challenges, and sometimes ethical challenges **(see Chapter 4)**. For example, in some cases actually gaining admittance to the social setting of interest may be difficult, especially where close-knit groups are involved. Having gained admittance to the setting, the question arises for the researcher as to whether to pose as a typical member of the group, whether to adopt a plausible disguise or persona (e.g. a 'journalist' or 'writer') or whether to admit to being a researcher.

Selection of informants is an issue to be addressed by the participant observer in the same way that sampling must be considered by the survey researcher. The members of the study group who are most friendly and talkative may be the easiest to communicate with, but may give a biased picture of the views and behaviour of the group as a whole.

In addition, there are practical problems to be faced over how to record information. When the researcher's identity as a researcher has not been revealed, the taking of notes in real time or the use of a recorder may be impossible. Even when the researcher has identified her- or himself as such, or has assumed a plausible identity, the use of such devices may interfere with the sort of natural relationship which the researcher is trying to establish. The taking of regular and detailed notes is, however, the basic data recording method. This may be supplemented by photographs and even video and sound recordings in some instances.

Analysing texts

Nature

The analysis of texts, such as plays and novels, is the very basis of some disciplines in the humanities, such as media studies and cultural studies. As researchers from these disciplines have turned their attention to sport issues, and as the relationships between sport and 'cultural products' have become recognised, the approach is playing an increasingly important role in sport research. The term *text* is now used to embrace not just printed material, but also pictures, posters, recorded music, film and television, and the Internet. Indeed, virtually any cultural product can, in the jargon, be *read* as *text*.

It is not proposed to outline analysis techniques in detail in this book, since approaches are very varied, including the qualitative, literary 'reading' of texts, the *interpretation* of texts sometimes referred to as *hermeneutics*, and the highly quantified form of analysis known as *content analysis*. The approach here is, rather, to introduce some examples of work in this area.

Novels and other literature

- Sönmez *et al.* (1993) examine the concept of sport as portrayed in the novels of Kenyan author Ngugi wa Thiong'o. The analysis provides a perspective on a non-Western view of sport and its place in a culture faced with the upheaval of the colonial and post-colonial experience.

- In two papers, Hultsman and Harper (1992; Harper and Hultsman, 1992) analyse a collection of 1930s essays on life in the 'Old South' of the United States to reveal new insights into sport and class at that time.

- One chapter in Paul Barry's (2006: 414–44) biography of Kerry Packer (former Australian media owner and originator of televised one-day cricket) provides a fascinating insight into one, very rich, man's approach to 'serious sport' (Stebbins, 1982) – in this case polo – illustrating the value of biographies as a source of material on sport.

Mass media coverage

Media coverage of selected topics can be studied quantitatively by measuring the column centimetres devoted to the topic in newspapers or the time devoted to the topic on television. Examples are the studies by:

- Brown (1995) and Rowe and Brown (1994): of press coverage of women's sport in Australian newspapers;
- Toohey (1990): analysis of the television coverage of the Barcelona Olympic Games;
- Cuneen and Lynch (1988) and Cuneen *et al.* (1989): analysis of the verbal and pictorial press coverage of a sporting event.

Film

- *Sport in Society* (2008): a special issue studying sport films;
- Baker (1998): sports, film, history and identity;
- Bora and Daimari (2012): sport films and social messages.

Internet

- Clavio and Eagleman (2011): gender and images in sports blogs.
- McKay and Dallaire (2012): sportswomen countering media portrayals.

Biographical research

Nature

Biographical research covers a range of techniques which involve researching all or a substantial part of the lives of individuals or groups of individuals. The most common example of such research is the conventional biography or autobiography, but the biographical approach includes a number of other research approaches and outputs, including: oral history; memory work; and personal domain histories. The term 'narrative research' is also sometimes used

(Armour and Chen, 2012). Detailed guidance on the conduct of biographical research is not given in this book, but a brief overview of the field is given here and sources of further information in the Resources section.

Biography/autobiography/personal narrative

There are many published accounts of lives of business leaders which, while often read for entertainment, also provide insight into how business and business leaders operate. Perhaps the most well known is the autobiography of Lee Iacocca (1984), the CEO of Chrysler during a turbulent period. In Australia, *The Rise and Rise of Kerry Packer* (media owner and originator of one-day cricket), by Paul Barry (1990, 2006), is a notable example of sport business biographies.

Oral history

Oral history involves recording eye-witness accounts of events and typically storing the files and/or a transcription of them in an archive as a source for research. While such accounts often range more widely than the interviewees' own lives, they are nevertheless personal accounts. In an ambitious project, Jobling, Naar and Hanley (2012) conducted a joint oral history project with people who had contributed to the Australian Paralympic Movement since the inaugural Paralympic Games in Rome, 1960. Through the use of multiple oral histories the paper concludes by analysing issues that arose from the interviews regarding the development of the Paralympic movement. In Britain, the 'Up and Under' rugby league oral history project includes 100 interviews with players, administrators and fans (see Resources section: websites). A database of oral histories of the lives of British sportsmen and women is provided on the British library website (see Resources section: websites).

Memory work

Memory work is a structured way of eliciting subjects' memories of events; it can be seen as a focus group aided by individual writing. Participants are asked to write a short account of an experience related to the research topic – for example power relationships in sport organisations. The written accounts are read aloud in focus group settings and discussed, and may be followed up with further writing and/or interviewing (see Markula and Friend, 2005; Onyx and Small, 2001).

Personal domain histories

In the 1980s, a technique termed 'personal leisure histories' was developed by Hedges (1986) to study the ways in which significant changes in life circumstances (marriage, birth of a child, change of job, health issues, etc.) impacted on patterns of leisure, including sport participation. A sport-related example can be found in Collins (2003: 182–3).

Ethnography and mixed methods

The ethnographic style of research is not one technique but an approach which may draw on a variety of techniques. Traditionally, ethnography has been the research methodology of anthropologists studying non-industrial communities, through observation and participant observation as well as interviewing. Thus, in discussing the early application of ethnography to sport, Robert Sands (2002: 4–5) notes studies of the games and sport activities of Native American tribes. Generally, as applied to sport research, it seeks to study people 'in the round' and to see the world through the eyes of those being researched, allowing them to speak for themselves, often revealed through extensive direct quotations in the research report. Often also, the aim is to debunk conventional, establishment, 'common sense' views of 'social problems', 'deviants', sexual and ethnic stereotypes, and so on. In sport studies the approach has become particularly associated with 'cultural studies', for example of youth subcultures and ethnic groups.

Ethnography can be seen as a 'mixed-method' approach **(see Chapter 5)**. In the qualitative research context, a term used for mixed methods is *bricolage*, a French word referring to craft-workers who are able to 'make do' with whatever materials or tools are at hand, as is quilt-making. The practitioner is then known as a *bricoleur* (Denzin and Lincoln, 2005: 4–6).

Validity and reliability, trustworthiness

The issues of validity – the extent to which research accurately represents what it is intended to represent – and reliability – the extent to which research is replicable – were discussed in Chapter 2, and it was noted there that some researchers prefer to use the term *trustworthiness* when discussing qualitative methods.

Internal validity is concerned with the processes by which information is gathered from the subjects of the study. A case could be made that information collected by qualitative methods has a greater chance of being internally valid than information gathered by means of, for example, a short questionnaire, since, in the qualitative data collection situation, more time and effort are generally taken to collect any one piece of information. Thus the exchange between interviewer and interviewee in an in-depth interview or the discussion in a focus group should increase the likelihood of interviewer/facilitator and interviewee/participants understanding one another.

External validity is concerned with the applicability of the findings beyond the subjects of the research. Typically, no formal claim of generalisability is made on the basis of qualitative study, but **(as noted in Chapter 2)** this strict rule is often implicitly ignored. It is noted that efforts are often made to select samples of subjects for qualitative research which have some semblance of representativeness, at least in terms of the qualitative diversity of the population being studied **(see Chapter 13)**. It would be strange if researchers conducting qualitative research projects did not believe that there were *some* implications beyond the limited sample of subjects studied. Thus the belief is that what has been found is true of *some people* among the population from which the study subjects were drawn, but the extent cannot be quantified. In theoretical terms, in cases where the findings of qualitative research are inconsistent with existing theory, it at least establishes that the theory is not *universally* valid. Furthermore, theoretical propositions arising from qualitative research *may* be more widely applicable.

Unlike the physical sciences, replicability of qualitative social research findings is clearly unlikely. However, accumulation of similar, or logically consistent, findings from a wide range of studies lends strength to the findings, not in a statistical sense, but in terms of the robustness of the findings in different settings. There is a parallel in quantitative meta-analyses, where it can be argued that similar, but statistically insignificant, findings from a number of studies may be given some cumulative support if the level of significance of individual studies was affected by sample sizes.

Thus, while qualitative research cannot offer the rigorous tests of validity and reliability of quantitative research, the issues can be discussed, and some form of assessment of *trustworthiness* arrived at.

Summary

This chapter introduces the role of qualitative approaches in sport research. One of the basic assumptions of qualitative research is that reality is socially and subjectively constructed rather than objectively determined. In this perspective, researchers are consciously seen as part of the research process seeking to uncover meanings and an understanding of the issues they are researching. In general, qualitative research involves the collection of a large amount of 'rich' information concerning relatively few people or organisations rather than the more limited information from a large number of people or organisations common in quantitative methods.

Qualitative methods generally require a more flexible, recursive, approach to overall research design and conduct, in contrast to the more linear, sequential approach used in most quantitative research. Hypothesis formation evolves as the research progresses; data collection and analysis take place concurrently and writing is also often an evolutionary process, rather than a separate process which happens at the end of the project.

There is a range of qualitative methods available to the researcher, including in-depth interviews, group interviews, focus groups, participant observation, textual analysis, biographical methods and ethnographic methods. The chapter outlines the nature and techniques involved in using each of these methods.

Validity and reliability of qualitative methods cannot be assessed using the rigorous, quantified tests of quantitative methods, but the issues can be addressed and assessed to give an assessment of what some have termed *trustworthiness*.

Test questions

1. Outline some of the merits of qualitative data.

2. Explain the difference between sequential and recursive approaches to research.

3. Outline Whyte's levels of interviewer intervention in an in-depth/informal interview.

4. In-depth interviews involve an interviewer: what is the equivalent in a focus group?

5. Name three types of biographical research.

Exercises

1. Use the checklist in Figure 9.4 to interview a willing friend or colleague. Assess your performance as an interviewer.

2. If you are studying with others, organise yourselves into groups of 5 or 6 and organise a focus-group interview, with one person as facilitator, choosing a topic of mutual interest, such as 'fitness versus the enjoyment of sport'. Take turns in acting as convenor and assess one another's skills as convenor.

Resources

Websites

- British Library: oral histories of the lives of British sportsmen and women: http://sounds.bl.uk/Oral-history/Sport

- 'Up and Under' rugby league oral history project: www.rugbyleagueoralhistory.co.uk

- Digital transcription software/services: search online for 'digital transcription in [your country name]

Publications

- Qualitative methods:

  - general: Lofland and Lofland (1984), Burgess (1982), Denzin and Lincoln (1994, 2005), Silverman (1993);

  - sports studies: Andrews *et al.* (2006);

  - sport management: Edwards and Skinner (2009); Skinner and Edwards (2005);

  - sport and exercise: *Qualitative Research in Sport and Exercise* (journal);

  - sport psychology: Biddle *et al.* (2001: 792–804);

  - physical education: Gerdes and Conn (2001).

- Auto-ethnography: Sparkes (2000), Humberstone (2009).

- Biography/autobiography/personal narrative: Atkinson (1998), Bale *et al.* (2004), Bertaux (1981), Roberts (2002); personal domain histories: Hedges (1986), Collins, 2003: 182–3); narrative research: Armour and Chen (2012); personal narratives: Denison (1996), Markula (2006), Mellick and Fleming (2010), Tsang (2000).

- *Bricolage*: Denzin and Lincoln (2005: 4–6).

- Content analysis: Biddle *et al.* (2001: 796–800), Kian *et al.* (2009); Pierce *et al.* (2012), Thomson *et al.* (2010).

- Ethnography in sport: Light (2010), Olive and Thorpe (2011), Sands (2002).

- Examples of qualitative research in sport studies:

  - motor sports, riots: Cuneen and Lynch (1988), Cuneen *et al.* (1989), Mariotti (2007), Pettinga and DeGaris (2011).

  - football fans: Gibson *et al.* (2002), Giulianotti (1995), Lock *et al.* (2012), Marsh *et al.* (1978).

- ○ sport/social club: Wynne (1986).

- ○ triathletes: Lamont and Kennelly (2012).

- Focus groups: Calder (1977), Greenbaum (1998, 2000), Krueger (1988), Morgan (1993), Reynolds and Johnson (1978), Slater and Tiggemann (2010), Stewart and Shamdasani (1990).

- Grounded theory: in general: Glaser and Strauss (1967), Strauss (1987), Strauss and Corbin (1994); in sport: Holt and Dunn (2004), Hutchison *et al.* (2010, 2011), Weed (2005), Weissensteiner *et al.* (2009).

- Informal/in-depth interviews: Dunne (1995), Thomson *et al.* (2010), Schulenkorf and Edwards (2012).

- Memory work: Johnson and Dunlap (2011), Markula and Friend (2005), Onyx and Small (2001).

- Narrative research: see Biography etc.

- Oral history: Cahn (1994).

- Participant observation: Giulianotti (1995), Xiao Yan and Chalip (2009).

- Qualitative-quantitative debate: see Chapter 2 Resources section.

- Textual/visual: Apostolis and Giles (2011), Plymire (2006); physical culture: Phoenix (2010); sport coaching: Jones *et al.* (2012); Olympic Games: *Visual Sociology* (2012) special issue; visual methods in physical cultures: *Qualitative Research in Sport and Exercise* (journal) (2010) special issue; sport blogs: Clavio and Eagleman (2011).

References

Andrews, D. L., Mason, D. S. and Silk, M. L. (eds) (2006) *Qualitative Methods in Sports Studies*. Oxford: Berg.

Apostolis, N. and Giles, A. R. (2011) Portrayals of women golfers in the 2008 issues of *Golf Digest*. *Sociology of Sport Journal*, 28(2), 226–38.

Armour, K. and Chen, H. (2012) Narrative research methods; where the art of storytelling meets the science of research. In K. Armour and D. Macdonald (eds) *Research Methods in Physical Education and Youth Sport*. London: Routledge, 237–49.

Atkinson, R. (1998) *The Life Story Interview*. London: Sage.

Baker, A. (1998) Sports, film, history and identity. *Journal of Sport History*, 25(2), 217–33.

Barry, P. (1999) *The Rise and Fall of Alan Bond*. Sydney: Bantam/ABC.

Barry, P. (2006) *The Rise and Rise of Kerry Packer – Uncut*. Sydney: Bantam/ABC.

Bertaux, D. (ed.) (1981) *Biography and Society*. London: Sage.

Biddle, S. J. H., Markland, D. and Gilbourne, D. (2001) Research methods in sport and exercise psychology: quantitative and qualitative issues. *Journal of Sports Sciences*, 19(10), 777–809.

Bora, A. and Daimari, P. J. (2012) Sports films for social message communication. *New Media and Mass Communication*, 6(1), 5–8.

Brewer, B., Vose, J., Raalte, J. V. and Petitpas, A. (2011) Metaqualitative reflections in sport and exercise psychology. *Qualitative Research in Sport, Exercise and Health*, 3(3), 329–34.

Brown, P. (1995) Women, sport and the media: an historical perspective on sports coverage in the Sydney Morning Herald, 1890–1990. In C. Simpson and B. Gidlow (eds) *Australian and New Zealand Association for Leisure Studies, Second Conference – Leisure Connexions*. Canterbury, New Zealand: Lincoln University, 44–50.

Burgess, R. G. (ed.) (1982) *Field Research: A Sourcebook and Field Manual*. London: Allen & Unwin.

Cahn, S. K. (1994) Sports talk: oral history and its uses, problems, and possibilities for sport history. *Journal of American History*, 81(2), 594–609.

Calder, B. (1977) Focus groups and the nature of qualitative marketing research. *Journal of Marketing Research*, 14, Aug., 353–64.

Clavio, G. and Eagleman, A. N. (2011) Gender and sexually suggestive images in sports blogs. *Journal of Sport Management*, 7(4), 295–304.

Collins, M. F. (2003) *Sport and Social Exclusion*. London: Routledge.

Cunneen, C. and Lynch, R. (1988) The social meaning of conflict in riots at the Australian Grand Prix motorcycle races. *Leisure Studies*, 7(1), 1–20.

Cuneen, C., Findlay, M., Lynch, R. and Tupper, V. (1989) *Dynamics of Collective Conflict: Riots at the Bathurst 'Bike Races'*. North Ryde, NSW: Law Book Co.

Darcy, S. and Dowse, L. (2012) In search of a level playing field – the constraints and benefits of sport participation for people with intellectual disability. *Disability and Society*, 1–15.

Denison, J. (1996) Sport narratives. *Qualitative Inquiry*, 2(3), 351–62.

Denzin, N. K. and Lincoln, Y. S. (eds) (1994) *Handbook of Qualitative Research*. Thousand Oaks, CA: Sage.

Denzin, N. K. and Lincoln, Y. S. (eds) (2005) *Handbook of Qualitative Research, Third edn*. Thousand Oaks, CA: Sage.

Dunne, S. (1995) *Interviewing Techniques for Writers and Researchers*. London: A & C Black.

Dupuis, S. (1999) Naked truths: towards a reflexive methodology in leisure research. *Leisure Sciences*, 21(1), 43–64.

Edwards, A. and Skinner, J. (2009) *Qualitative Research in Sport Management*. Oxford: Butterworth-Heinemann.

Gerdes, D. A. and Conn, J. H. (2001) A user-friendly look at qualitative research methods. *Physical Educator*, 58(4), 183–93.

Gibson, H., Willming, C. and Holdnak, A. (2002) 'We're Gators… not just Gator fans': serious leisure and University of Florida football. *Journal of Leisure Research*, 34(4), 397–425.

Giulianotti, R. (1995) Participant observation and research into football hooliganism: reflections on the problems of entrée and everyday risks. *Sociology of Sport Journal*, 12(1), 1–20.

Glaser, B. and Strauss, A. L. (1967) *The Discovery of Grounded Theory: Strategies for Qualitative Research.* Chicago: Aldine.

Greenbaum, T. L. (1998) *The Handbook for Focus Group Research, Second edn.* Thousand Oaks, CA: Sage.

Greenbaum, T. L. (2000) *Moderating Focus Groups: A Practical Guide for Group Facilitation.* Thousand Oaks, CA: Sage.

Harper, W. and Hultsman, J. (1992) Interpreting leisure as text: the whole. *Leisure Studies*, 11(3), 233–42.

Hastie, P., and Glotova, O. (2012) Analysing qualitative data. In K. Armour & D. Macdonald (eds), *Research Methods in Physical Education and Youth Sport.* London: Routledge, 309–20.

Hastie, P. and Hay, P. (2012) Qualitative approaches. In K. Armour and D. Macdonald (eds) *Research Methods in Physical Education and Youth Sport.* London: Routledge, 79–94.

Hedges, B. (1986) *Personal Leisure Histories.* London: Sports Council/Economic and Social Research Council.

Holt, N. L. and Dunn, J. G. H. (2004) Toward a grounded theory of the psychosocial competencies and environmental conditions associated with soccer success. *Journal of Applied Sport Psychology*, 16(3), 199–219.

Hultsman, J. and Harper, W. (1992) Interpreting leisure as text: the part. *Leisure Studies*, 11(2), 135–46.

Humberstone, B. (2009) Sport management, gender and the 'bigger picture': challenging changes in higher education – a partial auto/ethnographical account. *Sport Management Review*, 12(4), 255–262.

Hutchison, A. J., Johnston, L. H. and Breckon, J. D. (2010) Using QSR-NVivo to facilitate the development of a grounded theory project: an account of a worked example. *International Journal of Social Research Methodology*, 13(4), 283–302.

Hutchison, A. J., Johnston, L. H. and Breckon, J. D. (2011) Grounded theory-based research within exercise psychology: a critical review. *Qualitative Research in Psychology*, 8(3), 247–72.

Iacocca, L. A. (1984) *Iacocca: An Autobiography.* Toronto: Bantam Books.

Jobling, I. F., Naar, T. and Hanley, M. (2012) The Australian Paralympic oral history project: remembering, reflecting, recording and promoting disability in sport. *International Journal of Disability, Development and Education*, 59(3), 295–303.

Johnson, C. W. and Dunlap, R. (2011) 'They were not drag queens, they were playboy models and bodybuilders': media, masculinities and gay sexual identity. *Annals of Leisure Research*, 14(2–3), 209–23.

Jones, R., Santos, S., Mesquita, I. and Gilbourne, D. (2012) Visual methods in coaching research: capturing everyday lives. In K. Armour and D. Macdonald (eds) *Research Methods in Physical Education and Youth Sport.* London: Routledge, 263–75.

Kelly, J. R. (1980) Leisure and quality: beyond the quantitative barrier in research. In T. L. Goodale and P. A. Witt (eds) *Recreation and Leisure: Issues in an Era of Change.* State College, PA: Venture, 300–14.

Kian, E. T. M., Mondello, M. and Vincent, J. (2009) ESPN – the women's sports network? A content analysis of internet coverage of March madness. *Journal of Broadcasting and Electronic Media*, 53(3), 477–95.

Krueger, R. A. (1988) *Focus Groups: A Practical Guide for Applied Research.* Newbury Park, CA: Sage.

Lamont, M. and Kennelly, M. (2012) A qualitative exploration of participant motives among committed amateur triathletes. *Leisure Sciences*, 34(3), 236–55.

Light, R. L. (2010) Children's social and personal development through sport: a case study of an Australian swimming club. *Journal of Sport and Social Issues*, 34(4), 379–95.

Lock, D., Taylor, T., Funk, D. and Darcy, S. (2012) Exploring the development of team identification. *Journal of Sport Management*, 26(4), 283–94.

Lofland, J. and Lofland, L. H. (1984) *Analyzing Social Settings: A Guide to Qualitative Observation and Analysis, Second edn.* Belmont, CA: Wadsworth.

Mackay, S. and Dallaire, C. (2012) Skirtboarder net-a-narratives: young women creating their skateboarding (re)presentations. *International Review for the Sociology of Sport*, 48(2), 171–95.

Maguire, J. (1991) Human sciences, sport sciences, and the need to study people 'in the round'. *Quest*, 43(2), 190–206.

Mariotti, F. (2007) Learning to share knowledge in the Italian motorsport industry. *Knowledge and Process Management*, 14(2), 81–94.

Markula, P. (2006) Sport and personal narratives. In D. L. Andrews, D. S. Mason and M. L. Silk (eds), *Qualitative Methods in Sports Studies.* Oxford: Berg, 165–84.

Markula, P. and Friend, L. A. (2005) Memory-work as an interpretive methodology for sport management. *Journal of Sport Management*, 19(4), 442–63.

Marsh, P., Rosser, E. and Harré, R. (1978) *The Rules of Disorder.* London: Routledge.

McCall, G. J. and Simmons, J. L. (eds) (1969) *Issues in Participant Observation.* Reading, MA: Addison-Wesley.

Mellick, M. and Fleming, S. (2010) Personal narrative and the ethics of disclosure: a case study from elite sport. *Qualitative Research*, 10(3), 299–314.

Miles, M. B. and Huberman, A. M. (1994) *Qualitative Data Analysis, Second edn.* Thousand Oaks, CA: Sage.

Morgan, D. L. (ed.) (1993) *Successful Focus Groups: Advancing the State of the Art.* Newbury Park, CA: Sage.

Olive, R. and Thorpe, H. (2011) Negotiating the 'f-word' in the field: doing feminist ethnography in action sport cultures. *Sociology of Sport Journal*, 28(4), 421–440.

Onyx, J. and Small. J. (2001) Memory-work: the method. *Qualitative Inquiry*, 7(6), 773–86.

Peterson, K. I. (1994) Qualitative research methods for the travel and tourism industry. In J. R. B. Ritchie and C. R. Goeldner (eds) *Travel, Tourism and Hospitality Research, Second edn.* New York: John Wiley, 487–92.

Pettinga, D. M. and DeGaris, L. (2011) A case study for NASCAR driver sponsors: making greatest use of the character traits fans like and dislike in a driver. *International Journal of Motorsport Management*, 1(1), 18 pages, available at: http://scholar.wssu.edu/ijmm/vol1/iss1/4/ (Accessed May 2013).

Phoenix, C. (2010) Seeing the world of physical culture: the potential of visual methods for qualitative research in sport and exercise. *Qualitative Research in Sport and Exercise*, 2(2), 93–108.

Pierce, D., Petersen, J., Clavio, G. and Meadows, B. (2012) Content analysis of sport ticket sales job announcements. *Sport, Business and Management*, 2(2), 137–55.

Plymire, D. (2006) Qualitative methods in sport-media studies. In D. L. Andrews, D. S. Mason and M. L. Silk (eds) *Qualitative Methods in Sports Studies.* Oxford: Berg, 139–64.

Qualitative Research in Sport and Exercise (2010) Special issue: Visual methods in physical cultures, 2(2).

Reynolds, F. and Johnson, D. (1978) Validity of focus group findings. *Journal of Advertising Research*, 19(1), 3–24.

Roberts, B. (2002) *Biographical Research.* Buckingham, UK: Open University Press.

Rowe, D. and Brown, P. (1994) Promoting women's sport: theory, policy and practice. *Leisure Studies*, 13(2), 97–110.

Ryan, C. (2000) Tourist experiences, phenomenographic analysis, post-positivism and neural network software. *International Journal of Tourism Research*, 2(1), 119–31.

Sands, R. R. (2002) *Sport Ethnography.* Champaign, IL: Human Kinetics.

Schulenkorf, N. and Edwards, D. (2012) Maximizing positive social impacts: strategies for sustaining and leveraging the benefits of intercommunity sport events in divided societies. *Journal of Sport Management*, 26(4), 379–390.

Silverman, D. (1993) *Interpreting Qualitative Data: Methods for Analysing Talk, Text and Interaction.* London: Sage.

Skinner, J. and Edwards, A. (2005) Inventive pathways: fresh visions of sport management research. *Journal of Sport Management*, 19(4), 404–21.

Slater, A. and Tiggemann, M. (2010) 'Uncool to do sport': A focus group study of adolescent girls' reasons for withdrawing from physical activity. *Psychology of Sport and Exercise*, 11(6), 619–26.

Sönmez, S., Shinew, K., Marchese, L., Veldkamp, C. and Burnett, G. W. (1993) Leisure corrupted: an artist's portrait of leisure in a changing society. *Leisure Studies*, 12(4), 266–76.

Sparkes, A. (2000) Autoethnographies and narratives of self. *Sociology of Sport Journal*, 17(1), 21–43.

Sport in Society (2008) Special issue: Introducing sport in films, 11(2–3).

Stebbins, R. A. (1982) Serious leisure: a conceptual statement. *Pacific Sociological Review*, 25(3), 251–72.

Stewart, D. W. and Shamdasani, P. N. (1990) *Focus Groups: Theory and Practice.* Newbury Park, CA: Sage.

Strauss, A. and Corbin, J. (1994) Grounded theory methodology. In N. K. Denzin and Y. S. Lincoln (eds) *Handbook of Qualitative Research.* Thousand Oaks, CA: Sage, 273–85.

Strauss, A. L. (1987) *Qualitative Analysis for Social Scientists.* Cambridge: Cambridge University Press.

Thomson, A., Darcy, S. and Pearce, S. (2010) Ganma theory and third-sector sport-development programmes for Aboriginal and Torres Strait Islander youth: implications for sports management. *Sport Management Review*, 13(4), 313–30.

Toohey, K. (1990) A content analysis of the Australian television coverage of the 1988 Seoul Olympics. Paper to the *Commonwealth and International Conference of Physical Education, Sport, Health, Dance, Recreation and Leisure,* January, Auckland.

Tsang, T. (2000) Let me tell you a story: a narrative exploration of identity in high-performance sport. *Sociology of Sport Journal*, 17(1), 44–59.

Visual Sociology (2012) Special issue: Olympic Games, 10(1–2).

Weed, M. (2005) Sports tourism theory and method/concepts, issues and epistemologies. *European Sport Management Quarterly*, 5(3), 229–42.

Weissensteiner, J., Abernethey, B. and Farrow, D. (2009) Towards the development of a conceptual model of expertise in cricket batting: a grounded theory approach. *Journal of Applied Sport Psychology*, 21(3), 276–92.

Whyte, W. F. (1955) *Street Corner Society.* Chicago: University of Chicago Press.

Whyte, W. F. (1982) Interviewing in field research. In R. G. Burgess (ed.) *Field Research: A Sourcebook and Field Manual.* London: Allen & Unwin, 111–122.

Wynne, D. (1986) Living on 'The Heath'. *Leisure Studies*, 5(1), 109–16.

Xiao Yan, X. and Chalip, L. (2009) Marching in the glory: experiences and meanings when working for a sport mega-event. *Journal of Sport Management*, 23(2), 210–37.

Questionnaire surveys: typology, design and coding

Introduction

This chapter presents an overview of the range of types of questionnaire survey and questionnaire design. Questionnaire surveys involve the gathering of information from individuals using a formally designed *questionnaire* or *interview schedule* and are arguably the most commonly used technique in sport research.

The first part of the chapter discusses the merits of questionnaire methods and the distinction between the interviewer-completion and respondent-completion modes, followed by an overview of the characteristics of the various forms of questionnaire survey: the household questionnaire survey; the street survey; the telephone survey; the postal or mail survey; e-survey; on-site or user surveys; and captive group surveys.

The second half of the chapter considers the factors which must be taken into account in designing questionnaires for sport studies. First, the relationships between research problems and information requirements are examined. This is followed by consideration of the types of information typically included in sport-related questionnaires, the wording of questions, coding of questionnaires for computer analysis, the ordering and layout of questions and the problem of validity. Finally, some consideration is given to the special requirements of time-budget studies.

Definitions and terminology

A questionnaire can be defined as a written/printed or computer-based schedule of questions and a *pro forma* for recording answers to the questions. It is therefore both a means of eliciting information from respondents and a medium for recording answers.

The term *questionnaire survey* or *questionnaire-based survey* is used deliberately in this chapter to emphasise that the words *survey* and *questionnaire* mean two different things. There is a tendency in common parlance – and unfortunately in some research literature – to use the terms survey and questionnaire synonymously. For example, researchers have been known to make statements such as: '1000 surveys were distributed'. This is inappropriate: only *one* survey was involved – 1000 *questionnaires* were distributed. To distinguish the two terms:

- a questionnaire is a written/printed or computer-based schedule of questions;

- a survey is the *process* of designing and conducting a study involving the gathering of information from a number of subjects.

A 'survey' does not always include a questionnaire; thus, for example, a study could involve a visual survey of beach crowding or a documentary survey of the contents of organisations' annual reports.

Alternative terms for the word questionnaire are 'research instrument' or 'survey instrument', which reference the science laboratory context. In addition, 'survey form', 'question schedule', or 'interview schedule' are sometimes used.

Roles

Questionnaire surveys are used when a specified range of information is required from individuals or organisations. The most common form is based on a representative sample of a defined population of individuals or organisations, although in some cases the whole population is included, as in a national census of the population: in both cases the aim is to make statements about the characteristics of the population on the basis of the data from the sample, typically in the form of percentages, averages, relationships and trends.

Questionnaire-based surveys are generally used to collect responses to questions which have a limited number of possible answers, for example a person's gender or educational level, but some questions can be open-ended, with an unspecified range of answers – for example an open question on a visitor's complaints or suggestions regarding the management of a sport facility, programme or event.

Questionnaire-based surveys can play a role in the task of estimating the number of visits to sport facilities or events where visit numbers are not automatically gathered by administrative means, such as the sale of tickets. Examples include urban parks and tourism destinations with car-borne access.

As noted in Figure 7.2, information on visitor numbers may be gathered administratively (ticket sales, bookings), by direct counts/observation or wholly or in part by questionnaire-based survey.

Merits

Questionnaire surveys usually involve quantification – the presentation of results in numerical terms. This has implications for the way the data are collected, analysed and interpreted. In Chapter 9 a list of merits of qualitative methods is presented. The merits of questionnaire surveys can be similarly examined. Some of the qualities of questionnaire surveys which make them useful in sport-related research are set out below:

- Contemporary sport is often a mass phenomenon, requiring major involvement from governmental, non-profit and/or commercial organisations, which rely on quantified information for significant aspects of their decision-making. Questionnaire surveys are an ideal means of providing some of this information.

- While absolute objectivity is impossible, questionnaire methods provide a transparent set of research procedures such that the way information was collected and how it was analysed or interpreted is clear for all to see, although, it must be said, journal articles vary in the amount of detail provided. Questionnaire survey data, which are invariably available in digital form, can often be re-analysed by others if they wish to extend the research or provide an alternative interpretation.

- Quantification can provide relatively complex information in a succinct, easily understandable, form, including graphics.

- Methods such as longitudinal surveys and annually repeated surveys provide the opportunity to study change over time, using comparable methodology.

- Sport encompasses a wide range of activities, with a range of characteristics, such as frequency, duration and degree of organisation, expenditure, location, level of enjoyment and aspirations. Questionnaires are a good means of ensuring that a complete picture of a person's patterns of participation is obtained.

- While qualitative methods are ideal for exploring attitudes, meanings and perceptions on an individual basis, questionnaire methods provide the means to gather and record simple information on the incidence of attitudes, meanings and perceptions among a substantial sample of the population, thus indicating not only that certain attitudes exist but how widespread they are.

Comparison of this list and the one referring to qualitative methods at the beginning of Chapter 9 reinforces the view that each method has its merits and appropriate uses – the 'horses for courses' idea. Questionnaire surveys have a role to play when the research questions indicate the need for fairly structured data and generally when data are required from samples which are explicitly representative of a defined wider population. Examples of the role of questionnaire surveys versus other methods are shown in Figure 10.1.

Limitations

Questionnaire-based surveys have a number of limitations, related to the fact that they are based on self-reported data and generally on samples.

Self-reported data

Questionnaire surveys rely on information from respondents. The accuracy of what respondents say depends on their own powers of recall, on their honesty and, fundamentally, on the format of the questions included in the questionnaire. There has been relatively little research on the validity or accuracy of

Organisation	Topic	Questionnaire survey	Qualitative methods	Secondary analysis
Sport facility management	How to increase number of visitors	• User/visitor survey on what types of people use which services and when • Community survey on socio-demographic characteristics of users vs. non-users and perceptions of facility	• Observation and/or focus groups on experience of visiting the facility – quality, atmosphere, service	• Analysis of ticket sales and utilisation data re different activities/services
Sports Commission	Data for sport strategic plan	• National survey of sports participation, expenditure and socio-economic characteristics of participants	• In-depth interviews or focus groups on sport participation and constraints	• Analysis of international data
Individual researcher	The role of sport in a community	• Household survey of socio-demographic characteristics and numbers of sport participants	• In-depth interviews on meanings and importance of sport in individuals' lifestyles	• Analysis of official data on sport participation

Figure 10.1   The use of questionnaire surveys compared with other methods – examples

questionnaire data in sport studies. Problems of validity and accuracy arise from a number of sources, including exaggeration and under-reporting; accuracy of recall; and sensitivity.

● *Exaggeration/under-reporting:* Some research (see Resources section) has suggested that respondents exaggerate levels of participation in some activities and under-report others. This may be conscious or unconscious and may be for reasons of prestige or lack of it – what Oppenheim (2000: 138) calls 'social desirability bias' – or a desire to be positive and friendly towards the interviewer, at least in a face-to-face situation. For example, if the interview is about sport, respondents may tend to exaggerate their interest in, and involvement with sport just to be helpful.

● *Accuracy of recall:* Mistakes can be made in recalling events at all or in estimating frequency: for example, if someone claims to take part in an activity twice a week, is that equivalent to 104 times a year? Apart from seasonality, which could be addressed in the questionnaire, such factors as weather conditions, illness, public holidays, and family and work emergencies may all reduce the actual level of participation. Even if the question attempts to avoid this problem by asking respondents the actual number of occasions on which they have participated in a given time-period, respondents may be working from the 'once a week' notion and still overestimate. Where alternative sources of information, such as club records, are available, it is possible to check the accuracy of questionnaire-based information, but studies of this phenomenon suggest substantial overestimation in sporting/physical activity – examples are listed in the Resources section.

● *Sensitivity:* Sensitive topics can also give rise to underestimation or overestimation: for example, Nora Schaeffer (2000) provides information on responses regarding sexual activity and drug use.

This suggests the need for careful questionnaire design and cross-checking/triangulation where possible, but also that the researcher and the user of research results should always bear in mind the nature and source of the data and not fall into the trap of believing that, because information is presented in numerical form and is based on large numbers, it represents immutable 'truth'.

Samples

Questionnaire surveys usually, but not always, involve only a proportion, or *sample*, of the population in which the researcher is interested. For example, the national sport participation surveys **(see Chapter 7)** are based on samples of only a few thousand to represent tens of millions of people. How such samples are chosen, how the size of the sample is decided and the implications of relying on a sample to represent a population relates to the science of sampling **(see Chapter 13.)**

Interviewer-completion or respondent-completion?

Questionnaire surveys can take one of two forms:

- *Interviewer-completed:* the questionnaire provides the *script* for an interview; an interviewer reads the questions out to the respondent and records the respondent's answers on the questionnaire – the classic 'clipboard' situation, where the method may also be referred to as *face-to-face* interviewing. When telephone surveys are involved, the interviewer may record answers on a computer.

- *Respondent-completed*, often referred to as *self-completion:* respondents read and fill out the questionnaire for themselves, on paper or online.

Each approach has its particular advantages and disadvantages, as summarised in Figure 10.2. Interviewer-completion is more expensive in terms of interviewers' time (which usually has to be paid for) but the use of an interviewer usually ensures a more accurate and complete response. Respondent-completion can be cheaper and quicker but often results in low response rates, which can introduce bias into the results because those who choose not to respond or are unable to respond, perhaps because of language or literacy difficulties, may differ from those who do respond. When designing a questionnaire for respondent-completion, greater care must be taken with layout and presentation since it must be read and completed by 'untrained' people. In terms of design, respondent-completion questionnaires should ideally consist primarily of *closed* questions – that is, questions which can be answered by ticking boxes. *Open-ended questions* – where respondents have to write out their answers – should generally be avoided in such a situation, since they invariably achieve only a low response. For example, in an interview, respondents will often give expansive answers to questions such as 'Do you have any comments to make

	Interviewer-completion	**Respondent-completion**
Advantages	More accuracy	Cheaper
	Higher response rates	Quicker
	Fuller and more complete answers	Relatively anonymous
	Less 'user-friendly' design possible	
Disadvantages	Higher cost	Patchy response
	Less anonymity	Incomplete response
		Risk of frivolous responses
		More care needed in design

Figure 10.2   Interviewer-completion compared with respondent-completion

on the overall management of this facility?' But they will not as readily write down such answers in a respondent-completion questionnaire.

There may, however, be cases when respondent-completion is to be preferred, or is the only practicable approach – for example when the people to be surveyed are widely scattered geographically, which would make face-to-face interviews impossibly expensive and a mail or postal survey, which intrinsically involves respondent-completion, an obvious choice, or when it is felt that, on sensitive matters, respondents might prefer the anonymity of the respondent-completed questionnaire. Some of the issues connected with respondent-completion questionnaires are discussed more fully in the section on mail surveys.

It should be noted that some commentators, in discussions of research methods, draw a distinction between 'interview methods' and 'questionnaire methods'; this is clearly misleading because the interviewer-completed questionnaire-based survey clearly involves an interview, so the 'questionnaire method' may involve an interview and is therefore not distinct from the 'interview method'. What such comments are invariably referring to is a distinction between questionnaire-based methods and in-depth or semi-structured interviews **(see Chapter 9)**.

Types of questionnaire survey

Questionnaire surveys in the sport field can be divided into six types: household surveys; street surveys; telephone surveys; mail surveys; e-surveys; user/on-site/visitor surveys; and captive group surveys. Each of these is discussed in more detail below and some of their basic characteristics are summarised in Figure 10.3.

The household questionnaire survey

Nature

A significant amount of quantified data on sport participation is derived from household questionnaire surveys. While academics draw on the data extensively, the majority of such surveys are commissioned by government and commercial sport organisations for policy or marketing purposes. The advantage of household surveys is that they are generally representative of the community – the samples drawn tend to include all age-groups, above a certain minimum, and all occupational groups. They also generally represent a complete geographical area – a whole country, a state or region, a local government area or a neighbourhood. Household surveys are therefore designed to provide

Type	Interviewer or respondent completion	Cost	Sample	Possible length of questionnaire	Response rate
Household					
Standard	Either	Expensive	Whole population	Long	High
Time-use	Respondent	Expensive	Whole population	Long	High
Omnibus	Either	Medium per client	Whole population	Long	High
Street	Interviewer	Medium	Most of population	Short	Medium
Telephone	Interviewer	Medium	People with land-line telephone	Short	High but falling
Mail	Respondent	Cheap	General or special	Varies	Low
E-survey	Respondent	Cheap	People accessible via email/Internet	Medium	Medium
On-site	Either	Medium	Site users only	Medium	High
Captive	Respondent	Cheap	Captive group only	Medium	High

Figure 10.3　Types of questionnaire survey – characteristics

representative information on the reported sport behaviour of the community as a whole or a particular group drawn from the whole community – for example the population aged 65 and over, or young people aged 15–24.

While some household sport surveys are specialised, many are broad-ranging in their coverage. That is, they tend to ask, among other things, about participation in a wide range of sport, exercise and physical recreation activities. This facilitates exploration of a wide range of issues which other types of survey cannot so readily tackle.

Conduct

Normally, household questionnaire surveys are interviewer-completed. However, it is possible for a questionnaire to be left at a respondent's home for respondent-completion and later collection, in which case the fieldworker then has the responsibility of checking that questionnaires have been fully completed and perhaps conducting an interview in those situations where respondents have been unable to fill in the questionnaire, either because they have been too busy, have forgotten, have lost the questionnaire, or because of literacy or language problems or infirmity.

Being home-based, this sort of survey can involve quite lengthy questionnaires and interviews. By contrast, in the street, at a sport facility or over the telephone, it can be difficult to conduct a lengthy interview. General sport participation surveys in particular, with their wide range of possible activities, often involve a very complex questionnaire which is difficult to administer 'on the run'. With the home-based interview it is usually possible to pursue issues at greater length than is possible in other settings. An interview of three-quarters of an hour in duration is not out of the question and 20–30 minutes is quite common.

A variation on the standard household questionnaire interview survey is to combine interviewer-completed and respondent-completed elements: the interviewer conducts an interview with one member of the household about the household – how many people live there, whether the dwelling is owned or rented, perhaps information on recreational equipment, or anything to do with the household as a whole. Then an individual questionnaire is left for each member of the household to complete, concerning their own sport behaviour. The interviewer calls back later to collect these individual questionnaires.

The potential length of interviews, the problems of contacting representative samples and, on occasions, the wide geographical spread of the study area mean that household surveys are usually the most expensive to conduct, per interview. Costs of the order of £25 or £30 per interview are typical, depending on the amount of analysis included in the price. When samples of several thousands are involved, the costs can therefore be substantial.

Omnibus surveys

While considering household surveys, mention should be made of the *omnibus* survey. These are surveys conducted by a market research or survey organisation with various questions included in the questionnaire on behalf of different clients. The main costs of conducting the survey, which lie in sampling and contacting respondents, are therefore shared by a number of clients. The cost of collecting fairly standard demographic and socio-economic information – such as age, gender, family structure, occupation and income – is also shared among the clients. With regular omnibus surveys, many of the procedures, such as sampling and data processing, have become routinised, and interviewers are in place throughout the country already trained and familiar with the type of questionnaire and the requirements of the market research company – these factors can reduce costs significantly.

The British *Household Survey* (later *General Household Survey*) was an omnibus survey of 20,000 people run by the Office for National Statistics, the clients being government departments and agencies. In the years when sport questions were included, the clients for those questions were the various national sport/recreation agencies, such as the Sports Council and the Countryside Commission. A similar *General Social Survey* is conducted by the Australian Bureau of Statistics **(see Chapter 7)**.

Although discussed here as a sub-category of household surveys, omnibus surveys may also be conducted using other formats, notably telephone and e-surveys.

Time-use surveys

Time-use, or time-budget, surveys are designed to collect information about people's use of time. Such information is generally collected as the main or subsidiary part of a household survey, but in addition to answering a questionnaire, respondents are asked to complete a diary, typically covering a period of one to two days. Respondents are asked to record their waking hour activities in a time-use diary, including starting and stopping times, together with information on where the activity was done, with whom, and possibly whether the respondent considered it to be paid work, domestic work or leisure. Information on secondary activities is also generally gathered, for example listening to music while exercising.

Coding and analysis of time-use data presents a considerable challenge, since hundreds of sport and non-sport activities must be given a code and information processed for, say, 60 or 70 quarter-hour periods each day. Space does not permit a detailed treatment of this specialised topic here, but it can be followed up in the literature indicated in the Resources section.

National surveys

Chapter 7 discusses national sport and leisure participation surveys, typically conducted by government statistical agencies, as source of secondary data. These surveys are typically large-scale household or telephone surveys. Often their main secondary use is comparison with locally conducted surveys: the aim being to establish whether, on some participation measure, the local community is above or below the national average. If such comparisons are to be made, it follows that the local survey must be conducted in a similar way and the comparison questions in the questionnaire must be similarly worded. This clearly places a constraint on design, but, apart from the ability to make comparisons, it also has the advantage that the question format has been thoroughly tested.

The street survey

Nature

The street survey involves a relatively short questionnaire and is conducted, as the name implies, on the street – usually a shopping street or business area – or in squares or shopping malls, where a cross-section of the community might be expected to be found. The method can also be used to interview tourists to an area, including sport tourists, in which case the survey would be conducted at locations where such tourists are known to congregate, such as in relevant sport venues or their environs, near tourist accommodation areas, or at transport locations, such as airports or bus-stations. In the sport-tourism case the survey could be seen as having some of the characteristics of the on-site, user or visitor survey, as discussed below.

Conduct

Stopping people in the street or similar environments for an interview places certain limitations on the interview process. First, an interview conducted in the street cannot generally be as long as one conducted at someone's home – especially when the interviewee is in a hurry. Of course, there are some household interviews which are very short because the interviewee is in a hurry or is a reluctant respondent and there are street interviews which are lengthy because the respondent has plenty of time. As a general rule, however, the street interview must be shorter. In both the home and the street interview situation, before committing themselves to an interview, potential respondents invariably ask: 'How long will it take?' In the home-based situation a reply of '15–20 minutes' is generally acceptable but in the street situation anything more than '5 minutes' would generally lead to a marked reduction in the proportion of people prepared to cooperate. The range of topics/issues/activities which can be covered in a street interview is therefore restricted and this must be taken into account in designing the questionnaire.

The second limitation of the street survey is the problem of contacting a representative sample of the population. Certain types of people might not frequent shopping areas at all, or only infrequently – for instance people who are housebound for various reasons or those who have other people to do their shopping. Such individuals might be of particular importance in some studies, so their omission can significantly compromise the results. There is little that can be done to overcome this problem; it has to be accepted as a limitation of the method. The other side of this coin is that certain groups will be over-represented in shopping streets – notably full-time home/child carers, the retired and the unemployed in suburban shopping areas, or office workers in business areas. It might also be the case that certain areas are frequented more by, for example, young people than old people or by men rather than women, so any sample would be representative of the users of the area, but not of the local population or visitor population as a whole. One approach to overcoming these problems is *quota sampling*.

Quota sampling

The technique of *quota sampling* involves the interviewer being given a predetermined quota of different types of people – for example by age, sex, occupation – to interview. The proportions in each category in the target population must be known in advance – for example by reference to the Population Census **(see Chapter 7)**. For certain types of sport tourism, for example skiing, there may be information from booking data. When the survey is complete, if the sample is still not representative with regard to the key characteristics, further adjustments can be achieved through the process of *weighting* **(see Chapter 13)**. Where background information on the population is not known, it is not possible to use the quota sampling method to achieve representativeness.

The telephone survey

Nature

The telephone survey is particularly popular with political pollsters because of its speed and the ease with which a widespread sample of the community can be contacted. It is also used extensively in market and academic research for the same reasons.

An obvious limitation of the technique is that it excludes non-telephone subscribers – generally low-income groups and some mobile sections of the population. With telephones in virtually all homes in economically developed countries this is not now as serious a problem as it was in the past. In the case of relatively simple surveys like political opinion polls, where the researcher has access to previous results from both telephone and face-to-face interviews, this problem may be overcome by the use of a correction factor – for instance it might be known that inclusion of non-telephone subscribers always adds x per cent to the Labour vote. In certain kinds of market research the absence of the poorer parts of the community from the survey may be unimportant because they do not form a significant part of the market, but for much public policy and academic research this can be a significant limitation.

An emerging problem is the case of households which do not have land-line telephones, relying only on mobile phones, which are not listed in publicly available directories. This is likely to involve mainly young people, who are an important target of much survey work. Again, it may be possible to correct for this statistically if the characteristics of this group are known. In some cases, mobile phone numbers can be contacted randomly when the range of numbers used for domestic, as opposed to business, subscribers is known.

Conduct

Length of interview can be a limitation of telephone surveys – but not as serious as in the case of street interviews; telephone interviews of 10 or 15 minutes are acceptable.

The technique has its own unique set of problems in relation to sampling. Generally, the numbers to be called are selected at random from the telephone directory. Market research companies generally use computer-assisted telephone interviewing (CATI), involving equipment and software which automatically dials random telephone numbers from a digital database. CATI systems also enable the interviewer to key answers directly into a computer, so dispensing with the printed questionnaire. This speeds up the analysis process considerably and cuts down the possibility of error in transcribing results from printed questionnaire to computer. It also explains how the results of overnight political opinion polls can be published in the newspapers the next morning.

If a representative cross-section of the community is to be included then it is necessary for telephone surveys to be conducted in the evenings and/or at weekends if those who have paid jobs are to be included.

A limitation of the telephone interview is that respondents cannot be shown such things as lists or images, for example of activities or attitude dimensions. For long lists, of more than six or seven items, reading them out can be tedious.

It can be argued that telephones have an advantage over face-to-face interviews in that respondents may feel that they are more anonymous and may therefore be more forthcoming in their opinions. But it could also be argued that the face-to-face interview has other advantages in terms of eye-contact and body language which enable the skilled interviewer to conduct a better interview than is possible over the telephone.

The main advantage of the telephone survey is that it is quick and relatively cheap to conduct. However, in some countries there is growing reluctance on the part of the public to cooperate with telephone surveys, resulting in the need to make a number of calls to contact cooperative respondents, thus raising the costs and raising questions about representativeness. The solution being adopted in market research is the use of online methods, discussed below.

Representativeness and response levels

An increasing number of problems arise in the conduct of telephone surveys, including consumer-related, technological, legal and social factors.

Reference has already been made to problems caused by the consumer shift to mobile or cell phone technology: unlike land-line telephones, mobile phone numbers are not publicly listed and geographically identifiable, and people who rely entirely on mobile phones are not a cross-section of the whole community, so continued reliance on land-line telephones for surveys can result in biased samples. In developing countries the history is unfolding differently because the mobile phone has arrived in advance of universal access to land-line telephones.

Technological devices used to control and manage telephone access also present difficulties in contacting survey respondents, including user ID and answer machines/voice mail. Added to this, privacy legislation enables telephone subscribers to deny access for tele-marketing, although bona-fide social research calls are generally exempt.

In addition to consumer and technological change, surveyors note an increasing tendency for members of the public to refuse to cooperate with telephone surveys. Thus, one American organisation reports that, once contact is made, using standard survey techniques, while 58 per cent of contactees agreed to an interview in 1997, this had fallen to 38 per cent by 2003, although these figures were higher (at 74 per cent and 59 per cent, respectively) when more rigorous techniques, including call-backs, were used (Pew Research Center, 2004).

The result of these changes is increased costs for telephone surveys as well as increased concerns about representativeness, resulting in a trend towards e-surveys, as discussed below, typically involving a 'panel' of respondents, see Chapter 5.

National surveys

The comments about national surveys, made in relation to household surveys above, also apply to telephone surveys.

The mail survey

Nature

There are certain situations where the mail or postal method is the only practical survey technique to use. The commonest example is where members or customers of some national organisation are to be surveyed. The costs of conducting face-to-face interviews with even a sample of the members or customers would be substantial – a mail survey is the obvious solution. The mail survey has the advantage that a large sample can be included. In the case of a membership organisation, there may be advantages in surveying the whole membership, even though this may not be necessary in statistical terms. It can, however, be very helpful in terms of the internal politics of the organisation for all members to be given the opportunity to participate in the survey and to 'have their say'.

The problem of low response rates

The most notorious problem of postal surveys is low response rates. In many cases as few as 25 or 30 per cent of those sent a questionnaire bother to reply

1. The interest of the respondent in the survey topic
2. The length of the questionnaire
3. Questionnaire design/presentation/complexity
4. Style, content and authorship of the accompanying letter
5. Provision of a postage-paid reply envelope
6. Rewards for responding
7. Number and timing of reminders/follow-ups

Figure 10.4 Factors affecting mail survey response

and when surveys are poorly conceived and designed the response rate can fall to 3 or 4 per cent. Surveys with only 30 per cent response rates are regularly reported in the research literature, but questions must be raised as to their validity when 70 per cent of the target sample is not represented.

What affects the response rate in mail surveys? Seven different factors can be identified, as listed in Figure 10.4. The various factors and measures listed are discussed in turn below.

1. Interest of the respondent in the survey topic

A survey of a local community about a proposal to route a six-lane highway through the neighbourhood would probably result in a high response rate, but a survey of the same community on general patterns of sport behaviour would probably result in a low response rate. Variation among the population in the level of interest in the topic can result in a biased (that is, unrepresentative) response. For example, a survey on sport facility provision might evoke a high response rate among those interested in sport and a low response rate among those not interested – giving a false impression of community enthusiasm for sport facility provision. To some extent this can be corrected by weighting if the bias corresponds with certain known characteristics of the population. For example, if there was a high response rate from young people and a low response rate from older people, information from the Population Census on the actual proportions of different age-groups in the community could be used to weight the results.

2. Length of the questionnaire

It might be expected that a long questionnaire would discourage potential respondents. It can, however, be argued that other factors, such as the topic and the presentation of the questionnaire, are more important than the length of the questionnaire – that is, if the topic is interesting to the respondent and is well presented then length of questionnaire and the time taken to complete it may be less of an issue.

3. Questionnaire design/presentation/complexity

More care must be taken in design and physical presentation with any respondent-completed questionnaire. Typesetting, colour coding of pages, graphics and so on may be necessary. Sport surveys often present long lists of activities, which can make a questionnaire look very complicated and demanding to complete.

4. The accompanying letter

The letter from the sponsor or researcher which accompanies the questionnaire may have an influence on people's willingness to respond. Does it give a good reason for the survey? Is it from someone, or the type of organisation, whom the potential respondent trusts or respects?

5. Postage-paid reply envelope

It is usual to include a postage-paid envelope for the return of the questionnaire. Some believe that an envelope with a real stamp on it will produce a better response rate than a business reply-paid envelope. Providing reply envelopes with real stamps is more expensive because, apart from the time spent in sticking stamps on envelopes, stamps are effectively wasted on those who do not respond.

6. Rewards

The question of rewards for taking part in a survey can arise in relation to any sort of survey but it is a device used most often in postal surveys. One approach is to send every respondent some small reward, such as a voucher for a firm's or agency's product or service, or even money. A more common approach is to enter all respondents in a draw for a prize. Even a fairly costly prize may be money well spent if it results in a substantial increase in the response rate, particularly when considered in relation to the cost of the alternative methods, such as a household survey involving face-to-face interviews. It could, however, be argued that the introduction of rewards causes certain people to respond for the wrong reasons and that it introduces a potential source of bias in responses. It might also be considered that the inclusion of a prize or reward 'lowers the tone' of the survey and places it in the same category as other, commercial, junk mail that comes through people's letter boxes every day.

7. Reminders/follow-ups

Sensible reminder and follow-up procedures are perhaps the most significant tool available to the researcher. They can include postcard/email/phone reminders, supplying a second copy of the questionnaire and offering a telephone interview, indicated in the sequence suggested in Figure 10.5. Dillman *et al.* (2009) have conducted experiments with the offer of a telephone interview and note that this clearly increases the response rate but may provide different responses from the standard mail survey – this may be seen as a strength (a sort of triangulation) or a weakness.

An example of the effects of follow-ups can be seen in Figure 10.6, which relates to a mail survey of residents' recreational use of a river estuary (sailing, fishing, swimming). It can be seen that the level of responses peaked after only three days and looked likely to cease after about 16 days, which would have given a potential response rate of just 40 per cent. The surges in responses following the sending of the postcard and the second copy of the questionnaire can be seen and the net result was a 75 per cent response rate, which is very

Day		Attachments	Comment
1	Initial mail-out	Questionnaire	–
8	Postcard reminder	–	Email or telephone might be used if available and resources permit.
15	Letter reminder	Copy of questionnaire	Copy of questionnaire is enclosed 'in case the original has been mislaid'). Email might be used. Offer of telephone interview.
22	Final postcard reminder	–	As above, email or phone might be used and offer of telephone interview.

Figure 10.5   Mail survey follow-ups

Source: Dillman *et al.* (2009)

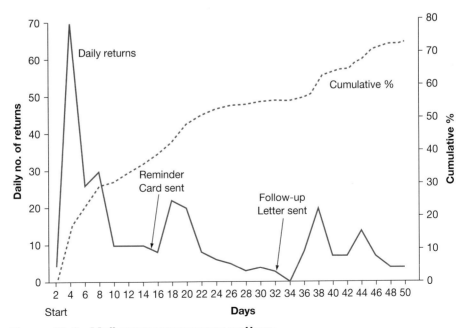

Figure 10.6   Mail survey response pattern

Source: Robertson and Veal (1987)

good for this type of survey. The need for follow-ups must be considered when budgeting for a postal survey, since postage and printing costs are often the most significant item in such budgets.

The sending out of reminders means that it must be possible to identify returned questionnaires, so that reminders are not sent to those who have already replied. This means that questionnaires or envelopes must have an identifying number which can be matched with the mailing list. Some respondents resent this potential breach of confidentiality but it cannot be avoided if only non-respondents are to be followed up. The confidentiality issue may be overcome if the identifying number is placed on the reply envelope rather than the questionnaire. A further possibility is for the replies to be sent to a 'neutral' party, such as a solicitor or accountant. However, there is often a further advantage to being able to identify responses in general terms; known information on respondents can be used to check the representativeness of the response. For instance, the questionnaire may not include respondents' addresses, but the geographical spread of the response can be examined if the identity of the responses is known, and any necessary weighting can be carried out.

It has been shown that sending final reminders with a personalised letter and sending it via certified/registered mail can significantly increase the response rate compared with non-personalised letters and ordinary mail (Gitelson and Drogin (1992)).

How much is enough?

What level of response is acceptable? One answer would be to say that an adequate response has been achieved if the characteristics of non-respondents and the responses they would have given are not significantly different from those of respondents. But how do you know the characteristics and responses of non-respondents? In some cases the researcher has access to some limited information on non-respondents – for example their geographical location and other information which might be held on the database from which addresses were drawn. This can be used to make comparisons.

One approach which covers both characteristics and question responses is to compare early responders with later responders – if there is no difference this may indicate that further pursuit of non-responders is not necessary. It would, of course, be helpful to the research community if results of such examinations were publicly available so that conclusions could be drawn as to whether there is a general response rate at which further response patterns stabilise, whether there is no such rate or whether it is variable. Just a few researchers have conducted experiments on this question **(see Chapter 11 in Case study 11.8)**.

Gitelson and Drogin (1992) used a user/site/visitor and mail survey combo (described below). Since the mail survey sample respondents and non-respondents had all been interviewed on-site, it was possible to compare the characteristics of the two groups in terms of the information from the on-site survey questionnaires.

Mail and user/site/visitor survey combos

A common practice is to conduct a brief face-to-face interview at a sport venue or event and ask respondents to complete a mail survey (or e-survey) questionnaire on their return home. This shortens the time taken to conduct the on-site interview but also means that respondents can give views about the facility or event when their visit has been completed in its entirety. In some cases the mail-back questionnaire may be provided after the on-site interview; in other cases addresses (or email addresses) may be obtained and the questionnaire mailed out. Of course, the mail or email part of the survey will be subject to the problems of non-response discussed under mail surveys.

Discussing/analysing non-response

However conscientious the researcher may be in taking efforts to maximise the response rate in a survey, there will still be a certain level of non-response. In analysing and writing up results this issue should be addressed and consideration given to the extent to which there is any reason to believe, or even evidence to show, that the non-respondents may be different from the respondents, suggesting the possibility of the sample being biased. Jordan *et al.* (2011) provide an analysis of the often inadequate discussion of these matters in sport management research. The issue is discussed further in the final chapter on research report preparation.

E-surveys

Nature and conduct

E-surveys, or electronic or online surveys, are conducted via the Internet. Standard 'hard copy' mail has been the traditional medium for mail surveys and is still popular, but costs, speed and response rates, as discussed above, are increasingly seen as drawbacks of the method. Similarly, the growing problems of traditional telephone surveys have been outlined above. The result has been increasing use of the electronic or e-survey. A number of formats exist, ranging from simply using an email to transmit a traditional questionnaire, to a fully electronic, online format, as summarised in Figure 10.7.

The first version simply uses email to replace the sending-out process. The second version uses email to send out and return, and uses a word-processor and/or spreadsheet rather than hard copy, but the questionnaire is still in traditional format. In the electronic versions the whole process takes place online and the questionnaire has become interactive. The questionnaire simplifies completion for the respondent so that, when 'filter' questions are involved,

Type	Request	Questionnaire	Completion	Return
Hybrid email/mail	Email	Attached text file	Manual on hard copy	Mail
Hybrid email	Email	Attached text file	Word-processor/ spreadsheet	Email + attached text file
Fully electronic: ad hoc	Email	Online, interactive	Online	Online submission
Fully electronic: panel	Panel member email	Online, interactive	Online	Online submission

Figure 10.7   Types of e-survey

which require the respondent to skip certain questions and jump to a particular section of the questionnaire, this takes place automatically.

Commercial survey organisations offer e-survey services in which the customer/researcher specifies the questions to be included, then asks survey participants to access the survey organisation's website to complete the survey. The customer/researcher can download the results on demand.

Many corporate organisations, such as banks, from time to time invite their online customers to complete online questionnaire surveys to obtain customer feedback on service quality. Similarly, while hotels still invite guests to complete a hard-copy feedback questionnaire on completion of their stay, it is now common for guests to receive an invitation to participate in an online survey via email some time after their return home.

An e-survey may be combined with a user/site/visitor survey in a similar way to the 'mail and user/site/visitor survey combo' discussed above.

Advantages and disadvantages

The advantages of e-surveys to the researcher are the low cost and the speed with which they may be conducted. The fully electronic versions are designed to be very user-friendly, as noted above.

The disadvantage of the e-survey is that it is confined to those with access to the Internet and, while the sending of reminders is cheap, the problem of low response may still be a problem for some surveys because they may be seen as part of the increasing volume of 'junk mail' received via email.

User/on-site/visitor surveys

Nature

The terms *on-site*, *site*, *user* or *visitor* survey are used to refer to this type of survey. *On-site* and *site survey* tend to be used in the context of outdoor studies, *user survey* in the context of indoor facilities, and *visitor survey* when tourists or day-trippers, including sport-tourists, are involved. The term user survey is utilised in this section to cover all these situations.

The user survey is the most common type of survey used by managers in sport. In general, this is a more controlled setting than the street survey; interviewers are seen by respondents to be part of the management of the facility and usually it is possible to interview users at a convenient time when they are not in a rush, as they may be in the street or shopping mall.

Conduct

User surveys can be conducted by interviewer or by respondent-completion. Unless carefully supervised, respondent-completion methods can lead to a poor standard in the completion of questionnaires and a low response level. And as with all low response levels, this can be a source of serious bias in that those who reply may be unrepresentative of the users or visitors as a whole.

The usual respondent-completion survey involves handing users a questionnaire on their arrival at the site and collecting them on their departure, or conducting the whole procedure upon departure. For situations where suitable breaks take place during a user's stay, for example half-time or quarter-time at a sports match, interviewing may take place during such breaks. Where respondent-completion is thought to be desirable or necessary, sufficient staff should be employed to check all users leaving the site, to ask for the completed questionnaires, to provide replacements for questionnaires which have been mislaid and to assist in completing questionnaires, including completion by interview if necessary. Leaving a pile of questionnaires with a busy receptionist to hand out and collect rarely works well.

Conducting user surveys by interview is generally preferable to respondent-completion for the reasons discussed earlier in this chapter. The use of interviewers obviously has a cost disadvantage but, depending on the length of the interview, costs per interview are usually comparatively low. Typically, a user-survey interview will take about five minutes, but in some longer-stay facilities, such as a beach or all-day event, significantly longer interviews are possible. Given the need to check through completed questionnaires, the gaps in user traffic and the need for interviewers to take breaks, it is reasonable to expect interviewers in such situations to complete about six interviews in an hour. Such estimates are, of course, necessary when considering project budgets and timetables.

The survey methods considered so far have been fairly multi-purpose – they could be used for market research for a range of products or services, by public agencies for a variety of policy-orientated purposes, or for academic research, which may or may not be policy or management orientated. User surveys are more specific. The most common use of such surveys is for policy, planning or management purposes. They are the type of survey which readers of this book are most likely to be involved with; they are the most convenient for students to 'cut their teeth' on; and they are the most common surveys for individual managers to become involved in. For these reasons the roles of user surveys are considered in some detail below.

The uses of user surveys

What can user surveys be used for? Four topics are discussed briefly below: catchment area; user socio-demographic profile; user opinions; and non-users.

Catchment area

What is the *catchment* or *market* area of the facility or service? That is, what geographical area do most of the users come from? This can be important in terms of advertising policy. Management can concentrate on its existing catchment area and focus its advertising and marketing accordingly or it can take conscious decisions to use marketing to attempt to extend its catchment area. But in order to take either of these approaches it is first necessary to establish the current catchment area. In some cases this information is already available from membership records, but this does not always reflect the pattern of actual use, so in most cases it can only be discovered by means of a survey, that is, by asking users where they live or where they have travelled from to use the facility.

User socio-demographic profile

What is the socio-economic/demographic profile of the facility users? It might be thought that a management capable of observation would be able to make this assessment without the need for a survey. This depends on the type of facility, the extent to which management is in continuous contact with users and the variability of the user profile. For example, the manager of a small gym might be very well informed on this because of the price of membership and the relatively narrow demographic characteristics of the clientele. But managers of large multi-use centres, while they may have an impression of the variety of different types of user groups, will be less informed, or even misinformed, about the detail.

Profile information can be used in a number of ways. As with data on catchment area, it can be used to consolidate or extend the market. Very often the commercial operator will opt to consolidate – to focus on a particular client group and maximise the market share of that group, by appropriate advertising, pricing and product development. In the case of a public sector facility the remit is usually to attract as wide a cross-section of the community as possible, so the data would be used to highlight those sections of the community not being catered for and therefore requiring marketing, pricing or product development attention. More broadly, a public agency responsible for a range of types of facility could use the data to check whether the community is being appropriately provided for by all its facilities taken together.

User opinions

What are the opinions of users about the design, accessibility and services quality of the facility? Such opinion data are invariably collected in user surveys and are usually of great interest to managers, but the interpretation of the data is not without its difficulties. If management is looking for pertinent criticisms, current users may be the wrong group to consult. Those who are most critical are likely no longer to be using the facility. Those using the facility may be reluctant to be very critical because it undermines their own situation – if the place is so poor, why are they there? Furthermore, those who are prepared to be critical may not be the sorts of clients for whom the facility is designed.

In some situations, people have little choice between facilities so criticisms are perhaps more easily interpreted. For example, parents' comments about the suitability of a local park for children's play can be particularly pertinent when it is the only play area available in the neighbourhood.

When opinion data have been collected it is often difficult to know precisely what to do with the results. Very often the largest group of users has no complaint or suggestion to make – either because they cannot be bothered to think of anything in the interview situation or because of the respondent selection process referred to above. Often the most common complaint is raised by as few as 10 per cent of users. If this is the most common complaint, then logically something ought to be done about it by the management – but it could also be said that 90 per cent of the users are not concerned about that issue, so perhaps there is no need to do anything about it! Very often, therefore, management can use survey results to suit their own preferences. If they want to do something about X, they can say that X was complained about by more users than anything else; if they do not want to do anything about X, they can say that 90 per cent of users are satisfied with X the way it is.

Managers mostly want to enhance and maximise the quality of the experience enjoyed by their visitors: it may not be criticism of specific features that is important but users' overall evaluations of the experience. Thus users can be asked to rate a facility or area using a scale such as: very good/good/fair/poor/very poor or very satisfied/satisfied/dissatisfied/very dissatisfied. The results of such an evaluation can be used to compare users' evaluations of one facility with another. Or they could be used to examine the same facility at different times to see if satisfaction has increased or declined. This is, of course, a feature of evaluative research **(see Chapters 1 and 2)**.

Non-users

User surveys by definition involve only current users of a facility or current visitors to an area. This is often cited as a limitation of such surveys, the implication being that non-users may be of more interest than users if the aim of management is to increase the number of users or visitors. Caution should, however, be exercised in moving to consider conducting research on non-users. For a start, the number of non-users is usually very large. For example, in a city of a million population, a facility which has 5,000 users has 995,000 non-users! In a country with a population of 50 million, a ski resort which attracts a million visitors a year has 49 million non-visitors, and if management is interested in international visitors, they have around 6 billion non-visitors! The idea that all non-users are potential users, and should therefore be researched, is therefore somewhat naive.

The user survey can, however, help in focusing any research which is to be conducted on non-users. For example, in the case of a local sport facility the user survey defines the catchment area and, unless there is some reason for believing that the catchment area can or should be extended, the non-users to be studied are those who live within that area. Similarly, the user profile indicates the type of person currently using the facility, and again, unless there is a conscious decision to attempt to change that profile, the non-users to be studied are the ones with that profile living within the defined catchment area. Importantly, comparison between the user profile and the profile of the population of the catchment area, as revealed by Population Census data **(see Chapter 7)**, can be used to estimate the numbers and characteristics of non-users in the area. Thus user surveys can reveal something about non-users!

User/site/visitor and mail/e-survey combo

In the discussion of mail surveys above, the idea of a 'mail and user/site/ visitor survey combo' is discussed, in which a short face-to-face on-site interview is followed by a request to the respondent to complete a mail survey or e-survey questionnaire on their return home.

Captive group surveys

Nature

The *captive group* survey is generally not referred to in other research methods texts. It refers to the situation where the people to be included in the survey comprise the membership of some group where access can be negotiated *en bloc*. Such groups include school children, adult education groups, clubs of various kinds and groups of employees – although all have their various unique characteristics.

Conduct

A roomful of cooperative people can provide a number of respondent-completed questionnaires very quickly. Respondent-completion is less problematic in captive situations than in less controlled situations because it is possible to take the group through the questionnaire question by question and therefore ensure good standards of completion.

The most common example of a captive group is schoolchildren, since the easiest way to contact children under school leaving age is via schools. The method may, however, appear simpler than it is in practice. Research on children for education purposes has become so common that education authorities are cautious about permitting access to children for surveys. Very often permission for any survey work must be obtained from the central education authority – the permission of the class teacher or head teacher is not sufficient.

The use of tertiary students for psychologically orientated research is very common and a considerable amount of research is conducted using sport teams.

While the most economical use of this technique involves using a respondent-completed questionnaire, interview methods can also be used. The essential feature is that access to members of the group is facilitated by their membership of that group and the fact that they are gathered together in one place at one time. It is important to be aware of the criteria for membership of the group and to compare that with the needs of the research. In some cases an apparent match can be misleading. For example, attendees at a retired people's club meeting do not include all retired people – it excludes 'non-joiners' and the housebound. While schools include all young people, care must be taken over their catchment areas, compared with the study area of the research, and with the mix of public sector and private schools.

Ethical research principles indicate that individuals in the above 'captive' situations should participate in research only on a voluntary basis and should not feel pressured to participate **(see Chapter 4.)**

Questionnaire design

Introduction – research problems and information requirements

The important principle in designing questionnaires is to take it slowly and carefully and to remember why the research is being done. Very often researchers move too quickly into 'questionnaire design mode' and begin listing all the things 'it would be interesting to ask'. In many organisations a draft questionnaire is circulated for comment and everyone in the organisation joins in. The process begins to resemble Christmas-tree decorating – nobody must be left out and everybody must be allowed to contribute their favourite bauble. This is not the best way to proceed!

The decision to conduct a questionnaire survey should itself be the culmination of a careful process of thought and discussion, involving consideration of all possible methods, not just surveys. The concepts and variables involved,

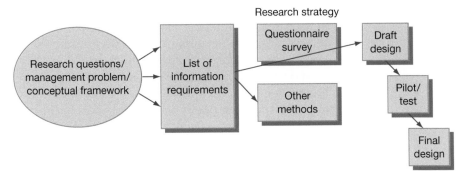

Figure 10.8 Questionnaire design process

and the relationships to be investigated, possibly in the form of hypotheses, theories, models or evaluative frameworks, should be clear and should guide the questionnaire design process, as illustrated in Figure 10.8. It is not advisable to *begin* with a list of questions to be included in the questionnaire. The starting point should ideally be an examination of the management, planning, policy or theoretical questions to be addressed, followed by the drawing up of a list of the information required to address the problems. This is outlined in Chapter 3 as elements 1–5 of the research process. Element 6, deciding the research strategy, involves determining which of the listed information requirements should be met by means of a questionnaire survey and which should be met by other methods. Questions should be included in the questionnaire only if they relate to requirements listed in element 5. This means that every question included must be linked back to the *research questions.*

In designing a questionnaire, the researcher should, of course, have sought out as much previous research on the topic or related topics as possible. This can have an effect on the overall design of a project. More specifically, if it is decided that the study in hand should have points of comparison with earlier studies, data will need to be collected on a similar basis to that in the earlier studies. Questionnaires from previous studies therefore become part of the input into the questionnaire design process.

Example questionnaires

Before considering questionnaire design in more detail, some examples of short questionnaires are presented in Case study 10.1, including typical questions used in household and site surveys, with interviewer-completed and respondent-completed examples:

- *Example A: site/street survey* is a questionnaire used to assess students' attitudes to sport on campus – it is labelled as a site/street survey questionnaire since, as it would be administered to students on-campus, it partly resembles a site or user survey, but since not all students may make use of the services being examined, it resembles a survey conducted in a street or shopping centre. It is presented as respondent-completed, but completion would probably best be conducted 'under supervision' – that is, completed and handed back to a survey worker at the time, rather than being handed out for later return, which would inevitably produce a low response rate. If the cooperation of the university authorities is obtained so that the questionnaire can be handed out and completed in class time, it becomes a 'captive group' survey.

- *Example B: household survey* is an interviewer-completed questionnaire for a household survey on sport/active holidays.

- *Example C: site survey* is an interviewer-completed questionnaire for a site survey of park users.

Annotations in the left-hand margin of these example questionnaires indicate the type of question involved, as discussed later in the chapter. These example questionnaires cannot, of course, cover all situations, but they give a wide range of examples of questions and appropriate formats.

General design issues

Wording of questions

In wording the questions for a questionnaire the researcher should:

- avoid jargon;
- simplify wherever possible;
- avoid ambiguity;
- avoid leading questions;
- ask only one question at a time (i.e. avoid multi-purpose questions).

Examples of good and bad practice in question wording are given in Figure 10.9.

Pre-coded vs. open-ended questions

As illustrated in Figure 10.10, an *open-ended* question is one where the interviewer asks a question without any prompting of the range of answers to be expected, and writes down the respondent's reply verbatim. In a respondent-completed questionnaire a line or space is left for respondents to write their answers. A closed or pre-coded question is one where the respondent is offered a range of answers to choose from, either verbally or from a show card or, in the case of a respondent-completed questionnaire, having the range of answers set out in the questionnaire and (usually) being asked to tick boxes.

Case study 10.1   Example questionnaires

A: Site/street survey respondent-completed

	Campus Sporting Life Survey 2013		Office Use
			# _____

1. Which of the following best describes your current situation?

Standard pre-coded

Full-time student with no regular paid work	☐ 1	
Full-time student with some regular paid work	☐ 2	__ status
Part-time student with full-time job	☐ 3	
	☐ 4	

2. Which of the following university sport-facilities have you used in the last 4 weeks?

Pre-coded
Multiple response
- dichotomous

Swimming pool	☐ 1	__ pool
Gym	☐ 1	__ gym
Squash court	☐ 1	__ squash
Attended a sports match as spectator	☐ 1	__ spectate

3. In thinking about your possible use of the sport facilities services, provided on campus what are the most important considerations for you? Please rank the items below in terms of their importance to you. Rank them from 1 for the most important to 5 for the least important.

Ranking

	Rank	
Free or cheap access	___	__ cheap
Convenient opening hours	___	__ hours
Quality of facilities	___	__ qual
Opportunities to socialise/meet people	___	__ meet
Available time	___	__ time

4. Approximately how much do you spend in an average week on leisure, sport and social activities on and off campus?

Numerical - uncoded

£_____

_____
spend

5. Please indicate the importance of the following to you in relation to your participation in sport

Likert scales

	Very important	Important	Not at all Important	
Relaxation	☐ 3	☐ 2	☐ 1	__ relax
Social interaction	☐ 3	☐ 2	☐ 1	__ social
Fitness	☐ 3	☐ 2	☐ 1	__ fitness

Open-ended
Multiple response
- categories

6. What suggestions would you make for improving campus sport?

__ sug1
__ sug2
__ sug3

_____

_____

Standard pre-coded

7. You are: Male ☐ 1   Female ☐ 2   __ gend

Numerical - uncoded

8. Your age last birthday was: ____ years   __ age

B: Household survey – interviewer-completed

Respondent No	**Short Stay Sport Holiday** ____#
	Introductory remarks: Hallo. We are from St. Anthony's College and we are conducting a survey on people's short-stay holidays involving sporting activity. Would you mind answering a few questions? It will take just a few minutes and the results will be kept confidential.
Pre-coded, factual	1. In the last year, have you been on a short holiday trip of one, two or three nights away from home involving a sporting activity? Yes 1 – go to Q.2 No 2 – end interview ____
Open-ended, factual, numerical	2. How many times did you go on such trips in the year? Number of times: ___ go to q. 2 ____
Open-ended, factual	3. On your last trip, where did you go? _____ ____

4. What were the main activities you engaged in on your visit?

Multiple response	a. Sightseeing	1	e. Golf	1	__ __
	b. Eating and drinking	1	f. Fishing	1	__ __
	c. Swimming	1	g. Skiing	1	__ __
	d. Walking	1	h. Other	1	__ __

5. To what extent do you agree with the following statements?

	Agree strongly	Agree	Neither	Disagree	Disagree strongly	
Simple pre-coded, factual	A short break is as valuable as long holiday	5	4	3	2	1	____
	Holidays make life worth living	5	4	3	2	1	____

6. Can you tell me which of the following age-groups you fall into?

Pre-coded with showcard factual	**Under 15**	**A**
	15-19	**B**
	20-29	**C**
	30-59	**D**
	60+	**E**

7. Which of the following best describes your current situation?

Pre-coded with showcard factual	**In full-time paid work**	**A**
	In part-time paid work	**B**
	In full-time education	**C**
	Full-time home/child care	**D**
	Retired	**E**
	Looking for work	**F**
	Other	**G**

Pre-coded, factual, observed	THANK YOU FOR YOUR HELP		
	Observe gender:	Male	1
		Female	2

C: Site survey – interviewer-completed

> The survey is being carried out for the local council to find out what users of the park think of the park, and what changes they would like to see. A total of 100 users of the park are interviewed at the only entrance, in batches of 10, at different days of the week, at different times of the day, and in different weather conditions.

Ramsey Street Park Survey
Excuse me: we are carrying out a survey for the council to find out what people think about the park.
Could you spare a few minutes to answer a few questions?

1. How often do you visit this park?

Every day	1
Several times a week	2
Once a week	3
Every 2 or 3 weeks	4
Once a month	5
Less often	6
First visit	7

Simple pre-coded

2. Where have you travelled from today?

Home	1
Work	2
School/college/univ.	3
Other	4

Simple pre-coded, factual

3. What suburb is that in?

_____

Open-ended, factual

4. How long did it take you to get here?

5 minutes or less	1
6–15 minutes	2
16–30 minutes	3
31 minutes or more	4

Simple pre-coded factual

5. How did you travel here?

Walk	1
Car	2
Motorbike	3
Bicycle	4
Bus/tram	5
Other	6

Simple pre-coded factual

6. What do you like most about the park?

_____

Open-ended, opinion / factual

7. What do you like least about the park?

_____

Open-ended, opinion

8. Looking at the card, where would you place this park, in relation to others you know?

A. Way below average	**1**
B. Below average	**2**
C. Average	**3**
D. Above average	**4**
E. Well above average	**5**

Attitude statement with show-card

9. Can you tell me which of these age-groups you fall into?

Under 15	**A**
15-19	**B**
20-29	**C**
30-59	**D**
60+	**E**

Pre-coded factual with showcard

10. How many people are there in your group here today, including your self?

Alone	1
Two	2
3–4	3
5 or more	4

Pre-coded factual

Open-ended, factual, numerical

11. How many vehicles did your group arrive in? ____

Observe, factual

THANK YOU FOR YOUR HELP

Observe:	Male	1
	Female	2

Principle	Bad example	Improved version
Use simple language	What is your frequency of utilisation of sports goods retailers?	How often do you use sports shops?
Avoid ambiguity	Do you play sport very often?	Have you played any of the following sports within the last four weeks? (show list)
Avoid leading questions	Are you against the extension of the airport?	What is your opinion on the extension of the airport? Are you for it, against it or not concerned?
Ask just one question at a time.	Do you use the local sports centre, and if so what do you think of its facilities?	1. Do you use the local sports centre? Yes/No 2. What do you think of the facilities in the centre?

Figure 10.9   Question wording: examples of good and bad practice

Open-ended
What is the main constraint on your ability to study?

_____

Pre-coded/closed
Which of the following/items listed on the card is the main constraint on your ability to study? (show card – if interviewer-completed)
A. My job $\Box_1$
B. Timetabling $\Box_2$
C. Child care $\Box_3$
D. Spouse/partner $\Box_4$
E. Money $\Box_5$
F. Energy $\Box_6$
G. Other _____ $\Box_7$

Card shown to respondent:

A. My job
B. Timetabling of the course
C. Child care
D. Spouse/partner
E. Money
F. Energy
G. Other _____

Figure 10.10   Open-ended vs. pre-coded questions – example

In the open-ended case there is no prior list. In the closed/pre-coded case there is a list which is shown to the respondent. A third possibility, in an interviewer-administered survey, is a combination of the two, where the question is asked in an open-ended manner, no card is shown to the respondent, but the answer is recorded by ticking the appropriate box on a pre-coded list. If the answer does not fit any of the items on the list, it is written in an 'other' category and may be given a code at the analysis stage.

The advantage of the open-ended question is that the respondent's answer is not unduly influenced by the interviewer or by the question wording and the verbatim replies from respondents can provide a rich source of varied material which might have been hidden by categories on a pre-coded list. Figure 10.11 gives an example of the range of responses which can result from a single open-ended question.

Pre-coded groups are often used when asking respondents about quantified information, such as age, income, expenditure, because of convenience and saving any embarrassment respondents may have about divulging precise figures. However, there is an advantage in using the open-ended approach for such data, that is, in obtaining actual figures rather than group codes, in that it permits the flexible option of grouping categories in alternative ways when carrying out the analysis. It also enables averages and other measures to be calculated and facilitates a range of statistical analysis not possible with groups. The actual figure is therefore often more useful for analysis purposes.

Open-ended questions have two major disadvantages. First, the analysis of verbatim answers to qualitative questions for computer analysis is laborious and may result in a final set of categories which are of no more value than a well-constructed pre-coded list. In the case of the answers in Figure 10.11, for example, for detailed analysis it may be necessary to group the answers into, say, six groups – this would be time-consuming and would involve a certain amount of judgement in grouping individual answers, which can be a source of errors. This process is discussed in more detail under coding below. Often, therefore, an open-ended question is used in a pilot survey, the results from which are then used to devise a coded list of categories for the main survey.

The second disadvantage of the open-ended approach is that, in the case of respondent-completed questionnaires, response rates to such questions can be very low: people are often too lazy or too busy to write out free-form answers and may have literacy or language problems. When to use open-ended or closed questions is therefore a matter of judgement.

Types of information

Generally, the information to be gathered from questionnaire surveys can be divided into three groups:

1. Activities/behaviour   What?

Question: Do you have any complaints about this (beach/picnic) area?
(Site survey in a beachside National Park with boating, swimming, fishing and camping. Number of responses in brackets)

Sand bars (22)

Parking (5)

Wild car driving (1)

Lack of beach area (1)

Too few shops (1)

Too few picnic tables (4)

No timber for barbecue (2)

Need more picnic space (3)

Need boat hire facilities (1)

Need active recn facilities (1)

Litter/pollution (74)

Urban sprawl (1)

Need wharf fishing access (1)

Lack of info. on walking trails (1)

Not enough facilities (3)

Slow barbecues (2)

Uncontrolled camping (1)

Lack/poor toilets (9)

Amenities too far from camp site (1)

Too much development (4)

(Speed) boats (44)

Need more trees for shade (1)

Yobbos drinking beer on beach (1)

Spear fishermen (1)

Water skiers (2)

Against nudism (3)

Loud music (1)

Dumped cars (1)

Traffic (1)

Poor roads (1)

Sand flies (1)

More barbecues (1)

Shells/oysters (1)

Need outdoor cafes (1)

Need more food places (1)

Water too shallow (1)

Uncontrolled boats (23)

Jet skis (39)

Surveys (1)

Should be kept for locals (1)

Seaweed (3)

Need showers (1)

Administration of National Park (1)

Maintenance and policing of Park (1)

Trucks on beach (2)

Anglers (1)

Crowds/tourists (26)

Having to pay entry fee (6)

Houses along waterfront (2)

Unpleasant smell (drain) (2)

Sales people (1)

Need electric barbecues (1)

Dogs (21)

No access to coast (1)

Park rangers not operating in interest of the public (1)

Behaviour of others (20)

Access – long indirect road (1)

Need more shops (2)

Navigation marks unclear (1)

Need more taps (1)

Need more swings (1)

No first-aid facilities (1)

Need powered caravan sites (1)

Allow dogs (1)

Private beach areas (1)

Lack of restaurant (1)

Need rain shelters (1)

Can't spear fish (1)

No road shoulders for cyclists (1)

Remove rocks from swim areas (1)

Dangerous boat ramp pollutant activities (1)

Figure 10.11 Example of range of replies resulting from an open-ended question
Source: Robertson and Veal, 1987

2. Respondent characteristics   Who?

3. Attitudes/motivations   Why?

Figure 10.12 lists some of the more common types of information collected under these three headings. The items covered are, of course, necessarily general in nature and do not cover all the specialised types of information which can be collected by questionnaire surveys. Some of these items of information require more intrusive questions than others – for example income. And some can be difficult to ascertain accurately – for example occupation or details of

---

1. Activities and events/places

Site/visitor surveys
- Activities while on site or in the area
- Use of site attractions/facilities
- Frequency of visit
- Time spent on site
- Expenditure per head – amounts/purposes
- Travel-related information
- Trip origin (where travelled from)
- Trip purpose
- Home address
- Travel mode
- Travel time
- Accommodation type used

Household/telephone/postal surveys
- Activities
- What, where, how often, time spent,
- When, who with?
- Use of particular facilities/sites
- Travel mode to out-of-home activities
- Expenditure patterns
- Past activities (personal sport histories)
- Planned future activities
- Sports equipment owned

2. Respondent characteristics – all survey types
- Gender
- Age
- Economic status (paid work, retired etc.)
- Occupation/social class (own or 'head of household')
- Previous employment history
- Income (own or household)
- Education/qualifications
- Marital/family status
- Household type/family size
- Life-cycle
- Ethnic group/country of birth
- Residential location/trip origin
- Mobility - driving licence, private transport
- Party/group size/type (site/visitor surveys)
- Self-assessed health status

3. Attitude/motivation information – examples

Site/visitor surveys
- Reasons for choice of site/area
- Meaning/importance/values
- Satisfaction/evaluation of experience/services
- Comments on facility
- Future intentions/hopes

Household/telephone/postal surveys
- Sporting aspirations/needs
- Evaluation of services/facilities available
- Psychological meaning of activities/satisfactions
- Reactions to development/provision proposals
- Values – re environment, competition, etc.

Figure 10.12   Range of information in sport questionnaires

expenditure while on a visit. They are not therefore all equally suitable for all survey situations.

Activity/events/places questions

Activity is at the core of sport research and the procedure for measuring it is far from simple. A variety of possible measures is indicated in Figure 7.2, including the participation rate, the number of participants, the volume of activity or visits, time and money spent and intensity of activity. In any study, consideration should be given as to which types of measure are necessary. The issues are discussed in turn below: in relation to sport participation and frequency separately.

In addition to *activity*, the terms *events* and *places* are used to reflect the scope of the phenomena being studied. For some research purposes it is only necessary to know that a person has engaged in a generic activity – for example 'played squash'. In yet other cases it is necessary to know the geographical location, or 'place', of the activity – for example 'visited a sport facility within/ outside the local government area', or the precise facility – for example 'visited X sport centre'. In other cases, it is not just the generic activity or the place that is of interest but also the specific organised event – for example 'swimming carnival at the pool'.

Devising questions to gather information on activities in sport participation surveys presents four main issues:

- operationalising the term 'sport';
- whether to use an open-ended or pre-coded format;
- the reference period for participation;
- intensity.

The scope of the term 'sport' should be clear from very early in the planning of a research projects; it is, after all, part of the process of defining and operationalising concepts **(see Chapter 3)**. This will have involved deciding how broad a concept of 'sport' to use; in particular, whether it encompasses non-organised activity and non-leisure exercise activity **(see Figure 1.1)**. This will need to be made clear to the respondent through the introductory remarks and the wording of questions.

An open-ended format question simply asks respondents to list the sporting activities they have engaged in over a specified period. Without any prompting of the range of activities intended to be included, respondents might have difficulty in recalling all their activities, and in any case may not understand the full scope of the word 'sport'. Providing people with checklists of activities to choose from may be unwieldy, but it ensures that all respondents consider the same range of options. The disadvantage of the checklist is that the length of the list may be daunting to some respondents, particularly the less literate, and activities later in the list may be under-represented. In the case of an interviewer-completed questionnaire the main problem may be the time it takes to read out the list and the problem of patience and tedium which it may entail, so a show-card may be used; but of course, this is not possible with telephone interviews. The UK *General Household Survey* compromised by offering a checklist of about a dozen 'types' of sport activity, such as home-based activities, and outdoor and indoor activity as an *aide-mémoire* for the respondent.

The reference period for recalling activities crucially affects the survey findings as noted in Chapter 7. For example, recent Australian survey data shows that the proportion of the adult population who claimed to have taken part in at least one exercise/recreation/sport activity over the year prior to interview was 82.3 per cent, but the proportion who had taken part in the two weeks prior to interview was just 69.6 per cent (SCORS, 2011). The shorter the time-period used the more accurate the recall of respondents is likely to be, but shorter time-periods exclude large proportions of participants in those activities which are engaged in relatively infrequently. This can be seen in Table 10.1 which refers to some older data on participation rates in Britain in 1987 and shows that the effect of the length of reference period varies for different activities. It should also be noted that a reference time-period shorter than a year necessitates conducting the survey at different times of the year in order to take account of seasonal variation in types and levels of participation.

In local surveys or in surveys focused on specific policy areas, it may be of interest to explore the use of specific, named, sport facilities or events using a variety of approaches to measuring use.

In the case of site/user surveys there is usually little problem in asking about activities, since the range of possible activities is limited to those available on the site. It is usual to ask people what activities they plan to engage in or have engaged in during their visit. Use of specific ancillary facilities – such as refreshment facilities – is also generally explored.

Table 10.1   Participation in sport/physical recreation activities by reference period, Britain, 1987

Activity	% of persons aged 16+ participating in:		
	A. year	B. four weeks	Ratio of A:B
Walking	68.2	44.5	1.5
Swimming: indoor	35.1	12.8	2.7
Swimming: outdoor	14.9	2.9	5.1
Keep fit/yoga	20.7	12.3	1.7
Golf	11.0	4.7	2.3
Tennis	7.1	2.0	3.3
Cricket	3.3	0.9	3.7
Skiing	2.6	0.3	8.7

Source: General Household Survey, adapted from Gratton (2005: 117)

Sport tourism activities/events/places

In the case of household questionnaire surveys concerned with sport tourism, the activity question concerns trips taken away from the home area over a specified time-period in regard to sport. As with local sport activities, a major consideration is the recall time-period. For major holidays a one-year recall period is not out of the question, but for short breaks, asking about trips during that length of time may lead to inaccuracies in recall, so a shorter time-period of, say, three months is often adopted. This means that a survey must be conducted at different times of the year to capture seasonal variation.

A second time-period issue concerns the definition of tourist 'trip'. The definition used in a survey may follow an accepted definition of tourism, for example a trip involving a stay away from home of one night or more. However, in some local tourism studies *day-trips* above a certain distance may also be of interest.

In addition to indicating trips taken, household sport-tourism questionnaires also generally include questions on the trip destination, activities at the destination (active or passive/spectator), length of stay, travel mode and type of accommodation used. Tourism surveys are usually much more concerned with economic matters than local sport surveys, so questions on the cost of the trip and of expenditure in various categories are often included.

For site surveys in a sport tourism context, the activity questions asked of tourists may be similar to those asked of locals but the reference period will of course be the period of their stay in the destination.

Media use

Questionnaires often include questions on media use, sometimes because viewing sport via the media is of interest, but also because such information can be useful when considering advertising policy. To obtain accurate information in this area would require a considerable number of questions on frequency of reading/viewing/listening and, in the case of electronic media, the type of programmes favoured. When the research is concerned with small-scale local facilities or services, television advertising is generally out of the question because of cost, so information on television watching may not be gathered. Similar considerations may apply to magazine and national newspaper reading. For many surveys, therefore, two questions are involved (show-cards with lists of publications would usually be used):

● What (local) newspapers do you read regularly, that is, at least weekly?

● What (local) radio stations do you listen to regularly, that is, at least twice a week?

Respondent characteristics

Age

Any examination of sport participation data will show the importance of age in differentiating patterns of behaviour and attitudes; it is therefore one of the data items most commonly included in questionnaires. The main decision to be made is whether to use pre-coded groups or ask for respondents' actual age. The advantages and disadvantages of the two approaches are discussed above, under pre-coded vs. open-ended questions. If using pre-coded groups, it is important to ensure that there are no overlapping age-categories. For example, in the following it would not be clear into which group a 14-year-old respondent would fall.

A 0–14
B 14–19

Note that, to ensure comparability with Population Census data, age-groups should be specified as: 15–19, 20–24, 25–29, etc., *not* 16–20, 21–25, 26–30 etc.

Economic status/occupation/socio-economic group/class

A person's economic and occupational situation clearly impinges on sport behaviour. Information on such matters is important for marketing and planning and also in relation to public policy concerns with equity. Economic status is a person's situation vis-à-vis the formal economy, as listed in Figure 10.13. In contemporary developed economies, only about half the population is engaged in the paid workforce.

Occupation typically denotes a person's type of paid work, so it is generally asked only of those identified from the economic status question as being in paid work. Others (e.g. unemployed or retired) are sometimes asked what their last paid job was or what the occupation of the 'main breadwinner' of the household is. Such questions can, however, become complex because of full-time students living with parents or independently, single parents living on social security and so on. In a household survey it may be possible to pursue these matters, but in other situations, such as site surveys, it may not be appropriate because it would seem too intrusive. For those in paid work the sorts of question asked are:

- What is your occupation?

- What sort of work do you do?

- Which of the groups on this card best describes your occupation?

Sufficient information should be obtained to enable respondents to be classified into an appropriate occupational category. Market researchers and official bodies, such as Office for National Statistics, tend to use slightly different classifications, as shown in Figure 10.13. Such groupings, along with economic status, are often referred to as a person's *socio-economic group* or SEG. This is closely

Economic status

- In full-time paid work
- In part-time paid work
- Full-time with home or child care
- In full-time education
- Retired
- Unemployed/looking for paid employment
- Other

Market research occupation/SEG classification

AB Managerial, administrative, professional (at senior or intermediate level)

C1 Supervisory or clerical (i.e. white collar) and junior managerial, administrative or professional

C2 Skilled manual

DE Semi-skilled, unskilled and casual workers and those entirely dependent on state pensions

National Statistics, Socio-Economic Classifications (NS-SEC)*

- Employers (large organisations) and senior managers
- Higher professionals
- Lower managerial and professional
- Intermediate (e.g. clerks, secretaries, computer operators)
- Small employers and own-account non-professional
- Supervisors, craft and related
- Semi-routine (e.g. cooks, bus-drivers, hairdressers, shop assistants)
- Routine (e.g. waiters, cleaners, couriers)
- Never worked, long-term unemployed

Figure 10.13 Economic status/occupational/socio-economic groupings

* The NS-SEC system was adopted by the UK Office for National Statistics in 1998 (Roberts, 2011: 20). Earlier editions of the book have used pre-1998 systems.

related to the idea of *class* or social class. Space does not permit a discussion of this complex concept here, but sources are given in the Resources section.

Because people can be vague in response to an open-ended question on occupation it is wise to include a supplementary question to draw out a full description. For example 'office worker', 'engineer' and 'self-employed' are not adequate answers because they can cover such a wide variety of grades of occupation. A supplementary question could be: 'What sort of work is that?' In a household survey it may be possible to ask additional questions to be absolutely sure of the respondent's occupation. Such questions would check on the industry involved and the number of staff supervised by the respondent.

Income

A typical wording of a question on income would be:

- What is your own personal gross income from all sources before taxes? or
- Which of the groups on the card does your own personal gross income from all sources before tax fall into?

Gross income is normally asked for, since it can be too complicated to gather information on income net of taxes and other deductions. Since there is often a major difference between gross and net income, this makes the variable a somewhat imprecise one. A further problem with income as a variable is that personal income is not a particularly useful variable for those who are not income recipients or who are not the main income recipients of the household. This can be overcome if all members of the household are being interviewed or if the respondent is asked about the 'main income earner' in the household. However, many teenage children, for example, do not know their parents' income and it might be seen as improper to ask them. Income is a sensitive issue and, in view of the limitations discussed above, is often excluded in site or visitor surveys.

Marital status

Since legal marital status fails to indicate the domestic situation of increasing numbers of people, the usefulness of this variable is declining. In terms of sport behaviour, whether or not a person has responsibility for children is likely to be a more important variable. Usual categories for marital status are:

- married;
- single – never married;
- widowed/divorced/separated.

Respondents who are not formally married but living in a *de facto* relationship can then decide for themselves how they want to be classified, or a separate category can be created.

Household type and group type and size

Household type is a useful variable for many sport studies but, except in the household interview situation, the data may be difficult to collect, because a number of items of information are required. In a household interview it is possible to ask 'Who lives here?' A simplified version would be to ask about the number of children of various ages in the household. Classifying the information into 'household type' must be done subsequently. Typical categories are as set out in Figure 10.14a.

In the case of user/site surveys it is more usual to ask about the size of the party or group and its composition – for example how many children and adults of various ages are present. Clearly such information is important for planning, marketing, managing and programming facilities. A typical categorisation of groups is as shown in Figure 10.14b.

It should be noted, however, that 'size of group' is not the same as 'vehicle occupancy', since some larger groups may arrive in several vehicles. So if the latter information is required for traffic management purposes, it must be asked separately.

a. Household type – Household survey

Question format: Can you please tell me who lives here?

Person	Relationship to Respondent	Gender M/F	Age	Occupation
1	Respondent			
2				
3				
4				
5				

Household type classification based on the above information:
A. Single parent and 1 dependent child
B. Single parent and 2 or more dependent children
C. Couple and 1 dependent child
D. Couple and 2 or more dependent children
E. Couple, no children
F. Related adults only
G. Unrelated adults only
H. Single person
I. Other.

b. Visitor groups – Site survey

Question format:
a. How many people are there in this group, including yourself?   ——
b. How many children aged under 5 are there in the group?   ——
c. How many children aged between 5 and 15?   ——
d. How many people aged 60 or over?   ——

Group classification based on the above information:
A. Youngest member aged 0–4
B. Youngest member aged 5–15
C. Lone adult
D. Two adults (under 60)
E. Older couple (60 and over)
F. 3–5 adults
G. 6 + adults.

Figure 10.14   **Household type and visitor group type**

A. Child/young single – dependent (on parents)
B. Young single – independent
C. Young married/partnered – no children
D. Parent – dependent children
E. Parent – children now independent
F. Retired – up to 70
G. Retired – over 70

Figure 10.15   Life-cycle stages

Life-cycle

Some researchers have argued that individual variables, such as age and marital status, are not good predictors of sport behaviour; rather, we should examine the composite variable *life-cycle* (Rapoport and Rapoport, 1975). As with household type, a person's stage in the life-cycle is not based on a single question but built up from a number of items of information, including age, economic status and marital/family status. A possible classification is as set out in Figure 10.15. Life*style* **(see Chapter 5)** is a further development of this idea, but generally involves collection of a considerable amount of additional data.

Ethnic group

Ethnic group is often included in sport surveys because ethnically based cultures influence sport behaviour and also because of policy concerns for equity between social groups. Everyone belongs to an ethnic group – that is, a social group that shares religious, language and other cultural values and practices and experiences – including sport. Ethnicity therefore becomes important in sport policy, planning and management, particularly as regards minority groups whose needs may not be met by mainstream facilities and services. A common approach to ethnicity in the past was to ask the respondent's country of birth, since most ethnic minority groups were migrant groups. But this, of course, does not identify members of ethnic minority groups not born overseas. Parents' place of birth identifies the second generation of migrant groups but not third and subsequent generations. Country of birth has therefore become less and less useful as an indicator of ethnic group membership in many countries. Observation is an obvious solution but is not reliable for many groups. The solution is to ask people what ethnic group they consider they belong to. While this may cause offence to some, it is the most satisfactory approach overall.

Residential location/trip origin

Where a person lives can be a significant determinant of access to sport facilities and is a reflection of socio-economic position and related patterns of consumption. Residential location and trip origin are also the basis of catchment area analysis for individual facilities. The situation varies depending on the survey type:

- Household survey: the residential location is already known by the interviewer and some sort of code – for street, suburb, local government area, county, as appropriate – can be recorded on the questionnaire.

- Street survey: home location is not always required, but if it is, a broad category, such as suburb, is usually adequate.

- Site/visitor surveys: in order to study the catchment area of the facility, it is necessary to ask people where they live or where they have travelled from. How much detail is required? This depends on the nature of the facility. For local facilities with small catchment areas it may be necessary to know the street (but not the number of the dwelling). For less local urban facilities the suburb is sufficient. For countryside facilities the town/city of residence will be required. For overseas visitors the country is usually adequate information, although there may be interest in where they are staying.

In Case study 14.4 an example is given of the use of home-location data to show the catchment area of a facility. In that example the information came from membership records, but it could equally well arise from a questionnaire survey of facility users.

Market research firms often record full addresses and/or telephone numbers of survey respondents in order to undertake subsequent quality checks on interviewers, to ensure that the respondents have in fact been interviewed.

Housing information

Information on the type of dwelling in which respondents live is usually collected in household surveys because it can easily be gathered by observation. The information is clearly relevant in sport research because of the implications of dwelling type for access to private recreational space – a phenomenon often referred to in policy documents but rarely researched. Whether or not people own their own home is an important socio-economic variable. Typical categories for these items of information are shown in Figure 10.16.

Type of dwelling	Tenure
Separate house	Owned outright
Semi-detached house	Being purchased
Terrace house	Rented
Flat/maisonette	Other
Caravan, houseboat	
Other	

Figure 10.16   Housing information

Transport

Because mobility is such an important factor in sport behaviour, questionnaires often include questions on ownership of and access to vehicles. People are sometimes asked if they possess a current driver's licence. In the case of site surveys, the mode of transport used to travel to the site, and vehicle occupancy as discussed under household/groups above, is often asked. If people claim to have used two or more modes of transport to reach a site, the various modes can all be recorded or respondents can be asked to indicate the one on which they travelled the furthest.

Attitude/opinion questions

Attitudes and opinions are more complex aspects of questionnaire design. A range of techniques exists to explore people's opinions and attitudes, as listed in Figure 10.17. The first three formats, direct, open-ended questions, checklists and ranking, are straightforward, but the other formats presented merit some comment.

Likert scales

Scaling techniques are sometimes known as 'Likert scales' after the psychologist who developed their use and analysis. In this technique, respondents are asked to indicate their agreement or disagreement with a proposition or the importance they attach to a factor, using a standard set of responses. One of the advantages of this approach is that the responses can be quantified, as discussed below under coding.

Ranking

Asking respondents to rank items in order of importance is a relatively straightforward process, provided the list is not too long: more than five or six items could test respondents' patience. Again, the responses can be quantified – for example in the form of average ranks.

Attitude statements

Attitude statements are a means of exploring respondents' attitudes towards a wide range of issues, including questions of a philosophical or political nature. Respondents are shown a series of statements and asked to indicate, using a scale, the extent to which they agree or disagree with them.

Responses to both Likert-scale questions and attitude statements can be scored, as indicated by the numerals beside the boxes in Figure 10.17. For example, 'agree strongly' could be given a score of 5, 'agree' a score of 4, and so on to 'disagree strongly' with a score of 1. Scores can then be averaged across a number of respondents. So, for example, a group of people who mostly either

a. Open-ended/direct: What attracted you to apply for this course?

_____

b. Checklist: Of the items on the card, which was the most important to you in applying for this course?

> A. Good reputation
> B. Easy access
> C. Curriculum
> D. Level of fees
> E. Easy parking

c. Ranking: Please rank the items on the card in terms of their importance to you in choosing a course. Please rank them 1 for the most important to 5 for the least important.

	Rank
A. Good reputation	___
B. Easy access	___
C. Curriculum	___
D. Level of fees	___
E. Easy parking	___

d. Likert scales: Looking at the items on the card, please say how important each was to you in deciding to visit this area; was it: Very important, Quite important, Not very important or Not at all important?

	Very important	Quite important	Not very important	Not at all important
Good reputation	$\square_4$	$\square_3$	$\square_2$	$\square_1$
Easy access	$\square_4$	$\square_3$	$\square_2$	$\square_1$
Curriculum	$\square_4$	$\square_3$	$\square_2$	$\square_1$
Level of fees	$\square_4$	$\square_3$	$\square_2$	$\square_1$
Easy parking	$\square_4$	$\square_3$	$\square_2$	$\square_1$

e. Attitude statements: Please read the statements below and indicate your level of agreement or disagreement with them by ticking the appropriate box.

	Agree Strongly	Agree	No opinion	Disagree	Disagree strongly
The learning experience is more important than the qualification in education	$\square_5$	$\square_4$	$\square_3$	$\square_2$	$\square_1$
Graduate course fees are too high	$\square_5$	$\square_4$	$\square_3$	$\square_2$	$\square_1$

f. Semantic differential: Please look at the list below and tick the line to indicate where you think this course falls in relation to each factor listed.

Difficult	|___|___|___|___|	Easy
Irrelevant	|___|___|___|___|	Relevant
Professional	|___|___|___|___|	Unprofessional
Dull	|___|___|___|___|	Interesting

Figure 10.17   Opinion/attitude question formats

'agreed' or 'agreed strongly' with a statement would produce an average score between 4 and 5, whereas a group who 'disagreed' or 'disagreed strongly' would produce a low score, between 1 and 2. Such scores enable the strength of agreement with different statements to be compared, and the opinions of different groups of people to be compared.

Semantic differential

The semantic differential method involves offering respondents *pairs* of contrasting descriptors and asking them to indicate how the activity facility, place or service being studied relates to the descriptors. This technique is suitable for a respondent-completion questionnaire, since the respondent is required to place a tick on each line. It would be difficult to replicate this exactly in an interview situation with no visual prompts, such as in a telephone survey; the effect would be to reduce the possible answers to three: close to one end or the other and 'in the middle'. The choice of pairs of words used in a semantic differential list should arise from the research context and theory.

Repertory grid

A further development of this approach is the *repertory grid* technique **(see Chapter 5)**. Here the pairs of words – called *personal constructs* – are developed by the respondent. This technique is not explored further here, but references to examples of its use in sport research are given in the Resources section.

Market segments

The idea of market segmentation or lifestyle studies is introduced in Chapter 1. This involves classifying survey respondents according to a mix of activity, socio-demographic and attitude variables. All the necessary data items for this have therefore been discussed above. Actually determining market segments or lifestyle groupings is then an analytical task **(this is discussed in Part III of the book, notable in Chapter 17 under factor and cluster analysis)**.

Ordering of questions and layout of questionnaires

Survey introductory remarks

Should a questionnaire include introductory remarks, for example explaining the purpose of the survey and asking for the respondent's assistance? In the case of a mail survey such material is generally included in the covering letter. In the case of other forms of respondent-completion questionnaire a short note at the beginning of the questionnaire is advisable, although fieldworkers handing out questionnaires will usually provide the necessary introduction and explanation. In the case of interviewer-administered questionnaires the remarks can be printed on the top of each questionnaire or can be included in the interviewers' written instructions.

In practice, interviewers are unlikely to approach potential interviewees and actually read from a script. When seeking the cooperation of a potential inter-viewee it is usually necessary to maintain eye contact, so interviewers must know in advance what they want to say. In the case of household surveys, potential interviewees may require a considerable amount of information and proof of identity from the interviewer before agreeing to be interviewed. But in the case of site interviews, respondents are generally more interested in knowing how long the interview will take and what sort of questions they will be asked – so only minimal opening remarks are necessary. For example, for a site survey the introduction could be as brief as: 'Excuse me, we are conducting a survey of users of the centre; would you mind answering a few questions?'

It is usually necessary for an interviewer to indicate what organisation they represent, and this can be reinforced by an identity badge. Market research or consultancy companies often instruct interviewers to indicate only that they represent the company and not the client who commissioned the research. This can ensure that unbiased opinions are obtained, although in some cases it can raise ethical considerations if it is felt that respondents have a right to know what organisation will be using the information gathered.

One function of opening remarks can be to assure the respondent of con-fidentiality. In the case of site surveys, where names and addresses are not generally collected, confidentiality is easy to maintain. In the case of house-hold and some postal surveys, respondents can be identified, so assurances are generally necessary. The issue of confidentiality, including practical means of ensuring it, is an ethical issue **(see Chapter 4)**.

Question order

It is important that an interview based on a questionnaire flow in a logical and comfortable manner. A number of principles should be borne in mind.

1. Start with easy questions.

2. Start with 'relevant' questions: for example, if the respondent has been told that the survey is about sport, begin with some questions about sport.

3. Personal questions, dealing with such things as age or income, are gener-ally best left to near the end: while they do not generally cause problems, and respondents need not answer those personal questions if they object, they are less likely to cause offence if asked later in the interview when a rapport has been established between interviewer and respondent. Similar principles apply in relation to respondent-completion questionnaires. It is sometimes suggested that this is an unethical practice, in that people might not agree to cooperate if they knew in advance that personal ques-tions would be asked. But since in sport surveys the personal information is

rarely deeply personal, and respondents can and do decline to answer such questions, the practice is widely seen as acceptable.

Layout

- General: A questionnaire should be laid out and printed in such a way that the person who must read it – whether interviewer or interviewee – can follow all the instructions easily and answer all the questions that they are meant to answer. In the case of respondent-completion questionnaires, extra care must be taken with layout because it can be very difficult to rectify faults once the survey process is under way. Clarity of layout, and the over-all impression given by the questionnaire, can be all-important in obtaining a good response. Mail surveys, where the researcher does not have direct contact with the respondent, are the most demanding. A professionally laid out, typeset and printed questionnaire will pay dividends in terms of response rate and accuracy and completeness of responses.

- Filtering: Layout becomes particularly important when a questionnaire contains filters – that is, when answers to certain questions determine which subsequent questions must be answered. An example, with alternative ways of dealing with layout, is shown in Figure 10.18.

- Length: A professionally laid out and typeset format can reduce the number of pages considerably, which may increase the response rate if the perceived length of the questionnaire is a factor. Even where interviewers are used, there are advantages in keeping the questionnaire as compact as possible for ease of handling. A two-column format, as used in Case study 10.1, example C, is worth exploring and can be easily achieved with word-processing packages.

- Tick boxes and codes: The questionnaire shown in Case study 10.1A is designed for respondent-completion and the layout therefore involves

---

Layout 1

1. a. Have you studied at this university before?

    Yes   □$_1$

    No   □$_2$

  b. If YES: How long ago did you study here? ____ years

Layout 2

1. Have you studied at this university before?

    Yes   □$_1$ Go to question 3

    No   □$_2$ Go to question 2

2. How long ago did you study here? ____ years

Figure 10.18 Filtering: examples

boxes for the respondent to tick. Boxes can, however, be laborious to type and layout, so where an interviewer is being used, as in examples B and C, the interviewer can circle codes.

● Office-use column: The 'office use' column is not always necessary in interviewer-administered questionnaires, but is included in examples A and B for exposition purposes. This type of layout can be used for respondent-completion in some situations – for example in certain 'captive group' situations or where respondents are known to be highly literate and are unlikely to be deterred by the apparent technicalities of the layout.

Coding

Most questionnaire survey data are now analysed by computer. This means that the information in the questionnaire must be coded – that is, converted into, generally numerical, codes and organised in a systematic, 'machine-readable', manner. Different procedures apply to pre-coded and open-ended questions and these are discussed in turn below.

Pre-coded questions

The principle for coding of pre-coded questions is illustrated in many of the questions in the example questionnaires in Case study 10.1. For example, for question 1 in example A, the codes are as shown beside the boxes. Only one answer is possible, so only one code is recorded as the answer to this question.

Where the answer is already numerical, there is no need to code the answer because the numerical answer can be handled by the computer. For example, in question 4 of example A, actual expenditure is asked for, which is a number and does not require coding.

Scaled answers, as in Likert scales and attitude statements, readily lend themselves to coding, as shown by the numerals in the examples given in Figure 10.17. In the case of the semantic differential, each of the sections of the response line can be numbered, say 1–4, so that answers can be given a numerical code, depending on where the respondent marks the line.

Open-ended questions

In the case of completely open-ended questions, quite an elaborate procedure must be followed to devise a coding system. As already suggested, the answers to open-ended questions can be copied from the questionnaires and presented in a report 'raw', as in Figure 10.11. If this is all that is required from the open-ended questions, there is no point in spending the considerable labour necessary to code the information for computer analysis: the computer will merely reproduce what can be more easily achieved manually.

Computer analysis comes into its own if it is intended to analyse the results in more detail – for example comparing the opinions of two or more socio-demographic groups. If such comparisons are to be made, it will usually be difficult to do so with, say, 50 or 60 different response groups to compare, especially if many of the responses are given by only one or two respondents. The aim then is to devise a coding system which groups the responses into a manageable number of categories.

If a large sample is involved, it is advisable that the coding system be devised using a pilot survey, so that open-ended questions become pre-coded, but if this is not considered desirable then a representative sub-sample of the responses, say 50 or 100, might be used for the purpose. All responses are written down, noting the number of occurrences of each answer as in Figure 10.19. Then individual codes are given for the most frequent responses and the others are grouped into meaningful categories, as indicated. This is a matter of judgement. The aim is not to leave too many responses in the 'other' category.

Recording coded information

Computer analysis is conducted using the coded information from a questionnaire. This is best illustrated by an example – a completed questionnaire from Case study 10.1A is set out in Figure 10.20.

Answers from 25 respondents to the question: 'What suggestions would you make for improving campus sporting life?'

More sport available ///	Better food ///
Upgrade gym facilities ////	Keep out non-students //
More weekday events //	Better spectator accommodation ///
More lunchtime events /	Better coaches/instructors //
More evening events //	More classes for women //
Better music in gym /	Lower membership costs //
Cheaper drinks ///	Warmer pool water //
Free transport from city //	Better control of facility users //

Suggested coding system code	
Comments on range of sport	1
Comments on timing	2
Comments on facilities	3
Comments on costs	4
Comments on organisation	5
Other	6

Figure 10.19 Coding open-ended questions – example

Campus Sporting Life Survey 2008

			Office Use
			# _1_

1. Which of the following best describes your current situation?

Full-time student with no regular paid work	☐ 1	
Full-time student with some regular paid work	☑ 2	_2_ status
Part-time student with full-time job	☐ 3	
Part-time student – other	☐ 4	

2. Which of the following university sport facilities have you used in the last 4 weeks?

Swimming pool	☑ 1	_1_ pool
Gym	☑ 1	_1_ gym
Squash court	☐ 1	_0_ squash
Attended sports match as spectator	☐ 1	_0_ spectate

3. In thinking about using the sport and social services provided on campus, what are the most important considerations for you? Please rank the items below in terms of their importance to you. Rank them from 1 for the most important to 5 for the least important.

	Rank	
Free or cheap access	_1_	_1_ cheap
Convenient opening hours	_4_	_4_ hours
Quality of facilities	_2_	_2_ unusual
Opportunities to socialise/meet people	_3_	_3_ meet
Available time	_5_	_5_ time

4. Approximately how much do you spend in an average week on sport and social activities on and off campus?

£ _100_   _100_ spend

5. Please indicate the importance of the following to you in relation to your participation in sport.

	Very important	Important	Not at all Important	
Relaxation opportunities	☑ 3	☐ 2	☐ 1	_3_ relax
Social interaction	☑ 3	☐ 2	☐ 1	_3_ social
Fitness	☐ 3	☐ 2	☑ 1	_1_ fitness

6. What suggestions would you make for improving campus sport?

Provide more lunchtime sessions

_1_ sug1
__ sug2
__ sug3

7. You are: Male ☐ 1   Female ☑ 2   _2_ gend

8. Your age last birthday was: _22_ years   _22_ age

Figure 10.20 Completed questionnaire

In the 'office use' column, *spaces* are provided into which the codes from the answers can be written. The 'variable names' in the office column – qno, crse, lib, etc. – are explained in more detail in the analysis chapter **(see Chapter 16.)**

- Questionnaire number, in the 'office use' column, is an identifier so that a link can be made between data in the computer and actual questionnaires – the example questionnaire is number 001

- Question 1 – only one answer/code can be given

- Question 2 – respondents can tick up to four boxes

- Question 3 – five ranks must be recorded

- Question 4 – asks for an actual number and this will be transferred into the computer without coding

- Question 5 – consists of three Likert-scale items

- Question 6 – an open-ended question. It is envisaged that some respondents might give more than one answer, so spaces have been reserved for three answers (although in the example, only one has been given). The answers have a coding system (devised as discussed above) as follows:

  - Comments on range of sport   1
  - Comments on timing   2
  - Comments on facilities   3
  - Comments on cost   4
  - Comments on organisation   5
  - Other   6

The data from this particular completed questionnaire therefore become a single row of numbers, as shown in the first row of Figure 10.21, which shows how data from 15 completed questionnaires would look. How such a set of data may be analysed by computer is discussed in the analysis chapter **(see Chapter 16.)**

Validity of questionnaire-based data

Threats to validity

Questionnaires are designed to gather information from individuals about their characteristics, behaviour and attitudes. Whether or not they actually achieve this depends on a number of possible threats to validity. Some of these are summarised in Figure 10.22.

The principles of questionnaire design discussed above and the principles of sampling outlined **(see Chapter 13)** are designed to minimise threats to

qno	status	pool	gym	squash	spectate	cheap	hour	qual	meet	time	spend	relax	social	fitness	sug1	sug2	sug3	gend	age
1	2	1	1	0	0	1	4	2	3	5	100	3	3	1	1			1	18
2	2	1	1	1	0	1	4	2	3	5	50	2	3	1	2	1		1	19
3	3	1	0	0	0	2	5	1	3	4	250	2	2	2	3	4		2	19
4	4	0	0	0	0	2	3	1	4	5	25	3	2	2	1	2	4	1	22
5	3	1	0	0	1	1	4	3	2	5	55	3	3	1				2	24
6	3	1	1	1	0	2	4	1	3	5	40	2	3	1	2			2	20
7	2	1	0	0	0	3	2	1	4	5	150	2	3	2	3			2	20
8	2	1	0	1	0	3	4	2	1	5	250	1	2	2	4	5		1	21
9	4	0	1	0	0	1	5	2	3	4	300	2	3	2				1	21
10	3	1	1	0	0	2	3	1	5	4	100	1	2	1	1	1		2	21
11	3	1	1	0	1	2	3	1	4	5	75	2	2	1	2	3		2	19
12	2	1	0	1	0	1	4	3	2	5	50	2	3	1				1	22
13	1	1	0	1	0	1	5	2	3	4	55	2	3	2	1	2		2	21
14	3	1	1	0	0	2	4	1	3	5	75	3	3	2	4			2	20
15	1	1	1	0	0	3	2	1	5	4	150	3	3	1	1	2	5	1	20

Figure 10.21 Data from 15 completed questionnaires

Threat	Nature
Non-response	Non-respondents may be significantly different from respondents, thus resulting in a biased sample.
Questionnaire design: lack of clarity	Leading questions, ambiguity, etc. result in inaccurate data.
Accuracy of recall	Respondents vary in their ability to recall activity or its timing/nature, especially over long time-periods.
Desire to impress	People have a natural desire to impress others, to give a good report of themselves, resulting in exaggeration of good points and downplaying of bad points.
Privacy concerns/sensitivity	People may be reluctant to provide information at all on private/ sensitive matters, or may provide incomplete or inaccurate information.
Language/accent	Respondent may have difficulty with the language of the questionnaire/interview and respondent or interviewer may have difficulty in understanding the other's accent.
Interviewee patience/fatigue	Interviews perceived to be excessively long or uninteresting may lead to incomplete responses.
Physical context	If interview or questionnaire completion takes place in a distracting environment, inaccuracies or incompleteness may result.
Interviewer-administered	
Interviewer–respondent rapport	Particularly good or poor interviewer–respondent rapport may affect the accuracy and completeness of responses.
Interviewer consistency	If interviewer does not consistently follow instructions, or different interviewers interpret instructions differently, inaccuracies may result.
Respondent-completed	
Literacy	Respondents have difficulty in understanding questions or, in case of open-ended questions, in writing answers.
Non-completion	For a variety of reasons, some questions are not answered.

Figure 10.22   Questionnaire surveys: threats to validity

validity. To some extent the researcher must simply live with the limitations of the survey method and hope that inaccuracies are not significant and that some of them cancel each other out. There are, however, some measures which can be taken to check on the presence of this type of problem.

Checking validity

Some aspects of validity can be checked. The possibility of random or systematic error in responses may be checked by: the use of dummy questions or answer categories; semi-disguised duplication of questions; comparing time-periods; and by referring to an alternative data source, where one exists. These possibilities are discussed in turn below.

Dummy questions or answer categories

In a survey of sport/recreation managers in Britain in the early 1980s, respondents were asked to indicate, from a list, what books and reports they had heard of and had read. Included in the list was one plausible, but non-existent, title. A significant proportion of respondents indicated that they had heard of the report and a small proportion claimed to have read it! Such a response does not necessarily mean that respondents were lying – they may simply have been confused about the titles of particular publications. But it does provide cautionary information to the researcher on the degree of error in responses to such questions, since it suggests that responses to the genuine titles may also include a certain amount of inaccuracy. For example, if 2 per cent of respondents claim to have heard of the non-existent report, this could suggest that all answers are subject to an error of plus or minus 2 per cent.

Semi-disguised duplication of questions

A similar approach is to include two or more questions in different parts of the questionnaire, which essentially ask the same thing. For example, an early question could ask respondents to rank a list of activities in order of preference. Later in the questionnaire, in the context of asking some detailed questions, respondents could be asked to indicate their favourite activity. In the analysis, the responses could be tested for consistency.

Rather than detecting error, it is possible that this approach can discover that the interview or questionnaire-completion experience itself has caused respondents to change their opinion, because it causes them to think through in detail something which they might previously have only considered superficially. In an Australian survey of gambling behaviour and attitudes towards a proposed casino development, Grichting and Caltabiano (1986) asked, at the beginning of the interview: 'What do you think about the casino coming to Townsville? Are you for it or against it?' At the end of the interview they asked: 'Taking everything you have said into consideration, what do you think now about the casino coming to Townsville? Are you for it or against it?' It was found that about 'one in six respondents changed their attitude toward the casino during the course of the interview'.

Comparing time-periods

Bachman and O'Malley (1981) used data from a survey of marijuana and alcohol use among senior high school students to explore apparent inconsistencies in reported use levels in the last month and in the last year. Except for seasonal activities, it might be expected that use levels in the last month would be about one-twelfth of use levels for the whole year. It was found that use levels reported for the last month were very much higher than this, suggesting that either the one-month figures were exaggerated or the one-year figures were under-reported.

Ideally, such findings should be followed up with additional research to confirm the patterns in the case of alcohol and drug use, investigate its prevalence in relation to other types of activity and suggest ways in which it might be taken into account in future survey work. There is little evidence of this being done.

Use of an alternative data source

Professional sport leagues typically keep records of spectator attendances which could be compared with estimates derived from survey research, although the latter would need to be designed to distinguish between spectating at professional games and other spectating. Some sports must keep data on registered amateur players for insurance purpose, and this could be compared with data from suitably designed surveys.

Two studies conducted at the University of Pennsylvania by David Chase and colleagues compared questionnaire survey results on estimated numbers participating in swimming and tennis over two seasons with club sign-in records. In the first study (Chase and Godbey, 1983) it was found that over 75 per cent of respondents in both swimming and tennis clubs overestimated their visits and in over 40 per cent of cases the error was greater than 100 per cent. The second larger-scale study of a swimming club (Chase and Harada, 1984) confirmed the general picture, with survey respondents' estimate of previous season visits averaging 30, while the club records indicated that the actual frequency was 17.

Taking account of validity problems

There is no indication in the research and policy literature that those organisations and researchers conducting and using questionnaire survey results in the sport area take the above findings on validity problems into account. The above discussions refer only to recall of factual information, but questions may also arise in regard to the validity of responses to questions on attitudes and aspirations. There does not seem to be much interest in exploring these problems among the sport research community. Some of the issues have, however, been addressed by researchers in the medical sector, as the volume of papers edited by Stone *et al.* (2000) demonstrates.

Conducting questionnaire surveys

Planning fieldwork arrangements

The scale and complexity of the data collection, or fieldwork, process in survey research can obviously vary enormously. At one extreme the process is largely a matter of personal organisation on the part of the researcher; at the

a. Seek permissions – to visit sites, obtain records, etc.
b. Obtain lists for sampling – e.g. membership lists
c. Arrange printing – of questionnaires etc.
d. Check insurance issues
e. Prepare written instructions for interviewers
f. Prepare identity badges/letters for interviewers
g. Recruit interviewers and supervisors
h. Train interviewers and supervisors
i. Obtain quotations for any fieldwork to be conducted by other organisations
j. Appoint and train data coders/processors

Figure 10.23   Fieldwork planning tasks

other extreme a staff of hundreds may need to be recruited, trained and supervised. Fieldwork must be organised in any empirical study involving primary
data collection, but because of the popularity of the survey method and the
likelihood that it will involve organisation of individuals other than the single
researchers, some attention is given to the task in this chapter.

Some of the items which need consideration are listed in Figure 10.23 and
brief notes are presented below.

a. Seek permissions

It is important to remember that permission is often needed to interview in public places, such as streets and beaches, because of local bye-laws. Many areas
which are thought of as 'public' are in fact the responsibility of some public
or private organisation – for example shopping centres and parks. Permission
must be sought from these organisations to conduct fieldwork. It is also good
practice to inform the local police if interviewing is being conducted in public
places, in case of complaints or queries from the public.

b. Obtain lists

Obtaining lists, such as voters or membership lists, for sampling may seem
routine, but often apparently straightforward tasks can involve delays, or the
material may not be quite in the form anticipated and it takes time to process.
Often research projects are conducted on very tight schedules and delays of a
few days can be crucial. Therefore the earlier these routine tasks are tackled
the better.

c. Arrange printing

Printing sounds straightforward, but the in-house print-shop has busy periods when it may not be possible to obtain a quick job turnround. Checking
on printing procedures and turnround times at an early stage is therefore
advisable.

d. Check insurance

When conducting fieldwork away from a normal place of work, insurance issues may arise, including public liability and workers' compensation for interviewers. In the case of educational institutions, staff and students are normally covered as long as they are engaged in legitimate university/college activities, but these matters should be checked with a competent legal authority in the organisation.

e. Prepare written instructions for interviewers

Provision of written instructions for interviewers is advisable and may cover:

- detailed comments on questionnaires and/or other instruments;
- instructions in relation to checking of completed questionnaires etc. for legibility and completeness;
- instructions on returning questionnaires etc.;
- dress and behaviour codes;
- roster details;
- 'wet weather' instructions, if relevant;
- instructions on what to do in the case of 'difficult' interviewees, etc.;
- details of time-sheets, payment, etc.;
- contact telephone numbers.

A note on questionnaire-based interviewing is appropriate here. The general approach to interviewing when using a questionnaire is that the interviewer should be instructed to adhere precisely to the wording on the questionnaire. If the respondent does not understand the question, the question should simply be repeated exactly as before; if the respondent still does not understand then the interviewer should move on to the next question. If this procedure is to be adhered to, the importance of question wording and the testing of such wording in one or more pilot surveys is clear.

The above procedure is clearly important in relation to attitude questions. Any word of explanation or elaboration from the interviewer could influence, and therefore bias, the response. In relation to factual questions, however, it may be less important – a word of explanation from the interviewer may be acceptable if it results in obtaining accurate information.

f. Prepare identity badges/letters

If working in a public or semi-public place, fieldworkers should be clearly identified. A badge with the institutional logo and the fieldworker's given name is advisable. A letter from the research supervisor indicating that the fieldworker is engaged in legitimate research activity for the organisation may also be helpful.

g. Recruit interviewers and supervisors

Where paid interviewers, supervisors or other fieldworkers are to be used it will be necessary to go through the normal procedures for employing part-time staff. Advice from the organisation's Human Resources Unit, or someone familiar with their procedures, will need to be sought.

h. Training

The length of training will vary with the complexity of the fieldwork and the experience of the fieldwork staff. Paid fieldworkers should be paid for the training session(s), and this should be budgeted for. A two- or three-hour session is usually sufficient, but more may be necessary for a complex project. It is advisable for interviewers to practise interviews on each other and report back on difficulties encountered.

i. Obtain quotations

In some cases, certain aspects of the project are to be undertaken by other organisations – for example data processing. Obtaining detailed quotations on price as early as possible is clearly advisable.

j. Appoint and train data processors

In some cases, the coding, editing and processing of data for computer analysis is a significant task in its own right, requiring staff to be recruited. Recruitment and training procedures will need to be followed as for fieldworkers.

Conducting a pilot survey

Pilot surveys are small-scale 'trial runs' of a larger survey. Pilot surveys relate particularly to questionnaire surveys, but can in fact relate to trying out any type of research procedure. It is always advisable to carry out one or more pilot surveys before embarking on the main data collection exercise. The purposes of pilot surveys are summarised in Figure 10.24. Clearly, the pilot can be used to test all aspects of the survey, not just question wording. Item e, 'familiarity with respondents', refers to the role of the pilot in alerting the researcher to any characteristics, idiosyncrasies or sensitivities of the respondent group with which he or she may not have been previously familiar. Such matters can affect the design and conduct of the main survey. Items h and i, concerned with the response rate and length of interview, can be most important in providing information to 'fine-tune' the survey process. For example, it may be necessary

---

a. Test questionnaire wording
b. Test question sequencing
c. Test questionnaire layout
d. Code open-ended questions
e. Gain familiarity with respondents
f. Test fieldwork arrangements
g. Train and test fieldworkers
h. Estimate response rate
i. Estimate interview etc. time
j. Test analysis procedures

Figure 10.24   Pilot survey purposes

to shorten the questionnaire and/or vary the number of field staff so that the project keeps on schedule and within budget.

In principle, at least some of the pilot interviews should be carried out by the researcher in charge, or at least by some experienced interviewers, since the interviewers will be required to report back on the pilot survey experience and contribute to discussions on any revisions to the questionnaire or fieldwork arrangements which might subsequently be made. The de-briefing session following the pilot survey is very important and should take place as soon as possible after the completion of the exercise, so that the details are fresh in the interviewers' minds.

Summary

This chapter provides an introduction to questionnaire surveys, arguably the most commonly used data collection vehicle in sport research. The merits of questionnaire surveys are discussed, including the ability to quantify, transparency, succinctness in data presentation, the ability to study change over time, comprehensive coverage of complex phenomena and generalisability to the whole population. The second part of the chapter is devoted to discussing the features of seven different forms of the questionnaire survey: the household survey, the street survey, the telephone survey, the mail survey, the e-survey, the user/on-site/visitor survey and the captive group survey. The third part of the chapter considers questionnaire design and coding. Finally, the chapter considers fieldwork arrangements for questionnaire surveys, including the conduct of pilot surveys.

Test questions

1. What are the merits of questionnaire surveys?

2. Seven types of questionnaire survey are discussed in the chapter; what are they?

3. List three of these questionnaire survey types and outline their characteristics in terms of: respondent or interviewer completion, cost, nature of the sample, possible length of questionnaire, and likely response rate.

4. What type of survey methodology would you use to conduct for a sample of 500 of the following:

    a. Skiers visiting a seaside resort

    b. Members of Greenpeace

    c. The users of a sport centre

    d. The sport users of a large urban park

    e. People visiting a country to attend a major international sport event

    f. People who do not play sport

    g. Members of a sport team

    h. Members of a gym

    i. People aged 14 and over living in the local council area

    j. Young people aged 11–13 living in the local council area

5. What is quota sampling?

6. What measures might be used to increase response rates in mail surveys?

7. What principles should be followed in wording questions in questionnaires?

8. What is the difference between pre-coded and open-ended questions and what are the advantages and disadvantages of the two formats?

Exercises

1. Design a questionnaire in relation to the study discussed in Case study 3.1, limiting the questionnaire to ten questions only.

2. Design a question on people's attitudes towards commercial sponsorship of sport, using three alternative question formats.

3. If you are a member of a sport studies class, invite members of the class to complete the questionnaire in Case study 10.1A and devise a coding system for the answers to the open-ended question based on the answers obtained.

4. Locate a published research report or thesis which includes a questionnaire survey and contains a copy of the questionnaire used (usually in an appendix) and provide a critique of the questionnaire design.

Resources

Websites

- Time-budget diaries/time-use surveys:
  - Australia: Australian Bureau of Statistics: 2006 Time Use Survey: www
    .abs.gov.au
  - UK: Office for National Statistics 2005 Time Use Survey: www.statistics
    .gov.uk
  - USA: Bureau of Labor Statistics: US Time Use Survey: www.bls.gov/
    tus/
  - Harmonised European Time Use Survey: www.h2.scb.se/tus/tus/
    default.htm
  - Centre for Time Use Research, University of Oxford: www.timeuse.org/

Publications

- Attitude measurement: Oppenheim (2000: Chapter 11), Pritchard and Funk
  (2010).
- Class: Chan and Goldthorpe (2007), Roberts (2011).
- E-surveys: Dillman *et al.* (2009).
- Large-scale, national household surveys: see Resources section in Chapter 7.
- Mail surveys: Dillman *et al.* (2009).
- Questionnaire design generally: Oppenheim (2000); Sirakaya-Turk *et al.*
  (2011); life-cycle: Rapoport and Rapoport (1975), Zuzanek *et al.* (1998).
- Repertory grid technique/personal constructs: Kelly (1955); sport team
  members: Feixas *et al.* (2007).
- Surveys generally: Bryman (2012), Keller (2012); limitations regarding opin-
  ions: Bourdieu (1978).
- Telephone surveys: Lavrakas (1993), Lepkowski *et al.* (2008).
- Time-budget diaries/time-use surveys: Australian Bureau of Statistics
  (2007), Gershuny (2000), Ham *et al.* (2009), Pentland *et al.* (1999), Szalai
  (1972), Tudor-Locke *et al.* (2009), Taniguchi and Shupe (2012).
- Validity: exaggerated/unreliable etc. responses to questionnaires: Chase
  and Godbey (1983), Chase and Harada (1984), Bachman and O'Malley
  (1981), Schaeffer (2000), Oppenheim (2000: 138–9).

References

Australian Bureau of Statistics (ABS) (2007) *How Australians Use their Time, 2006* (Cat. No. 4153.0). Canberra: ABS.

Bachman, J. G. and O'Malley, P. M. (1981) When four months equal a year: inconsistencies in student reports of drug use. *Public Opinion Quarterly*, 45(4), 536–48.

Biddle, S. J. H., Markland, D., Gilbourne, D., Chatzisarantis, N. L. D. and Sparkes, A. C. (2001) Research methods in sport and exercise psychology: quantitative and qualitative issues. *Journal of Sports Sciences*, 19(10), 777–809.

Bourdieu, P. (1978) Public opinion does not exist. In A. Mattelart and S. Siegelaub (eds) *Communication and Class Struggle 1. Capitalism, Imperialism*. New York: International General, 124–30.

Bryman, A. (2012) *Social Research Methods, Fourth edn.* Oxford: Oxford University Press.

Chan, T. W. and Goldthorpe, J. H. (2007) Class and status: the conceptual distinction and its empirical relevance. *American Sociological Review*. 72(3), 512–32.

Chase, D. R. and Godbey, G. C. (1983) The accuracy of self-reported participation rates. *Leisure Studies*, 2(2), 231–6.

Chase, D. and Harada, M. (1984) Response error in self-reported recreation participation. *Journal of Leisure Research*, 16(4), 322–9.

Dillman, D. A., Smyth, J. D. and Christian, L. M. (2009) *Internet, Mail, and Mixed-Mode Surveys: The Tailored Design Method, Third edn.* New York: Wiley.

Feixas, G., Marti, J. and Villegas, M. (2007) Personal construct assessment of sport teams. *International Journal of Personal Construct Theory*, 2(1), 49–54.

Gershuny, J. (2000) *Changing Times: Work and Leisure in Postindustrial Society.* Oxford: Oxford University Press.

Gitelson, R. J. and Drogin, E. B. (1992) An experiment on the efficacy of a certified final mailing. *Journal of Leisure Research*, 24(1), 72–8.

Gratton, C. (2005) Great Britain. In G. Cushman, A. J. Veal and J. Zuzanek (eds) *Free Time and Leisure Participation: International Perspectives*, Wallingford, UK: CABI, 109–26.

Grichting, W. L. and Caltabiano, M. L. (1986) Amount and direction of bias in survey interviewing. *Australian Psychologist*, 21(1), 69–78.

Ham, S. A., Kruger, J. and Tudor-Locke, C. (2009) Participation by US adults in sports, exercise, and recreational physical activities. *Journal of Physical Activity and Health*, 6(1), 6–14.

Hammitt, W. E. and McDonald, C. D. (1982) Response bias and the need for extensive mail questionnaire follow-ups among selected recreation samples. *Journal of Leisure Research*, 14(3), 207–16.

Jordan, J. S., Walker, M., Kent, A. and Inoue, Y. (2011) The frequency of nonresponse analysis in the *Journal of Sport Management. Journal of Sport Management*, 25(3), 229–39.

Keller, G. (2012) *Statistics for Management and Economics, Second edn.* Mason, OH: South-Western Cengage Learning.

Kelly, G. A. (1955) *The Psychology of Personal Constructs.* New York: Norton.

Lavrakas, P. K. (1993) *Telephone Survey Methods: Sampling, Selection and Supervision, Second edn.* Newbury Park, CA: Sage.

Lepkowski, J. M., Tucker, C., Brick, J. M. and de Leeuw, E. (eds) (2008) *Advances in Telephone Survey Methodology.* New York: John Wiley.

Oppenheim, A. N. (2000) *Questionnaire Design, Interviewing and Attitude Measurement: New edn.* London: Continuum.

Pentland, W. E., Harvey, A. S., Lawton, M. P. and McColl, M. A. (eds) (1999) *Time Use Research in the Social Sciences.* New York: Kluwer/Plenum.

Pew Research Center for the People and the Press (2004) *Polls Face Growing Resistance, But Still Representative, Survey Experiment Shows.* Washington, DC: Pew Research Center, available at: http://people-press.org/report/211/ (Accessed May 2013).

Pritchard, M. P. and Funk, D. C. (2010) The formation and effect of attitude importance in professional sport. *European Journal of Marketing*, 44(7), 1017–36.

Rapoport, R. and Rapoport, R. N. (1975) *Leisure and the Family Life Cycle.* London: Routledge.

Roberts, K. (2011) *Class in Contemporary Britain, Second edn.* Basingstoke, UK: Palgrave Macmillan.

Robertson, R. W. and Veal, A. J. (1987) *Port Hacking Visitor Use Study.* Sydney: Centre for Leisure and Tourism Studies, University of Technology, Sydney.

Schaeffer, N. C. (2000) Asking questions about threatening topics: a selective overview. In A. A. Stone *et al.* (eds) *The Science of Self-report: Implications for Research and Practice.* Mahwah, NJ: Lawrence Erlbaum, 105–22.

Siesmaa, E. J., Blitvich, J. D., White, P. E. and Finch, C. F. (2011) Measuring children's self-reported sport participation, risk perception and injury history: development and validation of a survey instrument. *Journal of Science and Medicine in Sport/Sports Medicine Australia*, 14(1), 22–26.

Sirakaya-Turk, E., Uysal, M., Hammitt, W. and Vaske, J. (2011) Survey research: sampling and questionnaire design. In E. Sirakaya-Turk, M. Uysal, W. E. Hammitt and J. J. Vaske (eds), *Research Methods for Leisure, Recreation and Tourism.* Wallingford, UK: CABI, 94–113.

Standing Committee on Recreation and Sport (SCORS) (2011) *Participation in Exercise, Recreation and Sport, Annual Report 2010.* Canberra: Australian Sports Commission, available at: www.ausport.gov.au/information/casro/ERASS (Accessed May 2013).

Stone, A. A., Turkkan, J. S., Bachrach, C. A., Jobe, J. B., Kurtzman, H. S. and Cain, V. S. (2000) *The Science of Self-report: Implications for Research and Practice.* Mahwah, NJ: Lawrence Erlbaum.

Szalai, A. (ed.) (1972) *The Use of Time: Daily Activities of Urban and Suburban Populations in Twelve Countries.* The Hague: Mouton.

Taniguchi, H. and Shupe, F. L. (2012) Gender and family status differences in leisure-time sports/fitness participation. *International Review for the Sociology of Sport.*

Tudor-Locke, C., Washington, T. L., Ainsworth, B. E. and Troiano, R. P. (2009) Linking the American Time Use Survey (ATUS) and the compendium of physical activities: methods and rationale. *Journal of Physical Activity and Health*, 6(3), 347–53.

Zuzanek, J., Robinson, J. P. and Iwasaki, Y. (1998) The relationship between stress, health and physically active leisure as a function of life-cycle. *Leisure Sciences*, 20(3), 253–75.

Experimental research

Introduction

The essence of the experiment is that the researcher aims to control all the relevant variables in the research environment. Selected variables related to the subjects or objects of the research are manipulated while others are held constant and the effects on subjects/objects are measured. The experimental approach is closely associated with the positivist paradigm and is consistent with the classic scientific model of testing hypotheses and seeking to establish cause and effect relationships **(see Chapter 2)**. It is also the methodology which seeks to capture the principles of causality **(Chapters 2 and 16)**.

Use of the experimental method is common on the sport science wing of sport studies, but is generally thought of as rare on the social science wing of the field, but when consideration is given to the full range of experimental and quasi-experimental methods used and the diversity of disciplinary contributions to the field, the body of experimental research is found to be quite substantial. The second part of the chapter therefore examines the use of experimental methods in a range of sport research contexts.

This chapter is located in Part II of the book which is concerned with data collection, while data analysis is addressed in Part III. In the case of experimental methods, however, there is no corresponding separate analysis chapter in Part III. This is because, in the sport context, experimental data are invariably collected via one of the standard social science methods, such as questionnaires, observation or the use of secondary data. So the analysis procedures outlined for these standard methodologies apply. Situations where data are gathered by means of observations from an experiment result in a data file of cases and values for variables, so analysis procedures are comparable to those followed for a data file from a questionnaire survey.

The first part of the chapter explores, in turn: the principles of experimental research; the issue of validity; and quasi-experimental designs.

Principles of experimental research

Components

The essence of the experiment is that selected variables are manipulated while others are held constant and the effects on subjects are then measured. In the terminology of experimental study the researcher is concerned with a *dependent variable*, an *independent or treatment variable*, a *treatment group* and a *control group*. There may be one or more of each of these components in any one study.

- *Dependent variable*: The dependent variable is a measurable outcome of the experiment. Participation in a sport activity, level of satisfaction with a service and level of fitness or health status could all be dependent variables.

- *Independent variable:* The independent variable or *treatment variable* represents a quality or characteristic that is varied or manipulated during the experiment. Some examples of independent variables are: provision of information/training or incentives, an exercise or training programme and variation in the level and/or quality of service received. The independent or treatment variable is manipulated during the experiment to examine its effect on the dependent variable.

- *Treatment or experimental group:* The group of participants or subjects receiving the treatment is referred to as the *treatment* or *experimental group.*

- *Control group:* In order to take account of the possible effects of other environmental variables on the outcome of the experiment, the researcher often uses a control group that is not subject to the treatment. The attributes of the control group may be matched with the attributes of the experimental or treatment group so that the two groups are as similar as possible, or subjects may be randomly assigned to the two groups.

The classic experimental design

The classic or true design for experimental research, the pre-test/post-test control group design, is summarised in Figure 11.1 and involves six steps:

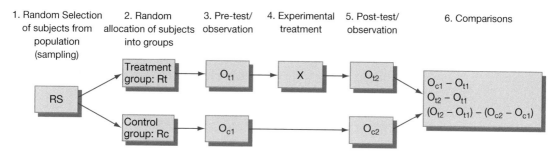

Figure 11.1   Classic experimental design

1. Selection of subjects from a population (sampling).

2. Subjects are *randomly allocated* to two groups: A, the treatment group, and B, the control group.

3. In the *pre-test observation*, subjects in both groups are measured with respect to the dependent variable.

4. The *experimental treatment*, E, is applied to the treatment group, A, but not to the control group, B.

5. In the *post-test observation*, subjects in both groups are measured again with respect to the dependent variable.

6. For the experimental treatment to be judged positive:

   ● there should be no significant difference between O_{t1} and O_{c1}

   ● there should be a significant difference between $(O_{t2} - O_{t1})$ and $(O_{c2} - O_{c1})$

Typically in Step 6 the calculations will be based on mean scores for each measurement for each group. The concept of significant difference is discussed **(see Chapter 17.)**

Validity

The aim of the classic design is to ensure, as far as possible, the *validity* of the research findings. Validity refers to the extent to which the information collected in a research study truly reflects the phenomenon being studied. There is generally a trade-off to be made between research validity and practicality and cost. While perfection is impossible, researchers should be aware of *threats to validity* and take these into account in the design of the experiment.

Internal validity	Aspects of the experimental design which raise doubts as to whether change in dependent variable can be attributed entirely to the independent variable/ treatment.
Maturation	Change occurs in study subjects during the study period – e.g. fatigue.
History	Change in the external environment affects the study – e.g. weather conditions.
Testing	The test/observation process itself may affect subjects – e.g. asking questions raises awareness of, and therefore changes in, behaviour.
Instrumentation	Inconsistency or unreliability in the measuring instruments or observation procedures during a study – e.g. change in the way a questionnaire is designed.
Selection bias	Treatment group and control group have significantly different characteristics – e.g. one group markedly older than the other.
Mortality	Attrition of subjects from a study – likely to happen if treatment process is spread over a long period of time.
External validity	Extent to which results may be generalised beyond the study subjects and setting.
Reactive effects of testing	Tests/observation may sensitise subjects and affect behaviour responses, which would not happen in 'real life' – e.g. subjects wish to impress the researchers.
Effects of selection	Subjects may not be representative of wider population – e.g. when experiments conducted with tertiary students or city centre dwellers. The very fact of involvement with a study may cause subjects to behave differently from people generally – the 'Hawthorne effect'.

Figure 11.2   Threats to validity of experiments

Threats to validity

Threats to the validity of experimental research fall into two main groups: *internal*, in which design components are compromised, and *external*, which relate to the application of the findings to the population to which the results are intended to apply. Some of these threats are summarised in Figure 11.2.

In Figure 11.2, reference is made to the 'Hawthorne effect', in which being part of a study affects people's behaviour. This was demonstrated many years ago in a study in the Hawthorne Plant of the Western Electric Company in the United States, which investigated the relationship between productivity and the brightness of lighting in the factory. As expected, productivity increased as illumination was increased. However, as brightness was decreased, productivity also rose. It was concluded that it was the attention the workers were receiving as a result of the study, rather than the level of lighting itself, that was affecting production.

Field experiments versus laboratory experiments

Field experiments take place 'in the field', that is, naturalistic, non-laboratory settings. There is a trade-off between laboratory experiments and field experiments in relation to external and internal validity. Exercise laboratories have an element of the 'natural' since they invariably contain the same sort of exercise equipment as seen in a public gym, and computers do not necessarily look out of place. In the case of social or psychological sport research, the equivalent of the 'laboratory' is often an office, meeting room or classroom where data are elicited from subjects. In general, field experiments undertaken in typical sport settings have greater external validity than laboratory-based experiments, but experimentation involves the researcher intervening to change something and if the subjects of the research are aware of this, there is an immediate loss of 'naturalness' and the subjects may therefore not behave in a normal way. Furthermore, there is always a chance of other uncontrollable, and unmeasured, external factors intervening to affect behaviour. Laboratory-based experiments, on the other hand, tend to have greater internal reliability than field experiments because the researcher has more control of extraneous variables in a laboratory. The decision should only be made after careful consideration of the threats to internal and external validity described above, and consideration of the objectives of the research. The 'obvious' approach may not in fact be ideal. For example, it might be thought obvious that it would be appropriate to gather data from sport participants at a sport facility, but if the interest is in general patterns of sporting behaviour, it might be best to avoid the possibility of subjects being over-influenced by any particular sport/facility experience.

Quasi-experimental designs

Types of quasi-experimental design

In a natural science experiment, the subjects will be identical specimens or samples of organic or inorganic matter, or laboratory animals that are as nearly as possible identical, and are treated identically except for the experimental treatment. This is not possible in the sorts of social or organisational contexts with which sport is involved. In such contexts, therefore, compromises must be made with the classic model and *quasi-experimental* designs must be devised.

Four common quasi-experimental designs are shown in Figure 11.3. Some designs simplify the classic model, for example by dispensing with a control group or the pre-test stage, while others complicate it, for example by adding

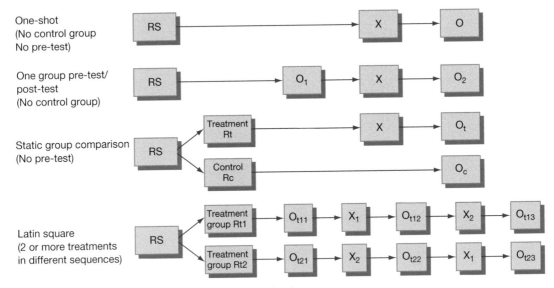

Figure 11.3 Quasi-experimental research designs

additional treatments. They are often used where time, cost and practicality are important considerations, but there is often a loss of validity associated with each design. The four designs are:

- the one-shot design;
- the one-group pre-test–post-test design;
- the static group design; and
- the Latin square.

Experiments and projects

There is a tendency in some references to the experimental method to equate 'experiment' with 'research project'. But typically a research project will comprise a series of experiments. In order to conduct an individual experiment it is necessary to define the relevant dependent and independent/treatment variables. But a project can comprise a number of experiments and the programme of experiments may evolve during the course of the project. Imagine a medical scientist searching for a drug to treat a virus: a number of possibilities may be explored before a successful treatment is discovered. This may take a number of experiments, even a number of projects. Thus an experimental project, or sequence of projects, may be much more exploratory, even inductive, than the formal hypothetical-deductive model of the single experiment.

Experimental methods in sport research

Experiments involve research in a controlled environment in which the researcher is able to vary the conditions of the environment for research purposes. Opportunities to do this exist in some sport contexts, for example, with the usual ethical provisos **(see Chapter 4)**, using 'captive groups' such as sport teams or athletes in a training programme. But when the general public, customers of a service or employees of an organisation are involved, the opportunities are limited, which explains the widespread use of non-experimental methods, notably questionnaire-based surveys. Experimental or quasi-experimental methods are nevertheless used in a variety of sport contexts, as indicated in Figure 11.4, and these are discussed in turn below.

Training/coaching

Athlete training/coaching is a research field in its own right: it investigates which exercise and pedagogical devices work most effectively in achieving the goals of fitness, skill acquisition and retention and individual and team performance. However, the training/coaching environment also provides a laboratory-type setting involving subjects, the athletes, who are accustomed to being told what to do, and an environment which can be substantially controlled by the coach or the researcher under the authority of the coach. The subjects are also 'captive' **(see Chapter 10)** for a prolonged period, thus facilitating 'before', 'after' and 'follow-up' measurement following single or multiple

Training/coaching	Studies of effectiveness of various training/coaching methods and athlete behaviour/responses in training/coaching contexts.
Sport policy/management pilot/trial projects	Innovations in policy or management practice are tested by experimental or pilot projects and evaluated using a variety of methods and with varying degrees of rigour.
Psychological/perceptual	Samples of subjects exposed to hypothetical situations/questions or images.
Equipment	Studies of equipment–athlete interaction.
Experimenting with research methods	Testing of innovative or alternative research methods or techniques, usually in the same setting, with the same subjects or split samples.
Children's physical activity/ play	Observational studies of children with different play equipment/ environments.
Other examples	Action research; Q methodology; qualitative methods; discrete choice experiments (DCE); mental mapping; and physical models.

Figure 11.4 Types and contexts of experiments in sport research

experimental interventions. Thus research in such an environment can also be used to investigate human sport/exercise behaviour unrelated to specific training/coaching goals. Examples of experiments in this type of setting are summarised in Case studies 11.1 to 11.3.

Case study 11.1   Training patterns and performance

A great deal of sport performance research is focused on approaches to improve coaching and training techniques. One issue is the effectiveness of, and balance between, substantial programmed periods of time devoted to practising particular skills (the 'block' approach) versus random switching from one skill to another for short bursts ('random' approach). Porter and Magill (2010) tested a new form of increased levels of coach intervention compared with traditional block and random scheduling. Experiment 1 used a golf putting exercise, and it was found that those who followed the increasing schedule of intervention had superior retention of performance level over those in the control group who were only exposed to traditional random scheduling. Experiment 2 used a number of different generalised motor programmes involving three different basketball passes and it was found that those subject to gradually increased coach intervention performed better than those in the control group. The outcome of the experiments indicated that gradually increasing frequency of coach intervention enhanced skill learning.

Case study 11.2   Visual and auditory cues and behaviour

Visual

There is body of research in behavioural psychology which examines the way people use visual cues in the environment in decision-making processes. This is relevant to areas such as road safety and child development, but can also be applied in various sporting contexts. An example is Cañal-Bruland's (2009) experimental study of soccer players' anticipation of opponents' movements. He explored Posner's *cueing paradigm*, which suggests that individuals' decision-making is improved if they are given cues as to where to focus their attention. *Visual cue* experiments can be used to test sport decision-making tasks through a series of exercises. Subjects were shown static slides of footballers coming towards them dribbling a ball. The slides were the last video frame before the player shot the ball. Subjects were asked to indicate, as quickly as possible, the direction they believed the player was about to kick. The slides were preceded by blank slides with a visual cue in the form of a red spot of varying size, directing the subject's eye to a large part of the screen, for example, covering the whole player, or small, 'information rich' part, such as the feet or hips. In the control situations there were no cues. The analysis focused on the speed and accuracy of the subjects' responses. It was found that the size/positioning of the cue had no significant effects on the results.

In another study, Cereatti *et al.* (2009) explored the question as to whether playing particular sports results in the development of particular visual skills. They therefore compared the visual skills of a mixed (control) group of physically fit individuals with a group of orienteers who require rapid visual recognition and interpretation skills to succeed in their sport. The experiments were computer-based, involving subjects responding to a series of recognition tests requiring quick responses. It was found that the orienteers did indeed have superior visual skills to those of the control group, suggesting that particular sports can develop a high level of visual skills.

Auditory

In reviewing the literature on the use of auditory stimulation in sport training, Murgia *et al.* (2012) found that most research in this area has focused on its use in aiding athletes in the correct timing of their movements. They explored another possible use of auditory stimulation: to trigger physiological arousal. Their experimental study involved 18 participants who bench-pressed three lifts with and without an auditory stimulus.

The auditory stimulus, delivered through headphones, involved an initial countdown, followed by a low-intensity sound corresponding to the down phase of the lift and a high-intensity sound associated with the pressing phase. Power exerted was measured by the weights equipment and its associated software. It was found that the lifts accompanied by auditory stimulation produced a 2.5 per cent higher level of power exerted.

> ### Case study 11.3   Pre-competition stress
>
> An example of a study of training techniques to enhance sport performance is that by Shaji, Verma and Khanna (2011), which used 'mindfulness meditation therapy' (a Buddhist practice) as a relaxation intervention to moderate pre-competition stress in shooters. The experimental intervention involved relaxation meditation sessions during five weeks of training, with pre-, post- and follow-up testing of shooting performance. The sample consisted of 96 elite competitive shooters, 48 in the meditation group and 48 in a control group. The conclusion of the study was that mindfulness meditation therapy reduced pre-competition stress and enhanced shooting performance.

Sport policy/management experimental projects

Conducting experiments, often called *pilot projects*, *pilot programmes* or *trials*, is popular in the government sport policy sector, partly for the overt reason that it is wise to test effectiveness of policies on a small scale before implementing them on a wide scale, but also because, to be somewhat cynical, they are much cheaper than rolling out a full-scale policy and can delay, possibly indefinitely, having to make a decision on the full roll-out. Invariably such projects include an evaluation component, although, in practice, this is not always adequately resourced or rigorously conducted.

In typical cases the declared policy-related experimentation is to increase levels of participation in sport and physical exercise among a target group. However, invariably the rationale behind the policy of boosting participation is related to other policy areas, notably health and crime reduction and, more recently in Britain, 'social inclusion': the notion that all groups should enjoy the rights of citizenship, including engagement with sporting, social and cultural activity (Collins, 2003). In these cases, the criterion for the success of a project is not just participation itself, but the resultant hoped-for improvements in health, crime reduction or social inclusion. The experimental model is therefore as shown in Figure 11.5. Two lots of measurements/observations are made, relating to participation and the social policy criterion, while the 'control' is often, in effect, the community at large, for example the general level of sport participation or crime rates, related to the whole population or, in some cases, youth.

Given its association with health, sport involves not just social scientists but also medical and human movement scientists. Thus both the researchers involved and the policy-makers, who commission such research and work with its results, are familiar with the experimental method and it is often accepted in this environment that evidence-based policy should be based on

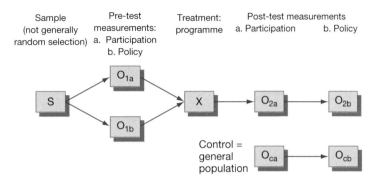

Figure 11.5 **Experimental model of policy projects**

rigorously conducted experiments. In order to provide such a basis for policy development, therefore, a number of reviews of available research have been carried out to establish what rigorous evidence exists on the effectiveness, or otherwise, of various types of experimental intervention. One of these is summarised in Case study 11.4. The paucity of research meeting strict experimental criteria illustrates the 'clash of cultures' among different research traditions. One theme of policy interventions in sport is the proposition that engaging 'at risk' young people in sport can reduce the likelihood of their engagement in delinquent or criminal activity. This is discussed in Case study 11.5.

Case study 11.4   Sport participation promotion projects: review

Priest *et al.* (2008) conducted a review of available literature on experiments/ projects/interventions conducted by sporting organisations and designed to increase community sport participation. The review involved the scanning of databases containing some 15,000 research publications. They noted that interventions to boost sport participation can take a variety of forms, including:

- mass media campaigns;
- information or education sessions;
- management or organisational change strategies;
- policy changes, for example to improve the socio-cultural environment to encourage people of specific age, gender or ethnicity to participate;
- changes to traditional or existing programmes, for example club- or association-initiated rule modification programmes;
- provision of activities beyond traditional or existing programmes, for example 'Come and Try' initiatives (teaser or taster programmes), skill improvement programmes, volunteer encouragement programmes (Priest *et al.*, 2008: no pagination).

The aim of the review was to identify suitable studies, to evaluate them methodologically and to draw conclusions about the effectiveness of various forms of intervention in promoting sport participation. Their conclusions were:

> We found no controlled studies that met the inclusion criteria. We identified no uncontrolled studies, with pre- and post-test data, suitable to be included in ... this review ... and therefore assessed no studies for methodological quality. Despite using the most comprehensive search methods to date, no studies were identified that employed a controlled evaluation design. (Priest *et al.*, 2008: no pagination)

This extraordinary finding indicates that, despite the involvement of health and sport scientists, along with social scientists, as discussed above, none of the studies identified conformed to the classic scientific model, with control groups and pre-intervention and post-intervention data. Even relaxing the requirement for a control group (uncontrolled studies), no studies were found with pre-test and post-test data.

This is an extreme example of a problem recognised by others in attempting to review this field of study. Blamey and Mutrie (2004: 748) noted one study which identified 253 publications for review but excluded 159 due to limitations in study design, and another where only 12 out of 254 papers satisfied the review criteria. Fred Coalter (2007: 27–9) notes that this situation is not unique to sport and refers to discussion in the policy literature which suggests that the rigorous experimental criteria used in the natural sciences may not be appropriate in social policy areas and that, in any case, there is an absence of theoretical understanding of the causes of sport participation and non-participation to inform the design and evaluation of programmes/projects/experiments (pp. 171–4). Pawson (2006) also subjects the critical review/meta-analysis approach **(see Chapter 6)** to critical analysis and suggests that its medical science-based rigour may not be appropriate for social policy applications.

Case study 11.5   Sport and crime reduction

In his book on *Sport and Crime Reduction*, Nichols (2007) presents eight case studies of projects designed to divert young people from engaging in crime through participation in a sport-related programme. Just one project, conducted in Britain, is described here. During a three-year period, 194 young people on probation volunteered to take part in a 12-week 'sport counselling' service which introduced them to a range of local council sporting facilities and courses such as life saving. No follow-up study was undertaken in relation to sport participation, but the social (crime) outcome was measured by tracking reconviction rates over the following two years. The reconviction rate for participants who completed the 12-week programmes was significantly lower than for those who completed less than 8 weeks and matched control groups who had not taken part in the programme at all. Programme participants' self-esteem was also measured, at the beginning and end of the programme, and participation in the full course was found to make a significant positive difference.

Psychological/perceptual studies

The study of some psychological and perceptual aspects of sport lends itself to experimental research, where subjects can be exposed to visual stimuli and their reactions or opinions recorded. Such studies provide an opportunity for research to examine a variety of interventions that may affect sport performance. Some visual and auditory examples are summarised in Case study 11.6.

Case study 11.6   Psychological/perceptual studies

a. Mood and physical activity

One of the reasons why participation in sport and other forms of physical activity is encouraged is because of the health benefits it brings. These can be physical or mental. One aspect of poor mental health is depression. Kanning and Schlicht (2010) conducted a study to examine the effect of physical activity on mood. A sample of 13 subjects kept diaries over a 10-week period, in which, on a daily basis, they recorded three randomly chosen distinct activities and how they felt before and after the activity. The researchers found a positive relationship between engagement in physical activity and mood level, with the greatest effect being when people started the activity in a depressed mood. In this quasi-experimental method the selection of the 'treatment' and the pre-test and post-test observations are under the control of the subjects. The method has some similarities with experience sampling method (ESM) **(see Chapter 5)**, but without the real-time external prompts and recording.

▶

b. Red jersey colour and success in combat sports

The proposition that contestants in sport competitions who wear red are more successful than contestants wearing other colours has been established on the basis of analysis of secondary data from the Olympic Games and English soccer league **(see Case study 14.6).** Dreiskaemper *et al.* (2013), however, noted that existing research had concentrated on contest results and had not examined whether the colour advantage arose from effects on the behaviour of athletes or referees, and decided to explore this issue using an experimental method. Male handball players engaged in the experiment during breaks in a training session. The players were randomly allocated red and blue body protectors and engaged in short bouts of an artificially devised combat contest involving heavily padded 'smash sticks'. Tractive force was measured using a leg dynamometer, before and after strapping on the protector, while heart rate was measured before, during and after the bout. It was found that the increase in heart rate during the bout was greater for players wearing red than for those wearing blue and they also showed an increase in tractive force following the strapping on of the body protector. Thus, the researchers concluded that wearing red appears to have a direct positive effect on athletes' physical parameters.

Equipment

Equipment is a key feature of many sports. Equipment manufacturers are engaged in extensive experimentation but the results are rarely publicly available. Generic, as opposed to brand-specific, experiments are, however, conducted and an example is shown in Case study 11.7.

Case study 11.7	Players and sporting equipment

Noting that elite tennis players are very particular about the tension at which their rackets are strung, Bower and Cross (2008) conducted experiments to examine the ability of elite players to detect differences in string tension and the efficiency of different string tensions in play. Participants in the study were 18 elite tennis players (i.e. nationally ranked or in the world top 1500, and aiming for a professional career) taking part in a tournament. Each participant compared two rackets with a string tension difference of 11 pounds, using each racket to return four balls projected by a machine. The test was conducted twice. If the player successfully detected a difference in the first test, it was repeated with two rackets with a string tension difference of 6 pounds; if unsuccessful, the repeat test involved rackets with a string tension difference of 17 pounds. The results were:

- of the 18 players, 5 detected the 11-pound difference: of these, only 2 could detect the 6-pound difference in the second test;
- 13 players could *not* detect the 11-pound difference: of these 11 could not detect even the 17-pound difference in the second test.

These findings were clearly at variance with the players' typical concern about string tension in their rackets. Other experiments, not summarised here, were conducted to test the rebound efficiency of rackets with different tensions.

Experimenting with research methods

The practice of conducting experimental research to test the efficacy of different research methods has a long history in the sport sector: for example, the report of one of the earliest research projects funded by the Sports Council in England, in the late 1960s, was entitled *Experiments in Recreation Research* (Burton, 1971). While the basic methods being examined in this type of study are not themselves experimental, the experimental quality of the studies lies in the practice of going beyond what would be normal practice, namely using multiple methods or variations on methods, in order to discover the effects of different research practices. Examples are presented in Case study 11.8.

Case study 11.8   Experiments with research methods

a. Response rate, follow-up and bias

Hammitt and McDonald (1982) conducted an on-site survey of users at two river recreation sites and followed up with a 15-page mail questionnaire to all who participated in the on-site survey. A response rate of 52 per cent was achieved with two reminders. Remaining non-respondents were sent a two-page reduced version of the mail questionnaire, resulting in an overall response rate of 75 per cent. They therefore had data from three different groups, as depicted in Figure 11.6. Because of the on-site interview they had data even on members of group C, who did not respond to either mail questionnaire.

▶

Respondent group	Data available from:			Total
	On-site qu're	15-page mail qu're	2-page mail qu're	
A. 15-page mail survey	A_1	A_2	–	A_t
B. 2-page mail survey	B_1	–	B_2	B_t
C. On-site survey only	C_1	–		C_t

Figure 11.6 Survey respondent groups – Hammitt and McDonald
From: Hammitt and McDonald (1982)

By comparing the results on the common data items between the three groups it was possible to determine whether the additional reminders made any difference to the pattern of responses. On one comparison using 17 data items, only four showed a significant difference, and on another, only one item out of 19 showed a significant difference. It was therefore concluded that there was no major benefit, in terms of representativeness, in pursuing a high response rate. Subsequent correspondence in the *Journal of Leisure Research* concerning this and similar studies cautioned that the findings were not necessarily universal, since they were contingent on the population being relatively homogeneous with respect to socio-demographic characteristics and affinity with the activity, which may not apply in all cases (Christensen, 1982).

b. Assessing event-visitor expenditure

Irwin *et al.* (1996) compared two methods of collecting data from sporting-event visitors on their expenditure allocation patterns – a key data item in economic impact studies. Most studies ask people to estimate their allocations of expenditure to such categories as travel, accommodation, entry fees, food and souvenirs, by means of a questionnaire survey conducted during the event. This involves an element of estimation of expenditures not yet incurred at the time of completing the questionnaire, and is therefore a possible source of error. The researchers therefore decided to experiment with a real-time diary approach. The research was conducted at two US National Collegiate Athletic Association championship events. From pre-booking data, one sample of attendees for each event was mailed diary forms and asked to keep a record of expenditures at the event and mail the completed forms back to the researchers after the event. Another sample was selected on-site during the event and asked to complete a questionnaire on estimated total expenditure patterns. At both sites it was found that the on-site survey respondent estimated average expenditure was between 11 and 23 per cent less than the diary-based estimates. The authors therefore suggest that the more costly diary method should be used where possible.

c. Movement measurement devices

Technological developments often provide the researcher with new types of equipment which may have advantages and disadvantages, which must be evaluated. One such development is satellite-based global positioning systems (GPS) which might replace camera-based systems in measuring, recording and analysing athlete movements for training purposes. Lightweight devices can be attached to athletes and can record and transmit data to computers equipped with appropriate software – such devices are sometimes used in sport broadcasts, providing viewers with information on such things as players' distance travelled. While numerous evaluations of the accuracy of GPS devices have been carried out in large spaces, such as football fields, Duffield *et al.* (2010) conducted an experiment in a relatively confined space – a tennis court – and tested their accuracy against traditional fixed-camera methodology. Four GPS devices were used simultaneously, two each with low (1 Hz) and high (5 Hz) resolution. A single athlete with the devices attached conducted a specified series of movements of varying speed and distance on a tennis court, with the activity being simultaneously recorded and analysed by a camera-based system. It was found that the GPS systems significantly underestimated both distance covered and peak and mean speeds, although the higher-resolution device performed better than the low-resolution device.

Children's play

The study of children's physical play can be pursued by experimental methods because young children in particular spend much of their time in play environments controlled to a greater or lesser degree by adults. The play environment can be modified and changes in the children's behaviour observed without children being aware that a controlled experiment is being conducted. An example is presented in Case study 11.9.

> ### Case study 11.9   Children's physical play experiments
>
> In what Quigg *et al.* (2012) described as a natural experimental design, they worked with a local council in New Zealand which was engaged in a programme to upgrade community playgrounds, to study the effects of the new equipment/design on children's physical activity. One upgraded playground was the intervention, and a playground which had not yet been upgraded was selected as the control. Physical activity was measured and recorded using an accelerometer worn by the children for eight days. The project also involved a respondent-completed questionnaire for parents/guardians to collect data on the perceptions of neighbourhood, how the children travelled to school, types of extra-curricular activities, ethnicity, caregiver age and gender, and household vehicle access and income. Some 184 children aged between 5 and 10 years were involved in this study, with 156 completing a one-year follow-up assessment (20 per cent attrition). The results of this study showed that there was a statistically significant increase in the total daily activity for the children in the upgraded playgrounds. One noticeable difference was that children with a lower body mass index showed a higher increase in activity than those with a higher body mass index. The study demonstrated the effectiveness of suitably designed playgrounds in promoting physical activity levels of children.

Other examples of use of experimental methods

Action research

Action research is discussed in Chapter 5 and it is noted there that it has some features of an experimental design. The approach is depicted in Figure 5.5 as comprising five steps and it can be seen that:

- Steps 1 and 2, which identify and assess a social problem, can be seen as the pre-test observation, with selection of a treatment group implied;

- Step 3, the campaign for and achievement of action, is the treatment;

- Step 4, researching the results of the action, is the post-test observation.

One of the features of the experimental method is that the researcher controls the experimental process. In action research, the researchers do not necessarily *control* the process but the philosophy of action research is that they are involved with, and therefore seek to have an *influence* on, the process.

Discrete choice experiments (DCEs)

In Chapter 5, reference is made to *conjoint analysis*, the analytical basis for *discrete choice experiments* (DCEs), which seek to explore people's decision-making processes in regard to choice of products or activities, including such phenomena as sport activities, services or facilities. The 'experimental' feature of this approach is that, rather than researching people's decision-making in the 'real world', it involves asking subjects to make choices among hypothetical alternative products defined in terms of various combinations of features. In some cases the information is presented via a questionnaire and subjects record their choices on the questionnaire, so the approach could be seen as a particular form of questionnaire-based survey. In other cases, subjects are presented with information on cards containing information on products with different combinations of features and are asked to sort them in order of preference. Either of these approaches can, of course, be operated via computer.

The technique is underpinned by the mathematical procedures such as conjoint analysis and multidimensional scaling **(see Chapter 17)**.

Case study 11.10	Discrete choice experiment: sport facility preferences of soccer attendees

Bjørnskov Pedersen *et al.* (2011) used a discrete choice experiment (DCE) to study soccer match attendees' facility preferences at a stadium in Denmark. The attributes included in the DCE were: ticket price differentiation related to the quality of opponents; wide screens behind the goals; sale of refreshments in the stand; fully covered stand; and cheerleaders. The results showed that the attendees were able to differentiate between the attributes, with statistically significant outcomes for all attributes except use of cheerleaders, where there was a great deal of heterogeneity among the attendees. Specifically, the advantage of the DCE method was in being able to differentiate between the strength of preference for each of the attributes. In this case, wide screens and fully covered stands were regarded to be of high importance, followed by the sale of refreshments in the stands. Cheerleaders were highly valued by some respondents but other respondents regarded their addition as being of little value, while others found that they detracted from the experience.

Q methodology

Q methodology, in which research participants arrange cards containing statements into a predetermined distribution, is also described in Chapter 5. While the approach can be seen as merely an elaboration of a questionnaire-based survey, the design and manipulation of the card-sorting process indicates a level of control which reflects features of the experimental approach.

Qualitative methods

In the bulk of experimental research in the sport field, quantitative research methods are used. However, where the planned outcomes of an experiment are qualitative, for example changing subjects' attitudes, qualitative methods could possibly be considered. An example is the project described by Suckling *et al.* (2009) which assessed changing attitudes of young people following involvement in a sport participation promotion programme.

More generally, qualitative research is typically presented as distinct from the classic, positivist scientific experimental method. This applies particularly to those qualitative methodologies in which the researcher engages actively with the subjects – such as some participant observation and non-standardised interviewing. However, such approaches have certain features of the experimental method. The researcher's involvement with the subject can be seen as paralleling the 'treatment' in an experiment, although, of course, it is not in a controlled environment.

Mind mapping with MRI (magnetic resonance imaging)

In the area of sport performance, technology is able to be used in an experimental design to literally map the mind of participants in experimental studies. Wright *et al.* (2010) examined the concept of anticipation in players of different-graded skill levels in badminton using MRI scans. The experiment sought to assess players' anticipated directional response from video clips immediately before and after racket shuttle contact. The scans showed that people at an expert level demonstrated additional enhancement in the frontal cortex areas of the brain, indicating that anticipation activity in experts could be verified through examination of brain function activity.

Summary

Experimental methods are closely associated with the *positivist paradigm* and are consistent with the classic 'scientific' model of testing hypotheses and establishing cause-and-effect relationships. The essence of the experiment is that the researcher ideally controls all the relevant variables in the experiment. Selected variables are manipulated, while others are held constant and the effects on subjects are measured. Components of the experiment are: the treatment or experimental group; the control group; dependent variable; and the independent or treatment variable. The independent or treatment variable is manipulated during the experiment to examine its effect on the dependent variable. Typically, variables are measured before the treatment (pre-test) and after the treatment (post-test). Quasi-experimental designs vary this model by, for example omitting a control group, omitting the pre-test or including more than one treatment group or treatment. Although *experimental methods* are usually associated with natural science and laboratories, it is possible to conduct some experiments in sport contexts. Among these contexts are: policy/management pilot or trial projects; training/coaching; equipment testing; experiments with research methods; psychological/perceptual studies, sport-related experiments and children's play.

Test questions

1. Explain the difference between an independent and dependent variable.

2. What are the defining characteristics of the experimental method?

3. What are the main threats to the validity of experimental research?

4. Outline two examples of quasi-experimental models and indicate how they deviate from the classic experimental model.

5. Give three examples of contexts where experimental methods have been used in sport research.

Exercises

1. Outline a true experimental research design to test the hypothesis that regular walking is a more effective way of achieving physical fitness than playing organised sport.

2. How could a sport organisation set up an experiment to test the effectiveness of two forms of advertising? What elements of the 'classic' experimental design would need to be sacrificed? What type of quasi-experiment would this be?

3. Regarding Case study 11.6b, concerning the colour of sportswear: explore the literature cited in Dreiskaemper *et al.* (2013) and identify other experiments which address this topic.

Resources

- The classic work on experimental research design is Campbell and Stanley (1972).

- Competition: effect on performance and cheating: Schwieren and Weichselbaumer (2010).

- Educational performance and sport participation: Rees and Sabia (2010).

- Emotions and sport performance: Woodman *et al.* (2009).

- Evidence-based policy and systematic reviews: Pawson (2006).

- Facility feature preferences: Bjørnskov Pedersen *et al.* (2011).

- Inclusion/exclusion and sport: Szymanski (2001), Collins (2003), Rooth (2011).

- Discrete choice experiments/stated choice method:

  - overview: Crouch and Louviere (2001), Louviere and Woodworth (1983), Louviere *et al.* (2000);

  - facility feature preferences: Bjørnskov Pedersen *et al.* (2011);

  - rock-climbing (and bibliography of environmental/recreation examples): Hanley *et al.* (2001);

  - sport fishery: Aas *et al.* (2000);

  - sport tourism: Chalip and McGuirty (2004), Wiebke *et al.* (2008).

- Policy-related experiments: Alexander (1994), Centre for Leisure and Sport Research (2002), Coalter (2007), Mazanov and Connor (2010); crime prevention: Nichols (2007).

- Research on research methods: Christensen (1982), Gitelson and Drogin (1992); survey follow-up methods and response rates: Hammitt and McDonald (1982); alternative methods of collecting expenditure data at sporting events: Faulkner and Raybould (1995), Irwin *et al.* (1996).

- Team and organisation identification and cause-related sport marketing: Lee and Ferreira (2013).

- Terrorism and sport fans: Dechesne *et al.* (2000).

References

Aas, Ø., Haider, W. and Hunt, L. (2000) Angler responses to potential harvest regulations in a Norwegian sport fishery: a conjoint-based choice modelling approach. *North American Journal of Fisheries Management*, 20(4), 940–50.

Alexander, K. (1994) Developing sport education in Western Australia. *Aussie Sport Action*, 5(1), 8–9.

Bjørnskov Pedersen, L., Kiil, A. and Kjær, T. (2011) Soccer attendees' preferences for facilities at the Fionia Park Stadium: an application of the discrete choice experiment. *Journal of Sports Economics*, 12(2), 179–99.

Blamey, A. and Mutrie, N. (2004) Changing the individual to promote health-enhancing physical activity: the difficulties of producing evidence and translating it into practice. *Journal of Sports Sciences*, 22(8), 741–54.

Bower, R. and Cross, R. (2008) Elite tennis player sensitivity to changes in string tension and the effect on resulting ball dynamics. *Sports Engineering*, 11(1), 31–6.

Burton, T. L. (1971) *Experiments in Recreation Research*. London: Allen & Unwin.

Campbell, D. T. and Stanley, J. C. (1972) *Experimental and Quasi-Experimental Designs for Research*. Chicago: Rand McNally.

Cañal-Bruland, R. (2009) Visual cueing in sport-specific decision making. *International Journal of Sport and Exercise Psychology*, 7(4), 450–64.

Centre for Leisure and Sport Research (2002) *Count Me In: The Dimensions of Social Inclusion through Culture and Sport*. Report to the Department for Culture, Media and Sport, Leeds: Centre for Leisure and Sport Research, Leeds Metropolitan University.

Cereatti, L., Casella, R., Manganelli, M. and Pesce, C. (2009) Visual attention in adolescents: facilitating effects of sport expertise and acute physical exercise. *Psychology of Sport and Exercise*, 10(1), 136–45.

Chalip, L. and McGuirty, J. (2004) Bundling sport events with the host destination. *Journal of Sport and Tourism*, 9(3), 267–82.

Christensen, J. E. (1982) On generalizing about the need for follow-up efforts in mail response surveys. *Journal of Leisure Research*, 14(3), 263–65.

Coalter, F. (2007) *A Wider Social Role for Sport: Who's Keeping the Score?* London: Routledge.

Collins, M. F. (2003) *Sport and Social Exclusion*. London: Routledge.

Crouch, G. I. and Louviere, J. J. (2001) A review of choice modelling research in tourism, hospitality and leisure. In J. A. Mazanec, G. I. Crouch, J. R. B. Ritchie and A. G. Woodside (eds) *Consumer Psychology of Tourism, Hospitality and Leisure, Vol. 2*. Wallingford, UK: CABI, 67–86.

Dechesne, M., Greenberg, J., Arndt, J. and Schimel, J. (2000) Terror management and the vicissitudes of sports fan affiliation: the effects of mortality salience on optimism and fan identification. *European Journal of Social Psychology*, 30(6), 813–35.

Dreiskaemper, D., Strauss, B., Hagemann, N. and Busch, D. (2013) Influence of red jersey color on physical parameters in combat sports. *Journal of Sport and Exercise Psychology*, 35(1), 44–9.

Duffield, R., Reid, M., Baker, J. and Spratford, W. (2010) Accuracy and reliability of GPS devices for measurement of movement patterns in confined spaces for court-based sports. *Journal of Science and Medicine in Sport*, 13(7), 523–5.

Faulkner, B. and Raybould, M. (1995) Monitoring visitor expenditure associated with attendance at sporting events: an experimental assessment of the diary and recall methods. *Festival Management and Event Tourism*, 3(2), 73–81.

Gitelson, R. J. and Drogin, E. B. (1992) An experiment on the efficacy of a certified final mailing. *Journal of Leisure Research*, 24(1), 72–8.

Haerens, L. and Tallir, I. (2010) Experimental research in physical education and sports. In K. Armour and D. Macdonald (eds) *Research Methods in Physical Education and Youth Sport*. London: Routledge, 149–62.

Hammitt, W. E. and McDonald, C. D. (1982) Response bias and the need for extensive mail questionnaire follow-ups among selected recreation samples. *Journal of Leisure Research*, 14(3), 207–16.

Hanley, N., Mourato, S. and Wright, R. E. (2001) Choice modelling approaches: a superior alternative for environmental evaluation? *Journal of Economic Surveys*, 15(3), 435–62.

Irwin, R. L., Wang, P. and Sutton, W. A. (1996) Comparative analysis of diaries and projected spending to assess patron expenditure behavior at short-term sporting events. *Festival Management and Event Tourism*, 4(1), 29–37.

Kanning, M. and Schlicht, W. (2010) Be active and become happy: an ecological momentary assessment of physical activity and mood. *Journal of Sport and Exercise Psychology*, 32(2), 253–61.

Lee, J. and Ferreira, M. (2013) A role of team and organizational identification in the success of cause-related sport marketing. *Sport Management Review*, 16, in press.

Louviere, J. J. and Woodworth, G. (1983) Design and analysis of simulated consumer choice or allocation experiments: an approach based on aggregate data. *Journal of Marketing Research*, 20(3), 350–67.

Louviere, J. J., Hensher, D. A. and Swait, J. D. (2000) *Stated Choice Methods: Analysis and Applications*. Cambridge: Cambridge University Press.

Mazanov, J. and Connor, J. (2010) Rethinking the management of drugs in sport. *International Journal of Sport Policy and Politics*, 2(1), 49–63.

Murgia, M., Sors, F., Vono, R., Muroni, A. F., Delitalia, L., Di Corrado, D. and Agostini, T. (2012) Using auditory stimulation to enhance athletes' strength: an experimental study in weightlifting. *Review of Psychology*, 19(1), 13–16.

Nichols, G. (2007) *Sport and Crime Reduction: The Role of Sports in Tackling Youth Crime*. London: Routledge.

Pawson, R. (2006) Systematic obfuscation: a critical analysis of the meta-analytic approach. Chapter 3 of: *Evidence-based Policy: A Realist Perspective*. London: Sage, 38–72.

Porter, J. M. and Magill, R. A. (2010) Systematically increasing contextual interference is beneficial for learning sport skills. *Journal of Sports Sciences*, 28(12), 1277–85.

Priest, N., Armstrong, R., Doyle, J. and Waters, E. (2008) Interventions implemented through sporting organisations for increasing participation in sport. *Cochrane Database of Systematic Reviews*, 3, no pagination.

Quigg, R., Reeder, A., Gray, A., Holt, A. and Waters, D. (2012) The effectiveness of a community playground intervention. *Journal of Urban Health*, 89(1), 171–84.

Rees, D. I. and Sabia, J. J. (2010) Sports participation and academic performance: evidence from the national longitudinal study of adolescent health. *Economics of Education Review*, 29(5), 751–9.

Rooth, D.-O. (2011) Work out or out of work – the labor market return to physical fitness and leisure sports activities. *Labour Economics*, 18(3), 399–409.

Schwieren, C. and Weichselbaumer, D. (2010) Does competition enhance performance or cheating? A laboratory experiment. *Journal of Economic Psychology*, 31(3), 241–53.

Shaji, D. J., Verma, D. S. K. and Khanna, D. G. L. (2011) The effect of mindfulness meditation on HPA-axis in pre-competition stress in sports performance of elite shooters. *National Journal of Integrated Research in Medicine*, 2(3), 15–21.

Suckling, S., Ryan, P. and Dent, M. (2009) Beliefs, barriers and control: a model for research into social exclusion. *International Journal of Public Sector Management*, 22(5), 423–31.

Szymanski, S. (2001) Income inequality, competitive balance and the attractiveness of team sports: some evidence and a natural experiment from English soccer. *Economic Journal*, 111(469), 69–84.

Wiebke, U., Ulrike, P. and Wolfgang, H. (2008) Trends in winter sport tourism: challenges for the future. *Tourism Review*, 63(1), 36–47.

Woodman, T., Davis, P. A., Hardy, L., Callow, N., Glasscock, I. and Yuill-Proctor, J. (2009) Emotions and sport performance: an exploration of happiness, hope, and anger. *Journal of Sport and Exercise Psychology*, 31(2), 169–88.

Wright, M. J., Bishop, D. T., Jackson, R. C. and Abernethy, B. (2010) Functional MRI reveals expert-novice differences during sport-related anticipation. *NeuroReport*, 21(2), 94–8.

The case study method

Introduction

A case study involves the study of an individual example – a case – of the phenomenon being researched. The aim is to seek to understand the phenomenon by studying one or more single examples in depth. To some extent, all social research is a case study at some level, since all research is geographically and temporally unique. Thus, for example, a survey of 500 visitors to a particular sport venue can be seen as a case study of the use of that venue, and even a nation-wide survey of the sport activities of thousands of people in a Western country carried out in 2010 could be viewed, in one sense, as a case study of the activities of the population of one affluent country in the early twenty-first century.

The case study *research method* should be distinguished from other uses of the concept of cases, including in the law, where it refers to an individual crime, arrest and trial and may be important in setting precedents, and in medicine, where cases refer to individual patients. In both these examples, the case – either live or as a written record – becomes a vehicle for teaching and in the business sector this is its exclusive use, the most well-known example being the Harvard Business School cases (Harvard Business School, nd) while sport business-related examples are presented by Chadwick and Arthur (2012).

This chapter considers in turn: the definition of the case study method; the merits of the case study method; types of case study; data collection; and data analysis. A number of examples of case study research in sport contexts are then presented.

Definitions

What is the case study method?

John Gerring (2007: 19–20) defines a *case* as 'a spatially delimited phenomenon (a unit) observed at a single point in time or over some period of time' and a *case study* as 'the intensive study of a single case'. He goes on to observe:

> Case study research may incorporate several cases, that is, multiple case studies. However, at a certain point it will no longer be possible to investigate those cases so intensively. At the point where the emphasis of a study shifts from the individual case to a sample of cases, we shall say that a study is *cross-case*. Evidently the distinction between case study and cross-case study is a matter of degree. The fewer cases there are, and the more intensively they are studied, the more the work merits the appellation 'case study'... All empirical work may be classified as either case study (comprising one or a few cases) or cross-case study (involving many cases). *(Gerring, 2007: 20)*

Thus, there is a continuum between the case study method and cross-case research rather than a sharp line of separation. Gerring goes on to express a hope that his book:

> will contribute to breaking down the rather artificial boundaries that have separated these genres within the social sciences. Properly constituted, there is no reason that case study results cannot be synthesized with results gained from cross-case analysis, and vice versa. *(Gerring, 2007: 13)*

What the case study method is not

The fact that research projects using the case study method typically involves only one or a few cases suggests some similarity with qualitative research methods and in some texts the case study method is subsumed under 'qualitative methods' (e.g. Finn *et al.*, 2000: 81) but, as leading authority Robert Yin states:

> ... the case study method is not just a form of 'qualitative research', even though some have recognised the case study as being among the array of qualitative research choices ... The use of a mix of quantitative and qualitative evidence ... are but two of the ways that case study research goes beyond being a type of qualitative research. *(Yin, 2014: 19)*

In fact, the use of a variety of types of data and types of analysis can be said to be a key feature of the case study method.

Some commentators (for example, Zikmund, 1997: 108) have implied that the case study method is used only for 'exploratory' purposes, but this is not the only possible purpose: as Yin (2014: 7) asserts: 'case study research is far from being only an exploratory strategy'. Indeed, case studies can be used at all stages of research, from exploratory to theory development (George and Bennett, 2005) and theory testing, as discussed below (see Figure 12.2). Thus, they can be the basis of substantive research projects in their own right, as the case studies listed later in the chapter demonstrate.

Scale

Cases can consist of individuals, communities (villages, towns, cities), whole countries, organisations and companies, places and projects or events. These demographic and geographic dimensions are illustrated in Figure 12.1.

A case study of an individual or small group, such as a sport team, can involve a range of qualitative and quantitative methods. As we move up in scale, the range of possible methods increases, in terms of both primary and secondary sources, including, for example, the use of information on a site and its environment and history and the social and demographic characteristics of the population of a community or country. Thus the sheer variety of types of data and types of data analysis would offer a 'rich' description of the *case* – the site or the country and its people. Furthermore, a case study at one level (for example of a community or an organisation) could involve a variety of quantitative and qualitative methods and data sources involving components at lower levels (for example, questionnaire surveys of residents or employees, or financial and membership data).

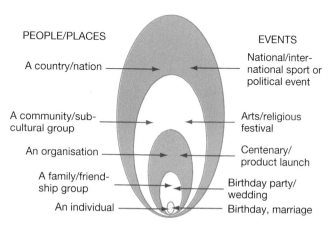

Figure 12.1 The case study method: demographic and geographic levels

Validity and reliability

Arguably, the multiple methodologies and data sources used by the typical case study method offer the possibility of achieving as high a level of internal validity as any single method discussed elsewhere in this book, since the limitations of one method or data source may be overcome by drawing on the qualities of another – a form of triangulation.

External validity – the extent to which findings apply beyond the specific case – may also be aided by the use of multiple data sources, such as the use of secondary data from the wider population for comparative purposes and to establish the extent to which the case study is typical or unique – drawing on cross-case research as suggested by John Gerring above. Because, in case study research, only one or a few cases are examined, the method does not typically seek to produce findings which are generally or universally representative. Thus a case study of an organisation does not include statements of the kind: 'this explains the behaviour of organisation X, therefore it will explain or predict the behaviour of the 50,000 similar organisations in similar situations or a significant proportion of them'. However, if research has *no* implications beyond the particular case at a particular time and place, there would be little point in conducting it. Referring again to Gerring:

> To conduct a case study implies that one has also conducted cross-case analysis, or at least thought about the broader set of cases. Otherwise, it is impossible for an author to answer the defining question of all case study research: what is this a case of? *(Gerring, 2007: 13)*

The relationship between case study research and the world beyond the case itself can be mediated by theory and policy issues, so conclusions might be in the form: 'this explains the behaviour of organisation X, which is inconsistent with theoretically based expectations, suggesting the possible need for some modification to the theory', or: 'this explains the behaviour of organisation X, suggesting that other types of organisation might be examined to see whether the explanation applies more widely'. Thus, while case study research may not result in generalisations about a population, it can have valid things to say in relation to theory in the case of explanatory research and in relation to policy in the case of evaluative research. Thus a number of scenarios can be envisaged in regard to theory and policy, as shown in Figure 12.2.

Using the typology discussed in the first chapter of this book: in the case of *explanatory* research a case study can be used to *test the applicability of an existing theory*. This might occur in situations where a theoretical proposition has never been tested empirically or where it has not been tested in a particular context. Thus, for example, a proposition about sport motivation may have been tested in regard to team sports but not individual sports. If the theory is found to be

Type of research	Research purpose	Case-study outcomes
Descriptive research	Identifying the characteristics of a particular phenomenon	Descriptions of and comparisons between phenomena, which may be used for education purposes or to inform corporate or public policy-making and decision-making or as input to other research.
Explanatory research	Testing a single existing theory	Case study *confirms* applicability of theory in at least one setting or, alternatively, *raises doubts* as to applicability of theory and suggests modification or alternatives.
	Testing alternative/competing theories	Case study demonstrates that one theory works better than the other in a particular situation, or that neither works.
	Develop theory where none exists	The case study can suggest *possible* theory and may also provide at least partial empirical testing.
Evaluative research	Testing effectiveness of a single policy	Case study *confirms* effectiveness of the policy in at least one setting or, alternatively, *raises doubts* as to effectiveness of the policy and possibly suggests modification or alternatives.
	Testing alternative/competing policies	Case study demonstrates that one policy is more effective than the other in a particular situation, or that neither works.
	Establish need for policy measures	The case study outlines the current policy problems and their likely causes and suggests the need for policy action.

Figure 12.2   **Case-study research: theory and policy**

non-applicable in a particular case study situation, this does not necessarily 'disprove' it, but can raise doubts as to its universality.

In the case of policy-related *evaluative* research the corresponding research task would be to test the effectiveness of a policy or type of management practice. For example, while the impact of promotional/advertising policy could be examined by use of aggregate national statistics on customer/participant numbers, it could also be examined by means of a case study of the experience in one or two communities or neighbourhoods, particularly if the results of the national statistical analysis were unclear or indicated an apparent lack of impact.

Reliability, in the sense of exact replication of research, is, of course, impossible in case study research, but the accumulation of evidence from a number of case studies may build a consensus around the findings of a programme of case study research and other evidence.

Merits of the case study approach

The particular merits of the case study method can be summarised as follows.

- The ability to place people, organisations, events and experiences in their social, cultural and historical context.
- Ability to treat the subject of study as a whole, rather than abstracting a limited set of pre-selected features.
- Multiple methods – triangulation – are implicit and seen as a strength.
- The single case, or limited number of cases, offers a manageable data collection task when resources are limited.
- Flexibility in data collection strategy allows researchers to adapt a research strategy as the research proceeds.
- There is no necessity to generalise to a defined wider population.

Design of case studies

While the case study method offers flexibility, it does not absolve the researcher from undertaking the usual initial preparatory steps – specifying research questions, reviewing the literature, establishing a theoretical/conceptual framework and determining data needs and sources **(see Chapter 3)**. As in any research, it is important to plan ahead to avoid the problem of having collected a lot of data and not knowing what to do with it. While flexibility is possible in some research environments, it is rarely unlimited – for example in some circumstances it may be possible to interview people, or ask them for data, a number of times as new issues emerge in the course of the research, but in other circumstances this may not be possible.

In addition to the general guidance on the planning of research projects set out in Chapter 3, three specific issues are discussed here: defining the unit of analysis; selection of cases and data gathering.

Defining the unit of analysis

While it might be a somewhat obvious point to make, it is necessary to be clear about the *unit of analysis* in case study research. For example, if the unit of analysis – the case – is a single sport facility owned by a large organisation, it is important to keep the analysis at the facility level. Thus, for example, the policies and practices of the parent organisation are inevitably relevant, but they are 'given' influences on the facility management; the research is not *about* the parent organisation. Conversely, data on individual staff of the facility will form part of the research, but only insofar as they contribute to an understanding of the operation of the facility as a unit.

Selecting the case(s)

Of key importance in the case study method is the selection of the case or cases. This is, of course, comparable to sampling in cross-case studies. Four types of case selection can be considered:

- *Purposive*: Where multiple cases are involved, the selection of cases is likely to be purposive – for example in selecting a range of organisations of similar or different sizes, in the same or different sectors, in comparable or contrasting geographical locations or of similar or contrasting levels of success or profitability.

- *Illustrative*: Often the case(s) will be deliberately chosen to increase the likelihood of illustrating a particular proposition – for example if the research is concerned with leadership success, *successful* organisations with high-profile leaders may be deliberately chosen.

- *Typical/atypical*: The case may be chosen because it is believed to be typical of the phenomenon being studied, or it may be deliberately chosen as an extreme or atypical case. Thus, a study examining the secrets of success in a particular sport might well select the *most* successful player, club or league for study.

- *Pragmatic/opportunistic*: In some cases the selection of cases may be pragmatic – for example when the researcher has ready access to an organisation, possibly because she or he is a member or employee of it.

Whatever the rationale for the selection of a case or cases, it should be clearly articulated in the research report, and the implications of the selection discussed.

Data gathering

A case study project generally uses a number of data sources and data-gathering techniques, including:

- documents;
- secondary data analysis;
- in-depth interviews;
- questionnaire surveys;
- observation;

- participant observation; and

- experimental methods.

The process of selecting data sources and collection techniques is the same as in any other research process **(see Chapter 3)**. In that chapter, the idea that different data sources might be used in the same project to address different research questions or aspects of research questions is discussed. It is noted that all data collection should be linked to the research questions – even in cases where the research questions are being modified as the research progresses.

When a number of disparate data types and sources are involved, two other issues should be borne in mind:

- *consistency of the unit of analysis* – if, for example, participation data are involved, it is important that the data relate to the same geographical unit;

- *temporal consistency* – ideally, except when the focus of the research is on change over time, all data should relate to the same time-period – this is related to the issue of the unit of analysis, since reorganisation – of, for example, a corporate body, administrative boundaries or the composition of a sports league – can result in changes in the size, composition and functions of organisations over time.

Analysis

To the extent that the design of the case study, or parts of it, resembles that of more formalised research projects, with fixed research questions and corresponding data collection and analysis procedures, the analysis process will tend to be deductive in nature; the data analysis will be designed to address the questions posed in advance. But a case study can involve qualitative methods with a recursive, more inductive format **(see Figure 9.1)**. Indeed, the flexibility of the whole case study approach suggests a more inductive approach. Thus the discovery, in the course of the research, of a previously unknown source of information might lead the researcher to ask the question: Can these data add something to the research? While the new data source might help in addressing the existing research questions in unanticipated ways, it could also suggest whole new research questions.

Five main methods of analysis are outlined by both Burns (1994: 324–5) and Yin (2014: 142–67):

- *pattern matching* – relating the features of the case to what might be expected from some existing theory;

- *explanation building* – often an iterative process whereby a logical/causal explanation of what is discovered (events, behaviour, etc.) is developed by to-and-fro referencing between theory/explanation and data;

- *time series analysis* – explanations are developed on the basis of observing patterns of change over time.

  George and Bennett (2005: 181–232) use the terms:

  - *logic models* – management/evaluation models based on the sequence: initial conditions, needs, problems, resources; action; outcomes; impacts – see Figure 1.5;
  - *cross-case synthesis* – where multiple cases are involved, cross-case comparison may be involved, sometimes using quantitative methods.
  - *congruence method* – the equivalent of correlation in quantitative research: events or characteristics A and B occur together, in the same or different case studies, suggesting some sort of relationship; and
  - *process tracing* – seeking one or more possible causal explanations from within the case study material, for the observed concurrence of A and B (similar to 'explanation building').

In fact, since all forms of data may arise in a case study, all forms of analysis are possible. It is the pulling together of the results of analyses of different sorts to form coherent conclusions which presents the challenge.

Case studies in practice

The rest of the chapter consists of summaries of five case studies. The examples provide brief details on each study, but further details can be followed up in the references provided. Additional examples are indicated in the Resources section.

Case study 12.1   Activity profile: swimming

In an 'activity profile' the 'case' is the activity. This case study is an example of descriptive research which, as suggested in Figure 12.2, may be of use in education or corporate or public policy-making and decision-making and as input to other research. The example presented here is quite limited and draws on one survey source, the annual Australian Exercise, Recreation and Sport Survey (**see Chapter 7**).

Figure 12.3 shows trends in organised and non-organised participation in swimming by Australian adults between 2001 and 2010. In 2010 the participation rate was 13 per cent, meaning that 87 per cent did not participate – a

▶

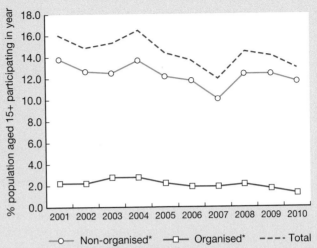

Figure 12.3   Trends in swimming participation, Australia, 2001–10

*Non-organised = persons who engage in only non-organised activity; organised includes some who engage in both organised and non-organised activity

Source: ERASS 2001–2010 (see Chapter 7 for details)

somewhat surprising figure given that the minimum criterion for inclusion is participation just once in the year prior to interview. With the exception of increases in 2004 and 2008 (the latter likely to be at least partly the result of a change in survey company), a steady decline is indicated. While the fall may not look dramatic, the reduction of 3 per cent in the overall participation rate is a fall of almost a fifth and in the case of organised participation, the fall is even more dramatic. The raw data upon which the diagram is based is shown in Table 12.1 (columns A–C), which also indicates (columns D–E) that the fall in *numbers of participants* **(see discussion of measurement in Chapter 7)** par-tially disguises the rate of reduction because of the underlying increase in the Australian population.

While the case study is descriptive only, it immediately gives rise to policy questions and research questions. Why do 87 per cent of Australian adults *not* swim even once in the course of a year, given that most Australians live near the coast in a pleasant climate? Why is there a decline in organised swimming activity? Is this due to a decline in demand and swimming club membership or a reduction in learn-to-swim programmes? Why has Australia's success in international swimming competitions not promoted more participation in swimming in the population as a whole? Are trends among children under 15 years old the same as for adults?

The case study could be extended with additional data from the ERASS and data from other surveys, the sport's governing body, Swimming Australia, and research literature.

Table 12.1 Trends in swimming participation, adults aged 15+, Australia, 2001–10

	Participation at least once in year prior to interview					
	A	B	C	D	E	F
	Non-organised*	Organised*	Total	Non-organised*	Organised*	Total
	%	%	%	'000s	'000s	'000s
2001	13.8	2.2	16.0	2083.0	332.5	2415.5
2002	12.7	2.2	14.9	1944.7	333.3	2278.0
2003	12.5	2.8	15.3	1948.7	434.4	2383.1
2004	13.7	2.8	16.5	2162.9	442.8	2605.7
2005	12.2	2.2	14.4	1965.4	345.8	2311.2
2006	11.8	1.9	13.7	1897.3	305.5	2202.8
2007	10.1	1.9	12.0	1661.1	305.1	1966.2
2008	12.4	2.1	14.5	2065.0	349.3	2414.3
2009	12.4	1.7	14.1	2126.8	292.3	2419.1
2010	11.7	1.3	13.0	2056.4	222.8	2279.2
% Change 2001–10	−15.2	−40.9	−18.8	−1.3	−33.0	−5.6

*Non-organised = persons who engage in only non-organised activity; organised includes some who engage in both organised and non-organised activity

Source: ERASS 2001–2010 (see Chapter 7 for details)

Case study 12.2   Nike, advertising and women

Victoria Carty's (1997) case study of the Nike sportswear company draws on a number of information sources and theoretical perspectives to explore and critique the *modus operandi* of the sports shoe and clothing company, particularly in regard to its treatment of women. The main information sources are existing accounts of the development of Nike from the academic and popular literature and examples of Nike advertising on television and in print. Theoretical perspectives include theories of globalization and postmodernism and the concept of 'global commodity chains', which geographically trace manufactured products from the point of consumption to the point of manufacture.

The thesis of the study is that Nike's advertising aimed at Western women consumers projects an image of the independent woman, while its manufacturing practices exploit Third World women who make up the majority of its manufacturing labour force employed at low wages and working in poor conditions in its own factories and those of its subcontractors. The research seeks to demonstrate the validity of well-established theoretical frameworks which are critical of the role of multinational global corporations, particularly in the production of fashion products where the costs of manufacturing are heavily outweighed by the costs of marketing and the retail mark-up. Thus, using a case study of a single firm, the study seeks to 'illustrate the interdependencies between production and consumption, or economics and culture, as organized in the global economy'. We have discussed, above, the proposition that, while conclusions from case studies can, strictly speaking, apply only to the 'case' involved in the study, they would be of limited use if they did not at least raise the possibility of wider implications. Here the implication is that Nike may not be unique among multinational companies in its exploitative approach to women.

| Case study 12.3 | Leisure, sport, lifestyle and the new middle class |

Derek Wynne's (1990, 1998) *Leisure, Lifestyle and the New Middle Class: A Case Study* demonstrates clearly the use of multiple methods in a case study. It is a study of the residents of 'The Heath', a new middle-class southern England development of some 250 dwellings with its own sport leisure centre and club. The author lived in the development for three years and based his research on: a questionnaire survey of all residents; in-depth interviews with selected residents; and participant observation/ethnography. He used the theoretical frameworks developed by Pierre Bourdieu in his book *Distinction* (1984) to explore the social class situation and lifestyles, including sporting activity, of the 500 or so adult residents of The Heath. While the current occupational and educationally shaped social class positions of the residents were similar, their origins (working-class or middle-class parents) differed and were reflected in differing leisure patterns and cultural states. And these differences were further reflected in the differences between two distinct user groups of the leisure centre/club, the 'drinkers' who mainly socialised in the club bar, and the 'sporters' who made use of the club's sporting facilities.

Case study 12.4 The Beckham brand

In their article, 'The multiple brand personalities of David Beckham', Vincent, Hill and Lee (2009) trace the sporting career of the English football/soccer star and his emergence, along with his pop-star wife, as a 'celebrity'. In particular, they note how he has appealed to various market segments, including: serious football fans because of his sporting skills; working-class groups because of his working-class background; the 'average' family because of his relatively conventional family life; the fashion world because of his sense of style; and the gay community because of his 'metrosexual' persona. This broad appeal is reflected in his market worth to football clubs as a player and to a wide range of companies as a sponsorship vehicle. The case study is presented in narrative style, drawing on media and biographical sources. Vincent *et al.* are not alone in focusing on Beckham, who has been the subject of a number of papers in academic sport journals (e.g. Cashmore and Parker, 2003; Gilmour and Rowe, 2010).

Case study 12.5 Sponsorship

A feature of sport sponsorship is that sponsoring organisations must typically expect to spend considerably more than their sponsoring fee to gain maximum marketing benefit from a sponsorship deal – referred to as 'activation' or 'leverage'. Such additional expenditure can be several times the sponsorship fee (the 'activation ratio') and can be on such things as hospitality, media advertising, special branded packaging and competition promotion and prizes. O'Reilly and Horning (2013) conducted a case study of the sport sponsorship activity of the Canadian arm of a large American company involved in dozens of sport sponsorship contracts and hundreds of activation programmes. The research covered a three-year period and involved examination of over 100 internal company documents on its sponsorship activity and interviews with 25 company employees from the vice-president down. The aim was to explore the motivation for sponsorship and activation programmes and the evaluation and decision-making processes involved. The case study involves a mix of quantitative and qualitative data collection and analysis and notes a relatively high activation ratio and above-trend increases in company sales revenue.

Summary

This chapter considers the case study method, which involves the study of a single case, or a small number of cases on the phenomenon of interest, which contrasts with other methods discussed in the book which generally involve *cross-case* methods. But cross-case research may be embedded in a case study – for example a study of a single community or club may involve a questionnaire-based survey of residents or members, respectively. These case studies often use multiple methods, including any or all of the other methods discussed in the book. The chapter examines tasks in the design and conduct of case studies, including definition of the unit of analysis and selection of cases. Five examples of contrasting sport case studies complete the chapter.

Test questions

1. Define case study research and cross-case research.

2. Discuss the external validity challenges involved in case study research.

3. What are the five approaches to selecting cases discussed in the chapter?

4. Three approaches to case study analysis have been suggested in the literature: name and describe these approaches.

Exercises

1. Consider a sport facility/attraction known to you and outline the elements which might be involved in setting up a case study to explore the reasons for its success.

2. Compile an activity profile, similar to that in Case study 12.1, using data on another activity and/or another country.

3. Read two of the example case studies listed in the Resources section below and identify the range of data sources used, methods of analysis and how the various types of information are drawn together to draw conclusions.

4. Select a national, state/provincial or local government organisation and, from information available on its website, compile a case study of its policies and actions devoted to promoting sport participation. The exercise could be extended to a comparison between two organisations.

Resources

Websites

- Australian Exercise Recreation and Sport Survey (ERASS): www.ausport .gov.au/information/casro

- Harvard Business School cases: http://hbsp.harvard.edu, search 'sport'.

- UK Active People Survey: www.sportengland.org/research/active_people _survey.aspx

Publications

- General: Bromley (1986), Burns (1994: 312–31), Byrne and Ragin (2009), Flyvbjerg (2006), George and Bennett (2005), Gerring (2007), Stake (1994, 1995), Thomas (2012), Yin (2014).

- In sport: Armour and Griffiths (2012).

- Business cases: Chadwick and Arthur (2012).

- Examples of case studies:

  - city sport policies: Leeds, UK: Bramham (2001); Antwerp, Belgium: Theeboom and de Knop (2001).

  - comparative case studies: women sport coaches: Shaw and Allen (2009); program fidelity: Pascual *et al.* (2011).

  - community sport: organisational capacity: Misener and Doherty (2009); sport policy: Phillpots *et al.* (2011).

  - history of an institution (UK Sports Institute): Theodoraki (2001).

  - lifestyle sports: Wheaton (2004) contains case studies of: skateboarding, mountain climbing, surfing, rock climbing, windsurfing, adventure racing, and frisbee.

  - organisations and companies: Reebok: Yu (2008); Nike: Carty (1997) (see Case study 12.2).

  - research ethics: Mellick and Fleming (2010).

  - single sport profile: Australian Bureau of Statistics (2011).

  - sponsorship: O'Reilly and Horning (2013) (see Case study 12.5).

  - sporting celebrities: David Beckham: Cashmore and Parker (2003), Gilmour and Rowe (2010) *et al.* (2009) (see Case study 12.4).

  - sport and city governance: Henry and Paramio Salcines (1998).

- o sport events: media coverage: Green *et al.* (2003), Gruneau (1989), Sanderson and Hambrick (2012); impact: Gratton *et al.* (2000), Henderson *et al.* (2010).

- o sporting/social club/community: Wynne (1986, 1998) (see Case study 12.3).

- o sport and social exclusion: four case studies: Collins (2003).

- o sport participation, national patterns: Nicholson *et al.* (2010).

- o urban revival through investment in sport: Trendafilova *et al.* (2012).

References

Armour, K. and Griffiths, M. (2012) Case study research. In K. Armour and D. Macdonald (eds) *Research Methods in Physical Education and Youth Sport.* London: Routledge, 204–16.

Australian Bureau of Statistics (2011) A serve of all things tennis. *Perspectives on Sport, June 2011* (Cat. No. 4156.0.55.001), available at www.abs.gov.au (Accessed May 2013) (search for 4156.0. 55.001).

Bourdieu, P. (1984) *Distinction: A Social Critique of the Judgement of Taste.* London: Routledge.

Bramham, P. (2001) Sports policy in the city: a case study of Leeds. In C. Gratton and I. P. Henry (eds) *Sport in the City: the Role of Sport in Urban Regeneration.* London: Routledge, 286–306.

Bromley, D. B. (1986) *The Case-Study Method in Psychology and Related Disciplines.* New York: John Wiley & Sons.

Burns, R. B. (1994) *Introduction to Research Methods, Second edn.* Melbourne: Longman Cheshire.

Byrne, D. and Ragin, C. C. (Eds) (2009) *The Sage Handbook of Case-Based Methods.* London: Sage.

Carty, V. (1997) Ideologies and forms of domination in the organization of the global production and consumption of goods in the emerging postmodern era: a case study of Nike Corporation and the implications for gender. *Gender, Work and Organization,* 4(4), 189–201.

Cashmore, E. and Parker, A. (2003) One David Beckham? Celebrity, masculinity and the soccerati. *Sociology of Sport Journal,* 20(3), 214–31.

Chadwick, S. and Arthur, D. (2012) *International Cases in the Business of Sport.* London: Routledge.

Collins, M. F. (2003) *Sport and Social Exclusion.* London: Routledge.

Fenn, C., Bridgwood, A., Dust, K., Hutton, L., Jobson, M. and Skinner, M. (2004) *Arts in England 2003: Attendance, Participation and Attitudes: Findings of a Study Carried out by the Social Survey Division of the Office for National Statistics.* London: Arts Council England.

Flyvbjerg, B. (2006) Five misunderstandings about case-study research. *Qualitative Inquiry*, 12(2), 219–45.

George, A. L. and Bennett, A. (2005) *Case Studies and Theory Development in the Social Sciences.* Cambridge, MA: MIT Press.

Gerring, J. (2007) *Case Study Research: Principles and Practices.* New York: Cambridge University Press.

Gilmour, C. and Rowe, D. (2010). When Becks came to Sydney: multiple readings of a sport celebrity. *Soccer and Society*, 11(3), 229–41.

Gratton, C., Dobson, N. and Shibli, S. (2000) The economic importance of major sports events: a case-study of six events. *Managing Leisure*, 5(1), 17–28.

Green, B. C., Costa, C. and Fitzgerald, M. (2003) Marketing the host city: analysing exposure generated by a sport event. *International Journal of Sports Marketing and Sponsorship*, 4(4), 335–53, reprinted in M. Weed (ed.) (2008) *Sport and Tourism: A Reader.* London: Routledge, 346–61.

Gruneau, R. (1989) Making spectacle: a case study in television sports production. In L. A. Wenner (ed.) *Media, Sports and Society.* Newbury Park, CA: Sage, 134–54.

Harvard Business School (nd) *Harvard Business School Case Studies.* Cambridge, MA: Harvard University, available at: http://hbsp.harvard.edu (Accessed May 2013).

Henderson, J. C., Foo, K., Lim, H. and Yip, S. (2010) Sports events and tourism: the Singapore Formula One Grand Prix. *International Journal of Event and Festival Management*, 1(1), 60–73.

Henry, I. and Paramio Salcines, J. L. (1998) Sport, culture and urban regimes: the case of Bilbao. In M. F. Collins and I. S. Cooper (eds) *Leisure Management: Issues and Applications.* Wallingford, UK: CAB International, 97–112.

MacPhail, A., Gorely, T. and Kirk, D. (2003) Young people's socialisation into sport: a case study of an athletics club. *Sport, Education and Society*, 8(2), 251–67.

Mellick, M. and Fleming, S. (2010) Personal narrative and the ethics of disclosure: a case study from elite sport. *Qualitative Research*, 10(3), 299–314.

Misener, K. and Doherty, A. (2009) A case study of organizational capacity in nonprofit community sport. *Journal of Sport Management*, 23(4), 457–82.

Nicholson, M., Hoye, R. and Houlihan, B. (2010) *Participation in Sport: International Policy Perspectives.* London: Routledge.

O'Reilly, N. and Horning, D. L. (2013) Leveraging sponsorship: the activation ratio. *Sport Management Review*, published online.

Pascual, C., Escarti, A., Llopis, R. and Gutierrez, M. (2011) Implementation fidelity of a program designed to promote personal and social responsibility through physical education: a comparative case study. *Research Quarterly for Exercise and Sport*, 82(3), 499–511.

Phillpots, L., Grix, J. and Quarmby, T. (2011) Centralized grassroots sport policy and 'new governance': a case study of county sports partnerships in the

UK: unpacking the paradox. *International Review for the Sociology of Sport*, 46(3), 265–81.

Sanderson, J. and Hambrick, M. (2012) Covering the scandal in 140 characters: a case study of Twitter's role in coverage of the Penn State saga. *International Journal of Sport Communication*, 5(3), 384–402.

Shaw, S. and Allen, J. B. (2009) The experiences of high performance women coaches: a case study of two regional sport organisations. *Sport Management Review*, 12(4), 217–28.

Stake, R. E. (1994) Case studies. In N. K. Denzin and Y. S. Lincoln (eds) *Handbook of Qualitative Research*. Thousand Oaks, CA: Sage, 236–47.

Stake, R. E. (1995) *The Art of Case Study Research*. Thousand Oaks, CA: Sage.

Suckling, S., Ryan, P. and Dent, M. (2009) Beliefs, barriers and control: a model for research into social exclusion. *International Journal of Public Sector Management*, 22(5), 423–31.

Theeboom, M. and de Knop, P. (2001) Sports policy research in the city of Antwerp. In C. Gratton and I. P. Henry (eds) *Sport in the City: The Role of Sport in Urban Regeneration*. London: Routledge, 278–85.

Theodoraki, E. (2001) The making of the UK Sports Institute. In C. Gratton and I. P. Henry (eds) *Sport in the City: The Role of Sport in Urban Regeneration*. London: Routledge, 240–58.

Thomas, G. (2012) *How to do Your Case Study: A Guide for Students and Researchers*. London: Sage.

Trendafilova, S., Waller, S. N., Daniell, R. B. and McClendon, J. (2012). 'Motor City' rebound? Sport as a catalyst to reviving downtown Detroit: a case study. *City, Culture and Society*, 3(3), 181–7.

Vincent, J., Hill, J. S. and Lee, J. W. (2009) The multiple brand personalities of David Beckham: a case study of the Beckham brand. *Sport Marketing Quarterly*, 18(3), 173–80.

Wheaton, B. (ed.) (2004) *Understanding Lifestyle Sports: Consumption, Identity and Difference*. London: Routledge.

Wynne, D. (1990) Leisure, lifestyle and the construction of social position. *Leisure Studies*, 9(1), 21–34.

Wynne, D. (1998) *Leisure, Lifestyle and the New Middle Class: A Case Study*. London: Routledge.

Yin, R. K. (2014) *Case Study Research: Design and Methods, Fifth edn*. Thousand Oaks, CA: Sage.

Yu, X. (2008) Impacts of corporate code of conduct on labor standards: a case study of Reebok's athletic footwear supplier factory in China. *Journal of Business Ethics*, 81(3), 513–29.

Zhang, L. and Zhao, S. X. (2009) City branding and the Olympic effect: a case study of Beijing. *Cities*, 26(5), 245–54.

Zikmund, W. G. (1997) *Business Research Methods, Fifth edn*. Orlando, FL: Dryden Press.

Sampling: quantitative and qualitative

Introduction

This chapter is an introduction to the principles of sampling and considers: the idea of sampling; samples and populations; representativeness and random sampling; sample sizes and their consequences in terms of 'confidence intervals'; weighting;.

The idea of sampling

In most research it is necessary to *sample*. Mainly because of costs, it is not usually possible to gather data from *all* the people, organisations or other entities which are the focus of the research. For example, if the aim of a research project is to study the sport participation behaviour of the adult population of a country, no one has the resources to conduct interviews with the millions of individuals who make up the adult population. The only time when the whole population of a country is interviewed is every 5 or 10 years, when the government statistical agency conducts the official Census of Population – and the cost of collecting and analysing the data can run into hundreds of millions of pounds or dollars.

At a more modest level, it would be virtually impossible to conduct face-to-face interviews with all the users of a large stadium, even in one event, since many thousands enter the site and leave in a short space of time. It might be possible to hand respondent-completion questionnaires to all visitors, but this approach has disadvantages in terms of quality and the level and representativeness of response **(see Chapter 10)**. The usual procedure is to interview a sample – a proportion – of the users. In Chapter 8, on observational methods, the problems of continuous counting of numbers of users of sport sites were discussed and it was noted that often available resources demand that sample counts be undertaken – that is, the numbers entering the site or present at the site are counted on a sample of occasions.

Sampling has implications for the way data are collected, analysed and interpreted.

Samples and populations

One item of terminology should be clarified initially. The total category of subjects which is the focus of attention in a particular research project is known as the *population*. A *sample* is selected from the population. The use of the term population makes obvious sense when dealing with communities of people – for instance when referring to the population of Britain or the population of London. But in social research the term also applies in other instances: for example, the users of a sport facility over a period of time are the *population of users* and the players registered with a sports league are the *population of players*.

The term *population* can also be applied to non-human phenomena – for example if a study of the physical characteristics of Australia's beaches found that there were 10,000 beaches in all, from which 100 were to be selected for study, then the 10,000 beaches can be referred to as the *population of beaches* and the 100 selected for study would be the sample. In some texts the word *universe* is used instead of population.

· If a sample is to be selected for study then two questions arise:

1. What procedures must be followed to ensure that the sample is representative of the population?

2. How large should the sample be?

These two questions are discussed in turn below, but they are related, since, other things being equal, the larger the sample, the more chance it has of being representative.

Representativeness

Random sampling

A sample which is not representative of the population is described as *biased*. The whole process of sample selection must be aimed at *minimising* bias in the sample. The researcher seeks to achieve representativeness and to minimise bias by adopting the principles of *random sampling*. This is not the most helpful term since it implies that the process is not methodical. This is far from the case – random does not mean haphazard! The meaning of random sampling is as follows:

> In random sampling all members of the population have an equal chance of inclusion in the sample.

For example, if a sample of 1000 people is to be selected from a population of 10,000, every member of the population must have a 1 in 10 chance of being selected. In practice, most sampling methods involving human beings can only approximate this rule. The problems of achieving random sampling vary with the type of survey and are discussed below in relation to: household surveys; site/user/visitor surveys; telephone surveys; street surveys; quota sampling; mail surveys; and sampling and random assignment selection in experimental research.

Sampling for household surveys

The problem of achieving randomness can be examined in the case of a household survey of the adult residents of a country. If the adult population of the country is, say, 40 million and we wish to interview a sample of 1000, every member of the adult population should have a 1 in 40,000 chance of being included in the sample. How would this be achieved? Ideally, there should be a complete list of all 40 million of the country's adults; their names or an identifying number should be written on slips of paper and placed in a revolving drum, physically or electronically, as in a Lottery draw, and 1000 names should be drawn out. Each time a choice is made, everyone has a one in 40 million chance of selection – since this happens 1000 times, each person has a total of 1000 in 40 million or one in 40,000 chance of selection.

This would be a very laborious process. Surely a close approximation would be to forget the slips of paper and the drum and choose every 40,000th name on the list. But where should the starting point be? It should be some random point between 1 and 40,000. There are published 'tables of random numbers' and random numbers can be produced from computers, as discussed under 'sampling for experiments' below. Strictly speaking, the whole sample should be chosen using random numbers, since this would approximate most closely to the 'names in a drum' procedure.

In practice, however, such a list of the population being studied rarely exists. The nearest thing to it would be the electoral registers of all the constituencies in the country. Electoral registers are fairly comprehensive because adults are required by law to register, but they are not perfect. Highly mobile/homeless people are often not included; many who live in multi-occupied premises are omitted. The physical task of selecting the names from such a list would be immense, but there is another disadvantage with this approach. If every 40,000th voter on the registers were selected, the sample would be scattered throughout the country. The cost of visiting every one of those selected for a face-to-face interview would be very high.

In practice, therefore, organisations conducting national surveys compromise by employing 'multi-stage' sampling and 'clustered' sampling. Multi-stage means that sampling is not done directly but by stages. For example, if the country had, say, four provinces or regions, the proposed sample of 1000 would be subdivided in the same proportions as the populations of the regions. Within each region, local government areas could then be divided into rural and urban and, for example, four urban and two rural areas would be selected at random – with the intention of selecting appropriate sub-samples, of perhaps 25, 40 or 50 from each area. These sub-samples could be selected from electoral registers, or streets could be selected and individuals contacted by calling on, say, every fifth house in the street. In any one street, interviewers may be instructed to interview, say, 10 or 15 people. By interviewing 'clusters' of people in this way, costs are minimised. But care must be taken not to reduce the number of clusters too much, since then the full range of population and area types might not be included. Once a house has been selected for interview, if just one person is to be interviewed, a procedure must be devised for selecting a respondent from the household members; this is discussed in relation to telephone surveys below.

Sampling for telephone surveys

The traditional process for sampling for telephone surveys from the public residential telephone directories and the move to computer-assisted telephone interviewing (CATI) methods is described in Chapter 9. Some of the emerging difficulties with this method, given the rise of mobile-only households **(see Chapter 10)**, threaten the representativeness of samples. Insofar as the resultant bias is age-related, this can be corrected by weighting, but if it reflects lifestyle differences, not much can be done about it. The printed or electronic directory is close to the list of people on the electoral register, as discussed above, except that, since there is typically only one land-line telephone per house, the list effectively refers to households rather than individuals.

As with household surveys, it is therefore necessary to use some procedure for selecting a respondent from among household members.

If, in face-to-face household surveys or telephone surveys, the interviewer were to interview the person who happened to answer the door or the telephone, this could result in bias, depending on local custom as to who in the household is more likely to answer the door or the phone. There is, of course, invariably a lower age limit for the survey, so persons under the prescribed age will not be selected. A typical procedure to 'randomise' the process of choosing among eligible household members is to ask to interview the person in the household whose birthday is nearest to the interview date.

Sampling for site/user/visitor surveys

Conditions at sport sites or facilities vary enormously, depending on the type and size of facility, the season, day of the week, the time of day or the weather. This discussion can only therefore be in general terms. To ensure randomness, and therefore representativeness, it is necessary for interviewers to adhere to strict rules. Site interviewers operate in two ways:

1. ISUM: the interviewer is stationary and the users mobile – for instance when the interviewer is located near the entrance/exit and visitors are interviewed as they enter or leave;

2. USIM: the user is stationary and the interviewer mobile – for instance when interviewing seated spectators at a sporting event.

In the ISUM case, the instructions they should follow should be something like:

> When one interview is complete, check through the questionnaire for completeness and legibility. When you are ready with a new questionnaire, stop the next person to enter the gate. Stick strictly to this rule and do not select interviewees on any other basis.

The important thing is that interviewers should not avoid certain types of user by picking and choosing whom to interview. Ideally, there should be some rule such as interviewing every fifth person to come through the door/gate, but, since users will enter at a varying rate and interviews vary in length, this is rarely possible.

In the USIM case, the interviewer should be given a certain route to follow on the site and be instructed to interview, say, every fifth group they pass. In seated venues, in some situations, a system of selecting bays/rows can be established and people sitting at the ends of rows can be interviewed; in other situations, interviewing may only be possible during breaks, and will typically take place in the circulation areas.

Where interviewers are employed, the success of the process will depend on the training given to the interviewers and this could involve observation of them at work to ensure that they are following the rules.

Sampling in site/visitor surveys, when users arrive throughout the day, leads inevitably to variation in the proportion of users interviewed at different times of the day **(see Chapter 10)**. Where users tend to stay for long periods – as in the case of beaches – this may not matter, but where people stay for shorter periods and where the type of user may vary during the course of the day or week, the sample will probably be unrepresentative – that is, biased. This should be corrected by weighting, as indicated at the end of the chapter.

When surveys involve the handing out of questionnaires for respondent-completion – as is sometimes done at active or spectator sport venues – field staff should be available to encourage their completion and return, otherwise respondents will be self-selected. Busy sport-venue receptionists can rarely be relied upon to do a thorough job in handing out and collecting in questionnaires, unless the survey is a priority of the management and therefore closely supervised. Normally, a significant proportion of the population will fail to return the questionnaire – but it is unlikely that this self-selection process will be random. For example, people with difficulties in reading or writing, or people who are in a hurry, may fail to return their questionnaires. Those with 'something to say', whether positive or negative, are more likely to return their questionnaires than people who are apathetic or just content with the service, thus giving a misleading impression of the proportion of users who have strong opinions. Thus it can be seen that this type of 'uncontrolled' sampling situation is at risk of introducing serious bias into the sample and should therefore be avoided if at all possible.

Sampling for street surveys and quota sampling

Although the technique of quota sampling can be used in other situations, it is most common in street surveys. The street survey is usually seen as a means of contacting a representative sample of the community but in fact it can also be seen as a sort of 'site survey', the site being the shopping area. As such, a street survey which involved a random sample of the users of the street would be representative of the users of the shopping area rather than of the community as a whole – in a suburban shopping centre it would, for instance, have a high proportion of retired people or full-time home/child carers.

If the aim is to obtain a representative sample of the whole community, then to achieve this interviewers are typically given 'quotas' of people of different types to contact, the quotas being based on demographic information about the community which is available from the census. For example, if the census indicates that 12 per cent of the population is retired, interviewers would be required to include 12 retired people in every 100 interviewed. Once interviewers have filled their quota in certain age/gender groups, they are required to become more selective in whom they approach in order to fill the gaps in their quotas.

The quota-sampling method can only be used when background information on the target population is known – as with community surveys. In most user surveys this information is not known, so the strict following of random sampling procedures must be relied upon.

Sampling for mail surveys

The initial list of people to whom the questionnaire is sent in a mail survey may be the whole study population or a sample. If a sample is selected it can usually be done completely randomly because the mailing list for the whole population is usually available.

The respondents to a mail survey form a sample, but it is not randomly selected but self-selected. This introduces sources of bias similar to those in the uncontrolled self-completion site surveys discussed above. There is little that can be done about this except to make every effort to achieve a high response rate. In some cases information may be available on the population which can be used to weight the sample to correct for certain sources of bias – for example in the case of a national survey the sample could be weighted to correct for any geographical bias in response because the geographical distribution of the population would be known. If, for example, the survey is of an occupational association and the proportion of members in various grades is known from records, then this can be used for weighting purposes. But ultimately, mail surveys suffer from an unknown and uncorrectable element of bias caused by non-response. All surveys experience non-response, of course, but the problem is greater with mail surveys because the level of non-response is usually greater. A number of measures are available to minimise the problem **(see Chapter 10 and Case Study 11.8a)**.

Sampling for complex events

Events with multiple ticketed and non-ticketed sites – for example a multisport festival – present particular challenges for the researcher, not least in the task of sampling. Typically, research is required to provide information on a number of matters, including: the number of visitors to the destination/host community; number of visitors and locals attending individual sites and individual events; and socio-demographic profile, expenditure patterns and satisfaction/evaluation of visitors and local participants. This information will be gathered by one or more of the methods discussed. The sampling task, then, involves considering the relevant protocols above. In addition, secondary data sources, such as ticket sales records, will be drawn upon. The unique challenge, therefore, is not the sampling and data collection per se but combining data from different sources to provide estimates for the whole event, particularly when an event involves large non-ticketed components and attracts significant numbers of tourists and day-trippers in addition to visitors.

Sampling and random assignment in experimental research

Often experimental subjects are, in effect, a 'convenience' sample, as used in qualitative research, discussed at the end of the chapter. The group of students or team/club members are selected on the basis of convenient accessibility. In this case, the sample can at best be seen as likely to be representative of people in a similar situation – for example, 18–19-year-old physical education students at a major urban university, mostly from middle-class backgrounds. But, of course, university environments vary, so the students may live different lifestyles from physical education students at other universities. The question of representativeness, or otherwise, is often established when experiments are replicated in other environments, and results are consolidated in systematic reviews of the research literature.

A sampling-related task in experimental research arises in relation to the random assignment of subjects to the experimental and control groups **(see Chapter 11)**. Typically, the overall sample is of manageable size, so a list of names is available. The truly random way of proceeding is to use random numbers. For example, if there are 234 individuals in the overall sample, and the aim is to allocate half to the experimental group and half to the control group, the subjects should be numbered from 1 to 234 and 117 random numbers should be used to select the experimental group. In the past, tables of random numbers, often published as an appendix in statistics textbooks, were used to do this, but now 'random number generators' are available online (e.g. <www.random.org>). In the example, the online generator would be requested to produce 117 random numbers between 1 and 234.

Sample size

There is a popular misconception that the size of a sample should be decided on the basis of its relationship to the size of the population – for example that a sample should be, say, 5 per cent or 10 per cent of the population. *This is not so.* What is important is the *absolute* size of the sample, regardless of the size of the population. For example, a sample size of 1000 is equally valid, provided proper sampling procedures have been followed, whether it is a sample of the British adult population (50 million), the residents of London (7 million), the residents of Brighton (100,000) or the students of a university (e.g. 15,000).

It is worth repeating: it is the *absolute size of the sample* which is important, not its size relative to the population. This rule applies in all cases, except when the population itself is small – this exception and its implications are discussed later in the chapter.

On what criteria, therefore, should a sample size be determined? The criteria are basically threefold: 1. the required level of *precision* in the results; 2. the level of *detail* in the proposed analysis; and 3. the available *budget.* These issues are discussed in turn below.

1. Level of precision – confidence intervals

The idea of the level of precision can be explained as follows. The question to be posed is: To what extent do the findings from a sample precisely reflect the population from which it is drawn? For example, if a survey was designed to investigate physical exercise participation and it was found that 50 per cent of a sample of 500 people had engaged in some form of physical exercise in the last two weeks, how sure can we be that this finding – this *statistic* – is true of the population as a whole? How sure can we be, having taken all appropriate measures to choose a representative sample that it is, indeed, representative, that the percentage of exercise participants in the population is not in fact, say, 70 per cent or 30 per cent?

This question is answered in terms of probabilities. If the true value is around 50 per cent, then, as long as random sampling procedures have been followed, the *probability* of drawing a sample which was so wrong that no one in the sample had exercised in the last two weeks would be very remote – almost impossible one might say. On the other hand, the *probability* of coming up with, say, 48 or 49 per cent or 51 or 52 per cent would, one would think, be fairly high. The probability of coming up with 70 or 30 per cent would be somewhere in between.

Statisticians have examined the likely pattern of distribution of all possible samples of various sizes drawn from populations of various sizes and established that, when a sample is randomly drawn, the sample value of a statistic has a certain probability of being within a certain range either side of the real value of the statistic. That range is plus or minus twice the 'standard error' of the statistic. The size of the standard error depends on the size of the sample and is unrelated to the size of the population. A properly drawn sample has a 95 per cent chance of producing a statistic with a value which is within two standard errors of the true population value, so, conversely, there is a 95 per cent chance that the true population value lies within two standard errors of the sample statistic. This means that, if a hundred samples of the same size were drawn, in 95 cases we would expect the value of the statistic to be within two standard errors of the population value; in five cases we would expect it to be outside the range. Since we do not generally actually know the population value, we have to rely on this theoretical statement of probability about the likely accuracy of our finding: we have a 95 per cent chance of being approximately right and a 5 per cent chance of being wrong.

This 'two standard errors' range is referred to as the '95 per cent confidence interval' of a statistic. The relationship between standard errors and level of probability is a property of the 'normal curve' – a bell-shaped curve with certain mathematical properties, which we are not able to pursue here. The idea of a normal curve and 95 per cent confidence intervals is illustrated in Figure 13.1. The idea of probabilities related to the properties of certain 'distributions' also arises in other types of statistical analysis **(see Chapter 17.)**

Tables have been drawn up by statisticians which give the confidence intervals for various statistics for various sample sizes, as shown in Table 13.1. Down the side of the table are various sample sizes, ranging from 50 to 10,000. Across the top of the table are statistics which one might find from a survey – for example 20 per cent play tennis. The table shows 20 per cent together with 80 per cent because if it is found that 20 per cent of the sample play tennis, then it has also been found that 80 per cent *do not* play tennis. Any conclusion about the accuracy of the statistic of 20 per cent also applies to the corresponding statistic of 80 per cent. In the body of the table are the *confidence intervals.*

An example of how the table is interpreted is as follows: suppose we have a sample size of 500 and we have a finding that 30 per cent of the sample have a certain characteristic – for example they have exercised in the last two weeks (so 70 per cent have *not* exercised). Reading off the table, for a sample size of 500, we find that a finding of 30 per cent (and 70 per cent) is subject to a confidence interval of plus or minus 4.0. So we can be fairly certain that the population value lies in the range 26.0 to 34.0 per cent.

An important point should be noted about these confidence intervals: to halve the confidence interval it is necessary to quadruple the sample size. In the example above, a sample of 2000 people (four times the original sample) would give a confidence interval of plus or minus 2.0 per cent (half the original confidence interval). The cost of increasing the precision of surveys by increasing the sample is therefore very high.

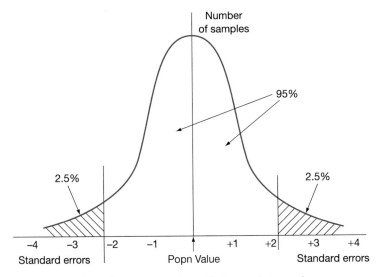

Figure 13.1   The normal curve and confidence intervals

Table 13.1 Confidence intervals related to sample size

Sample size	Percentages found from sample ('results')							
	50%	40 or 60%	30 or 70%	20 or 80%	10 or 90%	5 or 95%	2 or 98%	1 or 99%
	Confidence intervals (±%)							
50	±13.9	±13.6	±12.7	±11.1	±8.3	*	*	*
80	±11.0	±10.7	±10.0	±8.8	±6.6	*	*	*
100	±9.8	±9.6	±9.0	±7.8	±5.9	±4.3	*	*
150	±8.0	±7.8	±7.3	±6.4	±4.8	±3.5	*	*
200	±6.9	±6.8	±6.3	±5.5	±4.2	±3.0	±1.9	*
250	±6.2	±6.1	±5.7	±5.0	±3.7	±2.7	±1.7	*
300	±5.7	±5.5	±5.2	±4.5	±3.4	±2.5	±1.6	*
400	±4.9	±4.8	±4.5	±3.9	±2.9	±2.1	±1.4	±1.0
500	±4.4	±4.3	±4.0	±3.5	±2.6	±1.9	±1.2	±0.9
750	±3.6	±3.5	±3.3	±2.9	±2.1	±1.6	±1.0	±0.7
1000	±3.1	±3.0	±2.8	±2.5	±1.9	±1.3	±0.9	±0.6
2000	±2.2	±2.1	±2.0	±1.7	±1.3	±1.0	±0.6	±0.4
4000	±1.5	±1.5	±1.4	±1.2	±0.9	±0.7	±0.4	±0.3
10,000	±1.0	±1.0	±0.9	±0.8	±0.6	±0.4	±0.3	±0.2

*confidence interval greater than the percentage

Interpretation of table: for example, for a sample size of 400 a finding of 30% is subject to a confidence interval of ±4.5 (that is to say, we can be 95% certain that the population value lies in the range 25.5% to 34.5%). For formula to calculate confidence intervals see Appendix 17.2.

Note that for smaller samples the confidence intervals become very large – for instance for a sample of 50 the interval is plus or minus 13.9 per cent, meaning that a finding of 50 per cent can only be estimated to be within the range 36.1 to 63.9 per cent. For some statistics, for the smaller sample sizes, the confidence intervals are not calculable because the total margin of error is larger than the original statistic.

It should be noted that these confidence intervals apply only for samples which have been drawn using random sampling methods; other methods, such as multi-stage sampling, tend to produce larger confidence intervals, but the difference is generally small, so the matter is not pursued here.

The implications of the precision criterion for deciding sample size now become clear. A sample size of, say, 1000 would give a confidence interval for a finding of 50 per cent of plus or minus 3.1 per cent. If that margin of error was not considered acceptable then a larger sample size would be necessary. Whether or not it is considered acceptable depends on the uses to which the data will be put and is related to the type of analysis to be done, as discussed below.

An alternative way of considering these relationships between sample size and confidence interval is presented in Table 13.2. This presents, in the body of the table, the necessary sample size to achieve a given confidence interval.

Table 13.2 Necessary sample sizes to achieve given confidence intervals

Conf. Interval	Percentages found from sample ('results')						
	50%	40 or 60%	30 or 70%	20 or 80%	10 or 90%	5 or 95%	1 or 99%
	Minimum necessary sample size						
±1%	9600	9216	8064	6144	3456	1824	380
±2%	2400	2304	2016	1536	864	456	*
±3%	1067	1024	896	683	384	203	*
±4%	600	576	504	384	216	114	*
±5%	384	369	323	246	138	73	*
±6%	267	256	224	171	96	*	*
±7%	196	188	165	125	71	*	*
±8%	150	144	126	96	54	*	*
±9%	119	114	100	76	43	*	*
±10%	96	92	81	61	35	*	*

2. Level of detail of proposed analysis

The confidence intervals in Table 13.1 illustrate further the second criterion concerning the choice of sample size – the type of analysis to be undertaken. If many detailed comparisons are to be made, especially concerning small proportions of the population, then certain sample sizes may preclude very meaningful analysis. For instance, suppose a survey is conducted with a sample of 200 and it is found that 20 per cent of respondents went bowling and 30 per cent played tennis. The 20 per cent is subject to a margin of error of plus or minus 5.5 per cent and the 30 per cent is subject to a margin of plus or minus 6.3 per cent. Thus it is estimated that the proportions playing the two activities are as follows:

Bowling: between 14.5 and 25.5%   Tennis: between 23.7 and 36.3%

The confidence intervals overlap, so we cannot conclude that there is any 'significant' difference in the popularity of the two activities, despite a 10 per cent difference given by the survey. This is likely to be very limiting in any analysis. If the sample were 500 the confidence intervals would be 3.5 per cent and 4.0 per cent, respectively, giving estimates as follows:

Bowling: between 16.5 and 23.5%   Tennis: between 26.0 and 34.0%

In this case the confidence intervals do *not* overlap and we can be fairly certain that tennis *is* more popular than bowling.

The detail of the analysis, the extent of subdivision of the sample into sub-samples, and the acceptable level of precision will therefore determine the necessary size of the sample. By and large, this has nothing to do with the overall size of the original population, although there is a likelihood that the larger the population the greater its diversity and therefore the greater the need for subdivision into sub-samples.

Budget

A further point to be noted is that it could be positively wasteful to expend resources on a large sample when it can be shown to be unnecessary. For example, a sample of 10,000 gives estimates of statistics with a maximum confidence interval of ±1 per cent. Such a survey could cost, say, £200,000 to conduct. To halve that confidence interval to ±0.5 per cent would mean quadrupling the sample size to 40,000 at a cost of £800,000. There can be very few situations where such expenditure would be justified for such a small return.

Ultimately then, the limiting factor in determining sample size will be this third criterion, the resources available. Even if the budget available limits the sample size severely, it may be decided to go ahead and risk the possibility of an unrepresentative sample. If the sample is small, however, the detail of the analysis will need to be limited. If resources are so limited that the validity of quantitative research is questionable, it may be sensible to consider qualitative research which may be more feasible. Alternatively, the proposed research can be seen as a 'pilot' exercise, with the emphasis on methodology, preparatory to a more adequately resourced full-scale study in future.

Reporting sample size issues

How should the issue of sample size and confidence intervals be referred to in the report on the research? In some scientific research, complex statistical tests are considered necessary in reporting statistical results from surveys **(see Chapter 17)**. In much social science research, and sport research in particular, requirements are less rigorous. This is true to some extent in academic research, but is markedly so in the reporting of applied research. While it is necessary to be aware of the limitations imposed by the sample size and not to make comparisons which the data cannot support, explicit reference to such matters in the text of a consultancy/policy report is rare. A great deal of statistical jargon is not generally required: the lay reader expects the researcher to do a good job and expert readers should be given enough information to check the analysis in the report for themselves. It is recommended that an appendix be included in such reports indicating the size of the sampling errors. Appendix 13.1 gives a possible format.

In academic journals the rules are somewhat different and there is an expectation that statistical tests be 'up front'.

Confidence intervals applied to population estimates

The above comments are focused on confidence intervals applied to percentages of samples. Caution should be used when discussing population estimates based on sample surveys. But in many cases the sample statistics are applied to the population as a whole to obtain estimates of, for example, total visits to a facility, when even more care should be taken. A hypothetical worked example is outlined in Table 13.3. It might be thought that because the survey finding (12%) is subject to a confidence interval of ±2.0%, this also applies to the estimated number of persons visiting and to the number of visits. But this is not so, both the number of persons and the number of visits are subject to a confidence interval of ±16.7%. To obtain a confidence interval of ±2.0% of the number of persons/visits, that is to reduce it to an eighth of its current size, would require a sample size of at least 64,000.

Sample size and small populations

The above discussion of sample size assumes that the population is large – in fact the statistical formulae used to calculate the confidence intervals are based on the assumption that the population is, in effect, infinite. The relationship between the size of confidence intervals and the size of the population becomes noticeable when the population size falls below about 50,000, as shown in Table 13.4. The table presents sample sizes necessary to produce 95 per cent confidence intervals of ±5 per cent and ±1 per cent for a sample finding of 50 per cent for different population sizes. Only the sample sizes for a 50 per cent finding are presented since the 50 per cent finding is the most demanding in terms of sample size: for a given sample size, the confidence intervals for other findings – for example **30/70%** – is always smaller. The table first indicates the

Table 13.3 Confidence intervals applied to visit numbers

Item	Source	Number
Population	Census	500,000
Sample	Survey	1000
% visiting facility in a year	Survey	12%
Percentage confidence interval	Table 13.1	±2.0%
Estimated number of persons	12% of 500,000	60,000
Conf. interval in terms of persons	+2% of 500,000	±10,000
Confidence interval as % of no. of persons	(10,000/60,000) × 100	±16.7%
Frequency of visit, times per year	Survey	2.5
Estimated total visits	Calc.: (12% of 500,000) × 2.5	150,000
Confidence interval in terms of visits	Calc.: (2% of 500,000) × 2.5	+25,000
Confidence interval as % of visits	Calc.: (25,000/150,000) × 100	±16.7%

Table 13.4   Sample size and population size: small populations

Population size	Minimum sample sizes for confidence interval of ±5% and ±1% on a sample finding of 50%	
	±5%	±1%
Infinite*	384	9602
10,000,000	384	9593
5,000,000	384	9584
1,000,000	384	9511
500,000	384	9422
100,000	383	8761
50,000	381	8056
25,000	378	6938
20,000	377	6488
10,000	370	4899
5000	357	3288
2000	322	1655
1000	278	906
500	217	475
200	132	196
100	80	99
50	44	50

*as in Tables 13.1 and 13.2 and formula in Appendix 17.2

sample size for an infinite population and it can be seen that the sample sizes are the same as indicated for a ±5 per cent or ±1 per cent confidence interval in the first column of Table 13.2. The details of the formula relating confidence intervals to population size can be found in Krejcie and Morgan (1970).

Weighting

Situations where weighting of survey or count data may be required have been referred to at various points in the book. Here we discuss the principles involved. Take the example of the data shown in Table 13.5. In the sample of 45 interviews the number of interviews is spread fairly equally through the day, whereas more than half the actual users visit around the middle of the day (this information probably having been obtained by observation/counts). This can be a source of bias in the sample, since the mid-day users may differ from the others in their characteristics or opinions and they will be under-represented in the sample. The aim of weighting is to produce a weighted sample with a distribution similar to that of the actual users.

One approach is to 'gross up' the sample numbers to reflect the actual numbers – for example, the 9–11 a.m. group is weighted by **25 ÷ 10 = 2.5,** the 11–1 p.m. group is weighted by **240 ÷ 12 = 20,** and so on, as shown in Table 13.6.

The weighting factors can be fed into the computer for the weighting to be done automatically **(see Chapter 16)**. The initial weighting factors are equal to the number of users divided by the sample number for that time-period. The weighted sample therefore is made to resemble the overall user numbers. It should be noted, however, that the sample size is still 45, not 435! If statistical tests are to be carried out, it would be advisable to divide the weighting factors by 435 to bring the weighted sample total back to 45.

In this example the basis of the weighting relates to the pattern of visits over the course of the day, which happened to be information which was available in relation to this particular type of survey. Any other data available on the population could be used – for example if age structure is available from the census, then age-groups rather than time-periods might be used.

Table 13.5 Interview/usage data from a site/visitor survey

	Interviews		Actual users (counts)	
Time	**#**	**%**	**#**	**%**
9–11 a.m.	10	22.2	25	5.7
11.01 a.m.–1 p.m.	12	26.7	240	55.2
1.01–3 p.m.	11	24.4	110	25.3
3.01–5 p.m.	12	26.7	60	2.7
Total	45	100.0	435	100.0

Table 13.6 Weighting

	A	**B**	**C**	**D**
Time	**No. of interviews**	**No. of users**	**Weighting factors**	**Weighted sample No.**
Source	**Survey**	**Counts**	**B/A**	**CxA**
9–11 a.m.	10	25	2.5	25
11.01 a.m.–1 p.m.	12	240	20.0	240
1.01–3 p.m.	11	110	10.0	110
3.01–5 p.m.	12	60	5.0	60
Total	45	435		435

Sampling for qualitative research

Qualitative research generally makes no claim to quantitative representativeness and, by definition, does not involve statistical calculation demanding prescribed levels of precision. Generally, therefore, the quantitative considerations outlined above are not relevant to qualitative research. This is not to say that representativeness is ignored entirely. As Karla Henderson (1991: 132) puts it: 'the researcher using the qualitative approach is not concerned about adequate numbers or random selection, but in trying to present a working picture of the broader social structure from which the observations are drawn'. Thus if the population being studied includes young and old people, then both young and old people will be included in the sample, unless an explicit decision has been made to concentrate on one age-group only. But the sample will not necessarily reflect the *proportions* of young and old in the study population. Miles and Huberman (1994: 28) list 16 'strategies' for qualitative sampling. Some of these are presented in Figure 13.2.

In the research report on a qualitative research project the sampling methods used should be adequately described. In all cases, just how individuals are selected and contacted should be described. For example, if the 'criterion' sampling method was used, what was the criterion used and how were the people who met the criterion contacted? If a 'snowball' method was used, how was it started? If 'convenience' sampling was used, what was the convenience factor – friendship, family, colleagues, students, neighbours?

Method	Characteristics
Convenience	Use of conveniently located persons or organisations – e.g. friends. colleagues, students, organisations in the neighbourhood, spectators visiting a local sport venue.
Criterion	Individuals selected on the basis of a key criterion – e.g. age-group, membership of a club, purchasers of memorabilia.
Homogeneous	Deliberately selecting a relatively homogeneous sub-set of the population – e.g. university-educated male cyclists aged 20–30.
Maximum variation	Deliberately studying contrasting cases. Opposite of 'homogeneous'.
Opportunistic	Similar to 'convenience' but involves taking advantages of opportunities as they arise - e.g. studying major sporting event taking place locally.
Purposeful	Similar to 'criterion' but may involve other considerations, such as 'maximum variation', typicality.
Snowball	Interviewees used as source of suggestions for additional contacts.
Stratified purposeful	Selection of a range of cases based on set criteria, e.g. representatives of a range of age-groups or nationalities.
Theory-based	Sampling strategy driven by development of theory as the research proceeds (e.g. see Holt *et al.*, 2012: 288).

Figure 13.2 Selected qualitative sampling methods

There are no generally hard and fast rules for determining the appropriate sample size in qualitative research. One criterion used in quantitative research also applies, namely the available budget and time. Some of the sampling methods listed in Figure 13.2 point towards a minimum sample size, for example the range of groups to be covered in the criterion and stratified-purposeful methods. In grounded theory research, the sample size may be determined by the process of 'saturation', that is, the point at which further subjects stop producing new themes or theoretical categories (Charmaz, 2006: 113).

Summary

This chapter covers the topic of sampling, which is the process of selecting a proportion of the 'population' of subjects for study. It also examines the implications of sampling for data analysis. Two key issues are considered: *representativeness* of samples, and sample *size*. The researcher seeks representativeness by following the principles of *random sampling*, which means that, as nearly as possible, every member of the population has an equal chance of being selected. Different types of survey involve different practical procedures for achieving random sampling. If a sample has been randomly selected, the question still arises as to the extent to which the statistical findings from the sample truly reflect the population. Statistical procedures have been developed to assess the level of probability that a sample finding lies within a certain margin of the true population value. This margin is known as a *confidence interval* and its size is related to the size of the sample, regardless of the size of the population – the larger the sample the smaller the confidence interval or margin of statistical error. The necessary sample size for a study therefore depends on the precision required in the results, the detail of the analysis to be undertaken and the available budget. Finally, the chapter considers the practice of *weighting* to correct a sample for known bias, and methods for qualitative sampling.

Test questions

1. Define random sampling.

2. What is the opposite of a random/representative sample?

3. What is multi-stage sampling and why is it used?

4. What is a confidence interval?

5. What determines the size of the sample to be used in a study?

6. What is weighting?

7. Name three possible approaches to sampling for qualitative research.

Exercises

1. Examine two published research reports or journal articles related to empirical studies and identify the procedures used to ensure a random sample and how the sample sizes used are justified.

2. Using the report in exercise 1, produce confidence intervals for a range of percentage statistics occurring in the report.

3. In the example comparing bowling and tennis on page 396 above, what would the confidence intervals be if the sample size was 4000?

4. Examine the results from a national sport participation survey and produce confidence intervals for a number of the key findings.

Resources

Websites

Random number generator: www.random.org.

Publications

• Sampling and the statistical implications of sampling are addressed in numerous statistics textbooks, for example: Kidder (1981: Chapter 4), Spatz and Johnston (1989: Chapter 6), Thomas *et al.* (2011).

• Sampling for qualitative methods: Miles and Huberman (1994).

• Sampling for telephone interviews: Lepkowski *et al.* (2008).

• Small populations: Krejcie and Morgan (1970).

References

Charmaz, K. (2006) *Constructing Grounded Theory.* London: Sage.

Henderson, K. A. (1991) *Dimensions of Choice: A Qualitative Approach to Recreation, Parks, and Leisure Research.* State College, PA: Venture.

Holt, N. L., Knight, C. J. and Tamminen, K. A. (2012) Grounded theory. In K. Armour and D. Macdonald (eds) *Research Methods in Physical Education and Youth Sport.* London: Routledge, 276–94.

Kidder, L. (1981) *Selltiz, Wrightsman and Cook's Research Methods in Social Relations*. New York: Holt, Rinehart and Winston.

Krejcie, R. V. and Morgan, D. W. (1970) Determining sample size for research activities. *Educational and Psychological Measurement*, 30(4), 607–10.

Lepkowski, J. M., Tucker, C., Brick, J. M., de Leeuw, E. and Japec, L. (eds) (2008) *Advances in Telephone Survey Methodology*. New York: John Wiley.

Miles, M. B. and Huberman, A. M. (1994). *Qualitative Data Analysis, Second edn*. Thousand Oaks, CA: Sage.

Spatz, C. and Johnston, J. O. (1989) *Basic Statistics: Tales of Distribution, Fourth edn*. Pacific Grove, CA: Brooks/Cole Publishing.

Thomas, J. R., Nelson, J. K. and Silverman, S. J. (2011) *Research Methods in Physical Activity*. Champaign, IL: Human Kinetics.

Appendix 13.1 Suggested appendix on sample size and confidence intervals

This is a suggested wording for an appendix or note to be included in research reports based on sample data. Suppose the survey has a sample size of 500.

Statistical note

All sample surveys are subject to a margin of statistical error. The margins of error, or 'confidence intervals' for this survey, with a sample of 500, are as follows:

Finding from the Survey	95% Confidence interval
50%	± 4.4%
40% or 60%	± 4.3%
30% or 70%	± 4.0%
20% or 80%	± 3.5%
10% or 90%	± 2.6%
5% or 95%	± 1.9%
1% or 99%	± 0.9%

This means, for example, that if 20 per cent of the sample are found to have a particular characteristic, there is an estimated 95 per cent chance that the true population percentage lies in the range 20 ± 3.5, i.e. between 16.5 and 23.5 per cent. These margins of error have been taken into account in the analyses in this report.

Data Analysis

This part of the book considers analysis of data in various forms and from various sources and so each of the four chapters has particular links with specific chapters in Part II. Some Part II chapters, namely observation **(Chapter 8)**, experimental methods **(Chapter 11)**, the case study method **(Chapter 12)** and sampling **(Chapter 13)**, are linked to all four of the Part III chapters in various ways:

- Chapter 14: Secondary data analysis provides examples of the use of some of the types of data source discussed in Chapter 7.

- Chapter 15, Qualitative data analysis, considers both manual and computer-aided analysis of the type of data discussed in Chapter 9.

- Chapter 16, Survey analysis, continues where Chapter 10 left off, examining the use of both spreadsheet programs and a statistical computer package for the analysis of questionnaire-based survey data.

- Chapter 17, Statistical analysis, relates particularly to the questionnaire-based data discussed in Chapters 10 and 16, but is also particularly related to Chapter 11, Experimental methods.

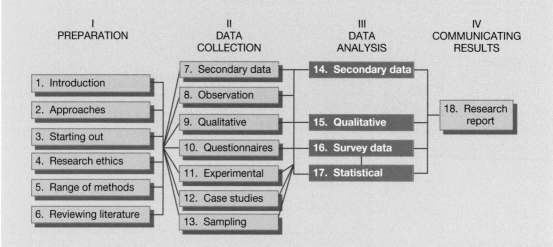

Analysing Secondary Data

Introduction

The secondary data phenomenon and its various forms and sources are described in Chapter 7. There are no specific analytical techniques or computer packages associated with such data, given its diversity. Most of the quantitative data is susceptible to relatively simple spreadsheet analysis. Where re-analysis of survey data is involved, the procedures outlined in Chapters 16 and 17 for the analysis stage of the primary project in which the data were gathered will apply. Similarly, for qualitative data, the procedures in Chapter 15 will apply. In this chapter, therefore, the aim is not to address the detail of analytical techniques, but to provide summaries of examples of practical and imaginative uses of secondary data for sport research purposes.

Examples of secondary data analysis

Case study 14.1   *The Spirit Level* and sport

In *The Spirit Level: Why More Equal Societies Almost Always do Better*, Richard Wilkinson and Kate Pickett (2009) use cross-national secondary data from the United Nations and other sources to make the case that the more equal the distribution of income in a country the more favourable are the outcomes on a range

▶

of indicators of human well-being, including life-expectancy, infant mortality, physical and mental health, educational performance and the level of crime.

The book concentrates mainly on the 21 countries with the highest per capita national incomes, with Portugal, Greece and Israel at the lower end (NI per capita ≤ $20K) and Norway and the United States at the upper end (NI per capita ≥$35K). For each country, inequality is measured by the ratio of the average share of income of the top 20 per cent of households to that of the bottom 20 per cent, income being net of income tax and benefits and adjusted for size of household. This measure identifies the United States, Portugal, the UK, New Zealand and Australia as the most unequal countries and Japan and the Scandinavian countries, Norway, Finland, Sweden and Denmark, as the most equal.

The Spirit Level does not include sport, but it is possible to remedy this deficiency with secondary data on sport participation, which is the purpose of this case study.

Country-specific secondary data on sport participation for European countries are obtainable from a Eurostat survey, as shown in Table 14.1. Using a presentation format similar to that used by Wilkinson and Pickett, their measure of income inequality for each country was plotted against sport participation rates in Figure 14.1. This was produced with the graphics facility of the Excel spreadsheet program and includes a plot of the data and a trend (regression) line and a measure of goodness of fit (R^2), **(see Chapter 17)**. It indicates quite strongly ($R^2 = 0.37$) that countries with more unequal incomes are less involved in active sport and physical recreation.

Table 14.1 Inequality and sport participation data, European countries, 2009

	Index of income inequality	Sport participation % of adults (15+) at least once/week
Austria	4.7	69
Belgium	4.5	57
Denmark	4.3	90
Finland	3.7	78
France	5.4	75
Germany	5.1	78
Greece	6.2	48
Ireland	6.0	74
Italy	6.6	37
Netherlands	5.2	84
Portugal	7.9	48
Spain	5.4	71
Sweden	3.9	84
Switzerland	5.6	80
UK	7.2	73

Sources: Income inequality, ratio of income of top 20% of households to that of bottom 20%: Wilkinson and Pickett (2009: Fig. 2.1, p. 17); sport participation: European Commission (2010)

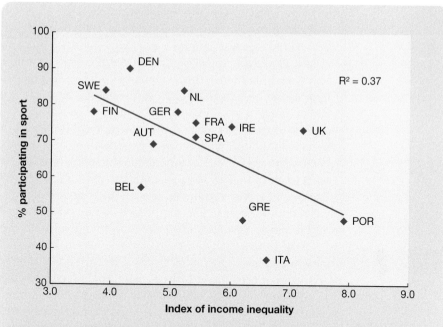

Figure 14.1 Income inequality and sport participation, European countries, 2009

Data sources: see Table 14.1

| Case study 14.2 | Estimating likely demand for a sport facility |

The problem

A developer or local council is considering whether to build a sport facility on a particular site in a suburban area, as part of a multi-purpose leisure/commercial complex. A feasibility study is to be undertaken examining various activities to determine the best combination of facilities to offer. Part of this process involves investigation of local demand and supply for different activities. This case study examines basketball to demonstrate a possible methodology to be used in this exercise. The town has a population of 100,000 and already has one public basketball complex with four courts. A range of possible approaches could be considered to investigate this question.

Possible approaches

The existing basketball facility could be examined to see whether it is overused or underused, that is, whether demand is already being adequately met by the existing facility. This, however, may not give the full answer, since it might be found that an underused facility is poorly managed, in poor condition or poorly located. It might also be difficult to obtain commercially sensitive data from potential competitors if the centre is privately run.

▶

An interview survey of local residents could be conducted to ask whether they would like to go to play basketball but do not do so at present because of lack of suitable facilities. Even if the time and money were available to conduct such a survey, the results could not be relied on as the main piece of information on which to base the decision because, while people's honesty and accuracy in recalling activities might be relied on to a certain extent in relation to their actual behaviour, asking them to predict their behaviour in hypothetical future situations is very risky.

Communities of similar population size and type could be examined to see what levels of basketball provision they have and how well it is used. Again, this may be a time-consuming process and somewhat 'hit-and-miss' because it is not always easy to find comparable communities and because some of the data required, being commercially 'sensitive', may not be readily available.

Using secondary data would involve drawing on an appropriate national survey and the Population Census, which could be used to provide an approximate estimate of likely demand for basketball in the area. The aim is to provide an estimate of the level of demand which a community of the size of that in the study area is likely to generate and compare that with the level of demand already likely to be catered for by the existing centre, to see whether or not there is a surplus of demand over current supply.

The approach

The general secondary data approach is represented diagrammatically in Figure 14.2. The steps A to H shown in the diagram are discussed in turn below.

A. Age-specific participation rates

One of the features of basketball participation is that it varies considerably by age: young people have much higher participation rates than older people. If, for example, the study town contains a higher than average proportion of young people, it would be expected that it would produce a higher than average demand for basketball, and vice versa. The national sport participation survey gives information on the percentage of people of different ages that play basketball, as shown in Table 14.2, column I.

B. Population by age-groups

Suppose the census gives the population of the town as 100,000, and the population aged 11 and over as 90,000. In Table 14.2, columns II and III, the age structure of the national population aged 10 and over is compared with that of the study town. Clearly the town has a much younger age profile than the national average. So it is clearly advisable to give consideration to the question of age structure in estimating demand for basketball.

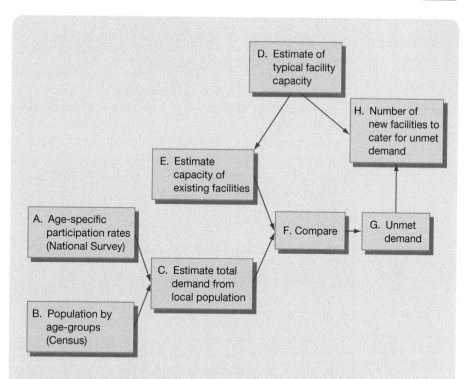

Figure 14.2   Estimating likely demand for a sport facility: approach

Table 14.2   Basketball participation by age

	I	II	III
Age-group	Proportions playing basketball in an average week	National population	Study town population
Source:	National survey	Census	Census
	%	%	%
10–14 years	7.5	10.7	13.8
15–19	14.9	11.2	16.8
20–24	5.5	10.6	16.4
25–29	4.6	9.5	12.2
30–39	0.5	17.9	18.2
40–49	0.2	12.7	7.8
50–59	0.0	10.5	6.6
60+	0.0	16.9	8.2
Total/average	3.5	100.0	100.0

Sources: Hypothetical data

C. Estimate total demand from local population

Table 14.3 indicates how demand for basketball would be estimated: attendances are estimated for each age-group and summed to give a total of 4600 attendances per week. As anticipated, the overall participation rate of 5.1 per cent is considerably higher than the national participation rate of 3.5 per cent. For this exercise, suppose that the national survey indicates that most basketball participants play once a week, and those who play more than once are cancelled out by those who miss a session for various reasons, so that the average visit rate is once a week, so 4600 participants generate a demand of 4600 visits per week.

D. Estimate of typical facility capacity

Assume that a typical basketball court accommodates 500 visits per week.

E. Estimate capacity of existing facilities

The town already has four courts, which should therefore accommodate 2000 visit per week.

F. Compare

The total estimated demand is 4600 visits per week, and the existing cinemas have a capacity of 2000 per week.

G. Unmet demand

Unmet demand can therefore be estimated as about 2600 visits per week.

H. Number of new facilities to cater for unmet demand

It would take five typical basketball courts to cater for the unmet demand.

Table 14.3 Estimating demand for basketball

	X % of age-group participating per week	Y Town population	Estimated demand (visits per week)
Data source:	National survey	Census	XY/100
10–14 years	7.5	12,414	931
15–19	14.9	15,129	2255
20–24	5.5	14,741	811
25–29	4.6	11,017	507
30–39	0.5	16,371	82
40–49	0.2	6983	14
50–59	0.0	5974	0
60+	0.0	7371	0
Total/average	3.5	90,000	4600 = 5.1%

Comment

The above approach does not predict demand precisely – it merely indicates a 'ball park' demand figure. A well-managed and programmed court complex might draw far more demand than is estimated. The national survey attendance rates relate to average attendances across the country, so clearly there are places where higher attendance rates occur as well as places where lower rates occur, affected by local supply conditions, demographics and traditions. What the exercise indicates is that, on the basis of data to hand, 4600 basketball attendances a week seem likely. This seems a very simple and crude calculation, but quite often investors – in the public and private sector – fail to carry out even this sort of simple calculation to check on 'ball park' demand figures; investments are made on the basis of personal hunch, and then surprise is expressed when demand fails to materialise. Sources for information on more detailed application of this sort of demand planning are indicated in the Resources section.

Forecasting note: to provide a simple forecast of future demand, for, say, the year 2020, it would be necessary merely to insert population forecasts for the year 2020 into column Y of Table 14.3 and rework the calculations.

Economic note: while the exercise here has been outlined in terms of 'number of participants or visits', use of household expenditure data (see Chapter 7), can convert the unit of analysis into expenditure.

Case study 14.3   Facility utilisation

Managers typically have information available on the use of facilities and this can be used as a source of data for management-related research. The level of utilisation of existing facilities is an important issue for managers and planners and this case study illustrates how existing data can be used to address this question.

Table 14.4 presents data which might be routinely collected on the level of

Table 14.4 Facility utilisation data

Usage	Area A		Area B		Area C	
	Number of users	% utilisation	Number of users	% utilisation	Number of users	% utilisation
Capacity:	300	100.0	120	100.0	500	100.0
Monday	120	40.0	60	50.0	310	62.0
Tuesday	150	50.0	40	33.3	210	42.0
Wednesday	180	60.0	30	25.0	180	36.0
Thursday	120	40.0	80	66.7	375	75.0
Friday	100	33.3	95	79.2	430	86.0
Saturday	210	70.0	110	91.7	420	84.0
Sunday	250	83.3	40	33.3	310	62.0
Week total	1130	53.8	455	54.2	2235	63.9

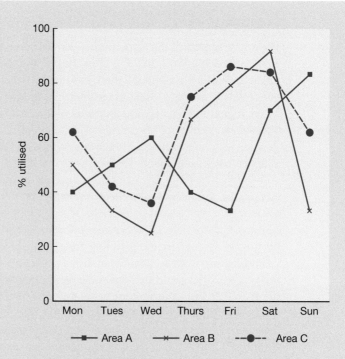

Figure 14.3   Facility utilisation

use of particular areas of a facility (e.g. various rooms or halls in an indoor sports centre). The daily usage levels might be averaged over a number of weeks. For each of the areas it is necessary to estimate the daily capacity: this is a reasonable assessment of the number of users which would equate to the facility being deemed 'fully used'. The numbers of users are related to the capacity in the form of percentages, and these are graphed in Figure 14.3.

The graph shows a different pattern of use for Area A, compared with the other two areas. Area A is underused on Monday, Thursday and Friday, while areas B and C are underused between Sunday and Wednesday. This suggests the need for different programming and marketing policies for the various areas.

Case study 14.4   Facility catchment area

Sport facilities often have available information on users' addresses which can be used to study the *catchment area* or *market area* – an important aspect of planning and management. Many sport facilities, for example, have member-ship or subscriber lists. Sport tourism businesses which provide residential facilities typically have details of home addresses of patrons.

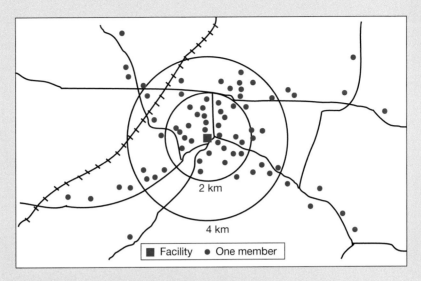

Figure 14.4   Catchment/market area

Sources: Membership/patron address records (hypothetical)

Figure 14.4 shows how such data can be plotted on a map to produce a visual representation of the catchment or market area of the facility. Such information can be used either to concentrate marketing to increase sales in the existing area, or to focus marketing outside the identified area in order to extend the catchment or market area.

When very large numbers are involved it may be necessary to sample membership or customer lists – for example selecting every fifth or tenth member or patron on the list.

While this case study is used to illustrate the use of secondary data, catchment areas can also be based on survey data, which will be necessary if existing information on client addresses is not available **(see Chapter 10, particularly discussion of user/site surveys)**.

Case study 14.5   Olympic medals

The Olympic Games and other major sporting contests offer data on participants and medals won, which provide an opportunity for secondary analysis to explore, among other issues, the criteria for judging the success of a team or country in the event. A number of published examples are indicated in the Resources section, but here we illustrate the idea by examining the 'medal table' for the London 2012 Olympic Games.

▶

The raw data are presented in Table 14.5, which includes the 28 countries which appear in the top ten in at least one of the various measures of performance used below.

Table 14.5 Medals, population and GDP, London 2012 Olympic Games, top ten* countries

	Medals			Popn, millions	GDP $bn	GDP, $'000 per head of population
	Gold	Silver	Bronze			
United States	46	29	29	305.0	14,988	48.1
China	38	27	23	1324.7	12,771	9.5
Great Britain	29	17	19	61.7	2397	38.2
Russia	24	26	32	140.7	2462	17.7
South Korea	13	8	7	48.4	1548	31.7
Germany	11	19	14	82.6	3212	39.3
France	11	11	12	64.1	2308	35.5
Italy	8	9	11	58.1	1938	31.7
Hungary	8	4	5	10.0	190	19.0
Australia	7	16	12	21.0	1026	47.1
Japan	7	14	17	127.3	4589	36.0
Ukraine	6	5	9	46.0	354	7.8
New Zealand	6	2	5	4.2	137	32.0
Cuba	5	3	6	11.2	64	5.7
Jamaica	4	4	4	2.8	28	9.9
North Korea	4	0	2	24.5	12	0.5
Ethiopia	3	1	3	88.0	77	0.8
Croatia	3	1	2	4.5	76	17.0
Kenya	2	4	5	37.9	61	1.4
Denmark	2	4	3	5.5	217	39.1
Georgia	1	3	3	4.6	28	6.0
Slovenia	1	1	2	2.0	58	29.2
Trinidad & Tob	1	0	3	1.2	39	31.9
Grenada	1	0	0	0.1	1	7.4
Mongolia	0	2	3	2.8	4	1.6
Armenia	0	1	2	3.0	9	3.0
Montenegro	0	1	0	0.6	4	6.5
Afghanistan	0	0	1	3.0	1	0.5

Sources: population/GDP: Conference Board (Groningen University, Sweden): www.conference-board.org/data/economydatabase/, medals: media sources.* Countries appearing in top ten in at least one measure of performance

The secondary data to be used here comprise, first of all, the 'medal tally', which was widely published in the media at the end of the Games and also in reference sources such as Wallechinsky and Louky (2012) (Note: medal tables are not available on the International Olympic Committee website since they are not seen as reflecting the true spirit of the Games.) Second, we use population and gross domestic product (GDP) data. These are available from numerous sources, but in this case from the University of Groningen Conference Board website (see Resources section). Data for all 85 countries (out of 200 competing) which won at least one medal are presented on the book's website.

The ranking in Table 14.5 is that used in the media listings during the Games, that is: in order of gold medals won. But there are at least nine measures which could be used, namely:

a. Gold medals won

b. Total medals, gold, silver and bronze, won

c. Points: for example: gold = 3 points, silver = 2 points, bronze = 1 point

d. Medals per million population

e. Points per million population

f. Medals per $billion GDP

g. Points per $billion GDP

h. Medals per $1000 GDP per head

i. Points per $1000 GDP per head.

These measures are presented in Table 14.6 and the rankings based on these scores are presented in Table 14.7. It can be seen that the rankings of the top ten countries, as conventionally assessed, decline dramatically when population and income are taken into account, while the rankings of lowly placed countries show an equally dramatic increase when we take into account low populations (Grenada, Trinidad and Tobago, New Zealand) or low income (North Korea, Ethiopia, Kenya).

▶

Table 14.6 Scores on nine measures of national performance, London 2012 Olympic Games

	Medals			Per million popn		Per $bn GDP		Per $'000 GDP/head	
	Gold	Total	Points	Medals	Points	Medals	Points	Medals	Points
	a	b	c	d	e	f	g	h	i
United States	46	104	225	0.3	0.7	0.007	4.7	2.16	4.7
China	38	88	191	0.1	0.1	0.007	20.1	9.26	20.1
Great Britain	29	65	140	1.1	2.3	0.027	3.7	1.70	3.7
Russia	24	82	156	0.6	1.1	0.033	8.8	4.62	8.8
South Korea	13	28	62	0.6	1.3	0.018	2.0	0.88	2.0
Germany	11	44	85	0.5	1.0	0.014	2.2	1.12	2.2
France	11	34	67	0.5	1.0	0.015	1.9	0.96	1.9
Italy	8	28	53	0.5	0.9	0.014	1.7	0.88	1.7
Hungary	8	17	37	1.7	3.7	0.090	1.9	0.89	1.9
Australia	7	35	65	1.7	3.1	0.034	1.4	0.74	1.4
Japan	7	38	66	0.3	0.5	0.008	1.8	1.06	1.8
Ukraine	6	20	37	0.4	0.8	0.057	4.7	2.55	4.7
New Zealand	6	13	27	3.1	6.5	0.095	0.8	0.41	0.8
Cuba	5	14	27	1.3	2.4	0.219	4.7	2.45	4.7
Jamaica	4	12	24	4.3	8.6	0.424	2.4	1.22	2.4
North Korea	4	6	14	0.2	0.6	0.486	27.8	11.90	27.8
Ethiopia	3	7	14	0.1	0.2	0.091	17.6	8.79	17.6
Croatia	3	6	13	1.3	2.9	0.079	0.8	0.35	0.8
Kenya	2	11	19	0.3	0.5	0.181	13.1	7.60	13.1
Denmark	2	9	17	1.6	3.1	0.042	0.4	0.23	0.4
Georgia	1	7	12	1.5	2.6	0.254	2.0	1.17	2.0
Slovenia	1	4	7	2.0	3.5	0.068	0.2	0.14	0.2
Trinidad & Tob	1	4	6	3.2	4.9	0.102	0.2	0.13	0.2
Grenada	1	1	3	9.6	28.8	1.294	0.4	0.13	0.4
Mongolia	0	5	7	1.8	2.5	1.098	4.3	3.08	4.3
Armenia	0	3	4	1.0	1.3	0.333	1.3	0.99	1.3
Montenegro	0	1	2	1.6	3.2	0.243	0.3	0.15	0.3
Afghanistan	0	1	1	0.3	0.3	0.670	2.0	2.00	2.0

Sources: see Table 14.5

Case study 14.6	The colour red and sporting success

Hill and Barton (2005a),† noting research that indicates that 'Red colouration is a sexually selected, testosterone-dependent signal of male quality in a variety of animals', and that anger in humans is associated with 'reddening of the skin due to increased blood flow', decided to explore the implications for sporting contests. To do this they used results data on combat sports (boxing, taekwondo, Greco-Roman and freestyle wrestling) from the 2004 Athens

Table 14.7 Rankings of nine measures of performance, London 2012 Olympic Games

	Medals			Per million popn		Per $bn GDP		Per $'000 GDP/head	
	Gold	Total	Points	Medals	Points	Medals	Points	Medals	Points
	a	b	c	d	e	f	g	h	i
United States	1	1	1	49	44	66	8	9	8
China	2	2	2	75	69	67	2	2	2
Great Britain	3	4	4	20	18	41	10	11	10
Russia	4	3	3	32	31	36	5	5	5
South Korea	5	9	9	33	30	47	20	26	20
Germany	6	5	5	37	34	54	15	17	15
France	7	8	6	38	33	50	22	23	22
Italy	8	10	10	41	37	53	26	25	T
Hungary	9	15	12	7	5	16	21	24	21
Australia	10	7	8	8	9	35	30	31	30
Japan	11	6	7	51	50	63	24	18	24
Ukraine	14	11	13	43	39	26	7	7	7
New Zealand	16	18	18	4	3	14	37	41	37
Cuba	15	17	17	16	15	9	6	8	6
Jamaica	18	21	22	2	2	5	12	15	12
North Korea	20	35	30	57	48	4	1	1	1
Ethiopia	24	33	29	71	67	15	3	3	3
Croatia	25	37	34	15	10	20	41	47	41
Kenya	27	23	24	52	51	10	4	4	4
Denmark	30	28	26	9	8	31	51	52	51
Georgia	39	32	35	12	12	7	19	16	19
Slovenia	44	45	46	5	6	21	62	60	62
Trinidad & Tob	45	43	47	3	4	13	68	66	68
Grenada	52	78	63	1	1	1	54	64	54
Mongolia	56	39	44	6	13	2	9	6	9
Armenia	58	54	53	22	27	6	31	21	31
Montenegro	81	74	75	10	7	8	56	57	56
Afghanistan	73	85	79	50	60	3	18	10	18

Sources: based on Table 14.6 scores

Olympic Games. In these sports contestants were randomly assigned red or blue outfits or body protectors. It was found that, across all four sports, contestants wearing red won consistently more fights. In a second study, Hill and Barton and other colleagues (Attrill, Gresty, Hill and Barton, 2008) used results data from the English soccer league going back to 1947 to explore the association between shirt colour and competition success. Again, it was found that red was significantly associated with success.

Rowe, Harris and Roberts (2005), however, challenge the findings of Hill and Barton, showing that in the same Olympic Games, in judo, where contestants are randomly allocated white and blue outfits, there is apparently a significant advantage to those wearing blue. They suggest that the factor at work may be visibility rather than the evolutionary and cultural significance of colour as argued by Hill and Barton. In their response, Hill and Barton (2005b) challenge the visibility argument, given the close proximity of the contestants and the typical bright lighting in the sports examined. Furthermore, they note that the significance of red relates particularly to males, with no apparent effect among women contestants. In a further note, Rowe *et al.* (2006) reported that it had been drawn to their attention that for some judo contests (25 out of 301 analysed) the blue outfit was not randomly assigned but was allocated to seeded players. They reported that re-analysis of the data excluding these cases confirmed their original findings.

The phenomenon of shirt colour and competitive success has also been explored using experimental methods, as indicated in Case study 11.6b.

† It should be noted that, on the website of the journal *Nature*, it is possible to download not only a copy of Hill and Barton's paper, but also a supplementary spreadsheet file of the raw data used and a file containing additional methodological information. This practice, of making raw data publicly available, is discussed in Chapter 4 in relation to research ethics, and is likely to become increasingly common in other journals.

Summary

The chapter presents six case studies demonstrating potential uses of secondary data in planning and management situations, including: cross-national examination of income inequality and sport participation; estimating demand for new sport facilities in a local community; assessment of levels of utilisation of parts of a sport facility; analysis of a sport facility catchment area; assessment of the medal success of competing countries in the London 2012 Olympic Games; and relationships between the colour red and success in sport.

Exercises

1. Select a sport activity of your choice and a community and, using data from a national leisure participation survey and from the Population Census (see Chapter 7), provide an estimate of the likely demand for the activity in the selected community, using the methodology outlined in Case study 14.2.

2. In relation to exercise 1, what would be the implications of a predicted increase of 15 per cent in the number of people aged 60 and over and a 15 per cent decrease in the number of people aged 25 and under, over the next five years?

3. Undertake an exercise similar to Case study 14.3 for a leisure facility for which you can obtain usage data.

4. Undertake an exercise similar to Case study 14.4 for a leisure facility for which you can obtain user/member address data.

5. Select an activity from a national leisure participation survey and provide a *profile* of the activity, indicating the overall level of participation and how participation is related to age, gender, occupation and education (this is similar to exercise 2 in Chapter 12, based on Case study 12.1, where it was viewed as an example of a case study).

Resources

Websites

- Demand/participation planning: www.leisuresource.net under 'U-Plan'.

- Data on national populations and GDP: Conference Board (Groningen University, Sweden): www.conference-board.org/data/economydatabase/

Publications

- See Chapter 7 Resources section for details of secondary data sources.

- Demand planning and other methods: Veal (2010).

- Olympic/Paralympic Games medal performance: Olympics: Balmer *et al.* (2003), Bernard and Busse (2004), Hogan and Norton (2000), Lyons (2012), Shibli and Bingham (2005, 2008), Shibli *et al.* (2012), Vagenas and Vlachokyriakou (2012), Veal (2012, search on [Medals]), Wallechinsky and Loucky (2012); Paralympics: Buts *et al.* (2013).

References

Attrill, M. J., Gresty, K. A., Hill, R. A. and Barton, R. A. (2008) Red shirt colour is associated with long-term team success in English football. *Journal of Sports Sciences*, 26(6), 577–82.

Balmer, N., Nevill, A. and Williams, A. (2003) Modelling home advantage in the Summer Olympic Games. *Journal of Sports Sciences*, 21(6), 469–78.

Bernard, A. B. and Busse, M. R. (2004) Who wins the Olympic Games? Economic resources and medal totals. *Review of Economics and Statistics*, 86(1), 413–17.

Buts, C., Du Bois, C., Heynels, B. and Jegers, M. (2013) Socioeconomic determinants of success at the Summer Paralympics. *Journal of Sports Economics*, 14(2), 133–47.

European Commission (2010) *Sport and Physical Activity, Special Eurobarometer 334.* Brussels: European Commission, available at: http://ec.europa.eu/public_opinion/archives/eb_special_en.htm (Accessed July 2012).

Hill, R. A. and Barton, R. A. (2005a) Red enhances human performance in contests. *Nature*, 435(19 May), 293.

Hill, R. A. and Barton, R. A. (2005b) Hill and Barton reply. *Nature*, 437(27 Oct), E10.

Hogan, K. and Norton, K. (2000) The 'price' of Olympic gold. *Journal of Science and Medicine in Sport*, 3(2), 203–18.

Lyons, K. (2012) Predicting gold medals at the Olympics. *The Conversation*, 23 July, Australian online publication, available at: http://theconversation.edu.au/pages/london-olympics (Accessed May 2013).

Rowe, C., Harris, J. M. and Roberts, S. C. (2005) Seeing red? Putting sportswear in context. *Nature*, 437(27 Oct), E10–E11.

Rowe, C., Harris, J. M. and Roberts, S. C. (2006) Corrigendum: Seeing red? Putting sportswear in context. *Nature*, 441(11 May), E3.

Shibli, S. and Bingham, J. (2005) Measuring the sporting success of nations. In I. Henry (ed.) *Transnational and Comparative Research in Sport.* London: Routledge, 59–81.

Shibli, S. and Bingham, J. (2008) A forecast of the performance of China in the Beijing Olympic Games 2008 and the underlying performance management issues. *Managing Leisure*, 13(3/4), 272–92.

Vagenas, G. and Vlachokyriakou, E. (2012) Olympic medals and demo-economic factors: novel predictors, the ex-host effect, the exact role of team size, and the 'population-GDP' model revisited. *Sport Management Review*, 15(3), 211–17.

Veal, A. J. (2010) *Leisure, Sport and Tourism: Politics, Policy and Planning.* Wallingford, UK: CABI.

Veal, A. J. (2012) *The Olympic Games: A Bibliography.* Business School, University of Technology, Sydney, On-line Bibliography 5, available at: www.olympic.uts.edu.au/downloads/olympic_bib_update2.pdf (Accessed May 2013).

Wallechinsky, D. and Loucky, J. (2012) *The Complete Book of the Olympics.* London: Aurum Press.

Wilkinson, R. and Pickett, K. (2009) *The Spirit Level: Why More Equal Societies Almost Always do Better.* London: Allen Lane.

Analysing qualitative data

Introduction

Data collection and analysis

This chapter addresses the task of analysing qualitative data. It is sometimes difficult to separate the collection and analysis processes for qualitative research, at least in a temporal sense; but there is nevertheless a clear difference between certain data collection activities, such as interviewing someone with a recorder, and certain analysis activities, such as poring over typed interview transcripts. While quantitative research can be inductive and qualitative research can be deductive **(see Chapter 2)**, the qualitative approach lends itself to a more inductive process, especially when conducted on a small scale. This difference is illustrated in Figure 15.1, which presents variations on the circular process of research depicted in Figure 2.3.

Traditionally qualitative data were analysed by manual means, and this continues, but in recent years computer software has become available to aid the process. Computers replicate and speed up some of the more mechanical aspects of the manual processes but, of course, the task of interpretation remains with the researcher. The chapter first discusses the question of data storage and confidentiality and then considers manual analysis methods and computer-based methods in turn. Since the most common form of qualitative data is interview or focus group transcripts or notes, the following discussions are based on this form of data. Most of the procedures nevertheless apply, in adapted form, to other forms of data, such as printed materials from organisational archives or the media.

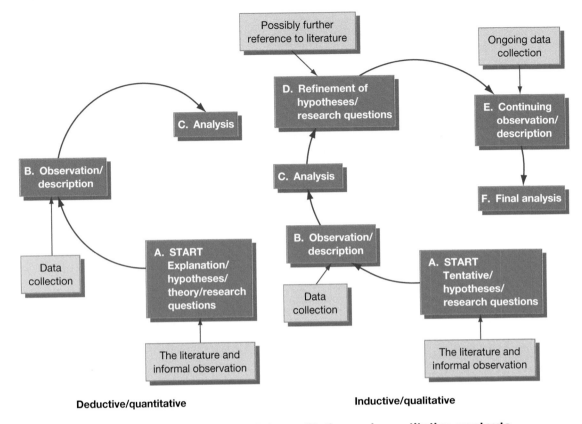

Figure 15.1   Circular model of research in qualitative and quantitative contexts

Data storage and confidentiality

Regardless of whether qualitative data are analysed manually or by computer, consideration should be given to the security and confidentiality of transcripts and recordings, particularly if sensitive material is involved. This raises ethical issues **(see Chapter 4)**.

As a precaution, research material should ideally not be labelled with real names of organisations or people. Fictitious names or codes should be created. If it is felt that it will be necessary to relate tapes and transcripts back to original respondents at some later date, for example for second interviews, the list relating fictitious identities to real identities should be kept in a separate, secure place. Of course, actual names mentioned by respondents on recordings cannot easily be erased, and it is a matter of judgement as to whether it is necessary to disguise such names in transcripts, although in most cases they should be disguised in any quotations of the material in the research report. In some cases, however, it is necessary to create transcripts which can be more anonymous than the original. For example, an interviewee might say: 'I find it difficult to get on with John' – the transcript might change 'John' to 'David', but may need to identify John/David's position – for example: 'I find it difficult to get on with David [Supervisor]'.

Digitised research material stored on computer hard drives and other storage media is subject to the security risks of any digitised information. Some software, including NVivo discussed in this chapter, offers password protection which may be a useful precaution.

Case study example

A case study of some in-depth interview data is used to illustrate qualitative data analysis – both manual and by computer, as shown in Case study 15.1.

Case study 15.1   Activity choice qualitative study

Figure 15.2 presents a very simple conceptual framework for studying leisure activity choice. It is based on a model presented by Brandenburg *et al.* (1982) and further developed in Veal (1995), and suggests that individuals' choice of leisure activity is influenced by background characteristics and experiences, present constraints and personal factors, but also by key events which trigger participation.

While this example is expressed in terms of leisure as a whole, the framework would be suitable for analysis of a sector of leisure, such as sport, or holiday-taking, or the arts. Thus the activity choices, X, Y, Z, could relate to the whole range of leisure activities or a restricted sector. The model could be explored quantitatively, for example, by means of a questionnaire, but that would be likely to require prior definition of the three sets of influences and a set of key events. Further, since any one of the three groups could involve a substantial list of items (e.g. background/experience, parental influence, school experience, higher education experience, geography/climate, activities experienced), the analysis task would be daunting. A qualitative approach

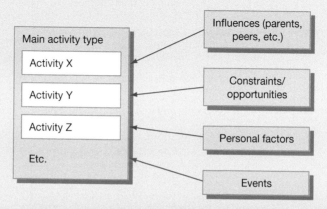

Figure 15.2 Outline conceptual framework for a qualitative study of activity choice

would enable the various factors and influences to be identified and analysed in a more exploratory manner. Interviews could be conducted using a checklist of the sort presented in Figure 9.4.

Figure 15.3 contains short extracts from three interviews with individuals about their leisure choices. The comments in the first column are explained below. These transcripts are used to illustrate manual and computer analysis of texts. The aim is to illustrate the mechanics of analysis in a way which could be readily replicated by the student. The length of the transcripts extracts and their number has therefore been limited. The substantive outcomes are therefore incidental and not particularly meaningful taken in isolation. In a complete research exercise, full transcripts, running to many pages, would be involved and, although we are dealing with qualitative research, the number of interviews/transcripts in a study of this type would normally be more than three.

Mark (Age 22, Male, Student, Income £8K)

Q. What would you say is your most time-consuming leisure activity outside of the home at present?

Act.: Sport –
football
Constraint:
Commitments,
Need to keep fit,
Time, Money

Well, I would say it's playing football, at least during the season. While the football's on, because of training twice a week and needing to be fairly serious about keeping fit I don't do much else: I probably only go to a pub once – or at most twice – a week. I don't have the time or the money to do much more.

Q. How were you introduced to football?

Influence:
Parent+
Teacher ++
Event:
Coaching clinic

Oh, I've always played … since I could run around I suppose. My dad says he spotted my talent – so-called – when I was a toddler, but it was one of the teachers at primary school that really encouraged me. He persuaded my mum to take me to a coaching clinic when I was about 8 or 9, then I got into the local under-11s.

Q. Why do you think you are attracted to football?

Personal:
Competitive,
Team
oriented, Active

Well, I'm pretty competitive – so I like sport generally. I like the team-spirit thing with football – I don't think I could do an individual sport where you didn't have a team around you. You make good friends. And it's fast and you're involved the whole time … I get bored playing cricket where you're standing around half the time.

Donna (Age 27, Female, FT Employed, Income £19K)

Q. What would you say is your most time-consuming leisure activity outside of the home at present?

Act.: Socialising
Sport: gym,
swimming –

Just socialising I would say … you know, going out for a meal or a drink with friends … I go to the gym once or twice a week … and I like to swim a bit in the summer, but they don't take up much time overall.

Figure 15.3 Interview transcript extracts

Q. When did you first start going out socially on a regular basis?

Event: Job/
earning money
Influence: Peers

I was about 16, I guess: the parents were a bit restrictive, but once I started earning a bit of money at weekends I managed to go out at least twice a week – to parties and to the cinema and stuff … my mum and dad didn't have any money to give me, so it wasn't until I started to work part-time that I could go out, sort of regularly. I've always had a fairly close-knit group of friends, girlfriends, about the same age as me, who've always gone out together … even with boyfriends – and one husband – arriving on the scene and disappearing from time to time!

Q. What limits the number of times you go out socialising in a week?

Constraint:
Time, Job/money

Time and money! But mostly it's time these days – cos we don't always spend a lot.

Q. What are the essential ingredients for a good night out?

Personal:
Social – informal
Constraint: Time

It's all about people … people you know and people you might meet! Things like good food – and drink – or good music are important, but the enjoyment comes from doing it with your friends and knowing they have the same sorts of tastes and the same sense of fun. I am serious enough at work, I couldn't imagine myself spending a lot of time with some team sport with serious training and all that: I just don't have the time – or the inclination!

Lee (Age 23, Male, FT Employed, Income £22K)

Q. What would you say is your most time-consuming leisure activity outside of the home at present?

Event: Girlfriend
Personal:
Anti-routine

It varies. I don't have any set pattern. Up until a couple of weeks ago I was going out with this girl and, apart from going round each other's house, we spent a lot of time going out, one way or another – to the pub, cinema, walking, shopping – it varied. Now that's stopped, it's still a bit of a mixture, but with various friends. I hate routine, so I don't get involved with anything regular.

Q. So what single thing – from among the mixture of things you do – would you say you spent most time doing in the last week?

Act.: Cinema

In the last week? Well, I haven't been out that much: it would have to be the movies: I went twice and one of them was one of those late-night double billers – about four hours.

Q. Are you a movie buff?

Event:
Good review

I wouldn't go that far, but I like movies. I read reviews and that. The movie I saw on Tuesday had a lot of hype and I saw two or three good reviews. For once, the hype was justified: it was really good. Really good: better than the reviews – and that doesn't happen often.

Figure 15.3 (*continued*)

Manual methods of analysis

Introduction

There are various ways of analysing interview transcripts or notes. The essence of any analysis procedure must be to return to the terms of reference, the conceptual framework and the research questions or hypotheses of the research **(see Chapter 3)**. The information gathered should be sorted through and evaluated in relation to the concepts identified in the conceptual framework, the research questions posed or the hypotheses put forward. In qualitative research, those original ideas may be tentative and fluid. Questions and/or hypotheses and the definition and operationalisation of concepts may be detailed or general; the more detailed and specific they are, the more likely it is that they will influence the initial stages of the analysis. Conversely, the more general and tentative they are the more likely it is that the data analysis process will influence their development and refinement. Data gathering, hypothesis formulation and the identification of concepts is a two-way, evolving process. Ideas are refined and revised in the light of the information gathered, as described in relation to the *recursive* approach and *grounded theory* approach discussed in Chapter 9 and summarised in Figure 9.1. In Chapter 3 it is noted that the development of a conceptual framework and of research questions or hypotheses is the most difficult and challenging part of a research project.

In addition to the problem of ordering and summarising the data conceptually, the researcher is faced with the very practical problem of just how to approach the pile of interview notes or transcripts.

Reading

The basic activity in qualitative analysis is *reading* of notes, transcripts, documents or *listening* to or *viewing* audio and video materials. In what follows, it is assumed that the material being analysed is text – while practical adaptations are necessary for audio and video material, the principles are the same. The reading is done initially in light of initial research questions and/or hypotheses and/or those which have evolved during the data collection process.

Emergent themes

A typical approach to qualitative analysis is to search for *emergent themes* – the equivalent of *variables* in quantitative research. Indeed, it has been argued, for example by Sherry Dupuis (1999), that the practice mimics too closely the positivistic approach to research which many proponents of qualitative methods disparage. There is certainly the temptation to begin adopting a quasi-quantitative approach to the process, identifying as themes only those which arise from the transcripts of a number of subjects. Clearly this would be inconsistent with the qualitative approach: a theme which emerges from just one subject is as valid as one which emerges from ten subjects. The criterion for identification should be the extent to which the theme appears to be salient to the interviewee.

The themes may arise from the conceptual framework and research questions, and therefore be consciously searched for in a deductive way, or they may emerge unprompted in a more inductive way. Typically, both processes will be at work.

Themes which emerge from the transcripts are 'flagged' in the left-hand margin of the transcripts in Figure 15.3. The researcher's judgement of the strength with which the views are expressed is indicated here with one or more plus or minus signs. It is clear that other themes might be identified and alternative terms might be used for the items which are identified, illustrating the personal and subjective nature of qualitative analysis.

The 'developed' conceptual framework presented in Figure 15.4 shows how some of the themes/concepts/factors and relationships emerging from the interviews might begin to be incorporated into the conceptual framework. On the basis of information from short abstracts from three interviews, the conceptual framework is *developed* but not *fully* developed; it represents work in progress. The 'levels' referred to relate to discussion of computer-aided analysis discussed later in the chapter.

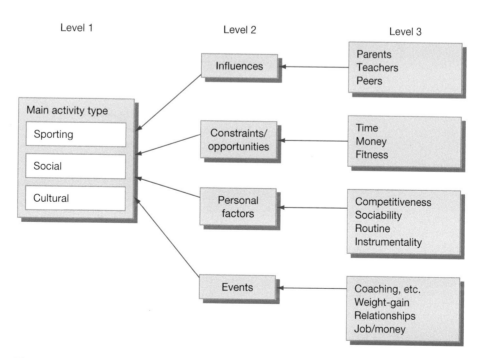

Figure 15.4 Developed conceptual framework for qualitative study of activity choice

Mechanics

The initial steps in qualitative analysis involve fairly methodical procedures to classify and organise the information collected.

Analysis can be done by hand on hard-copy transcripts, which should have a wide margin on one side to accommodate the 'flagging' of themes as discussed above. Colour coding can be used in the flagging process and 'Post-It' notes may also be used to mark key sections.

Standard word-processing packages can be of considerable assistance in the analysis process. The space for flagging can then be secured using the 'columns' or tables facility in the word-processor. Word-processing packages also have facilities for:

- adding 'Comments' (e.g. in the Tracking facility in Word);

- blocking text with colour, underlining or bold;

- 'searching' to locate key words and phrases;

- paragraph and/or line numbering;

- coding and cross-referencing using indexing or cross-referencing procedures.

It can be seen, therefore, that standard word-processing packages have a number of features to assist the analysis.

These can help to keep track of topics across a number of interviews, and of topics which are covered several times in the same interview. A particular focus of the analysis may be related not only to particular substantive topics raised by the interviewer, and therefore related to particular questions, but also to, for example, underlying attitudes expressed by interviewees, which might arise at any time in an interview.

The index becomes the basis for further analysis and writing up the results of the analysis: being able to locate points in the transcripts where themes are expressed enables the researcher to check the wording used by respondents and explore context and related sentiments and facilitates the location of suitable quotations to illustrate the write-up of the results.

Analysis

In qualitative data analysis it is possible to use techniques and presentation methods that are similar to those used in quantitative analysis. For example, in Figure 15.5 an analysis similar to a crosstabulation is shown, with twelve hypothetical interviewees 'plotted' on a two-dimensional space based on two variables derived from the interviews referred to above. The placing of the respondents depends on a qualitative assessment based on the interview transcripts. It can be seen that, in the example, the respondents fall into four groups. Given that this is a qualitative survey and the sample of interviewees

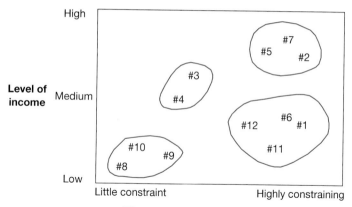

Figure 15.5 'Crosstabulation' of qualitative data

is unlikely to be statistically representative, the *numbers* in each group are not important, but simply the identification of the existence of three groups. Such a grouping would provide the basis for further analysis of the transcripts (see Huberman and Miles, 1994: 437).

Thus analysis of qualitative data has certain parallels with quantitative analysis, with themes corresponding to variables and relationships explored in ways which parallel crosstabulation and correlation. But they are parallels only, not equivalents. Whereas quantitative analysis generally seeks to establish whether certain observations and relationships are generally true in the wider population on the basis of statistical probability, qualitative analysis seeks to establish the existence of relationships on the basis of what individual people say and do. If only one person or organisation in the study is shown to behave in a certain way as a result of certain forces, this is a valid finding for qualitative research – the question of just how widespread such behaviour is in the wider society becomes a matter for other types of research.

Miles and Huberman (1994) offer a range of data sorting, presentation and analysis techniques, for individual subjects – 'within-case' – and for grouping or comparing a number of subjects – 'cross-case'. In a number of cases they emulate quantitative analysis, as in the example of 'crosstabulation' above. For example, subjects' various experiences or actions may be grouped into a typology and further grouped by the time-period in which they took place. This may be done diagrammatically or in tabular form and may be deductive, relating experience patterns of a theoretically derived conceptual framework, or inductive, with conceptual frameworks, models or networks being developed from the data.

Detailed analysis may be less important when the purpose of in-depth or informal interviews is to provide input into the design of a formal questionnaire. In that case the interviewer will generally make a series of notes arising from the interview which are likely to be of relevance to the questionnaire design process, and can also provide input to the design process from memory, as long as the questionnaire design work is undertaken fairly soon after the interviews.

Qualitative analysis using computer software – introduction

When the researcher is faced with a substantial number of lengthy documents to analyse, the decision may be made to ease the laborious process of coding and analysing by making use of one of the computer-aided qualitative data analysis software (CAQDAS) packages now available. As with statistical packages, it takes time to learn how to use qualitative analysis packages and to set up a system for an individual project, so a decision has to be made, on the basis of the size and complexity of the documentary material to be analysed, as to whether that investment of time will result in a net time saving, compared with manual analysis. Consideration should, however, be given to the fact that, once an analysis system has been set up, more analysis can be relatively quickly undertaken, possibly resulting in better quality of output than may have been possible using manual methods. Further, looking to the future, a computerised analysis system can more easily be returned to at future dates for additional interrogation. Finally, even if the amount of data in a given project does not justify setting up a computerised analysis system, a smaller project may be an easier vehicle for learning to use and gain experience with a package. Familiarity and experience with a computer package merits an entry on a *curriculum vitae*.

It has been noted above that standard word-processing packages such as Microsoft Word offer such facilities, which can aid in sorting and locating material in transcripts. The standard word-processing package is, however, limited in its capabilities for this purpose. A number of purpose-designed CAQDAS packages are now on the market. One of the most commonly used, and which is demonstrated here, is NVivo, part of a stable of packages from QSR (Qualitative Solutions and Research Pty Ltd), which includes N6, an updated version of the well-known NUD*IST, and XSight designed for market researchers. Details of these and other packages can be found on the QSR website, the address for which is given at the end of the chapter.

Interview transcripts

As with the manual analysis discussed above, the extracts of interview transcripts from the Activity Choice project as outlined in Case study 15.1 (Figure 15.3) are used to demonstrate operation of NVivo here. An ideal way for readers to engage with this section is to replicate the processes outlined on a computer. In what follows it is assumed that the reader has access to a computer with NVivo installed.

Readers who wish to replicate the procedures should first either type the text of the transcripts into three files or download them from the book's website. They should be in files named (a small font and wide margins are advised for ease of viewing on the NVivo screen): Mark.doc; Donna.doc; and Lee.doc. The suffix .doc (or .docx) indicates Word format, but NVivo will also accept text format (suffix .txt), rich text format (.rtf) or portable document format (.pdf). The files are introduced via the procedure 'Importing internal documents' below.

NVivo

Introduction

NVivo is the one of the most widely used CAQDAS packages. The software enables the researcher to index and coordinate the analysis of text stored as computer files. This includes primary material, such as interview transcripts and field notes, and other material such as newspaper clippings, company reports and video clips. In addition, it assists in shaping and understanding data and in developing and testing theoretical assumptions about the data.

It is not possible in a short summary such as this to present all the features of the package – this is done in the online tutorials and 'Help' built into the package and in other specialist texts, such as that by Patricia Bazeley (2007). Details of support materials are provided on the QSR website (see Resources section). Just a few NVivo procedures, considered to be sufficient to get started with the package, are outlined here, as shown in Figure 15.6.

Starting up

The NVivo opening window is divided into two section, 'Get started' and 'Community, the latter containing news, tips and videos. The Get started section includes a list of 'Recent Projects', where a demonstration environmental change project is already installed, and where your project(s) will in due course be listed. It also includes 'New Project', which is where we begin.

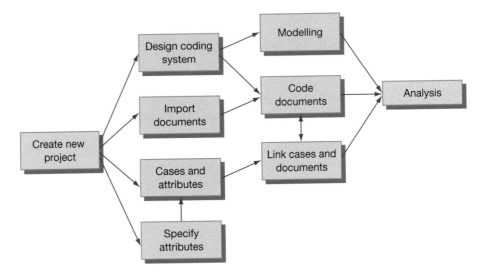

Figure 15.6 NVivo procedures covered

Creating a new project

To demonstrate the system, we start with **New Project.** This involves creating a named location for a research project, into which the documents to be analysed, such as interview transcripts, will be added. The NVivo procedures to create a project for the Activity Choice project are shown in Figure 15.7.

Saving

During an NVivo session, the program will periodically remind the user to save the current version of the project. Backup copies should also be created at the end of a session.

Attributes

Attributes of subjects/cases involved in a study can be recorded as for variables in a quantitative study. At the top of the transcripts we have four items of information for each respondent: age; gender; employment status; and income (see Figure 15.3) and these can be recorded as a set of attributes in the NVivo system, as shown in Figure 15.8.

Cases and their attributes

We can now introduce our three interviewees as *cases* and record their individual socio-demographic attributes. Procedures are shown in Figure 15.9.

1. Click on *New Project*
2. In the Title box enter: ActivityChoice
3. A file name *ActivityChoice.nvp* automatically appears in the *File Name* box – it will have a default 'My documents' location on your computer but this can be altered by clicking on *Browse* and specifying a location of choice.
4. Click on *OK*.
5. The screen appears, as shown below.
6. Along the top of the screen is a menu ribbon with a number of 'tabs'. All of the procedures that are noted in Figures 15.8 to 15.17 can be undertaken by clicking on the icons under these tabs.
7. The rest of the screen is divided into three areas:
   - Left-hand side: *Navigation View* – clicking on one of the items in the bottom half (main menu) brings up a menu in the top half
   - Right-hand-centre: *List View* – contents of folders
   - Right-hand-lower: *Detail View* – contents of files: not shown below, but see Figure 15.9.

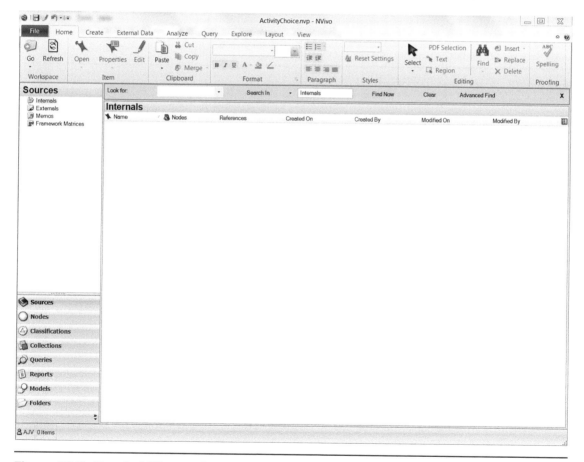

Figure 15.7   Create NVivo project – procedure

1. Click on *Classifications* on the main menu (bottom left of the screen): the *Source Qualifications* screen appears.
2. Under the *Create* tab click on *Node Classification*: a *New Classifications* dialogue box appears. Enter the name *Case*, then click on OK.
3. Right click on the new *Case* node classification that now appears in the List View and select *New Attribute*. (This can also be done from the menu ribbon: *Create > Attribute*.)
4. In the *New Attribute* dialogue box enter the name *Gender*.
5. Click on the *Values* tab:
   - 'Unassigned' and 'Not applicable' default values are already in place:
   - click on *Add* and type in the value *Male*
   - click on *Add* again and type in *Female*, then click on *OK*
   - the attribute *Gender* should now be seen listed under *Attributes.*
6. Repeat steps 3–5 for attribute *Empstat* (employment status), with values *FT Employed* and *Student.*
7. Repeat step 3 and 4 for attribute *Age* and *Income*, changing the *Type* from *Text* to *Integer.* Step 5 is not necessary because these are uncoded numerical variables.
8. The four attributes, *Age, Empstat, Gender, Income*, should now be seen listed under *Case.* The attributes can be sorted alphabetically by clicking the header: *Name.*

Figure 15.8   Attributes – procedure

1. Click on *Nodes* in the bottom left hand corner of the screen, then right click *Nodes* in the Navigation View and select *New Folder*. (*Create > New Folder*)
2. In the *New Folder* dialogue box enter *Cases*, then click on *OK.*
3. Click on *Cases* in the Navigation View. Right click in the *Cases* List View area of the screen and select *New Node*. (*Create > Node*)
4. In the New Node dialog box enter the name *Mark.*
5. Still in the New Node dialog box, click on the *Attribute Values* tab, then select *Case* classification. The four attributes are listed:
   a. for *Age* and *Income*: key in Mark's age in years (22) and income in £'000s (8)
   b. from the drop-down lists of values for *Gender* and *Empstat*, select *Male* and *Student* respectively. Then click on *OK.*
6. Repeat steps 3–5 for Donna and Lee.
7. Save the project to disk using *File > Save* on the menu ribbon.
8. Click *Explore > Node Classification Sheet*, then select *Case*: the three cases and their attributes appear in a spreadsheet-style table as below.
9. The Case/Attributes data can be presented in spreadsheet format, so if the information is already held in spreadsheet format, the spreadsheet can be imported into NVivo, replacing the above procedure. This is achieved via: *External Data > Classification Sheets > Browse* where the location of the spreadsheet file is stored.
10. Conversely, the Casebook can be exported to a spreadsheet file via the same *External Data* tab but selecting the furthest right *Classification Sheets* icon.

Figure 15.9   Cases and attributes – procedure

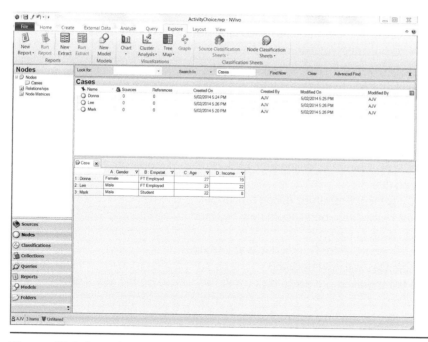

Figure 15.9 (*continued*)

Importing documents

Information on the interviewees and their attributes have been imported into the Activity Choice project system and the three transcript files must also be imported, as shown in Figure 15.10. It will be seen that other types of material can be incorporated, including sound and video material and external material such as links to websites. This demonstration is confined to dealing with text documents generated internally as part of the research project.

Linking cases and documents

The interview transcript files must now be linked with the three interviewees/cases, Mark, Donna and Lee, already identified in the system, as shown in Figure 15.11.

Setting up a coding system

As with questionnaires, documents such as interview transcripts must be *coded* in order to be analysed by computer. This involves setting up a *coding system.* A coding system can develop and evolve as the research progresses, but it has to start somewhere. In the section on manual coding above, the 'flagging' process is similar to the coding process involved here. On the basis of an initial

1. In the Navigation View area, click on *Sources.*
2. In the menu which now appears above, click on *Internals.*
3. On the menu ribbon click *Create > Folder.*
4. In the *New Folder* dialog box enter the Name *Interviews* and click *OK.*
5. *Interviews* now appears as a sub-folder to the *Internals* folder in the *Sources* menu to the left.
6. Click on *Interviews*, then on the menu ribbon click *External Data > Documents.*
7. In the *Import Internals* dialog box: click on *Browse* to locate Mark.doc and click on *OK.*
8. The *Document Properties* dialog box appears: click on *OK.*
9. The file name Mark.doc should now be listed in the *Internals* List View area, with its date of creation.
10. Repeat steps 6–9 for Donna.doc and Lee.doc.
11. All three files will now be listed.
12. Save the modified project to disk using *File > Save* on the menu ribbon.

Figure 15.10   Importing documents – procedure

1. In the Navigation View area, click on *Sources*, then *Internals> Interviews* on the menu, so that the three files appear in List View, under the heading *Internals.*
2. Click on the file icon on the left of the *Mark* file to highlight it.
3. On the menu ribbon, select *Analyze > Existing Nodes.*
4. The *Select Project Items* dialog box appears under *Nodes*: select *Cases* and the list of three files will appear.
5. Check *Mark* and click on *OK.*
6. Repeat steps 2–5 for Donna and Lee.
7. The three cases/interviewees, with their attributes, are now linked with their respective interview transcripts – if you go to *Nodes> Cases* and click on one of the files, you will see in the Display View area that the link is noted on the top of the transcript.

Figure 15.11   Linking documents and cases – procedure

conceptual framework (Figure 15.2) and reading short extracts from three interview transcripts, it was possible to develop a coding system which is displayed in the side notes in Figure 15.3 and reflected in the more developed conceptual framework in Figure 15.4. In a fully fledged project the researcher would go on to read and code the full interview transcripts of the three example interviewees and other interviewees as well, and would apply the flagging/coding system to the other text read and would further develop the system in an inductive way. Coding systems using NVivo are developed in the same way. In the example below, the codes developed in the manual process are entered into the Activity Choice project to demonstrate the beginnings of a coding system.

The grouping of related concepts, as shown in Figure 15.4, is referred to in NVivo as *Tree Nodes*. Free-floating concepts, which have not been linked to any tree structure, are referred to as *Free Nodes*. The procedures in Figure 15.12 describe the process for entering information presented in Figure 15.4 into the NVivo project file. The relevance of the three *levels* mentioned in Figure 15.4 should become apparent in this process.

Modelling

The coding system can be depicted diagrammatically as a *model*. The procedures and output are shown in Figure 15.13. Here the model is depicted generically. Later it is shown how the way the model works for an individual case can be depicted.

Coding text

Once a coding system has been set up, documents, such as interview transcripts, can be coded. This process is outlined in Figure 15.14.

This illustration uses the coding system developed above, which arose from the manual analysis and theoretical framework outlined earlier in the chapter, but the coder is not restricted to this framework: additional codes/nodes can be added as you go along. This reflects the qualitative methodology and is, of course, very likely to arise with longer interview transcripts. The procedure involves selecting 'At new node' at Step 5b in Figure 15.14.

Project summary

The Activity Choice project information is now assembled and coded, as summarised in Figure 15.15. Analysis involves exploring the content of the coded interview transcripts and the cases and their attributes.

Analysis

Software packages invariably include a wide range of procedures which it is impossible to cover in a short summary such as this. Here we cover two very basic analysis procedures/issues which will be sufficient to get the researcher started. In reality, these procedures do not encompass data analysis as such, which is concerned with identifying relationships and meanings, discussed in a limited way in the manual analysis section above. The procedures covered here are related to data processing so that the analysis can begin. Two procedures are described below: *Coding Query* and *Matrix Coding Query*.

1. In the Navigation View area, click on *Nodes*
2. Click on *Nodes* in the sub menu, then *Create > New Folder*.
3. In the *New Folder* dialogue box enter *Free Nodes*, then click on *OK*.
4. Repeat steps 2–3 again, this time enter *Tree Nodes*.
5. In the *Nodes* menu click on *Tree Nodes*.
6. Right click in the List View area and select *New Node* (or, *Create > Node*). Type in the name *Main Activity* and click on *OK*. Main Activity is now listed under *Tree Nodes*.
7. Highlight *Main Activity* and, holding the pointer on *Main Activity*, click *Create > Node*, then in the *New Node* dialog box type in the name *Activity type* and click on *OK*. *Activity type* should now be listed under *Main Activity*.
8. Highlight *Activity type* and click *Create > Node*, enter *Sporting* and click on *OK*.
9. Repeat step 8, adding *Social and Cultural* – Cultural, Social, Sporting should now be listed under *Activity type*.
10. Repeat step 7 for: Influences, Constraints, Personal and Events.
11. Repeat steps 7–8 for:
    a. *Influences: Parents, Teachers, Peers*
    b. *Constraints: Time, Money, Fitness*
    c. *Personal: Competitive, Social-non-social, Anti-routine, Instrumental*
    d. *Events: Parents, Teachers, Peers.*

The screen should then appear as follows.

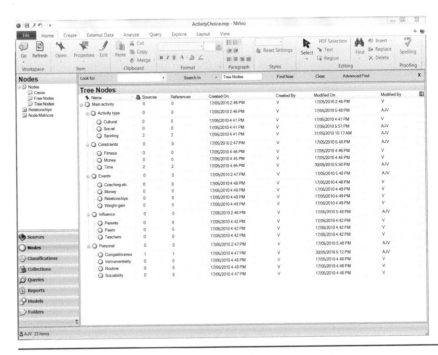

Figure 15.12   Setting up a coding system – procedure

The following NVivo procedures show how the coding system can be presented diagrammatically as a *model*.

1. In the Navigation View area select *Nodes* and then *Tree Nodes* from the menu: the *Main Activity* node specified in Figure 15.12 will appear in the List View area.
2. In the Navigation View are, select *Models*, which will now replace *Tree Nodes* in the List View area.
3. Right click in the List View area and from the menu, select *New Model*. (*Explore > New Model*)
4. In the *New Model* dialog box enter a name for the model eg. *Mode1 1*, and click on *OK*.
5. A workspace for *Model 1* appears below in the Detail View area. A new *Model* tab is also available with a selection of shapes. NB. The workspace can be expanded to full screen by clicking *View > Undock All* (and clicking on *View > Dock All* to reverse).
6. Before working with the model click *Click to edit* in the top of the work space.
7. Right click in the work space and, from the drop-down menu, select *Add Project Items*. (*Model > Add Project Items*)
8. In the *Select Project Items* dialog box, click on box next to *Nodes* to bring up extra options. Highlight *Tree Nodes* (not the adjacent tick-box for this exercise)
9. *Main Activity* appears in the space to the right: check the tick box and click on *OK*.
10. The first part of the graphic, a circle containing *Main Activity*, should appear in the workspace. Drag it to the centre, top of the workspace.
11. Click *Model > Add Associated Data*, check *Children*, then click on *OK*.
12. The five factors (Personal, Activity type, Events, Events, Influence and Constraints) appear, as shown below.
13. Click on *Influence* and repeat step 11: the three influences, teachers, peers, parents, appear as below.
14. Click on *Events* and repeat step 11.
15. This can be repeated for all factors, but it will be necessary to click and drag the shapes around to fit them appropriately into the work space. The sizes of the shapes and the font can be increased or reduced.

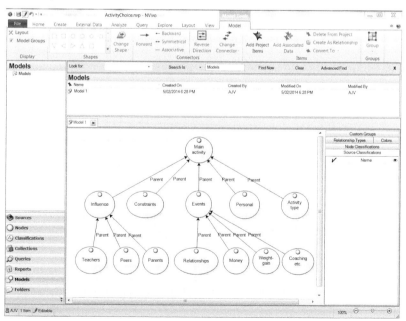

Figure 15.13   Modelling – procedure

1. In the Navigation View area select *Nodes* and then *Tree Nodes* from the sub-menu: the *Main Activity* node specified in Figure 15.12 will appear in the List View Area.

2. Double click on *Mark* and the transcript should appear below in the Display View area.

3. A section of text is coded by highlighting: to have this highlighting indicated visually on the text after it has been coded: on the Windows menu, select *View > Highlight > Coding for selected items.*

4. The coding can also be indicated visually with *Coding stripes* which appear in the space to the right of the text. To activate this select: *View > Coding Stripes > Nodes Most Coding.* (It will be noted that two coding stripes are already in place: one indicates that the Mark transcript as a whole is coded to the *Case* Mark and the other is a 'coding density' stripe which relates to the amount of coding.)

5. To code the activity 'playing football' in Mark's transcript:
   a. Highlight *playing football.*
   b. On the menu ribbon, select *Analyze > Existing Nodes* – the *Select Project Items* dialog box should appear.
   c. In the *Select Project Items* dialog box: select *Tree Nodes – Main Activity* should appear.
   d. Click on the + on the left of the *Main Activity* listing and factors, *Personal, Influence, Activity type*, etc. will be listed below.
   e. Click on the + on the left of *Activity type* and *Sporting, Social, Cultural* will be listed below.
   f. Select *Sporting* using the tick-box and click *OK.*
   g. The text should appear highlighted (if in step 3 you chose to highlight the *Sporting* node) and a *Sporting* stripe should appear in the right-hand space.

6. Repeat step 5 for:
   - text 'While the football's on, because of training twice a week and needing to be fairly serious about keeping fit I don't do much else: I probably only go to a pub once – or at most twice – a week', which is coded as *Constraints > Time;*
   - text: 'I'm pretty competitive – so I like sport generally' coded: *Personal > Competitive*

7. The result should appear as below.

8. Repeat steps 2–7 for Donna and the statement 'I go to the gym once or twice a week' (result not shown below).

Figure 15.14   Coding text – procedure

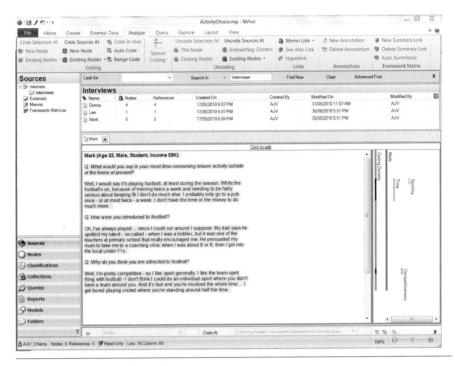

Figure 15.14 (*continued*)

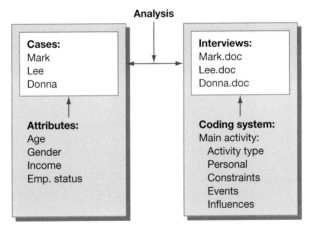

Figure 15.15   **Activity Choice project summary**

Coding query

One of the simplest forms of analysis is simply to obtain a listing of all the sections of text coded in a certain way. Thus a listing of all passages in the transcripts coded with Sporting as the Main Activity is obtained as shown in Figure 15.16.

Rather than searching for text coded as a node in the coding system it is possible to search for any item of specified text. This would involve selecting Text Search instead of Coding at Step 2 in Figure 15.16.

To select the text which has been coded *Sporting* as *Main Activity:*

1. In the Navigation View area, select *Queries:* the List View area will now be headed *Queries.*
2. Right click in the List View area and select *New Query > Coding* (or *Query > Coding* from the menu ribbon).
3. A *Coding Query* dialog box appears offering selection by *Node* or by *Any node where* (which refers to attributes).
4. To select by the *Node* 'Sporting': click on *Select* and click on the + to the left of *Nodes.* Then click on *Tree Node > Main Activity > Activity Type > Sporting > OK.*
5. Click on *Run* and a listing will appear in the Detail View area with the names of the cases, Mark and Donna, and a printout of the relevant text, as shown below.
6. The results of this query can be saved for future reference: *Click Query > Store Query. Results* and type in a name, e.g. Query_Sporting. This material can subsequently be accessed when required via the Navigation View area: *Queries > Results.*

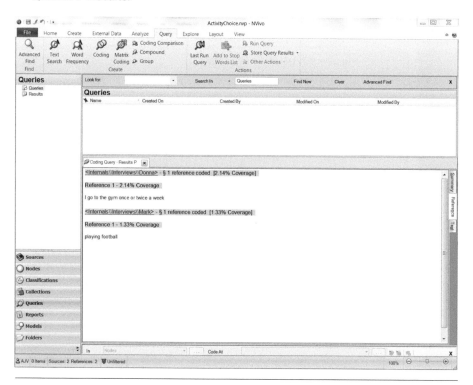

Figure 15.16   Coding query – procedure

To divide interviewees engaging in sporting activities into males and females:

1. In the Navigation View area, select *Queries*: the List View area will now be headed *Queries*.
2. Right click in the List View area and select *New Query > Matrix Coding* (or *Query > Matrix Coding* from the menu ribbon).
3. In the *Matrix Coding Query* dialog box, under *Matrix Coding Criteria* and *Rows* and *Define More Rows: Selected Items* will be displayed.
4. Click on the *Select* button on the right. *The Select Project Items* dialog box will appear.
5. In the *Select Project Items* dialog box click on the + to the left of *Nodes*, then highlight *Tree Nodes* to bring up *Main Activity*, then check the box next to *Sporting* (as in Figure 15.14 steps 5d–f) and click on *OK*.
6. On returning to the *Matrix Coding Query* dialog box, click on *Add to List* and *Nodes\\Tree Nodes\\Main Activity\Activity Type\Sporting* will appear under *Name*.
7. Click the *Columns* tab and under *Define More Columns* select *Attribute Condition > Select*.
8. In the *Coding Search Item* dialog box click on *Select*.
9. In the *Select Project Items* dialogue box click on *Node Classifications > Case > Gender > OK*.
10. The *Coding Search Item* dialogue box automatically indicates the *Gender* Attribute condition as 'equals value' and 'Male'. Click on *OK*.
11. On returning to the *Matrix Coding Query* dialog box click on *Add to List* and *Case:Gender = Male* will appear under name.
12. Repeat steps 7–11 but in step 10 change the value to 'Female'.
13. Click on *Run* and the results will be displayed in a table as follows (it may be necessary to widen the columns to display the labels in full):

	A: Case:Gender = Male	B: Case:Gender = Female
Sporting	1	1

14. This shows one male and one female coded as taking part in sport as their main activity: double clicking in the cells containing the numbers will bring up the relevant coded text.

Figure 15.17 Matrix coding query – procedure

Matrix coding query

The *Coding Query* can be seen as the equivalent of a frequency count in questionnaire survey analysis; the equivalent of a crosstabulation is a *Matrix Coding Query*. Figure 15.17 shows the procedure for conducting such an analysis in the Activity Choice project to separate sport participants by gender.

Case study

The case study research used to demonstrate the NVivo package is deliberately simple. Real research projects are generally considerably more complex, with more subjects, much lengthier interview transcripts and hence more involved analysis processes. Case study 15.2 is included to give some idea of the potential complexity.

Case study 15.2   Using psychological contract to understand volunteer management in community sport clubs

In dealing with large amounts of qualitative data, qualitative data analysis software can be used to help both quantify the coding structures and assist in locating relevant examples of quotations to use within the construction of the narrative of the article. This case study is part of a research project conducted by Taylor *et al*. (2006) to examine the human resource management practices used to manage volunteers in community sport clubs. The context was a national sport governing body which had identified volunteer management issues in Australian Rugby Union as a strategic issue for future growth across its 800 clubs. Theoretically the study sought to explain how Liao-Troth's (2001) 'psychological contract theory' could be applied to better understand volunteer responses to human resource management practices. It did so by examining attitudes towards the four components of the psychological contract (1. transactional; 2. in good faith and fair dealing; 3. intrinsic volunteer characteristics; and 4. working conditions) and their sub-themes and how these differed between the individual volunteers and club administrators, most of whom were themselves volunteers. The study involved 16 club-based focus-group discussions involving a total of almost 100 persons and an online questionnaire survey. From the latter, 49 respondents took part in a follow-up interview, originally planned via telephone, but in practice administered by emailing a list of questions calling for open-ended responses. All email texts were uploaded into an NVivo project file.

Table 15.1 presents the comparison of the proportions of the coded email interview texts that could be attributed to each component and sub-theme. It can be seen, therefore, that, despite the material being qualitative in nature, the scale of the project meant that a certain amount of quantification was used in the reporting. There were three areas where substantial differences between administrators and volunteers emerged: transactional elements; good faith and fair dealing; and intrinsic job characteristics. NVivo was also used to retrieve specific examples of the coded text, and Table 15.2 gives just a few examples of contrasting quotations from administrators and volunteers. Analyses of these findings were then used to make suggestions in regard to improvement of human resource management practices within club management, as indicated in the article.

Table 15.1 Psychological contract framework classification

	% of transcript content	
	Administrators %	Volunteers %
1. Transactional		
Job descriptions	4.5	0.9
Strategic planning and policies	8.8	4.0
Regulatory and legal issues	8.4	0.9
Funding from union and sponsors	3.0	1.2
Professionalism and grassroots rugby	5.5	2.1
Volunteer recruitment and turnover	15.2	0.0
Evaluation and appraisal	3.6	0.0
Subtotal	49.0	9.2
2. Good faith and fair dealing		
Fair and honest treatment	0.4	2.8
Communication	5.7	8.6
Cooperative work relationship	1.0	3.4
Management by superiors	0.7	5.5
Subtotal	7.8	20.3
3. Intrinsic volunteer characteristics		
Interesting work	0.0	0.0
Meaningful work	0.3	1.8
Challenging work	0.0	0.6
Rewarding work	0.4	12.3
Social environment and networking	3.0	10.1
Committing to work	1.6	0.0
Time restrictions	3.8	7.4
Motivation	3.3	0.3
Recognition and appreciation	7.7	9.5
Subtotal	20.0	42.0
4. Working conditions		
Resources and tools needed to do job	1.3	3.4
Training and skill development	8.1	2.8
Opportunity to learn	2.4	1.2
Safe working conditions	0.9	0.6
Number of people to do the work	3.3	10.7
Issues with people not involved	1.3	4.0
Support from committee or union	4.7	5.8
Expense reimbursement	1.3	0.0
Subtotal	23.2	28.5
Total	100.0	100.0

Table 15.2   Examples of psychological contract quotations

Components/sub-themes	Quotations: examples for first three sub-themes in each component
1. Transactional	
Job descriptions	I'd say it would be a lot easier to get someone into a position if someone had written down on paper the exact role and their responsibility. (A)
Strategic planning/policies	Not sure we have any strategies. (V) The club is professionally run. There is a plan in place for the future. (V)
Regulatory and legal issues	The changes in the Occupational Health and Safety laws make it very hard to get people involved unless they hold some sort of certificate. (A)
2. Good faith and fair dealing	
Fair and honest treatment	It was my wife that made me realise something about volunteers, I used to go and whinge to her and she said to me, 'don't compare yourself to everyone else cause they don't have the same passion as you and remember, you don't pay them, they're volunteers'. I went 'der ... you're exactly right' and I've changed my whole attitude. (A)
Communication	My club is particularly bad at interacting with its volunteers. This is no criticism of the club, rather a reflection that it is an amateur sport that is run by limited people in their spare time. (V) The club has made changes this year which have allowed volunteers a greater say, and generally they are fairly happy with the future directions. (V)
Cooperative work relationship	A lack of consultation from the committee regarding important issues which affect all members. (V) We have an excellent Club President/Club Secretary who has a 'can do' attitude. It becomes infectious and therefore things will happen. As a strategy: reserve time after training for decision-making (not in family time); utilise email for communication; minimise formal meetings; empower small committees to perform important projects. (V)
3. Intrinsic volunteer characteristics	
Meaningful work	Seeing the children develop into young players and young people. (V)
Challenging work	The sense of putting something back into the sport allied to the camaraderie and sense of potential achievement. (V)

Components/sub-themes	Quotations: examples for first three sub-themes in each component
Rewarding work	Without volunteers (coaches, managers etc.) the amateur game would not continue to survive. (A)
4. Working conditions	
Resources/tools needed to do job	From doing the registrar's job for the last 2 years the ARU have made that job [online database] very hard. So much more time-consuming and so much more difficult. I don't know whether it saves time for them, but from our club base level it has been an absolute nightmare in terms of getting the data into the system, maintaining it and keeping it, they loose it on us, year in, year out. (A)
Training/skill development	Provision of training in those elements required to make a successful contribution e.g. assistance towards gaining coaching qualifications or basic book-keeping courses, etc. (V)
Opportunity to learn	As a volunteer, although I played rugby and attended courses, I spent a lot of time gathering training resources from websites as I saw the need and dedicated the time to this. There are sites that provide tremendous access to training resources, however geared to senior levels. Could the ARU provide a resource section aimed at different age levels – providing age-appropriate drills to help coaches, plus tips on team tactics/strategies? (V)

Note: A = Administrator; V = Volunteer. ARU = Australian Rugby Union

Summary

The chapter is divided into two sections dealing respectively with manual and computer-aided analysis methods.

Manual methods of data analysis involve 'flagging' issues or themes which emerge in texts such as interview transcripts. Such issues or themes may relate to an existing draft conceptual framework, to research questions and/or hypotheses or, in a 'grounded theory', to an inductive approach; they may be used to build up a conceptual framework from the data. Since texts are invariably available as word-processed files, it is noted that certain features of word-processing packages, such as 'search' and 'list' or 'index', can be used to assist in the 'flagging' process. This provides a link to the custom-made computer-aided qualitative data analysis software (CAQDAS) packages.

The second part of the chapter introduces the NVivo package, covering the setting up of a project file and a coding system, coding of data and some elementary analysis procedures. While the package has a large range of capabilities – including the handling of data other than interview transcripts – just a limited range of analysis procedures is presented in this short outline; but it is believed this is adequate for the qualitative researcher to make a start with computer-aided data analysis.

Test questions

1. What are the two major activities involved in manual analysis of qualitative data?

2. What word-processing procedures might be used in 'manual' analysis of qualitative data?

3. What is the difference between a 'Node' and a 'Document' in NVivo?

4. What is the difference between a 'Tree Node' and a 'Free Node' in NVivo?

Exercises

1. Download from the book's website the three transcript files for the 'Activity Choice' project used above – or type them out from Figure 15.3 – and replicate the coding and analyses presented above. This can be done manually or by using NVivo.

2. Run the NVivo tutorials included with the package, particularly exploring features of NVivo not presented in this chapter.

3. Select an example of a quantitative and a qualitative research report from a recent edition of one of the sport journals and consider whether the qualitative research project could have been approached using quantitative methods and whether the quantitative project could have been approached using qualitative methods.

4. Using the issues of a newspaper for one week, provide a qualitative and quantitative analysis of the coverage of a topic of interest, such as: sport and the environment, ethnic minorities, or women and sport.

Resources

Websites

- NVivo website: www.qsrinternational.com – includes a downloadable bibliography on qualitative data analysis sources.
- CATPAC – text analysis package: www.galileoco.com/N_catpac.asp.
- *Qualitative Research* journal: http://qrj.sagepub.com.
- The Qualitative Report (portal): www.nova.edu/ssss/QR/web.html.

Publications

- Analysis of qualitative data generally: Miles and Huberman (1994).
- Qualitative methods in sport studies: Andrews *et al.* (2006).
- Qualitative methods in sport management: Edwards and Skinner (2009).
- Use of computer software packages in qualitative data analysis: Miles and Weitzman (1994), Richards and Richards (1994); in grounded theory and physical activity: Hutchison *et al.* (2010, 2011).
- Use of NVivo software: Bazeley (2007), Gibbs (2002 – does not include latest version of NVivo).

References

Andrews, D. L., Mason, D. S. and Silk, M. L. (eds) (2006) *Qualitative Methods in Sports Studies.* Oxford: Berg.

Bazeley, P. (2007) *Qualitative Data Analysis with NVivo.* Thousand Oaks, CA: Sage.

Brandenburg, J., Greiner, W., Hamilton-Smith, E., Scholten, H., Senior, R. and Webb, J. (1982) A conceptual model of how people adopt recreation activities. *Leisure Studies*, 1(3), 263–76.

Dupuis, S. (1999) Naked truths: towards a reflexive methodology in leisure research. *Leisure Sciences*, 21(1), 43–64.

Edwards, A. and Skinner, J. (2009) *Qualitative Research in Sport Management.* Oxford: Butterworth-Heinemann.

Gibbs, G. R. (2002) *Qualitative Data Analysis: Explorations with NVivo.* Maidenhead, UK: Open University Press.

Huberman, A. M. and Miles, M. B. (1994) Data management and analysis methods. In N. K. Denzin and Y. S. Lincoln (eds) *Handbook of Qualitative Research.* Thousand Oaks, CA: Sage, 428–44.

Hutchison, A. J., Johnston, L. H. and Breckon, J. D. (2010) Using QSR-NVivo to facilitate the development of a grounded theory project: an account of a worked example. *International Journal of Social Research Methodology*, 13(4), 283–302.

Hutchison, A. J., Johnston, L. H. and Breckon, J. D. (2011) Grounded theory-based research within exercise psychology: a critical review. *Qualitative Research in Psychology*, 8(3), 247–72.

Liao-Troth, M. A. (2001) Attitude differences between paid workers and volunteers. *Nonprofit Management and Leadership*, 11(4), 423–42.

Miles, M. B. and Huberman, A. M. (1994) *Qualitative Data Analysis, Second edn.* Thousand Oaks, CA: Sage.

Miles, M. and Weitzman, E. (1994) *Computer Programs for Qualitative Data Analysis.* Thousand Oaks, CA: Sage.

Richards, T. J. and Richards, L. (1994) Using computers in qualitative research. In N. K. Denzin and Y. S. Lincoln (eds) *Handbook of Qualitative Research,* Thousand Oaks, CA: Sage, 445–62.

Taylor, T., Darcy, S., Cuskelly, G. and Hoye, R. (2006) Using psychological contract theory to explore issues in effective volunteer management. *European Sports Management Quarterly*, 6(2), 123–47.

Thomas, J., Harden, A. and Oakley, A. (2004) Integrating qualitative research with trials in systematic reviews. *British Medical Journal*, 328(7446), 1010–12.

Veal, A. J. (1995) Leisure studies: frameworks for analysis. In H. Ruskin and A. Sivan (eds) *Leisure Education: Towards the 21st Century.* Provo, Utah: Brigham Young University Press, 124–36.

Analysing quantitative and survey data

Introduction

In this chapter the analysis of questionnaire survey data is addressed using two types of computer package:

- *Spreadsheets:* the most widespread computer application used for general data analysis – Microsoft Excel is used to demonstrate certain analysis procedures.

- *Statistical packages:* used to analyse statistical data in a research context – one of the most widely used packages is the Statistical Package for the Social Sciences (SPSS) and this is used here for demonstration purposes. Other packages include *Minitab*, *BMD* (Biomedical Data analysis), *SAS* (Statistical Analysis System) and *Turbostats.*

Figure 10.20, in Chapter 10, contains a copy of a simple questionnaire which is used to demonstrate analysis processes in this chapter. Chapter 10 dealt with the procedure for coding the data from this questionnaire in a form suitable for computer analysis, as shown in Figures 10.21 and 10.22.

Before addressing the mechanics of data analysis, however, the typology of research **(see Chapter 1)** is discussed in relation to the analysis process.

Survey data analysis and types of research

In Chapter 1 it was noted that research might be of three kinds: descriptive, explanatory and evaluative. Before considering the process of analysing questionnaire survey data, these types of research and their relationship to survey analysis are discussed in turn below and summarised in Figure 16.1.

Descriptive research

Descriptive research usually involves the presentation of information in a fairly simple form. Of the analytical procedures described in this chapter, the two most appropriate for descriptive research are:

● *frequencies*, which present counts and percentages of responses for single variables; and

● *means*, which present averages for numerical variables.

Explanatory research

Descriptive data do not, of themselves, *explain* anything. To explain the patterns in data or relationships between phenomena represented by the data it is necessary to consider the question of *causality* – how to determine whether A is caused by B. In Chapter 3 it was noted that to establish causality it is necessary to fulfil four criteria: association, time priority, non-spurious relation and rationale:

● *Associations* between variables can be explored using such procedures as *crosstabulations* **(described in this chapter)** and *regression* **(described in Chapter 17)**.

● *Time priority* – involves establishing that, for A to be the *cause* of B, A must take place *before* B – this is sometimes testable in social science research and

Research type	Analytical procedures
Descriptive	Frequencies, Means
Explanatory	Crosstabulation, Comparison of means, Regression
Evaluative	Frequencies – compared with targets or benchmarks
	Crosstabulations – comparing user/customer-groups
	Means – compared with targets or benchmarks

Figure 16.1   Research types and analytical procedures

is sometimes obvious, but is generally more appropriate for the conditions of the natural science laboratory.

- *Non-spurious* relationships are those which 'make sense' theoretically (that is, the relationship between A and B is not mediated by a third, extraneous variable C), and are not just a 'fluke' of the data. This can be approached using survey analysis techniques. For example, suppose it is found that expenditure on sport is inversely related to age for the whole sample. If this relationship is also found for, say, men and women separately, and for other sub-groups – even random sub-samples – this suggests the likelihood of a non-spurious relationship.

- *Rationale*, or *theory*, is of course not produced by computer analysis but should be integral to the research design. The research may be *deductive* in nature, with pre-established hypotheses which are tested by the data analysis, or it may be *inductive*, in which development of theory and explanation-building take place to a greater or lesser extent as part of the data analysis process. Either way, *explanation*, or the establishment of causality, is not complete without some sort of rational, conceptual explanation of the relationships found.

The example questionnaire **(see Figure 10.20)** offers only limited scope for *explanatory* research. For example, differences in attitudes between the various student groups – full-time and part-time or different age-groups for example – may indicate that varying expectations from campus sporting life may be a function of student group characteristics.

The particular procedures which are appropriate for explanatory analysis and which are covered in this chapter are the production of *crosstabulations*, which facilitate examination of the relationship between two or more variables based on frequencies, and the examination of the *means* of two or more variables. These procedures can establish whether or not statistical relationships exist between variables, but whether or not they are spurious and/or supported by theory involves reference to the theoretical or conceptual framework.

Evaluative research

Evaluative research basically involves comparisons between survey findings and some benchmark derived from expectations, past figures, other similar facilities or programmes or target performance standards. The analysis called for, therefore, is relatively simple, generally involving comparisons between findings from the survey and some benchmark value.

The example questionnaire could be used for evaluative purposes – for example a low level of use of any of the services listed in question 2 could imply that the existing service is not performing well in meeting the demands of students and low levels of use by particular groups could indicate a failure to meet the needs of all groups.

Overlaps

Analysis does not always fall exclusively into one of the above three modes. For example, in presenting a descriptive account of the example Campus Sporting Life survey results, it would be natural to provide a breakdown of the participation patterns and preferences of the four student groups included. While this could be descriptive in form, it would begin at least to hint at explanation, in that any differences in the groups' patterns of behaviour or opinions would seem to call for explanation; the analysis would be saying 'these groups are different' and would be implicitly posing the question 'why?'. Insofar as the providers of campus services aimed to serve all sections of the student community, the data could be used in evaluating management.

Reliability

In Chapter 2 reference was made to questions of *validity* and *reliability*. It has been noted that some attempt at testing validity – whether the data are measuring what they are intended to measure – can be achieved in the design of questionnaires. Reliability – whether similar results would be obtained if the research were replicated – is a difficult issue in the social sciences, but an approach can be made at the analysis stage. While statistical procedures are well suited to establishing the magnitude and strength of associations, the question of the reliability of such associations is more complex. Unlike the natural sciences, it is not always possible, for practical or resource reasons, to replicate research in the social sciences to establish reliability. While reference to previous research reported in the literature can be relevant and helpful in this respect, in fact the changing patterns of human behaviour over time and space means that consistency with previous research findings is by no means a guarantee of reliability – indeed, it is the tracking of *change* which is often the aim of social research.

 If the sample is large enough, one approach to reliability is to split the sample into two or more sub-samples on a random basis, or on the basis of a selected variable, and see if the results for the sub-samples are the same as for the sample as a whole. In the *SPSS* package this can be achieved using the procedure *split file:* the procedure is not covered here but is relatively straightforward to operate.

Spreadsheet analysis

Since most users of this book will be familiar with spreadsheet use, this section does not provide a guide to elementary spreadsheet procedures, but only to procedures specific to analysis of the type of data produced from questionnaire surveys.

 The shaded part of Figure 16.2 reproduces in spreadsheet format the data for 15 completed questionnaires in the Campus Sporting Life survey from

	A	B	C	D	E	F	G	H	I	J	K	L	M	N	O	P	Q	R	S	T	U	V
1	qno	status	pool	gym	squash	spectate	cheap	hour	qual	meet	time	relax	social	fitness	sug1	sug2	sug3	gend		age		spend
2	1	2	1	1	0	0	1	4	2	3	5	3	3	1	1			1		18		100
3	2	2	1	1	1	0	1	4	2	3	5	2	3	1	2	1		1		19		50
4	3	3	1	0	0	0	2	5	1	3	4	2	2	2	3	4		2		19		250
5	4	4	0	0	0	0	2	3	1	4	5	3	2	2	1	2	4	1		22		25
6	5	3	1	0	0	1	1	4	3	2	5	3	3	1				2		24		55
7	6	3	1	1	1	0	2	4	1	3	5	2	3	1	2			2		20		40
8	7	2	1	0	0	0	3	2	1	4	5	2	3	2	3	5		2		20		150
9	8	2	1	0	1	0	3	4	2	1	5	1	2	2	4			1		21		250
10	9	4	0	1	0	0	1	5	2	3	4	2	3	2				1		21		300
11	10	3	1	1	0	0	2	3	1	5	4	1	2	1	1	1		2		21		100
12	11	3	1	1	0	1	2	3	1	4	5	2	2	1	2	3		2		19		75
13	12	2	1	0	1	0	1	4	3	2	5	2	3	1				1		22		50
14	13	1	1	0	1	0	1	5	2	3	4	2	3	2	1	2		2		21		55
15	14	3	1	1	0	0	2	4	1	3	5	3	3	2	4	2		2		20		75
16	15	1	1	1	0	0	3	2	1	5	4	3	3	1	1	2	5	1		20		150
17																						
18	Code	Freq	Freq	Freq	Freq	Freq	Freq	Freq	Freq	Freq	Freq	Freq	Freq	Freq	Freq	Freq	Freq	Freq	Cat.	Freq	Cat.	Freq
19	0	0	2	7	10	13	0	0	0	0	0	0	0	0	0	0	0	0	19	4	74	6
20	1	2	13	8	5	2	6	0	8	1	0	2	0	8	5	2	0	7	21	8	100	4
21	2	5	0	0	0	0	6	2	5	2	0	8	5	7	3	3	0	8	23	2	200	2
22	3	6	0	0	0	0	3	3	2	7	0	5	10	0	2	1	0	0	25	1		3
23	4	2	0	0	0	0	0	7	0	3	0	0	0	0	2	1	1	0				
24	5	0	0	0	0	0	0	3	0	2	5	0	0	0	0	1	1	0				
25	Total	15	15	15	15	15	15	15	15	15	15	15	15	15	12	8	2	15		15		15
26	Averages																			20.5		115

Figure 16.2 Questionnaire survey data: spreadsheet analysis

Figure 10.21. There is one change: the expenditure variable (*spend*) has been shifted to the end to sit alongside *age*, since both are uncoded numerical variables which are treated individually below. The unshaded part is produced by the FREQUENCY procedure provided in Excel. This procedure is described in Figure 16.3.

Spreadsheet analysis is suitable for a small data set when simple frequency tables are required. But for larger data sets, particularly longer questionnaires and more complex analyses, a statistical software package, as outlined below, is advisable.

Statistical Package for the Social Sciences (SPSS)

The main part of the chapter is organised as a step-by-step introductory manual for operating the SPSS package in the analysis of questionnaire survey data. It is envisaged that the reader will have access to a computer with SPSS available on it, so that the procedures described here can be tried out in practice.

The question arises, at what point is it worthwhile to invest time and energy in mastering a computer package for survey analysis, rather than relying on a spreadsheet program, with which many people are already familiar? This, of course, depends on the scale and complexity of the task in hand and the likely future career path of the researcher. It is clear that a specialist survey package has far more capabilities than a spreadsheet, as this chapter and the next demonstrate. It should be noted that basic coding and data preparation are identical for both approaches and the basic data file is interchangeable between a spreadsheet and a survey analysis package such as SPSS. It is also the case (as noted in Chapter 15) that familiarity and experience with a computer package merits an entry on a *curriculum vitae*.

SPSS for Windows is the version of the package which is available for IBM-compatible personal computers using the Microsoft *Windows* system. Version 18 of the package is referred to here. Most universities provide access to the software and further details and information on specialist guides can be found on the SPSS Inc. website (see Resources section).

A full list of SPSS procedures can be found in the online *SPSS* manual which is included in the software package. In this chapter, only five analysis procedures are described:

- *Descriptives* – key descriptive statistics for specified variables;
- *Frequencies* – counts and percentages of individual variables;
- *Crosstabs* – the crosstabulation of two or more variables;
- *Means* – obtaining means/averages of appropriate variables;
- *Graphs* – the production of charts and graphs.

1. Type **Code** in cell A18.
2. Type **Freq** in cell B18.
3. Type the codes **0, 1, 2, 3, 4, 5** in cells A19 to A24 respectively (0–5 covers all the codes used by variables *status* to *gend*).
4. Select cells B19 to B24 (the cells in which the results of the frequency counts will be placed).
5. Type the following 'array formula' in the 'formula bar' (not shown in Fig. 16.2):
   a. =**FREQUENCY(B2:B16,$A19:$A24)** and then press Ctrl+Shift+Enter together.
   b. The results will appear as shown in cells B19 to B24 in Fig. 16.2.
   c. Note: When you have typed =**FR** Excel will offer you a pop-up FREQUENCY which you can select with a double click.
      - You can *select* the cells B2:B16 rather than typing the cell references manually.
      - The $A format is used in $A19:$A24 because the codes in cells A19:A24 will be utilised for all 17 coded variables, so in spreadsheet parlance, and absolute rather than a relative column location must be specified.
      - General instructions on the use of the FREQUENCY formula are provide by the Excel Help facility.
6. The heading in cell B18 and the formulae in cells B19:B24 can now be copied to produce the frequencies for the other 16 variables: copy cells B19:B24 as one array and paste into cells C19:C24 in one 'copy and paste' operation.
7. Create totals in row 25 using normal spreadsheet procedures.
8. Example results, for *status*, are as follows:

Category	No.
Full-time student with no regular paid work	2
Full-time student with some regular paid work	5
Part-time student with full-time job	6
Part-time student – other	2
Total	15

9. For each variable percentages can be created from the frequencies, and graphics can be created from the frequencies or the percentages using normal spreadsheet procedures.
10. Type category groupings for the non-coded variables, *age* and *spend*, in cells S19:S21 and U19:U20 respectively.
    - cell S19: 19 indicates a group aged 19 and under
    - cell S20: 21 indicates a group aged 20–21
    - cell S21: 23 indicates a group aged 22–23
    - cell S22: 25 indicates a group aged 24–25 (if blank, indicates '24 and over')
11. Select cells T19:T22, then type the following 'array formula' in the 'formula bar' (not shown in Fig. 16.1):
    - =FREQUENCY(T2:T16, S19:S22) (note: $S is not required, because the information is only being used for one variable) and then press Ctrl+Shift+Enter together.
    - The results will appear as shown in cells T19 to T22 in Fig. 16.1.
12. Results for *age* are therefore:

Age	No.
18–19	4
20–21	8
22–23	2
24–25	1

13. A similar process can be followed for the variable *spend*.
14. Totals, percentages and graphics can be produced as for the other variables. In addition, for the two non-coded variables, averages may be calculated.

Figure 16.3 Questionnaire survey data: spreadsheet analysis steps

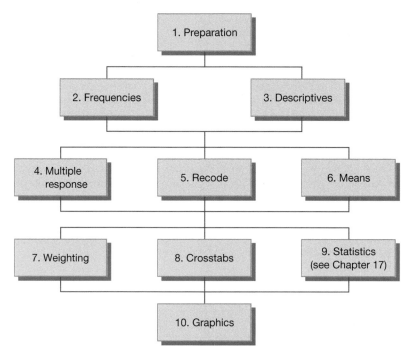

Figure 16.4   Survey analysis – overview

The areas covered in this chapter and the statistical procedures covered in Chapter 17 are summarised in Figure 16.4.

The chapter deals with the analysis of data from questionnaire surveys. But SPSS can be used to analyse data from other sources also. And although the package is ideally suited to dealing with numerical data, it can also handle non-numerical data. Any data organised on the basis of *cases* and a common range of *variables* for each case can be analysed using the package (*cases* and *variables* are defined below).

The chapter does not deal with procedures for logging into a computer, file handling or the installation of the SPSS software onto the computer; it is assumed that SPSS for Windows is already installed on a computer available to the reader. The information in the chapter provides an introduction to the basics only.

Preparation

Cases and variables

Statistical analysis packages deal with data which are organised in terms of *cases* and *variables*.

● A *case* is a single example of the phenomenon being studied and for which data have been collected – for example an individual member of a community who has been interviewed, a participant in a sport, an employee of a company, a visitor to a country, a sporting organisation or a country for which data are available. So a *sample* is made up of a number of *cases*.

- A *variable* is an item of information which is available for all or some of the cases, which can take on different values or categories – for example the *gender* of an individual, which can take on the category 'male' or 'female'; the *salary* of an employee, which can be any monetary value; the *number of employees* of a company; the *population* of a country.

The use of *variables* is further discussed here, while *cases* arise when entering data, as discussed later in the chapter.

Specifying variables

In order to communicate with the program it is necessary to identify each item of data in the questionnaire by a *variable name*. The questionnaire (Figure 10.20) is *annotated with variable names* in the 'Office Use' column. The question numbers and corresponding variable names are listed in Figure 16.5, together with an additional nine items of information for each variable, which are required by the software. These items are discussed in turn below.

1. Question no.

The question number from the questionnaire (Figure 10.20).

2. Name

- In addition to variables related to the eight questions in the questionnaire, there is a variable *qno* to record a reference number for each case or questionnaire.

- Every item of information on the questionnaire is given a *unique* name (no two variables with the same name).

- The length of variable names is limited to 64 letters/numbers (no spaces), beginning with a letter or @, #, $. It is not permitted to use any of the following for variable names, because the SPSS program already uses these names for other purposes and would get confused!

  ALL   AND   BY   EQ   GE   GT   LE   LT   NE   NOT   OR   TO   WITH

Three possible systems for naming variables are:

- the practice adopted here, which is to use variable names which are full or shortened versions of how the item might be described – for example *status* for student status, and *sug1* for improvement suggestion 1;

- use a generalised name such as *var* for variable; so a questionnaire with 5 variables would have variable names: *var1, var2, var3, var4, var5*;

- use of question numbers – for example *Q1, Q2a, Q2b*, and so on.

1 Question No.*	2 Name*	3 Type	4 Width	5 Decimal places	6 Label	7 Values/Value labels	8 Missing values	9 Columns	10 Alignment	11 Measure/Data type
–	qno	Numeric	4	0	Questionnaire number	None	None	4	Right	Scale
1.	status	Numeric	1	0	Student status	1 F/T student – no work 2 F/T student – working 3 P/T student – F/T job 4 P/T student – other	None	4	Right	Nominal
2.	pool	Numeric	1	0	Campus pool in last 4 wks	1 Yes 0 No	None	4	Right	Nominal
	gym	Numeric	1	0	Campus gym in last 4 wks	as for pool	None	4	Right	Nominal
	squash	Numeric	1	0	Campus squash in last 4 wks	as for pool	None	4	Right	Nominal
	spectate	Numeric	1	0	Spectator on campus in last 4 wks	as for pool	None	4	Right	Nominal
3.	cheap	Numeric	1	0	Free/cheap (rank)	None	None	4	Right	Ordinal
	hours	Numeric	1	0	Opening hours (rank)	None	None	4	Right	Ordinal
	qual	Numeric	1	0	Quality of facilities (rank)	None	None	4	Right	Ordinal
	meet	Numeric	1	0	Socialising (rank)	None	None	4	Right	Ordinal
	time	Numeric	1	0	Time available (rank)	None	None	4	Right	Ordinal
4.	spend	Numeric	4	0	Expenditure on sport etc./month	None	None	4	Right	Scale
5.	relax	Numeric	1	0	Relaxation – importance	3 Very important 2 Important 1 Not at all important	None	4	Right	Scale
	social	Numeric	1	0	Social interaction – importance	as for relax	None	4	Right	Scale
	fitness	Numeric	1	0	Fitness – importance	as for relax	None	4	Right	Scale
6.	sug1	Numeric	2	0	Improvement suggestion – 1	1 Programme content§ 2 Timing 3 Facilities 4 Costs 5 Organisation	None	4	Right	Nominal
	sug2	Numeric	2	0	Improvement suggestion – 2	as for sug1	None	4	Right	Nominal
	sug3	Numeric	2	0	Improvement suggestion – 3	as for sug1	None	4	Right	Nominal
7.	gend	Numeric	1	0	Gender	1 Male 2 Female	None	4	Right	Nominal
8.	age	Numeric	2	0	Age	None	None	4	Right	Scale

Figure 16.5   Variable names, labels and values

* From Figure 10.20

§ See Figure 10.19 for derivation of coding system

Question 6 should be noted. It is an open-ended question and respondents might wish to give any number of answers. In this case the designer of the questionnaire has assigned three variables to record up to three answers (*sug1*, *sug2* and *sug3*), on the assumption that a maximum of three answers would be given by any one respondent. Not all respondents will necessarily give three answers – this is no problem, because *sug2* and/or *sug3* can be left blank. Some may, however, give *more* than three answers, in which case it would not be possible to record the fourth and subsequent answers and that information would be lost. If more than a handful of respondents give more than three answers then a fourth variable (*sug4*) could be added. The decision on how many answers to allow for must depend on a preliminary scanning of the questionnaires. As an open-ended question, the coding system for question 6 applies to all three variables and was devised from the range of free-form answers as discussed in Chapter 10 (Figure 10.19).

3. Type

All the variables in the Campus Sporting Life survey questionnaire are *numeric* – that is, they can only be numbers. A number of other possibilities exist, including *date* and *string*, the latter meaning text comprising any combination of letters and numbers, but these options are not pursued here.

4. Width

Width specifies the maximum number of digits for the value of a variable. In the Campus Sporting Life survey questionnaire, all variables are single-digit except two:

- *qno:* width will depend on the size of the sample – here a width of four digits is indicated, indicating a maximum possible sample size of 9999;
- *cost:* width has been put at four, suggesting maximum possible individual weekly expenditure on sport and social activity of £9999 – which should accommodate all respondents!

5. Decimal places

None of the variables in the Campus Sporting Life questionnaire includes *decimal* places, so the number of decimal places is set to zero for all of them. Many variables could, however, include decimals or dollars/cents, pounds/pence – for example a person's height, or a tourist's expenditure per day.

6. Label

The variable *label* is fuller and more descriptive than the variable *name*, and there is no restriction on content or length. It can be included in output tables, making them more readily understandable by the reader. This is often helpful with long questionnaires with many variables, and particularly when the short variable *names* are not immediately recognisable.

7. Value labels

Value labels identify the codes used for each variable – e.g. for *gend*, 1 = male and 2 = female. In the case of the Campus Sporting Life:

- The questionnaire number is just a reference number so it has no value labels.

- Variables based on questions 1, 2 and 5 have specific codes or values (1, 2, 3 etc.) with value labels as specified in the questionnaire.

- Variables based on question 3 are ranks from 1 to 5 – they have therefore been specified in Figure 16.4 as having no value labels. In fact, the values for these variables *could* be given value labels as follows: 1 = 'First', 2 = 'Second', 3 = 'Third', 4 = 'Fourth', 5 = 'Fifth'.

- The variable *spend* is an uncoded numerical sum of money and *age* is a number of years – they therefore have no value labels.

- The values/labels for the open-ended question, 6, were derived as shown in Chapter 10 (Figure 10.19).

8. Missing

If a respondent does not answer a question in a questionnaire, the data entry may be left blank, or a 'No answer' or 'Not applicable' code may be provided. The software will automatically treat a blank in the data as a 'missing value', but specific 'No answer' and 'Not applicable' codes can be provided and specified as *missing values*. The implications are that missing values are excluded when means and percentages are being calculated. In the Campus Sporting Life data set, the phenomenon of missing values becomes apparent in the case of variables *sug1*, *sug2* and *sug3*, since some respondents offer no suggestions at all, many offer only one and very few offer three – so there are usually numerous blanks in the data, particularly for *sug2* and *sug3*. In the case of the four variables associated with question 2, it would be possible for non-use of services to be left as a blank, giving rise to missing values, but in this case non-use has been coded as a zero. The *missing value* phenomenon is not pursued in detail in this chapter but is apparent in a number of the outputs from SPSS provided in this and the next chapter.

9. Columns

The number of columns or digits per variable is a presentational matter concerning the layout of the 'Data view' screen discussed below. A variable can be *displayed* with any number of columns regardless of the specified *width* of the underlying variable. In the Campus Sporting Life example, the specification is four columns for all variables, enabling all the data to be seen on the 'Data view' screen at once, without scrolling on most computer screens.

10. Alignment

Alignment is also presentational. As in a spreadsheet, or table, numerical data are easier to read if aligned to the right, while text is often more suitably aligned to the left.

11. Measure

Data can be divided into *nominal, ordinal* and *scale* types.

- *Nominal data* are made up of non-numerical *categories,* such as the status categories in question 1 and 'Yes/No' in question 2 of the example questionnaire. In this situation, while numerical codes are used in computer analysis, they have no numerical meaning – for example, code 2 is not 'half' of code 4. The 1 and 0 codes could equally well be 6 and 7, A and B, or X and Y. It does not make sense, therefore, to calculate, for example, an average or mean of *nominal data* codes.

- *Ordinal data* reflect a *ranking,* as in question 3 of the example questionnaire; the 1, 2, 3 in this question represent the *order of importance,* but rank 3 cannot be interpreted as being '3 times as high as' rank 1. It is, however, possible to take an average or mean rank – for example to speak of an 'average ranking'.

- *Scale data*[1] are fully numerical – as in questions 4 (*spend*) and 8 (*age*) of the example questionnaire. Numerical information, such as a person's age, expenditure or frequency of participation in an activity, are *scale data.* In this case an answer of 4 *is* twice as high as an answer of 2 and averages or means are clearly appropriate.

The data type, or type of measure, of a variable affects the range of statistical analysis which can be performed and the appropriate formats for graphical presentation; **these are discussed later, particularly in Chapter 17**.

In Figure 16.5 each variable is identified as nominal, ordinal or scale, as follows:

- *qno* is identified as a *scale* variable, although it will not be used in analysis;
- variables from questions 1, 2, 6 and 7 are *nominal;*
- variables from question 3 are *ordinal;*
- the question 4 variable, *spend,* and question 8 variable, *age,* are *scale* variables;
- question 5 variables are 'Likert-style' variables, specified as *scale* variables for the reasons discussed below.

12. Attitude/Likert variables

Variables arising from *Attitude/Likert variables* have been used extensively in psychological and market research and have come to be seen almost as *scale* variables when, in reality, they are just ordinal. Means are therefore accepted as an appropriate form of analysis when using such variables. The scores of 1 to 3 in question 5 in the Campus Sporting Life questionnaire can be treated as numerical indicators of the level of importance respondents attach to the items listed. The means can be interpreted as average 'scores' on importance. It is possible to add scores in some circumstances.

13. Role

The default setting for all variables is *input*. This need not concern us here. The idea of an *output* variable will be apparent when the *Recode* procedure is discussed below.

Starting up

To start an *SPSS Statistics* session on a computer, activate the program as indicated in Figure 16.6. Switch to the *Variable View* screen to start the process outlined below.

Entering information about variables – Variable View window

The information about the variables arising from a questionnaire, as shown in Figure 16.5 above, must be typed into the *Variable View* window. The result of this exercise for the Campus Sporting Life questionnaire is as shown in Figure 16.8. It should be noted that for variables with identical value labels, the value labels can be copied and pasted.

---

1. Start *SPSS Statistics* on your computer using the appropriate screen icon or *Start* and *All Programs*.
2. The dialog box headed *SPSS Statistics*, with the question *What would you like to do?* is presented.
3. Click on *Type in data* then *OK*.
4. The *Data View* window, which will receive the data, and *Variable View* window, which will receive information about the variables, should now be available, as in Figure 16.7, and you can switch between them using the tab at the bottom of the screen.

Figure 16.6 Starting an *SPSS Statistics* session

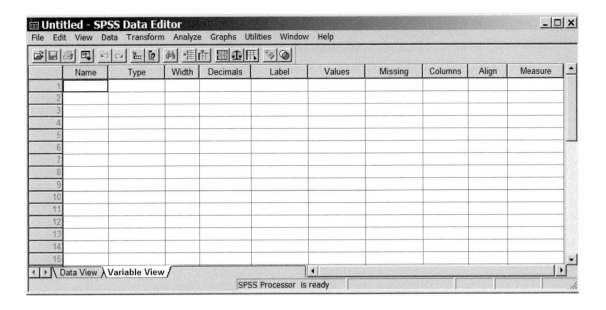

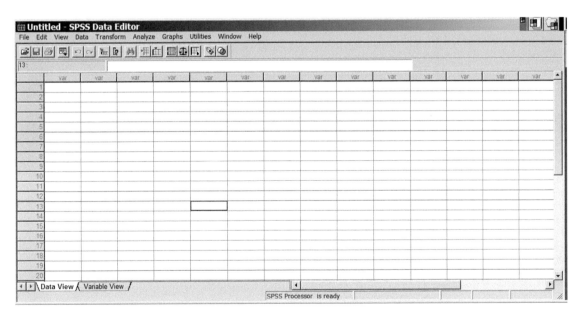

Figure 16.7   Blank Variable View and Data View windows

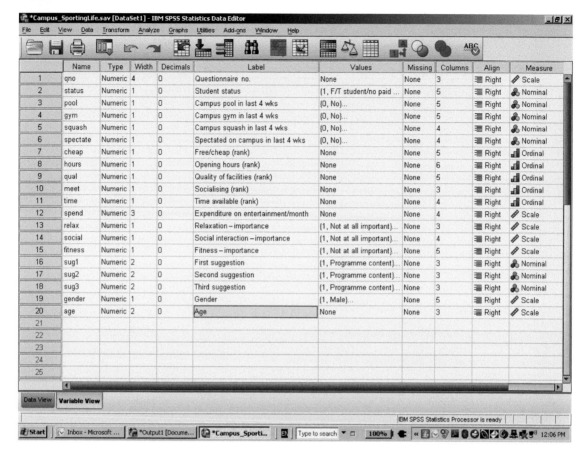

Figure 16.8   Variable View window with variable names and labels

Saving work

As with any computer work, the file should be saved to hard disk or a memory stick from time to time during the course of preparation and when completed, and a backup copy should also be made. The suffix for an SPSS data file is .sav, so the example file could be called CampusSportingLife.sav. Once the file is *saved* the title 'CampusSportingLife' appears at the top of the screen.

Entering data – Data View window

Switching to the *Data View* window reveals that the variable names entered via the *Variable View* window have automatically been put in place, and the system is ready to receive data. Data from the questionnaires can now be keyed in: one row on the screen per questionnaire, or *case*. Figure 16.9 shows the *Data View* window with data from the 15 cases/questionnaires shown in Figure 10.21. While a sample of 15 would generally be seen as too small for a typical leisure/ tourism survey, it is used here for demonstration purposes.

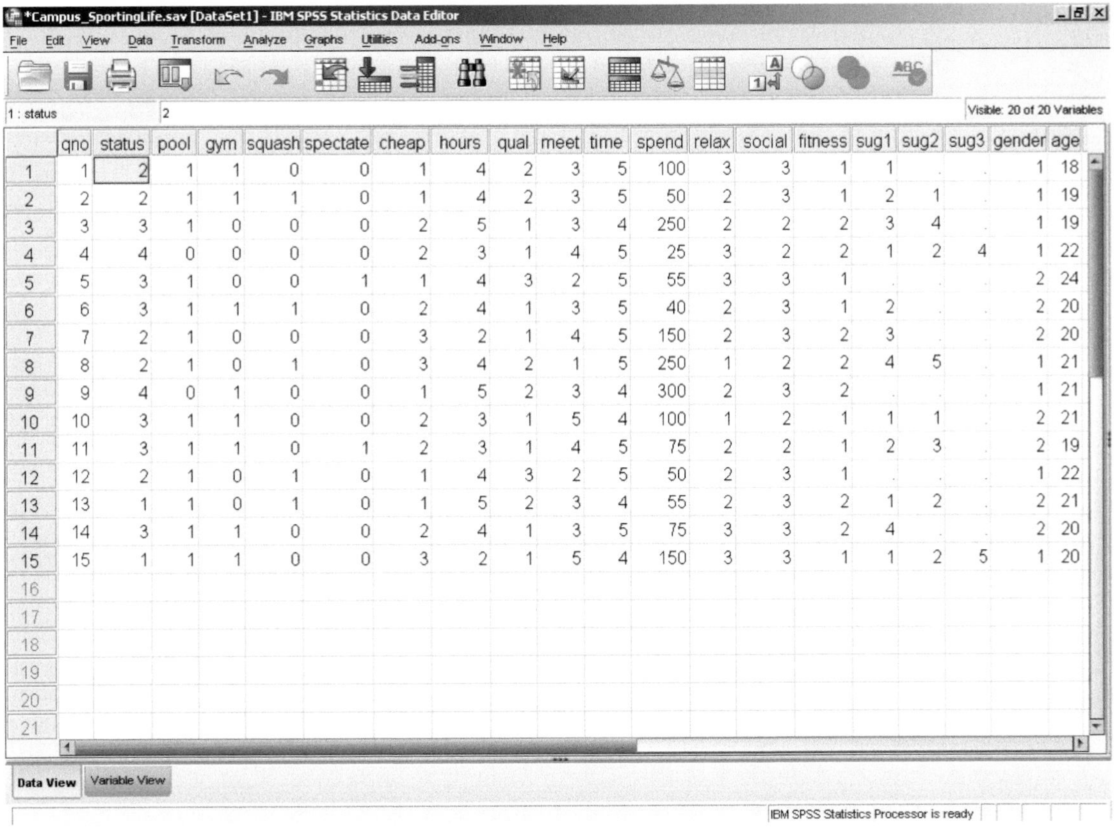

	qno	status	pool	gym	squash	spectate	cheap	hours	qual	meet	time	spend	relax	social	fitness	sug1	sug2	sug3	gender	age
1	1	2	1	1	0	0	1	4	2	3	5	100	3	3	1	1	.	.	1	18
2	2	2	1	1	1	0	1	4	2	3	5	50	2	3	1	2	1	.	1	19
3	3	3	1	0	0	0	2	5	1	3	4	250	2	2	2	3	4	.	1	19
4	4	4	0	0	0	0	2	3	1	4	5	25	3	2	2	1	2	4	1	22
5	5	3	1	0	0	1	1	4	3	2	5	55	3	3	1	.	.	.	2	24
6	6	3	1	1	1	0	2	4	1	3	5	40	2	3	1	2	.	.	2	20
7	7	2	1	0	0	0	3	2	1	4	5	150	2	3	2	3	.	.	2	20
8	8	2	1	0	1	0	3	4	2	1	5	250	1	2	2	4	5	.	1	21
9	9	4	0	1	0	0	1	5	2	3	4	300	2	3	2	.	.	.	1	21
10	10	3	1	1	0	0	2	3	1	5	4	100	1	2	1	1	1	.	2	21
11	11	3	1	1	0	1	2	3	1	4	5	75	2	2	1	2	3	.	2	19
12	12	2	1	0	1	0	1	4	3	2	5	50	2	3	1	.	.	.	1	22
13	13	1	1	0	1	0	1	5	2	3	4	55	2	3	2	1	2	.	2	21
14	14	3	1	1	0	0	2	4	1	3	5	75	3	3	2	4	.	.	2	20
15	15	1	1	1	0	0	3	2	1	5	4	150	3	3	1	1	2	5	1	20

Figure 16.9 Data View window with data from 15 questionnaires/cases

It can be seen that this is similar to the spreadsheet data file as shown in Figure 16.2. Indeed, if the data have already been typed into a spreadsheet and saved in a file, this file can be uploaded directly by SPSS. Go to File> Open> Data and, in the 'Open Data' dialog box, locate the file and change the 'Files of type' to the appropriate type – e.g. Excel.

Once the Data View and Variable View windows have been completed and the file saved, you are ready to begin analysis.

SPSS Statistics procedures

Starting an analysis session

The data file with which you are dealing may already be on screen (as in Figure 16.9) if you have just completed typing in data. If not, and in subsequent sessions, you will need to open the file, as shown in Figure 16.10.

1. Start SPSS *Statistics* on your computer using the appropriate screen icon or *Start* and *All Programs*.
2. The dialog box headed *SPSS Statistics*, with the question *What would you like to do?* is presented.
3. If this is the computer on which you set up your *SPSS* file it may be listed in the *Open an existing data source* window – e.g. CampusSportingLife.sav – and you can select by clicking on it. If your file is not displayed, select *More files...* and locate your file in the appropriate location.
4. The completed *Data View* and *Variable View* windows should now be available.

Figure 16.10 Starting an SPSS analysis session

Descriptives

The *Descriptives* procedure produces a range of statistics for specified variables. It is a useful initial procedure to run as a check on certain minimal information for all variables. The details for running the procedure and an example of the resultant output are shown in Figure 16.11. In the example used, five statistics are produced for each variable (except *qno*).

N – total count

The total count is 15 for all variables except the second and third suggestion since only 12 respondents offered a second suggestion and only 8 offered a third; for the others these variables were blank.

Minimum and maximum

For coded variables, this is a check that nothing has been miscoded outside the coding range, e.g. 1–3. For the non-coded numerical variables, the maximum and minimum provided may be a useful finding.

Mean

The mean or average is the sum of all the values for that variable divided by the number of responses (N) for that variable. It is one measure of the idea of the 'middle' – or 'central tendency' – of the values for a variable for this sample; other *measures of central tendency* are discussed under the *Frequencies* procedure below.

The mean is generally a useful statistic for:

- numerical variables – in this case, mean Expenditure is £115 and the mean *age* of the sample members is 20.47 years;

- ordinal variables – for example the average rank for the *cheap* variable is 1.8.

Procedure

1. Select *Analyze* then *Descriptive Statistics* then *Descriptives*.
2. Select all variables except *qno* and transfer them to the *Variable(s)* box
3. Select *Options* and ensure that the following are ticked: *Mean, St. Deviation, Minimum, Maximum* then click on *Continue*.
4. Click on *OK* to produce the following output.

Output

Descriptive Statistics

	N	Minimum	Maximum	Mean	Std. Deviation
Student status	15	1	4	2.53	.915
Campus pool last 4 wks	15	0	1	.87	.352
Campus gym last 4 wks	15	0	1	.53	.516
Campus squash last 4 wks	15	0	1	.33	.488
Spectator on campus last 4 wks	15	0	1	.13	.352
Free/cheap (rank)	15	1	3	1.80	.775
Daytime events (rank)	15	2	5	3.73	.961
Not available elsewhere (rank)	15	1	3	1.60	.737
Socialising (rank)	15	1	5	3.20	1.082
Quality of presentation (rank)	15	4	5	4.67	.488
Expenditure on sport etc./month	15	25	300	115.00	87.076
Relaxation opportunities – importance	15	1	3	2.20	.676
Social interaction – importance	15	2	3	2.67	.488
Fitness – importance	15	1	2	1.47	.516
First suggestion	12	1	4	2.08	1.165
Second suggestion	8	1	5	2.50	1.414
Third suggestion	2	4	5	4.50	.707
Gender	15	1	2	1.47	.516
Age	15	18	24	20.47	1.506

Figure 16.11 Descriptives procedure and output

In general, this is not a useful statistic for nominal/coded variables, but there are exceptions:

- Likert scales – Relaxation, Social interaction, Fitness – the score can be seen as an index of importance **(see Chapter 10)**, so the mean is an indicator of the average level of importance for the sample: thus in this example, Social interaction (mean 2.67) is the most important and Fitness (Mean 1.47) is the least important.

- variables Campus pool to Spectator: since non-users score zero, the mean is effectively the number of users divided by the total, which is the proportion of users: thus, for example, the proportion of users of the cafe/bar is 0.87 or 87%.

Standard deviation

The standard deviation is a measure of the spread of values around the mean. In this example, among the variables which respondents were asked to rank, for the Quality of presentation, the standard deviation is 0.488, while that for Socialising is 1.082: this makes sense when we see from the maximum/minimum that for the former all responses were either 4 or 5, whereas for the latter they ranged from 1 to 5. **The standard deviation is discussed further in Chapter 17.**

Frequencies

The *Frequencies* procedure is the simplest form of descriptive analysis: it merely produces counts and percentages for individual variables – for example the numbers and percentages of respondents registered in each student status group. The procedure can be run for one variable at a time or for a number of variables.

Frequencies for one variable

The steps to obtain a table for the variable *status* are set out in Figure 16.12, together with the resultant output. The *Output* window presents two tables. The first, *Statistics*, indicates the number of 'valid cases' on which the analysis is based – in this case 15. The second table, headed *Student status*, shows:

- *Frequency* – count of the numbers of students in each status group;
- *Percent* converts frequency numbers into percentages;
- *Valid Percent* is explained above under 'missing'; and
- *Cumulative Percent* adds percentages cumulatively – which may be useful for a variable like *spend* or *age*, but is not particularly useful for the variable *status*.

Frequencies for a number of variables

Frequency tables for all the variables can be obtained, by transferring all the variables (except *qno*) into the *Variable(s)* box in Step 2 in Figure 16.12. Running frequency tables for all variables is a common early instruction in survey analysis: it is a good way of obtaining an overview of the results, and checking that all is well with the data. The results of this exercise for the example questionnaire are in Appendix 16.1.

It should be noted that the list of variables in the *Frequencies* dialog box can appear in the form of variable *names* or the longer variable *labels* and can be arranged in the order they appear in the Variable View window or alphabetically. To change these settings, go to *Edit> Options> General> Variable Lists*. Changes to the format of output tables can also be made here. The changes

Procedure

1. Select *Analyze* from the menu bar at the top of the screen, then *Descriptive Statistics*, then *Frequencies*. This opens the *Frequencies* dialog box.
2. In the *Frequencies* dialog box:
   a. select the variable *status* by highlighting it. Then click on the right arrow to transfer it to the *Variable(s)* box for analysis.
   b. make sure that *Display frequency tables* is ticked.
   c. select *OK* and the results will appear in a new *Output* window as shown below.

Output

Frequencies

Student status

N	Valid	15
	Missing	0

Student status

		Frequency	Percent	Valid Percent	Cumulative Percent
Valid	F/T student/no paid work	2	13.3	13.3	13.3
	F/T student/paid work	5	33.3	33.3	46.7
	P/T student - F/T job	6	40.0	40.0	86.7
	P/T student/Other	2	13.3	13.3	100.0
	Total	15	100.0	100.0	

Figure 16.12   Frequencies for one variable: procedure and output

will not be implemented until the file has been saved and closed and then re-started.

Checking for errors

After obtaining the *Descriptives* and/or *Frequencies* printout for all variables, check through the results to see if there are any errors. This could be, for example, in the form of an invalid code or an unexpected missing value. The error must be traced in the data file and corrected, perhaps by reference back to the original questionnaire. The data must then be corrected on the data window and the *Frequencies* table for that variable run again. *The corrected, 'clean' data file should then be saved to disk.*

Multiple response

Questions 2 and 6 in the example questionnaire are *multiple response* questions. They are single questions with a number of possible responses and must be analysed using a number of variables. 'Multiple response' analysis procedures are available in SPSS to handle their particular characteristics. There are two types of multiple response question:

● *Multiple response – dichotomous:* question 2 on campus sport activity is a dichotomous variable, because each answer category is essentially a yes/no (two values) variable; any one respondent could tick one, two, three or all four boxes, so each is a separate variable.

● *Multiple response – categories:* question 6 on suggestions for improvements has three variables, sug1, sug2, sug3, each coded with the same five category values, as discussed earlier.

It can be seen from Appendix 16.1 that the normal *Frequencies* procedure produces output for these questions in a rather inconvenient format – four tables for question 2 and three tables for question 6. The *Multiple Response* procedure combines multiple responses into a single table for each question. The procedure is operated as shown in Figure 16.13, together with the results – one table each for questions 2 and 6. It should be noted that percentages are given related to the number of respondents and to the number of responses – which of these to use depends on the aims of the research.

Recode

As the name implies, *Recode* is a procedure which can be used to change the codes or values of variables. The procedure can be applied to scale, ordinal or nominal variables. This might be done for a number of reasons:

● presentational purposes, when there are a large number of categories and several contain small numbers of responses;

● theoretical purposes, when different parts of the analysis call for different groupings of response categories;

● for comparative reasons, when comparisons with previous research require different groupings;

● for statistical reasons **(see Chapter 17.**

Recode with scale and ordinal variables

Scale and ordinal variables are not pre-coded – the actual value given by respondents is recorded in the data file. In the case of scale variables in particular, this means that the *Frequencies* procedure outlined above produces a table with one line for every value in the data set – as can be seen in Appendix 16.1

Procedure

1. Select *Analyze*, then *Multiple Response* then *Define Variable Sets*

Multiple response – dichotomous	**Multiple response – categories**
2. Transfer *pool, gym, squash* and *spectate* into the *Variables in Set* box	2. Put *sug1, sug2, sug3* into the *Variables in Set* box
3. Under the *Variables are coded as...* box, select *Dichotomies*	3. Under *Variables are coded as...*, select *Categories*
4. Enter *1* in the *Counted value* box	4. Enter *Range 1* through *5*
5. Give the 'set' a *Name* – e.g. *Sports*	5. Add *Name*, e.g. *sugs*
6. Add a *Label* – e.g. *Sport facilities used*	6. Add *Label*, e.g. *Suggestions for improvement*
7. Select *Add*	7. Select *Add*
8. A new variable, *$sports*, is listed automatically	8. A new variable *$sugs* is listed automatically
9. Select *Close*	9. Select *Close*

To produce a table:
1. Select *Analyze*
2. Select *Multiple Response*
3. Select *Frequencies* and use the new variables

Output

Multiple Response

Group: $Sports – Sport facilities used (Value tabulated = 1)

Dichotomy label	Name	Count	Pct of Responses	Pct of Cases
Campus pool in last 4 wks	pool	13	46.4	92.9
Campus gym in last 4 wks	gym	8	28.6	57.1
Campus squash in last 4 wks	squash	5	17.9	35.7
Spectate on campus in last 4 wks	spectate	2	7.1	14.3
Total responses		28	100.0	200.0

1 missing cases; 14 valid cases

Group: $Sug – Suggestions for improvement

Category label	Code	Count	Pct of Responses	Pct of Cases
Programme content	1	7	31.8	58.3
Timing	2	6	27.3	50.0
Facilities	3	3	13.6	25.0
Costs	4	4	18.2	33.3
Organisation	5	2	9.1	16.7
Total responses	22	100.0	183.3	

3 missing cases; 12 valid cases

Figure 16.13 Multiple Response procedure and output

for variables *spend* and *age*. With large samples this can produce impractically large tables with possibly hundreds of lines, which would be unreadable and unmanageable, particularly for crosstabulation (discussed below). A *Recoded*, grouped, version of such variables can be produced using the method demonstrated in the first part of Figure 16.14.

Ordinal variables, such as those in question 3, can be recoded – for example ranks first and second could be grouped together, and third and fourth could be grouped together, and so on. Similarly, Likert-type variables, as in question 5, can be recoded – for example grouping 'very important' and 'important' together.

It might be asked: if the variable is to be grouped anyway, why not present groupings in the questionnaire, where respondents can tick a box? This is often done, but the advantage of not having the variable pre-coded is that it is possible to be flexible about what groupings are required and it is also possible to use such procedures as *Means* and *Regression*, which is not generally possible with pre-coded or nominal variables.

Recode with nominal/pre-coded variables

It is also possible to change the groupings of nominal or pre-coded variables using *Recode*. For instance, analysis could be conducted comparing all full-time students and all part-time students – that is, two groups rather than four. This is illustrated in the second part of Figure 16.14.

Mean, median and mode – measures of central tendency

We have already considered the idea of measures of central tendency and the mean in the discussion of *Descriptives* above. As noted there, a *mean* is the same as an *average* and is only appropriate for scale or ordinal data, not for nominal variables with codes which represent qualitative categories, except for the exceptions discussed above.

Here we also consider two other measures of central tendency:

- the *median*, which is the value for which there are as many members of the sample above as there are below; and

- the *mode*, which is the value which contains the largest number of sample members.

Two procedures are available in SPSS for producing means, as shown in Figure 16.15.

- Method 1 uses a feature of the *Frequencies* procedure:
- Example 1a shows that

  – mean expenditure on sport etc. among the sample is £115

Part 1. For a scale or ordinal variable

Example: recode the variable *spend* as follows:

Proposed groupings	New code	Value labels
0–50	1	£0–50
51–100	2	£51–100
101–200	3	£101–200
201+	4	£201 and over

Procedure

1. From the top of the screen, select *Transform*, then *Recode into Different Variables*.
2. Select the variable to be recoded, *spend*, and transfer to the *Numeric variable --> Output variable* box
3. In the *Output Variable* box, add a *Name* (e.g. *spendr*) and *Label* (e.g. *Spend on sport etc. – recoded*).
4. Select *Old and New Values*.
5. In the *Old Value* box select *Range*. In the first box enter *1* and in the second box, enter *50*.
6. In the *Value* box, enter *1*, then click on *Add*. The *Old–New* box should now contain '1 thru 50 --> 1'.
7. Repeat steps 5 and 6 for: *51* through *100* – *Value 2*; and 101 through 200 – *Value 3*
8. Select *Range through Highest*: enter *201*. In the *Value* box enter *4*, then click on *Add*.
   The *Old–New* box should now contain: 1 thru 50-->1, 51 thru 100 --> 2, 101 thru 200 --> 3, 201 thru Highest --> 4.
9. Select *Continue*
10. Select *Change*, then *OK*. The new variable now appears on the Data View and Variable View screens.
11. Add *Value Labels*, as above, via the *Variable View* window, as for any variable.
12. *Save* the data file with the new variable, if you will want to use it again.
13. Produce a *Frequencies* table for the recoded variable *spendr* in the usual way, to produce the output below.

Output: Spend recoded

	Frequency	Percent	Valid Percent	Cumulative Percent
£ 0–50	4	26.7	26.7	26.7
£ 51–100	6	40.0	40.0	66.7
£ 101–200	2	13.3	13.3	80.0
£ 201+	3	20.0	20.0	100.0
Total	15	100.0	100.0	

Part 2. For a string (pre-coded) variable

Example: recode the variable *status* as follows:

Current coding	New code	Value labels
1. F/T student – no work	1	Full-time student
2. F/T student – working		
3. P/T student – F/T job	2	Part-time student
4. P/T student – other		

Procedure

1–4. Repeat steps 1–3 above, using variable *status*, recoded variable name *statusr* and label *Status – recoded*.
5. In the *Old Value* box select *Range*. In the first box enter *1* and in the second box, enter *2*.
6. In the *Value* box, enter *1*, then click on *Add*. The *Old–New* box should now contain '1 thru 2--> 1.
7. Repeat steps 5 and 6 for: *3* through *4* – *Value 2*. The *Old–New* box also now contains '3 thru 4--> 2.
8. Select *Continue*
9. Select *Change*, then *OK*. The new variable now appears on the Data View and Variable View screens.
10. Add *Value Labels*, as above, via the *Variable View* window, as for any variable.
11. *Save* the data file with the new variable, if you will want to use it again.
12. Produce a *Frequencies* table for the recoded variable *statusr* in the usual way, to produce the output below.

Output: Status recoded

	Frequency	Percent	Valid Percent	Cumulative Percent
Full-time student	7	46.7	46.7	46.7
Part-time student	8	53.3	53.3	100.0
Total	15	100.0	100.0	

Figure 16.14 Recode procedure and output

Method 1. Using *Frequencies* procedure

a. Scale variable

1. Select *Analyze*, then *Descriptive Statistics* then *Frequencies*.
2. Select *spend* and transfer to the *Variable(s)* box.
3. Select *Statistics* and click on *Mean*, *Median* and *Mode*.
4. Select *Continue*.
5. Select *OK* to run the *Frequencies* in the normal way.

Output (Frequency table not reproduced)

Statistics: Expenditure on sport etc./month

N Valid	15
Missing	0
Mean	115.00
Median	75.00
Mode	50*

* Multiple modes exist. The smallest value is shown

b. Attitude statements/Likert scales

Using the procedure as in *a.*, above, to produce means for the three variables: *relax*, *social* and *fitness*, results in output is as follows.

Output (Frequency table not reproduced)

	Relaxation opportunities – importance	Social interaction – importance	Fitness – importance
N Valid	15	15	15
Missing	0	0	0
Mean	2.20	2.67	1.47
Median	2.0	3.0	1.0
Mode	2	3	1

Method 2. Using *Means* procedure

a. Scale variable

1. Select *Analyze*, then *Compare Means*, then *Means*.
2. Select *status* and put it into the *Independent list*** box.
3. Select *spend* and put it into the *Dependent list*** box.
4. Select *OK*. Means and standard deviations for each course group are produced, as below, showing different values for different groups.

Output – Report

Expenditure on sport etc./week

Student status	Mean	N	Std. Deviation**
F/T student/no paid work	102.50	2	67.175
F/T student/paid work	120.00	5	83.666
P/T student – F/T job	99.17	6	76.643
P/T student/Other	162.50	2	194.454
Total	115.00	15	87.076

Figure 16.15   Means procedures and output

(** The idea of dependent and independent variable and standard deviations are discussed in Ch. 11.)

- the median value is £75, which is lower than the mean because there are more people in the lower expenditure categories than in the higher categories
- the mode is £50, £75, £100, £200 and £250, since all these values have two responses.

- Example 1b demonstrates the use of the procedure for producing mean scores for Likert-type scales – the median does not have a lot of meaning, but the mode, which is the most popular value for each variable, may be meaningful and useful in some situations.

- Method 2 uses the *Means* procedure which produces means for sub-groups as well as for the whole sample. For example, in Figure 16.12, mean expenditures on entertainment are shown for students of different statuses. Note that this moves beyond description into the area of possible *explanation*, since it reveals that a student's full-time/part-time and employment status may lead to different levels of expenditure.

Presenting the results: statistical summary

The layout of the frequency tables produced by the software contains more detail than is necessary for most reports. It is recommended that a *Statistical Summary* be prepared for inclusion in any report, rather than include a copy of the computer printout. The summary must be prepared with a word-processor, either typing it out afresh or editing the saved *SPSS Output* file. For example, the output from the *Frequencies, Recodes, Multiple response* and *Means* analysis covered so far could be summarised as in Figure 16.16.

The following should be noted about the summary:

- The results from *Multiple response* variables are presented in single tables.

- Recoded versions of *spend* and *age* are included.

- The mean *spend* and *age* and the mean scores for the attitude/Likert-type variables come from the *Means* procedure discussed above.

- It is generally not necessary to include raw frequency counts as well as percentages in reports, since the sample size is indicated: readers of the summary can work out the raw numbers for themselves if required.

Crosstabulation

Introduction

After calculation of frequencies and means, the most commonly used procedure used in survey analysis is probably crosstabulation. This relates two or more variables to produce tables of the sort commonly encountered in social research. In analysing the relationships between variables, crosstabulation marks the move from purely descriptive to explanatory analysis. The *SPSS Crosstabs* procedure and output are demonstrated in Part 1 of Figure 16.17.

Sample size	15

Student status	%
F/T student/no paid work	13.3
F/T student/paid work	33.3
P/T student – F/T job	40.0
P/T student/Other	13.3
Total	100.0

Campus sport activity in the last 4 weeks	%
Pool	86.7
Gym	53.3
Squash	33.3
Spectating	13.3

Importance of factors in campus services	Average rank
Cheap	1.8
Opening hours	3.7
Quality of facilities	1.6
Opportunities for socialising	3.2
Time available	4.7

Expenditure on entertainment/month	%
£0–50	26.7
£51–100	40.0
£101–200	13.3
Over £200	20.0
Average expenditure/week	£115.00

Suggestions for improvements	% of cases
Comments on programme content	58.3
Comments on timing	50.0
Comments on facilities	25.0
Comments on costs	33.3
Comments on organisation	16.7

Gender	%
Male	53.3
Female	46.3
Age	%
18–19	26.7
20–21	53.4
22 and over	20.0

Importance of factors in campus services

	Very important	Important	Not Important	Mean score*
	%	%	%	%
Relaxation	33.3	53.3	13.3	2.2
Social interaction	66.7	33.3	0.0	2.7
Fitness	0.0	46.7	53.8	1.5

(* 3 = very important 2 = important 1= not important)

Figure 16.16   Campus Sporting Life Survey 2011: statistical summary

Rows and columns

Having been specified as the *row* variable in Figure 16.17 Part 1, *status* appears down the side of the table, while the *column* variable, *gym*, appears across the top. Specifying the two variables the other way round would produce a table with *status* across the top and *gym* down the side.

Percentages

In most cases, percentages are required in tables rather than just the raw figures. The Part 1 procedure includes percentages only for the row and column totals (which are the same as the percentages in the *Frequencies* tables for the individual variables). The cells in the body of the table contain only counts of the raw data, not percentages. To produce percentages in the body of the table it is necessary to specify the 'cell contents'. There are four relevant options for individual cell contents:

- counts;

- row percentages – where percentages add to 100 going across a row;

- column percentages – where percentages add to 100 going down the column;

- total percentages – where all cell percentages add to 100.

The choice of which percentages to use depends on the context and the purpose of the analysis – it generally becomes apparent in the course of discussing the contents of a table; often 'trial and error' is involved in testing out the use of particular percentages in particular situations. The procedures for producing percentages in *Crosstabs* are as shown in Part 2 of Figure 16.17.

Three-way crosstabulations

Often three-way crosstabulations are required. For example, the above table could be further subdivided by gender. This is demonstrated in Part 3 of Figure 16.17. Further subdivision is possible, although often sample size places limits on how far this can go.

Weighting

The weighting of data to correct for biased samples is discussed in Chapter 13, where the procedure for calculating a weighting factor is discussed. The simplest way of introducing a weighting factor to the SPSS process is to include the weights as an additional variable. For example, the 'weighting' variable might be called *wt* and the weights typed into the data file like any other item of data. To weight data, select *Data* and use the *Weight Cases* feature, specifying the appropriate variable (e.g. *wt*) as weighting variable. To save having to type in the weights for every respondent, SPSS provides a logical procedure. For example, if all master's course students are to be given a weight of 1.3, it is possible to indicate this in the *Weight cases* procedure. It is not intended to explain

Part 1 Crosstabs – Counts only

Procedure

1. Select *Analyze*, then *Descriptive Statistics*, then *Crosstabs*.
2. Transfer *gym* to the *Columns* box.
3. Transfer *status* to the *Rows* box.
4. Select *OK*. Output is as below.

Output

Student status * Campus gym in last 4 wks Crosstabulation

		Campus gym in last 4 wks		Total
		No	Yes	
Student status	F/T student/no paid work	1	1	2
	F/T student/paid work	3	2	5
	P/T student – F/T job	2	4	6
	P/T student/Other	1	1	2
Total		7	8	15

Part 2 Crosstabs – with percentages

Procedure

1–3. Repeat steps 1–3 above.
4.   In the *Crosstabs* dialog box select *Cells*. The *Crosstabs: Cell Display* dialog box is presented.
5.   In the *Counts* box click on the tick in the *Observed* box to make it disappear (NB. omit this step if you wish to retain counts as well as percentages).
6.   In the *Percentages*, select *Row*.
7.   Select *Continue*, then *OK*. Output appears as follows.

Output

Student status * Campus gym in last 4 wks Crosstabulation

		Campus gym in last 4 wks		Total
		No	Yes	
Student status	F/T student/no paid work	50.0%	50.0%	100.0%
	F/T student/paid work	60.0%	40.0%	100.0%
	P/T student – F/T job	33.3%	66.7%	100.0%
	P/T student/Other	50.0%	50.0%	100.0%
Total		46.7%	53.3%	100.0%

Part 3 Three-way crosstabulation

Procedure

1. Repeat steps 1–3 in Part 1 above.
4. In the *Crosstabs* dialog box: transfer *gender* into the *Layer* box.
5. Select *OK* to produce output as follows.

Output

Student status * Campus gym in last 4 wks* Gender Crosstabulation

Gender			Campus gym in last 4 wks		Total
			No	Yes	
Male	Student status	F/T student/no paid work	1	1	2
		P/T student – F/T job	2	3	5
		P/T student/Other	0	1	1
	Total		3	5	8
Female	Student status	F/T student/paid work	3	2	5
		P/T student – F/T job	0	1	1
		P/T student/Other	1	0	1
	Total		4	3	7

Figure 16.17   Crosstabs procedures and output

the detail of this procedure here – the reader is referred to the Help facility in the *Weight Cases* dialog box.

Graphics

Graphical presentation of data is an aid to communication in most situations: for example, most people can see trends and patterns in data more easily in graphic form. Computer packages generally offer the following graphic formats for data presentation:

- bar graph;
- stacked bar graph;
- pie chart;
- line graph.

Computers can produce all four formats from any one set of data. But all formats are not equally appropriate for all data types: the appropriate type of graphic depends on the type of data or level of measurement involved. The three data types therefore lend themselves to different graphical treatment. The relationships between these types of data and permitted graphical types are summarised in Figure 16.18.

- The *bar graph* or *histogram* deals with *categories* for each bar, so any scale variable must first be divided into groups – using the *Recode* procedure. The 'stacked' bar graph includes information on two variables – the graphical equivalent of the crosstabulation.

- The *pie chart* is just that: it divides something into sections like a pie. The segments making up the pie chart must therefore add up to some sort of meaningful total – often the total sample or 100 per cent.

	Data type		
	Nominal	**Ordinal**	**Scale**
Data characteristics	Qualitative categories	Ranks	Numerical
Example questions in Fig. 10.21	1, 2, 6	3, 5	4
Mean/average possible	No	Yes	Yes
Types of graphic			
Bar graph	Yes	Yes	Yes*
Pie chart	Yes	Yes	Yes*
Line graph	No	No	Yes
Scattergram	No	No	Yes

Figure 16.18 Data types and graphics

* Grouped

- The *line graph* is the most constrained and is used more generally in more quantified research. Strictly speaking, it should only be used with *scale* variables.
  - A line graph with a single scale variable indicates the distribution of a variable although, for the type of data in the example survey, this is probably best done by means of a bar chart.
  - A line graph can be used to show the relationship between two *scale* variables – with one variable on each axis. However, a fitted *regression* line **(see Chapter 17)** is generally more meaningful than a line traced through all observation points, as would happen with a line graph.
- A *scattergram* is based on two *scale* variables, but involves just plots of the observation points, rather than drawing a line through them. This may be overcome by use of a 'best fit' line based on *regression* **(see Chapter 17)**.

Graphics are easily produced in SPSS using an optional feature of the *Frequencies* command, but this is not very flexible. A better option is the *Graphs* facility. Examples of graphics output from this facility are shown in Figure 16.19. It is not proposed to consider graphics procedures in detail here; details can be found in the SPSS Graphs Help facility.

a. Bar chart
1. Select *Graphs* at the top of the screen, then *Legacy Dialogs*.
2. Select *Bar* and then *Simple* then *Define* to produce the dialog box: *Define Simple Bar: Summaries for Groups of Cases*.
3. Transfer *status* to the *Category Axis* box.
4. Select *N of cases* or *% of cases*. In example here, *% of cases* has been selected.
5. Select *OK* to produce the bar chart.

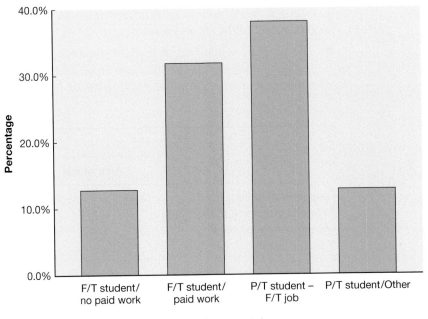

Figure 16.19   Graphics procedures and output

b. Stacked bar chart

1. Select *Graphs* at the top of the screen, then *Legacy Dialogs*.
2. Select *Bar* and then *Stacked* then *Define* to produce the dialog box: *Define Stack Bar: Summaries for Groups of Cases*.
3. Transfer *status* to the *Category axis* box and *gender* to the *Define Stacks by* box.
4. Select *N of cases* or *% of cases*. In the example here, *N of cases* has been selected.
5. Select *OK* to produce the stacked bar chart.

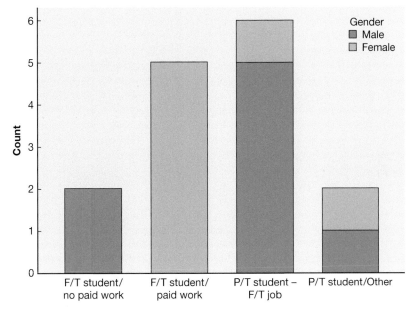

c. Pie chart

1. Select *Graphs* at the top of the screen, then *Legacy Dialogs*.
2. Select *Pie* and then *Summary for Groups of Cases* then *Define* to produce the dialog box: *Define Pie: Summaries for Groups of Cases*.
3. Transfer *status* to the *Define slices by* box.
4. Select *N of cases* or *% of cases*. In the example here, *N of cases* has been selected.
5. Select *OK* to produce the pie chart.

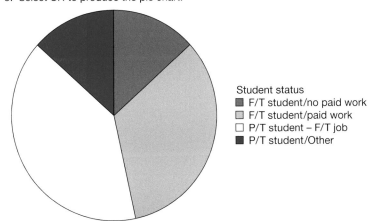

Figure 16.19 (*continued*)

d. Line graph

1. Select *Graphs* at the top of the screen, then *Legacy Dialogs*.
2. Select *Line* and then *Simple* then *Define* to produce the dialog box: *Define Simple Line: Summaries for Groups of Cases*.
3. Transfer *age* to the *Category axis* box.
4. Select *N of cases* or *% of cases*. In the example here, *N of cases* has been selected.
5. Select *OK* to produce the graphic d.

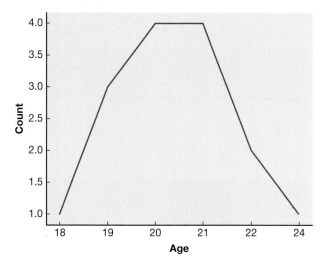

e. Scattergram

1. Select *Graphs* at the top of the screen, then *Legacy Dialogs*.
2. Select *Scatter/Dot* and then *Simple Scatter,* then *Define* to produce the dialog box: *Simple Scatterplot*.
3. Transfer *spend* to the *Y-axis* box and *age* to the *X-axis* box.
4. Select *OK* to produce graphic e.

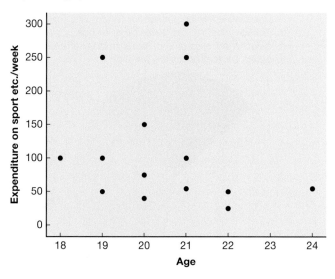

Figure 16.19 (*continued*)

The analysis process

The above is only a brief introduction to the mechanics of survey data analysis. While SPSS is capable of much more sophisticated analyses, mastery of the procedures presented here can provide a sound basis for a viable programme of analysis.

Summary

Following a discussion of the relationship between types of research and types of data analysis and an introduction to spreadsheet analysis of survey data, this chapter provides an introduction to the use of the *SPSS* software package for analysis of data from a questionnaire survey. Based on the introduction to coding in Chapter 10, the process of introducing survey data and information on variables into the *SPSS* package is demonstrated. This includes a discussion of levels of measurement and three corresponding variable types: nominal, ordinal and scale. The chapter covers six *SPSS* analysis procedures, as follows.

- *Frequencies* provides counts and percentages for individual and multiple variables.

- *Multiple response* creates single tables for the two or more variables arising from questions with multiple responses.

- *Recode* is used to create groups for scale variables and regroup pre-coded variables.

- *Means* calculates the means, or averages, of variables and compares means for sub-samples.

- *Crosstabs* creates crosstabulations or frequency tables showing the relationships between two or more variables.

- *Weight* is used to weight data according to some criterion variable **(see Chapter 10)**.

- *Graphs* produces graphical representations of data in various forms, including bar charts, pie charts, line graphs and scattergrams.

Test questions

1. Explain the difference between nominal, ordinal and scale variables and give examples.

2. What is the advantage of using an uncoded format for a scale variable in a questionnaire, rather than coding it into groups?

3. Outline the characteristics of the two types of multiple response question.

4. Why might an analyst wish to recode variables?

5. What are the two procedures for obtaining means in SPSS?

Exercises

1. The major exercise for this chapter is to replicate the analyses presented in the chapter. This can be done by typing the data and variable definition data in Figures 16.8 and 16.9 or downloading it from the book's website, and carrying out the instructions for the various procedures in the chapter.

2. Repeat each of the procedures in exercise 1 using at least one different variable in each procedure.

3. Conduct a survey of students using the questionnaire in Figure 10.20; and analyse the data using SPSS, following the analysis procedures outlined in this chapter.

Resources

Regarding SPSS:

- Access and guidance: It is envisaged that most readers will have access to a teacher/tutor to assist as problems arise. The SPSS package itself includes a tutorial for beginners and there are numerous books available on the use of SPSS, as indicated below. In higher education institutions, SPSS, as with other computer packages, is generally made available in computer laboratories on licence. Further training is available in SPSS, and other survey packages, through universities, commercial computer training organisations and the SPSS company itself in major centres around the world.

- The SPSS website is at: http://www-01.ibm.com/software/uk/analytics/spss.

- A number of guides to the use of SPSS exist, for example: Carver and Nash (2005), Coakes and Steed (2010), George and Mallery (2010), Pallant (2010).

  Regarding questionnaire survey analysis generally:

- It is difficult to locate published research reports which give full details of questionnaire surveys and their analysis. While many journal articles are based on survey research, they typically do not provide a copy of the questionnaire and provide only a brief summary of the analysis process – often only part of the analysis arising from the data.

- Few commercially published books are based primarily on questionnaire survey data and, even when they are, full details are not always provided.

- Government-sponsored survey reports, by the government statistical agency or other agencies, often contain these details – although inevitably they are generally either purely descriptive or related in a fairly straightforward manner to policy issues. Such reports are inconsistently available in libraries, but are often available on the Internet **(as indicated in the Resources section of Chapter 7)**.

- For an international review of survey evidence on sport participation surveys, see: Cushman *et al.* (2005) and Nicholson *et al.* (2010).

References

Carver, R. H. and Nash, J. G. (2005) *Doing Data Analysis with SPSS Version 12.0*. Belmont, CA: Thomson/Brooks/Cole.

Carver, R. H. and Nash, J. G. (2011) *Doing Data Analysis with SPSS Version 18.0*. Pacific Grove, CA: Duxbury Press.

Coakes, S. J. and Steed, L. G. (1999) SPSS *Analysis Without Anguish: (Version 11.0 for Windows)*. Brisbane: John Wiley & Sons.

Cushman, G., Veal, A. J. and Zuzanek, J. (eds) (2005) *Free Time and Leisure Participation: International Perspectives*, Wallingford, UK: CABI.

George, D. and Mallery, P. (2010) *SPSS for Windows Step by Step: A Simple Guide and Reference, 18.0 Update*. Boston, MA: Prentice Hall.

Nicholson, M., Hoye, R. and Houlihan, B. (eds) (2010) *Participation in Sport: International Policy Perspectives*. London: Routledge.

Pallant, J. F. (2010) *SPSS Survival Manual: A Step by Step Guide to Data Analysis Using SPSS, Fourth edn*. Sydney: Allen & Unwin.

Appendix 16.1 Frequencies output file

Statistics (only scale and ordinal variables included here)

	Cheap	Hours	Qual	Meet	Time	Spend	Relax	Social	Fitness
N Valid	15	15	15	15	15	15	15	15	15
Missing	0	0	0	0	0	0	0	0	0
Mean	1.8	3.73	1.6	3.2	4.67	115	2.2	1.67	1.47

Student status

		Frequency	Percent	Valid Percent	Cumulative Percent
Valid	F/T student/no paid work	2	13.3	13.3	13.3
	F/T student/paid work	5	33.3	33.3	46.7
	P/T student – F/T job	6	40.0	40.0	86.7
	P/T student/Other	2	13.3	13.3	100.0
	Total	15	100.0	100.0	

Campus pool in last 4 wks

		Frequency	Percent	Valid Percent	Cumulative Percent
Valid	No	2	13.3	13.3	13.3
	Yes	13	86.7	86.7	100.0
	Total	15	100.0	100.0	

Campus gym in last 4 wks

		Frequency	Percent	Valid Percent	Cumulative Percent
Valid	No	7	46.7	46.7	46.7
	Yes	8	53.3	53.3	100.0
	Total	15	100.0	100.0	

Campus squash facilities in last 4 wks

		Frequency	Percent	Valid Percent	Cumulative Percent
Valid	No	10	66.7	66.7	66.7
	Yes	5	33.3	33.3	100.0
	Total	15	100.0	100.0	

Spectated sport on campus in last 4 wks

		Frequency	Percent	Valid Percent	Cumulative Percent
Valid	No	13	86.7	86.7	86.7
	Yes	2	13.3	13.3	100.0
	Total	15	100.0	100.0	

Free/cheap (rank)

		Frequency	Percent	Valid Percent	Cumulative Percent
Valid	1	6	40.0	40.0	40.0
	2	6	40.0	40.0	80
	3	3	20.0	20.0	100.0
	Total	15	100.0	100.0	

Opening hours (rank)

		Frequency	Percent	Valid Percent	Cumulative Percent
Valid	2	2	13.3	13.3	13.3
	3	3	20.0	20.0	33.3
	4	7	46.7	46.7	80.0
	5	3	20.0	20.0	100.0
	Total	15	100.0	100.0	

Quality of facilities (rank)

		Frequency	Percent	Valid Percent	Cumulative Percent
Valid	1	8	53.3	53.3	53.3
	2	5	33.3	33.3	86.7
	3	2	13.3	13.3	100.0
	Total	15	100.0	100.0	

Socialising (rank)

		Frequency	Percent	Valid Percent	Cumulative Percent
Valid	1	1	6.7	6.7	6.7
	2	2	13.3	13.3	20.0
	3	7	46.7	46.7	66.7
	4	3	20.0	20.0	86.7
	5	2	13.3	13.3	100.0
	Total	15	100.0	100.0	

Time available (rank)

		Frequency	Percent	Valid Percent	Cumulative Percent
Valid	4	5	33.3	33.3	33.3
	5	10	66.7	66.7	100.0
	Total	15	100.0	100.0	

Expenditure on sport etc./week

		Frequency	Percent	Valid Percent	Cumulative Percent
Valid	25	1	6.7	6.7	6.7
	40	1	6.7	6.7	13.3
	50	2	13.3	13.3	26.7
	55	2	13.3	13.3	40.0
	75	2	13.3	13.3	53.3
	100	2	13.3	13.3	66.7
	150	2	13.3	13.3	80.0
	250	2	13.3	13.3	93.3
	300	1	6.7	6.7	100.0
	Total	15	100.0	100.0	

Relaxation – importance

		Frequency	Percent	Valid Percent	Cumulative Percent
Valid	Very important	2	13.3	13.3	13.3
	Important	8	53.3	53.3	66.7
	Not at all important	5	33.3	33.3	100.0
	Total	15	100.0	100.0	

Social interaction – importance

		Frequency	Percent	Valid Percent	Cumulative Percent
Valid	Important	5	33.3	33.3	33.3
	Not at all important	10	66.7	66.7	100.0
	Total	15	100.0	100.0	

Fitness – importance

		Frequency	Percent	Valid Percent	Cumulative Percent
Valid	Very important	8	53.3	53.3	53.3
	Important	7	46.7	46.7	100.0
	Total	15	100.0	100.0	

First suggestion

		Frequency	Percent	Valid Percent	Cumulative Percent
Valid	Programme content	5	33.3	41.7	41.7
	Timing	3	20.0	25.0	66.7
	Facilities	2	13.3	16.7	83.3
	Costs	2	13.3	16.7	100.0
	Total	12	80		
Missing	System	3	20		
Total		15	100.0		

Second suggestion

		Frequency	Percent	Valid Percent	Cumulative Percent
Valid	Programme content	2	13.3	25.0	25
	Timing	3	20.0	37.5	62.5
	Facilities	1	6.7	12.5	75
	Costs	1	6.7	12.5	87.5
	Organisation	1	6.7	12.5	100.0
	Total	8	53.3	100.0	
Missing	System	7	46.7		
Total		15	100.0		

Third suggestion

		Frequency	Percent	Valid Percent	Cumulative Percent
Valid	Costs	1	6.7	50.0	50
	Organisation	1	6.7	50.0	100.0
	Total	2	13.3	100.0	
Missing	System	13	86.7		
Total		15	100.0		

Gender

		Frequency	Percent	Valid Percent	Cumulative Percent
Valid	Male	8	53.3	53.3	53.3
	Female	7	46.7	46.7	100.0
	Total	15	100.0	100.0	

Age

		Frequency	Percent	Valid Percent	Cumulative Percent
Valid	18	1	6.7	6.7	6.7
	19	3	20.0	20.0	26.7
	20	4	26.7	26.7	53.3
	21	4	26.7	26.7	80
	22	2	13.3	13.3	93.3
	24	1	6.7	6.7	100.0
	Total	15	100.0	100.0	

Statistical analysis

Introduction

This chapter provides an introduction to statistics, building on the outline of sampling theory presented in Chapter 13 and the introduction to the Statistical Package for the Social Sciences (SPSS) package outlined in Chapter 16. It *is* only an introduction: it is not intended to be a complete course in statistics. There are many textbooks covering approximately the same ground as covered here, but in more detail and more depth, and reference to some of these texts is given in the Resources section. The outline of survey analysis in Chapter 16 deals with quantification and the generation and analysis of statistical information, but this chapter is concerned with more than just quantification. Given that **(see Chapter 13)** data based on samples are subject to a margin of error when generalising to the population from which they were drawn, this chapter examines how the accuracy of sample-based statistical data can be assessed and in particular how relationships between variables might be analysed and their statistical significance determined.

After dealing with some general concepts related to the statistical method, the chapter covers a number of statistical tests which are appropriate for different types of data. These tests are: the chi-square test, the t-test, analysis of variance, correlation, linear and multiple regression and multivariate analysis. In each case the SPSS procedures for carrying out the tests are described. At the end of the chapter some analysis procedures which are not covered in detail here but are used in some sport research are discussed in general terms, including: odds ratios, multidimensional scaling and structural equation modelling.

The statistics approach

Before examining particular statistical tests, some preliminary statistical concepts and ideas should be discussed, namely: the idea of probabilistic statements; the normal distribution; probabilistic statement formats; statistical significance; the null hypothesis; and dependent and independent variables.

Probabilistic statements

In general, the science of 'inferential statistics' seeks to make *probabilistic* statements about a *population* on the basis of information available from a *sample* drawn from that population. The statements are *probabilistic* because **(see Chapter 13)** it is not possible to be absolutely sure that any randomly drawn sample is truly representative of the population from which it has been drawn, so we can only estimate the *probability* that results obtained from a sample are true of the population. The 'statements' which might be made on the basis of sample survey findings can be descriptive, comparative or relational:

- descriptive: for example, 10 per cent of adults play tennis;

- comparative: for example, 10 per cent play tennis, but 12 per cent play golf;

- relational: for example, 15 per cent of people with high incomes play tennis but only 7 per cent of people with low incomes do so: there is a positive relationship between tennis-playing and income.

If they are based on data from samples, such statements cannot be made without qualification. The *sample* may indicate these findings, but it is not certain that they apply precisely to the population from which the sample is drawn, because there is always an element of doubt about any sample. Inferential statistics modifies the above example statements to be of the form:

- we can be 95 per cent confident that the proportion of adults that plays tennis is between 9 and 11 per cent;

- the proportion of golf players is *significantly* higher than the proportion of tennis players (at the 95 per cent level of probability);

- there is a positive relationship between level of income and level of tennis playing (at the 95 per cent level).

The normal distribution

Descriptive statements and 'confidence intervals' are discussed in general terms in Chapter 13 in relation to the issue of sample size. The probability or confidence interval statement is based on the *theoretical* idea of drawing repeated samples of the same size from the same population. The sample drawn in any one piece of research is only one of a large number of *possible* samples which might have been drawn. If a large number of samples *could* be drawn, such an exercise would produce a variety of results, some very unrepresentative of the population but most, assuming *random sampling* procedures are used, tending to produce results close to the true population values. Statistical theory – which we are unable to explore in detail here – is able to quantify this tendency, so that we can say that, in 95 or 99 out of 100 of such samples, the values found from the sample will fall within a certain range either side of the true population value – hence the idea of 'confidence intervals'.

The theory relates to the bell-shaped 'normal distribution' which would result if repeated samples were drawn and the values of a statistic (for example the proportion who play tennis) plotted, as shown in Figure 17.1. The 'normal curve' which would result if a very large number of samples were drawn was shown in Figure 13.1 in Chapter 13. The population value of a statistic (such as a percentage or the average of a variable) lies at the centre of the distribution and the value of the statistic found from a sample in a particular research project is just one among the many sample possibilities. The probabilistic statement is made on the basis of this distribution, which has theoretically known properties for different samples and measures, such as percentages and means.

This idea of levels of probability about the accuracy of sample findings based on the theoretical possibility of drawing many samples is common to most of the statistical procedures examined in this chapter.

Probabilistic statement formats

It is customary in social research to use probability levels of 95 or 99 per cent – and occasionally 90 or 99.9 per cent. As probability estimates these can be interpreted exactly as in everyday language – for example when we say '90 per cent certain', '50:50' or '9 times out of ten', we are making probabilistic statements. So, if a survey finding is *significant* (a concept discussed further below) at the '99 per cent level', we are saying that we believe that there is a 99 per cent chance that what we have found is true of the population – there is therefore, conversely, a 1 per cent chance that what we have found is *not* true. If we can only say that something is significant at the lower 95 per cent level, we are less confident – there is a 5 per cent chance that what we have found is not true. Thus the terminology *highly significant* is sometimes used in relation to findings at the 99 per cent level and *significant* for the 95 per cent level.

In some cases, instead of the computer-generated results of statistical tests using these conventional cut-off points, they present the exact probability – for example it might be found that a result is significant at the 96.5 per cent level or the 82.5 per cent level. It is then left up to the researcher to judge whether such levels are acceptable.

Note also that sometimes the result is expressed as 1 per cent and sometimes as 99 per cent, or as 5 per cent rather than 95 per cent. A further variation is to express the probability as a proportion rather than a percentage – for example 0.05 rather than 5 per cent, or 0.01 rather than 1 per cent. Similarly, the exact

a. Drawing repeated samples

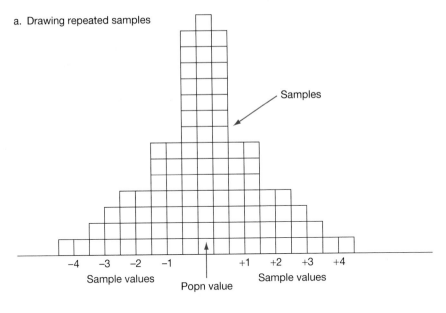

b. Normal distribution/curve

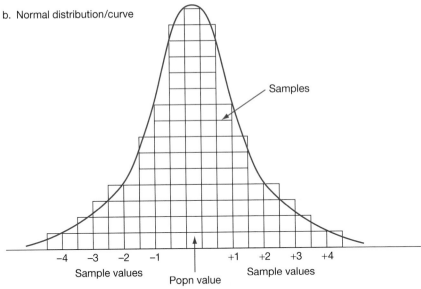

Figure 17.1 Drawing repeated samples and the normal distribution

calculations may be expressed as proportions, for example 0.035 rather than 3.5 per cent or 96.5 per cent.

In the following, therefore, in each row the three forms are equivalent.

5%	95%	0.05
1%	99%	0.01
0.1%	99.9%	0.001
3.5%	96.5%	0.035
7.5%	92.5%	0.075

In computer printouts from SPSS, if the probability is below .0005 it some-times comes out as .000 because it is printed only to three decimal places. In some research reports and computer printouts, results which are significant at the 5 per cent level are indicated by * and those significant at the 1 per cent level are indicated by **.

In the examples and discussions in the chapter, the 5 per cent/95 per cent value is used as the criterion level of tests of significance.

Significance

The second common feature of statistical tests and procedures is that they deal with the idea of *significance*. A *significant* difference or relationship is one which is *unlikely to have happened by chance*. So, for example, the bigger the difference between two sample percentages the more likely it is that the difference is *real* and not just a statistical chance happening.

For example, if it was found from a sample that 10 per cent of women played tennis and 11 per cent of men played tennis, we would be inclined, even from a common-sense point of view, to say that the difference is not sig-nificant. If another sample were selected, we would not be surprised to find a larger difference between the two figures, for them to be exactly the same or even the opposite way round: it is 'too close to call'. However, whether or not such a small difference is *statistically* significant depends on the sample size. If the findings were based on a small sample, say around 100 people, 50 men and 50 women, the difference would not be significant – the chances of getting a different result from a different sample of 100 people from the same population would be high – one person more or less in each group would change the percentage difference by two. But if the sample were large – say 1000 men and 1000 women – then it might be found to be statistically signifi-cant: it would take changes of ten persons to change the percentages by one. So if the result is based on such a large sample we can be much more confi-dent that it is 'real' and would be reproduced if another sample of similar size were drawn.

Statistical theory enables us to quantify and assess 'significance' – that is, to say what sizes of differences are significant for what sizes of sample.

Statistical significance should not, however, be confused with *social, theoreti-cal* or *managerial* significance. For example, if the above finding about men's and women's tennis-playing was based on a sample of, say, 10,000 people, it would be *statistically* significant, but this does not make the difference signifi-cant in any social sense. For all practical purposes, on the basis of such find-ings, we would say that men's and women's tennis-playing rates are the same or very similar. This is a very important point to bear in mind when reading research results based on statistics: large samples can produce many 'statisti-cally significant' findings, but that does not necessarily make them 'significant' in any other way.

The null hypothesis

A common feature of the statistical method is the concept of the *null hypothesis*, referred to by the symbol H_0. It is based on the idea of setting up two mutually incompatible hypotheses, so that only one can be true. If one proposition is true then the other is untrue. The null hypothesis usually proposes that there is *no difference* between two observed values or that there is *no relationship* between variables. There are therefore two possibilities:

H_0 – Null hypothesis: there is *no* significant difference or relationship.
H_1 – Alternative hypothesis: there *is* a significant difference or relationship.

Usually it is the *alternative* hypothesis, H_1, that the researcher is interested in, but statistical theory explores the implications of the *null* hypothesis.

In terms of the types of research approach discussed in Chapter 2, this is very much a *deductive* approach: the hypothesis is set up in advance of the analysis. However **(as noted in Chapter 2)**, this may be set in the context of an exploratory or even inductive project in which a number of relationships are explored, but the testing of each relationship is set up as a deductive process.

The use of the null hypothesis idea can be illustrated by example. Suppose, in a study of sport participation patterns, using a sample of 1000 adults, part of the study focuses on the relative popularity of golf and tennis. The null hypothesis would be that the participation levels are the same.

H_0 – tennis and golf participation levels are the same.
H_1 – tennis and golf participation levels are significantly different.

Suppose it is found that 120 (12 per cent) play tennis and 120 (12 per cent) play golf. Clearly there is no difference between the two figures; they are consistent with the null hypothesis. The null hypothesis is accepted and the alternative hypothesis is rejected.

But suppose the numbers playing tennis were found to be 121 (12.1 per cent) and the number playing golf was 120 (12.0 per cent). Would we reject the null hypothesis and accept the alternative, that tennis and golf participation levels are different? From what we know of samples, clearly not: this would be too close to call. Such a small difference between the two figures would still be consistent with the null hypothesis. So how big would the difference have to be before we reject the null hypothesis and accept that there is significant difference? A difference of 5, 10, 15? This is where statistical theory comes in, to provide a test of what is and is not a significant difference. And this is basically what the rest of this chapter is all about: providing tests of the relationship between sample findings and the null hypothesis for different situations. The null hypothesis is used in each of the tests examined.

Dependent and independent variables

The terminology *dependent variable* and *independent variable* is discussed in Chapter 1 and is frequently used in statistical analysis. If there is a significant

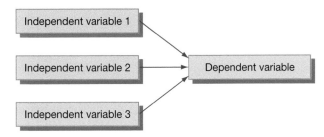

Figure 17.2 Dependent and independent variables

relationship between a dependent and an independent variable, the *implication* is that changes in the former are caused by changes in the latter: the independent variable *influences* the dependent variable.

For example, if it is suggested that the level of golf participation is influenced by a person's income level, golf participation is the *dependent* variable and income is the *independent* variable. Even though a certain level of income does not *cause* people to play golf, it makes more sense to suggest that level of income facilitates or constrains the level of golf participation than to suggest the opposite. So it makes some sense to talk of golf participation being *dependent* on income. One variable can be dependent on a number of independent variables, as illustrated in Figure 17.2 – for example it may be hypothesised that golf participation is dependent on income *and* occupation *and* age.

Statistical tests

Types of data and appropriate tests

The idea of levels of measurement, or types of data, was introduced in Chapter 16, when nominal, ordinal and scale data were discussed. The higher the level of measurement the greater the range of analysis that can be carried out on the data. For example, it is possible to calculate means/averages of ordinal and scale measures, but not of nominal data. Consequently, different statistical tests are associated with different levels of measurement. The rest of the chapter sets out different statistical tests to be used in different situations, as summarised in Figure 17.3. The tests all relate to comparisons between variables and relationships between variables. The appropriate type of test to be used depends on the format of the data, the level of measurement and the number of variables involved.

In what follows:

● Data from a questionnaire survey similar to that used in Chapter 16 are used to illustrate the various tests, but with a larger sample and additional sport and other leisure participation variables added.

Task	Format of data	No. of variables	Types of variable	Test
Relationship between two variables	Crosstabulation of frequencies	2	Nominal	Chi-square
Difference between two means – paired	Means: for a whole sample	2	Two scale/ordinal	t-test – paired
Difference between two means – independent samples	Means: for two sub-groups	2	1. scale/ordinal (means) 2. nominal (2 grps only)	t-test – independent samples
Relationship between two variables	Means: for 3+ sub-groups	2	1. scale/ordinal (means) 2. nominal (3+ groups)	One-way analysis of variance
Relationship between three or more variables	Means: crosstabulated	3+	1. scale/ordinal (means) 2. Two or more nominal	Factorial analysis of variance
Relationship between two variables	Individual measures	2	Two scale/ordinal	Correlation
Linear relationship between two variables	Individual measures	2	Two scale/ordinal	Linear regression
Linear relationship between three or more variables	Individual measures	3+	Three or more scale/ordinal	Multiple regression
Relationships between large numbers of variables	Individual measures	Many	Large numbers of scale/ordinal	Factor analysis/Cluster analysis

Figure 17.3   Types of data and types of statistical test

- Listings of the added questions, variables and data used can be found in Appendix 17.1.

- The variable *statusr* in the data set is produced as shown in Figure 16.13 part 2.

- As in Chapter 16, the examples have been created using SPSS for Windows, Version 18.

- For readers who are mathematically inclined, formulae for various of the test statistics are shown in Appendix 17.2.

Chi-square

Introduction

The chi-square test (symbol: χ^2, pronounced ky, to rhyme with sky) can be used in a number of situations, but its use is demonstrated here in relation to crosstabulations of two *nominal* variables – the familiar tables produced from such packages as SPSS. When examining crosstabulations it is possible to use 'common sense' and an underlying knowledge of the size of confidence intervals **(see Chapter 13)** to make an approximate judgement as to whether there is any sort of relationship between the two variables involved in the table. However, unless the pattern is very clear, it can be difficult to judge whether the overall differences are *significant*. The chi-square test is designed to achieve this.

Null hypothesis

The example chosen relates student full-time/part-time status (*statusr*) to gender (*gender*). The null hypothesis is that *there is no difference in student full-time/part-time status between male and female respondents;* that is:

H_0 – there is *no* relationship between student status and gender in the population of students.
H_1 – there *is* a relationship between status and gender in the population of students.

Note that the proposition being tested can therefore be expressed in three ways, as shown in Figure 17.4.

Procedures

Figure 17.5 shows the SPSS procedures to obtain a crosstabulation with a chi-square test, and the resultant output. The interpretation of this output is discussed below.

Expected frequencies

The cells of the table include counts and column percentages **(as discussed in relation to crosstabulations in Chapter 16)**. But they also include *expected counts*. These are the counts which *would be expected* if the null hypothesis were true – that is, if there were no difference between males and females in their full-time/part-time status. In this case we have an equal number of men and women in the sample, so the expected values show a 50:50 split for each status.

Option 1	Option 2	Option 3
H_0 There is *no* relationship between full-time/part-time status and gender in the population of students	H_0 Male and female full-time/part-time status in the population of students is the same	H_0 Observed and expected values are not significantly different
H_1 There *is* a relationship between full-time/part-time status and gender in the population of students	H_1 Male and female full-time/part-time status in the population of students is different	H_1 Observed and expected values are significantly different

Figure 17.4 Alternative expressions of hypotheses

Procedure

1. Select *Analyze*, then *Descriptive Statistics*, then *Crosstabs*.
2. Transfer the variable *statusr* to the *Row(s)* box and *gender* to the *Column(s)* box.
3. Select *Statistics*, then, in the *Crosstabs: Statistics* dialog box, select *Chi-square* then *Continue*.
4. Select *Cells*, then, in the *Crosstabs: Cells Display* dialog box:
   - in *Counts:* select *Observed* and *Expected*
   - in *Percentages:* select *Column* then *Continue*.
5. Select *OK* to produce the output below (*Case Processing Summary* table omitted).

Output

Student status recoded* Gender Crosstabulation

			Gender		Total
			Male	Female	
Student status recoded	Full-time	Count	18	9	27
		Expected Count	13.5	13.5	27.0
		% within Gender	72.0%	36.0%	54.0%
	Part-time	Count	7	16	23
		Expected Count	11.5	11.5	23.0
		% within Gender	28.0%	64.0%	46.0%
Total		Count	25	25	50
		Expected Count	25.0	25.0	50.0
		% within Student status recoded	50.0%	50.0%	100.0%

Chi-Square Tests (key items highlighted)

	Value	df	Asymp. Sig. (2-sided)	Exact Sig. (2-sided)	Exact Sig. (1-sided)
Pearson Chi-Square	6.522[a]	1	.011		
Continuity Correction[b]	5.153	1	.023		
Likelihood Ratio	6.676	1	.010		
Fisher's Exact Test				.022	.011
Linear-by-Linear Association	6.391	1	.011		
N of Valid Cases	50				

a 0 cells (.0%) have expected count less than 5. The minimum expected count is 11.50.

b Computed only for a 2 × 2 table

Figure 17.5 Chi-square test – procedures

The value of chi-square

Chi-square is a statistic based on the sum of the differences between the counts and the expected counts: the greater this sum the greater the value of chi-square. However, if the differences between the observed and expected counts in the table are simply added, it will be found that the positives cancel out the negatives, giving zero. Chi-square is therefore based on the sum of the *squared* values of the differences. The SPSS package calculates the value of chi-square, so it is not necessary to know the details of the formula. It is sufficient to understand that chi-square is a statistical measure of the difference between the observed and expected counts in the table.

In the example in Figure 17.5, the value of chi-square is 6.522. We are using the 'Pearson' value, devised by the statistician Karl Pearson – the other values (continuity correction, likelihood ratio, Fisher's exact test and linear-by-linear association) do not concern us here.

Interpretation

How should this value of chi-square be interpreted? We have noted that the greater the difference between the observed and expected values the greater the value of chi-square. Our null hypothesis is that there is *no* difference between the two sets of values. But clearly, we would accept some *minor* differences between two sets of values and still accept the null hypothesis. But just how big would the differences have to be before we would reject the null hypothesis and conclude that there *is* a difference between male and female full-time/part-time status?

For a given size of table (in this case two cells by two) statisticians have been able to calculate the likelihood of obtaining various values of chi-square when the null hypothesis is true. As with the normal distribution **(see Chapter 16)**, this is based on the theoretical possibility of drawing lots of samples of the same size. This is shown in Figure 17.6. It shows that, for a particular table size, if the null hypothesis is true, some differences in observed and expected counts can be expected from most samples drawn from a given population, so a *range of values* of chi-square can be expected. Most values of chi-square would be expected to be fairly small; some larger values would occur, but only rarely – they are unlikely.

Therefore, if any value of chi-square is in the range to the right of the 5 per cent point in the diagram it is considered unlikely and *inconsistent* with the null hypothesis: we *reject* the null hypothesis. If it is in the range to the left of the 5 per cent point we *accept* the null hypothesis.

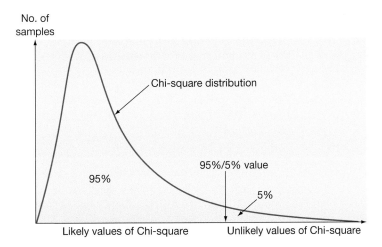

Figure 17.6 Distribution of chi-square assuming null hypothesis is true

In Figure 17.5, the output tells us the value of chi-square for the table: 6.522. It also indicates the likelihood, or probability, of this value: 0.011, or 1.1 per cent. Our value of chi-square is therefore an unlikely one (it has a likelihood less than 5 per cent), so we reject the null hypothesis and conclude that there *is* a significant difference between the proportion of full-time/part-time status for male and female students.

Degrees of freedom

The values of chi-square depend on the table size, which is indirectly measured by the *degrees of freedom*. Degrees of freedom are calculated by: *the number of rows minus one* multiplied by *the number of columns minus one*. So, for the table in Figure 17.5, the degrees of freedom are: **(2–1) × (2–1) = 1 × 1 = 1.** This is shown in the output table under *df*.

Expected counts rule

One rule for the application of chi-square is that there should not be more than one-fifth of the cells of the table with expected counts of less than five, and none with an expected count of less than one. The output indicates whether such cells exist. Note that the bottom of the table indicates that no cells have an expected count of less than five and the minimum expected count is 11.5, so there is no problem. Grouping of some of the values by recoding can be used to reduce the number of cells and thus increase the expected frequencies. In fact this was done in the example with the recoded variable – if the analysis is run with the original *status* variable the test infringes the expected counts rule and is invalid.

Reporting

How should the results of statistical tests such as chi-square be reported? Four solutions can be considered, as follows:

1. Include the results of the test in the table in the research report, as in Figure 17.7. The commentary might then merely say: 'The relationship between full-time/part-time status and gender was significant at the 5 per cent level'.

2. Include the test results in the text, for example: 'The relationship between full-time/part-time status and gender was significant at the 5 per cent level ($\chi^2 = 6.5$, 1 DF)'.

3. Make the statistics less intrusive by including a note in the report or paper indicating that all tests were conducted at the 5 per cent level and that test values are included in the tables, or are listed in an appendix, or even excluded altogether for non-technical audiences.

4. Use the starring approach (* and **) to indicate significant and highly significant results in tables, as discussed above.

Table 1 Full-time/part-time status by gender

	Male	Female	Total
Status	%	%	%
Full-time student	72.0	36.0	54.0
Part-time student	28.0	64.0	46.0
Total	100.0	100.0	100.0
Sample size:	25	25	50

$\chi^2 = 6.52$, DF 1, significant at the 5% level

Figure 17.7   **Presentation of chi-square test results**

Comparing two means: the t-test

Introduction

So far we have dealt only with proportions or percentages, either singly or in crosstabulations, but many research results are in the form of averages – for example the average age of a group of participants in an activity, the average expenditure of visitors from different countries, or the average score of a group on a Likert scale. In statistical parlance an average is referred to as a *mean*. Means can only be calculated for *ordinal* and *scale* variables, not for nominal variables.

The simplest form of analysis is to compare two means to see whether they are significantly different. For example, we might want to test whether the average age of golf players in a sample is significantly different from that of the tennis players, or whether the average amount spent on sport by a group of people is greater or less than the amount they spend on cinema attendance. In this situation the null hypothesis is expressed as follows:

H_0 – Null hypothesis: there is *no* difference between the means
H_1– Alternative hypothesis: there *is* a difference between the means.

For this situation, rather than chi-square, a statistic referred to as 't' is calculated – but the interpretation is similar. This is based on a formula involving the sample size and the two means to be compared. If there is *no difference* between two means in the population (H_0) then, for a given sample size, t has a known 'distribution' of likely values, as illustrated in Figure 17.8 in comparison with the chi-square distribution. High values are rare, so if the value from a sample is high – in the top 5 per cent of values for that sample size – then we reject H_0 and accept H_1; that is, we conclude that there *is* a significant difference at the 5 per cent level of probability respectively. Note that, because 't' can take on negative or positive values, there are two 'tails' to its distribution – hence the reference to 'two-tailed test' in some of the output discussed below.

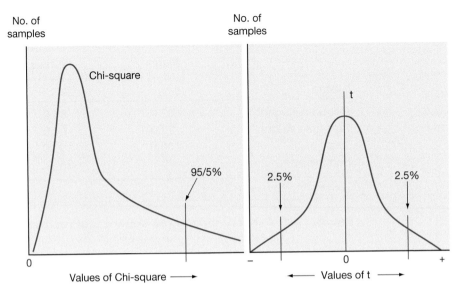

Figure 17.8 Chi-square and t distributions

There are two situations where we might want to compare means:

A To compare the means of two variables which apply to the whole sample – for example comparing the average amount spent on sport with the average income (for everybody in the sample). This is known as a *paired samples test*.

B To compare the means of one variable for two sub-groups – for example comparing the average age of men in the sample with that of women. The sample is divided into two sub-groups, men and women; this is known as a *group* or *independent samples* test.

A. Paired samples test

Figure 17.9 presents two examples of the paired samples test. The SPSS output provides a range of statistics with which we are not concerned here – including a correlation, which is discussed later in the chapter. The items we are interested in are depicted in bold in Figure 17.9.

Example 1 compares the frequency of playing sport with the frequency of visiting parks:

● the people in the sample play sport on average 12.2 times in three months and visit parks on average 9.8 times, a difference of 2.4 – the question is whether this difference is significant;

● the value of t is 1.245 and its (2-tail) significance is 0.219 or 21.9 per cent;

● the result is consistent with the null hypothesis (0.219 is much higher than 0.05);

● so we accept the null hypothesis, that the difference between the level of sport-playing and the level of visits to parks is *not* significant.

Procedure

1. Select *Analyze*, then *Compare Means*.
2. Select *Paired Samples T-Test*.
3. Highlight the first variable to be compared and transfer to the *Paired variables* box, then transfer the second variable.
4. Select *OK* to obtain t-test output.

Output

Example 1: Playing sport vs. visiting parks

Paired Samples Statistics

		Mean	N	Std. Deviation	Std. Error Mean
Pair 1	**Play sport**	**12.20**	50	13.095	1.852
	Visit park	**9.80**	50	8.804	1.245

Paired Samples Correlations (IGNORE)

		N	Correlation	Sig.
Pair 1	Play sport and Visit park	50	.274	.054

Paired Samples Test

		Paired Differences					t	df	Sig. (2-tailed)
		Mean	Std. Deviation	Std. Error Mean	95% Confidence Interval of the Difference				
					Lower	Upper			
Pair 1	**Play sport Visit park**	**2.400**	13.631	1.928	−1.474	6.274	**1.245**	49	**.219**

Example 2: Visit parks vs. going out for a meal
Paired Samples Statistics

		Mean	N	Std. Deviation	Std. Error Mean
Pair 1	**Visit park**	**9.80**	50	8.804	1.245
	Go out for meal	**6.54**	50	3.157	0.446

Paired Samples Correlations (IGNORE)

		N	Correlation	Sig.
Pair 1	Visit park and Go out for meal	50	−.044	.759

Paired Samples Test

		Paired Differences					t	df	Sig. (2-tailed)
		Mean	Std. Deviation	Std. Error Mean	95% Confidence Interval of the Difference				
					Lower	Upper			
Pair 1	**Visit park Go out for meal**	**3.26**	9.484	1.341	0.565	5.955	**2.431**	49	**.019**

Figure 17.9 Comparing means: t-test: paired samples: procedures

Example 2 compares the frequency of visiting parks and going out for a meal. In this case:

- the difference in the mean frequencies is 3.26;
- the value of t is 2.431;
- its significance level is 0.019, which is below 0.05;
- so we reject the null hypothesis and conclude that there *is* a significant difference between the frequency of visiting parks and going out for meals.

B. Independent samples test

Figure 17.10 compares levels of expenditure on sport etc. by male and female students:

Procedure
1. Select *Analyze* and then *Compare Means.*
2. Select *Independent Samples T-Test.*
3. Select the variable for which the mean is required (*spend*) and transfer to *Test variables* box.
5. Select variable to be used to divide the sample into two groups (*gender*) and transfer to *Grouping variable* box.
6. Select *Define groups* and enter the values used to divide the sample into two groups (in the example: 1 for Male and 2 for Female). Select *Continue* and the two values appear in brackets following the name of the grouping variable: *gender*(1,2).
7. Select *OK* to obtain t-test.

Output
Group Statistics

	Gender	N	Mean	Std. Deviation	Std. Error Mean
Expenditure on sport etc. £	**Male**	25	**110.00**	77.607	15.521
	Female	25	**138.60**	84.613	16.923

Independent Samples Test

	Levene's Test for Equality of Variances		t-test for Equality of Means						
	F	Sig.	t	df	Sig. (2-tailed)	Mean Difference	Std. Error Difference	95% Confidence Interval of the Difference	
								Lower	Upper
Equal variances assumed	.431	.514	**−1.245**	48	**.219**	−28.600	22.963	−74.770	17.570
Equal variances not assumed			−1.245	47.646	.219	−28.600	22.963	−74.779	17.579

Figure 17.10 Comparing means: t-test: independent samples – procedure

- for males expenditure is £110 and for males it is £138.60, a difference of £28.60;
- t has a value of –1.25 and a significance level of 0.219;
- since 0.219 is above 0.05, this is consistent with the null hypothesis, so we accept that there is no significant difference between the two expenditure figures.

A number of means: one-way analysis of variance (ANOVA)

Introduction

The t-test was used to examine differences between means two at a time. *Analysis of variance* (ANOVA) is used to examine *more than two* means at a time. This begins to resemble the crosstabulation process, but with *means* appearing in the cells of the table instead of counts. An example is shown in Figure 17.11, which compares mean activity participation levels and sport expenditure for the various student status groups. Here the question which we seek to answer with ANOVA is whether, for each item, the mean for the different groups of students are different from the overall mean – that is, whether participation/expenditure is related to student status.

Procedure

To obtain a table showing the means to be compared:
1. Select *Analyze* and then *Compare Means.*
2. Select *Means.*
3. Select the variable for which the mean is required (*sport, spectate2, park, meal, sportexp*) and transfer to the *Dependent list* box.
4. Select variable for grouping (*status*) and transfer to the *Independent list* box.
5. In *Options* ensure that *Mean* and *Number of cases* are in the *Cell statistics* box.
6. Select *OK* to produce the output.

Output

Student status		Play sport	Watch sport	Visit park	Go out for meal	Sport expenditure
F/T student/no paid work	Mean	9.69	2.62	9.77	6.46	328.46
	N	13	13	13	13	13
F/T student/paid work	Mean	9.64	2.93	8.64	4.00	342.50
	N	14	14	14	14	14
P/T student – F/T job	Mean	19.06	2.25	8.63	8.19	425.63
	N	16	16	16	16	16
P/T student/Other	Mean	6.29	3.29	14.86	8.00	752.86
	N	7	7	7	7	7
Total	Mean	12.20	2.68	9.80	6.54	422.90
	N	50	50	50	50	50

Figure 17.11 Comparing ranges of means – procedures

Null hypothesis

The null hypothesis is therefore: that all the group means are equal to the overall (total) mean. How different must the group means be from the overall mean before we reject this hypothesis?

Variance

Whether or not the means are in effect from *one* population (with *one* mean) or from *different* sub-populations (with *different* means) depends not only on the differences between the means but also on the 'spread', or *variance*, of the cases upon which they are based. Figure 17.12 shows four examples of three means, with the associated spread of cases around them:

● A the means are well spaced and there is very little overlap in the cases – there *is* a significant difference between the means;

● B the means are closer together and there is considerable overlap, suggesting that they may be from the same population;

● C the means are spaced as in A, but the spread around the means is greater and so overlap is considerable, suggesting uncertainty as to whether or not the means are significantly different;

● D the worst case of overlap – so we can be fairly certain that the three sets of data are from the same population.

A visual presentation of this type of information, although in a different format, can be obtained using the *Boxplot* feature within the *Graphics* procedure of SPSS.

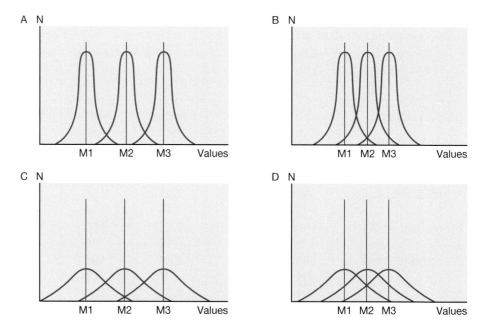

Figure 17.12 Comparing means and variances

The 'spread' of sample values is referred to as the *variance* and can be measured by adding up the differences between the scores of individual cases and the mean score.

Analysis of variance

Whether or not the means are significantly different from the overall mean depends on:

1. the spread of the separate sub-group means around the overall mean – the *between groups* variance – the greater the between groups variance the *greater* the likelihood of significant difference; and

2. the spread of each of the sub-group cases around the sub-group mean – the *within groups* variance – the greater the within groups variance the *less* the likelihood of significant difference.

Analysis of variance is based on the ratio of these two measures, which produces a statistic referred to as F. As with the other statistics examined, values of F for a given number of degrees of freedom (based on sample sizes and number of groups) have a known probability distribution in the null hypothesis situation. High values are unlikely and result in the rejection of the null hypothesis.

Procedures for analysis of variance

The SPSS procedures for analysis of variance and examples of output are shown in Figure 17.13.
    Figure 17.13 shows the following:

● In the ANOVA table:
    – for the first three activities significance is above 0.05, so the null hypothesis is accepted and it is concluded that participation in these activities is not related to student status;
    – for the last two activities, going out for a meal and sport expenditure, significance is below 0.05 so the null hypothesis is rejected and we conclude that there is a relationship between these activities and student status.

● The *Post hoc* test table identifies the between-group differences for those variables for which there is a statistically significant difference: and is presented here for going out for a meal. In the 'mean difference' column an * denotes that the mean difference is significant at the 0.05 level, and this is the case for four comparisons.

Procedure

1. Select *Analyze* and then *Compare Means*.
2. Select *One-way ANOVA*.
4. Select variables for which means are required (*sport, spectate2, park, meal, sportexp*) and put in the *Dependent list* box.
5. Select variable for grouping (*status*) and put in the *Independent list* box.
6. Select *Post Hoc* and click the *Tukey* checkbox and leave Significance level at 0.05.
7. Select *Options* and click *Descriptive, Homogeneity of variance test, Brown-Forsythe, Welsh and Means* plot checkboxes.
8. Select *OK* to produce the output.

Output

ANOVA

		Sum of Squares	df	Mean Square	F	Sig.
Play sport	Between Groups	1171.650	3	390.550	2.485	.072
	Within Groups	7230.350	46	157.182		
	Total	8402.000	49			
Watch sport	Between Groups	6.446	3	2.149	.411	.746
	Within Groups	240.434	46	5.227		
	Total	246.880	49			
Visit park	Between Groups	219.871	3	73.290	.942	.428
	Within Groups	3578.129	46	77.785		
	Total	3798.000	49			
Go out for meal	Between Groups	148.752	3	49.584	6.715	.001
	Within Groups	339.668	46	7.384		
	Total	488.420	49			
Annual sport exp	Between Groups	968661.162	3	322887.054	6.644	.001
	Within Groups	2235593.338	46	48599.855		
	Total	3204254.500	49			

POST-HOC TEST

Go out for a meal					95% Conf. interval	
(I) Student status	(J) Student status	Mean Difference (I-J)	Std. Error	Sig.	Lower Bound	Upper Bound
F/T student/no paid work	F/T student/paid work	2.462	1.047	.101	−.33	5.25
	P/T student – F/T job	−1.726	1.015	.335	−4.43	.98
	P/T student/Other	−1.538	1.274	.625	−4.93	1.86
F/T student/paid work	F/T student/no paid work	−2.462	1.047	.101	−5.25	.33
	P/T student – F/T job	−4.188*	.994	.001	−6.84	−1.54
	P/T student/Other	−4.000*	1.258	.014	−7.35	−.65
P/T student - F/T job	F/T student/no paid work	1.726	1.015	.335	−.98	4.43
	F/T student/paid work	−4.188*	.994	.001	1.54	6.84
	P/T student/Other	.188	1.231	.999	−3.09	3.47
P/T student/Other	F/T student/no paid work	1.538	1.274	.625	−1.86	4.93
	F/T student/paid work	−4.000*	1.258	.014	.65	7.35
	P/T student – F/T job	−.188	1.231	.999	−3.47	3.09

* in the mean difference column an* notes that the mean difference is significant to the 0.05 level

Figure 17.13 One-way analysis of variance – procedures

A table of means: factorial analysis of variance (ANOVA)

Introduction

As with one-way analysis of variance, factorial analysis of variance deals with *means*. But while the former deals with means of groups determined on the basis of *one* variable, the latter is designed for sets of means grouped by more than one classifying variable, or 'factor'. An example is shown in Figure 17.14,

---

Procedure

1. Select *Analyze* then *Compare Means* then *Means*.
2. Select *sport* and transfer to the *Dependent list* box.
3. Select *status* and transfer to the *Independent list* box.
4. Click on *Next* to get *Layer 2 of 2*, then *gender* and transfer to the *Independent list* box.
5. Select *OK* to obtain the output.

Output

Watch sport

Student status	Gender	Mean	N	Std. Deviation
F/T student/no paid work	Male	3.11	9	1.833
	Female	1.50	4	2.380
	Total	2.62	13	2.063
F/T student/paid work	Male	1.56	9	1.130
	Female	5.40	5	2.191
	Total	2.93	14	2.433
P/T student – F/T job	Male	1.40	5	2.074
	Female	2.64	11	2.730
	Total	2.25	16	2.543
P/T student/Other	Male	3.50	2	2.121
	Female	3.20	5	1.643
	Total	3.29	7	1.604
Total	Male	2.24	25	1.786
	Female	3.12	25	2.587
	Total	2.68	50	2.245

How the above might be presented in a report

Table 1: Frequency of watching sport, by status and gender

Course	Mean number of visits in three months		
	Male	Female	Total
F/T student/no paid work	3.1	1.5	2.6
F/T student/paid work	1.6	5.4	2.9
P/T student – F/T job	1.4	2.6	2.3
P/T student/Other	3.5	3.2	3.3
Total	2.2	3.1	2.7

Figure 17.14   A table of means – procedures

which presents a table of mean frequency of sport-spectating by status and gender, with no statistical test at this stage. It can be seen that:

- there is little difference in frequency of spectating by status, with the lowest mean frequency 2.6 and the highest 3.3;
- there is little difference in frequency of spectating by gender (male 2.2, female 3.1);
- but when the two variables are put together, considerable differences emerge, with the lowest mean frequency at 1.4 and the highest at 5.4.

Analysis of variance examines this 'crosstabulation of means' and determines whether the differences revealed are significant. As with the one-way analysis of variance, the procedure examines the differences *between* group means and the spread of values *within* groups.

Null hypothesis

The null hypothesis is that there is no interaction between the variables – that the level of sport-spectating of the students in the various categories is not affected by gender. A table of 'expected counts' consistent with the null hypothesis could be produced as for the chi-square example, but the values would be means rather than numbers of cases.

Procedures for factorial analysis of variance

Figure 17.15 shows the results of a factorial analysis of variance on the above data. The F probabilities in bold indicate that the relationship between:

- sport-spectating and status alone is not significant (Sig. = 0.250);
- sport-spectating and gender is not significant (Sig. = 0.242);
- sport-spectating and course and gender together is significant at the 5 per cent level (Sig. = 0.019) – so the null hypothesis is rejected: the interaction between gender and status with regard to sport-spectating is significant at the 5 per cent level.

Correlation

Introduction

Correlation can be used to examine the relationships between two or more *ordinal or scale* variables. If two variables are related in a systematic way they are said to be *correlated*. They can be:

- *positively* correlated (as one variable increases so does the other);
- *negatively* correlated (as one variable increases the other decreases); or
- *un-correlated* (there is no relationship between the variables).

Procedure

1. Select *Analyze* then *General Linear Model*.
2. Select *Univariate*.
3. Select the *Dependent* variable – the one for which the means are to be calculated (*spectate2*).
4. Select the *Fixed Factors* – the two variables affecting the dependent variable (*status* and *gender*).
5. Click on the *Post Hoc* box and in the dialog box transfer *status* and *gender* to the *Post Hoc tests for:* box, then select *LSD*, then click *Continue*.
6. Select *OK* to obtain the output.

Output

Tests of Between-Subjects Effects

Dependent Variable: Watch sport (key items in bold)

Source	Type III Sum of Squares	df	Mean Square	F	Sig.
Corrected Model	66.523(a)	7	9.503	2.213	.052
Intercept	299.090	1	299.090	69.650	.000
status	18.308	3	6.103	**1.421**	**.250**
gender	6.041	1	6.041	**1.407**	**.242**
status * gender	47.424	3	15.808	**3.681**	**.019**
Error	180.357	42	4.294		
Total	606.000	50			
Corrected Total	246.880	49			

a R Squared =.269 (Adjusted R Squared =.148)

Figure 17.15   Factorial analysis of variance – procedures
Relating to data in Figure 17.14.

It is often helpful to think of correlation in visual terms. Relationships between income and four variables are shown in Figure 17.16, illustrating a variety of types of correlation. The graphics were produced using the *SPSS* graphics *Scatterplot* procedure (**see Chapter 16**). Each dot represents one person (or case or observation). The correlation coefficients, r, are explained below.

Correlation coefficient (r)

Correlation can be measured by means of the *correlation coefficient*, usually represented by the letter r. The coefficient has the following characteristics:

- zero if there is no relationship between two variables;
- + 1.0 if there is perfect positive correlation between two variables;
- −1.0 if there is perfect negative correlation between two variables;
- between 0 and +1.0 if there is *some* positive correlation;
- between 0 and −1.0 if there is *some* negative correlation;

- the closer the coefficient is to 1.0, the higher the correlation, e.g.:
  - 0.9 is a *high positive* correlation;
  - 0.2 is a *low positive* correlation;
  - −0.8 is a *high negative* correlation.

a. **Watch sport increases with income – a weak positive correlation (r = 0.46)**

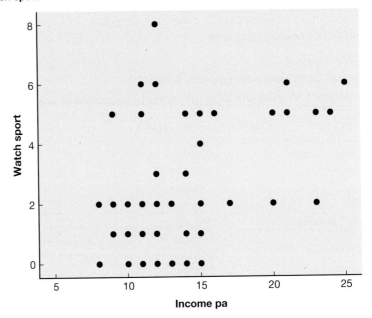

b. **Play sport participation declines with income – a moderate negative correlation (r = −0.44)**

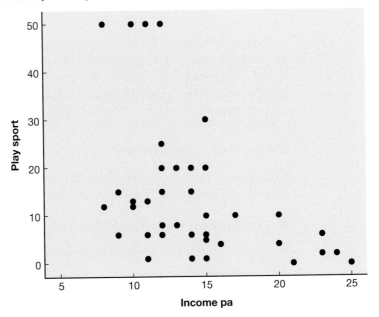

Figure 17.16 Relationships between variables

c. **No apparent relationship between park visiting and income – almost zero correlation (r = 0.024)**

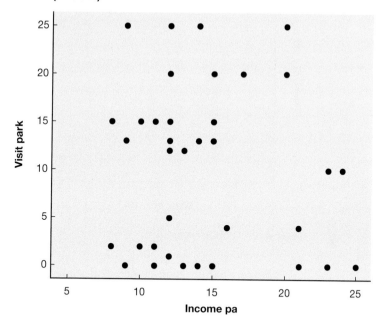

d. **Sport expenditure clearly increases with income – very strong positive correlation (r = 0.91)**

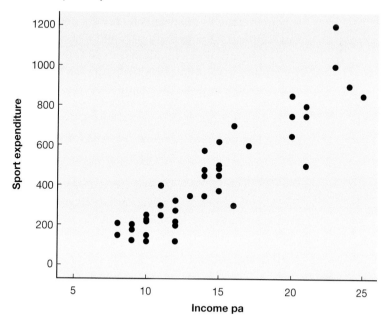

Figure 17.16 (*continued*)

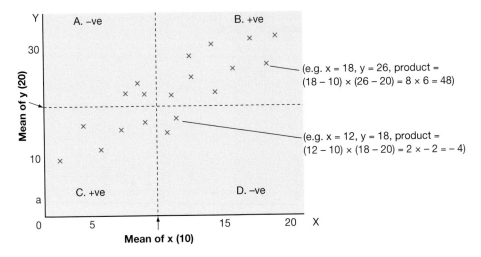

Figure 17.17 Correlation

The correlation coefficient is calculated by measuring how far each data point is from the mean of each of the two variables and multiplying the two differences. In Figure 17.17 it can be seen that the result will be a positive number for data points in the top right-hand and bottom left-hand quadrants (B and C) and negative for data points in the other two quadrants (A and D). The calculations are shown for two of the data points by way of illustration. If most of the data points are in quadrants B and C a positive correlation will result, while if most of the data points are in A and D a negative correlation will result. If the data points are widely scattered in all four quadrants, the negatives cancel out the positives, resulting in a low value for the correlation. This explains in very broad terms the basis of the positive and negative correlations, and high and low correlations. It is beyond the scope of this book to explain how the 'perfect' correlation is made to equal one, but, for those with the requisite mathematics, this can be deduced from the formula for r, which is given in Appendix 17.2.

Significance of r

The *significance* of a correlation coefficient depends on its size, as discussed above, and also the sample size, and is assessed by means of a t-test.

Null hypothesis

The null hypothesis is that the correlation is zero. The t-test therefore indicates only whether the correlation coefficient is *significantly different from zero*. Quite low coefficients can emerge as 'significant' if the sample is large enough.

Procedures for correlation

The SPSS procedures for producing correlation coefficients between pairs of variables are shown in Figure 17.18. The output is in the form of a symmetrical

Procedure

1. Select *Analyze*
2. Select *Correlate*
3. Select *Bivariate*
4. Select variables to be included (*inc, sport, spectate2, park, meal, sportexp*) and transfer to the *Variables* box
6. Select *OK* to produce output.

Output

Correlations

		Income pa	Play sport	Watch sport	Visit park	Go out for meal	Sport expenditure
Income pa	Pearson Correlation	1.000	−.439**	.460**	.024	.076	.915**
	Sig. (2-tailed)	.	.001	.001	.866	.598	.000
	N	50	50	50	50	50	50
Play sport	Pearson Correlation	−.439**	1.000	−.679**	.274	.454**	−.368**
	Sig. (2-tailed)	.001	.	.000	.054	.001	.008
	N	50	50	50	50	50	50
Watch sport	Pearson Correlation	.460**	−.679**	1.000	−.292*	−.286*	.379**
	Sig. (2-tailed)	.001	.000	.	.039	.044	.007
	N	50	50	50	50	50	50
Visit park	Pearson Correlation	.024	.274	−.292*	1.000	−.044	.058
	Sig. (2-tailed)	.866	.054	.039	.	.759	.688
	N	50	50	50	50	50	50
Go out for meal	Pearson Correlation	.076	.454**	−.286*	−.044	1.000	.119
	Sig. (2-tailed)	.598	.001	.044	.759	.	.410
	N	50	50	50	50	50	50
Annual sport exp.	Pearson Correlation	.915**	−.368**	.379	.058	.119	1.000
	Sig. (2-tailed)	.000	.008	.007	.688	.410	.
	N	50	50	50	50	50	50

Figure 17.18   Correlation matrix – procedures

** Correlation is significant at the 0.01 level (2-tailed).

* Correlation is significant at the 0.05 level (2-tailed).

matrix, so that, for example, the correlation between playing sport and income is the same as between income and playing sport. For each pair of variables, the output includes the correlation coefficient, the significant/probability of the t-test and the sample size (N). The starring system discussed above is used to indicate significance at the 5 per cent and 1 per cent levels. As with other tests, if the probability is below the 0.05 or 0.01 levels we reject the null hypothesis and conclude that the correlation is significantly different from zero, at the 5 per cent or 1 per cent level, respectively.

Linear regression

Introduction

Linear regression takes us one step further in this type of quantitative analysis – in the direction of 'prediction'. If the correlation between two variables is consistent enough, one variable can be used to predict or estimate the other. In particular, easily measured variables (such as age or income) can be used to predict variables which are more difficult or costly to measure (such as participation in sport activities). For example, knowledge of the relationship between age and sport participation can be used in planning sport facilities for a community: the future age-structure of the community can be relatively easily estimated and with this information future demand for sport activities can be estimated.

The procedures described here are just one format in which the relationships between variables of interest can be examined. If the variables can be quantified, the techniques enable the strength and nature of the relationship to be quantified also.

Regression model

To predict one variable on the basis of another, a *model* or equation is needed of the type:

Sport participation = *some number* times AGE

Suppose sport participation is measured in terms of the number of days' participation over the course of a year. Regression analysis produces an equation of the form:

Sport participation (days) = a + b * AGE (years)

The *coefficients* or *parameters*, a and b, are determined from examination of existing data, using regression analysis. The process of finding out the values of the parameters or coefficients is referred to as *calibration* of the model.

In general terms this is represented by the equation: **y = a + bx,** where y stands for participation and x stands for age. Note that here *Sport participation* is the *dependent* variable and AGE is the *independent* variable.

In visual terms this describes a 'regression line' fitted through the data, with 'intercept' or 'constant' of *a* and 'slope' of *b*, as shown in Figure 17.19. The regression procedure finds the 'line of best fit' by finding the line which minimises the sum of the (squared) differences between it and the data points, and specifies this line by giving values for a and b.

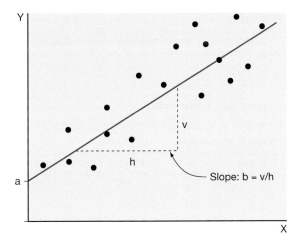

Figure 17.19   Regression line

Procedures for regression

Examples of regression output from SPSS, using income as the independent variable, are shown in Figure 17.20. The program produces a large amount of output with which we are not concerned here – only the items in bold are discussed. However, the output illustrates the point that regression is an involved process and only the broad outlines are dealt with in this book. The output relates to *multiple* regression, which involves more than one independent variable, as discussed in the next section – but here we have only one independent variable, income.

The items we are interested in are the value of the regression coefficient, R (similar to the correlation coefficient, r), the value of R^2, which is an indicator of how well the data fit the regression line, its test of significance, and the coefficients listed under B. For Example 1 in Figure 17.20, the relationship between income and sport expenditure:

- the value of R is 0.915;

- R^2 is 0.836;

- probability (as measured by an F test) is 0.000 which makes it highly significant;

- the *constant* (a) is –323.493 and the *coefficient* of *slope* (b) for income is 52.563.

  The regression equation is therefore:

  Sport expenditure (£ pa) = –323.493 + 52.563 * income (in £'000s pa)

This regression line can be plotted onto a graph, as shown in Figure 17.21, using the SPSS *Curve estimation* procedure.

Procedure

1. Select *Analyze* then *Regression.*
2. Select *Linear.*
3. Select *dependent* and *independent* variables.
4. Select *OK* to produce the output.

Output (key items in bold)

Example 1: Income (independent) by sport expenditure (dependent)

Model Summary

Model	R	R Square	Adjusted R Square	Std. Error of the Estimate
1	.915	.836	.833	104.51

a Predictors: (Constant), Income pa

ANOVA

Model		Sum of Squares	df	Mean Square	F	Sig.
1	Regression	2679971.336	1	2679971.336	245.361	.000
	Residual	524283.164	48	10922.566		
	Total	3204254.500	49			

a Predictors: (Constant), Income pa. b Dependent Variable: Holiday expenditure

Coefficients

Model		Unstandardized Coefficients		Standardized Coeffs	t	Sig.
		B	Std. Error	Beta		
1	(Constant)	−323.493	49.890		−6.484	.000
	Income pa	52.563	3.356	.915	15.664	.000

a Dependent Variable: Sport expenditure

Example 2: Income (independent) by play sport (dependent)

Model Summary

Model	R	R Square	Adjusted R Square	Std. Error of the Estimate
1	.439	.193	.176	11.88

a Predictors: (Constant), Income pa

ANOVA

Model		Sum of Squares	df	Mean Square	F	Sig.
1	Regression	1618.566	1	1618.566	11.453	.001
	Residual	6783.434	48	141.322		
	Total	8402.000	49			

a Predictors: (Constant), Income pa. b Dependent Variable: Play sport

Coefficients

Model		Unstandardized Coefficients		Standardized Coeffs	t	Sig.
		B	Std. Error	Beta		
1	(Constant)	30.543	5.675		5.382	.000
	Income pa	−1.292	.382	−.439	−3.384	.001

a Dependent Variable: Play sport

Figure 17.20   Regression analysis – procedures

Procedure

1. Select *Analyze* then *Regression* then *Curve Estimation*
2. Select *sportexp* then transfer to *Dependents* box and *inc* and transfer to *Independents* box
3. Select *OK* to produce output

Output

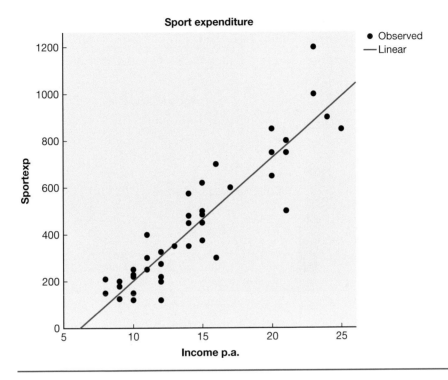

Figure 17.21 Regression line – curve fit – procedure

With this equation, if we knew a student's income we could estimate their level of sport expenditure, either by reading it off the graph or calculating it. For example, for a student with an income of £10,000 a year:

Sport expenditure = –323.49 + 52.56 * 10 = –323.49 + 525.60 = £202.11

So we would estimate that such a student would spend £202 on sport in a year. Of course, we are not saying that *every* student with that income will spend this sum: the regression line/equation is a sort of average; it is not precise.

Example 2 in Figure 17.20 produces comparable output for the relationship between sport participation and income, but with a negative relationship. In this case the resultant regression equation would be:

Playing sport (frequency in 3 months) = 30.5 – 1.3 * income (in £'000s pa).

Procedure

1. Select *Analyze* then *Regression* then *Curve Fit*.
2. Select *dependent* and *independent* variables (*sportexp* and *inc*).
3. Under *Models* select *Cubic*.
4. Select *OK* to produce output.

Output

Independent: inc

Dependent	Mth	Rsq	d.f.	F	Sigf	b0	b1	b2	b3
sportexp	Cubic	.843	46	82.43	.000	494.351	−113.10	10.5471	−.2118

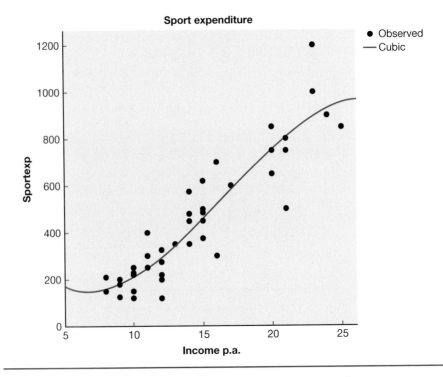

Figure 17.22 Regression: curve fit, non-linear – procedures

Non-linear regression

In Figure 17.22 the relationship between the two variables is *non-linear* – that is, the relationship indicated is curved, rather than being a straight line. The SPSS *Curve fit* procedure offers a number of models which may produce lines/curves which fit the data better than a simple straight line. Theory or trial and error may lead to a suitable model. In Figure 17.22 a 'cubic' model is presented, in which the independent variable is raised to the power of three – this results in the curved line indicated and a small increase in the value of R^2 to 0.843.

This emphasises the importance of examining the data *visually*, as done here, and not relying just on correlation coefficients.

Multiple regression

Multiple regression is linear regression involving more than one independent variable. For example, we might hypothesise that sport participation is dependent on income and age. Thus our model, or regression equation, would be:

$$\text{Sport participation} = a + b \times \text{income} + c \times \text{age}$$

In *linear* regression, as discussed above, the procedure fits a straight line to the data – the line of *best fit*. In *multiple* regression the procedure fits a *surface* to the data – the surface of best fit. It is possible to visualise this in three dimensions (one dependent and two independent variables), with the axes forming a three-dimensional box, the observations suspended in space and the regression surface being a flat plane somewhere within the box (SPSS offers a 3-D graphical option to represent this in the *Scattergram* procedure.) When additional variables are included, four, five or 'n' dimensions are involved and it is not possible to visualise the process, but the mathematical principles used to establish the regression equation, in principle, are the same.

An example, in which playing sport is related to income and age, is shown in Figure 17.23. It will be noticed that the value of R has risen from 0.44 in the single variable case (Figure 17.20, Example 2) to 0.5799, indicating an improvement in the 'fit' of the data to the model. The model equation is now:

$$\text{Sport-spectating (per 3 months)} = -0.3.49 + 0.056 * \text{income} + 0.0227 * \text{age}$$

It is possible, in theory, to continue to add variables to the equation. This should, however, be done with caution, since it frequently involves *multicollinearity*, where the independent variables are themselves intercorrelated. The 'independent' variables should be, as far as possible, just that: independent. Various tests exist to check for this phenomenon. Often, in sport, a large number of variables are involved, many intercorrelated, but each contributing something to the sport phenomenon under investigation. Multivariate analysis procedures, such as cluster and factor analysis, discussed below, are designed partly to overcome these problems.

Structural equation modelling

A technique often used in sport research is *structural equation modelling* (SEM), or *path analysis*, in which a network of equations is established to model a particular social process. An example is shown in Figure 17.24, relating to health and fitness. This suggests that a person's exercise regime affects the person's fitness which in turn affects the person's health. But engaging in exercise might also affect health directly because it produces a sense of well-being. There are direct and indirect influences among the variables and SEM seeks to identify and quantify them using regression equations.

Procedure

1. Select *Analyze* then *Regression* then *Linear.*
2. Transfer *sport* to *dependent* box and *age, income* to *independents* box.
3. At *Method*, select *Enter* for all the selected variables to be included immediately, or *Stepwise* for the program to select and include variables in order of influence.
4. Select *OK* to produce the output.

Output

Variables Entered/Removed[b]

Model	Variables Entered	Variables Removed	Method
1	**Age, Income pa**[a]	.	Enter

a All requested variables entered. b Dependent Variable: Watch sport

Model Summary

Model	R	R Square	Adjusted R Square	Std. Error of the Estimate
1	**.580**[a]	**.336**	.308	1.87

a Predictors: (Constant), Age, Income pa

ANOVA[b]

Model		Sum of Squares	df	Mean Square	F	Sig.
1	Regression	83.023	2	41.512	**11.907**	**.000**[a]
	Residual	163.857	47	3.486		
	Total	246.880	49			

a Predictors: (Constant), Age, Income pa. b Dependent Variable: Watch sport

Coefficients[a]

		Unstandardized Coefficients		Standardized Coefficients	t	Sig.
Model		B	Std. Error	Beta		
1	(Constant)	**−3.493**	1.316		−2.654	.011
	Income pa	**.056**	.084	.111	.662	.511
	Age	**.227**	.076	.497	2.969	.005

a Dependent Variable: Watch sport

Figure 17.23 Multiple regression – procedures

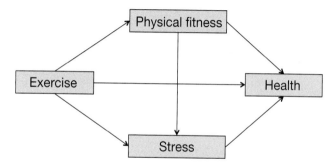

Figure 17.24 Structural equation modelling

One form of SEM is *hierarchical modelling* which recognises that data sets are often structured hierarchically – for example, players in a sport belong to teams, which have features in common, then teams belong to regional leagues which in turn belong to national leagues. While team and league membership can be seen as variables attached to individual players, statistically and conceptually it is advisable to recognise the existence of groups of players with common characteristics. Special computer packages and procedures are available to undertake SEM and hierarchical modelling, as indicated in the Resources section.

Challenges are presented in two statistical analysis situations which often arise in sport research: binary data and nominal data. Solutions are offered by *binary logistic regression* and *multiple classification analysis*, respectively. These are discussed briefly below.

Binary logistic regression analysis and odds ratios: Data in binary form – for example male/female or participant/non-participant – can be quantified by use of one and zero. Mathematically, statistics such as means and correlation coefficients can be calculated, but they violate some of the principles behind statistical tests, such as the assumption that data are normally distributed. The oddity of the data can be seen in Figure 17.25, which portrays one scale variable and one binary variable, with a regression line and correlation coefficient indicated. If the scale variable were to be replaced by a second binary variable, all the cases would be located at four points only: 0,0; 0,1; 1,1; and 1,0.

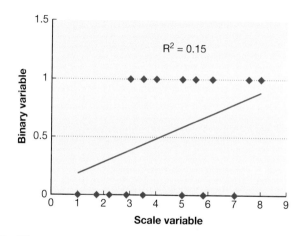

Figure 17.25 Binary and scale variable graphic

Binary logistic regression is designed to cope with these situations. The relationship is described by the *odds ratios*. An odds ratio describes the relative strength of the association between an independent variable and categories of the dependent variables. For example, in examining the relationship between sport participation (yes/no) and gender (male/female), an odds ratio of 1.4 for males and 0.6 for females would indicate that males are 1.4 times more likely to participate in sport than females and females are 0.6 times as likely to participate as males. The advantage of binary logistic regression over, for example, a series of chi-square tests is that all independent variables can be modelled in a single procedure with the odds ratios for each being considered against each other. Sources/examples are provided in the Resources section.

Multidimensional scaling

Nominal data can be handled in combination with scale/ordinal data, as indicated in Figure 17.3, but when relationships between a number of nominal variables are involved, *multidimensional scaling* is one solution. It typically creates a visual representation of the pattern of proximities (i.e. similarities or distances) among variables. Sources and examples are indicated in the Resources section.

Multivariate analysis

Introduction

A number of analytical techniques are used when the number of independent variables is large and there is a desire to group them in some way. The theoretical counterpart to this is that there are some complex phenomena which cannot be measured by one or two variables, but require a 'battery' of variables, each contributing some aspect to the make-up of the phenomenon. Examples are:

- a person's 'lifestyle' or 'psychographic' group (made up of variables such as sport, leisure and work patterns, income and expenditure patterns, values, age, and family/household situation);

- a person's characteristics as a sport tourist (made up of variables such as travel experience, expenditure patterns, sport product desired and satisfactions sought).

Each of these is often researched using a large number of data items – for example lifestyles/psychographics have been measured by asking people as many as 300 questions about their attitudes to work, politics, morals, sport and leisure, religion and so on. The procedures discussed below may be:

- *exploratory* – the analytical process is used to discover any factors/clusters which may exist in the data; or

- *confirmatory* – the analytical process is used to test the existence of one or more hypothesised clusters or factors.

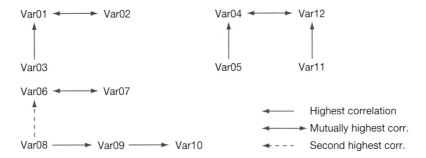

Figure 17.26 Simple manual factor analysis

Factor analysis

Factor analysis is based on the idea that certain variables 'go together', in that people with a high score on one variable also tend to have a high score on certain others, which might then form a group – for example people who play sport are also likely to watch sport; people with strong pro-environment views might be found to favour certain types of outdoor activity. Analysis of this type of phenomenon can be approached using a simple, manual technique involving a correlation matrix of the variables, as illustrated in Figure 17.25. Groupings of variables can be produced by indicating which variables have their highest and second-highest correlations with each other. In Figure 17.26 three groupings of variables are shown.

This procedure only takes account of the highest and second-highest correlations, as indicated. But variables will have a range of lower-order relationships with each other which are difficult to take account of using this manual method. A number of lower-order correlations may, cumulatively, be more significant than a single highest correlation. Factor analysis is a mathematical procedure which groups the variables taking account of *all* the correlations. The details of the method are beyond the scope of this book, but sources are indicated in the Resources section.

Cluster analysis

Cluster analysis is another 'grouping' procedure, but it focuses on the individuals directly rather than the variables. Imagine a situation with two variables, age and some behavioural variable, and data points plotted in the usual way, as shown in Figure 17.27. It can be seen that there are three broad 'clusters' of respondents – two young clusters and one older cluster. Each of these clusters might form, for example, particular market segments. With just two variables and a few observations it is relatively simple to identify clusters visually. But with more variables and hundreds of cases this would be more difficult.

Cluster analysis involves giving the computer a set of rules for building clusters. It first calculates the 'distances' between data points, in terms of a range of specified variables. Those points which are closest together are put into a

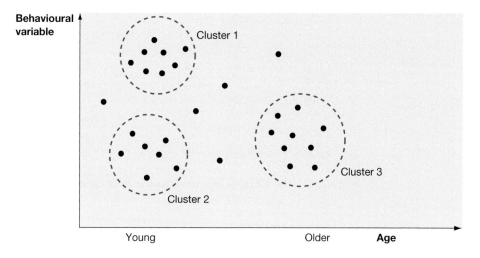

Figure 17.27   Plots of 'clusters'

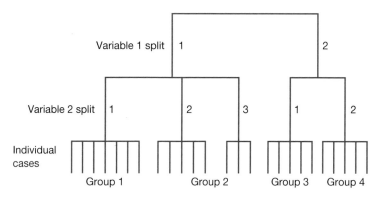

Figure 17.28   Dendrogram

first-round 'cluster' and a new 'point' halfway between the two is put in their place. The process is repeated to form a second round of clustering, and a third and fourth and so on, until there are only two 'points' left. The result is usually illustrated by a 'dendrogram', of the sort shown in Figure 17.28.

In conclusion

Much sport research, even of a quantitative nature, is conducted without the use of the techniques covered in this chapter. This is a reflection of the descriptive nature of some of the research in the field **(see Chapter 1)**, the nature of the data involved and the needs of the audience or client for the research. Often in sport the need is for 'broad brush' research findings: accuracy is required but not a high level of precision. Contrast this with medical research, where precision can be a matter of life or death. To some extent the use of statistical techniques is related to disciplinary traditions, and this is reflected in the variety of journals in the field. Some sport researchers could therefore find that they rarely make use of the techniques presented in this chapter, but they may wish to be able to interpret research reports which do make use of them, and they should be able to utilise them if called upon.

As has been stressed throughout this book, data collection and analysis should be determined by a theoretical, conceptual or evaluative framework. At the analysis stage the researcher should, ideally, not be wondering what to relate to what, and choosing variables and analyses in an ad hoc manner. While a certain amount of inductive exploration and even serendipity is inevitable, ideally there should be a basic analysis plan from the beginning. Key variables and the question of relationships between them should have been thought about in advance, for example as a result of an early 'concept mapping' exercise. Thus, while the examples given in this chapter may appear ad hoc and 'data driven', in a real research project the procedures used should be theory driven or problem or hypothesis driven.

Summary

This chapter builds on Chapter 13, which introduces the idea of sampling and its effects, and on Chapter 16, which deals with the analysis of questionnaire survey data using the package SPSS. Here, the principles and processes involved in statistical analysis are introduced. The phenomenon of statistics, in this context, does not refer just to quantification, but to the processes required to generalise from sample findings to the wider population. Statistical concepts are initially introduced, including: the idea of probabilistic statements; the normal distribution; significance; the null hypothesis; and dependent and independent variables. The chapter then outlines SPSS procedures and presents outputs for a number of statistical tests, as follows.

- chi-square – for examining the relationship between two variables in frequency table;

- the t-test – for comparing the significance of the difference between two means;

- one-way analysis of variance (ANOVA) – for examining the relationship between two variables as expressed by a set of means;

- factorial analysis of variance (ANOVA) – for examining the relationship between one dependent variable and two independent variables based on means;

- correlation – the relationship between two scale variables;

- linear regression – which establishes the 'line of best fit' between two variables;

- multiple regression – which examines the relationship between one dependent variable and two or more independent variables;

- cluster and factor analysis – which deal with summarising the relationships among large numbers of variables.

Test questions

1. What is a probabilistic statement?

2. Explain the nature and purpose of the 'null hypothesis'.

3. If two measures from a study are described as statistically different at the .05 level, what does this mean?

4. Outline the three main types of measure applied to variables and the implications of each for undertaking statistical tests.

5. What statistical tests can be used for nominal variables?

Exercises

1. Replicate all or a selection of the analyses set out in this chapter using the data in Appendix 17.1 (downloadable from the book website).

2. Using your own questionnaire developed in Chapter 16, add a range of scale variables to the questionnaire, similar to those listed in Appendix 17.1, conduct supplementary interviews covering these variables and replicate some of the analyses set out in this chapter.

Resources

Websites

- SPSS: http://www-01.ibm.com/software/analytics/spss

- Structural equation modelling (SEM):

○ Semnet discussion group: www2.gsu.edu/~mkteer/semnet.html

○ Amos software: www.spss.com/amos

○ Lisrel software: www.ssicentral.com/lisrel/index.html

Publications

- Statistical analysis generally: There are many excellent statistics textbooks available which cover the range of techniques included in this chapter and, of course, much more. Texts vary in terms of the degree of familiarity with mathematics they assume on the part of the reader, so readers with limited mathematical knowledge should 'shop around' to find a text which deals with the topic in conceptual terms rather than in detailed mathematical terms. However, a certain amount of mathematical aptitude is, of course, essential.

- Binary data analysis, logistic analysis, odds ratios: Cox and Snell (1989), Pampel (2000); sport example: Lera-Lopez and Rapun-Garate (2005).

- Cluster analysis: Downward and Riordan (2009).

- Factor analysis: Kim and Mueller (1978).

- Hierarchical modelling: Todd *et al.* (2005).

- Modelling: sport participation demand: Downward and Rasciute (2010); consumer sport and recreation expenditure: Pawlowski and Breuer (2011).

- Multidimensional scaling: Borg and Groenen (2005); sport example: Brackenridge *et al.* (2008).

- Multi-level modelling: Luke (2004); sport examples: Todd *et al.* (2005), Wicker *et al.* (2013).

- SPSS texts: see Chapter 16, Resources section.

- Structural equation modelling (SEM): general: Kline (2005); sport examples: Kokolakakis *et al.* (2012), Van Tuyckom *et al.* (2010).

References

Borg, I. and Groenen, P. J. F. (2005) *Modern Multidimensional Scaling.* New York: Springer.

Brackenridge, C. H., Bishopp, D., Moussalli, S. and Tapp, J. (2008) The characteristics of sexual abuse in sport: a multidimensional scaling analysis of events described in media reports. *International Journal of Sport and Exercise Psychology*, 6(4), 385–406.

Cox, D. R., and Snell, E. J. (1989) *Analysis of Binary Data*. Boca Raton, FL: Chapman Hall/CRC.

Downward, P. and Rasciute, S. (2010) The relative demands for sports and leisure in England. *European Sport Management Quarterly*, 10(2), 189–214.

Downward, P. and Riordan, J. (2009) Social interactions and the demand for sport: cluster demand in economics. In D. Byrne and C. C. Ragin (eds) *Sage Handbook of Case-based Methods*. London: Sage, 392–409.

Kim, J-O. and Mueller, C. W. (1978) *Factor Analysis: Statistical Methods and Practical Issues*. Thousand Oaks, CA: Sage.

Kline, R. B. (2005) *Principles and Practice of Structural Equation Modelling, Second edn*. New York: Guilford Press.

Kokolakakis, T., Lera-López, F. and Panagouleas, T. (2012) Analysis of the determinants of sports participation in Spain and England. *Applied Economics*, 44(21), 2785–98.

Lera-Lopez, F. and Rapun-Garate, M. (2005) Sports participation versus consumer expenditure on sport: different determinants and strategies in sports management. *European Sport Management Quarterly*, 5(2), 167–86.

Luke, D. A. (2004) *Multilevel Modelling*. Thousand Oaks, CA: Sage.

Pampel, F. C. (2000) *Logistic Regression: a Primer*. Thousand Oaks, CA: Sage.

Pawlowski, T. and Breuer, C. (2011) The demand for sports and recreational services: empirical evidence from Germany. *European Sport Management Quarterly*, 11(1), 5–34.

Todd, S. Y., Crook, T. R. and Barilla, A. G. (2005) Hierarchical linear modelling of multilevel data. *Journal of Sport Management*, 19(4), 387–403.

Van Tuyckom, C., Schveerder, J. and Bracke, P. (2010) Gender and age inequalities in regular sports participation: A cross-national study of 25 European countries. *Journal of Sports Sciences*, 28(10), 1077–84.

Wicker, P., Hallmann, K. and Breur, C. (2013) Analyzing the impact of sport infrastructure on sport participation using geo-coded data: evidence from multi-level models. *Sport Management Review*, 16(1), 54–67.

Appendix 17.1 Details of example data file used – questionnaire, variable details and data

Additional questions (added to the questionnaire in Figure 10.20)

What is your approximate gross income in £ per year: £ | ___inc

Approximately how many times have you engaged in the following activities
in the last 3 months:

a. Sporting activity   ____times | ____sport
b. Watch sport live   ____times | ____ spectate2
c. Visited a park   ____times | ____ park
d. Gone out for a meal   ____times | ____ meal

Approximately how much did you spend on sport,
including equipment and fees, in the last year?   £____ | ____ sportexp

Variable details

Name	Type	Width	Decimals	Lab	Values	Missing	Columns	Align	Measure
qno	Numeric	5	0	Questionnaire number	None	None	8	Right	Scale
status	Numeric	5	0	Student status	1 Undergrad. 2 Grad. Dip. 3 Masters 4 Other	None	8	Right	Nominal
pool	Numeric	5	0	Campus pool in last 4 wks	0 No 1 Yes	None	8	Right	Nominal
gym	Numeric	5	0	Campus gym in last 4 wks	0 No 1 Yes	None	8	Right	Nominal
squash	Numeric	5	0	Campus squash in last 4 wks	0 No 1 Yes	None	8	Right	Nominal
spectate2	Numeric	5	0	Spectated on campus in last 4 wks	0 No 1 Yes	None	8	Right	Nominal
cheap	Numeric	5	0	Free/cheap (rank)	None	None	8	Right	Ordinal
hours	Numeric	5	0	Opening hours (rank)	None	None	8	Right	Ordinal
qual	Numeric	5	0	Quality of facilities (rank)	None	None	8	Right	Ordinal
meet	Numeric	5	0	Socialising (rank)	None	None	8	Right	Ordinal
time	Numeric	5	0	Time available (rank)	None	None	8	Right	Ordinal
spend	Numeric	5	0	Expenditure on sport/ entertainment per month	None	None	8	Right	Scale
relax	Numeric	5	0	Relaxation – importance	1 Not Important 2 Important 3 Very Important	None	8	Right	Scale
social	Numeric	5	0	Social interaction – importance	As above	None	8	Right	Scale
fitness	Numeric	5	0	Fitness – importance	As above	None	8	Right	Scale

Name	Type	Width	Decimals	Lab	Values	Missing	Columns	Align	Measure
sug1	Numeric	5	0	First suggestion	1 Programme content 2 Timing 3 Facilities 4 Costs 5 Organisation	None	8	Right	Nominal
sug2	Numeric	5	0	Second suggestion	As above	None	8	Right	Nominal
sug3	Numeric	5	0	Third suggestion	As above	None	8	Right	Nominal
age	Numeric	5	0	Age	None	None	8	Right	Scale
gender	Numeric	5	0	Gender	1 male 2 Female	None	8	Right	Nominal
inc	Numeric	5	0	Income pa, $'000s	None	None	8	Right	Scale
sport	Numeric	5	0	Play sport – times in last 3 months	None	None	8	Right	Scale
spectate2	Numeric	5	0	Watch sport – times in last 3 months	None	None	8	Right	Scale
park	Numeric	5	0	Visit park – times in last 3 months	None	None	8	Right	Scale
meal	Numeric	5	0	Go out for meal – times in last 3 months	None	None	8	Right	Scale
sportexp	Numeric	5	0	Annual sport exp	None	None	8	Right	Scale
statusr	Numeric	5	0	Student status – recoded	1 Full-time 2 Part-time	None	7	Right	Nominal

Data

Qno	status	pool	gym	squash	spectate	cheap	hours	qual	meet	time	spend	relax	social	fitness	sug1	sug2	sug3	age	gender	inc	sport	spectate2	park	meal	sportexp
1	2	1	1	0	0	1	4	2	3	5	100	3	3	1	1	.	.	18	1	12	25	1	5	8	220
2	2	1	1	1	0	1	4	2	3	5	50	2	3	1	2	1	.	23	1	15	30	0	15	10	485
3	3	1	0	0	0	2	5	1	3	4	250	2	2	2	3	4	.	28	2	15	5	4	20	2	450
4	4	0	0	0	0	2	3	1	4	5	25	3	2	2	1	2	4	35	2	21	0	5	4	12	750
5	3	1	0	0	1	1	4	3	2	5	55	3	3	1	.	.	.	29	2	20	4	5	25	4	650
6	3	1	1	1	0	2	4	1	3	5	40	2	3	1	2	.	.	29	1	14	20	0	0	8	480
7	2	1	0	0	0	3	2	1	4	5	150	2	3	2	3	.	.	23	2	11	6	6	0	3	250
8	2	1	0	1	0	3	4	2	1	5	250	1	2	2	4	5	.	22	1	12	8	0	12	1	120
9	4	0	1	0	0	1	5	2	3	4	300	2	3	2	.	.	.	22	2	15	10	2	20	6	450
10	3	1	1	0	0	2	3	1	5	4	100	1	2	1	1	1	.	19	2	12	50	0	15	10	220
11	3	1	1	0	1	2	3	1	4	5	75	2	2	1	2	3	.	20	1	11	13	1	2	9	300
12	2	1	0	1	0	1	4	3	2	5	50	2	3	1	.	.	.	19	1	14	6	3	13	5	575
13	1	1	0	1	0	1	5	2	3	4	55	2	3	2	1	2	.	21	2	11	1	5	0	7	300
14	3	1	0	0	0	2	2	1	3	5	75	3	3	2	4	.	.	35	2	25	0	6	0	9	850
15	1	1	1	1	0	3	4	1	5	4	150	3	3	1	1	2	5	22	1	9	15	1	25	6	200
16	2	1	0	0	0	3	4	1	2	5	200	1	2	2	4	5	.	28	2	12	6	8	1	2	220
17	1	0	0	0	0	1	5	2	3	4	175	2	3	2	.	.	.	20	2	12	20	0	20	11	275
18	1	1	1	1	0	2	3	1	5	4	100	1	2	1	1	2	.	21	1	8	12	2	2	8	150
19	4	1	1	0	1	2	3	1	4	5	105	2	3	1	1	3	4	32	2	23	2	5	10	10	1200

sportexp	meal	park	spectate2	sport	inc	gender	age	sug3	sug2	sug1	fitness	social	relax	spend	time	meet	qual	hours	cheap	spectate	squash	gym	pool	status	Qno
300	0	4	5	4	16	1	23	.	.	2	1	2	2	50	5	2	3	4	1	0	1	0	1	1	20
250	3	0	2	6	11	1	18	.	.	3	2	3	2	150	5	4	1	2	3	0	0	0	1	1	21
325	1	12	2	8	12	1	25	.	5	4	2	2	1	250	5	1	2	4	3	0	1	0	1	2	22
600	6	20	2	10	17	2	22	.	.	.	2	3	2	300	4	3	2	5	1	0	0	1	0	4	23
400	12	15	0	50	11	2	29	.	1	1	1	2	1	100	4	5	1	3	2	0	0	1	1	3	24
230	9	2	1	13	10	1	23	.	3	2	1	2	2	75	5	4	1	3	2	1	0	1	1	3	25
125	5	13	5	6	9	2	19	.	.	.	1	3	2	50	5	2	3	4	1	0	1	0	1	2	26
350	7	0	5	1	14	1	21	.	2	1	2	3	2	55	4	3	2	5	1	0	1	0	1	1	27
500	9	0	6	0	21	2	35	.	.	4	2	3	3	75	5	3	1	4	2	0	0	1	1	3	28
200	6	25	1	15	12	1	22	5	2	1	1	3	3	150	4	5	1	2	3	0	0	1	1	1	29
850	4	25	5	4	20	1	29	.	.	.	1	3	3	55	5	2	3	4	1	1	0	0	1	3	30
350	8	0	0	20	13	1	20	.	.	2	1	3	2	40	5	3	1	4	2	0	1	1	1	3	31
1000	3	0	2	6	23	1	23	.	.	3	2	3	2	150	5	4	1	2	3	0	0	0	1	2	32
275	4	12	6	8	12	2	25	.	5	4	2	2	1	250	5	1	2	4	3	0	1	0	1	2	33
750	6	20	2	10	20	1	22	.	.	.	2	3	2	300	4	3	2	5	1	0	0	1	0	4	34
150	10	15	0	50	10	2	19	.	1	1	1	2	1	100	4	5	1	3	2	0	0	1	1	3	35
250	9	2	1	13	10	2	20	.	3	2	1	2	2	75	5	4	1	3	2	1	0	1	1	3	36
450	5	13	1	6	15	1	19	.	.	.	1	3	2	50	5	2	3	4	1	0	1	0	1	2	37

Case																									
38	1	1	0	1	0	1	5	2	3	4	55	2	3	2	1	2	.	21	1	15	1	5	0	7	500
39	3	1	1	0	0	2	4	1	3	5	75	3	3	2	4	.	.	35	2	21	0	6	0	9	800
40	1	1	1	0	0	3	2	1	5	4	150	3	3	1	1	2	5	22	2	14	15	1	25	6	450
41	1	0	0	0	0	1	5	2	3	4	175	2	3	2	.	.	.	20	2	15	20	0	20	11	375
42	1	1	1	1	0	2	3	1	5	4	100	1	2	1	1	2	.	21	1	10	12	2	2	8	220
43	4	1	1	0	1	2	3	1	4	5	105	2	3	1	1	3	4	32	1	24	2	5	10	10	900
44	1	1	0	1	0	1	4	3	2	5	50	2	2	1	2	.	.	28	1	16	4	5	4	4	700
45	2	1	0	0	0	3	2	1	4	5	150	2	3	2	3	.	.	23	2	9	6	2	0	3	180
46	2	1	0	1	0	3	4	2	1	5	250	1	2	2	4	5	.	25	1	13	8	2	12	1	350
47	4	0	1	0	0	1	5	2	3	4	300	2	3	2	.	.	.	22	2	15	10	2	20	6	620
48	3	1	1	0	0	2	3	1	5	4	100	1	2	1	1	1	.	19	2	8	50	0	15	10	210
49	3	1	1	0	1	2	3	1	4	5	75	2	2	1	2	3	.	20	2	10	13	1	2	9	120
50	2	1	0	1	0	1	4	3	2	5	50	2	3	1	.	.	.	19	1	12	6	3	13	5	220

Appendix 17.2 Statistical formulae

95% Confidence interval for normal distribution for percentage p

$$\text{C.I.} = 1.96\sqrt{\frac{p(100-p)}{n-1}}$$

Where n = sample size

Chi-square

$$\chi^2 = \sqrt{\Sigma((O - E)/E)^2}$$

t for difference between means

$$t = \sqrt{\frac{(\bar{x}_1 - \bar{x}_2)}{(s_1^2/n_1 + s_2^2 + n_1)}}$$

Standard deviation

$$SD = \sqrt{\frac{\Sigma(x-\bar{x})^2}{n}}$$

Correlation coefficient

$$r = \sqrt{\frac{\Sigma(x - \bar{x})(y - \hat{y}))^2}{(s_1^2/n_1 + s_2^2 + n_2)}}$$

Value of t for correlation coefficient

$$t = r\sqrt{(N - 2)/(1 - r)^2}$$

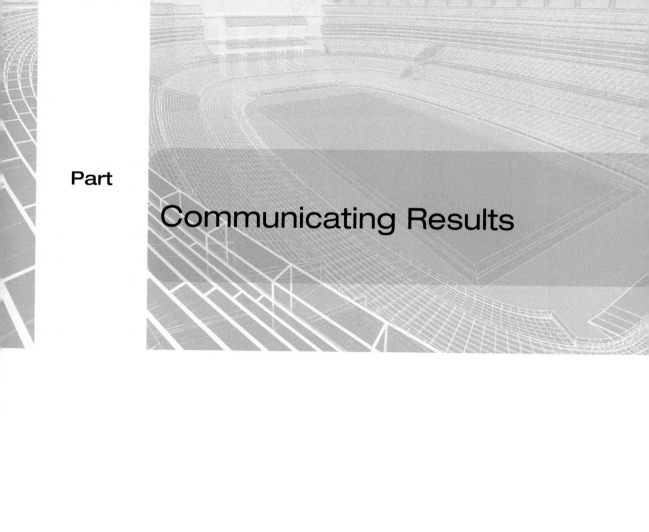

Part

Communicating Results

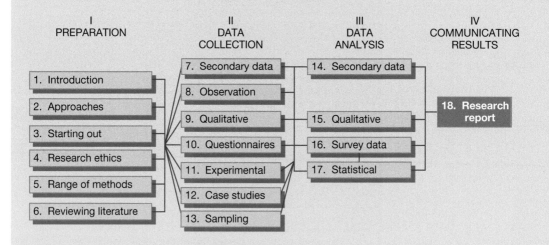

I PREPARATION	II DATA COLLECTION	III DATA ANALYSIS	IV COMMUNICATING RESULTS
1. Introduction	7. Secondary data	14. Secondary data	
2. Approaches	8. Observation		**18. Research report**
3. Starting out	9. Qualitative	15. Qualitative	
4. Research ethics	10. Questionnaires	16. Survey data	
5. Range of methods	11. Experimental	17. Statistical	
6. Reviewing literature	12. Case studies		
	13. Sampling		

Research reports and presentations

Introduction

This chapter outlines key aspects of the reporting of research results. It concentrates primarily on the preparation and presentation of written reports, including discussion of content, structure and layout, and considers the varying requirements and conventions of different reporting formats, including academic articles, consultancy reports, books and theses. It concludes with a consideration of non-written formats, particularly oral presentations.

Written research reports

Written reports of research are a key element of the world of research, management and planning. Applied studies of the sort discussed in Chapter 1, namely feasibility studies, marketing plans, sport and recreation needs studies, sport development plans, market research studies and performance appraisals, all tend to be presented in the form of written reports. The results of academic studies are produced in the form of articles, reports, books, or theses/dissertations. In this chapter we deal with three format groups: management/planning/project reports, academic articles and theses. The first of these may arise in a management/planning context or may arise from a funded academic project when the researcher reports to the funding body; this style of report is referred to as a *project report* in the discussion below. Project reports prepared for a policy or practitioner readership are referred to as *management reports*. In North America the word dissertation is generally used rather than thesis. The main distinguishing characteristics of the three styles of report are summarised in Figure 18.1.

The 'medium is the message' is a term coined by Marshall McLuhan, particularly in relation to electronic media, but in this case the medium is the written report. The ability to prepare a report and to recognise good-quality and poor-quality reports should be seen as a key element in the skills of the researcher and manager. While form is no substitute for good content, a report which is poorly presented can undermine or even negate good content. While most of the researcher's attention should, of course, be focused on achieving high-quality substantive content, the general presentational and structural aspects raised in this chapter also merit serious attention.

Getting started

In discussing research proposals in Chapter 3 it was noted that researchers invariably leave too little time for report writing. Even when adequate time has been allocated in the timetable, this is often whittled away and the writing of the report is delayed, leaving too little time. There is a tendency to put off report writing because it is difficult and it is often felt that, with just a little more data analysis or a little more reading of the literature, the process of writing the report will become easier. This is rarely the case – it is invariably difficult!

A regrettably common practice is for writers of research reports to spend a great deal of their depleted time, with the deadline looming, writing and preparing material which could have been attended to much earlier in the process. There are often large parts of any report which can be written before data analysis is complete, or even started. Such parts include the introduction, statement of objectives, outline of theoretical or evaluative framework, literature review and description of the methodology. In addition, time-consuming activities such as arranging for maps, illustrations and cover designs to be produced need not be left until the last minute! One way to start the process is to open files for each section/chapter of the report, including 'preliminaries' (acknowledgements, preface etc.) and 'end matter' (appendices, bibliography, etc.) and begin placing relevant material (notes, drafts, illustrations) in them from the beginning.

Report components

Reports generally include certain standard components, although some are unique to certain report styles, as shown in Figure 18.2. The components listed are discussed in turn below.

Characteristic	Management/planning/ project report	Academic article	Thesis
Authors	In-house staff, external consultants or funded academics	Academics	Honours, master's or doctoral students
Content	Report of commissioned or grant-funded project	Report of academic research	Report of academic research
Brief	Provided by commissioning organisation or outlined in grant application	Generally self-generated (although may arise from commissioned work)	Generally self-generated (although may arise in part from grant-funded project)
Quality assurance	In-house: internal Consultants/academics: reputation of consultants/ researchers	Anonymous refereeing process (see Chapter 1)	Supervision plus examination by external examiners
Readership	Professional managers/ planners and possibly elected or appointed board/council/committee members	Primarily academics	Primarily academic
Published status	May or may not be publicly available	Publicly available (often online) in published academic journals	Publicly available in libraries and, recently, online; findings generally published in summary form in one or more academic articles
Length	Varies	In the social/ management sciences, including sport studies, generally 5000–7000 words	In the social/management sciences, including sport studies: Honours: c. 20,000 words; Masters: c. 40,000 words; PhD: c. 70,000 words +
Emphasis	Emphasis on findings rather than links with the literature/theory and methodology (although the latter must be described)	Methodology, theory, literature as important as the findings	Methodology, theory, literature as important as the findings

Figure 18.1 Types of research report

Component	Content	Management/Planning/ Research report	Academic article	Thesis
Cover	– Title of report – Author(s) – Institution/publisher – ISBN (if published), back cover	All items	Not applicable	Prescribed by university regulations
Title page	– Title of report – Author(s) – Institution/publisher, including address, phone, fax numbers, email, website* – Sponsoring body (e.g. 'Report to the Sports Commission') – Date of publication* – If the report is for sale: ISBN*. (* sometimes on reverse of title page)	All items	Submitted article includes cover page containing: – Title of article – Author(s) – Institutional affiliation – Contact details (Page omitted by editors when article is sent for anonymous refereeing)	Prescribed by university regulations
Contents page(s)	See Figure 18.3 for example	As in Figure 18.3	Not applicable	As in Figure 18.3 but less detailed section numbering
Summary	Summary of **whole** report, including background, aims, methods, main findings, conclusions and (where applicable) recommendations	Executive Summary: Length: 20 pp report: ½–1 page 21–50 pp report: 3–4 pp 50–100 pp report: 5–6 pp	Abstract: Length: typically about 300 words	Synopsis: Length: typically 3–5 pages
Preface/Foreword	Optional. Contains background information, sometimes an explanation of authors' involvement with the project. Or may be by a significant individual not directly involved in the project. Not applicable in academic article, where such information may be included in an endnote.			
Acknowledgements	– Funding organisations – Liaison officers of funding organisations – Members of steering committees – Organisations/individuals providing access to information etc. – Staff employed (e.g. including interviewers, coders, computer programmers, secretaries, word processors) – Individuals (including academic supervisors) who have given advice, commented on report drafts, etc. – (Collectively) Individuals who responded to questionnaires, etc.			
Main body of report	Discussed separately			
Appendices	Text/statistical material included for the record but which, because of its size, would interrupt the flow if included in the main body of the report			

Figure 18.2　Report style and components

Cover

For a project report the cover should include minimal information, such as title, author(s) and publisher or sponsor. The lavishness and design content will vary with the context and the resources available.

If the report is available for sale it should include an International Standard Book Number (ISBN) on the back cover. The ISBN is a 13-digit product identifier for books and other published materials used by publishers, booksellers and libraries. The ISBN system is overseen by the London-based International ISBN Agency and registered with the International Organization for Standardization (ISO) in Geneva. ISBNs are allocated by National ISBN Agencies, which are often national libraries which, under national legislation, generally receive free deposit copies of all publications produced in their respective countries. The ISBN makes it easy to order publications through booksellers and ensures that the publication is catalogued in library systems and databases around the world.

Title page

The title page is the first page inside the cover of a project report. It may include much the same information as the cover or considerably more detail, as indicated in Figure 18.2. In some cases, as in commercially published books, some of the detail is provided on the reverse of the title page.

List of contents

A list of contents is required in project reports and theses and may include just chapter titles, but will also usually include full details of sub-sections. An example of a contents list is shown in Figure 18.3. Word-processing packages include procedures for compiling tables of contents and lists, such as tables and diagrams.

Summary – executive summary/abstract/synopsis

A summary is required for all three styles of report except for very short project reports. The summary is called *executive summary* (in a management report), *abstract* (in a journal article) or *synopsis* (in a thesis), depending on the context. The typical length also varies, depending on the context.

An executive summary is sometimes thought of as the summary for the 'busy executive' who does not have time to read the whole report, but really refers to the idea that it should contain information necessary to take *executive action* on the basis of the report.

A summary is *not* the introduction; as indicated in Figure 18.2, it should contain a summary of the *whole* report, article or thesis, including aims, method and results/conclusions. The summary should, of course, be written *last*.

CONTENTS

                                                Page

Executive Summary .... (i)
Preface .... (iii)
Acknowledgements .... (iv)

1. INTRODUCTION 1
   1.1 Background to the study 1
   1.2 The nature of the problem 3
   1.3 Aims of the study 4
   1.4 Outline of the report 4

2. LITERATURE REVIEW 5
   2.1 Research on youth and sport generally 5
   2.2 Research on student sport 8
   2.3 Conclusions: the state of knowledge on students and sport 10
   2.4 Questions still to be answered 12

3. METHODOLOGY 13
   3.1 Data requirements 13
   3.2 Selection of methods 15
   3.3 Secondary data: sources and proposed analysis 16
   3.4 In-depth interviews 18
   3.5 Questionnaire survey 19
   3.6 Pilot survey 21

4. STUDENT SPORT IN THE 1990s 22
   4.1 Data sources 22
   4.2 Students at school 22
   4.4 Students at college/university 25
   4.5 Conclusions 27

5. STUDENT WORK AND SPORT/LEISURE 29
   5.1 Sample characteristics 29
   5.2 Attitudes towards academic work 30
   5.3 Attitudes towards paid work 32
   5.4 Attitudes towards sport and leisure 34
   5.4 Work, leisure and sport: a synthesis 37

6. SUMMARY AND CONCLUSIONS 40
   6.1 Summary 40
   6.2 Conclusions 42

REFERENCES 44

APPENDICES
1. Copy of questionnaire 49
2. In-depth interview checklist 51
3. Census data on student population 53
4. Survey statistical summary 56

LIST OF TABLES
1.1   Title xx
1.2   Title xx
Etc.

LIST OF DIAGRAMS/ILLUSTRATIONS
1.1   Title .... yy
1.2   Title .... yy
Etc.

Figure 18.3   Example list of contents for a research report on student sport

Preface/foreword

Prefaces or forewords are used for a variety of purposes. Usually they explain the origins of the study and outline any qualifications or limitations. Acknowledgements of assistance may be included if there is no separate 'acknowledgements' section. Sometimes a significant individual is asked to write a foreword, such as the director of an institution, a minister or an eminent academic.

Acknowledgements

It is clearly a matter of courtesy to acknowledge any assistance received during the course of a research project. People and institutions who might be acknowledged are listed in Figure 18.2.

Main body of the report – technical aspects

Clearly the main body of the report is its most important component. The substantive content is discussed in the next section; here we consider a number of technical aspects of organisation and presentation, as listed in Figure 18.4.

Section numbering

In project reports it is usual to number not only the major sections/chapters, but also sub-sections within chapters, as shown in the example in Figure 18.3. Once a numbering system is established it should be carried through consistently throughout the report. Word-processing packages provide 'style' templates to facilitate this process.

In project reports, section numbers may extend to several levels; for example, within section 4.2, there could be sub-sections: 4.2.1, 4.2.2, etc. Further levels can become cumbersome and are generally not required throughout the report, so if there is an occasional need for further sub-sections it is often advisable to use a simple a., b., c. or (i), (ii), (iii), etc.

Journal articles rarely include section numbering; when it is included it is typically one level only.

In theses, chapters are numbered, and possibly one level of sections within chapters, but sub-section numbering is not generally used.

Paragraph numbering

In some reports, notably government reports, paragraphs are individually numbered, although this is rare. This can be useful for reference purposes when a report is being discussed in committees, etc. Paragraphs can be numbered in a single series for the whole report or chapter by chapter: in chapter 1: paragraphs 1.1, 1.2, 1.3, etc.; in chapter 2: paragraphs 2.1, 2.2, 2.3 etc., and so on.

- Section numbering
- Paragraph numbering
- 'Dot-point' lists
- Page numbering
- Headers/footers
- Heading hierarchy
- Typing layout/spacing
- Tables and statistical tests
- Presentation of tables and graphics
- Referencing
- Which person?

Figure 18.4   Main body of report: technical aspects

'Dot-point' lists

'Dot-point' lists are very common in project reports, and quite common in the other reporting formats. This device can assist the reader to understand the structure of the material and assists in visual scanning of a document. Project reports are often discussed in committee or written comments are offered in various consultation exercises, and this process is eased by dot-point lists, although numbered lists may be even more helpful: it is easier to refer to and to locate 'item 5' than 'the fifth dot point'.

Where possible, grammatical rules should be followed in dot-point lists. For example, in Figure 18.5, the introduction and the whole dot-point list are, in effect, all one sentence. There are therefore no capital letters at the beginning of each item, there are semi-colons at the end of each list item, 'and' after the pen-ultimate item and a full-stop at the end of the list. This principle is difficult to follow when the individual dot points are lengthy, perhaps themselves involving more than one sentence: in this case each dot point in a sequence should be treated as one or more complete sentences with capital letters and full-stops. Some publishers' 'house-styles', however, now omit the semi-colons, in effect treating the dot points grammatically as a series of headings.

In preparing a research report, the author should take account of:

- the likely readership;
- the requirements of the funding agency, as indicated in the study brief;
- printing or other distribution format;
- likely costs; and
- delivery of a clear message.

Figure 18.5   Dot-point list example

Page numbering

One problem in putting together long reports, especially when different authors are responsible for different sections, is to organise page numbering so that it follows on from chapter to chapter. This can be eased by numbering each chapter separately, for example: Chapter 1: pages 1.1, 1.2, 1.3, etc.; Chapter 2: pages 2.1, 2.2, 2.3, etc. and so on. Such a numbering system can also aid readers in finding their way around a report. Word-processors can be made to produce page numbers in this form.

It is general practice for the title page, contents page(s), acknowledgements and the executive summary pages to be numbered as a group using roman numerals (as in this book) and for the main body of the report to start at page 1 with normal numbers. Word-processors can facilitate this.

Headers/footers

Word-processing packages provide the facility to include a running header or footer across the top or bottom of each page. This can be used to indicate sections or chapters, as in this book, or, in the case of a consultancy report, to indicate title and authorship of the report, perhaps even displaying the consultancy logo on each page.

Heading hierarchy

In the main body of the report a hierarchy of heading styles should be used, with the major chapter/section headings being in the most prominent style and with decreasing emphasis for sub-section headings. For example:

1. Chapter Titles
1.1 Section Headings
1.1.1 Sub-section Headings

Such a convention helps readers to know where they are in a document. When a team is involved in writing a report it is clearly sensible to agree these heading styles in advance. Word-processing systems provide a number of and report 'styles' which standardise heading formats and section numbering systems, linked to the assembly of lists of contents.

Typing layout/spacing

Essays and books tend to use the convention of starting new paragraphs by indenting the first line. Report style is to separate paragraphs by a blank line and not to indent the first line. Report style also tends to have more headings. For a document in report style it is usual to leave wide margins, which raises the question as to whether it is necessary to print documents in 1.5 or double space format or whether single spacing is adequate (and more environmentally friendly!). Different journals have different format specifications for submission of articles, usually indicated in the journal itself and/or on the journal website. Universities provide their own guidelines for the layout of theses.

Tables and statistical tests

When presenting the results of quantitative research, an appropriate balance must be struck between the use of tables, graphics and text. In most cases, very large or complex tables are consigned to appendices and simplified or graphical versions included in the body of the report. It may be appropriate to place *all* tables in appendices and provide only 'reader-friendly' graphics in the body of the report. The decision on which approach to use depends partly on the complexity of the data to be presented, but mainly on the type of audience.

Tables, graphics and text each have a distinctive role to play in the presentation of the study findings:

● tables provide information;

● graphics illustrate that information so that patterns can be seen in a visual way;

● the text should be telling a story or developing an argument and 'orchestrating' tables and graphics to support that task.

There seems to be little point in the text of a report simply repeating what is in a table or graphic. At the least the text should highlight the main features of the data; ideally it should develop an argument or draw conclusions based on the data. In the example in Figure 18.6, Commentary A does little more than repeat what is in the table: it says nothing to the reader about the difference between men's and women's participation patterns, which is presumably the purpose of the exercise. Commentary B, on the other hand, is more informative, pointing out particular features of the data in the table.

In the more quantitative disciplines there is a convention that, in academic reports such as journal articles and theses, the detailed results of statistical tests should be mentioned in the text, even if the information is also available in a table. Thus, for example, a sentence in the text might read: 'Mean weekly frequency of participation by men (2.1) is significantly higher than for women (1.7, $t = 5.6$, $p > 0001$, see Table 2).' Clearly the information in brackets 'clutters' the text and makes it less 'reader-friendly' if there are a number of such insertions; it seems unnecessary to include it in the text if it can be seen in the table; and the information on the t-test may be meaningless to readers without statistical knowledge. In less quantitative fields it is not necessary to include the information in brackets, particularly the t-test result, in the text if it is available in a table. In management reports, results of statistical tests are often not included at all, although they may have been carried out, although such terms as 'significantly different' or 'not significantly different' may be used.

Presentation of diagrams and tables

Diagrams and tables should, as far as possible, be complete in themselves. That is, the title should be informative and the columns, rows or axes should be fully labelled so that the reader can understand them without necessarily referring

Table X. Participation in top 5 sports/physical activities, persons aged 16+, Great Britain, 1986

Activity	% Participating in four weeks prior to interview (most popular quarter)	
	Males	Females
Walking	21	18
Football	6	*
Snooker/billiards	17	3
Swimming – indoor	9	10
Darts	9	3
Keep fit/yoga	1	5

Source: General Household Survey, OPCS

* less than 0.05%

Commentary A

The table indicates that the top five sports and physical recreation activities for men are walking, with 21% participation, snooker/billiards (17%), indoor swimming (9%), darts (9%), and football (6%), whereas for women the five most popular activities are walking (18%), indoor swimming (10%), keep fit/yoga (5%), snooker/billiards (3%) and darts (3%).

Commentary B

Men and women may have more in common in their patterns of leisure activity than is popularly imagined. The table indicates that four activities – walking, swimming, snooker/billiards and darts – are included in the top five most popular sport and physical recreation activities for both men and women. While in general men's participation levels are higher than those of women, the table shows that women's participation rate exceeds that of men for two of the activities, namely keep fit/yoga and swimming.

Figure 18.6 Table and commentaries

to the text. The table in Figure 18.6 follows these principles. Thus tables or graphics presenting data from sport participation surveys or other data sources should include information on:

- the geographical area to which the data refer;
- the year to which the data refer or the year collected;
- gender and age-range of the sample or population to which the data relate;
- sample size, where relevant; and
- units of measurement.

Reproductions of secondary data should indicate the source of data, but tables or graphics presenting results from the primary data collection of the study, such as a survey, do not need to indicate this on every table and diagram – however, some consultants tend to do this for intellectual property reasons so that if a user copies just one table or diagram, its source is still indicated.

Referencing

References to the literature and other sources in academic reports should follow the referencing conventions as set out in Chapter 6. This may, however, be inappropriate for the non-academic readerships of management reports. While sources should be acknowledged in such reports, it is generally appropriate to do so in an unobtrusive manner – for example by use of the endnote or footnote rather than author/date reference style. In some management reports the 'review of the literature' is relegated to an appendix with just the conclusions being presented in the body of the report.

Which person?

In academic reports, it is conventional to report the conduct and findings of research in an 'impersonal style' – for example to say: 'A survey was conducted' rather than 'I/we conducted a survey'; and 'It was found that…' rather than 'I/we found that…'. Some believe that this attempt to appear 'scientific' is inappropriate in the social sciences, particularly in qualitative research where the researcher personally engages with the research subjects. First-person accounts are therefore sometimes, but not commonly, used in some sport research reports. The first person plural is also quite commonly used by consultants in management reports, especially when the consultants wish to convey the impression that they are bringing particular personal and team skills and experience to bear on a project.

The impersonal style can appear odd or pretentious when authors refer to their own work. Thus for us to say: 'Veal and Darcy (2002) have observed that sport participation is related to inequality' seems odd, and for us to say: 'The authors have observed that sport participation is related to inequality (Veal and Darcy, 2002)' seems pretentious. The solution in such a situation is either to use the first person – 'We have observed that sport participation is related to inequality (Veal and Darcy, 2002)' – or to 'de-centre' the authors – 'It has been observed that sport participation is related to inequality (Veal and Darcy, 2002)'.

Main body of the report – structure and content

Structure

It could be said that the three most important aspects of a research report are: 1. structure, 2. structure, and 3. structure! The *structure* of a report is of fundamental importance and needs to be thoroughly considered and discussed, particularly when a team is involved. While all reports have certain structural features in common, the important aspects of any one report concern the underlying argument and how that relates to the objectives of the study and any data collection and analysis involved. This is linked fundamentally to the *research objectives*, the *theoretical or evaluative framework* and the *overall research strategy* **(see Chapter 3)**.

Before writing starts, it can be useful to decide and agree not only the report structure and format, but also target word-lengths for each chapter or section. While an agreed structure is a necessary starting point, it is also necessary to be flexible. As drafting gets under way it may be found that what was originally conceived as one chapter needs to be divided into two or three chapters, or what was thought of as a separate chapter can be incorporated into another chapter or into an appendix. Throughout, consideration needs to be given to the overall length of the report, in terms of words or pages.

When a questionnaire survey is involved, there is a tendency for some authors to structure the report according to the sequence of questions in the questionnaire and, correspondingly, the sequence of tables as they are produced by the computer. This is not an appropriate way to proceed! Questionnaires are structured for ease of interview, for the convenience of interviewer and/or respondent: they do *not* provide a suitable sequence and structure for a report. The report should be structured around the substance of the research problem.

The table of contents, as shown in Figure 18.3, indicates the formal broad structure of the report to the reader. The example relates to project reports and theses, which tend to be lengthy and to be divided into chapters and to have tables of contents.

Journal articles are shorter and do not have tables of contents, but structure is, of course, still important. There is a conventional overall structure for journal articles involving about seven sections, as shown in Figure 18.7. This structure is not hard and fast: in particular, not all articles are empirical, so 'methods' and 'results' sections relating to data collection are not universal.

In the case of a project report, while the contents page indicates the general organisation of the report and should make the reader aware of the structure, this is rarely enough: it must be *explained* – often more than once. Being clear in your own mind about structure is one thing; conveying it to the reader can be quite

---

- Background/introduction/justification for the research/nature of the problem/ issue
- Review of the literature
- Specific outline of problem/issue/hypotheses
- Methods
- Results
- Conclusions
- References

Figure 18.7 Conventional academic article structure

another. Thus it is good practice, particularly in the case of a lengthy report/ thesis, to provide an outline of the structure of the whole report in the introductory chapter, *and* outlines of each chapter in the introduction to each chapter. Summaries are useful at the end of each chapter and these can be revisited and summarised at the end of the report when drawing conclusions together. It is advisable to provide numerous references backwards and forwards, as reminders to readers as to where they are in the overall 'story' of the report.

When a list of 'factors', 'issues' or 'topics' is about to be discussed, one by one, it is useful to list the factors or issues to be discussed, and then summarise at the end of the section to indicate what the review of factors or issues has achieved.

Articles are, of course, shorter, so organising the structure is less of a logistical challenge. There is no table of contents as such, although the abstract – typically just a paragraph – is usually printed at the beginning of an article and can give some impression of structure. But the logic and structure should, of course, also be explained within the article proper.

Between methods and results

All empirical research reports, regardless of format, should include a clear summary of the methods used to gather data. In journal articles the description is often quite short, because of the limitation of word-length. In management reports the description may be short in the body of the report because of the type of readership, but there is scope to provide more detail in appendices. In a thesis an extensive and explicit description of methods used is essential.

In all formats, but particularly in a thesis, the *choice* of methods should also be discussed. Why was a particular method selected? What alternatives were considered and why were they rejected? Such a discussion should be related to the nature of the research questions/hypotheses. It is not sufficient merely to list the characteristics and merits of the methods chosen, but to indicate why those *particular* characteristics were appropriate in *this particular project*. Factors to consider in selecting a research method are discussed at the end of Chapter 5 and these should be referred to in justifying the choice of method.

Part of the reporting of results of empirical research involves provision of some very basic information on the success of the chosen data collection method in achieving a suitable sample of subjects for study. Since this is technical in nature and not concerned directly with the substantive findings, it can be reported in the 'methods' section, although it is often reported as the first part of the 'results' section. This component of the report should provide information on:

- the size of the sample achieved;

- response rates and an indication as to whether they are deemed to be acceptable or likely to have caused bias;

- characteristics of the sample, particularly where they indicate the representativeness of the sample – thus a sample from a household or community survey might be compared with the known age/gender structure of the local population from the Population Census data for the area, while the age-structure of a site-survey sample might be compared with junior/adult ticket sales ratios or information from other similar surveys;

- any measures taken to correct sample bias by means of weighting, and a description of that process **(see Chapter 13)**.

While these comments relate particularly to quantitative research involving surveys, the same *principles*, concerning information on the nature of the sample of subjects under study, apply in all forms of empirical research, qualitative as well as quantitative and non-survey based as well as survey based.

Audiences and style

The style, format and length of a report are largely influenced by the type of audience at which it is aimed. The amount of technical jargon used and the detail with which data are presented will be affected by this question of audience. Audiences may be of three kinds:

- *Popular audience:* consisting of members of the general public who might read a report of research in a newspaper or magazine – full research reports are therefore not generally written for a popular readership.

- *Decision-makers:* groups, such as members of boards of companies or clubs, elected members of councils, government ministers or senior executives, who may not have a detailed knowledge of a particular field, or may have a particular knowledge, which might be technical, managerial or political.

- *Experts:* professionals or academics who are familiar with the broad subject matter of the research.

Report functions: record and narrative

A research report can be thought of in two ways: first the report as *narrative* and, second, the report as *record*. Balancing these demands as the report is being put together can be a major challenge.

The report as narrative. Narrative refers to the idea that a report has to tell a story to the reader. The writer of the report therefore needs to think of the flow of the argument – the 'story' – in the same way that the writer of a novel has to consider the flow of the plot. The report as narrative may call for presentation of only simplified factual information or key features of the data, possibly in graphical form, to demonstrate and illustrate the argument. The narrative of a research report usually develops as indicated in Figure 18.8. The items listed may emerge in a variety of chapter-section configurations. For example, sections A and B could be one chapter/section or three or four, depending on the complexity of the project.

- *A. Introduction.* The introductory section(s) should reflect the considerations which emerged in the initial steps in the planning stages of a project

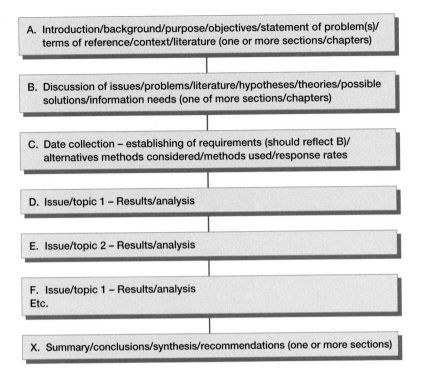

Figure 18.8   Report as narrative – structure

(components 1, 2 and 6 in Figure 3.1). The term 'context' is used to include the environment in which the research is situated, including any initial literature review which may be involved. Section(s) B should reflect components 2–6 in the research planning process and may include further reference to the literature.

- *B. Discussion of issues etc.* It is important that the relation between data requirements and the research questions and theoretical or evaluative framework be explained **(see Chapter 3)**. It should be clear from the discussion why the data are being collected – and how this relates to the planning/management/theoretical issues raised, how it was anticipated that the information collected would solve or shed light on the problems/issues raised, or aid decision-making.

- *C. Data collection/methodology.* This should be described in detail; it should be clear why particular techniques were chosen, how samples or subjects were selected, and what data collection instruments were used. Where sample surveys are involved, full information should be given on response rates and sample sizes obtained and some indication given of the consequences in terms of confidence intervals **(see Chapter 13)**. These technical aspects of the results of any survey work can be included in the methodology section of the report or in the first part of the results sections, and in some cases in appendices.

- *D., E., F., etc. results/analysis sections.* These should ideally be structured by the earlier conceptual or theoretical discussion (B) around issues and elements of the research problem.

- *X. Summary/conclusions.* Sometimes conclusions are fully set out in the results/analysis section(s) and all that is required in the final conclusions section is to reiterate and draw them together. In other cases the final section includes the final stage of analysis and the drawing of conclusions from that analysis. In writing the final section it is vital to refer back to the terms of reference/objectives of the study to ensure that all objectives have been met. Not all research reports include 'recommendations'. Recommendations are most likely to arise from evaluative research and in management research where the brief has explicitly asked for them. It should, of course, be clear to whom such recommendations are addressed.

The report as record. The report as 'record' means that a report is often also a reference source where future readers may wish to look for information. Being a good record may involve including extensive detailed information which would interfere with the narrative. The report as record is likely to call for the presentation of detailed information – even data which were collected but did not prove particularly relevant for the overall study conclusions.

It is wise to think beyond the immediate readership and use of a research report, and think of it also as the definitive record of the research conducted. It should therefore contain a summary of all the relevant data collected in a form which would be useful for any future user of the report. This means that, while data may be presented in the main body of the report in a highly condensed and summarised form in order to produce a readable narrative, it should *also* be presented in as much detail as possible 'for the record'. To avoid interfering with the narrative, data included for record purposes can be placed in appendices or, when large amounts of data are involved, in a separate statistical volume, or on a website.

In the case of questionnaire survey data, it can be a good idea to provide a statistical appendix which includes tables from all the questions in the order they appear in the questionnaire **(see Figure 16.16)**. Any reader interested in a specific aspect of the data is then able to locate and use it. The main body of the report can then be structured around issues and need not be constrained by the structure of the questionnaire.

The possibility arises that some of the recording functions discussed above can be devolved to a website. In some disciplines **(see Chapter 1)**, publications require original data to be publicly available online, so such online repositories could also include items such as summary results and copies of research instruments.

Research reports: conclusion

Ultimately the writing of a good research report is an art and a skill which develops with practice. Reports can be improved enormously as a result of comments from others – often because the writer has been 'too close' to the report for too long to be able to see glaring faults or omissions. The researcher/writer can also usually spot opportunities for improvement if he or she takes a short break and returns to the draft report with 'fresh eyes'.

Finally, checking and double-checking the report for typing, spelling and typographical errors is well worth the laborious effort!

Other media

While the written report is still the most common medium for the communication of research results, this is likely to change in future. In particular, the researcher is often required to present final or interim results of research in person and some sort of audio-visual aids are usually advisable, including: handouts, posters, computers and audio-visual devices. The most common other medium is the oral presentation aided by computer-based visuals using such packages as Microsoft 'PowerPoint'.

Oral presentations

An important point to bear in mind is the obvious fact that the audio-visual presentation is *not* the same as a written report. The presentation must be designed as a medium/message in its own right. The information to be presented must:

- fit into the time allotted; and

- be suitable for the medium and the audience.

Therefore a conscious selection of material must be made. This will normally be explained at the beginning of the presentation, but constant references to what is *not* being covered in the presentation because of lack of time are an indication of an unprofessional approach. For example, if there are six 'key findings' from a study, rather than rushing to cover all six, it is in most cases better to say to an audience: 'There are six findings from the study and in this presentation I am going to concentrate on the three most important.'

It goes without saying that the presenter should *practise* presenting the material to ensure that it fits into the time allotted. Such practice sessions can be seen as the equivalent of various drafts of the written report. Typically, it is necessary to be selective in making a presentation. Judgement must be used in deciding what to include and what to leave out. As with the writing of abstracts and synopses, this can be a considerable challenge. Practice-runs help in this process and programs such as PowerPoint include a 'rehearse timings' facility which helps in deciding how long to spend on particular parts of the presentation and what to leave out on grounds of time.

Reading from a prepared script is rarely as successful as talking directly to an audience. However, if a prepared script *is* being used, then practising the presentation, so that the presenter is very familiar with the script, is even more advisable, so that frequent eye-contact can be maintained with the audience.

Arranging and reviewing audio-visual recordings of practice-runs of a presentation can pay dividends (a recording facility is available in PowerPoint).

Use of 'PowerPoint'-type software

Most of the readers of this book are students, who sit through hundreds of PowerPoint-type presentations during the course of their studies. Students are therefore experienced judges of what is and is not a good presentation. These notes distil just a few of the 'dos and don'ts'.

- Do *not* stand in front of the screen!

- Do not overcrowd slides. The standard slide templates available in presentation programs provide a default font size and a default number of 'dot points' on a slide. This is for a good reason. Viewing an image when preparing it on a personal computer screen from less than a metre is different from viewing the same image projected on a screen in a lecture hall or meeting room. Thus, while a table or graphic with 30 lines of data may be readable in a printed report and on a personal computer screen, it may not be readable to someone 20 metres from a projection screen. In such a situation the most important, say, ten lines of the table or items in the graphic must be selected, or the table or graphic must be divided into two or more sequential slides. As an example, the PowerPoint slides available for this book include 8 slides for Figure 18.3: one containing the main chapter/section headings only (the headings in capital letters) and one each for the detail of each chapter/section and the references, appendices, etc. One of the worst things to hear from a presenter is: 'you probably won't be able to read this from the back of the room but…'. A practice run-through with a full-size screen viewed from the back of a room is advisable.

- Lots of text is not a good idea: if members of the audience are busy reading, they won't be listening to you!

- Use graphics. The PowerPoint-type presentation is a visual medium. Ideally, therefore, graphical images should be mixed with verbal material. Photographs, and even video material, from the research process and/or relating to the research subject can make a presentation 'come alive'. On the other hand, excessive use of such material can be a distraction and may limit time available for presentation of key material. A balance must be struck.

- Be careful about colour. Maximum contrast aids viewing. Yellow lettering on an orange background may look effective in close-up on a computer screen but could be unreadable when projected. Lighting conditions in rooms vary and projector colour definition can also vary: it is better to play it safe. Similarly, photographs which look good on a small screen may not impress when projected in large format.

● Use the *dynamic* features of the program. PowerPoint-type programs include 'animation'. While items flying into view from all directions may be a distraction, the sequential appearance of, for example, items in a dot-point list at least concentrates the viewer/listener on the item which the presenter is talking about. This works even more effectively with graphics. Again, using an example from the PowerPoint slides made available with this book: in the case of Figure 3.1, which summarises the ten components of the research process, the ten boxes appear sequentially, so that the presenter can talk about each component in turn as it appears.

Summary

This chapter considers the preparation of what is generally the final outcome of a research project, namely a written report. It considers the varying demands of three types of report: the management/planning/research project report, the academic journal article and the thesis, each with different audiences, different constraints and different conventions. The chapter reviews the various ancillary components of a report, including the cover, cover page, title page, list of contents, synopsis/abstract/executive summary, preface/foreword and acknowledgements. It then considers the main body of the report in terms of technical aspects, largely to do with format, and structure and content. Structure is emphasised as the key feature of a research report, particularly in their longer formats. The substance of the report is discussed in relation to its role as *narrative* and as *record*. Finally, advice is offered in regard to computer-aided oral presentations.

A final comment

Research is a creative process which, in the words of Norbert Elias with which we began this text, aims to 'make known something previously unknown to human beings … to advance human knowledge, to make it more certain or better fitting … the aim is … discovery'. It is hoped that this book will provide some assistance in that process of discovery and that the reader will enjoy some of the satisfactions and rewards which can come from worthwhile research.

Test questions/exercises

No specific exercises are offered here. By now the reader should be capable of venturing into the world of research by carrying out a research project from beginning to end.

Resources

The best reading relevant to this chapter is the critical reading of research reports. As regards non-print media, most readers of this book have ample opportunity in the course of their academic and/or professional lives to see good and bad examples of audio-visual presentations from which they can discern good and bad practice!

- General: Miles and Huberman (1994, Chapter 12, 298–306).

- Qualitative research: Wolcott (2008).

References

Miles, M. B. and Huberman, A. M. (1994) *Qualitative Data Analysis, Second edn.* Thousand Oaks, CA: Sage.

Wolcott, H. F. (2008) *Writing up Qualitative Research, Third edn.* Thousand Oaks, CA: Sage.

Index

Aas, Ø. 364
Abuse of research results 122
academic research 15–16, 20
accuracy of recall 281
ACORN – A Classification of Residential
    Neighbourhoods 144
action research 52, 135, 137, 157, 360
Active People survey (UK) 209, 210, 212, 221, 383
Adler, P. 246
aerial photography 243
age as a variable 314
Ahlfeldt, G. 158
Alexander, K. 364
Allen, J. 383
Allender, S. 192
Allwood, C. 53
American Psychological Association (style manual)
    181, 193
Amos software 537
Anderson, C. 137, 157
Andrew, D. 52, 98, 99
Andrews, D. 53, 252, 270, 453
anthropology 33
Antonio, R. 37, 52
Antwerp, 383
Apostolis, N. 271
applied vs theoretical research 27, 41
Armour, K. 157, 266, 270, 383
Arnberger, A., 246
Arthur, D. 369, 383
Athens 2004 Olympic Games 421
Atkinson, M. 27, 45, 53, 98
Atkinson, R. 270
attitude measurement 338, 320
attitude statements 320–1
Attrill, M. 422
Aughey, R. 246
Australian Bureau of Statistics (ABS) 90, 201, 13, 221,
    214, 338, 383

Australian Longitudinal Study on Women's Health 157
Australian Sports Commission 59, 62, 90, 94, 95, 99
authenticity 50
author/date system 184–5
authorship ethics 121
autoethnography 270
automatic counters 203, 24102, 246

Bachman, J. 338
Baker, A. 265
Baker, J. 142, 158
Balduck, A. 158
Bale, J. 178, 270
Balmer, N. 423
Barnes, C. 95
Barry, P. 264, 266
Bartlett, R. 172
Barton, R. 421, 422
Bauman, A. 27
Bazeley, P. 453
BBC – British Broadcasting Corporation 214
beaches 192, 233, 246
Beckham, David 381
Bell, E. 53, 158, 159, 246
Bennet, A. 371, 377, 383
Berger, I, 158
Bernard, A. 423
Bertaux, D. 270
bibliographies 168, 174
Biddle, S. 53, 270
Big data 137, 157
Billings, A. 158
Bingham, J. 215
biographical methods 109, 265–7
Birenbaum, A. 246
Bjørnskov Pederson, L. 361, 364
Blamey, A. 353
Blodgett, A. 157
BMD software 455

Bora, A. 265
Borg, I. 537
Borman, K. 53, 158
Botkin, M. 157
Bourdieu, P. 338, 380
Bower, R. 356–7
Brackeridge, C. 537
Bradbury, H. 157
brainstorming 59, 63
Bramham, P. 383
Brandenburg, J. 99, 427
Breuer, C. 192, 537
bricolage 40, 52, 267, 270
briefs for research 11, 91
Bromley, D. 383
Brown, P. 265
Brown, W. 157
Brownson, R. 59, 62, 98, 99
Brukner, P. 172
Bruner, G. 147, 148
Bryman, A. 53, 158, 159, 246, 338
budget 82
Bureau of Labor Statistics (USA: Time-use survey)
    338
Burgess, R. 270
Burke, S. 52, 180
burnout in sport 192
Burns, R. 53, 376, 383
Burton, T. 357
Busse, M. 423
Buts, C. 423
Buzan, T. 158
Byrne, D. 383

CACI Ltd. 145, 158
Cahn, S. 271
Caltabiano, M. 331
Calder, B. 271
Camarino, O. 53, 158, 246
Campbell, D. 364
Campus Sporting Life Survey questionnaire 304, 327,
    458ff
Cañal-Bruland, R. 350
Capranica, L. 157
captive group surveys 112, 300–1
Card, N. 158
Carlson, J. 158
Carrol, J. 157
Carty, V. 158, 379, 383
Carver, R. 491
case-study method 134, 369ff.
    analysis 376–7
    case selection 375
    data gathering 376–7
    definition 134, 370
    design 374–6

examples
    community sport 380
    David Beckham 381
    Nike and women 379–80
    sport sponsorship 381
    swimming profile 377–9
    also see Resources section 383
merits 374
scale 371
unit of analysis 374–5
validity and reliability 372
Cashman, R. 90, 95
Cashmore, E. 381, 383
Castellano, J. 246
catchment areas 298
CATPAC 453
Caudwell, J. 98
causality 38, 456–7
census of population 216–18, 387
Centre for leisure and Sport Research (UK) 364
Centre for Time Use Research 157, 338
Cereatti, L. 351
Chadwick, R. 383
Chadwick, S. 369
Chalip, L. 157, 271, 364
Chan, T. 338
Charmaz, K. 404
Chartered Institute of Public Finance and Accountancy
    (CIPFA) 221
Chase, D. 332, 338
Chaumette, P. 246
checklist
    for in-depth interview 258–9
    for research proposals 88, 93
Chen, H. 266, 270
Child, E. 246
Children
    and research ethics 112
    play 227, 246, 359
    play equipment 359
    play experiments 358–9
Christensen, J. 125, 358, 364
Christensen, K. 172
Christensen, M. 178
Cieslak, T. 246
circular model of the research process 43, 426
class – see social class
Clavio, G. 265, 271
Claxton, J. 157
climate change 122, 125, 143
coaching 109 (case study) , 246, 271
Coakes, S. 491
Coalter, F. 27, 52, 353, 364
Cochrane Collaboration 157
coding of questionnaires 325–8
Collins, M. 270, 352, 364, 384

commercial research
communication of findings 84
community studies 157
competition 364
computer-aided qualitative data analysis software
    (CAQDAS) 434
computer-aided telephone interviewing (CATI) 281,
    390
concept maps 53, 98
concepts 70–1, 98
conceptual framework 67–76, 98
    as models 73, 78
conference papers/presentations 21
confidence intervals 395–8, 406
conjoint analysis 137, 157
Conn, J. 270
Connor, J. 364
Connor, T. 140, 157
Conolly, I. 90
consensus studies 143
consultants 18
content analysis 138, 157, 176, 270
continuous counts 235
control groups 344
conversion studies 138, 157
Corbin, J. 271
Cordell, H. 207
cordon surveys 139
Cosper, R. 157
counting heads 150, 157, 202–4, 228
    by automatic counters 203, 241–2, 246
countryside recreation observation research
coupon surveys 138, 157
Cox, D. 537
Cresswell, J. 53, 157, 158
critical approach 36
Cross, R. 356–7
Crouch, G. 364
Crowe, M. 53, 158
Csiksentmihayli, M. 59, 140, 157
Cukiers, K. 157
Culver, D. 53
Cunneeen, C. 231, 246, 265, 270
Cus, A. 89
Cushman, G. 27, 208, 210, 213, 221, 491

Daimara, P. 265
Dallaire, C. 265
Darcy, S. 95, 96
data
    access to 122
    bases 170
    storage 85, 117–20
Davies, C. 41, 53
Dawson, J. 246
Dayton, T. 143

DCITA 193
De Bosscher, V. 99, 192
De Knop, P. 383
Dechesne. M. 364
deduction vs induction 43–7
DeGaris, L. 270
Delaney, K. 158
Delphi technique 139, 157
Denison, J. 60, 270
Denzin, N. 39, 267, 270
Department for Culture, Media and Sport (DCMS, UK)
    209, 210, 222
dependent variable 344, 502–3
descriptive research 6–7, 33, 37
deviant behaviour 230–1
Dillman, D. 292, 338
disability and sport (case study) 94–5
disciplines 31–3, 52, 67
    vs field of study
        multi-disciplinary research 32
        inter-disciplinary research 32
        cross-disciplinary research 32
discourse analysis 139, 157
discrete choice experiments 361, 364
documentary sources 218, 222
Doherty, A. 27, 383
Donne, K. 53, 109
Donohue, H. 139
Douglas, J. 246
Downward, P. 27, 52, 192, 537
Dreiskaemper, D. 356
Drogin, E. 294, 364
Duffield, R. 246, 358
Duffy, M. 149, 158
Dunlop, R. 271
Dunn, J. 271
Dupuis, S. 133, 158, 260, 430

Eagleman, A. 265, 271
EBSCO 170
eclecticism 52
Eckstein, R. 158
economics 33
Eder, R. 246
education and sport performance 364
Edwards, A. 270
Edwards, D. 271
Ekland, R. 157
electronically activated recorder (EAR) 140
Elias, N. 5
elite sport performance 215
emancipatory theory 52
Embrey, L. 99
Emerson, E. 95
empirical research 42
en route surveys 139, 157

endnote system – see footnote system
Endnote software 174, 192
Enemoto, A. 246
epidemiology 140, 157
epistemology 35
equipment 356–7
Ernst and Young 18
e-surveys 295, 338
ethics 105–26, 383
    captive group surveys and 112
    clearance 82
    codes of 106–7
    committees 106, 125
    guidelines 116, 125
    in sport 125
ethnicity 192, 318
ethnography 34, 40, 52, 270
Eurobarometer 220, 222
European Commission 208, 220, 410
European Platform for Sport Innovation 62, 99
evaluative research 6, 8, 27, 37, 373, 457
events expenditure 358, 364
everyday life 233
evidence-based policy 27, 364
Excel software 458–60
exclusion – see inclusion
Exercise, Recreation and Sport Survey (ERASS, Aust.)
        91, 95, 209, 210, 221, 378, 379, 383
expenditure on sport 192, 216
experience sampling method (ESM) 140, 157, 355
experimental method 46–7, 134, 343ff.
    action research 360
    classic design 344–5
    dependent and independent variables 502–3
    discrete choice experiments 361, 364
    examples:
        alternative research methods 357–8
        auditory cues 351
        children's play 358–9
        coaching/training 349–52
        equipment 356–7
        jersey colour and performance 356
        mental/mind mapping 362
        movement measurement 358
        pre-competition stress 352
        terrorism 364
        visual cues 350
    field vs laboratory experiments 347
    policy/management-related 352–5, 364
    psychological/perceptual 355
    Q methodology 146, 157, 158, 362
    qualitative methods 362
    quasi-experimental design 347–8
    sport-related 52, 349–60
    treatments/experimental & control groups 344
    validity 345–7

explanatory research 6, 7, 33, 37, 373, 456–7
exploratory research 6, 27, 33

facility catchment area (case study) 416–17
facility demand (case study) 411–15
facility use in UK 221
facility utilisation (case study) 415–16
facility preference 364
factor analysis 145
Farquhar, L. 158
Faulkner, B. 364
feasibility studies 22, 27
Feixas, G. 158, 338
Ferreira, M. 364
film as text 265
Findling, J. 172
Finn, M. 370
Fishing 364
Fiske, J. 233, 246
Fleming, S. 125, 270, 383
Flyvbjerg, B. 383
focus groups – see qualitative research
footnote system 186–8
forecasting 23
Foucault, M. 61
Friend, I. 266, 271
Frisby, W. 157
Frosdick, S. 246
Fullerton, S. 99
Funk, D. 27, 99, 338

Gartner, W. 157
Gauvian, L. 157
Geary, C. 192
Gee, C. 246
Gee, J. 157
General Household Survey (GHS, UK) 207, 212, 285, 312
General Social Survey (Aust.) 285
generalisability 153
geography 33
George, A. 371, 383, 371
George, D. 491
Gerdes, D. 270
Gerring, J. 370, 372, 383
Gershuny, J. 338,
Giacobbi, P. 53
Gobbs, G. 453
Gibson, H. 270
Giddens, A. 36
Giles, A. 271
Gilmour, C. 381, 383
Gitelson, R. 294, 364
Giulianotti, R. 270, 271
Glaser, B. 254, 271
Glass, G. 158, 193
global positioning systems (GPS) 228, 242–3, 246, 358

Glotova, O. 253
goals in planning 14
Godbey, G. 332, 338
Goffman, I. 233
Goldthorpe, J. 338
Google Scholar 171
Graham, D. 53
Grant, D. 233, 246
Gratton, C. 98, 172, 209, 210, 221, 384
Green, B. 384
Greenbaum, T. 271
Greenwood, D. 52, 53, 137, 157
Gresty, K. 422
Grichting, W. 331
Griffiths, M. 383
Groenen, P. 537
Groningen Growth & Development Centre, 418, 419, 423
grounded theory 34, 254, 271
group interviews – see focus groups
Gruneau, R. 384
Guba, E. 36, 40, 47, 50, 53

Haerens, L. 52
Hagedorn, R. 38
Hagger, M. 193
Haggerty, K. 107, 125
Hägglund, M. 140, 157
Hale, B. 53
Ham, S. 338
Hambrick, M. 384
Hammersley, M. 52
Hammitt, W. 357–8
Hanley, M. 266
Hanley, N. 364
Harada, M. 332, 338
Hargreaves, J. 171
harm to research subjects, risk of 116
Harmonised European Time Use Survey 220, 338
Harper, W. 264
Harris, J. 422
Hartsock, N. 37, 53
Hartwig, T. 246
Harvard Business School cases 369, 383
Harvard referencing system 184–5
Hastie, P. 53, 253
Hawthorne effect 346
Hay, P. 53, 125
Hedges, B. 266, 270
Hektner, J. 157
Henderson, K. 37, 50, 53, 68, 158
Henry, I. 383
Hensel, G. 147, 148
hermeneutics 138, 176
Heron, J. 53
Hill, J. 381

Hill, R. 421, 422
Hillier, J. 246
Hindson, A. 90
Historical research 141, 157
history 33
Hogan, K. 90, 423
Holistic approach 47
Holt, N. 271, 403
honesty and rigour in analysis 120
honesty in reporting results 120
Hopkins, N. 271
Horne, J. 158
Horning, D. 381, 381
household expenditure 192, 216
household surveys 283–6
household type/size 316–17
housing type 319
Howat, G. 27, 99
Howe, K. 53
Hsu, C. 157
Huberman, A. 67, 68, 98, 254, 403, 405, 433, 453, 569
Hultsman, J. 264
Humberstone, B. 270
Hunt, J. 157
Hunter, J. 157
Hurst, F. 157
Hutchison, A. 193, 271, 453
hypotheses 34–6, 39, 44–6, 70, 77
hypothetical-deductive model 39, 44

Iacocca, L. 266
Ideology 65
impact studies 23
importance-performance analysis 13, 27, 99
inclusion/exclusion 364, 383, 384
income 314
independent variable 344
in-depth interviews 256–61
    standardised 260
    informal/unstructured 260
induction vs deduction 39, 43
Informaworld 170
informal interviews 256
information requirements 79
informed consent 113, 125
Ingenta 170
intercept surveys 139
inter-disciplinary research 32
inter-library loans 173
International Assn for Time-Use Research 157
international sport participation 208
internet references 182
internet searching 171
interpretive approach 36
intersubjectivity 34, 42
interview checklist 258–9

interviewer vs respondent completion 282
interviewer recruitment and training 335
interviewing process 259
introductory remarks in questionnaires 322
Irwin, R. 27, 358, 364
ISBN – International Standard Book Number 552–3
ISI Web of Knowledge 170, 171
Iso-Ahola, S.
Israel, M. 125

James, J. 99, 148
James, K. 99, 148
Jarman, B. 157
Jenkins, C. 158
Jenkins, J. 27
Jennings, D. 246
Jersey colour and performance 356
Jennings, G. 27
Jobling, I. 266
Johnson, D. 271
Johnson, R. 158
Johnston, J. 405
Johnston, L. 98
Jones, I. 98, 271
Jones, R. 109, 157, 246
Jordan, F. 125
Jordan, J. 295
journals 20

Kamphorst, T. 208
Kanning, M. 355
Kasprzyk, D. 158
Kellehear, A. 130, 222, 226, 246
Keller, S. 147
Kelly, G. 146, 158, 338
Kelly, J. 158, 252
Kennelly, M. 270
key performance indicators (KPIs) 74–5
Khan, K. 172
Khanna, D. 352
Kian, E. 270
Kidder, L. 405
Kim, J.-O. 537
Kim, Y. 99
Kincheloe, J. 52
King, S. 52
Kinsley, B. 157
Kline, R. 46, 537
Kokolakakis, T. 537
Kosinski, M. 147
Kozinets, R. 158
Krahnstoever, N. 246
Krejcie, R. 405
Krenz, C. 53, 158
Kron, J. 172
Krueger, R. 271

Labovitz, S. 38
Lamont, M. 99, 270
Larson, R. 140, 157
Lavrakas, P. 338
Lee, A. 37
Lee, J. 364, 381
Lee, R. 144
Leeds, 383
Lenskyj, H. 65
Lepkowski, J. 338, 405
Lera-Lopez, F. 537
Levenson, H. 148
Levin, M. 52, 53, 137, 157
Levinson, D. 172
library catalogues 169
life cycle 318
Life Satisfaction Index 148
lifestyle 22, 27, 144, 158, 192
    see also psychographics
Light, R. 270
Likert scales 320, 473
Lincoln, Y. 36, 39, 40, 47, 50, 53, 65, 107, 125, 267, 270
Lisrel software 537
literature
    review 66, 129
    as basis for research 168
    conduct 177
    roles of 168
    types of 175
Little, J. 192, 193
Little, J. 158
Liu, Y. 95
Lock, D. 270
Lock, T. 157
Locus of Control Scale 148
Lofland, J. 246, 270
London 2012 Olympic Games (case study) 417–21
Long, J. 98
longitudinal studies 141, 157
Longitudinal Studies Centre 157
Looking (observation research) 244
Loue, S. 105, 125
Louky, J. 419, 423
Louviere, J. 364
Lowe, A. 52
Luke, D. 537
Lyle, J. 158
Lynch, R. 246, 265, 270
Lyons, K. 423

Macdonald, D. 157
Mackay, S. 265
Magill, R. 350
magnetic resonance imaging (MRI) 362
Maguire, J. 252

mail surveys 290–5, 338
    response rates 290–5
Mallen, C. 157
Mallery, P. 491
Mallios, W. 27
management
    data 206
    definition of 9
    information systems 206
Mann, M. 122, 125
mapping techniques 141
Mariotti, F. 270
marital status in questionnaires 315
market:
    areas 298
    profiles 22
    research 22
    segmentation 22
marketing 364
Market Research Society 124
Markula, P. 60, 266, 270, 271
Mars, G. 246
Marsh, P. 233, 246, 270
Marshall, S. 193
Martilla, J. 27
Martin, D. 148, 252
Martin, J. 158
Mason, D. 52, 157
Masteralexis, L. 98
Mayer-Schönberger, V. 157
Mazanov, J. 364
Mazodier, M. 99
McCall, G. 259
McDaniel, S. 157
McDonald, C. 357–8, 364
McFee, G. 125
McGuirty, J. 364
McKenzies, T. 227, 246
McKeown, B. 158
McLaughlin, O. 42
McNiff, J. 157
measurement of sport 200, 221
Measuring and Observation Tool in Sport (MOTS)
    246
media:
    reader/viewer/listener surveys 142
    use 313
Meeds, R. 158
Mehl, M. 141
Mellick, M. 270, 383
memory work 266, 271
Mendeley program 174, 192
mental maps 53, 158
Mertens, D. 27, 37, 53
Merz, G. 99
meta-analysis 142, 157, 158, 175, 179, 193

methodology 35, 158-
methods
    choice of 151
    range of 127ff
Microsoft Excel – see spreadsheet analysis
Miles, M. 67, 68, 98, 403, 405, 433, 453, 569
Miller, Richard K. and Asstes 216, 221
mind maps – see mental maps
Minitab software 455
Misener, K. 383
Misener, L. 192
mixed methods 53, 149, 151, 158
modelling 537
Moeller, G. 125
Mondello, M. 98
monitoring/evaluation 14
Montford, A. 122, 125
Morgan, D. L. 271
Morgan, D. W. 405
motor sports 270
movement measurement 246, 359
Moxham, C. 246
Mueller, C. 537
Mullin, B. 27
multi-disciplinary research 32
multi-stage sampling 390
multiple methods – see mixed methods
Murgia, M. 351
Murray, W. 157
Mutrie, N. 353
Myers-Briggs type indicators 147
mystery shopping 232, 246

Naar, T. 266
Nash, J. 491
National Council on Public Polls 110
National Health & Medical Research Council
    (NHMRC, Aust.) 106, 107, 124
national sport participation surveys 202–14, 221
naturalistic methods 46–7
Needham, R. ,139
netnography 143, 158
network analysis 143, 158
Neugarten, P. 148
Newland, B. 246
Newman, I. 99
Nicholls, A. 98
Nichols, G. 354, 364
Nicholson, M. 27, 208, 221, 384, 491
Nike (case study) 379–80, 383
Non-empirical research 42
non-users and user surveys 299
normal curve/distribution 396, 498, 500
Norton, K. 90, 423
Ntoumanis, N. 98
NVivo 435 (for procedures see Detailed Contents)

objectivity 48, 279
observation 48, 130, 225ff.
  children's pla 227, 246
  complementary role 232
  deviant behaviour 230–1
  ethics and 113
  everyday life 233
  fans 246
  looking 244
  movement patterns 246
  mystery shopping 232
  qualitative 233, 241, 246
  sampling 235
  security 246
  site choice 234
  social behaviour 233
  spatial use of sites 229
  spot counts 235
  steps in 233–41
  structural/systematic 226
  technology, use of 241–3, 246
  types of method 226
  unstructured/naturalistic/qualitative 228, 233, 241
  usage numbers 228, 239
  viewing points 234
  zones 237
occupation – see social class
Office for National Statistics (UK) 215, 217, 221, 314,
      338
Olive, R. 253, 270
Olivier, S. & A. 125
Olympic Games 65, 89–91, 158, 192, 215, 246, 265, 271,
      356
Olympic medals 417–21 (case study)
O'Malley, P. 338
O'Neill, M. 148
omnibus surveys 285
on-site surveys – see visitor surveys
ontology 35, 252
Onyx, J. 266, 271
Oppenheim, A. 143, 158, 281, 338
opportunism 59, 63, 219
oral history 266, 270, 271
oral presentations 566–8
O'Reilly, N. 381, 383
outdoor adventure (case study) 109
Oxford University Press (style guide) 181, 193
Owen, N. 99, 193

Packer, Kerry 264, 266
Pallant, J. 491
Pan, D. 142
Panel studies 144, 158
Paralympic Games 192, 266, 423
Paramio Salcines, J. 383
Parasuraman, A. 76

Parker, A. 381, 383
Parsons, W. 27
participant observation 263–4, 271
participation in sport 192
  age range 213
  intensity 201
  mass 192
  measurement 200–1
  rate 201
  social/demographic 214
  trends 27
participation reference period 211–13, 312
participatory research 53
Pascual, C. 383
Patton, M. 53
Pawlowski, T. 194, 537
Pawson, R. 193, 354, 364
Pearson, G. 246
Pederson, P. 98
Pelle, K. 172
Pelletier, I. 148
Pentland, W. 148, 158, 222, 338
perceptual mapping 158
Perdue, R. 157
performance evaluation 74
personal constructs – see repertory grid
Peterson, K. 253
Pettinga, D. 270
Phillpots, L. 383
phenomenography 34
phenomenology 34
Phoenix, C. 246, 271
photography 243, 246
physical activity interventions (case study) 180, 355
physical exercise 4
physical and mental health scale 148
Piano Clark, V. 158
Pickett, K. 409
Pierce, D. 270
Pikora, T. 99, 157
pilot surveys 335–6
Pitts, B. 27
plagiarism 122
planning/policy 9–14
  implementation 14
  methods/approaches 13
  monitoring/evaluation 14
  options 13
  rational-comprehensive model of 11
plans, definition of 9
Plymire, D. 53, 271
policies, definition of 9
policy/management-related research 9–14, 21, 33, 60
political science 33
Pollard, W. 27
popular/media issues 62

populations and samples
population census 216–18, 221
Porter, J. 350
position statements 21
positivism 36, 260
postal surveys – see mail surveys
post-positivism 36
Powell, J. 178
PowerPoint presentations 567–8
Pragmatism 40, 53
pre-coded vs open-ended questions 303, 307–9
prediction 38
presentations – see oral presentations
PricewaterhouseCoopers 18
Priest, N. 158, 192
primary data 48
Prior, L. 158
Pritchard, M. 338
Pro-Cite program 174
professional journals 21
projective techniques 144, 158
psychology 33
psychographics 22, 27, 144, 158
push polls 110

Q methodology 146, 157, 158, 362
qualitative data analysis – see qualitative methods
qualitative vs quantitative research 38, 53
qualitative methods 131–2, 252ff., 425ff.
  advantages and disadvantages 267, 270
  biographical 265–8, 270
  bricolage 267, 270
  conceptual framework 427, 431
  computer-aided qualitative data analysis software
    (CAQDAS) 434
  data storage and confidentiality 426–7
  definition 252
  digital transcription 270
  emergent themes 430–1
  ethnography 267, 270
  examples of 270
  and the experimental method 362
  film 265
  focus groups 262–3, 271
  grounded theory 254, 271
  in-depth interviews 256–61
  internet 265
  interview checklist 258
  interviewing 258–61
  mass media 265
  memory work 266, 271
  merits of 252
  NVivo processes – 435ff. see detailed contents
  oral history 266, 270, 271
  participant observation 263–4, 271
  personal domain histories 266

  personal narrative 266
  process 254
  range of 254
  recording 261
  recursive nature 255
  sampling for
  sport and 53, 270, 453
  texts 264–5, 271
  timetable 82
  uses in market research 253
  validity/reliability/trustworthiness 267–8
qualitative Report (online portal) 453
Qualitative Research journal 453
quantitative vs qualitative research – see qualitative vs
    quantitative
quantitative approaches 53
quantitative modelling 146
questionnaire-based surveys 132–4, 277ff.
  captive group surveys 300–1
  conduct/planning 332–6
  e-surveys 295–6
  household 283–6
  interviewer vs respondent completion 282
  limitations 280–1
  mail surveys 290–5, 338
    response rates 290
  merits 279
  omnibus 285
  pilot surveys 335–6
  quota sampling and 287
  reliability 458
  response rate 290
  roles 278
  spreadsheet analysis 458–60
  street surveys 286–8
  telephone surveys 288–90, 338
  terminology 278, 283
  time-use surveys 286
  types of 283–4
  user/visitor/on-site surveys 296–300
  validity 328–33, 338
questionnaire design and layout of 301–25, 338
  activity questions 311–13
  age 314
  attitude questions 320–2, 338
  coding 325–8
  ethnicity 318
  life cycle 316
  household type/size 316–17
  housing information 318
  income 314
  layout 324
  marital status 315
  participation reference period 312
  pre-coded vs open-ended questions 303, 307–9
  process 302

question order 322–4
question wording 307
residential location 318
respondent characteristics, 314–20
socio-economic group/class 314–15, 338
transport 302
questionnaires:
  coding of 325–8
  definition 278
Quigg, R. 360
quota sampling 287
quotations and references

Ragin, C. 383
Ramsey Street Park Survey questionnaire 306
Rapoport, R. 318, 338
Rapun-Garate, M. 537
Rasciute, S. 192, 537
rational-comprehensive model 11
Raybould, M. 361
real world research 85
Reason, P. 53, 157
recursive approach 255
refereed journals 20
Reebok 383
Rees, R. 193, 364
refereeing process 20
references 181–2
referencing systems 182ff.
  footnote system 186–7
  Harvard/author-date system 184–5
reflexivity 41, 53
RefWorks software 174, 192
reliability 49, 50, 53, 153, 210, 267, 372, 458
remote sensing
repertory grid 146, 158, 322, 338
report formats, types 551–2
report preparation 549ff.
  academic articles 552
  acknowledgements 554
  audiences and style 563
  as narrative or record
  cover page 553
  dot-point lists 556
  executive summary 553
  layout 557
  list of contents 553, 555
  management/policy report 552
  narrative vs record 563–4
  page numbering 557
  preface 553
  section numbering 554
  structure 560–2
  tables and diagrams/graphics 558
  theses 552
  title page 553

representativeness 389–94
research:
  by academics 15–16
  agendas 59, 62, 99
  approaches 98
  budget 82
  communicating findings 549ff.
  by consultants 18
  definition 5
  descriptive 6–7, 33, 37
  dissemination 24
  elements of 58
  ethics 105–26
  evaluative 6, 8, 33, 37
  explanatory 6, 7, 33, 37
  exploratory 6
  funding of 18–19
  information requirements 79
  by managers 17
  methods, mixed 53, 149, 151, 158
  methods, range of 127ff
  objectives 78
  outputs 19
  participatory 41
  in policy/planning/management 11
  process, circular model of 45, 426
  proposals 86–96
  purpose 64, 99
  questions 76–9
  in real world 86
  reports – see report preparation
  scientific 5
  social scientific 5
  stages 58, 98
  strategy 80, 99
  by students 16
  subjects 24
  terminology 24, 27, 34
  topic selection 59, 63
  why study? 8
researcher competence 111
response rates 290–5, 357–8
responsive research 91
Reynolds, F. 271
Reynolds, J. 158
Rial, A.. 27, 99
Rice, K. 221
Richards, T. & L. 453
Riddick, C. 27
Ridley, K. 158
Riordan, J. 537,
risk of harm 116
Roberts, B. 270
Roberts, K. 208, 315, 338
Roberts, S. 422
Robertson, J. 95

robertson, R. 293, 309
Rock-climbing 364
Rohm, A. 53, 158
Rohmann, G. 174
Rojek, C. 158
Rolf, C. 172
Ronkainen, I. 138
Rooth, D. 364
Rose, D. 158
Rosenthal, R.
Roth, D. 74
Rowe, C. 422
Rowe, D. 158, 265, 381, 383
Rudd, A. 158
Ruiz, J. 27
Ryan, C. 261
Ryan, T. 27

Sabia, J. 364
Sagarin, E. 246
Saito, H. 246
Salome, L. 27
Sallent, O. 158
sample size 394–401
    and confidence intervals 395–8, 406
    and national surveys 211
    and small populations 400, 405
samples and populations 388
sampling
    complex events/destinations and 393
    convenience 403
    experimental method and 394
    household surveys and 389–90
    mail surveys and 393
    multi-stage 390
    qualitative research and
    quota 392–3
    random 389
    representativeness 389–94
    site/user/visitor surveys and 391–2
    snowball 403
    street surveys and 392–3
    telephone surveys and 390–1, 405
    Sanderson, J. 384
Sandford, B. 157
Sands, R. 267, 270
SAS siftware 455
Saunders, M. 125
Sax, G. 53, 158
scales 147
Scanlan, T. 148
Schaeffer, N. 281, 338
Schlicht, W. 355
scholarship 128
Scholl, H. 159
Schulenkorf, N. 271

Schwarz, E. 157
Schwieren, C. 364
second-hand references 189
secondary data 48, 130, 199ff.
    advantages and disadvantages 205
    case studies of 409–22
    population census 216–18, 221, 412–13
    types 206
security at events 246
SEG – see socio-economic group
segmentation 22, 27
self-completion – see respondent completion
self-generated research 87
self-reported data 48, 53, 280
semantic differential 322
semi-structured interviews
Semeneoff, B. 158
Semnet discussion group 537
sensitive topics 281
serious leisure 27, 200, 201, 265
SERVQUAL 75
Shadish, W. 27
Shaji, G. 352
Shamdasani, D. 271
Shaw, S. 383
Sheppard, I. 53, 158
Sherrow, V. 172
Shibli, S. 215, 423
Short-term Sport Holiday Survey questionnaire 305
Shupe, F. 338
Significance 501
Silk, M. 52, 53, 252
Silverman, D. 270
Simmons, J. 259
Sirakaya-Turk, E. 338
site surveys – see user surveys
Skinner, J. 270, 453
Slater, A. 271
Small, J. 266, 271
Smith, M. 192
Smyth, J. 140
Snell, E. 537
social behaviour, observation of 233
social benefits and ethics 110
social class 314–15, 338
social concern 62
social psychology 33
Social Research Association 124
Social Sciences Citation Index 170
Society for Ambulatory Assessment 156
socio-economic group – see social class
sociology 33
sociometry – see network analysis
Solesbury, W. 27
Sönmez, S. 264
Spaaij, R. 233

Sparkes, A. 270
Spatz, C. 405
Spirit Level (case study) 409–10
sport:
    activity patterns 228
    adolescent girls and 99
    celebrities 383
    centre observation 237
    city policies 383, 384
    crime reduction and 354, 364
    definition 4
    engagement typology 200
    elite 99
    environmental influences 99
    employment in 202
    equipment 356–7
    events 99, 384
    expenditure 192, 201
    facilities – informal 228
    fans 231, 233, 270
    forecasting 27
    history 383
    inclusion and 364
    income inequality and 409–11
    leisure and 4
    lifestyle 383
    measurement 200, 221, 246
    needs studies 23
    organisations 383
    participation 352, 384
    policy experiments 352
    program fidelity 383
    psychology 99
    qualitative research on 270
    skills 99
    sponsorship 99, 383
    tourism 193, 364
    women and 383
Sport Commitment Model 148
sport consumption/motivation scale 148
sport events scale 148
Sport England 174, 212
sport for all project (case study) 89–91
Sport in Society (jnl) 265
Sport Industries Research Centre (UK) 216, 221
sport motivation scale 148
sport/social club 270
sport spectators scale 148
SPORTDiscus 170
sporting performance/success:
    education and 364
    emotions and 364
    jersey colour and 356
    Olympic medal count 417–21 (case study)
spot counts 235
spreadsheet analysis 458–60

SPSS: xxx, 46ff.
    analysis: see Detailed Contents Ch. 16
    data entry 470
    mean, median, mode 478
    overview 462
    presentation of results 481
    statistical tests – see statistics
    weighting 483
squash 158
Stake, R. 383
stakeholder consultation 11–13
Standing Committee on Recreation and Sport (SCORS, Aust.) 209, 312
standpoint research 53
Stanley, J.
stated choice method – see discrete choice experiments
statistics 497ff.
    analysis: see Detailed Contents Ch. 17
    cluster analysis 533, 537
    dependent and independent variables 502–3
    factor analysis 533, 537
    logistic regression 531, 537
    multi-dimensional scaling 534, 537
    multi-level/hierarchical modelling 531, 537
    multiple classification analysis 531
    normal distribution 498, 500
    null hypothesis 502
    odds ratios 531, 537
    probabilistic statements 498, 499
    significance 501
    structural equation modelling (SEM) 45, 529, 531, 536
Statistical Package for the Social Sciences – see SPSS
Stebbins, R. 27, 200, 201, 265
Steed, L. 491
Steen, I. 139
Stein, G. 157
Stekler, H. 27
Stephenson, W.
Stewart, B. 27
Stewart, D. 271
Stokowski, P. 144, 158
Stone, A. 49, 53, 140
Stone, J. 158
Strategic Business Insights 145, 158
Strauss, A. 254, 271
street surveys 286–8
structural equation modelling (SEM) 45, 529, 531, 536
student research 15
style manuals 193
subjectivism 34, 37, 48
subsidiary methods 135
Suckling, S. 362
Sullivan, C. 157
surveys – see questionnaire-based surveys

Sust, F. 90
Sydney 2000 Olympic Games 90
Sykes, H. 52
symbolic interaction 34
System for Observing Fitness Instruction Time (SOFIT) 227
systematic reviews 47, 129, 142, 179, 192, 352, 364
Szabo, A. 157
Szalai, A. 148, 158, 214, 335
Szymanski, S. 364

Tallir, I. 52
Taniguchi, H. 338
Taking Part survey (UK) 213, 221
Tashakkori, A. 53
Taylor, T. 182, 193, 448
team identification scale 148
Teddlie, C. 53
telephone surveys 288–90, 338
terms of reference for research 11
terrorism 364
texts, analysis of 158
Theeboom, M. 383
themes in qualitative research 430–1
Theodoraki, E. 383
Theodorakis, N. 148
theoretical framework – see conceptual framework
theoretical vs applied research 67–76
theses 15
thinking 129
Thomas, A. 270, 271
Thomas, C. 95
Thomas, D. 158
Thomas, G. 383
Thomas, J. 192, 405
Thorpe, H. 254, 270
Tice, A. 211
Tiggenbaum, M. 271
time-budget surveys – see time-use surveys
time-priority 38, 456
time-reference period – see reference time-period
time-lapse photography 243
time-use surveys 148, 158, 214–15, 222, 286, 338
timetable
Todd, S. 537
Tomlinson, A. 59, 99, 125
Toohey, K. 157, 265
topic selection 59, 63
Torres, C. 42
Trail, G. 99, 148
training – see coaching
transformative paradigm 53
treatment group 344
Trendafilova, S. 384
triangulation 149–50, 159
triathletes 270

Trost, S. 221
trustworthiness 49, 50, 53, 153, 267
Tsang, T. 270
Tudor-Locke, C. 338
Turbostats software 455
Tyler Eastman, S. 158

United Nations Inter-governmental Panel on Climate Change 175
University of Technology, Sydney 124
unobtrusive methods 49
unpublished research 173
'Up & Under' rugby league oral history project 270
U-plan 423
user opinions 299
user profile 298
user surveys, on-site 296–300

Vagenas, G. 423
validity 49–50, 53, 153, 210, 267, 338, 345–7, 372
VALS 145
values 11
Van Bottenburg, M. 27
Vanden Heuvel, A. 90
Van Tuyckom, C. 537
variables
    definition of 24
    dependent/independent 344, 502–3
Veal, A. 12, 13, 23, 27, 89, 99, 157, 192, 209, 219, 221, 293, 309, 423
Vergeer, I. 158
Verma, D. 352
video in observation research 243, 246
Vincent, J. 381
visitor
    expenditure 358–9
    profiles 230
    surveys – see user surveys
Visual Sociology 243, 246, 271
Vlachokyriakou, E. 423
volunteering in sport (case study) 448–51
VO2max 201
volume of activity 200

Wagner, U. 246
Waldren, J. 157
Walker, J. 182, 193
Wallechinsky, D. 419, 423
walking as exercise 193
Ware, J. 147, 148
Wäsche, H. 99, 144, 158
Web-based research 148, 159
website xxx
Weichselbaumer, D. 364
Weed, M. 52, 59, 98, 158, 181, 192, 193, 271
weighting 232, 240

Weissensteiner, J. 99, 271
Weitzman, E. 453
Welk, G. 221, 246
Westerbeek, H. 27
Wheaton, B. 145, 383
Whitehead, J. 157
Whyte, W. 261, 263
Wicker, P. 537
Wiebke, U. 364
Wiggins, D. 52, 157
Wikipedia 171
Wilkinson, R. 409
Wiseman, F. 246
Wolcott, H. 569
Woll, A. 99, 144, 158
Woodman, T. 364
Woodside, A. 138
Woodworth, G. 364

Wright, M. 362
Wynne, D. 157, 380, 384

Xiao, H.
Xiao Yan, X. 271
Xun, J. 158

Yin, R. 370, 371, 383
Young, C. 141, 157
young people 193
Yu, X. 383

Zhang, J. 27, 99
Zikmund, W. 371
zoning of observation sites
Zotero program 174, 192
Zuzanek, J. 158, 338